TOURISM BUSINESS AND PRODUCTS

TRAVEL AND TOURISM MANAGEMENT

(In 4 Volumes)

TRAVEL AND TOURISM

(Volume-1)

Editor

Prakash Talwar

ISHA

ISHA BOOKS

DELHI-110033

Travel and Tourism

Rs. 2700 (Set)

ISBN: 81-8205-330-7 (Set)
ISBN : 81-8205-331-5 (Vol.1)

Published in 2006 in India by
Isha Books
D-43, Prithviraj Road,
Adarsh Nagar, Delhi-110033
e-mail : ishabooks@hotmail.com

Laser Typesetting at : Shiva Infosystem, Delhi
Printed at : Mehra Offset Press, Delhi

Preface

Tourism comprises the activities of persons travelling to and staying places outside their usual environment for not more than one consecutive year for leisure, business and other purposes. It really counts as one of the economic and social phenomena of the last century and undoubtedly will retain its position for centuries to come. It has found a niche for itself as an effective instrument for generating employment, earning revenue and foreign exchange, enhancing environment preserving culture and tradition thereby facilitating overall development.

The travel and tourism industry bundles diverse products and services to provide for the recreational as well as business needs of both domestic and international travellers. In the last two decades, an increasing number of destination economies have come to rely on the travel, tourism and hospitality industry. Economic diversification and technological improvement have created a conducive environment for tourism development in the present age of globalisation.

The current trends in travel and tourism industry are discussed in this book elaborately. The emerging opportunities and challenges in this field are discussed with appropriate case studies. This book will be very useful for tour operators, students, policy makers, planners, marketers and other general readers interested in travel and tourism.

Editor

Contents

	Preface	*v*
1.	Emerging Patterns of Travel and Tourism	1
2.	Travel and Tourism in India	24
3.	Growth of Aviation Travel	35
4.	Tourism and Air Travelling in a Globalised World	63
5.	Travelling and Sustainable Tourism	83
6.	Tourism and Environmental Issues	119
7.	Travel-related Risks	151
8.	Air Travelling: Health Considerations	171
9.	Careers in Travel and Tourism	188
10.	Employment Issues	211
11.	Training in Travel and Tourism Sector	245
	Bibliography	263
	Index	265

1

Emerging Patterns of Travel and Tourism

Travel and tourism is one of the largest industry in the world. It is able to contribute to development which is economically, ecologically and socially sustainable, because it:

— has less impact on natural resources and the environment than most other industries;

— is based on enjoyment and appreciation of local culture, built heritage, and natural environment, as such that the industry has a direct and powerful motivation to protect these assets;

— can play a positive part in increasing consumer commitment to sustainable development principles through its unparalleled consumer distribution channels; and

— provides an economic incentive to conserve natural environments and habitats which might otherwise be allocated to more environmentally damaging land uses, thereby, helping to maintain bio-diversity.

Travel & Tourism depends on a wide range of infrastructure services - airports, air navigation, roads, railheads and ports, as well as basic infrastructure services required by hotels, restaurants, shops, and recreation facilities (e.g. telecommunications and utilities). It is the combination of tourism and good infrastructure that underpins the economic, environmental and social benefits. It is important to balance any decision to develop an area for tourism against the need to preserve fragile or threatened environments and cultures.

However, once a decision has been taken where an area is appropriate for new tourism development, or that an existing tourist site should be developed further, then good infrastructure will be essential to sustain the quality, economic viability and growth of Travel & Tourism. Good infrastructure will also be a key factor in the industry's ability to manage visitor flows in ways that do not affect the natural or built heritage, nor counteract against local interests.

Travel & Tourism takes many different forms - from a trip only a few hours away from home to long distance travel overseas. A common belief is that most Travel & Tourism involves large numbers of visitors from developed countries travelling by air to destinations in emerging countries. In fact, in most countries, the domestic tourism market is larger than the inbound market. Of course, the social and cultural impact of inbound visitors is often greater than that of domestic tourists.

Whether tourism is domestic or international, it involves visiting a destination away from the area in which one lives and using the services available in that destination. Therefore, tourists' requirements are for travel services to reach their destinations and once there, for services such as shelter, water, food, sanitation and entertainment. What makes tourism special is that, many of these different products and services are often supplied by different operators: usually small or medium sized businesses in local ownership. This makes tourism a highly fragmented and diverse industry and so co-ordinated, industry-wide action is difficult to achieve.

The influence of Travel & Tourism's demand also extends far beyond traditional tourism companies, into upstream suppliers like aircraft manufacturers or food producers and into the downstream service providers for travellers, like retail shops. Despite the difficulties caused by fragmentation and lengthy supply chains, there has been a steady growth in environmental good practice across the industry in recent years. There are examples of - airlines and airports reducing pollution and noise impacts; cruise liners practising marine conservation; hotels implementing energy consumption and waste disposal programs; car rental companies investing in increasingly fuel efficient fleets and railways sound proofing to dampen noise. The result is that there are a number of excellent initiatives in place designed to improve the environmental management of Travel & Tourism businesses. Of course, more needs to be done.

World Trade Tourism Council (WTTC) with 105 members is the global business leaders' forum for the Travel & Tourism industry. The WTTC have set in place an extensive strategy to promote a culture of sustainable development and have put in place a three-tiered structure for its achievement. In 1996 the WTTC, the World Tourism Organization and the Earth Council, joined together to launch an action plan entitled "Agenda 21 for the Travel & Tourism Industry: Towards Environmentally Sustainable Development" - a sectional sustainable development program based on the results of the Rio Earth Summit in 1992.

Since the launch of the document, the three organisations have begun a series of regional seminars to increase awareness of the conclusions, and to adapt the program for local implementation. The program has held regional seminars in London and Jakarta in 1997 and Victoria Falls and Dominica in 1998. WTTC has recently introduced a major addition to the program - the "Alliance for Sustainable Tourism", which invites public and private sector Travel & Tourism organisations to record their Agenda 21 based activities on a central web site and commit to co-operation with all other partners. In order to develop the program from global principles to community based action, WTTC is also discussing with the International Council for Local Environment Initiatives (ICLEI) on how the principles of "Agenda 21 for Travel & Tourism" can be built into Local Agenda 21 programs. Furthermore, WTTC is considering pilot projects in 5 cities around the world to serve as models for other destinations.

In 1994, WTTC initiated the "GREEN GLOBE", an Agenda 21 based industry improvement program, which provides guidance material and a certification process linked to both ISO standards and Agenda 21 principles. There are now 500 "GREEN GLOBE " members in 100 countries dedicated to improving environmental practice. The first certification has commenced with hotels groups in Jamaica and Manchester (UK).

"GREEN GLOBE" has also developed a specific Destination Program, which provides a methodology for Travel & Tourism destinations to implement sustainable development. The ultimate aim is that "GREEN GLOBE" will become the primary global standard of environmental commitment by the global Travel & Tourism industry and will be recognised by the public as such. Currently, "GREEN GLOBE" has the support of over 20 international industry organisations representing thousands of businesses world-wide and the support of the World Tourism Organization, the United Nations Environment Program and the Earth Council.

WTTC have also developed "ECoNETT", a web-site containing advice and data on good practice and sources of help and advice. "ECoNETT" is increasingly recognised as a focal point for environmental information, good practice, new techniques and technologies. The International Hotel & Restaurant Association (IH&RA), based in Paris, represents over 700,000 establishments in more than 150 countries. Its membership comprises some 50 national and international hotel and restaurant chains, over 110 national hotel and restaurant associations, independent hotel operators and restaurateurs, industry suppliers and 130 hotel schools.

The IH&RA has offices in Asia-Pacific and Latin America. It is also the voice of the world's hotels and restaurants and plays a global role in representing, protecting, promoting and informing the industry to enable its members to achieve their business objectives. The IH&RA has:

— raised environmental awareness and developed programs through joint workshops with national hotel associations and regularly encourages them to develop their own environmental awareness programs;

— established an annual Environmental Award sponsored by American Express and judged by the United Nations Environment Program (UNEP) that recognises efforts by independent and chain hotels to "green" the industry;

— published advice including practical publications such as the "Environmental Action Pack for Hotels" with the International Hotel Environment Initiative and UNEP and "Environmental Good Practice in Hotels" with UNEP;

— supported regional initiatives such as the Caribbean Action for Sustainable Tourism; and

— joined forces with UNEP and the International Hotel School Directors' Association to develop an

"Environmental Teaching Resource Package for Hospitality Educational Institutes".

The International Hotel Environment Initiative (IHEI), based in London, England, is a program of The Prince of Wales Business Leaders Forum. Founded in 1992 by a consortium of chief executives from 10 multinational hotel groups, IHEI is an educational charity designed to encourage continuous improvement in the environmental performance of the global hotel industry. It does this through:

— raising environmental awareness in the hotel industry by promoting good practice internationally;

— developing hotel-specific guidance, enabling hotels of all sizes to implement environmental programs; and

— multiplying the reach and impact of IHEI by working with partners, including hotel associations, governments, NGOs, tourism bodies and businesses.

IHEI is a catalyst and conduit for hotels to pool their resources and to share experience via a noncompetitive platform. In 5 years it has evolved into an organisation with global impact. IHEI has worked in 111 countries, stimulating and assisting with the establishment of local initiatives such as New Zealand's "Environmental Hotels of Auckland, the Asia Pacific Hotel Environment Initiative" and the Caribbean Action for Sustainable Tourism. Member hotels now represent over 1 million guest rooms and more than 8,000 hotels on 5 continents. The Co-operative Research Centre for Sustainable Tourism, based in Australia, was established in 1997 to enhance the strategic knowledge available to the Travel & Tourism industry through:

— long-term high-quality scientific and technological research which contributes to the development of an internationally competitive tourism industry;

— strengthening the links between research and its commercial and other applications;

— promoting co-operative research; and

— stimulating education and training, particularly in graduate programs, through active involvement of researchers from outside the higher education system in educational activities, and of graduate students in major research programs.

The number of initiatives undertaken by individual companies is large. The hotel has undertaken measures in the following areas to ensure that its operations are more sustainable:

— cultural and social - hotel employment, providing community infrastructure and development;

— natural environment - soil erosion measures and planting forests;

— pollution - sewage, solid waste and noise pollution reduction programs; and

— environmental communication - construction of an Eco Park where all waste is treated within the park, a dry debris sorting centre, a lecture room to promote environmental awareness and a sustainable development library.

Agents and Partnerships

The public sectors, particularly national and local government, have an important role to play by setting the agenda and providing the framework in which action should take place. The regulatory environment also plays an important role in creating the conditions suitable for sustainable tourism. Self-regulation involving the agreement and co-operation of industry is always likely to be the most effective solution. Therefore, the role of

trade associations and industry organisations in distributing information among their members and encouraging participation is essential. The major partnerships to be formed are between:

— *industry and the public sector*: to ensure consistency with the framework;

— *industry and the voluntary sector*: to tap into the enormous resources of expertise and good will that this sector is able to generate; and

— *industry and the public*: both travellers themselves and the people who live in the places they visit to develop more sustainable forms of tourism.

The industry is already doing much to improve its performance in terms of sustainable development. The challenge for the new millennium is to move from the existing ad hoc approach to a more systematic one. To do this will involve a partnership between industry and national governments to deliver the following:

(i) Governments:

— Integration of travel and tourism policy into broader government policies, especially the environment;

— Incentives for the Travel & Tourism industry, backed up where necessary by effective regulation.

(ii) Public/Private partnership:

— Infrastructure planned and developed with a long-term view and within a reference framework based on Agenda 21;

— Indicators and environmental impact assessment tools to enable effective local management and appropriate development.

(iii) International bodies:

- — Co-ordination at an international level of environmental action undertaken by all sectors of the Travel & Tourism industry;
- — Review of existing voluntary initiatives to improve the quality of reporting, their transparency and credibility, and the assessment of their contribution to sustainability.

(iv) Companies:

- — Commitment to place sustainable development issues at the core of the management structure;
- — Innovation of process and application through new technology;
- — Commitment to education and environmental training of staff.

Role of Consumer Behaviour

At the 1998 World Travel Market, WTTC hosted, as a part of its Environmental Awareness Day, a seminar entitled "Does the Consumer Care?" At this event, MORI presented the latest findings from their Business and the Environment survey - an annual UK survey devoted to public attitudes to the environment. The survey is now in its tenth year and illustrates the challenge facing the Travel & Tourism industry in influencing consumer behaviour to promote sustainable tourism. Travel & Tourism is now more associated with environmental damage than it has been in the past.

The industry's economic success is not dependent on its green record - public sensitivity to environmental problems on holiday/business trips has not increased and is no more of a deterrent to repeat travel than it was previously. There is a downward trend in the public's willingness to pay extra for environmental protection and environmentally friendly products, including "green" Travel & Tourism. Awareness of companies making environmental commitments is only marginally up. Therefore, the challenge is to persuade the consumer that it is in their interests to adopt and promote a sustainable approach in their activities and purchasing decisions.

Education programs and the development and widespread acceptance of codes of conduct are useful tools in achieving this step. Once this message has been conveyed, it is then important to back this up with the necessary information to enable consumers to make informed choices. It is here that "ecolabels" and award programs have value.

Education Programs

The Foundation for Environmental Education in Europe (FEEE) seeks to promote environmental education by carrying out campaigns and improving awareness of the importance of environmental education. It is composed of a network of international organisations. The FEEE (headquarters in Denmark) runs three major campaigns in Europe for providing safe and clean beaches and marinas. The award itself is given annually to beaches and marinas that satisfy a number of essential criteria in three separate areas: water quality; beach management and safety; and environmental information and education.

"GREEN GLOBE"'s Dodo Campaign, is based on a cartoon character, who features in 65 Travel & Tourism videos. Dodo explains and promotes the actions that visitors can take to reduce the impacts of their travels. The videos are aimed at children and are designed to be fun, whilst conveying important messages about sustainable Travel & Tourism. The aim is to have these videos shown on inflight and in-room television channels to raise awareness and influence consumer behaviour.

Codes of Conduct

Codes of conduct are also used to try and influence consumer behaviour. For example, "Guidelines for Responsible Environmental Tourism" are prepared and distributed by the American Society of Travel Agents to all customers who book holidays through their members' branches. The Guidelines aim to "encourage the growth of peaceful tourism and environmentally responsible travel" and include 10 recommendations to encourage tourists to act responsibly and show respect for their hosts and the environment of their destination(s). The Pacific Asia Tourism Association (PATA) is an industrial association, which promotes the Pacific Asia area's Travel & Tourism destinations, products and services. PATA also serves as a central resource of information and research, travel industry education and training, as well as quality product development with sensitivity for culture, heritage and environment.

In 1992, PATA introduced its "Code for Environmentally Responsible Tourism" to strengthen the principles of preservation in the region. Businesses, organisations and individuals wishing to affirm their support for the PATA Code are encouraged to participate in the PATA Green Leaf program. The Africa Travel Association has produced "Responsible Traveller Guidelines"; the Japanese Association of Travel Agents has produced the "Declaration of Earth Friendly Travellers" and there are many more examples of industry codes aimed at educating and influencing their customers.

Labelling Schemes

There are numerous examples of industry sponsored labelling schemes, whose aim is to recognise good industry practice and influence consumer behaviour into purchasing the labelled products. For example, the "Green Key,

Denmark" certificate operated by the Hotel, Restaurant and Leisure Industry Association (HORESTA) has 56 criteria that includes environmental information, water & energy consumption and waste management. Special features also include ecological food products, outdoor areas, non-smoking rooms, and adaptations for access by disabled persons.

Awards

There are a number of industries that runs and sponsors award programs to highlight and promote examples of good practice. For example, British Airways has run the "Tourism for Tomorrow" awards since 1992 to encourage action to protect the environment. The awards are directed at tour operators, hotels, national parks and heritage sites, and other activities associated with tourism. By selecting projects showing best practice in their field as role models, others are encouraged to follow suit and consider the environment in the everyday running of their tourism business.

The awards are run annually, with a winner selected from each of five regions and an overall winner. In addition, two special awards are made for mass tourism destinations. The awards are run in association with the British Tourist Authority, the Association of British Travel Agents, the Pacific Asia Travel Association and the American Society of Travel Agents. Entries to the awards have been increases every year. American Express also sponsors a variety of environmental awards for international tourism organisations.

Agents and Partnerships for Change

A broad based approach is called for which requires Travel & Tourism to work with:

- — national governments to raise the profile of environmental and social issues within the education system;
- — NGOs to raise awareness of tourism issues in their work and activities and provide feedback to the Travel & Tourism industry;
- — development organisations to communicate with host communities to understand their needs and requirements;
- — local authorities to engage local people through the inclusion of tourism issues in Local Agenda 21 plans;
- — national and international trade associations, labour representative organisations and training providers to increase awareness and training of staff in environmental and social issues;
- — Travel & Tourism publications (such as travel guides);
- — Travel & Tourism journalists to raise the profile of reporting environmental and social impacts of tourism among consumers and tourism businesses; and
- — the Internet as a source of information for potential travellers.

Protection of Natural and Cultural Resources

The Travel & Tourism industry has a vested interest in protecting the natural and cultural resources that are the core of its business. Travel & Tourism has less impacts on natural resources and the environment than other sectors and it has already done much to address the issues arising from its activities. There are examples, however, from around the world where the impact of Travel & Tourism has been damaging to the local environment and people. Some of the factors which contributes to the harmful impact of tourism are:

— a lack of awareness on the part of those making decisions about tourism development of the social, economic and environmental balance to be pursued in achieving sustainable development;

— a lack of commitment by tourism operators and travellers to contribute to the maintenance of the local environment and culture of the host destination;

— a weak institutional framework with inadequate controls can lead to tourism development which is both inappropriate and intrusive;

— unfairly traded tourism, whereby local communities are unable to share in its benefits;

— large flows of visitors in remote or sensitive locations can place considerable strains on local resources (particularly water) and supply systems. Travellers' expectations of the goods and services, which should be available, can lead to these items or services, being imported from outside or local supply chains, being distorted to meet demands; and

— tourism can change a destination's cultural make-up and, if poorly developed, can increase crime, prostitution and other social problems.

In order for tourism to realise its potential to achieve broad-based sustainable development, an effective partnership between Government and all sectors of the industry will be required. The following illustrates what is being done:

International Co-operation

IH&RA and the United Nations Organisation for Education, Science and Culture (UNESCO) have signed a co-operation agreement to encourage world-wide hotel chains to sponsor UNESCO cultural heritage sites and attract tourism to them via their marketing campaigns.

National Governments

In India, the government is pump priming local "eco-tourism" activities, which are primarily driven by local women. In Mexico, the government is kick starting village development for "eco-tourism" lodges in the Chiapas region involving the whole community. In England, the government has recently held a national consultation on sustainable tourism and, as a result, is developing a new strategy for tourism, which incorporates the principles of sustainable development as a core component. The Caribbean Tourism Organisation has developed a comprehensive strategy to develop "eco-tourism" in the Caribbean region. This strategy is closely integrated with the goals of the Association for Caribbean States (ACE) for a green Caribbean.

"GREEN GLOBE" has developed a specific "Destinations" program to recognise those tourist destinations where there is a concerted effort by all those involved in the local tourism industry to improve the quality of the environment. The Destinations process provides a framework to guide tourist locations towards achieving sustainable development based on the principles of Agenda 21. The Destinations programs are tailor made to reflect local circumstances, such as the level of environmental awareness, action taken to date and available resources. Each program is based on achieving progressive environmental improvements.

Targets are set within a realistic timetable and are developed by a steering group made up of key partners. The island of Jersey has become the first "GREEN GLOBE" Destination. Vilamoura in Portugal, Dominica in the Caribbean and 3 destinations in the Philippines have also entered the Destination program. For example, in 1996 Lusotour SA, a tourism development company, enacted a management plan for Vilamoura whereby employees are given responsibility for individual environmental tasks. The company has invested money into rehabilitating the surrounding natural environment, which includes pine forests and a lake that has significance to local wetland areas.

Guests are provided with a copy of the environmental policy and are encouraged to participate in the scheme through specialised brochures. The campaign includes recycling; treating diseased pine areas; regular cleaning of the beaches and marinas; development of a sewage treatment plant and new buildings in the resort are designed to minimise visual and environmental impacts. For its work in Vilamoura, Lusotour SA is also a winner of the British Airways Tourism for Tomorrow Awards.

The "Afrikatourism" brand has been developed by the Open Africa Foundation to encourage products, which embraces sustainable ecological, economic and social development based on Africa's unique cultural, natural and wildlife heritage. "Open Africa" is also developing a continuous network of "Afrikatourism" routes from the Cape to Cairo, known as the "African Dream". The Dream helps to create awareness of the many rural and environmental projects, which exist throughout Africa. "Team Africa", a transcontinental alliance of governments, corporations, institutions, professionals and individuals, provides leadership and motivation in the development of the "African Dream".

"Whale Watch Kaikoura" is an initiative of local Maori people from a small town on the East Coast of New Zealand's South Island. Within a kilometre of the Kaikoura shore is an area ideal for whales, where visitors are guaranteed to see them all year round. The Whale Watch began 11 years ago and is now a booming tourist destination, run by indigenous people with a strong sense of heritage and a view of the future based on strong principles of sustainability.

Jordan Tourism Investments, has revitalised the traditional village of Taybeh, in Jordan, into a cultural tourist resort, with the help and agreement of villagers. With many of the younger generation moving to the cities, the village was losing its character. By restoring its 19th century buildings and reviving old crafts, the village is now thriving again. The village lies 9km south east of the historic city of Petra. Opened in July 1994, the village now accommodates around 60,000 guests each year.

Uluru and Kakadu National Parks are both owned by indigenous Australians, the local Aboriginal communities, and jointly run with the National Parks and Wildlife Service. They are both major tourism destinations and involve indigenous participation in planning, management, and ownership of tourism infrastructure, as well as interpretation for visitors. They bring significant economic, social and cultural benefits to the local indigenous communities. The Conservation Corporation in Africa has established a series of high quality game parks in which local communities are major stakeholders and beneficiaries of tourism. This initiative is also helping to re-invigorate local crafts.

The challenge facing the tourism industry in moving towards a more sustainable future is set out in "Agenda 21 for the Travel & Tourism Industry". Working together in close co-operation such partnerships should aim to deliver the following:

— Close co-operation between the public and private sectors to deliver a regulatory regime, which encourages voluntary action but supplement, where necessary, with regulation in areas such as land-use and waste management.

— Agreed common standards and tools to enable the measurement of progress towards achieving sustainable development.

- — Certification criteria developed and more widely applied to industry initiatives.
- — A commitment to the controlled expansion, where appropriate, of infrastructure.
- — Environmental taxes, where applied, should be fair and non-discriminatory. They should be carefully thought out to minimise their impact on economic development, and revenues should be allocated to Travel & Tourism associated environment improvement programs.
- — International, national and local funding bodies should include sustainable development as a part of their criteria, so that in time, all funding would be dependent on sound environmental practice.
- — Contemporary research into sustainable tourism needs to be funded and developed. Issues requiring attention include design, carrying capacity, tour operator activities, environmental reporting, auditing and environmental impact assessments.
- — Environmental education and training should be increased, particularly in schools, for future hotel and tourism staff.
- — Greater investment and commitment to the use of new technology.

Coastal Tourism

Tourism provides an essential lifeline for many coastal communities. Faced with the prospect of increasing financial hardship, more and more coastal communities have turned to tourism as a means of generating income and survival. Tourism's impact on the coastal zone has, therefore, been largely positive. Of course, as in any area, if Tourism is not properly managed and developed, it can be harmful. Impacts arise from the construction of infrastructure (hotels, marinas, transport, waste treatment facilities, groynes etc.) and from recreation (golf courses, water sports, theme parks etc).

Coastal communities are now faced with tourism on a considerable scale, and the host to guest ratio can be very high in such areas. At the same time, coastal communities must try to maintain the resort's attraction as tourist demands change, sometimes quite rapidly. With coastal regions being primary tourist destinations, sensitive marine and coastal environments can suffer dramatically. For example, as a result of large-scale sea-front tourist development, considerable beach and dune erosion can occur. Tourism also impacts on environmental quality in the following ways:

— ribbon development, infrastructure requirements, particularly transport links;

— the treatment and disposal of solid and/or liquid wastes, particularly during peak tourist seasons, may be inadequate or at worst non-existent; and

— water is often consumed excessively, not only for drinking but for showers, laundry, swimming pools, maintenance of golf courses etc. This can affect the quantity and quality of fresh water available to indigenous coastal populations.

Recreational activities can also have a significant impact on the coastal zone:

— golf course's impact can be considerable, with those situated directly on coastal habitats (especially sand dunes) in particular;

— erosion of reefs and coral from divers and swimmers;

— pollution from boats and jets skis; and

— noise from motor boats and jet skis, cars and buses, nightlife and other activities.

Solutions

The development of a sustainable tourism industry in the coastal zone offers numerous opportunities. Opportunities includes, those for nature conservation - which, given the increasing interest in high quality natural and cultural experiences, can help to reverse the decline in market share of many coastal destinations. Tourism also provides important opportunities for strengthening local industries. Where industries are in decline, tourism ventures can help supplement declining income. The following examples illustrate what can be done to make the most of the opportunities offered by tourism in the coastal zone:

Calvia is a Municipality on the Mediterranean coast that has undertaken an Agenda 21 project to assist the sustainable development of its tourism sector, in order to counter the negative impact of short-term tourism development since the 1960s. The local council has now implemented a transferable policy aimed at modernising, improving and diversifying the local tourist industry, involving all stakeholders, including the local population. A Project Plan was enacted, and achievements so far include:

— indigenous development, based on the sustainable use of available resources;

— high quality services and an appropriate bed night capacity;

— a ban on new development on 1,700 acres;

— active participation of the residents in community life; and

— environmental management of municipality buildings, waste recycling, reduction in spending on electricity, and use of environmentally friendly materials for office use.

Quicksilver Tours, Queensland, Australia, is owned by one of the largest tourism operators to the Great Barrier Reef. Quicksilver have five large catamarans, which take about 1,000 tourists a day to dive on the reef. They have their own reef site with fixed diving platforms. They employ a team of biologists, both for environmental management and assessment as well as widespread environmental interpretation. Recent assessment of the reef, in the vicinity of the operation, shows that it is being maintained in pristine condition.

Kingfisher Bay Resort is found at Fraser Island, Queensland. It is a large five star "ecotourism" resort built in a beautiful, but fragile environment off the Queensland coast. Its concept, design, construction and management were conceived using the latest ecologically sustainable principles. It is a state-of-the-art "ecotourism" resort, which has won Australia's top tourism awards, and its economic and environmental success has influenced new coastal tourism developments.

Maho Bay's camps and studios in the US Virgin Islands have based their product on a commitment to minimise impact on the environment, conserve natural resources, engage in active and passive environmental education of their guests, and contribute to the local economy. Specific initiatives introduced at Maho Bay include the following: use of new technology; purchasing policies; waste management; environmental education; energy and water conservation; and support for local communities and culture. These initiatives show an appreciation of the need for alternative solutions to issues such as packaging and waste disposal through landfill. These are issues, which as the industry grows, will be increasingly important for the Travel & Tourism industry as a whole to address.

A number of issues do, of course, have particular importance for the coastal zone. Above all, the key to success is better participation at destination level among all the stakeholders concerned (such as at Calvia). In the case of the coastal zone, there are a number of additional organisations with an interest in coastal policy, marine conservation, shipping etc., which needs to be identified and included in partnerships for the coastal zone.

Successful planning for tourism is very important for the future of the industry in coastal regions, because a significant percentage of tourism occurs within the geographical parameters of the definition of a coastal zone. Concerted support from all countries involved (and the industries within them) is vital to protect the shared natural resources that coastal zones represent. Historically, the influence most hoteliers have on the environmental impact of their business is limited to working within existing buildings, or after a new site has been completed.

In April 1998, the IHEI convened a group of hoteliers, tour operators, architectural firms and sustainable development specialists with the goal of creating a partnership to be called the "Siting and Design Programme". The new initiative's mission will be to define responsible planning and design specifications that will cause minimal environmental damage at new sites.

Particular attention will be paid to sites located within ecologically sensitive areas and upon waterfronts. The "Siting and Design Programme" will strive to reach hotel owners, investors and developers to bring these issues to the attention of the entire industry. Linkages with government authorities that uphold responsible development standards would complete the partnership.

Future Challenges

Travel & Tourism creates jobs and wealth and has tremendous potential to contribute to economically, environmentally and socially sustainable development in both developed countries and emerging nations. It has a comparative advantage in that its start up and running costs can be low compared to many other forms of industry development. It is also often one of the few realistic options for development in many areas.

Therefore, there is a strong likelihood that the Travel & Tourism industry will continue to grow globally over the short to medium term. Of course, if Travel & Tourism is managed badly, it can have a detrimental effect - it can damage fragile environments and destroy local cultures. The challenge is to manage the future growth of the industry so as to minimise its negative impacts on the environment and host communities whilst maximising the benefits it brings in terms of jobs, wealth and support for local culture and industry, and protection of the built and natural environment.

2

Travel and Tourism in India

The tourism sector has immense backward and forward linkages in terms of both income and employment and can contribute significantly to the economy. An imaginative and innovative approach keeping in view the socio-demographic changes taking place world-wide and an efficient information system would yield better results. At the same time, the need for sound perspective planning with local participation is imperative.

In India, however, the sector has failed to receive due importance on the country's development agenda. Employing only 2.4% of the Indian workforce, the vast potential of tourism as an instrument of employment generation and poverty alleviation has tended to remain largely unutilized. Of the 625 million world tourist arrivals in 1998, India received a meagre 2.36 million or 0.38% of the total world tourist arrivals and only 0.62% of world tourist receipts.

Compared to other countries in the region India's performance in the sector has been rather poor. Major causes cited for the low performance are lack of professionalism, unhygienic conditions, poor infrastructure, lack of easily accessible information, lack of safety, poor visitor experience, restrictive air transport policy, inadequate facilitation services, multiplicity of taxes and the low priority accorded to tourism. However, despite its tiny share of world tourist arrivals, tourism in India has emerged the second largest foreign exchange earner for the country even though the mainstay of the Tourism industry in India continues to be domestic tourism.

Domestic tourists, who stayed in accommodation establishments, increased from 109.2 million in number in 1993 to 159.9 million in 1997, registering an annual rate of growth of 10%. That growth rate declined to 9.35% in 1999 when an estimated 175.4 million domestic tourist visits were recorded. The foreign tourist arrivals to India grew from 1.82 million in 1992-93 to 2.33 million in 1996-97, registering an average annual growth rate of 6.37% during the Eighth Five Year Plan Period. In first two years of the Ninth Plan, the growth rate declined to 1.49% and an estimated 2.40 million foreign tourist arrivals were recorded in 1998-99.

The international tourist arrivals at world's top tourism destinations in comparison with India are given at table 1. A very large proportion of the foreign tourists, i.e. around 91.7%, visited India for holidaying and sightseeing, followed by business travellers who constituted approximately 5.1% of the visitors.

Table 1. World top tourism destinations in comparison with India, International Tourists Arrivals

Rank			Countries	Arrivals (in million)	%change	% of Total
1990	1995	1998		1998	1998-97	1998
1	1	1	France	70	4.70%	11.20%
3	3	2	Spain	47.7	10.00%	7.60%
2	2	3	Unites States	47.1	-1.30%	7.50%
4	4	4	Italy	34.8	2.20%	5.60%
7	5	5	United Kingdom	25.5	-0.20%	4.10%
12	8	6	China	24	1.00%	3.80%
8	7	7	Mexico	19.3	-0.30%	3.10%

27	9	8	Poland	18.8	-3.60%	3.00%
10	11	9	Canada	18.7	7.90%	3.00%
6	10	10	Austria	17.3	3.80%	2.80%
9	13	11	Germany	16.5	4.20%	2.60%
16	12	12	Czech Republic	16.3	-3.00%	2.60%
17(1)	18	13	Russian Federation	15.8	3.00%	2.50%
5	6	14	Hungary	14.7	-15.00%	2.30%
14	17	15	Portugal	11.8	16.00%	1.90%
13	16	16	Greece	11.1	10.00%	1.80%
11	14	17	Switzerland	11	4.00%	1.80%
19	15	18	China (Hongkong)	9.6	-7.70%	1.50%
24	20	19	Turkey	9.2	1.80%	1.50%
21	21	20	Thailand	7.7	6.90%	1.20%
		40+	India	2.4	-0.50%	0.40%
			Sub Total	449.3		71.90%
			Other Countries	175.9		28.10%
			World Total	625.2	2.40%	100.00%

Although international arrivals are a small proportion of world tourist arrivals, international tourists have the longest stay of 29 days in India. This is reflected in the proportion of revenues being higher than percentage of world tourist arrivals. The foreign exchange earnings during the Eighth Plan period surged from Rs. 6,060 crore in 1992-93 to Rs 10,231 crore in 1996-97, achieving an annual growth rate of 13.99%. The growth rate declined to 10.99% in the first two years of the Ninth Plan and earnings in 1998-99 were estimated at Rs. 12,604 crore.

The sector provided direct employment to about 14.79 million people during 1998-99. The Ninth Plan envisages the Government playing a role of facilitator for private sector participation in the development of tourism. The Plan seeks to diversify the tourism product by encouraging rural and village tourism, pilgrim and spiritual tourism, adventure and eco tourism, indigenous and natural health tourism, heritage tourism and youth and senior citizens' packages.

The outlay for the Central Sector in the Ninth Plan is Rs. 793.75 crore, comprising a budgetary support of Rs. 485.75 crores and internal and extra budgetary resources of Rs. 308 crores. The main schemes of the Ministry of Tourism relate to infrastructure development, human resource development and publicity and marketing.

Ministry of Tourism has identified 21 circuits and 12 destinations for development. Financial assistance is provided to State/Union Territory (UT) Governments for developing tourist infrastructure at these places. In first three years of the Ninth Plan, 779 projects have been taken up. It has been observed that many States, particularly in the North-Eastern region, could not avail themselves of the financial assistance provided under the scheme because they could not find the required matching contribution for projects prioritized under the scheme. There is a need for modifying the pattern of funding under the scheme to enable all such States to benefit from it.

The scheme stipulates transfer of land ownership in respect of those projects in the name of the Central Government. The stipulation is acting as a deterrent in the operation of the scheme as the States face legal difficulties in transferring the land ownership. Ministry of Tourism needs to take urgent action to waive the condition. The Ministry has envisaged an equity scheme for attracting funds from financial institutions but the scheme has not made much headway because the State Governments have not been able to put up financially viable projects. There is a need to evaluate the scheme.

Human Resource Development

The hospitality and service sector has assumed high priority with the growth of tourism and the diversification of tourism activities. At present, the Ministry of Tourism is running 21 Institutes of Hotel Management (IHMs) and

Catering Technology and 14 Food craft Institutes (FCIs). The IHMs provide 3-year Diploma in Hotel Management, 1-½ year Post-Graduate Diploma in Accommodation Operations, 1-1/2 year Post-Graduate Diploma in Dietetics and Hospital Food Science, 1-1/2 year Certificate course in Food Production, 6- month Certificate course in Food & Beverage Services, 6- month Certificate course in Hotel and Catering Management, 1-1/2-year Post Diploma in Hotel Administration and P.G. Diploma in Fast Food Operations.

The FCIs are engaged in providing the craft Diploma in Cookery, Food & Beverage Service/ Restaurant & Counter service, Reception & Book Keeping, House Keeping and Bakery & Confectionery. The trained manpower released during the Eighth Plan period was 7168 persons. The tentative target in the Ninth Plan is to produce 12000 Diploma holders in Hotel Management and 16000 manpower in other crafts courses. A majority of Institutes operated by the Ministry have attained self-sufficiency in meeting the revenue expenditure. No new IHMs are proposed to be set up in the Ninth Plan period. In view of the employment generation potential of the craft level trained manpower, 15 new FCIs are to be set up in the Ninth Plan. The training courses run by the Institutes should be designed to suit the needs of the various target groups.

Marketing and Publicity

There is fierce competition in tourist generating markets from several nations for attracting traffic to their countries. Ministry of Tourism conducts overseas publicity through a network of 18 Government of India Tourist Offices located abroad. The promotional expenditure on the overseas offices, which was Rs. 47 crore in the terminal year of the Eighth Plan increased in the Ninth Plan period to Rs. 52.2 crores in 1999-2000, accounting for 47.45% of the total plan allocation in that year.

There is a need to examine cost effectiveness of the expenditure incurred on overseas publicity. The Ministry of Tourism also provides financial assistance to the State Governments for promotion of select fairs and festivals and rural craft Melas in the country. These fairs and festivals play a positive role in developing tourism by providing cultural glimpses of the States to tourists and generate local income and employment.

Corrective Measures

Restrictive Air Transport Policy: Air seat capacity constraints have been noticed on several international sectors connecting India. Air India, however, has not been able to take full advantage of the capacity available to it under the various bilateral agreements due to fleet limitations and low level of efficiency. A number of foreign airlines have shown interest in expanding seat capacities on the various sectors. Ministry of Civil Aviation, however, is denying international carriers additional flights for fear of diverting traffic away from Air India.

The non-availability of adequate air seat capacity is constraining the growth of tourism in the country. In the interest of the development of tourism and trade, a liberal policy of allowing capacity expansions by scheduled airlines needs to be followed.

Inadequate Facilitation Services: The facilitation services in the country are quite inadequate. The poor airport facilities are a constraint in the development of tourism. The airport infrastructure services need to be improved and modernized. The Ministry of External Affairs and the Ministry of Home Affairs can consider liberalisation of the system for issue of visa/permit. Streamlining the process of migration/customs clearance and prevention of touting and misguiding of tourists are also essential.

Multiplicity of Taxes: A multiplicity of taxes exists in the tourism sector. The quantum of taxes also varies from place to place. This creates hurdle in packaging of the tourism product and is also irksome to the tourist; it makes the product expensive as well. The taxes in the sector, therefore, need to be rationalized and reduced for end-customer to make the destination competitive. Further, some uniformity in taxes on tourist transport should be adopted to facilitate free flow of tourist traffic across the State borders.

Need for Publicity through Internet: In order to make effective use of the resources for overseas publicity, the application of information technology needs to be promoted in the sector. It may be advantageous to close the Government of India Tourist Offices overseas and promote publicity through the Internet and television. The Ministry of Tourism launched a website in January 1999. The tourist offices abroad are likely to become redundant with the improvement of the website.

Priority for Tourism: In spite of the repeated role of tourism in employment generation and socioeconomic development in the country, tourism has not attracted the desired priority. It is necessary to focus attention on the potential role of tourism as an effective instrument of employment generation, particularly in backward areas.

Haphazard and uncontrolled growth can destroy the very base on which tourism is built and poor planning can cause considerable damage as noticed at the places of tourist interest in States of Himachal Pradesh, Goa and Jammu & Kashmir. Tourism development should be based on perspective plans prepared with appropriate technical and professional assistance. The plans/projects must include environmental impact studies, carrying capacity studies, instruments of spatial and land use planning, instruments of architectural controls, strategy for preparing the local community to safeguard its cultural identity and awareness programmes for local participation and local commitment to the project.

Village and Rural Tourism

Rural tourism needs to be given an impetus by earmarking funds for pilot projects on the basis of a model plan for each State for the purpose. These villages can be taken up for priority development particularly if the projects can be linked with the restoration of heritage properties in the area. This would provide a boost to local performing arts and help conserve the local culture apart from preventing rural-urban migration.

Local people in the rural areas should be encouraged to participate in tourism related projects, which may preferably be formulated by the tourist officials in consultation with locals and NGOs. These projects could be in the nature of providing glimpse of the village ambience and the tourists presented with local cuisine, art and culture by persons in local costumes engaging in the daily activities of cooking, weaving, dancing etc..

Moderate, but clean, accommodations for tourists should be constructed by villagers in traditional design and architecture. Bank finances should be made available at attractive terms and conditions for promotion of such projects. Although the North-East could be developed as a tourist haven by virtue of its topographic advantages, diverse cultures and its pristine areas unspoilt by pollution, tourism development has tended to elude it. The Plan expenditure incurred on the schemes operated in the N.E. States has been only about 30% of the amount sanctioned during first three years of the Ninth Plan. The concept of non-lapsable funds, introduced to ensure utilization of the funds, is meaningless if it does not translate into concrete development. A revision in policy is required.

India Tourism Development Corporation Ltd. (ITDC)

The financial performance of ITDC improved during the Eighth Plan period and the net profit after tax increased from Rs. 10.05 crore in 1992-93 to Rs. 55.80 crore in 1996-97. In first two years of the Ninth Plan the profit after tax declined from Rs.43.30 crore in 1997-98 to Rs. 10.81 crore in 1998-99. ITDC would be required to intensify its efforts for economy in expenditure and grabbing more business through new initiatives in the face of competition by private sector. On the recommendations of Disinvestment Commission, the Government has taken a decision to disinvest in ITDC. Expeditious action is required in this direction.

Policy for Tourism Promotion

— A National Policy on Tourism was formulated in 1982 focusing on the development of travel circuits and assigned the responsibility of promoting international tourism to the Central Government and domestic tourism to the State Governments.

— Tourism was given the status of an 'industry' in 1986 and became eligible for several incentives and facilities including tax incentives, subsidies, priorities in the sanctioning of loans by the State financial institutions and preferences in providing electricity and water connections.

— Tourism was made a priority sector for foreign direct investment in 1991 making it eligible for automatic approvals upto 51% of the equity.

— A National Strategy for Tourism Development was evolved in 1996, which advocated the strengthening of an institutional set-up in human resource development, setting up of an Advisory Board of Tourism Industry and Trade (which has since been set up), the integrated development of tourist destinations and the promotion of private sector in tourism development.

— Tourism was granted 'Export House' status in 1998 making hotels, travel agents, tour operators and tourist transport operators eligible for such recognition entitling them to various incentives.

— In order to take advantage of the liberalised economic regime and the developments taking place around the world, a new National Tourism Policy is under consideration of the Government.

Action Points in Tourism Development

— Liberalise India's skies to increase air seat capacity.

— Have a visa-less/visa-on-arrival facility for tourists from selected countries.

— Improve and modernize airport infrastructure and services.

— Allow free inter-State tourist vehicle movement.

— Rationalise and reduce taxes for end customer to make destination competitive.

— Close down Government of India Tourist Offices located overseas and make publicity increasingly through Inter-net and other electronic media.

— Make tourism a national strategic priority for employment generation.

— Incorporate sustainability perspective in tourism development plans/projects to prevent the kind of environmental degradation that have taken place at Himachal Pradesh, Goa and Jammu & Kashmir.

— Provide impetus to rural tourism by linking village development with restoration of heritage properties.

— Create public awareness about economic and social benefits of tourism.

3

Growth of Aviation Travel

We are living during the end of the "age of oil" raises concerns about the wisdom of the increasing use of this non-renewable resource largely for non-essential transport and travel. Furthermore, the "embodied" greenhouse emissions associated with the increasing production of aircraft and consumer oriented commercial developments located at airports are substantial.

To fully account for all the issues and associated ramifications of aviation, a systems approach as used in life-cycle assessment (LCA) is required. Such an assessment would encompass issues such as the use of natural resources (particularly non-renewable forms such as oil); materials and energy use, for example in the manufacturing of aircraft and associated infrastructure construction and maintenance; waste generation (solid, waterborne and air emissions); ecological health; and human health and safety. Only through such a process, linked to protocols for allocating consumption and emission quotas, can one accurately assess the sustainability of an industry or sector.

The systems analysis approach used in life cycle assessment is nevertheless useful here at a conceptual level in emphasising the large socio-technical system surrounding aviation that is supported to a considerable extent by economic subsidies from governments. The key components of this system are shown in Figure 1 and encompass a wide variety of materials including aluminium, steel and plastic (aircraft), concrete (roads, airports and runways), and computers and satellites (for navigation, air traffic control and administration).

The social and cultural aspects of the system include, for example, the way in which aircraft production, operation and maintenance have become integrated within global and local economies, and the value and meaning of personal mobility for the various leisure and business users of the system. In a study focused specifically on the total requirements of energy and greenhouse gases associated with Australian transport, the indirect requirements of energy and greenhouse gases linked to a given transport task were found to be a significant proportion of the total energy and greenhouse gases. The direct requirements are linked to fuel use, whereas the indirect requirements are those incurred during the extraction, mining, storage and distribution of these fuels as well as those embodied in the goods and services necessary for the transport mode under consideration.

In the case of an aircraft, for example, this includes not only the energy and greenhouse gases required for manufacturing the aircraft, but also for mining and producing the iron and steel, aluminium and titanium, as well as other materials. For most modes of transport, Lenzen found that energy consumption and greenhouse gases associated with the operation of transport are about a third of the total. However, in the case of general, regional and domestic aviation, operational (indirect) requirements exceed fuel requirements.

For example, domestic aviation has a total greenhouse intensity of 0.49 kg CO_2 equivalent per passenger-kilometre (pkm), made up of 0.22 kg CO_2-e/pkm for direct fuel requirements and 0.26 kg CO_2-e/pkm from indirect operational requirements. On the other hand, international aviation has a total greenhouse gas intensity of 0.25 kg CO_2-e/pkm, made up of 0.16 kg CO_2-e/pkm for direct fuel and 0.09 kg CO_2-e/pkm for operational requirements. These data therefore show that especially operation requirements, and also fuel requirements per passenger-kilometre, decrease with increasing passenger task and average journey length.

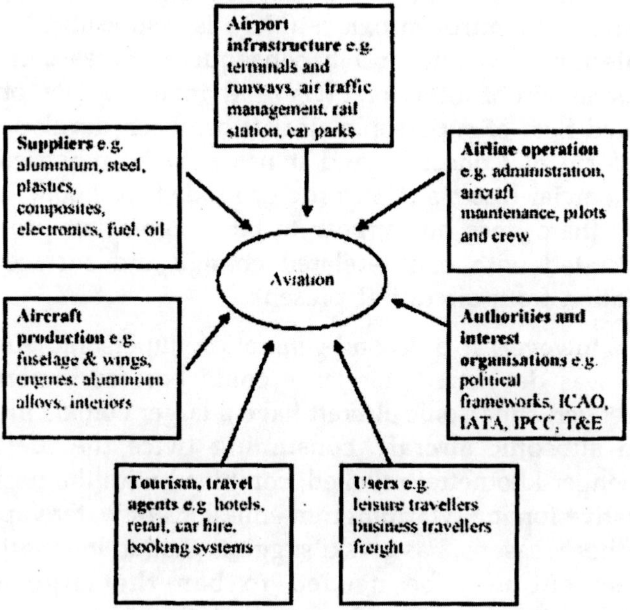

Figure 1. Key components of aviation's socio-technical system.

The dynamics and scale of growth in the aviation sector are clearly moving in an unsustainable direction. Trend analysis is used to provide a basis for investigating this increasing consumption, using various indicators for monitoring changes in "key resources" such as energy, and in "consumption clusters" such as mobility (United Nations Commission on Sustainable Development). Specific examples include, in the case of energy, emissions of greenhouse gases in gigagrams of CO_2 equivalent, and for mobility, distance travelled per capita by mode of transport.

Depletion of the ozone layer is another environmental issue that has been linked to aviation, but supersonic aircraft are implicated in this case. At the altitude at which these aircraft cruise (17 to 20 km above ground level), the chemistry of nitrogen oxides (NO_x) is responsible for the depletion of ozone and a consequent increase in the transmission of ultraviolet (UV) radiation. To date, only a limited fleet of supersonic aircraft has been developed in the form of Concorde, and it has now been retired for commercial reasons (Concorde grounded for good, 2003). Thus there does not appear to be a significant problem associated with ozone-related change and surface UV radiation from aircraft at present.

However, if a second-generation supersonic aircraft fleet was developed this issue could become important. Moreover, supersonic aircraft have a larger climate impact than subsonic aircraft, consuming twice the fuel per passenger-kilometre travelled, combined with the positive radiative forcing (warmingrom emissions of water vapour. For these reasons, Pastowski suggests that an international agreement may be needed to ban the large-scale introduction of supersonic civil air transport.

Across all categories of transport, external costs (excluding congestion) amounted to 530 billion Euro for 1995, this being 7.8% of total Gross Domestic Product (GDP). The most important cost categories are accidents (29% of total cost), air pollution (25%), and climate change (23%). The most important mode is road transport, causing 92% of total cost, followed by air transport, causing 6% of total external costs. A trend forecast is made between 1995 and 2010 with total costs projected to increase by 42%. Transport growth, and in particular aviation growth, and the increased valuation of environmental damages are seen as significant drivers.

For aviation, climate change is a dominant factor. Out of the total average cost for aviation of 48 Euro per 1,000 passenger-kilometre, climate change contributes a cost of 35 Euro per 1,000 passenger-kilometre. In the freight sector, the average external costs for aviation are significantly higher than the costs of other means of transport. The study found average external costs for aviation freight in 1995 totalling 205 Euro per 1,000 tonne-kilometre, with climate change contributing 154 Euro per 1,000 tkm of the total. An additional smaller but still significant contribution to climate change is attributed to an upstream processing component linked to factors such as the production and maintenance of aviation infrastructure.

Of significance here is the prominence being given to air pollution and climate change as important and increasing factors in externality costs. Monetary valuation to avoid or accept damage is considered inappropriate for the valuation of systems people cannot live well without, such as a relatively stable climate, a healthy level of air quality or a quiet environment.

One way in which the concept of sustainable transport has been addressed is by the application of generic sustainability principles such as those developed by the OECD (Organisation for Economic Cooperation and Development) and those used in the Natural Step system. For example, a sustainable transport (aviation) system is one for which ecosystem integrity is not significantly threatened and one where polluting substances emitted to the environment shall not exceed its assimilative capacity. A corollary to this principle is that potentially irreversible effects are avoided and adverse global phenomena such as climate change and stratospheric ozone depletion are not aggravated. General criteria for a more sustainable transport system flow out of such generic considerations. For example, Whitelegg lists the following:

— minimise dependence on fossil fuels

— cut consumption of raw materials

— reduce emissions of CO_2 and other greenhouse gases

— cut pollution to ground water and oceans

— minimise land use requirements

— reduce impact on habitats

— reduce soil erosion caused by transport infrastructure o stop the use of ozone-depleting substances.

However, more specific considerations then arise in relation to the scale of the changes needed, the required timeframe, the dynamics leading to the possible unsustainability and the nature of the urgency for achieving the sustainability focus. This is reflected in critical thresholds and environmental targets in order to meet objectives set for "how far and how fast?". In the case of climate change, for example, the Royal Commission on Environmental Pollution recommends that atmospheric concentrations of carbon dioxide should not exceed a limit of 550 parts per million by volume (ppmv), this being a level approximately double the pre-industrial level and above which dangerous and destructive climate change would be likely.

Others have suggested much lower precautionary threshold limits such as 350 ppmv. However, if 550 ppmv is selected as the upper limit, the Royal Commission on Environmental Pollution concludes that UK carbon dioxide emissions would still have to be reduced from their current level by almost 60% by 2050, and by almost 80% by 2100. The issue is complex given the international nature of the industry and the variety of actors involved, as well as whether other sectors will be willing or able to make more stringent emissions reductions to compensate for the forecast increase in emissions from aviation.

Relation Between Aviation and Climate Change

In relation to aviation and climate change, a major contribution was the publication in 1999 of the Intergovernmental Panel on Climate Change (IPCC) report, Aviation and the Global Atmosphere. Over 100 experts contributed to the report, and it was peer reviewed by another 150 experts worldwide. It concluded that although aviation contributes less to global warming than many other human activities, it does nevertheless generate a significant and fast growing percentage of human generated greenhouse gases. This IPCC report used a range of scenarios to estimate future air passenger travel demand, and the concept of radiative forcing to estimate the climate changing potential of emissions. Positive radiative forcing leads to global warming.

Whereas the aviation-induced proportion of human induced climate change was 3.5% of the total in 1992, by 2050 it is projected to be up to 7% of the total for the mid-range scenarios, and up to 15% for the high-range scenarios (taking the expected technological improvements into account, such as more fuel efficient engines, and better airframe designs). A significant issue for aviation concerns the combined effects of all aircraft emissions at the level subsonic aircraft normally fly (10 to 11 kilometres above ground), which are estimated to be about two to four times that based on carbon dioxide alone.

In addition to the direct radiative forcing effects of carbon dioxide, indirect greenhouse gases such as nitrogen oxides (NO_x) are linked to the formation of ozone in the upper troposphere, giving an additional greenhouse warming effect. Further, contrails (line-shaped condensation trails) are triggered by the water vapour emitted from aircraft and are linked to positive radiative forcing effects. The IPCC report also attributes small warming effects to the impacts of water vapour, sulphate and soot particles. Considerably more uncertainty surrounds the state of knowledge for the warming effects of emissions other than carbon dioxide.

Nevertheless, an increase in cirrus cloud cover is associated with aircraft emissions (in particular persistent contrails), and is associated with positive radiative forcing. Evidence provided to the Royal Commission on Environmental Pollution suggests that the relationship between air traffic and cirrus cloud is becoming more certain. In addition, further support for the positive radiative forcing effects of contrails is provided by a recent study that took advantage of the three-day grounding of commercial aviation in the USA following the 11 September 2001 terrorist attacks.

Over the period 11 to 14 September 2001, an anomalous increase of 1°C to 2°C in the daily temperature range was observed. The authors attribute this observation to the absence of contrails in this period, by suggesting that contrails reduce the daily temperature range by reducing the transfer of both incoming and outgoing infrared radiation. These characteristics of aviation's emissions have ramifications at both the policy level, and at the personal level in considering the idea of a personal "greenhouse budget". At the policy level, the IPCC report notes that aviation is an example of an industry that needs to take account of greenhouse gas emissions and the climate impacts of ozone and aerosols/clouds when evaluating the industry as a whole.

A more specific way of expressing this uses the notion of the Radiative Forcing Index (RFI)-the ratio of total radiative forcing to that from CO_2 emissions alone. With an RFI of about 3, the IPCC report acknowledges that aviation's role in climate change involves several important contributions beyond that from the release of carbon dioxide alone. The policy significance of aviation's augmented climate impacts is also acknowledged in a US General Accounting Office report that evaluated the IPCC report, and which was prepared for the Committee on Transportation and Infrastructure in the US House of Representatives.

Of significance at the personal level is the Centre of Sustainable Transportation's (CST) analysis of the impacts of a 12,000 km return trip between Toronto and Paris. Given the slightly greater fuel use per passenger-km and the greater impact of burning that fuel at an altitude of 11 km rather than at sea level, each kilometre a person travels in the air is assumed to have the warming impact of three kilometres travelled by car. Assuming average occupancies of cars and aircraft, the global warming contribution of the 12,000 km aircraft flight is therefore concluded to be similar to driving a car for 36,000 km.

As the average Canadian travels about 16,000 km per year by car, CST estimates that one such trans-Atlantic round trip is equivalent in global warming impact per passenger to more than two years of average car travel. When equity and sustainability criteria are applied to the consumption of aviation, the conclusions are striking. Apportioning the same right to pollute to everyone on the planet in a way that leads to the stabilisation of carbon dioxide emissions suggests that about 3.3 to 3.5 tonnes of carbon dioxide equivalent emissions per year per capita can be released.

A study on aviation's impact on the environment by the European Federation for Transport and Environment, used a figure of 1.5 tonnes of CO_2 per capita per year as a sustainable and equitable "greenhouse gas budget". Taking account of the energy required for household purposes and heating leaves approximately a quarter, that is about 400 kg of CO_2, for personal mobility. Based on the fuel used multiplied by a greenhouse effect factor of five, the authors conclude that a Frankfurt-New York return flight (12,400 km in total) translates into six years of climate equivalent car driving, or the using up of one's climate related transport budget for the next 10 years.

The greenhouse effect factor of five seems unduly high, but the example nevertheless makes a useful point in underlining how just one long haul flight can use up a personal greenhouse budget for several years. Websites are available to allow easy calculation of greenhouse gases associated with a planned trip based on distance, load factors and type of aircraft (e.g. http://www.chooseclimate.org/flying/index.html), with ignorance of the problem being identified as a significant issue.

Evolution of Aviation

Now we can see the scale and extent of aviation growth. For some, other concerns are paramount, such as the costs of aviation delays and the increasing congestion at major airports. For example, the World Travel and Tourism Council (WTTC) asserts that the economic costs of these delays are enormous-as much as US$6 billion a year at European airports for example. In addition, the environmental costs as measured by unnecessary extra fuel consumption, are considered to be equally high. In WTTC's assessment, these consequences of aviation growth should be addressed by urgently investing in new aviation infrastructure such as additional airport capacity and the expansion of runways and terminals at existing airports.

For others questioning the unconstrained growth of aviation, on the other hand, such forecasts lead to unrealistic and absurd conclusions. For example, the mid-range air traffic forecasts for the United Kingdom show passenger numbers at UK airports rising from 160 million in 1998 to 400 million in 2020, with aviation consultation documents projecting this forward to 500 million in 2030. Sewill considers these forecasts for demand in 2030 to be quite unrealistic, as aviation would be growing at the rate of a new Gatwick airport every 18 months, or a new Heathrow airport every three years. Similarly Graham acknowledges that assuming demand is purely a function of time can be very misleading, and argues that limits to air transport growth must occur at some future stage.

Air travel has grown almost 100-fold since 1950, at an average annual rate of 9%. This rate of growth is 2.4 times the average Growth Domestic Product (GDP) growth rate. Freight traffic, approximately 80% of which is carried on passenger aircraft, has also grown at 11% per annum since 1960. International air traffic has steadily increased its share of total world traffic (international plus domestic), increasing from 35% of the total in 1971 to 50% in 1992, to the current 60% of total world traffic. For example, of a total 3,017 billion passenger-kilometres performed in the year 2000, 1,778 billion were for international services.

Inversely, only about a third of the total (international plus domestic) passengers carried on world-scheduled services are international passengers (e.g. 538 million international passengers of a total of 1,656 million passengers in 2000). The rate of growth of air traffic has slowed from the earlier 9% per annum rate to about 5% per annum. Forecasts about future aviation traffic levels come from a number of sources. Some forecasts are short to medium term in nature (five to 20 years), whereas others use a 50- or 100-year timeframe. Typical of the shorter-term forecasts are those released by ICAO in June 2001 for the period through to 2010.

The ICAO forecasts in terms of scheduled passenger traffic (in passenger-km) suggested an average annual rate of growth of 4.5% over the period 1999 to 2010, similar to the growth rate for the period 1989 to 1999. International traffic is projected to grow faster than total traffic, at 5.5% per annum for passenger-kilometres and 6.5% per annum for freight tonne-kilometres. Over the period 1999 to 2010, the annual total number of domestic and international aircraft departures on scheduled services is projected to rise by almost a third and the number of aircraft-kilometres flown by almost a half.

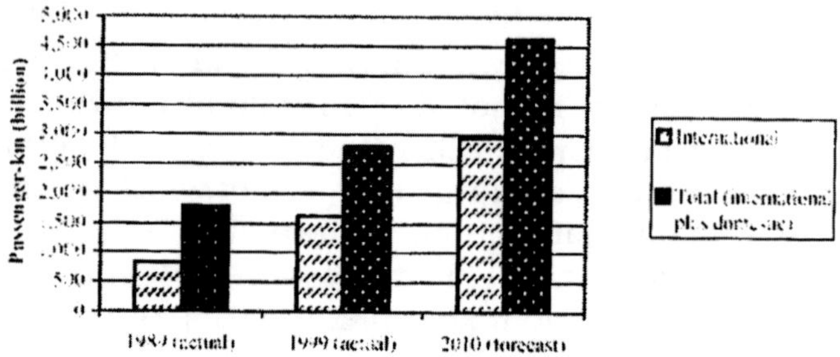

Figure 2. Air traffic forecasts worldwide for the year 2010 using passengerkilometres travelled Based on data in International Civil Aviation Organization.

Aviation industry projections generally are guided by "adaptive planning within the myth of predictability" leading to a "surprise-free expectation of the future, accepting maturity" and calling for "only incremental change to the established system". Such forecasts are usually based on the premise that the demand for air transport is determined primarily by economic development, with statistical analysis showing that growth in GDP explains about two-thirds of air travel growth. This is reflected in increased business activity and increasing incomes. Aviation demand is strongly linked to rising incomes, with people in higher income brackets showing a much higher per capita demand level. Growth in air travel is thus facilitated by rising incomes, and also by penetration into lower income groups. The latter occurs with the trend to lower fares and the increasing prevalence of low-cost airlines.

Demand for air freight is similarly a function of economic growth, and is further stimulated by increasing trade and the globalisation of business. An increasing demand for overseas products, and in particular, perishable goods such as flowers, exotic plants, fruit and vegetables is being observed, with civil aviation being used to transport such products over long distances. Fawcett notes that the procurement of such goods, often via the Internet, combined with rapid international air freight to enable fast delivery, is being celebrated as a new high value service sector. However, she considers this development as another example where the economic justification is strongly at odds with the ecological and resource implications.

Gillingwater, Humphreys and Watson analyse the environmental dimensions of the dramatic increase in air freight volumes linked to global supply chains dependent on air transport. In order to meet time sensitive movements, there is an increasing trend to use all-freighter air freight services. Typically older noisier aircraft such as the narrowbodied Boeing 727 are used, and these are flown predominantly at night. The nighttime impact of such cargo aircraft operations has been increasingly resisted by local communities because of noise nuisance and sleep disturbance, resulting in the imposition of curfews at airports.

The fundamental underlying assumptions of neoliberalism, namely continuing economic growth and rising GDP and incomes, are apparent in Current Market Outlook, the assessment of world air travel demand issued by Boeing each year. Even after the shocks to the airline industry of the terrorist events of 11 September, 2001 and the significant financial losses sustained, Boeing declares in its 2002 Current Market Outlook that "cycles are a regular part of the industry" and that "basic airline industry dynamics have not changed. The globalization of world economies and societies continues". Further it emphasises that "the major driver of long-term air travel growth is economic growth.

International trade, airline service improvements, and declining fares explain additional portions of traffic expansion". Boeing's 2002 Current Market Outlook's 20-year projections include the following:

— World GDP is forecast to grow by an average 2.9% per annum. GDP growth in developing regions may average over 4%, with China forecast to have the fastest growing GDP at 5.9% per annum.

— World revenue passenger kilometres (RPKs) are expected to grow at 4.9% per annum (two percentage points more than GDP), with regional forecasts varying from 2% to 9% per annum growth. For example, air travel (RPKs) in China is expected to grow at 7.6% per annum, with globalisation considered a major driver of China's international travel demand. Oceania (including Australia and New Zealand) is projected to have an average traffic growth rate of 3.4% per annum.

— Cargo traffic growth is expected to grow at 6.4% per annum. o The number of commercial aircraft (passenger and cargo) is expected to more than double from 15,271 in 2001 to 32,495 in 2021. Of the total number of 23,929 aircraft needed, 6,705 aircraft are expected to be replacements for aircraft retired from service, and a further 17,224 new aircraft are expected to be needed for passenger and cargo traffic growth (that is, about three quarters of the total number of new aircraft required). The largest share of aircraft deliveries is expected to be single aisle (57% of the total in 2021), with the market for B747 and larger aircraft considered to be small (4% of the total number in 2021).

— Where possible, it is considered that airlines will focus on frequent, non-stop services providing point-to-point services. Additional city pairs and frequencies are likely to be added to networks, demanding the maintenance of or reduction in aircraft size, as RPKs grow overall. Low-cost airlines are projected to increase their proportion of market share.

The impact of the low-cost airlines is strong now. An example concerns the passenger traffic across the English Channel to and from the UK. Ferry companies are currently facing a great challenge, as the low-cost airlines have significantly affected their market share. In 1996, 34% of cross-Channel travellers made the crossing by air; by 2000, the proportion crossing by air had doubled to 69% of the total. This significant shift was facilitated by the low-cost airlines challenging the higher pricing for short-haul flights previously set by the established scheduled airlines.

The low-cost airlines achieved this by filling their aircraft fully, rather than accepting the 70% load factor9 used by the scheduled airlines. The strong growth trend of the low-cost airlines is demonstrated by the fact that in the UK, for example, 29% of London Stansted airport passenger traffic was on low-cost airlines in 1998; in 2002, three-quarters of passengers were travelling on low-cost airlines such as Buzz, Ryanair and Go. On this basis, Stansted airport has been given approval for a GBP250 million expansion, including for a new terminal, to increase passenger capacity from 15 million passengers per annum to 25 million.

The models discussed so far are more or less sophisticated extrapolations of past trends, and thus have the disadvantage of not being able to predict turning points. In his extensive analysis of a range of forecasting approaches, including qualitative methods, time-series projections and causal models, Doganis concludes that qualitative or causal techniques are more likely to achieve better outcomes and to better predict turning points than time-series methods. Nevertheless, he acknowledges that there are "so many exogenous and unpredictable factors that may affect air transport demand that forecasts beyond 3-5 years ahead must be thought of as being very tentative".

The central problem confronting forecasting efforts is that no one can predict the future with any certainty and the only certainty about the future is that the unexpected will happen. As Faulkner observed, the mechanistic assumptions on which econometric and time series approaches to forecasting are based, are analogous to Newtonian physics in assuming constancy and linearity of relationships. Instead, he argues for the relevance of chaos theory to the forecasting process, and asserts that the new developments in physics parallel the construction of socio-economic systems as open rather than closed, and as dynamic rather than static.

These include the terrorist events of 11 September 2001, ongoing terrorist threats since then, the impacts of the war in Iraq and the worldwide transmission of Severe Acute Respiratory Syndrome (SARS). This series of events resulted in falling demand and increased security costs for airlines, with the world's scheduled airlines recording an estimated net loss of US$12 billion in 2001. Even the short-term forecast of.1% growth in world aviation passenger traffic in 2003 faltered, because of the significant negative impacts of SARS on the aviation industry.

Understanding the trends in the consumption of Australian transport (and in particular aviation) is instructive not only because Australia is a developed nation, but also because of its already high per capita greenhouse emissions by world standards. Analyses of projected energy use and greenhouse emissions from Australian transport have been produced by the Apelbaum Consulting Group, the Australian Greenhouse Office, and the Bureau of Transport and Regional Economics, the latter being an update of earlier work by the then Bureau of Transport and Communications Economics.

An overview from the Bureau of Transport and Regional Economics describes a range of approaches across agencies, including "bottom-up" methods (modelling transport sub-sectors) and "top-down" models (working down to the sector as a part of the total economy). The results from the recent 2002 Bureau of Transport and Regional Economics Report 107 are primarily discussed here-its "bottom-up" projections are more conservative than the Australian Greenhouse Office projections that incorporate "top down" approaches.

The increasing energy use and fuel consumed by transport are indicators of increasing consumption. In 2002, the Bureau of Transport and Regional Economics (BTRE) revised its base case, or "business as usual" projections of fuel use (and the associated greenhouse emissions). For example, an outline of the current and projected increases in fuel end-use by domestic Australian transport is shown in Table 1. The amounts of oil and gas used by the various modes of transport have been converted to gigalitres of petrol (i.e. automotive gasoline) equivalent in order to allow meaningful comparisons.

Table 1. Projected increases in fuel end use by domestic Australian transport

Sub-sector	1998 (GL petrol equivalent)	2020 (GL petrol equivalent)	Increase 1998-2020 (%)
Cars	16.9	21.5	27
Trucks	5.0	7.3	46

Light commercial vehicles	3.7	6.3	70
Aviation	2.0	4.9	142
Other	2.1	2.5	23
Total	29.7	42.5	43

The comparisons show that total domestic fuel use is forecast to grow by 43% over the 1998-2020 period. Although fuel use by cars dominates in both 1998 and 2020, there is a decline in their proportional contribution to the total transport fuel use by 2020. Aviation exhibits the greatest modal increase in fuel use over the period with a 142% increase. The modal energy share for civil aviation increases from 6.7% of the total in 1998 to 11.5% in 2020. Another study by the Australian Bureau of Agricultural and Resource Economics on Australia's energy projections to 2019-20 confirms these projected trends. It shows the transport sector to be the largest end user of energy in the Australian economy in comparison with the other sectors used including agriculture, mining, manufacturing, commercial and services, and residential.

The projected growth in energy use for transport is 2.3% per annum from 1998-99 to 2019-20. Over this period, the transport sector is forecast to account for around 82% of the total increase in final consumption of petroleum, and 41% of the total increase in final energy consumption across the economy as a whole. In relation to air transport, its share of fuel requirements for the transport sector as a whole is projected to rise from 14.5% in 1998-99 to almost 23% in 2019-20, an annual growth of 4.5%. Strong growth is expected in both the domestic and international air transport sectors, with growth in energy use averaging 4.4% and 4.6% per annum respectively.

By 2010 (the middle year of the first budget period of the Kyoto greenhouse targets i.e. 2008 to 2012), the total transport emissions under base case or "business as usual" assumptions are projected to be 87.4 million tonnes or 47% above the level for 1990 (the Kyoto target base year). The modelling is based on the fact that Australian transport demand has been shown to be highly dependent on economic growth and population growth. In addition, trends in improving fuel efficiencies are included (e.g. it is assumed that by 2020 domestic aviation will improve its fuel efficiency by 28% in the base case scenario).

More optimistic and pessimistic estimates than the base case are also made. Transport has an inherently high rate of growth in emissions, in contrast to the calls made for "deep cuts" in greenhouse emissions. An example of the latter is the recommendation from the Royal Commission on Environmental Pollution for a 60% reduction from current annual carbon dioxide emissions by 2050. The other feature of particular significance here is that within the aggregate forecast growth in domestic transport emissions to 2020 (about 1.7% per annum), aviation is projected to have the strongest rate of growth (averaging about 4.4% per annum).

Of particular importance from a policy perspective for the strong growth in aviation emissions is the way in which greenhouse gases are taken into account. Indirect greenhouse gases like carbon monoxide, oxides of nitrogen other than nitrous oxide, and non-methane volatile organic compounds influence the atmosphere concentrations of the direct greenhouse gases, the earlier reported CO_2 equivalent emissions tend to be 10 to 20% higher than those calculated for the three direct gases (carbon dioxide, methane and nitrous oxide) used in the most recent projections. The latter change was in response to the requirements of the Australian Greenhouse Office, for which the recent report was compiled.

Moreover, when international aviation linked to Australia is taken into account the ramifications are wider still. Air transport accounts for around 14% of total carbon dioxide emissions (CO_2-e) from Australian fuel use. Of this share of total emissions, bunker fuel use (international aviation) accounts for 66% and domestic aviation accounts for 34%. However, emissions from international aviation are not included within the targets agreed under the Kyoto protocol, and there is no agreement on how to attribute emissions from international aviation to individual countries.

The Bureau of Transport and Regional Economics makes its projections for such emissions from the fuel uplifted in Australia. Around 42% of the fuel required for international air passenger movement to and from Australia is uplifted in Australia. The familiar upward trending projections over time are apparent for aviation, with total domestic aviation projected to increase its carbon dioxide equivalent emission levels by 139% from 1999-2000 to 2019-20, mainly due to the scheduled airline market. The comparable value for international aviation emission levels (using fuel uplifted from Australia) is an increase of 258% over the same period.

Without including aviation's enhanced radiative forcing component, total civil aviation emissions are projected in 2020 to be 36% of the value for total domestic transport emissions. To the extent that Australia is a representative country in world greenhouse gas emissions trends, the combination of the rapid growth in the consumption of aviation transport and the approximately three-fold radiative forcing effects from aviation at altitude underlines this mode's significant and increasing contribution to global warming. The projections made rely strongly on the assumptions made.

Higher incomes, for example, lead to increased demand for travel, resulting in higher fuel consumption and emissions. Increased load factors and larger aircraft, however, would partially counteract this increase in fuel consumption. This is partially addressed by sensitivity analyses that were undertaken, where the values for the underlying variables (such as economic growth, population growth and fuel intensity) and the resulting emissions projections are different from those used in the base case. However, the Bureau of Transport and Regional Economics also acknowledges that the projections do not include any constraints on growth.

If demand behaviour changes markedly, for example by changes in consumer confidence, habits or travel modepreference, or if telecommuting replaces a significant share of business travel, then the projected growth in aviation emissions would be unlikely to reach the levels forecast. Predictions of traffic demands and emissions beyond the year 2015 are less certain because the probability of unforeseeable changes in key factors increases with time. The IPCC report presents a range of possible scenarios to investigate long-term projections to the year 2050, with a scenario being described as a set of assumptions devised to reflect the possible development of a particular situation over time.

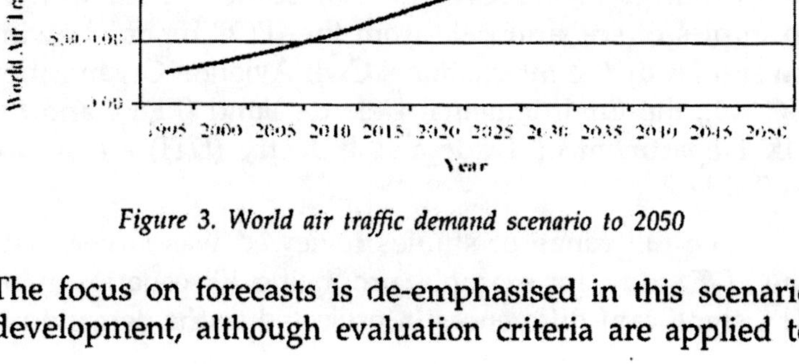

Figure 3. World air traffic demand scenario to 2050

The focus on forecasts is de-emphasised in this scenario development, although evaluation criteria are applied to check the plausibility of the various scenarios under consideration. An example of a medium-range scenario for aviation demand from the IPCC report, prepared by the Forecasting and Economic Analysis Sub-Group (FESG) of the International Civil Aviation Organization (ICAO), is given in Figure 3.

This scenario (labelled 'Fe' by ICAO) is based on higher growth rates than their base case scenario, but is given here as an example as it is consistent with industry projections, and is below the higher projections of the US Environmental Defense Fund scenarios. Detailed analysis and evaluation of a range of scenarios from a variety of sources are covered in the IPCC report, with gradients flatter and steeper than the curve illustrated here. Although more exacting approaches than simple linear correlations between explanatory variables are used, the difficulties of constructing long-term scenarios are clearly acknowledged:

Long-term (beyond 20 years) projection of aviation traffic demand, fleet fuel burned, and fleet emissions are inevitably speculative. Difficulty in forecasting technological developments that might be appropriate for the long term, possible shifts in traffic demand, and myriad uncertainties resulting from human society's development over the period in question all conspire to make long-term projections unreliable-sometimes astoundingly so. Nevertheless, some representative examples of scenario data from the IPCC report drawing on studies by the International Civil Aviation Organization (ICAO), the Environmental Defense Fund (EDF), and the UK Department of Trade and Industry (DTI) are shown in Table 2.

The full range of studies reviewed was larger, with the EDF study, for example, producing 10 scenarios in all. The significant differences in projected traffic demand are explained by the varying underlying assumptions, for example in relation to economic growth and population growth. The ICAO Forecasting and Economic Analysis Sub-Group (FESG) study calculated three air traffic demand scenarios, which when combined with two different engine technology scenarios, produced a total of six emissions projections.

Table 2. Summary data for the year 2050 from some long-term aviation scenarios

Scenario name	Traffic demand (10^9 RPK)	Calculated fuelburned (Tg yr^{-1})	Calculated CO_2(as C) (Tg yr^{-1})	Calculated NO_x (as NO_2) (Tg yr^{-1})
Base case ICAO (Fa1)	13,934	471.0	405.1	7.2
UK Dept of Trade and Industry (DTI)	18,106	633.2	544.6	4.5
ICAO high (Fe1)	21,978	744.3	640.1	11.4
ICAO high (Fe2)	21,978	772.1	664.0	8.8
Environmental Defense Fund base case (Eab)	23,257	1,143.0	983.0	7.9
Environmental Defense Fund high (Edh)	33,655	1,689.4	1,452.8	11.6

All of the 2050 scenarios suggest large increases in fuel consumption by aircraft with their associated carbon dioxide and other emissions. For example, the high ICAO scenario (Fe2) has fuel consumption increasing from 139 to 772 Tg yr^{-1} over the period 1992 to 2050. This would account for 13% of the total transport energy usage in 2050 and need 15% of the world's liquid fossil fuel production.

The high EDF (Edh) scenario shown in Table 2 has an increase in fuel consumption from 179 Tg yr^{-1} in 1990 to 1,689 Tg yr^{-1} in 2050. A still higher EDF scenario (Eeh) has fuel consumption increasing from 179 Tg yr^{-1} in 1990 to 2,297 Tg yr^{-1} in 2050. The latter case would imply aircraft accounting for 39% of transport energy usage and 45% of the world's liquid fuel production.

In evaluating the range of scenarios, an investigation by the US General Accounting Office found that experts in the aviation, scientific and environmental communities all agree that the aviation industry will continue to grow globally and contribute increasingly to human-generated greenhouse gas emissions. However, they differ in their estimates of the rates of growth. Whereas some of the aviation industry representatives interviewed consider the mid-range scenarios for traffic projections and emissions to be too high, environmental groups like the Environmental Defense Fund in the USA, and environmental think tanks such as the Centre for Sustainable Transportation in Canada, argue that the medium and high-range scenarios are more consistent with industry projections, and with the energy projections of agencies such as the National Aeronautics and Space Administration (NASA). Thus, the ICAO scenario (Fe) shown in Figure 3 and Table 2 is closer to the projections of the UK Department of Trade and Industry than the base case ICAO scenario (Fa).

The IPCC report used three plausibility checks to evaluate the range of scenarios. These were: (a) the fleet size required to carry the projected traffic in 2050; (b) the possible constraints on airport and infrastructure development (the scenarios assumed that sufficient infrastructure and capacity would be available); and (c) the implications of the demand for aviation fuel. On this basis, the authors conclude that the highest EDF scenarios are less plausible, as they would require radical developments in aircraft fleet size and associated infrastructure.

Similarly, low-growth scenarios are likely to be exceeded given the present state of the industry and its planned development. The ICAO (FESG) scenarios are considered to fall within the plausible range of outcomes. In agreement with this assessment, Whitelegg, a prominent academic in the transport field who has put the "no growth" case for aviation, considers that the most likely growth path is in the range between the ICAO base case (Fa in Table 2) and the higher EDF base case (Eab in Table 2). A more recent study, using an entirely different methodology from the IPCC report studies, provides further collaboration for the judgments above. Here, the methodology draws on relationships between the sales of bunker jet fuel, world crude oil prices and global GDP.

Four scenarios were used to investigate the increase in CO_2 emissions from international aviation from 1995 to 2050. Three of these, with varying degrees of global development, are exemplified at one extreme by a Schumpeterian world globalisation model in the narrow economic sense (GDP growth of 3.1%; Trade to GDP in 2050 of 39.4%). A fourth Ecological scenario focused on environmental issues in contrast to the other three scenarios, and gave priority to energy efficiency and sustainability issues, with less emphasis on economic growth (GDP growth of 1.6%; Trade to GDP in 2050 of 19.8%).

The range of increases in global CO_2 emissions from jet fuel consumption from 1995 to 2050 vary from a 187% increase for the Ecological scenario to a 513% increase for the Schumpeter (globalisation/liberalisation) model scenario. Olsthoorn notes this is a similar finding to that from the UK Department of Transport and Industry (DTI) study. The latter study estimates the CO_2 emissions from world aviation would increase by 100-500% from 1995 to

2050. Again, the high growth estimates from the EDF study (up to 1,100% increase from 1990 to 2050) are brought into question, although the lower growth base case EDF scenarios are comparable.

Using a model that addresses regional and global long-term scenarios, Schafer and Victor have examined "how much people will move around in the distant future" and "what modes of transport they will use". They used their model to project future mobility for 11 world regions between 1990 and 2050. Their estimates of historical and future global mobility (measured in passenger-kilometres, pkm) for each transport mode for the years 1960, 1990, 2020 and 2050 are shown in Figure 4. The model is an integrated one, in the sense that it takes into account competition between the various modes of transport (buses, trains, cars, and aircraft).

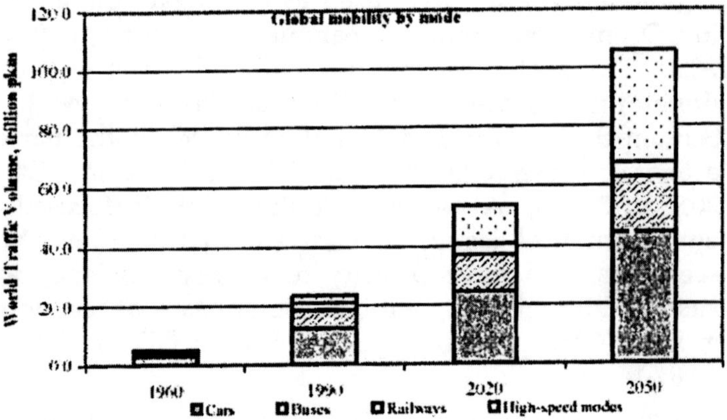

Figure 4. Historical and estimated future total global mobility by mode of transport.

Of particular interest in relation to aviation futures, is the model's use of a significant travel theory that assumes that budgets exist for both travel time and money. Thus, if people spend a constant share of money on travelling, rising incomes will predictably lead to a rising demand for mobility. Surveys from various cities and countries throughout the world confirm that people commonly spend a constant share of time on travel, typically a little over one hour per person per day. As total mobility rises, travellers switch to faster modes of travel to remain within this fixed travel time budget.

The model suggests that all transport modes except for aircraft will be in relative decline by 2050, when aircraft will provide 36% of global mobility and cars 42%. Although some modes are in relative decline, the absolute mobility for all modes will increase. These researchers claim that high-speed mobility in 2050 will be 18 times its 1990 level. In North America, high-speed transport (mainly aircraft, but also high speed trains) is projected to supply 71% of the mobility share by 2050. This study concludes that high-speed modes of transport will replace slower modes. This follows from the underlying theory related to growing economies in each region stimulating greater travel demand, with the fixed travel time budget requiring travellers to shift to faster modes of transport.

Shafer and Victor's model assumes that transport systems behave in a deterministic fashion, with increasing mobility following access to higher speed modes of transport. Of course, their conclusions depend on the validity of the travel time budget theory. Although some researchers have questioned this theory, Mokhtarian and Salomon (2001), in considering both sides of the debate, conclude that the empirical evidence supports at least a modified version of the travel time budget theory. Schafer and Victor's model is also technologically deterministic, with visions of large subsonic aircraft carrying 1,000 people progressing to craft travelling at supersonic and hypersonic speeds.

The world would essentially become a global city, the subcenters of which are connected by high-speed links. In essence, the conclusions from this particular avenue of research point to future societies with very high levels of mobility-"hypermobile" societies by current standards. The notable modal shifts that have been going on in passenger transport since the end of the Second World War provide collaboration for the above theory, as shown in the modal shares of Australian non-urban travel since that time.

The total mobility for all modes has increased with time, with rail losing out to cars as motor vehicles became widespread and as the road system was developed. At the same time, air travel has grown rapidly. This shift to air travel accelerated further in the 1990s when air travel was deregulated. Analyses of the recent and projected contributions to global warming from various modes of transport worldwide indicate that aviation will surpass the global warming impact of cars by 2030.

4

Tourism and Air Travelling in a Globalised World

The consumption of aviation travel and tourism became integrally linked during the latter half of the twentieth century. After the Second World War, developments in aircraft technology, including the introduction of commercial jet aircraft in the 1950s, were an important driver in the growth of tourism. The expansion of tourism by air has been described as being "beyond the wildest expectations of travellers at the beginning of the twentieth century". Thus, international tourist arrivals increased from 25 million in 1950 to 664 million in 1999, corresponding to an average annual growth rate of 7%. Wheatcroft, writing for the World Tourism Organization (WTO), states that the WTO has long recognised that aviation and tourism are interdependent segments of a single travel and tourism industry.

Further, "aviation and tourism must continue to work together for the optimum development of world travel". The tourism industry operates as an interrelated network of the following, mostly transnational, businesses and organisations within the context of economic globalisation:

— airlines and other linked modes of travel

— travel agents and tour operators

— international hotels and other accommodation

— theatres and entertainment

— a diverse range of businesses that provide supplies and services to the above.

Consequently, the boundaries between tourism, travel, leisure and accommodation are now quite unclear. For example, airline passengers are encouraged to join frequent flyer programs with rewards related to distance travelled, and "fly-buy" schemes linked to credit cards underline the link between the consumption of both travel and non-travel items. The driving force behind such travel and tourism developments is primarily the global economic system, with the process of globalisation also being facilitated by forces of social and cultural change that are linked to the development and impact of information technology and the mass media.

Indeed, increased economic globalisation assumes increasingly mobile societies. Local, previously relatively isolated and inaccessible places are now subject to global processes, and these have diverse economic, cultural and ecological consequences. Thus, the context for changes in tourism and travel is one of globalisation and international business motivation, supported in turn by compliant political systems. The World Travel and Tourism Council (WTTC) estimated that the travel and tourism industry:

— contributed 11.7% to the world's GDP in 1999

— directly or indirectly accounted for almost 200 million jobs worldwide, or 8% of the world's total employment in 1999

— will employ 254 million people by 2010.

In a position statement on air transport and freer world trade, the WTTC calls for a liberalisation of trade, transport and telecommunications. In relation to air transport in particular, the Council states: "a freeflowing [sic], competitive air transport system is fundamental to this development. It will fuel markets through price competition and service innovation". A more recent statement says: "we must look beyond the immediate outlook, towards a future vision of substantial air travel growth and to make the investments essential for its achievement".

Some elements of the associated WTTC action plan to achieve this vision include the presentation of persuasive arguments to show how air travel can be part of a sustainable economy without penal taxation; putting the case for the urgent need for new aviation infrastructure, including long-term airport plans for the next 20 to 30 years for all regions; and a worldwide public relations campaign to gain the support of "opinion formers" for such an action plan, including support from the policy agendas of governments. In the early 1990s, air arrivals accounted for 70% of tourist arrivals in at least 20 major countries that are popular with tourists, with 10 such countries (including Australia, New Zealand and Japan) reporting almost all international arrivals by air. This relationship is not as strong in Europe, where cars are more commonly used to make the relatively short trips across borders, and air travel accounts for only a quarter of international arrivals.

In keeping with the World Tourism Organization's bias towards the "economic objectives of tourism policies as paramount", the same author concludes that many governments are recognising the need to modify protectionist aviation policies in order to facilitate the growth of tourism, both domestically and internationally. Understandably, the terrorist events of 11 September, 2001 in the USA had a strong negative impact on travel and tourism, although the World Travel and Tourism Council's longer-term forecasts after 11 September were still very strong. Nevertheless, perceived threats to tourism led to the formation of an industry coalition, with the WTTC, of travel and tourism associations from around the world (representing airlines and airports, manufacturers, hotels and restaurants, tour operators and retail agents, travel related services, and credit card and rental companies). Thus, the tragic events of 11 September have both made more transparent and galvanised the web of business and economic interests surrounding aviation travel in the context of a global economic system.

More recently, just as the tourism and travel industry was beginning to overcome the downturn linked to the events of 11 September, 2001, it was challenged by the ramifications of further significant reductions in travel related to the 2003 war in Iraq and the spread of the disease Severe Acute Respiratory Syndrome (SARS). International travel fell 15 to 20% during the war, and US airlines sought US$3 billion from the US government in order to survive financially. Other airlines, for example Qantas and British Airways, announced job cuts in response to the downturn. The SARS related reduction in tourism to tourism-intensive economies such as China, Hong Kong and Singapore also significantly affected a variety of tourism, travel, entertainment and retail businesses. Global financial analysts at Morgan and Stanley expressed this in April 2003 as a 0.4% reduction to their Asian growth forecast for 2003.

Travel and Tourism Forecasting

The use of tourist arrivals and tourist receipts as indices of global travel forecasts is one way of estimating demand in the future and of understanding past trends, and the World Tourism Organization collects these for this purpose. These data show that the number of international tourist arrivals (i.e. arrivals from abroad) has increased by an average annual growth rate of 6.9% since 1950, from 25 million international arrivals in 1950 to 664 million in 1999 (Figure 1). Parallelling this increase is the increase in tourism receipts from $US 2.1 billion in 1950 to $US 455 billion in 1999.

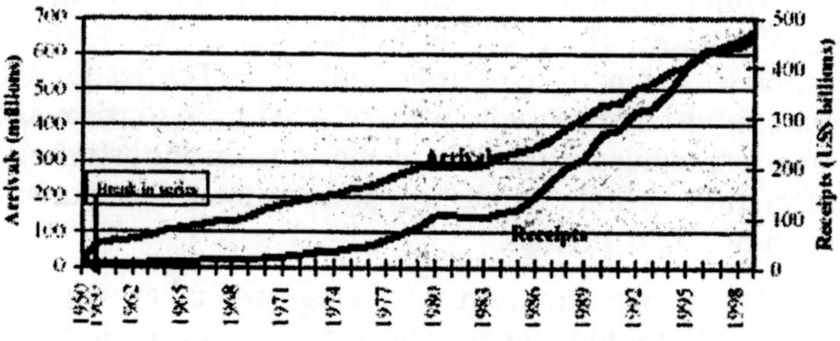

Figure 1. International tourist arrivals and tourism receipts, 1950-1999.

The usual upward trending graph of international arrivals and receipts from tourism followed an anomalous path after the terrorist events of 11 September, 2001, the Bali attack on 12 October, 2002, and the war in Iraq and the spread of SARS in 2003. The World Tourism Organization commented that "it is difficult to find a concrete confidence crisis that can compare with what the world experienced in 2001".

However, WTO still tends to promote an optimistic assessment of future trends, reporting that the 693 million international tourist arrivals in 2002 corresponds to a decrease of 0.6% or 4 million down from the 697 million arrivals in 2000. The general tenor of argument used by business driven interests is that after terrorist shocks and other such events, recovery occurs relatively quickly, and air travel rises eventually to new heights of activity, as pent-up demand due to postponed travel is observed. Even with such setbacks it is argued that tourism proves to be a resilient and stable economic sector with confidence that the growth of tourism will return to normal.

The World Tourism Organization's Tourism 2020 Vision program of research is an extension of its earlier work on tourism forecasting, which produced a series of forecasting reports for each of six WTO regions and a global volume. The 2020 Vision program analysed survey responses from 85 countries and 50 WTO-designated tourism "visionaries", who were selected from tourism and travel companies, suppliers to the tourism industry, and researchers, writers, publishers and academics in tourism, economics and politics.

For the medium term, an average annual growth rate of international tourism arrivals of 4.1% for the period 1995 to 2020 is forecast, with the numbers of international tourism arrivals expected to reach one billion by 2010 and 1.6 billion by 2020 (Figure 2). This forecast was reaffirmed despite the events of 11 September, 2001.

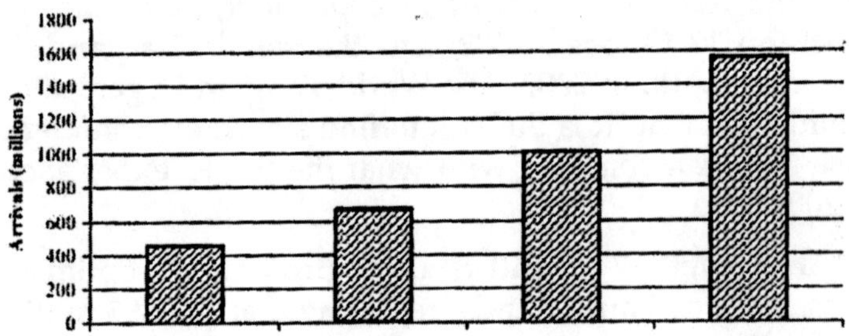

Figure 2. Actual and projected international tourist arrivals worldwide.

The Vision program also predicts that from 1995 to 2020 there will be a rise in the long-haul share of arrivals, with tourists travelling further afield. Hence the intraregional/ long-haul travel ratio is expected to increase from 82:18 in 1995 to 76:24 in 2020. Of the 1.6 billion worldwide arrivals in 2020, 1.18 billion are expected for intraregional travel and 377 million are expected to be long-haul travellers. This corresponds to an average worldwide annual growth rate of 3.8% for intraregional travel and 5.4% for long-haul travel.

As foreshadowed above, an aspect of tourism forecasting that is problematic concerns the long-term volatility of tourism demand related to a variety of shocks from external events. Examples include the worldwide petroleum shortages in 1973-74 and 1979-80; the Chernobyl nuclear accident in 1986 coupled with the US-Libyan conflict; the Gulf War in 1991; the terrorist events of 11 September, 2001 in the USA; and the 2003 war in Iraq and the global spread of the disease SARS. These events significantly reduced international travel and tourism following their occurrence, as well as impacting on domestic tourism. Such sporadic events are usually impossible to forecast, and their potential effects are obscure.

Nevertheless Frechtling's work encompasses a range of qualitative and quantitative methods that extend beyond extrapolative or time series methods, and adopts a view of the future as being neither totally predictable nor unpredictable. In his view, forecasts are seen to be useful and feasible by considering the future to be somewhat predictable and somewhat alterable. Further, complexity is acknowledged in that tourism demand is seen at times to be volatile, with a wide range of factors influencing tourism behaviour. Of particular relevance to Australia is the WTO region labelled East Asia and the Pacific. This covers the subregions of North Eastern Asia, South Eastern Asia and Oceania.

Tourist arrivals in the East Asia and Pacific region grew at an average of 7.4% per year in the decade 1990-2000, in spite of financial crises and violence in many countries. This puts growth in the East Asia and Pacific

Region well above the world average growth rate of 4.3% per year. Looking ahead, WTO forecasts 195 million arrivals in this region by 2010 and 397 million arrivals by 2020, corresponding to an average increase of about 6.5% per year from 2000 to 2020, the highest regional growth rate. Of the 1.56 billion tourist arrivals forecast worldwide for 2020, the East Asia and Pacific region is expected to contribute about 25%. These projections are driven by expected large increases in China, Hong Kong and Macau and by strong growth in South East Asia.

In the case of Australia, international tourist arrivals are closely linked with the global international tourist market (although Australia occupies a comparatively minor quantitative position in the world travel market). Further, an expected increase in the Asia and Pacific region over the next decade is likely to benefit Australia through intraregional travel. In the ten years from 1989 to 1999, international tourist arrivals to Australia more than doubled from 2.1 million to 4.5 million visitors. However, although numbers increased by 10.6% to 4.9 million arrivals in 2000, subsequent years had decreases (2001 was -1.5% from 2000; 2002 was -0.3% from 2001) as a result of travellers' reluctance to travel in times of uncertainty.

As a result of the series of negative shocks to the travel sector since 2001, the Tourism Forecasting Council (TFC) expected international travel to Australia to fall by 5.3% to around 4.6 million visitors in 2003, the lowest since 1999 and the third year in a row that inbound travel has contracted. Nevertheless, the TFC suggested that inbound travel to Australia would increase by 9.8% to just over 5 million visitors in 2004, assuming that confidence for international travel returns. Further, assuming a continuation of the previous "normal" trend, international tourist arrivals are expected to grow at about 5% per annum to reach 6.8 million visitors in 2010. This represents a significant downward shift from the forecast 9.4 million visitors for 2010, as made in the similar TFC report immediately after 11 September.

Outbound travel was similarly forecast to fall significantly by 4.2% in 2003, but is expected to strongly recover in 2004, increasing by 8.7% assuming the usual confidence levels to travel return. Outbound travel is projected to reach 4.6 million resident departures by 2012, with average growth of 2.9% between 2002 and 2012. To put this trend in perspective in relation to its resource and greenhouse implications, a related CSIRO study of Australian tourism trends estimates that international air departures in 2020 would require about 230 petajoules per year for fuel. This represents about one quarter of the current requirements for the total transport task (passenger plus freight) for the Australian economy.

Projecting further ahead, the study suggests that by the year 2050, the energy required for international departures could exceed 400 PJ per year. Another study conducted by the CSIRO investigated Australian inbound tourism to 2020, but used a different set of modelling assumptions than the Tourism Forecasting Council. The more conservative forecast of 11.2 million arrivals by 2020 (compared with 4.2 million in 1996) serves to highlight the variability in visitor numbers that could be created by a worldwide economic recession, or sudden increases in oil prices.

Given the range of factors involved in forecasting tourism demand, it is not surprising to find quite different forecasts depending on the models and variables used. For example, the earlier mentioned forecast for Australian inbound tourism by the Tourism Forecasting Council projected 9.4 million tourist arrivals by 2010. This can be compared with the figure of 11.2 million arrivals by 2020 in the CSIRO study. The CSIRO study recognised the dangers of simple models in such a complex area, suggesting that the problem of unrepresented variables is often severe. Nevertheless it used a relatively simple model that explains about 90% of the variations in visitor numbers using GNP per capita, population, and settler ratios, to make projections for 2020. However, the authors comment: "at best, statistical models can find strong patterns in the data consistent with expert views on the nature of the industry and which may have some predictive value".

RAMIFICATIONS

Aviation travel is clearly inextricably bound up with larger economic and political processes, including that of economic globalisation-and in particular the globalisation of tourism. However, transport, and in particular aviation travel, as a subsystem of tourism, has been largely unexamined systemically, especially in relation to ecological sustainability. Rather, aviation is often viewed simply as a strong instrument for the promotion of economic globalisation. An analysis of the tourism literature suggests that it is primarily constructed within a framework emphasising business and economics.

Tourist travel (including air travel) is a major source of environmental problems, thus linking the notions of sustainable tourism and sustainable mobility. 40 to 60% of the environmental loads linked to tourism are from the transport of tourists between their homes and the tourist region, as well as from local transport within the destination area. In the case of aviation, Hoyer argues for strong measures, including environmental taxes, to reduce the volume of international tourist travel by aircraft. This is because of the increase in the global impacts of such activity and the large tourism contribution to such international and long-distance flights.

More radically, Hoyer argues for new forms of tourism other than those based on auto- and aeromobility, as well as questioning the priority given to time efficiency as a value. Such measures naturally are inimical to the objectives of the aviation industry. For example, the Scandinavian Airlines System (SAS) opposes the use of environmental taxation in spite of its notable efforts to reduce environmental impacts. Nevertheless, the management of SAS admits that future growth in air transport, largely linked to tourism, will only increase environmental impacts.

Later work focuses on the issue of increasing travel to international meetings and conferences as "one of the environmentally most worrying changes in the mobility of post-industrial society". The authors contrast the globalisation and regional competition issues that encourage cities and institutions to put themselves on the conference map, with the environmental and social consequences involved. The radiative forcing index for aviation points to a multiplier effect of at least 2.7 for CO_2 emissions from aircraft, meaning that for each individual conference participant a global warming impact results that is typically equivalent to at least one, if not two or more years of total mobility for all other purposes in terms of comparative impact, depending on the distance travelled.

Another study on international passenger travel to New Zealand found that national energy use would increase by 6% if international air travel were to be included in national inventories. This energy use corresponds to an additional 1.9 million tonnes of carbon dioxide emissions. Although concentrating on energy use and CO_2 emissions per se because of the uncertainties associated with the full impact of aircraft emissions, she does acknowledge that her approach is a conservative one and that the impacts on the atmosphere are possibly considerably underestimated. Recent policy discussion in the UK involving the Departments of Transport and Treasury and the Royal Commission on Environmental

Pollution confirms the likely underestimation inherent in Becken's methodology.

As part of a study by CSIRO on the opportunities and challenges for Australian tourism in the longer term, the primary energy and greenhouse gas emissions for the tourism sector were estimated at the national level. In 1995, tourism contributed around 80 million tonnes of CO_2 equivalent of greenhouse emissions. For comparative purposes, total industrial activity and personal consumption in Australia contributed 575 million tonnes of CO_2 equivalent greenhouse gases. Across a range of consumption categories linked to tourists, the largest category for primary energy consumption for both international and domestic tourists is air transport.

Two categories of tourist consumption, "air transport" and "recreation and other services" each account for around 23% of the total domestic and international tourist greenhouse emissions (or 46% of the total for both categories). The authors underline the significance of these findings given that the externalities of world greenhouse issues are increasingly likely to be internalised in the structure of every industry, and especially one in which transport and air travel are integrally involved. "Sustainable tourism" is therefore becoming a contested concept like sustainability, being interpreted differently by different groups with opposing values.

The latter challenge the paradigm on which economic, social and political development is based, questioning the values of society as much as those of tourism. Organisations such as the World Tourism Organization (WTO) are associated with the pole concerned with mass tourism and strong economic growth, and especially with the globalisation of economic activities such as the growth of international tourism and long-haul tourist travel. It is true of course that some of the language used by WTO is typical of the "reassurance" and "balance" orientation characteristic of sustainable development and sustainable tourism discourses.

For example, in a document on international tourism, WTO speaks of "the continued need to combine sound economic development with the protection of natural resources". Similarly, the need for limits on tourism development is acknowledged by reorienting the industry's priorities and practices towards an acceptable balance between viable growth and environmental sustainability over the long term. Tourism clearly counts as one of the most remarkable economic and social phenomena of the last century. It will undoubtedly keep this position for the century to come. Every year a bigger portion of the world population takes part in tourism activity and for the majority of countries tourism has developed as one of the most dynamic and fastest growing sectors of the economy.

Even after the events of 11 September, 2001, the World Tourism Organization looked forward to "a return of consumer confidence in the travel industry" as the desire to travel for leisure or business reasons is a "social paradigm ... now deeply embedded in our modern lifestyles". Nevertheless since the 1990s, the image of tourism has been changing, to some extent, from a "smokeless industry" to one implicated in an array of global and local ecological concerns. This is reflected in terms such as "eco-tourism", "green tourism", and "sustainable tourism" and in a number of recent books e.g. Holden and journals e.g. Journal of Sustainable Tourism.

Although some are anxious to present these alternative forms of tourism as more sustainable by labelling them "appropriate", "responsible", and "soft", Wheeller has argued that such labelling distracts us from addressing "the real problem of mass tourism-the massive volume and, globally, the growing absolute number of tourists", with all of its associated cultural and ecological impacts. The issue of the volume of tourists as an aspect of the transport subsystem within tourism is depicted in Figure 3.

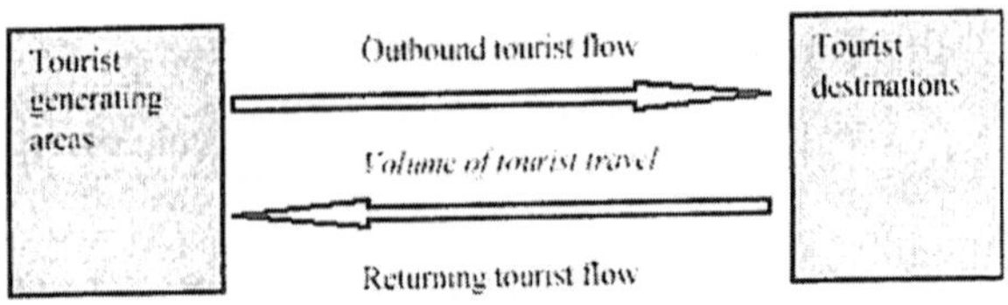

Figure 3. The tourism system: a transport perspective with volume of tourist travel.

Moreover, an OECD case study on tourism travel argues that the scale and extent of tourism-related travel are integrally linked with the rising number of air departures to far-off destinations. Combining the significant volume of people and demand pressure with an increasing propensity to travel further, as with long-haul holidays, is thus a prescription for significant ecological impact.

On the other hand, the Royal Commission on Environmental Pollution has also drawn attention to the particular problems associated with short-haul flights (800 km or less), which have a much higher proportional fuel use per passenger than medium- and long-haul flight distances.

The high rate of fuel burn during take-off and landing represents a disproportionate fuel usage for short flights, with for example, 20% of the fuel used for a 500 km flight between Stansted and Edinburgh, being required to get airborne and land. Such profligate fuel use is used to support policy arguments encouraging modal shifts, for example to rail, given the considerable environmental benefits achievable. The Commission suggests this approach both for domestic travel within the UK and for the shorter journeys to Europe. Sustainable tourism scenarios and principles as generally framed to date therefore do not appear to be getting to grips with the ecological ramifications of growth scenarios for the future.

Conventional Oil

Another major energy issue that has significant implications for aviation, in addition to the question of climate change, is the continuing availability of conventional oil. There is a growing literature pointing to a near to medium term supply problem. The main source of this view is a group of retired oil geologists freed from corporate commercial and political constraints e.g. Campbell and Laherrere, Deffeyes. Such a perspective is also increasingly appearing in a range of popular social and scientific analyses e.g. Heinberg, Rifkin. It is further supported by specialist groups such as the Oil Depletion Analysis Centre associated with the University of Reading in the UK, and in Australia at Murdoch University.

The above analyses essentially point to a near to medium term rapid decline in conventional oil production, a relatively modest contribution from non-conventional oils to partially offset conventional oil's decline, and a decline in conventional gas production from about 2020. Another experienced geoscientist Les Magoon has coined the term, the "Big Rollover", for the point in time when the world demand for conventional oil outstrips the capacity to produce it. This peak in production followed by a steady decline is generally estimated to be around the 2010 or thereabouts, although various estimates between 2003 and 2020 have been suggested.

Given the central role of oil in modern economies, and given that oil currently provides 90% of transport fuel, Magoon and others conclude that the arrival of such a time will be a major turning point in history. The critical issue is not an immediate running out of oil but rather the discontinuity created when humankind's ascent up the "oil production" mountain flips over to the descent down the mountain. A complex range of issues surrounds this issue, including the reliability of forecasting. For example, when M. King Hubbert in 1956 predicted correctly that oil production in the USA would peak in the early 1970s, almost everyone inside and outside the oil industry rejected his analysis.

Similarly, now that analysts have applied Hubbert's method to world oil production with an increasing consensus on an emerging oil crisis, such questions seem to be ignored by the popular press and mainstream politicians. This is partly due to the word "decline" being politically incorrect in the present culture of continuing growth. Against this contention, however, is the often-put argument that the cause of the 2003 war in Iraq was linked in part to an interest in longer-term influence over oil supplies and to the US transportation sector's heavy dependence on oil. With the arrival of the "Big Rollover", the geopolitical consequences of rising oil prices and the fact that demand will not be met, are likely to be far-reaching.

They include the likelihood of inflation, recession, and international tension, given that the remaining reserves are primarily in the Middle East. In addition, definitional problems including the reliability of official statistics, have been critiqued. Thus the notion of "proved reserves", for example, gives rise to "reserve growth", with OPEC misreporting its oil reserves because its quotas depend upon reported reserves. The Association for the Study of Peak Oil, a network of scientists in universities and government departments, particularly in Europe, is focusing on such complexity, and two international workshops have now been held, one in 2002 with a second one held in May 2003.

In contrast, a group of interests advising the US Government, including for example, the US Geological Survey, are still giving official projections for global oil supply for the next 25 years that are regarded as absurdly optimistic by the sources described above. Others in the "anti" group e.g. Adelman have critiqued the work of Campbell and Laherrere and Bentley, suggesting that their conclusions cannot be tested, as they draw on the proprietary and unpublished data base of Pertroconsultants (now called IHS). Nevertheless, it is significant that conservatively inclined bodies such as the International Energy Agency (IEA) prepared a paper for the G8 Energy Ministers' Meeting in 1998 that adopted a position akin to the Campbell and Laherrere work.

It forecast a peak in conventional oil of 78.9 million barrels per day in 2012. The IEA analysis assumes that the use of non-conventional oil expands rapidly after 2015 to meet the increase in demand for liquid fuels and to compensate for the decline in conventional oil production. However, the agency recognises that to produce large and increasing volumes of oil from non-conventional sources would require many major multi-billion dollar projects.

Those raising concerns most strongly about oil and gas depletion, on the other hand, argue that there are significant constraints preventing nonconventional oil from fully offsetting conventional oil's decline. These include: (a) non-conventional sources not coming on stream fast enough to fully compensate for the decline, (b) the sheer scale and cost of the mining and processing required, (c) significant environmental problems including a relative increase in greenhouse gases, and (d) questions related to net energy analysis.

In relation to aviation in particular, the Centre for Sustainable Transportation (CST) in Canada considers that the two factors likely to curtail the aviation growth envisaged by the industry are the need to curb greenhouse gas emissions and the lack of availability of low-cost aviation fuel, a consequence of the end of cheap oil. A more recent projection as part of the airport's new masterplan predicts a near trebling in passenger numbers between 2003 and 2023 to 68.3 million, with an associated 412,000 aircraft movements a year.

Further, Fleay is sceptical about the ongoing viability of tourism and the associated hospitality industry, given that these industries depend on cheap transport. The ramifications of rising oil prices for transport and tourism, including international air travel, are likewise highlighted in a CSIRO study of Australian tourism to the year 2020. The outcome of a detailed evaluation of aviation by the Intergovernmental Panel on Climate Change in relation to fuel options was that "there would not appear to be any practical alternatives to kerosene-based fuels for commercial jet aircraft for the next several decades".

In addition, this report and others indicate that the average fuel cost across the industry is about 11-15% of operating costs, but has been higher during times of high fuel prices (e.g. nearly 30% in the early 1980s). The high cost of fuel has also been a significant factor in poor operating profits. The global oil crisis in the early 1970s had long-term effects on the aviation industry, particularly in stimulating the development of more fuel-efficient aircraft, and it is acknowledged that the availability and cost of fuel will continue to exert strong pressures for fuel efficiency.

However, the growth in demand for commercial aviation has consistently exceeded increases in fuel efficiency, with the problems becoming more serious as efficiency improvements become more difficult to achieve. Based on past trends, further improvements in engine and airframe efficiency are likely to reduce fuel consumption per revenue passenger kilometre by 1% per year for the next 15 to 20 years. This contrasts with the anticipated long-term growth in commercial airline revenue passenger kilometres of 3 to 5% per year.

The crude oil shortfall is likely to restrict aviation traffic and growth, particularly in the next 50 years. In the shorter term (the next two decades), another study by the Institute of Air Transport suggests that the rising demand for jet fuel could exceed the maximum quantity obtainable by simple distillation, and that it may become necessary to produce part of the jet fuel required by the market by cracking heavy fuel. Hence, the production cost would inevitably go up. In summary, the report states: "there is a strong likelihood not only that the price of crude oil will increase, but the price of jet fuel will go up at an even faster rate".

The combination of the need to reduce greenhouse gas emissions, and the likely impact of oil depletion in the next two decades, is therefore likely to act as a very significant constraint on the growth of aviation. If, as often mooted, concerns about greenhouse gas emissions result in the application of a commercial aviation fuel tax in order to internalise the environmental costs of air travel, then the end of cheap oil would clearly further exacerbate the economic viability of airlines. Current aviation growth scenarios begin to look problematic, as the technology is so tied to oil, and in addition the introduction of alternatives such as hydrogen-powered aircraft, is likely to take decades. This is because of the lead-time required for new aircraft designs, incorporating, for example, the larger fuel tanks required for hydrogen.

In addition, new infrastructure for the production and supply of hydrogen would be required, and existing aircraft have a typical life expectancy of at least 25 years. The latter issue suggests that both kerosene and hydrogen fuel systems would need to be in operation simultaneously for a certain transition period. Although many industries may be able to adapt to ever-increasing oil prices, aviation appears to be particularly vulnerable and unable to substitute alternative fuel sources or to put new technologies in place in the necessary timeframe.

In the early 1970s, studies on alternative fuels were carried out by most of the major aircraft manufacturers in the USA, Europe and the former USSR. As the main driving force for these efforts was the oil price crisis in the 1970s, most of the activities were discontinued when oil prices declined again in the 1980s. Such activities have resumed in recent years with projects such as the German-Russian Project Cryoplane, inspired by the foreseeable depletion of oil and concerns about greenhouse gas emissions. It has been argued that liquid hydrogen produced on a renewable energy basis is the only candidate aviation fuel known today that would completely eliminate CO_2 emissions by aviation.

However, in addition to the unsolved questions related to new aircraft designs for hydrogen, the massive implications in regard to hydrogen production, storage and distribution are considered a major obstacle, likely to impede the introduction of hydrogen aircraft for several decades.

5

Travelling and Sustainable Tourism

The term 'consumption' is being increasingly incorporated into academic environmental discourse; the reports of international bodies; policy statements and documents by learned societies. Although sustainable consumption is not a popular concept with governments because of its potential threat to competitiveness and profitability, there has been some attention to the issue. The major cause of the continued deterioration of the global environment is the unsustainable pattern of consumption and production, particularly in industrialized countries, which is a matter of grave concern, aggravating poverty and imbalances.

In the UK and Europe, governments have initiated programs to build pro-environmental behaviours in households, capitalising on the work of the Global Action Plan (GAP). Again, the threatening nature of substantive changes in consumption patterns appears, as in the critique of the positivist assumptions underlying social-marketing techniques and educational-information campaigns, and the lack of attention to structural factors and institutional responsibilities. In 2001, the Organisation for Economic Cooperation and Development concluded that the environmental effects of current consumption patterns "remain a peripheral issue in most OECD countries, treated in an ad-hoc fashion".

Its OECD Environmental Outlook report provides an analysis of likely environmental changes to the year 2020 using data collected from across OECD countries (Organisation for Economic Cooperation and Development). Drawing on a Pressure-State-Response (PSR) framework for its analysis of environmental changes, the report uses a traffic light analogy to signal the degree of urgency for a range of pressures on the environment. The most urgent "red light" issues are those where recent trends have been negative and are expected to continue to be so to 2020.

Climate change as a result of greenhouse gas emissions is classified as one of the most important "red light" issues faced by OECD countries, with increased energy use and transport being prime contributors to greenhouse gas emissions. With transport, for example, the report concludes that motor vehicle kilometres travelled in OECD countries are expected to increase by 40% from 1997 to 2020 and that passenger air kilometres are expected to triple.

Transport is the growing in all regions of the world, with air travel generally growing faster than road travel. It is asserted that it is the fastest-growing source of greenhouse gas emissions and the area that most policy-makers find difficult to address. At a more macro level, the Environmental Outlook report acknowledges the underlying economic, social and technological factors driving the pressures on the environment. It concludes that the most significant drivers of environmental change (having both negative and positive effects) will be continued economic growth, the use of new technologies and changes in consumption patterns.

A more recent study on Household Tourism Travel across OECD countries underlines the fact that a narrow sectoral approach to consumption is more complex than a neat categorisation suggests. Thus tourism related travel is a significant source of transport energy use and carbon dioxide emissions, with the projected growth in such travel-especially long distance air travel-being expected to significantly increase the environmental impacts from this sector over the next 20 years.

Economic globalisation processes have engendered changes in tourism and travel markets, and the boundaries between tourism, travel, leisure and accommodation are now unclear. Thus airlines are increasingly part of global alliance groupings, with partners including international hotel groups, car rental companies, travel agents, leisure and entertainment businesses, and a range of other services including credit cards. The consumption web has become complex.

SUSTAINABILITY AND COMPLEXITY

Sustainable consumption is multifactorial and multidimensional in character, and requires for its understanding a transdisciplinary approach rather than a single discipline approach. The relationship between consumption and environment involves not only the physical aspects (often linked to environmental consequences), but also involves social, political, cultural and ethical questions. At a broader level, issues related to worldviews, pluralism and "paradigm co-existence" are important for facing the question of complexity. At the disciplinary level, the environmental and physical sciences thus describe consumption in terms of the transformation of energy and matter.

They emphasise the material implications of consumption, in view of the ecological limits to growth and concepts such as carrying capacity; conventional economists promote the maximisation of a person's consumption of goods and services, through the spending of money as the goal of life and as a means to happiness; and sociologists and anthropologists emphasise the social, symbolic and cultural meanings of consumption. As consumption is increasingly framed using a variety of discourses, there has been an associated interdisciplinary exchange of ideas on the issue.

At the conceptual level, the idea of "sustainable consumption" necessarily is part of the highly contested nature of the meaning of the concept "sustainability". The term "sustainable development" gained widespread support in 1987 with the publication of the Brundtland report A survey of the Web of Science database revealed an eightfold increase in the use of the term "sustainability" in journal articles published from 1990 to 1999. In contrast, in the researchers' own field of tourism the use of pertinent descriptors such as "tourism" only doubled over the same period.

The philosophical and ethical differences being expressed appear in the contrasting approaches taken in neoclassical (or conventional) economics and ecological economics. The maximally technocentric position seeks to maximise economic growth through unfettered free markets and resource exploitation. In contrast, the maximally ecocentric position is associated with a strong preservation ethic and with a reduced scale of economy being seen as imperative. This latter position, which is associated with deep ecology and social ecology, challenges values and principles underlying capitalist societies and attempts to tackle the root causes of unsustainability.

In between these extreme positions, a range of weak to strong sustainability positions has been posited, corresponding to various "light green" to "dark green" constructions of our relationships with nature. Here, modified economic growth characteristic of an accommodating position is more typical. One typical scheme for showing a range of conceptual positions along a spectrum of thought and practice is that used by harper , shown in Figure 1. The major attitudinal division is between "environmentalists" and "contrarians".

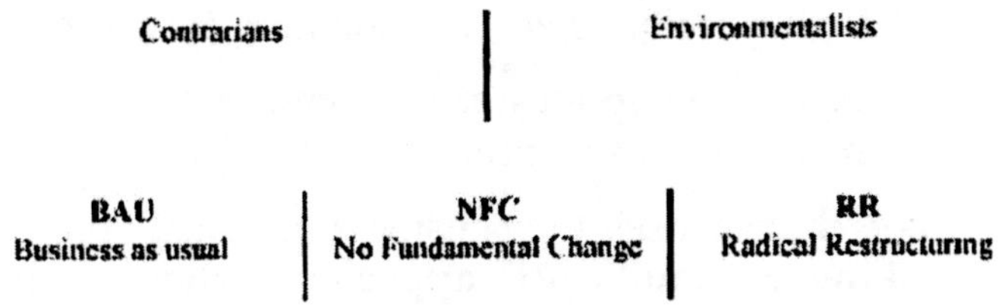

Figure 1. Map of "faultlines" between contrasting perceptions of our relationships with nature

In policy terms, there is common ground between the moderate wings of each side, giving three broad policy classes, namely: business as usual, no fundamental change, and radical restructuring. On the contrarian side, Harper cites several leading "prophets of boom" who are advocates of economic growth and contend that technological progress, increased economic efficiency, and new substitution opportunities will overcome any constraints and their implications for business e.g. Kahn, Beckerman, and Simon.

Most governments support economic growth, including the growth of affluence, and technological innovation, without fundamental challenge to the modern consumerist project. On the environmental side, Harper draws a policy faultline between the "respectable" mainstream majority seeking solutions broadly within the present framework of consumer culture and those who believe that radical restructuring (RR) of the basic fabric and aspirations of modern societies is necessary.

The latter group generally seeks limits on the principal factors underlying the environmental impact of human activity. Well-known RR names associated with particular factors include for example:

— population growth

— changing technology and economic structure

— changing conceptions of economic growth and levels of material consumption.

Harper characterises the "business as usual" proponents as taking a "hands off" approach, whereas the "no fundamental change" supporters tend to ignore population and consumption, and focus on technological innovation. In contrast, "radical restructuring" theorists highlight consumption, putting them at odds with the "modern project". These various analyses of sustainability and economics reflect the current range of environmental discourses.

How the debate on sustainability is framed in each discourse, as well as the key metaphors underlying the various storylines, determine how the problem is defined, which agents are valued, and where the solutions lie. For example, the concept "sustainable development", although considered by many to be an oxymoron, is most often linked to a more technocratic form of "environmentally benign growth". Related to this is the idea of ecological modernisation of industrial economies, which redefines the ecological crisis as a problem to be overcome by "technical and procedural innovation".

Eco-efficiency becomes the driving force for industrial innovation, and continued growth is regarded as part of the solution. The associated discourse thus involves a "rhetoric of reassurance" where we can have it all, including economic growth, environmental conservation and social justice. Thus, sustainable development may be regarded as "the late twentieth century expression for 'progress' ". Such a view tends to be the position of most in governments and business.

The economist's and technologist's approaches to sustainable consumption have been overly influential in policymaking processes. One reason is that such disciplines mirror the discourse, and therefore only people using these frameworks are seen as legitimate contributors to policy discussions. However, these disciplines underestimate the complexity of the world, and are politically attractive by virtue of being able to provide what appear to be easy solutions.

In contrast, Murphy and Cohen argue for more holistic policymaking, without eschewing technological innovation as one valuable way of tackling consumption related issues. On the other hand, the conservative sustainable development approach to be ethically "weak" as it clings to a modernist view of progress. This position accepts trade-offs between economic growth and environmental protection, and sustainability objectives are founded on more efficient energy and resource use and ecologically benign technologies.

The difference between the dominant (light green) and alternative (deep green) paradigms has been characterised as involving a radical ethical shift in the way humans relate to technology and the natural environment. It is the vast difference between these contrasting paradigms that is at the heart of many environmental controversies. To emphasise this difference, the economic strategy underlying the deep green approach has been characterised by various scholars as "authentic development", "ecodevelopment", "reverential development", and "alternative development", in order to redefine the term "development".

Another useful schema arguing for an expanded view of sustainability acknowledges not only the physical and socio-political aspects of sustainability, but also its non-material dimensions, which are often neglected. Such schemes have also been used to broaden frameworks of change to include personal and psychological issues as well as social and environmental aspects.

A further related and pertinent area of literature promotes the idea that the evolution of human consciousness is a critical determinant of sustainability. For example, the case for a new consciousness is argued in 3rd Millennium, the first report of the Club of Budapest. The often quoted Einstein remark that we cannot solve a problem with the same kind of thinking that gave rise to the problem, underlines the need for "new ways of perceiving and visioning ourselves, others, nature and the world around us". Without a new consciousness, the report asserts that it is unlikely that human beings will be able to avert deepening economic, social and cultural conflicts and ecological breakdowns. In broad terms the Club's report calls for:

— consciousness evolution by evolving human consciousness, with habit and inertia no longer being appropriate to the critical choices facing humanity

— evolution not just of technologies, but also of human perceptions, empathies, values and priorities

— a shift in the nature of human attention, empathy and concern from an ego-, business-, and nation-centred approach to a broader human-, nature-, and planetcentred one.

This shift in human consciousness is well underway, and that the most distinctive feature of an emerging paradigm is not technological change, but a change in human consciousness. On the one hand is a materialistic worldview that excludes ideas of spirituality and the sacred from consciousness, and where "human beings are ravishing the earth and massacring one another with instruments of ever greater technological sophistication in the quest for power, dominance, and material satisfaction".

On the other hand is a transpersonal vision that "enables human beings to discover their inseparability from all life" and where "we may again discover the sacred in ourselves and nature". Similarly, Harman considers that at the present time humanity is in the middle of a shift in its prevailing assumptions from an M-1 metaphysic to an M-3 metaphysic, more closely allied to the "perennial philosophy" of the world's spiritual traditions. To simplify discussion, Harman uses three possible metaphysics:

— M-1 Materialistic monism (matter giving rise to mind),

— M-2 Dualism (matter plus mind), and

— M-3 Transcendental monism (mind giving rise to matter).

Rather than setting out to prove the validity of a metaphysic, however, he argues that an M-3 metaphysic seems to provide the best fit for understanding the totality of human experience.

One significant objection reflects postmodern theorists' suspicions of any grand narrative, with their possible totalitarian leanings and associated dangers of naïvely Utopian frameworks. Defending the countervailing concept of diversity, Galtung and Inayatullah compare and contrast the work of 20 macrohistorians, encompassing theories of linear, cyclical and spiral patterns of change.

In the USA, a national survey in 1995 identified what was described as a new force for cultural change, using the term "integral culture". A core group of "cultural creatives" constituting about 10% of the population subscribe to values encompassing ecological sustainability, self-actualisation and spiritual practice, and issues of social conscience for the making of a better world.

Another group of "green cultural creatives", comprising 13% of the US adult population, share similar high levels of ecological and social concern with the "core cultural creatives", but give lower priority to spiritual or psychological growth. Although it is not entirely clear to what extent such changes in values are translated into behavioural changes, studies on downshifting indicate that an increasing number of people are willing to pursue voluntary, long-term, lifestyle changes that involve accepting significantly less income and consuming less.

An Australia Institute survey conducted in 2002 found that 23% of Australian adults aged 30-59 have downshifted in the last 10 years. The various reasons downshifters give include the desire to lead a more balanced and fulfilled life, wanting more quality time with their families, and the desire to live a less materialistic and more sustainable lifestyle.

The field of critical futures studies is in accord with these changes occurring at the individual level, and notes the changing ideas across the range of institutional, civilisational and global fronts. The broad shift in ideas underlying an emerging paradigm is typically that shown in table 1.

Table 1. Comparison between declining and resurgent worldviews Adapted from Slaughter

Ideas in decline	Resurgent ideas
Industrial worldview	Renewed worldview
Nature a resource	Nature a community
Full employment	Redefine employment
Development = progress	Revised model of development
Growth is good	Qualitative growth

Exploitation	Sustainability
Technology is neutral	Technology has embedded social and political interests
Dominance of nation state	Decline of nation state
Subject/object	Unity of subject and object
Loss of sacred	Recovery of sacred
Short-term thinking	Long-term thinking
Lack of foresight	Wide implementation of foresight

Similarly, from a range of possible, probable and preferable futures, a report of the Global Scenario Group posits a "great transition" scenario of a sustainable and desirable future emerging from new values, a revised model of development and the active engagement of civil society. Such a scenario assumes conscious (as opposed to conspicuous) consumption sensitive to ecological concerns. It suggests an "economics of permanence" in keeping with ecological sustainability, and replaces the concept of "consumers" with that of "layered beings" having a variety of material and non-material needs.

Given the complexity of the issues raised so far, it is useful to consider two models for thinking about these issues in a more holistic way, and for subsequently evaluating arguments from policy analysis and futures studies. Wilber's four quadrant classification applies to the interior and exterior of the individual and collective as shown in Figure 2. Although the figure shown has been simplified so as to exclude the stages of the holarchies linked to each of the four quadrants, one of Wilber's key claims is that all the quadrants are linked and cross-correlated.

Thus, higher or deeper stages of consciousness development will be reflected in behavioural, cultural and social system areas as well. People may be sitting in their favourite quadrant, so to speak, and miss the wider transformations being manifested in all four quadrants.

	INTERIOR	EXTERIOR
INDIVIDUAL	Interior-individual (consciousness) (experiential) I	It Exterior-individual (behaviour) (physical)
COLLECTIVE	We Interior-collective (worldviews) (cultural)	It Exterior-collective (social systems) (socio-political)

Figure 2. Wilber's four quadrant model of the cosmos

Wilber acknowledges the progress associated with modernity, normally equated with Western scientific civilisation since the Enlightenment, but considers that one downside of the Enlightenment paradigm has been its preoccupation with the right-hand column of exterior considerations. This is reflected in an inflated concern with the physical, behavioural and "objective". Wilber's model provides a more inclusive approach, by also addressing sustainability in the non-material sense. This includes both the individual or experiential aspects (upper left quadrant), and the collective interior or cultural aspects (lower left quadrant).

The integrative nature of the model implies that the emerging paradigm involves both a change in consciousness and a change in institutions-and in the sense that "trans" means beyond, it is both trans-rational and trans-industrial. That is, modes of consciousness beyond rationality are also reflected in techno-economic structures that move beyond industrialisation. Further, Tarnas suggests that "the evolution of paradigm shifts is an archetypal process, rather than merely either a rational-empirical or a sociological one", and therefore such shifts occur both subjectively and objectively.

In an analogous way, pathology in any one quadrant reverberates through all four quadrants. As Wilber states: "we are fast approaching an understanding that sees individual 'pathologies' as but the tip of an enormous iceberg that includes worldviews, social structures, and cultural access to depth". A second valuable model is Norgaard's framework for understanding development as a coevolutionary process between social and environmental systems (Figure 3). The social systems encompass the knowledge, values, organisation and technology systems, which coevolve with each other, and with the environmental systems.

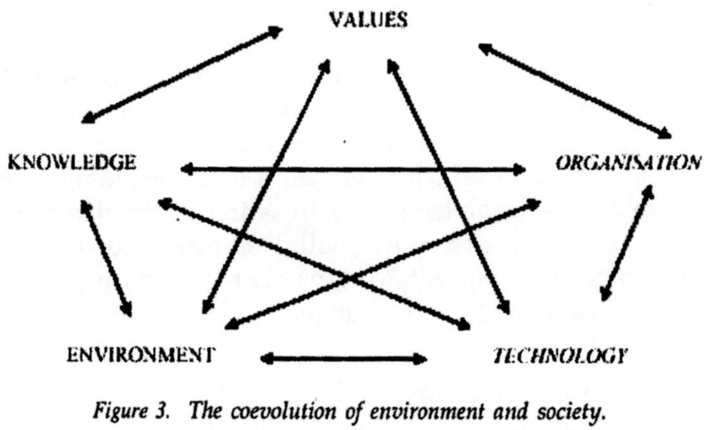

Figure 3. The coevolution of environment and society.

A number of observations from this model are useful in thinking about sustainable consumption. First, each system is related to each of the others, but is also changing and interacting with the others. Thus the coevolving nature of these systems and their relationships means that change occurs in unforeseeable ways. The model thus challenges the thinking underlying modernity, given that it does not facilitate prediction and control.

Second, there is currently an overemphasis on institutional structures such as global economics and the use of technologies (symbolised by the labels in italics in Figure 3), thus compromising a consideration of values. Norgaard believes that all the systems need to be considered. Further, he also argues that there is denial of the interconnections between people and nature and declares that "the whole Western construct of choice, of weighing options, and of conflict between the individual and the group follows from the premise of atomism and individualism".

Hence efforts to promote "green consumption" at the individual level can fail to see the broader picture or appreciate the structuring of "choice" itself. A third way in which the coevolutionary framework facilitates a critique of modernity is in acknowledging that industrial social systems have coevolved with the use of fossil hydrocarbons. The effect of this strong emphasis on fossil hydrocarbons has been to transfer the environmental impacts to other people, and "expanded the temporal and spatial dimensions of our interactions and coevolution with nature". Thus knowledge, organisation, technology and value systems are now being challenged by the ramifications of our interactions with nature, especially with the issue of climate change.

IPAT and Consumption

A useful, although overly simplified, identity (I = PAT) provides a helpful starting point for discussing a range of factors that are determinants of environmental pressure. The equation states that environmental impact (I) is a product of population size (P), affluence or consumption per capita (A) and technology (T). Although the formula and its limitations continue to stimulate debate, it is valuable for considering the multiplicative effect of population, consumption and technology in determining environmental impact, and in considering the relative roles of consumption and production.

For example, if population increases by 42% and consumption by 100%, then the equation can be used to calculate the reduction in T required to hold the environmental impact constant. That is, if P = 1.42 and A = 2.00, then I = 1 requires T = 0.35. In the case of car exhaust emissions, emissions per kilometre would need to fall 65% to accommodate increased numbers of people driving further distances. In the USA, the rising population of about 1% per year continues to offset roughly the efficiency gains of motor vehicles.

Thus, the issue of demand for products and services continuing to increase (A) often more than offsets the efficiency and productivity gains (T). Jevons foresaw this effect in 1865, suggesting that making coal burning more efficient would result in increased coal use, as the improved efficiency led to more economic uses of coal. The Jevons Principle is now used to describe this effect of technological advances more generally.

However, when population (P) and rising incomes (A) are taken into account over the same period, the reductions in resource use brought about through improved energy efficiency (T) are offset by the adverse environmental impacts of population and per capita consumption. A review of sustainable consumption and production for the Earth Summit in 2002 concludes that globally, many of the environmental and resource impacts of production and consumption have worsened in the last 25 years.

Especially in industrial countries, that environmental problems are increasingly linked to consumption rather than production patterns. That is, the technological solutions applied in industry have been offset by rising global incomes per capita (A), with more resource use and pollution caused by activities in the transport, residential and commercial sectors.

Aggregate materials use is more or less stable for some types of materials, but is rising with others such as paper, plastic and composites. Michaelis acknowledges that one of the most environmentally significant trends is the rapid growth in road and air traffic and the associated greenhouse gas emissions-in spite of the energy efficiency improvements in both cases. Even advocates of economic growth and the use of eco-efficiency measures such as Kageson acknowledge that one of the most difficult environmental problems to bring under control in the next 20 years is that of curbing carbon dioxide emissions.

Transport is a sector where particularly strong policies are needed, with the aviation sector putting considerable pressure on the environment in spite of its small share of overall passenger traffic. The I = PAT equation thus underlines the fact that although technology (T) has a significant role to play in policy development, consumption related issues (A) need to be understood in their own terms and not as determined by technology. For example, Potter and Skinner critique a technological perspective often taken in studies of transport futures. Drawing on an OECD study exploring the reduction of transport emissions to sustainable levels by 2030, they note that 30-40% of the reduction could be achieved by technical measures.

The remaining 60-70% reduction needs to come from demand management approaches, which depend on political, cultural and social innovation. In other words, the eco-efficiency discourse is tied primarily to supply-side and production debates. Discussion of consumption issues, however, addresses the long-standing denial of the social dimensions of environmental problems, and is concerned, for example, with issues such as identity creation and the structural/infrastructural constraints on consumption.

With respect to technology, the trend towards "radical resource productivity" using Factor Ten and Factor Four strategies is clearly an important part of future approaches to systems change in production and consumption. The fields of industrial ecology and what is described as industrial transformation research are investigating revolutionary advances in design and technology in the areas of energy and material flows and in the ways in which information and communication can substitute for energy and materials.

Underpinning the technological worldview, however, is often an uncritical technological optimism. Ausubel, for example, has catalogued the vast technological improvements in the last 100 years in fields such as computing, communications, transport and energy and asserts that the global warming debate has neglected and underestimated the importance of technical change in reducing greenhouse gases and adapting to climate change.

In the same way that propulsion of aircraft has improved by one hundred thousand times in 90 years, these researchers are optimistic about technological trajectories linked to decarbonisation and "envision a transport system producing zero emissions and sparing the surface landscape". They support the prospects for 21st century "green mobility" based on historical evolution and declare: "We can clearly see its elements: cars, powered by fuel cells; aeroplanes, powered by hydrogen; and maglevs, powered by electricity, probably nuclear. The future looks clean, fast, and green".

Conversely, others strongly critique the "technological dynamic that acknowledges no limits" and believe that "a combination of low-level human motivations and highpowered technology" is likely to be "a continuing disaster". The unquestioned assumption that constantly evolving technology is critical to the future and "progress" needs to be balanced by asking questions such as "Is technological change taking us where we want to go?" and "What effect does it have on our social, political and moral imagination?".

Orr further highlights the complexity of the Earth and its life support systems, and argues that such complexity can never be safely "managed" with science and technology. Rather, advances in knowledge carry with them the risks of advances in ignorance, as occurred with the initial discovery of chlorofluorocarbons (CFCs) in 1929 and the much later discovery of their impact on stratospheric ozone.

The initial ignorance of the potential impacts of these chemicals became "a critical life-threatening gap in human understanding of the biosphere". More pragmatically, Geels and Smit have identified a range of pitfalls linked to future explorations of technological developments. For example, initial promises are often set high to attract attention from financial sponsors and to stimulate agenda setting promises as part of strategic gains. A case in point is the impact of tele-conferencing on business travel with expectations of much decreased travel as a result of the contacts made by tele-conferencing.

However, both substitution and generation effects have been noted with tele-conferencing, so that the initial societal gains promised by the technology then need to be scaled down. The technologically optimistic claims that more and more hydrogen will fuel aircraft need to be contrasted with a major study by the Intergovernmental Panel on Climate Change, which underlines the difficulty of any easy "technical fix" for air travel.

The technology is still tied to oil, and there do not appear to be any practical alternatives to kerosene-based fuels for several decades. In the medium term, the future growth in air traffic is expected to far outstrip any efficiency gains. In addition, the specialist National Research Council Committee on Aeronautics Research and Technology for Environmental Capability notes that the rate of technological innovation is insufficient to address the aircraft noise, carbon dioxide (CO_2) and nitrogen oxide (NOx) emissions generated by increasing aircraft movements.

With respect to the use of hydrogen in aircraft, hydrogen engines are still in the R&D stage and it is not clear when or whether they will be introduced on a larger scale. Some suggest that large scale hydrogen in aviation is not likely in the next 50 years, and that the pressure on declining oil stocks may lead to the manufacture of a kerosene-like fuel from other sources such as oil shales and natural gas. Hence the high expectations in relation to this technology may need to be scaled down.

Even if effective substitution strategies such as hydrogen powered aircraft could be produced on a broad scale, this approach may still not get to grips with Orr's question above: "Is technological change taking us where we want to go?" For example, such aircraft, although not producing climate changing carbon dioxide emissions, could leave existing tourism and consumption patterns in place, or still have significant global warming consequences from the water vapour contrails left in their paths, as water vapour acts as a greenhouse gas too.

With respect to the population (P) factor in the IPAT equation, it is significant that for the past 25 years many affluent nations, backed by a number of professional scientific associations, have framed global environmental problems as arising from high rates of population growth. This allowed the industrialised countries to place the prime responsibility for remedying environmental dilemmas with the developing countries, thus diverting attention from the environmental consequences of lifestyles (A) in the rich countries.

The United Nations Development Program, on the other hand, highlighted global inequalities in consumption and resource use as the central issue, rather than overpopulation per se. Thus, this report asserts that 20% of the world's people in the highest income countries account for 86% of total private expenditure, with the poorest 20% of people accounting for a tiny 1.3%. The pattern is reflected in a range of statistics. The richest fifth:

— consume 45% of all meat and fish, the poorest fifth 5%

— consume 58% of total energy, the poorest fifth less than 4%

— have 74% of all telephone lines, the poorest fifth 1.5%

— consume 84% of all paper, the poorest fifth 1.1%

— own 87% of the world's vehicle fleet, the poorest fifth less than 1%.

Others have characterised the differences in consumption patterns by dividing the world's population into three socioecological classes. The richest 20% ("overconsumers") typically travel by car and air, eat high fat, meat based diets, and use pre-packaged and disposable products; another 20% live in absolute deprivation, travel by foot or donkey, eat nutritionally inadequate diets and drink contaminated water; the remaining 60% of the world's people are classified as "sustainers", living relatively lightly.

They typically travel by bicycle and public service transport; eat healthy diets of grains, vegetables and some meat; and drink clean water and generally use unpackaged foods. These inequitable consumption patterns have also been expressed numerically using the ecological footprint concept. Illustrative national averages in hectares (ha) per person are USA (9.6), Australia (9.4), Canada (7.2), Germany (4.6), Italy (4.2), China (1.4), India (1.0), and Bangladesh (0.7). If everyone at present on Earth adopted the same lifestyle as the average North American or Australian, Rees concludes that the land required to support this level of resource use would require three more planets.

The challenge facing the North and South in the decades to come in order to avoid "overshoot and collapse" lies in answering the question: "How can all people enjoy satisfying lives within an average of no more than 1.8 ha per person?". The scale and patterns of development are an important component of answering such a question. 20% of the world's people in rich countries account for 53% of carbon dioxide emissions, whereas the poorest fifth of the world's people contribute only 3%.

Brazil, China, India, Indonesia and Mexico are among the developing nations with the highest emissions, although their large populations mean that their per capita emissions are still small. The USA and Australia represent the extreme of overconsumption at more than 20 tonnes of carbon dioxide per person per year, whereas China's per capita emissions are less than three tonnes and India's less than one tonne. Thus, Australia's per capita emissions are more than 20 times higher than India's emissions.

The inequities of the patterns of global consumption highlight the need for the richest 20% of people to significantly reduce their resource consumption and for the poorest 20% to achieve consumption levels that will adequately contribute to human development. Wackernagel suggests that the richest segment of humanity needs to reduce its resource throughput by 6% every year-a reduction much more rapid than the Kyoto Protocol CO_2 reduction targets.

On the other hand, the South's carbon dioxide emissions, propelled by both population growth and expanding industrialisation, are raising the carrying capacity dilemmas revealed by ecological footprint analysis. China's fossil fuel emissions are second to the USA, and India's emissions have surged by nearly 50% since 1990.

In relation to the consumption of aviation travel, industrialised country airlines accounted for 80% of air traffic in 1995 and are the primary focus here. Nevertheless, it is pertinent to note that developing country contributions are growing rapidly. For example, Boeing projects that China will continue its rapid aviation development in the 21st century and will eclipse all other aviation markets except the United States. Specifically, a market for 1,790 new aircraft valued at $US 137 billion is forecast for the next 20 years. This is linked to a forecast average growth rate of 9% per year for China's domestic market over the 20 year period, compared with an average growth rate of 4.8% per year for world air travel.

Although it has been argued that the effects of population growth can be offset by changes in consumption habits and more efficient technologies, an Australia Institute study shows that Australia's population growth has been one of the main factors driving growth in domestic greenhouse gas emissions. A large proportion of Australia's recent population growth can be attributed to high rates of immigration. What is relevant for Chinese industrialisation processes (and in particular the aviation growth example) are the difficulties created when both population and resource use are increasing.

As Turton and Hamilton comment: "Changing energy-dependent lifestyles and shifting away from fossil fuels are hard enough without the added pressure of a rapidly growing population". For China, the probability of reaching a peak population within the next two decades is still low owing to its relatively young age structure. However, improvements in probabilistic forecasting indicate that by 2040 the probability of the population peaking becomes greater than 50%.

Globalisation, in its often-used sense of "economic globalisation", is strongly associated with the processes of expanded commodification and consumer capitalism, furthering the "growth of transworld capitalism". Although the instrumental processes of globalisation are often referred to-such as the spread of trade, the growth of transnational corporations, and the power of international financial markets-some e.g. Hamilton contend that the ideology of growth and consumer capitalism are central defining characteristics. As he says:

> Globalisation represents not just the export and imposition of economic policies built on neo-liberal orthodoxy. It represents the export of a culture and a psychological disposition based on growth, compulsive consumption and the exploitation of the natural world.

An example pertinent to this thesis concerns tourism. In contrast to "travellers" of earlier generations, vastly greater numbers of "tourists" are encouraged to buy packaged and branded products, with the advertising of "exotic" places regarded as an important tool of the capitalist enterprise. Air transport has been critical for the expansion of tourism on such a large scale, and shopping malls attached to airports have helped embed shopping as a core ritual of tourism.

Advertising is promulgated through transnational mass media, and a global event such as the Olympic games has become as much a "gathering of the brands" as a "gathering of the nations". From another perspective, social democrats argue that although "globophobia may constitute a satisfying political response to the complex challenges of globalisation for some ... it does not constitute a credible policy response".

This position does not uncritically accept neo-liberal economic ideology, but does acknowledge "the positive contribution that economic globalisation is delivering to global security, development and society". In doing this, Rudd notes that the "real multiplier" of economic globalisation has been the revolution in transport and communications technologies. Hence, "the global compression of transaction time and space is acting to create a genuinely global market, arguably for the first time in economic history". This stance also acknowledges the negative impacts of globalisation, and favours a reformist policy approach.

Scholte's approach is similar, but acknowledges the significant challenge such a pathway represents, given the deep ideological and material roots underpinning laissez-faire, market led globalisation. More radical critiques of globalisation are not supported, given that a reversal of globalisation looks impractical in the short or medium term, and given that such critiques offer only "fairly vague and insufficiently convincing visions of alternative futures".

More specific reform policy measures draw on other meanings given to the term "globalisation". Thus "public order globalisation" refers to governments working together to solve common problems, and could include, for instance, suprastate mechanisms to reduce environmental degradation that go well beyond the existing measures. Another example is the introduction of progressive global taxes, such as the so-called "Tobin tax", which would impose a charge on foreign exchange transactions.

A further connotation for globalisation, "popular globalisation", points to a much greater role for global civil society. Although "free trade" and "trade liberalisation" are very much part of neo-liberal orthodoxy, an "ecological trade" approach based on ecological economics, questions "the whole project of free trade". If growth is to occur, it has to be "decoupled" from growth practices that are contrary to ecological sustainability and social justice.

Consumption Environmental Issues

The issues of ecological thinking and values, and behaviour change in relation to sustainable consumption constitute extensive areas of research. One pertinent example is an OECD project conducted on sustainable consumption and individual travel behaviour. A strong message from the report is that travel behaviour is only marginally related to fundamental values and preferences. Rather, travel patterns and levels are more likely to result from a combination of habits and circumstances.

The individual behavioural aspects of travel were de-emphasised in the report, with individual travel behaviour seen as constrained within a wider socio-cultural web of institutions such as the media, the retail sector, industry and governments. Thus the report concludes that these higher-order actors are best targeted, as policy measures focusing only on individuals in these networks will most likely fail to bring about substantial shifts in travel behaviour.

The difficulties in tackling consciousness change as a change strategy are also borne out by comparing models used to understand responsible environmental behaviour on the one hand, and the travel decision process on the other. Responsible environmental behaviour has been linked to a variety of personality factors, and also depends on the individual knowing that a problem exists, before he or she can intentionally act on a particular environmental problem.

In addition, an individual must possess knowledge of the courses of action available to address the problem. Further, there are a variety of situational factors such as economic constraints, and social pressures to choose differing actions, which may counteract or strengthen other variables in the model. A typical "consumer behaviour" model of the travel decision process, on the other hand, frames the issues in terms of customer goals, travel opportunities, communications effort, and other variables such as the cost and time involved, assessment of travel risks, and previous travel experience.

Comparison of these models reveals the range of issues involved in decision-making processes. For example, the consumer behaviour model includes as an important element various travel stimuli such as advertising and promotion, and indicates where marketing action can be used to influence the decision-making process. The responsible environmental behaviour model in contrast raises the question: At what point will a person forego economic and other personal benefits to preserve the integrity of the environment? Some social science research on environmental consciousness and behaviour reveals that there is a dilemma between the common good and individual cost-benefit calculations, and that this has an effect on environmental behaviour.

Brand contends that the classical assumption that a high level of environmental knowledge leads to high environmental consciousness, and consequently to matching environmental behaviour, is not supported by the empirical findings. Rather, because of a variety of situational and infrastructural factors, environmental consciousness has been shown to account for not more than 10-20% of variance of (mostly) self-reported behaviour.

Thus, for example, the lifestyles of a number of older, immobile, traditionally thrifty people who show no pronounced environmental consciousness, is better (at least in terms of impact), than those of environmentally conscious, in many ways ecologically correct, academics who are highly mobile in pursuit of work or leisure. Similarly, Gatersleben and Vlek's study of Dutch consumers in the context of household metabolism and consumption in Europe found that:

— Dutch consumers will keep on buying consumer goods as long as they have the (increasing) opportunity and ability to do so.

— Most respondents considered household consumer behaviour should become more environmentally sound, except for moving to a smaller house and taking holidays closer to home. However, this generally did not motivate them to change their behaviour, even in those people who were more aware than others of the environmental impacts of their behaviour. For example, respondents agreed that it was necessary to reduce use of the car, but judged it only slightly possible to do so.

— Income and household composition were shown to be the most important variables influencing consumer behaviour, with level of education having a minimal effect.

The effect of positive environmental values is constrained by the influence of prevailing incentives or disincentives to adopt sustainable practices. Environmental attitudes have much less effect on behaviour when external incentives or disincentives are strong. That is, the more difficult, time-consuming or costly the behaviour, or if the behaviour is not required or tangibly rewarded, the less the influence of pro-environmental attitudes is on that behaviour being adopted.

For example, forgoing the convenience of a private car, especially in cities constructed around this form of transport, is a disincentive in conflict with pro-environmental desires to use more sustainable public transport forms. Therefore, as suggested in Maskit's critique of deep ecology and the problem of consumption, policy changes appear to be needed to force even those who "know better" to behave in a way that is commensurate with their beliefs.

Because "the practical effects of Self-realisation may lag behind the transformations in a way that Naess does not acknowledge", Maskit argues that policy changes are necessary for modifying our behaviours. This returns the emphasis to politics, as expressed in particular in the sixth point of the deep ecology platform (DEP), namely the need for deep changes in policies affecting basic economic, technological and ideological structures.

The relationship between policy changes and people's consciousness can be further clarified by considering a typical model for environmental education, which usually focuses on factors such as awareness, understanding, values, and taking action. The understanding segment of the four-stage environmental education model is important, as such an understanding influences the potential remedies for problems. It also demonstrates the disadvantages of incorrect perceptions.

For example, an extensive study of mental and cultural models of people in the USA, especially in relation to climate change, revealed the common misconception that such change is caused by the ozone hole. Similarly, energy efficiency was poorly understood and rarely mentioned as part of the solution to global warming. Surveys in Europe, on the other hand, have demonstrated a better understanding of renewable energy and energy conservation, but as in the USA, find the misapplication of the ozone hole model to global climate change. If most people support a cultural model inappropriately, majorities then support policies that are unlikely to be effective.

For example, banning CFC spray cans is incorrectly seen as more effective than energy efficiency in preventing global warming. It is apparent that although environmental educators have enjoyed successes, often their messages have limited success, or even fail. The complex nature of global environmental problems such as global warming is one barrier, with the causes and consequences being large in scope and distant across time and space, which obscures individual and social perceptions.

Burke thus concludes that the "dilemma of the commons", where the dilemma is between maximising individual benefits and avoiding collective ruin, does not arise, because of users' lack of knowledge of the collective costs. Rather, the costs of modern resource use are likely to be misinterpreted and marginalised in daily behaviour, if not altogether ignored. Although committed to a social learning approach, Milbrath also acknowledges the strong barriers to social learning and social change.

Given the deeply embedded nature of belief systems together with the reinforcement of dominant belief systems every day through activities such as modern advertising, he concludes that the presentation of research findings and reasoning is insufficient for social learning. Although a rational approach is helpful, it is seldom persuasive in itself. Hobson similarly critiques programs based on filling the public "information deficit" surrounding environmental issues as offering an "impoverished view of the complexity of human-social engagement", and suggests that the assumed direct link between information and behaviour is based on positivist models of behaviour change.

These observations were borne out in the earlier mentioned survey of initiatives to promote sustainable consumption in Australia. The levels of success for initiatives that relied on information alone were low, although the use of promotion combined with educational efforts improved outcomes to a degree. Success levels were high with obligatory or coercive initiatives where compliance was mandatory (or perceived to be so), or avoidance was difficult, as people had no choice but to act in an environmentally responsible way.

A more sophisticated way of initiating change at the social learning level is found in the Global Action Plan (GAP) groups involving discussion and support within community networks over a number of months. What is critical here is a shift from "practical consciousness" to "discursive consciousness". Routine and habitual consumption is likely to involve practical consciousness that is rarely questioned, whereas a change in consumption practices is facilitated by debate about behaviours taken for granted.

For example, the global warming issue can include discussion of the implications for those in industrialised countries of the current internationally inequitable pattern of greenhouse gas emissions. This leads to the idea of a "greenhouse gas budget" that is both ecologically sustainable and globally equitable. Lenzen and Smith's arguments to achieve global equity imply a figure of 3.5 tonnes of carbon dioxide per capita per year, thus requiring drastic reductions in Australia and the USA. Questions about what is responsible travel behaviour confront firstly the increasing number of tourists and their environmental impacts, as expressed in the equation E = NB, where E is environmental impact, N is the number of people, and B is their behaviour.

Further, the complex nature of global environmental problems such as global warming and the range of situational and infrastructural barriers to appropriate action underline the difficulties involved in targeting individual actions. With respect to individual change, intensive community based programs that involve deeper questioning, and a discursive review of habitual consumption patterns, appear to be the most effective. In addition to initiatives such as the Global Action Plan, transformative learning experiences of this deeper kind have been associated with fundamental changes in perspectives, feelings, values and ways of living, as evidenced in a four month course on global futurés with a group of adult learners and graduate students at the University of Toronto.

At the collective level, new alliances working for cultural change might include schools, universities, religious institutions, community groups and local governments. Ideally governments, the media, and business might be involved as well, but it is clear that few liberal democracies have advanced propositions that seriously challenge current consumption patterns, thereby endangering the prevailing economic growth agendas. As Murphy and Cohen say:

> The use of fossil fuels is so central to lifestyles in affluent countries, and the amount of change required over a relatively short time-scale is so great that it is difficult to imagine publics acting quickly enough without leadership and coercion.

Inevitably, normative issues about the definition and nature of sustainable development as a general goal sit along side more policy-oriented issues such as how sustainable consumption is to be achieved and what instruments are best used for this purpose. Typically the complexity of the issue is framed with an agenda like the following one from the OECD, quoted in Cohen. It catalogues a series of tasks including:

> The need for better knowledge of present consumption patterns; the challenges remaining to define a framework and set of goals for government to address consumption patterns as a coherent issue; the opportunities to influence lifestyles and consumption through practical, value-neutral measures; the importance of influencing the broader network of actors and institutions which shape individual consumption patterns; government measures to empower the individual consumer to make positive changes; and the need for the underlying macro-economic framework to

> encourage rather than obstruct progress towards more sustainable consumption and production patterns.

However, a closer examination of the consumption issue is potentially threatening as it confronts the fact that profound changes in consumption are required to achieve a sustainability transition. The emergence of global environmental issues that are challenging governments, and the recognition that such issues require more than technological solutions, raises basic questions about the nature of societies and the social dimensions of these ecological dilemmas.

Nevertheless, because of potential threats to economic growth mechanisms, Cohen believes that it is "unreasonable to expect the prevailing discourse around sustainable consumption to include in the foreseeable future unequivocal calls for restraint". These dilemmas appear in the initial policy formulation phase of the policy cycle too. Rist, for example, is a proponent of the value of qualitative research in identifying, understanding and defining policy problems. He also notes, however, that the "the pressures and structural incentives in the policy system all go in the other direction.

Develop short-term proposals with quick impacts to show responsiveness and accommodate all the vested interests in the iron triangle". The short-range orientation of policy analysis contrasts with the long-range theoretical and action orientation of futures studies. Whereas policy analysis is concerned with analysing the viability of particular policies, futures studies, especially in its critical dimensions, is concerned with making basic assumptions problematic. Where policy analysis is goal oriented, futures studies is vision oriented, examining a range of futures.

Where policy analysis often takes a limited view of knowledge approaches, futures studies attempts to acknowledge the differing ways in which individuals construct the world. "Policy Reform" is one of a series of futures scenarios proposed by the Global Scenario Group, with aspects of all the scenarios put forward currently in evidence. These scenarios vary in their underlying philosophies and responses:

— "Market Forces" depends on market optimism, assumes a world of accelerating economic globalisation, and regards well functioning markets as the key to resolving social, economic and environmental problems.

— "Policy Reform" depends on government action to constrain markets, with sustainability policy shaping a planetary transition. This is the perspective that informed the Brundtland report, and which generally influences policy discussions on sustainability.

— "Breakdown" envisions a world calamity, with population and economic growth leading to ecological collapse, international conflict and institutional disintegration.

— "Fortress World" is a variant of "Breakdown". In this case, authoritarian leadership and the armed forces are used to re-establish order and to prevent a collapse into "Breakdown".

— "Great Transition" is guided by sustainability philosophy and progressive global social evolution, with an involved global citizenry advancing a new development paradigm encompassing quality of life and a strong ecological sensibility. New roles for business and government, new values and participation by citizens, and the importance of civil society organisations are characteristic features.

One possibility the Global Scenario Group envisages is the phased emergence of a "Great Transition" as time proceeds. Initially, the "Market Forces" scenario still dominates until its internal contradictions lead to a global crisis. "Policy reform" ascends in the wake of the crisis, particularly in the period after 2015.

Eventually, the "Great Transition" scenario asserts itself more strongly as the gestating popular desire for changes in lifestyle, values and technology becomes widespread. This portrayal of futures transitions serves to highlight the issue that the "Policy Reform" scenario is eclipsed by the "Great Transition" era, signifying more fundamental shifts in consciousness and values. This sequence of the rise and fall of the strength of each scenario suggests that broad transformations in policy will be matched by changes in consciousness.

Applying Wilber's quadrant model (Figure 2) shows that making the needed social and economic changes to address global problems such as global warming requires not only the setting of national policies and the implementation of international treaties by governments, but also the understanding and active support of civil society. Further, the constructive synergies between the quadrants necessary for sustainability, avoids the contradiction of environmentally beneficial beliefs and actions being opposed by barriers to action such as structural constraints or ineffective financial incentives.

However, in the shorter term, given that progressive "Policy reform" can begin to have a positive impact on various indicators of sustainability, and given that governments have more tools at their disposal than other actors, a consideration of the various policy instruments that can be used to influence sustainable consumption is relevant. These instruments fall into four broad groups:

1. Regulatory (command and control) instruments are typically applied to producers e.g. pollution control, product standards, and extended producer responsibility. Legislation directed at "consumers" is less common ("thou shall consume in a sustainable

way"), but includes, for example, restrictions on water use in times of drought.

2. Economic instruments include full-cost pricing, environmental taxes and charging, green tax reform, and the removal of environmentally harmful subsidies. The use of price incentives to influence individual behaviour is typically strongly favoured by economists, although price is only one of a number of factors influencing people's behaviour. With respect to producers, significant subsidies provided to airlines, for example, are strongly questioned by environmental groups, with a recent study estimating that three of Europe's top airlines receive around 20% of their operating revenue from subsidies.
3. Social (information) instruments include awareness raising and information directed at "consumers", and voluntary eco-labelling schemes used by "producers". As discussed earlier, this approach works well for the so-called "easy choices" such as joining recycling schemes. It is much less effective, however, when the disadvantages to "consumers" increase, as in the case of getting people to switch from private cars to public transport.
4. Provision of physical alternatives and rearrangements, and using design for sustainability includes the development of ecologically benign technologies, and infrastructure changes that facilitate people taking sustainability into account in their decision-making.

These four general strategies can be directed at individual "consumers", at organisations in industry and public services, and also at the more macro-level of states and international organisations. An OECD study recommends that a mix of instruments is generally used to best advantage. The necessary political will and the value positions underlying the application of these instruments strongly affects their effectiveness. Governments strongly aligned with a "Market Forces" scenario are unlikely to pay attention to widespread social and environmental externalities, thus sending a message to the public that it is acceptable to continue consuming along present lines. Similarly, top-down informational campaigns directed at individual behaviour change enable such governments to avoid confronting the contradictions between ecological stewardship and economic growth. That is, "consumers" in a sense inherit the regulatory responsibilities that the state has cast off.

On the other hand, governments founded on Social Democratic and Green Party value orientations can apply these instruments in more progressive ways. Influencing the context of consumption could, for example, include changes to educational curricula, and the encouragement of public debate on the relationship between consumption and quality of life. Confronting, and perhaps regulating, advertising that portrays unsustainable behaviour as desirable is another possible strategy.

The design for sustainability approach is preventive rather than remedial in focus, and can bring progressively greater environmental benefits as an expanded view of design is applied. Design concepts based on "shallow" adaptive or substitutive change need to be distinguished from those based on "deep" more fundamental change. Thus some strategies redesign what is consumed, or make existing products more resource efficient; others reorganise the way consumption takes place; and others question the need fulfilled by the object, service or system.

6

Tourism and Environmental Issues

Tourism is not just a potential victim of climate change. It also contributes to its causes. Beyond seeking a zero emission form of travel for holidaymakers, a significant capping of emissions from air travel could be achieved through the introduction of an aviation fuel tax. Aviation fuel is currently exempt from tax, unlike other transport options which are less carbon intensive.

While the International Civil Aviation Organisation (ICAO) is strongly opposed to the introduction of a tax, WWF supports the introduction of an aviation tax. Revenues from such a tax should at least be partially invested in sustainable transport options. Another intermediate solution is presented by schemes such as Climate Care which offer tour operators or holidaymakers the opportunity to pay a voluntary levy on air travel into a fund that supports renewable energy projects and forest sequestration projects. The levy is calculated on a kilometre travelled basis and the investment aims to offset air travel CO_2 emissions by implementing reductions in other areas of energy usage.

Large tourist developments can put substantial pressure on local energy supplies, especially through air conditioning or heating. Energy requirements are often met by fossil fuel plant thus increasing the greenhouse gas emissions of the host country. In addition, the energy efficiency of buildings is often poor. Through improved standards at the development stage, or through retrofitting, it is possible to achieve considerable reductions in emissions.

Climate Change on Tourism

The tourism industry heavy reliance on the local environment and climate to sell holidays means that it could face serious challenges as a result of climate change. Global and regional temperatures are rising. The hottest year of the millennium was 1998 and the 1990s were the warmest decade.

Climate models suggest a future warming of 0.2-0.3°C per decade and sealevels are expected to rise at a rate of 4 to 10 centimetres per decade. An increase in extreme weather events such as floods and storms is also expected. While the impacts of climate change on tourism will vary, it is already clear that small island states such as the Maldives in the Indian Ocean, an increasingly popular tourist destination, will be particularly vulnerable to sea-level rise.

Climate change is also expected to increase the risk of illness in several parts of the world and this may lead to a falling-off of tourism. More frequent periods of extreme heat will cause discomfort in many eastern Mediterranean resorts, where the number of days above 40°C is expected to increase. A decline in cloud cover in Australia will increase exposure to the sun s harmful rays and malaria is likely to re-emerge in Spain, the most popular Mediterranean destination.

Winter tourism may also be affected, as the Alps and other European skiing destinations experience less snowfall and shorter skiing seasons. These impacts will be especially pronounced in lower-lying ski resorts, and in places where commercial ventures are already marginal. Tour operators and countries that rely on tourism for foreign revenue need to take into account the potential impacts of climate change, not only in planning new resorts or upgrading current facilities, but also in terms of the long-term future of their business.

WWF believes that action must be taken now by governments, individuals, and the tourism industry to reduce the threat of climate change. Governments worldwide should meet, and ideally go beyond, the commitments made through the Kyoto Protocol. The tourism industry itself must take action to reduce its contribution to global greenhouse gas emissions. For example, in destinations, changes to energy supply should be introduced, creating a shift from fossil fuel to renewable sources of energy such as wind, biomass and solar power. This needs to be coupled with changes to planning procedures and laws, so that more opportunities for renewable energy sources can be developed.

More stringent efficiency standards and a compulsory energy rating scheme could also be employed in buildings, such as hotels. Transport to, from, and around resorts and within destinations, is another key area where changes could be made. The tourism industry should incorporate public transport and cycling infrastructure in resort plans as well as alternative low impact vehicle technology. Offering customers the opportunity to make a contribution to renewable energy schemes as a way of offsetting air travel emissions would also be an important step. Finally, an international aviation fuel tax should be introduced, and local or short-haul holidays may be preferable in certain instances.

Air Travel and Environment

Travel by air is becoming almost as commonplace in the

21st century as walking was for our ancestors. Whether on business or for pleasure we fly, at the click of a mouse, to the four corners of the earth. Furthermore, thanks to travel search engines and low cost airlines, we even decide to go, not to a place of choice, but to where the cost is least. These are extraordinary freedoms. Air travel and airfreight are, at the same time, sinews of a growing, internet-linked, just-in-time, global economy. The growth is explosive. Since 1949, the birth year of the first passenger jet, air travel has grown seventy-fold. Britain has always been a world leader in aviation.

Today through its airlines, aerospace industries, its role in new thinking about air safety and security, and the great international hub of Heathrow, the country is a global player. But this position has not been won without cost to the environment. Britain's skies are noisy, its airports are hotspots of pollutants emitted by both planes and surface vehicles and as the number of flights increases, so do the acres dedicated to and blighted by aircraft operations. Yet compared with many of our Continental neighbours, where airports have been built or expanded to match demand, we have used operational efficiency to squeeze more and more use from existing runways. Since the end of the Second World War, the only completely new runway to have been built is Manchester's number two.

The London airport system is, as a result, one of the most constrained in the world. Constraint means congestion and with it delays, unreliable services, reduced efficiency, increased pollution and waste. Airlines lose revenue and costs rise for travellers, airports and all involved in flying. Such a situation is dangerous. Unless congestion is met by investment in new airport capacity there is a risk that Britain's air transport industry will become less competitive leading to damage to the economy. The forthcoming aviation White Paper will provide Government with an opportunity, for the first time in twenty years, to set out a new direction for air transport policy and to make long-term provision for airport capacity.

Aviation contributes to the British economy via air transport industries that employ over 500,000 and through firms, ranging from exporters of medical technology to travelling businessmen, which make use of their services. Aviation's growth has been the result, in turn, of the expansion of national and global economies which has led first to the movement of more goods and people, and, second to a fall, in real terms, of freight tariffs and travel costs.

The emergence in Britain of Europe's largest set of air charter firms is just one reflection of this growth. Wider benefits include stronger international trade links, wider transfer of research findings and speedier responses to natural disasters. A more detailed examination of how aviation affects the national economy reveals that airlines, airports and their supporting services make direct contributions; indirect contributions are made by off-airport activities such as hotels and tour operators; while decisions, for instance, to place investment in Britain because of its air links, count as contributions that are induced.

It is particularly noteworthy that "knowledge-based" jobs - a highly significant component in the new economy - tend to be those that can locate anywhere and are thus highly responsive to the availability of a good air transport hub. It should, furthermore, be noted that growth in air transport in the UK has taken place in a more open market than on the Continent.

— *Aviation jobs*: Reference has already been made to the 500,000 jobs that depend directly or indirectly on aviation. Expansion in air transport can be expected to cause this total to increase or, at least, to remain stable. But should Britain lose ground to France, Holland or Germany then a decline in such jobs must be a possibility.

— *Aviation Passengers*: The Government forecasts that demand for air travel in southeast England will rise from 117 million passengers in 2000 to about 200 million in 2015 and 300 million in 2030. Despite larger aircraft and developments in air and ground traffic control, it is not expected that this growth could be handled on existing runways. Additional capacity at Heathrow, Gatwick and Stansted, or even a new airport in the Thames Estuary, are therefore under consideration. Britain, as a gateway to Europe for the Americas, India and elsewhere, handles multitudes of transit passengers who in turn help raise the occupancy (and profitability) of connecting European and domestic flights.

Nearly 200 million passengers transited in 2002 and over a third passed through Heathrow. London's hub airport, and the operating base of British Airways, accordingly handles more international passengers than any other airport in the world. Paris, Amsterdam and Frankfurt, all of which have recently seen heavy investment, eye this business jealously.

— *Aviation and Commerce*: About a third of Britain's exports, worth some £60 billion, are air freighted every year while businessmen and women make about 6 million flights. Both activities contribute to the country's gross domestic product. Reliance on air transport has, furthermore, increased steadily over the years and there is little reason to expect this trend to turn. It follows that Britain's interests are best served by a prosperous aviation sector that seeks to meet demand for its services. To what extent the White Paper will enable this growth to be met and how its environmental impacts will be abated, will therefore be central to the long-term health of the British economy.

Technical Solutions

Everyone accepts that aviation's environmental damage must be minimised and its further growth made 'sustainable'. Emissions trading within and between industries is, meanwhile, increasingly seen as the best way to internalise the external costs of air transport all other activities. Trading promises to reduce pollution overall by eliminating first those sources that can be most inexpensively terminated while leaving those responsible for hard-to-treat emitters, such as aircraft, with time to develop the means to do so.

Environmental issues are, however, becoming ever more pressing. Not only is aircraft noise at airports generating increased opposition but pressure on governments and industry to cut greenhouse gasses mounts apace. Today's jet engines may be less noisy and more fuel efficient than their predecessors but, because there are so many more of them, fuel consumption and the noise affecting people living near airports are greater. It is thus far from true to say that technical progress has cut the overall environmental impact of aviation.

Reducing noise: The most contentious aspect of airport expansion is noise. Airports both attract and repel. Over time people are attracted by the prospect of jobs to live nearby. Meanwhile flight numbers grow and airport owners, in order to maximise the use of their costly assets, push as far as they can for 24 hour operation. None of this makes them good neighbours as demonstrated by recent legal actions against night noise in London.

Engines themselves are one source of aircraft noise but, as an airliner comes in to land, so is the roar of turbulent air over flaps and, above all, landing gear. The International Air Transport Association can claim that the average aircraft is now 20 decibels quieter than 30 years ago but if, on landing, the interval between successive flights shrinks, the exposure to noise of those underneath remains at best constant and at worst it is increased.

Containing noise is a major challenge for air transport. Three kinds of action are possible.

— Land use planning may be used to put distance between people and flight paths.

— Air traffic control can be used to route aircraft via the least populated flight paths - though this can increase fuel consumption and carbon emissions.

— Noise can be reduced at source by changes in engine design and aircraft aerodynamics.

Noise prospects: Future aircraft are forecast to be substantially quieter than the quietest models of today. NASA's 'Quiet Aircraft Technology' programme, for instance, aims to reduce the perceived noise of future subsonic aircraft by 50 per cent in ten years and 75 per cent in 25. But noise could be cut more quickly by reducing the age of the aircraft fleet. Given that the 'noise footprint' of today's new jets is less than 15 per cent of the oldest in use, updating the fleet would be highly effective. However this would cost money and is not happening. Although the world aircraft fleet has tripled in size over the past 25 years its average age has remained at about 11 years.

Reducing fuel consumption and emissions. Modern jets burn kerosene and together consume 3 to 4 per cent of fossil fuel production. When burnt in a jet engine kerosene produces carbon particles, water vapour and nitrogen oxides. These pollutants help to turn airports, and any communities adjacent to them, into hotspots of emissions. Aero engine pollutants are an added concern because, emitted at high altitude, they make a particularly powerful contribution to climate change.

Fuel consumption per passenger mile has been cut by 70 per cent since the dawn of the jet age thanks to larger and sleeker aircraft and to less thirsty engines. More economical turbines account for half this gain. Airlines welcome such efficiency, as much because it saves them money and reduces their exposure to oil price fluctuations, as for its green contribution but is an illustration of how profits and environmental protection can go hand in hand. However there is no gainsaying the statement that, given continuing growth in air travel, reducing the local and global environmental risks of aircraft emissions is a profound challenge.

Economy and pollution prospects: New technologies are in train that offer some prospect that carbon and water vapour emissions can be reduced. Three developments in particular are worth mentioning.

- New communications, navigation and traffic management technologies could enable aircraft to take more direct routes, avoid the waste of stacking and time spent with engines running on the ground.
- New lightweight materials promise both to cut aircraft weight and allow the forming of more aerodynamic wings and fuselages. Modifications such as wing tip extensions can also contribute to economy.
- Replacing fossil fuel is the third possibility. In the longer term hydrogen engines may power radically different aircraft from those of today - an event that America's desire to free itself from dependency on foreign oil may hasten. In the meantime there is scope for using electric fuel cells, already used in unmanned military aircraft, as auxiliary power sources for, say, aircraft equipment and lighting,

Meanwhile the International Civil Aviation Organisation is looking at emissions trading, environmental taxes and other economic instruments because of their promise to more effective in the near future than other forms of regulation or new technologies.

Congestion: Congestion in the air and on the tarmac, because it prolongs engine running, adds to noise and gas emissions and to inefficiency in general. Delays to aircraft can result from:

— Restrictions as ordered by traffic managers on the use of air space

— Lack of runway space and taxiways, or other constraints, on the ground.

— Security controls at aircraft terminals.

Government agencies and aviation regulators are increasingly aware that they, as managers of airports and their associated traffic management systems, have a role in reducing congestion and, with it, environmental impacts. This is leading to the design of air traffic control systems that allow aircraft to fly safely at closer intervals and traverse inhospitable terrain. On the ground better surface radar, mixed-mode operation of parallel runways and techniques that replace the downtime needed to keep runways clear of debris, can all increase the efficiency of operations.

Another useful innovation is the use of Lidar to plot the atmospheric vortices created by large jet engines. This enables the distance between successive aircraft to be reduced. Delays at terminals due to security checks can, likewise, be reduced by technologies that enable passengers to be scanned for hidden weapons while they are walking. Another antidote to the delay of queuing is automatic check-ins. The equipment needed for such procedures is, of course, expensive, but, to the extent that it can get more use from existing terminals may, by postponing the need for airport expansion, bring environmental benefits.

Emerging Options

— *No case for inaction*: The Government has made clear that, when considering Britain's lack of airport capacity, 'doing nothing is not an option'. Meanwhile growth in air travel is putting increasing pressure on existing airports and creating demand for additional runways - particularly in southeast England. If, as seems likely, the idea of a new airport on the north Kent coast is rejected, Ministers will have to reconcile elsewhere conflict between demand for travel and protection of the environment.

— *Responding to demand*: While new airports, runways and their associated technologies all expand the supply of air travel, the demand side is the best place to tackle their environmental impacts. The growth of low cost airlines, for instance, has led to a boom in flying. Why not use pricing to internalise its environmental damage? Putting the growth of air travel into a market context that includes the cost of environment damage is the fairest way of responding to demand. The frequent suggestion that take-off and landing slots be auctioned however needs to be treated with caution: if the UK acted alone there would be an asymmetry in its impacts on airline costs using UK airports.

— *More runways*: BAA, the owner and operator of Heathrow, Gatwick and Stansted, has proposed the construction of three new runways (from a choice of four) and rejected, on economic and environmental grounds, the idea of a new airport at Cliffe on the Thames Estuary. Whether this would meet demand for travel and enable Britain to compete in the long term with Paris, Charles de Gaulle and Schipol at Amsterdam is unclear but it is hard to see why not.

— *Airport to city links*: Airports have to be linked by roads and railways to the places they serve. If Cliffe is rejected in favour of expanding some or all of London's existing airports, some existing railway and motorway links will have to be expanded and upgraded. Whichever airports are chosen for expansion, it will be important to set their added capacity in the context of policies for multi-modal surface access.

The growing environmental impact of air transport has, in recent decades, been minimised by means of new aircraft technologies and operating procedures. The industry has, at the same time, recognised that actions which reduce the waste and costs associated with congestion in the air and on the ground are not only commercially beneficial but, by increasing the use of existing airports, reduce the need for new sites that would further spread the nuisances of noise and air pollution.

Further technological innovation is thus a key to meeting demand for air travel. Britain, as exemplified by its pioneering role in radar and commercial jet aircraft, has a good track record in this field. No opportunity should therefore be lost to promote research that will lead to the development of other technologies. Only by technical leadership can commercial leadership be assured.

Environmental Health Risks

Travellers often experience abrupt and dramatic changes in environmental conditions, which may have detrimental effects on health and well-being. Travel may involve major changes in altitude, temperature and humidity, and exposure to unfamiliar species of animals and insects. The negative impact of sudden changes in the environment can be minimized by taking simple precautions.

At high altitude, atmospheric pressure is reduced. The consequent reduction in oxygen pressure can lead to hypoxia (i.e. reduced supply of oxygen to the tissues). At altitudes of 1500-3500 metres, exercise tolerance is reduced and ventilation is increased. At 3500-5500 metres, there is hypoxia and altitude sickness may occur. Rapid ascent may lead to acute hypoxia: the affected person becomes faint and may lose consciousness. Acute mountain sickness may occur after 1-6 hours at high altitudes.

Headache is followed by anorexia, nausea and vomiting, and insomnia, fatigue, lassitude, and irritability. The outcome is fatal in some cases due to the development of pulmonary and cerebral oedema. Travellers with pre-existing cardiovascular or pulmonary disease or anaemia are highly sensitive to changes in altitude, which can be dangerous and even lifethreatening.

- Avoid direct travel to high altitudes if possible. Break the journey for 2-3 nights at 2500-3000 metres to help prevent acute mountain sickness.
- If direct travel to a high altitude cannot be avoided, the traveller should avoid overexertion, large meals, and alcohol after arrival.
- Travellers making a rapid ascent to high altitude (>3000 metres) can consider taking prophylactic medication (acetazolamide).
- Travellers planning to climb or trek at high altitude will require a period of gradual adaptation.
- Travellers with pre-existing cardiovascular or pulmonary disease or anaemia should seek medical advice before deciding to travel to a high altitude.

Heat and Humidity

Sudden changes in temperature and humidity may have adverse effects on health. Exposure to high temperature and humidity results in loss of water and electrolytes (salts) and may lead to heat exhaustion and heat stroke. In hot dry conditions, dehydration is particularly likely to develop unless care is taken to maintain adequate fluid intake. The addition of a little table salt to food or drink (unless this is contraindicated for the individual) can help to prevent heat exhaustion, particularly during the period of adaptation.

Consumption of salt-containing food and drink helps to replenish the electrolytes in case of heat exhaustion and after excessive sweating. Older travellers should take particular care to consume extra fluids in hot conditions, as the thirst reflex diminishes with age. Care should be taken to ensure that infants and young children drink enough liquid to avoid dehydration. Irritation of the skin may be experienced in hot conditions (prickly heat). Fungal skin infections such as tinea pedis (athlete's foot) are often aggravated by heat and humidity.

A daily shower, wearing loose cotton clothing and applying talcum powder to sensitive skin areas help to reduce the development or spread of these infections. Exposure to hot, dry, dusty air may lead to irritation and infection of the eyes and respiratory tract.

Ultraviolet Radiation

The ultraviolet (UV) radiation from the sun includes UVA (wavelength 315-400 nm) and UVB (280-315 nm) radiation, both of which are damaging to human skin and eyes. The intensity of UV radiation is indicated by the Global Solar UV Index, which is a measure of skin-damaging radiation. The Index describes the level of solar UV radiation at the

Earth's surface and is often reported as the maximum 10-30-minute average for the day.

The values of the Index range from zero upwards-the higher the Index value, the greater the potential for damage to the skin and eyes, and the less time it takes for harm to occur. The Index values are grouped into exposure categories, with values greater than 10 being "extreme". In general, the closer to the equator the higher the Index. UVB radiation is particularly intense in summer and in the 4-hour period around solar noon. UV radiation may penetrate clear water to a depth of 1 metre or more.

The adverse effects of ultraviolet radiation from the sun are the following:

— Exposure to UV radiation, particularly UVB, can produce severe debilitating sunburn and sunstroke, particularly in light-skinned people.

— Exposure of the eyes may result in acute keratitis ("snow blindness"), and long-term damage leads to the development of cataracts.

— Long-term adverse effects on the skin include:

  — the development of skin cancers (carcinomas and malignant melanoma), mainly due to UVB radiation;

  — accelerated ageing of the skin, mainly due to UVA radiation, which penetrates more deeply into the skin.

— Adverse reactions of the skin result from interaction with a wide range of medicinal drugs that may cause photosensitization and result in phototoxic or photoallergic dermatitis. A variety of different types of therapeutic drugs as well as oral contraceptives, some prophylactic antimalarial drugs and certain antimicrobials may cause adverse dermatological reactions on exposure to sunlight. Phototoxic contact reactions are caused by topical application of products, including perfumes, containing oil of bergamot or other citrus oils.

— Exposure may suppress the immune system, increase the risk of infectious disease, and limit the efficacy of vaccinations.

Precautions

— Avoid exposure to the sun in the middle of the day, when the UV intensity is greatest.

— Wear clothing that covers arms and legs (summer clothing is UV-protective and generally more effective than even good-quality sunscreen).

— Wear UV-protective sunglasses of wrap-around design and a wide-brimmed sun hat.

— Apply a broad-spectrum sunscreen of sun protection factor (SPF) 15+ liberally on areas of the body not protected by clothing and reapply frequently.

— Take particular care to ensure that children are well protected.

— Take precautions against excessive exposure on or in water.

— Check that medication being taken will not affect sensitivity to UV radiation.

— If adverse skin reactions have occurred previously, avoid any exposure to the sun and avoid any products that have previously caused the adverse reactions.

Foodborne and Waterborne

Many important infectious diseases (such as brucellosis, cholera, cryptosporidiosis, giardiasis, hepatitis A and E, legionellosis, leptospirosis, listeriosis, schistosomiasis and typhoid fever) are transmitted by contaminated food and water. For travellers, the main health problem associated with contaminated food and water is "travellers' diarrhoea", which can be caused by a wide range of infectious agents. Travellers' diarrhoea is the most common health problem encountered by travellers and may affect up to 80% of travellers to high-risk destinations.

Even a brief episode of severe diarrhoea may spoil a holiday or ruin a business trip. Diarrhoea may be accompanied by nausea, vomiting, and fever. Travellers' diarrhoea is primarily the result of consumption of contaminated food, drink, or drinking-water. Contamination in such cases is due to the presence of diseaseproducing microorganisms. A wide range of different bacteria, viruses, and some parasitic and fungal infections may cause travellers' diarrhoea. Illness is also caused by certain biological toxins found in seafood. The main diseases in this group are caused by poisoning from:

— paralytic shellfish

— neurotoxic shellfish

— amnesic shellfish

— ciguatera toxin

— scombroid fish

— puffer fish.

The toxins involved in these poisonings come from microorganisms consumed by or otherwise contaminating the fish. Poisonous chemicals may also contaminate food and drink. However, the illeffects are generally the result of long-term exposure and do not represent a significant health risk for travellers. Sporadic misuse of chemicals also occurs, such as the use of textile dyes in foodstuffs, which may give an unusually bright colour to the contaminated food.

The safety of food, drink and drinking-water depends mainly on the standards of hygiene applied locally in their preparation and handling. In countries with low standards of hygiene and sanitation and poor infrastructure for controlling the safety of food, drink and drinking-water, there is a high risk of contracting travellers' diarrhoea. In such countries, travellers should take precautions with all food and drink, including that served in good-quality hotels and restaurants, to minimize any risk of contracting a foodborne or waterborne infection. While the risks are greater in poor countries, locations with poor hygiene may be present in any country.

Another potential source of waterborne infection is contaminated recreational water, particularly sewage-polluted seawater or fresh water in lakes and rivers, as well as water in swimming pools and spas where filtering and disinfection are inadequate or even non-existent. Bathing in contaminated water may result in ingestion of diarrhoea-producing microorganisms and other infectious agents. It is particularly important that people in more vulnerable groups, i.e. infants and children, the elderly, pregnant women and people with impaired immune systems, take stringent precautions to avoid contaminated food and drink and unsafe recreational waters.

Travellers should:

- avoid consumption of potentially contaminated food or drink;
- avoid contact with potentially contaminated recreational waters;
- know how to treat diarrhoea;
- carry oral rehydration salts and water-disinfecting agents.

Precautions for avoiding unsafe food and drink

- Avoid cooked food that has been kept at room temperature for several hours.
- Eat only food that has been cooked thoroughly and is still hot.
- Avoid uncooked food, apart from fruit and vegetables that can be peeled or shelled, and avoid fruits with damaged skins.
- Avoid dishes containing raw or undercooked eggs.
- Avoid food bought from street vendors.
- Avoid ice cream from unreliable sources, including street vendors.
- In countries where poisonous biotoxins may be present in fish and shellfish, obtain advice locally.
- Boil unpasteurized (raw) milk before consumption.
- Boil drinking-water if its safety is doubtful; if boiling is not possible, a certified, well-maintained filter and/ or a disinfectant agent can be used.
- Avoid ice unless it has been made from safe water.
- Avoid brushing the teeth with unsafe water.
- Bottled or packaged cold drinks are usually safe provided that they are sealed; hot beverages are usually safe.

Precautions for avoiding unsafe recreational waters

- Seek information locally about the quality of recreational waters in the area.
- Avoid beaches obviously polluted by sewage.
- Avoid bathing in sewage-contaminated water.
- Avoid swallowing any sewage-contaminated water.

Treatment of diarrhoea

— Most diarrhoeal attacks are self-limiting, with recovery in a few days. It is important, especially for children, to avoid becoming dehydrated.

— As soon as diarrhoea starts, more fluids should be taken, such as bottled, boiled or treated water, or weak tea. If diarrhoea continues for more than one day, oral rehydration salt (ORS) solution should be taken and normal food consumption should continue. Amounts of ORS solution to drink:

  — Children under 2 years ¼-1/2 cup (50-100 ml) after each loose stool

  — Children 2-10 years ½-1 cup (100-200 ml) after each loose stool

  — Older children and adults Unlimited amount

If ORS solution is not available, a substitute containing 6 level teaspoons of sugar plus 1 level teaspoon of salt in 1 litre of safe drinking-water can be used, in the same amounts as for ORS. (A level teaspoon contains a volume of 5 ml.) Medical help should be sought if diarrhoea lasts for more than 3 days and/or there are very frequent watery bowel movements, blood in the stools, repeated vomiting or fever.

When no medical help is available and there is blood in the stools, a course of ciprofloxacin may be taken by adults. For children and pregnant women, azithromycin is recommended. Prophylactic use of antimicrobials is not recommended. Antidiarrhoeal medicines, e.g. loperamide, are not recommended for general use but may be used exceptionally, in addition to fluids and by adults only, for symptomatic relief. Antidiarrhoeal medicines should never be used to treat children. If there are other symptoms, medical advice should be sought.

Recreational Waters

The use of coastal waters and freshwater lakes and rivers for recreational purposes has a beneficial effect on health through exercise, and rest and relaxation. However, various hazards to health may also be associated with recreational waters. The main risks are the following:

- Drowning and injury.
- Physiological:
  - chilling, leading to coma and death;
  - thermal shock, leading to cramps and cardiac arrest;
  - acute exposure to heat and ultraviolet radiation in sunlight: heat exhaustion, sunburn, sunstroke;
  - cumulative exposure to sun (skin cancers, cataract).
- Infection:
  - ingestion or inhalation of, or contact with, pathogenic bacteria, fungi, parasites and viruses;
  - bites by mosquitoes and other insect vectors of infectious diseases.
- Poisoning and toxicoses:
  - ingestion or inhalation of, or contact with, chemically contaminated water, including oil slicks;
  - stings or bites of venomous animals;
  - ingestion or inhalation of, or contact with, blooms of toxigenic plankton.

Immersion hypothermia

Cold, rather than simple drowning, is the main cause of death at sea. When the body temperature falls (hypothermia), there is confusion followed by loss of consciousness, so that the head goes under water leading to drowning. With a life jacket capable of keeping the head out of water, drowning is avoided, but death due directly to hypothermic cardiac arrest will soon follow. However, wearing warm clothing as well as a life jacket can greatly prolong survival in cold water. Children, particularly boys, have less fat than adults and chill very rapidly in cool or cold water.

Swimming is difficult in very cold water (around 0°C), and even good swimmers often drown suddenly if they attempt to swim even short distances in water at these temperatures without a life jacket. Life jackets or some other form of flotation aid should always be worn in small craft, particularly by children and young men, when the water is cold. Alcohol, even in small amounts, can cause hypoglycaemia if consumed without food and after exercise. It causes confusion and disorientation and also, in cold surroundings, a rapid fall in body temperature.

Unless sufficient food is eaten at the same time, small amounts of alcohol can be exceedingly dangerous on longdistance swims, as well as after rowing or other strenuous and prolonged watersports exercise. Those engaging in winter activities on water, such as skating and fishing, should be aware that whole-body immersion must be avoided. Accidental immersion in water at or close to freezing temperatures is dangerous because the median lethal immersion time (time to death) is less than 30 minutes for children and most adults.

Immediate treatment is much more important than any later action in reviving victims of immersion hypothermia. A hot bath (the temperature no higher than the immersed hand will tolerate) is the most effective method of achieving this. In case of drowning, cardiac arrest and cessation of breathing should be treated by tipping water out of the stomach and giving immediate external cardiac massage and artificial ventilation. Cardiac massage should not be applied unless the heart has stopped. People who have inhaled water should always be sent to hospital to check for pulmonary complications.

Infection

In coastal waters, infection may result from ingestion or inhalation of, or contact with, pathogenic microorganisms, which may be naturally present, carried by people or animals using the water, or present as a result of faecal contamination. The most common consequences among travellers are diarrhoeal disease, acute febrile respiratory disease and ear infections. In fresh waters, leptospirosis may be spread by the urine of infected rodents, causing human infection through contact with broken skin or mucous membranes. In areas endemic for schistosomiasis, infection may be acquired by penetration of the skin by larvae during swimming or wading.

In swimming pools and spas, infection may occur if treatment and disinfection of the water is inadequate. Diarrhoea, gastroenteritis and throat infections may result from contact with contaminated water. Appropriate use of chlorine and other disinfectants controls most viruses and bacteria in water. However, the parasites Giardia and Cryptosporidium, which are shed in large numbers by infected individuals, are highly resistant to routine disinfection procedures. They are inactivated by ozone or eliminated by filtration.

Contamination of spas and whirlpools may lead to infection by Legionella and Pseudomonas aeruginosa. Otitis externa and infections of the urinary tract, respiratory tract, wounds and cornea have also been linked to spas. Direct person-to-person contact or physical contact with contaminated surfaces in the vicinity of pools and spas may spread the viruses that cause molluscum contagiosum and cutaneous papillomas (warts); fungal infections of the hair, fingernails and skin, notably tinea pedis (athlete's foot), are spread in a similar manner.

Precautions

— Adopt safe behaviour in all recreational waters.

— Avoid consumption of alcohol before any activities in or near recreational waters.

— Provide constant supervision of children in the vicinity of recreational waters.

— Avoid temperature extremes in spas, saunas, etc.; this is particularly important for users with pre-existing medical conditions, pregnant women and young children.

— Avoid excessive exposure to sunlight.

— Avoid contact with contaminated waters.

— Avoid swallowing any contaminated water.

— Obtain advice locally about the presence of potentially dangerous aquatic animals.

— Wear shoes when walking on shores, riverbanks and muddy terrain.

Animals and Insects

Mammals

Animals tend to avoid contact with humans and most do not attack unless provoked. Some large carnivores, however, are aggressive and may attack. Animals suffering from rabies often become aggressive and may attack without provocation. Wild animals may become aggressive if there is territorial intrusion, particularly when the young are being protected. Animal bites may cause serious injury and may also result in transmission of disease.

Rabies is the most important infectious health hazard from animal bites. In many developing countries, rabies is transmitted mainly by dogs, but many other species of mammals can be infected by the rabies virus. After any animal bite, the wound should be thoroughly cleansed with disinfectant or with soap or detergent and water, and medical or veterinary advice should be sought about the possibility of rabies in the area. Where a significant risk of rabies exists, the patient should be treated with post-exposure rabies vaccination and immunoglobulin.

A booster dose of tetanus toxoid is also recommended following an animal bite. Travellers who may be at increased risk of exposure to rabies may be advised to have pre-exposure vaccination before departure. Pre-exposure rabies vaccination does not eliminate the need for treatment after the bite of a rabid animal, but it reduces the number of vaccine doses required in the postexposure regimen.

Precautions

— Avoid direct contact with domestic animals in areas where rabies occurs, and with all wild and captive animals.

— Avoid behaviour that may startle, frighten or threaten an animal.

— Ensure that children do not approach, touch, or otherwise provoke any animal.

— Treat any animal bite immediately by washing with disinfectant or soap and seek medical advice.

— If a significant risk of exposure to rabies is foreseen, seek medical advice before travelling.

Travellers with accompanying animals should be aware that dogs (and, for some countries, cats) must be vaccinated against rabies in order to be allowed to cross international borders. A number of rabies-free countries have additional requirements. Before taking an animal abroad, the traveller should ascertain the regulatory requirements of the countries of destination and transit.

Snakes, scorpions and spiders

Travellers to tropical, subtropical and desert areas should be aware of the possible presence of venomous snakes, scorpions and spiders. Local advice should be sought about risks in the areas to be visited. Most venomous species are particularly active at night. Venom from snake and spider bites and from scorpion stings have various effects in addition to tissue damage in the vicinity of the bite. Neurotoxins are present in the venom of both terrestrial and aquatic snakes, and also often in the venom of scorpions and spiders.

Neurotoxins cause weakness and paralysis and other symptoms. Venom contacting the eyes causes severe damage and may result in blindness. Most snake venoms affect blood coagulation, which may result in haemorrhage and reduced blood pressure. Toxins in the hair of spiders such as tarantulas may cause intense irritation on contact with the skin. Poisoning by a venomous snake, scorpion or spider is a medical emergency requiring immediate attention.

The patient should be moved to the nearest medical facility as quickly as possible. First-aid measures call for immobilizing the entire affected limb with splints and firm, but not tight, bandaging to limit the spread of toxin in the body and the amount of local tissue damage. However, bandaging is not recommended if local swelling and tissue damage are present in the vicinity of the bite.

Other traditional first-aid methods (incisions and suction, tourniquets and compression) are harmful and should not be used. The decision to use antivenom should be taken only by qualified medical personnel, and it should be administered in a medical facility. Antivenom should be given only if its stated range of specificity includes the species responsible for the bite.

Precautions

— Obtain local advice about the possible presence of venomous snakes, scorpions and spiders in the area.

— Avoid walking barefoot or in open sandals in terrain where venomous snakes, scorpions or spiders may be present; wear boots or closed shoes and long trousers.

— Avoid placing hands or feet where snakes, spiders or scorpions may be hiding.

— Be particularly careful outdoors at night.

— Examine clothing and shoes before use for hidden snakes, scorpions or spiders.

Aquatic animals

Swimmers and divers may be bitten by certain aquatic animals, including conger and moray eels, stingrays, weever fish, scorpionfish, stonefish, piranhas, seals and sharks. They may be stung by venomous cnidaria-jellyfish, fire corals, sea anemones-and other invertebrate aquatic species including octopus. Severe and often fatal injury results from attack by crocodiles, which inhabit rivers and estuaries in many tropical countries, including the tropical north of Australia. Injuries from dangerous aquatic organisms occur as a result of:

— passing close to a venomous organism while bathing or wading;

— treading on a stingray, weever fish or sea urchin;

— handling venomous organisms during sea-shore exploration;

— invading the territory of large animals when swimming or at the water's edge;

— swimming in waters used as hunting grounds by large predators;

— interfering with, or provoking, dangerous aquatic organisms.

Precautions

— Obtain local advice on the possible presence of dangerous aquatic animals in the area.

— Adopt behaviour that will avoid provoking attack by predatory animals.

— Wear shoes when walking on the shore and at the water's edge.

— Avoid contact with jellyfish in water and dead jellyfish on the beach.

— Avoid walking, wading or swimming in crocodile-infested waters at all times of year.

— Seek medical advice after a sting or bite by a poisonous animal.

Treatment

In the case of envenomings by aquatic animals, treatment will depend on whether there is a wound or puncture or a localized skin reaction (e.g. rash). Punctures caused by spiny fish require immersion in hot water, extraction of the spines, careful cleaning of the wound and antibiotic therapy (and antivenom in the case of stonefish).

If punctures were caused by an octopus or sea urchin the treatment is basically the same but without exposure to heat. In the case of rashes or linear lesions, contact with cnidaria should be suspected; the treatment is based on the use of 5% acetic acid, local decontamination and corticosteroids (antivenom for the box jellyfish Chironex fleckeri), with adequate follow-up for eventual sequelae.

Insects and other vectors of disease

Vectors play an essential role in the transmission of many infectious diseases. Many vectors are bloodsucking insects, which ingest the disease-producing microorganism during a blood meal from an infected host (human or animal) and later inject it into a new host at the time of another blood meal.

Mosquitoes are important insect vectors of disease, and some diseases are transmitted by bloodsucking flies. In addition, ticks and certain aquatic snails are involved in the life cycle and transmission of disease. The principal vectors and the main diseases they transmit are shown in Table 1.

Water plays a key role in the life cycle of most vectors. Thus, the transmission of many vector-borne diseases is seasonal as there is a relationship between rainfall and the existence of breeding sites. Temperature is also a critical factor, limiting the distribution of vectors by altitude and latitude. Travellers are at lower risk of exposure to vector-borne diseases in urban centres, especially if they sleep in air-conditioned rooms. They may, however, be exposed to the vectors of dengue which bite mostly during the day.

Travellers to rural areas or to areas with low standards of hygiene and sanitation are usually at higher risk of exposure to disease vectors and personal protection is therefore essential. Evening/night-time activities outdoors may increase exposure to malaria vectors.

Table 1. Principal disease vectors and the diseases they transmita

Vectors	Main diseases transmitted
Aquatic snails	Schistosomiasis (bilharziasis)
Blackflies	River blindness (onchocerciasis)
Fleas	Plague
Mosquitoes	
Aedes	Dengue fever
Rift	Valley fever
	Yellow fever
Anopheles	Lymphatic filariasis
	Malaria
Culex	Japanese encephalitis
	Lymphatic filariasis
	West Nile fever
Sandflies	Leishmaniasis
	Sandfly fever (Phlebotomus fever)
Ticks	Crimean-Congo haemorrhagic fever
	Lyme disease
	Relapsing fever (borreliosis)
	Rickettsial diseases including spotted fevers and Q fever
	Tick-borne encephalitis
	Tularaemia
Triatomine bugs	Chagas disease
Tsetse flies	Sleeping sickness

Protection against vectors

Travellers may protect themselves from mosquitoes and other vectors by the means outlined in the following paragraphs. Insect repellents are substances applied to exposed skin or to clothing to prevent human/vector contact. The active ingredient in a repellent repels but does not kill insects. Choose a repellent containing DEET (N,N-diethyl-m-toluamide), IR3535 (3-[N-acetyl-N-butyl]-

aminopropionic acid ethyl ester) or Bayrepel® (1-piperidinecarboxylic acid, 2-(2-hydroxyethyl)-, 1-methylpropylester). Insect repellents should be applied to provide protection at times when insects are biting.

Care must be taken to avoid contact with mucous membranes. Insect repellents should not be sprayed on the face or applied to the eyelids or lips. Always wash the hands after applying the repellent. Insect repellents should not be applied to sensitive, sunburned or damaged skin or deep skin folds. Repeated applications may be required every 3-4 hours, especially in hot and humid climates. When the product is applied to clothes, the repellent effect lasts longer. Repellents should be used in strict accordance with the manufacturers' instructions and the dosage must not be exceeded, especially for young children.

Mosquito coils are the best known example of insecticide vaporizer, usually with a synthetic pyrethroid as the active ingredient. One coil serves a normal bedroom through the night, unless the room is particularly draughty. A more sophisticated version, which requires electricity, is an insecticide mat that is placed on an electrically heated grid, causing the insecticide to vaporize. Such devices can also be used during daytime if necessary.

Aerosol sprays intended to kill flying insects are effective for quick knockdown and killing. Indoor sleeping areas should be sprayed before bedtime. Treating a room with an insecticide spray will help to free it from insects, but the effect may be short-lived. Spraying combined with the use of a coil, a vaporizer or a mosquito net is recommended. Aerosol sprays intended for crawling insects should be sprayed on surfaces where these insects walk.

Protective clothing can help at times of the day when vectors are active. The thickness of the material is critical, and no skin should be left exposed unless treated with a repellent. Insect repellent applied to clothing is effective for longer than it may be on the skin. Extra protection is provided by treating clothing with permethrin or etofenprox, to prevent mosquitoes from biting through clothing. Label instructions should be followed to avoid damage to certain fabrics. In tick- and flea-infested areas, feet should be protected by appropriate footwear and by tucking long trousers into the socks. Such measures are further enhanced by application of repellents to the clothing.

Mosquito nets are excellent means of personal protection while sleeping. Nets can be used either with or without insecticide treatment. However, treated nets are much more effective. Pretreated nets may be commercially available. Nets should be strong and with a mesh size no larger than 1.5 mm. The net should be tucked in under the mattress, ensuring first that it is not torn and that there are no mosquitoes inside. Nets for use with cots and small beds are available, affording protection for babies whenever they are sleeping. Travellers camping in tents should use a combination of mosquito coils, repellents and screens. The mesh size of tent screens often exceeds 1.5 mm, so that special mosquito screens have to be deployed.

— Screening of windows, doors and eaves reduces exposure to flying insects. Accommodation with these features should be sought where available.

— Air-conditioning is a highly effective means of keeping mosquitoes and other insects out of a room. In air-conditioned hotels, other precautions are not necessary indoors.

— Avoid contact with freshwater bodies such as lakes, irrigation ditches and slowrunning streams in areas where schistosomiasis occurs.

7

Travel-related Risks

The risks associated with international travel are influenced by characteristics of the traveller (including age, sex and health status) and by characteristics of the travel (including destination, purpose and duration). Forward planning, appropriate preventive measures and careful precautions can substantially reduce the risks of adverse health consequences.

Although the medical profession and the travel industry can provide a great deal of help and advice, it is the traveller's responsibility to ask for information, to understand the risks involved, and to take the necessary precautions for the journey.

Factors in Determining the Risks

Key factors in determining the risks to which travellers may be exposed are:

— destination

— duration of visit

— purpose of visit

— standards of accommodation and food hygiene

— behaviour of the traveller.

Destinations where accommodation, hygiene and sanitation, medical care and water quality are of a high standard pose relatively few serious risks for the health of travellers, unless there is pre-existing illness. This applies to business travellers and tourists visiting most major cities and tourist centres and staying in good-quality accommodation.

In contrast, destinations where accommodation is of poor quality, hygiene and sanitation are inadequate, medical services do not exist, and clean water is unavailable may pose serious risks for the health of travellers. This applies, for example, to personnel from emergency relief and development agencies or tourists who venture into remote areas. In these settings, stringent precautions must be taken to avoid illness.

The duration of the visit and the behaviour and lifestyle of the traveller are important in determining the likelihood of exposure to many infectious agents and will influence decisions on the need for certain vaccinations or antimalarial medication. The duration of the visit may also determine whether the traveller may be subjected to marked changes in temperature and humidity during the visit, or to prolonged exposure to atmospheric pollution.

The purpose of the visit is critical in relation to the associated health risks. A business trip to a city, where the visit is spent in a hotel and/or conference centre of high standard, or a tourist trip to a well-organized resort, involves fewer risks than a visit to remote rural areas, whether for work or pleasure. However, behaviour also plays an important role; for example, going outdoors in the evenings in a malaria-endemic area without taking precautions may result in the traveller becoming infected with malaria. Exposure to insects, rodents or other animals, infectious agents and contaminated food and water, combined with the absence of appropriate medical facilities, makes travel in many remote regions particularly hazardous.

Medical Consultation

Travellers intending to visit a destination in a developing country should consult a travel medicine clinic or medical practitioner before the journey. This consultation should preferably take place 4-6 weeks before the journey, particularly if vaccination(s) may be required. However, last-minute travellers can also benefit from a medical consultation, even as late as the day before travel.

This consultation will determine the need for any vaccinations and/or antimalarial medication, as well as any other medical items that the traveller may require. A basic medical kit will be prescribed or provided, supplemented as appropriate to meet individual needs. A dental check-up is advisable before travel to developing countries or prolonged travel to remote areas. This is particularly important for people with chronic or recurrent dental problems.

Medical advisers base their recommendations, including those for vaccinations and other medication, on an assessment of risk for the individual traveller, which takes into account the likelihood of catching a disease and how serious this might be for the traveller concerned. Key elements of this risk assessment are the destination, duration and purpose of the visit, as well as the conditions of accommodation and the health status of the traveller. For each disease being considered, an assessment is also made of:

- availability of prophylaxis, possible side-effects and suitability for the traveller concerned;
- any associated public health risks (e.g. the risk of infecting others).

Collecting the information required to make a risk assessment involves detailed questioning of the traveller. A checklist or protocol is useful to ensure that all relevant information is obtained and recorded. The traveller should be provided with a personal record of the vaccinations given (patient-retained record) as vaccinations are often administered at different centres. A model checklist, reproducible for individual travellers, is provided.

Medical Kit and Toilet Items

Sufficient medical supplies should be carried to meet all foreseeable needs for the duration of the trip. A medical kit should be carried for all destinations where there may be significant health risks, particularly those in developing countries, and/or where the local availability of specific medications is not certain. This kit will include basic medicines to treat common ailments, first-aid articles, and any special medical items that may be needed by the individual traveller.

Certain categories of prescription medicine should be carried together with a medical attestation, signed by a physician, certifying that the traveller requires the medication for personal use. Some countries require not only a physician but also the national health administration to sign this certificate. All medicines should be carried in the hand luggage to minimize any risk of loss during the journey. A duplicate supply carried in the checked luggage is a safety precaution in case of loss or theft.

Toilet items should also be carried in sufficient quantity for the entire visit unless their availability at the travel destination is assured. These will include items for dental care, eye care including contact lenses, skin care and personal hygiene.

Basic Medical Kit

First-aid items:

— adhesive tape
— antiseptic wound cleanser
— bandages
— emollient eye drops
— insect repellent
— insect bite treatment
— nasal decongestant
— oral rehydration salts
— scissors and safety pins
— simple analgesic (e.g. paracetamol)
— sterile dressing
— clinical thermometer.

Additional items according to destination and individual needs:

— antidiarrhoeal medication
— antifungal powder
— antimalarial medication
— condoms
— medication for any pre-existing medical condition
— sedatives
— sterile syringes and needles
— water disinfectant
— other items to meet foreseeable needs, according to the destination and duration of the visit.

Travellers with Pre-existing Medical Conditions

Health risks associated with travel are greater for certain groups of travellers, including infants and young children, pregnant women, the elderly, the disabled, and those who have pre-existing health problems. For all of these travellers, medical advice and special precautions are necessary. They should be well informed about the available medical services at the travel destination.

Age

Infants and young children have special needs with regard to vaccinations and antimalarial precautions. They are particularly sensitive to ultraviolet radiation and become dehydrated more easily than adults in the event of inadequate fluid intake or loss of fluid due to diarrhoea. A child can be overcome by dehydration within a few hours. Air travel may cause discomfort to infants due to changes in cabin air pressure and is contraindicated for infants less than 7 days old.

Infants and young children are more sensitive to sudden changes in altitude. They are also more susceptible to many infectious diseases. Advanced age is not necessarily a contraindication for travel if the general health status is good. Elderly people should seek medical advice before planning longdistance travel.

Pregnancy

Travel is not generally contraindicated during pregnancy until close to the expected date of delivery, provided that the pregnancy is uncomplicated and the woman's health is good. Airlines impose some travel restrictions in late pregnancy and the neonatal period.

There are some restrictions on vaccination during pregnancy. Pregnant women risk serious complications if they contract malaria. Travel to malaria-endemic areas should be avoided during pregnancy if at all possible. Medication of any type should be taken during pregnancy only in accordance with medical advice. Travel to high altitudes or to remote areas is not advisable during pregnancy.

Disability

Physical disability is not usually a contraindication for travel if the general health status is good. Airlines have regulations on the conditions for travel for disabled passengers who need to be accompanied. Information should be obtained from the airline in advance.

Pre-existing illness

People suffering from chronic illnesses should seek medical advice before planning a journey. Conditions that increase health risks during travel include:

- cardiovascular disorders
- chronic hepatitis
- chronic inflammatory bowel diseases
- chronic renal disease requiring dialysis
- chronic respiratory diseases
- diabetes mellitus
- epilepsy
- immunosuppression due to medication or to HIV infection
- previous thromboembolic disease

— severe anaemia

— severe mental disorders

— any chronic condition requiring frequent medical intervention.

Any traveller with a chronic illness should carry all necessary medication for the journey and for the entire duration of the trip in their hand luggage. The name and contact details of their physician should be carried on their person with other travel documents, together with information about the medical condition and treatment, and details of medication (generic drug names included) and prescribed doses. A physician's letter certifying the necessity for any drugs or other medical items (e.g. syringes) carried by the traveller that may be questioned by customs officials should also be carried.

Insurance for Travellers

International travellers should be aware that medical care abroad is often available only at private medical facilities and may be costly. In places where good-quality medical care is not readily available, travellers may need to be repatriated in case of accident or illness. If death occurs abroad, repatriation of the body can be extremely expensive and may be difficult to arrange.

Travellers should be advised to

— seek information about possible reciprocal health care agreements between the country of residence and the destination country, and

— obtain special travellers' health insurance for destinations where health risks are significant and medical care is expensive or not readily available.

This health insurance should include coverage for changes to the itinerary, emergency repatriation for health reasons, hospitalization, medical care in case of illness or accident and repatriation of the body in case of death. Travel agents and tour operators usually provide information about travellers' health insurance.

It should be noted that some countries now require proof of adequate health insurance as a condition for entry. Travellers should know the procedures to follow to obtain assistance and reimbursement. A copy of the insurance certificate and contact details should be carried with other travel documents in the hand luggage.

Travel Industry Professionals

Tour operators, travel agents, and airline and shipping companies each have an important responsibility to safeguard the health of travellers. It is in the interests of the travel industry that travellers have the fewest possible problems when travelling to, and visiting, foreign countries. Contact with travellers before the journey provides a unique opportunity to inform and advise them of the situation in each of the countries they are visiting. The travel agent or tour operator should provide the following health-related guidance to travellers:

— Advise the traveller to consult a travel medicine clinic as soon as possible after planning a trip to any destination where significant health risks may be foreseen, particularly those in developing countries, preferably 4-6 weeks before departure.

— Advise last-minute travellers that a visit should be made to a travel medicine clinic, even up to the day before departure.

— Advise travellers if the destination presents any particular hazards to personal safety and security and suggest appropriate precautions.

- Encourage travellers to take out comprehensive travellers' health insurance and provide information on available policies.
- Inform travellers of the procedures for obtaining assistance and reimbursement, particularly if the insurance policy is arranged by the travel agent or company.
- Provide information on:
  - mandatory vaccination requirements for yellow fever;
  - the need for malaria precautions at the travel destination;
  - the existence of other important health hazards at the travel destination;
  - the presence or absence of good-quality medical facilities at the travel destination.

Responsibility of the Traveller

Travellers can obtain a great deal of information and advice from medical and travel industry professionals to help prevent health problems while abroad. However, travellers must accept that they are responsible for their health and well-being while travelling and on their return. The following are the main responsibilities to be accepted by the traveller:

- the decision to travel
- recognition and acceptance of any risks involved
- seeking health advice in good time, preferably 4-6 weeks before travel
- compliance with recommended vaccinations and other prescribed medication and health measures

— careful planning before departure
— carrying a medical kit and understanding its use
— obtaining adequate insurance cover
— health precautions before, during, and after the journey
— responsibility for obtaining a physician's letter pertaining to any prescription medicines, syringes, etc. being carried
— responsibility for the health and well-being of accompanying children
— precautions to avoid transmitting any infectious disease to others during and after travel
— careful reporting of any illness on return, including information about all recent travel
— respect for the host country and its population.

Medical Examination after Travel

Travellers should be advised to have a medical examination on their return if they:

— suffer from a chronic disease, such as cardiovascular disease, diabetes mellitus, chronic respiratory disease;
— experience illness in the weeks following their return home, particularly if fever, persistent diarrhoea, vomiting, jaundice, urinary disorders, skin disease or genital infection occurs;
— consider that they have been exposed to a serious infectious disease while travelling;
— have spent more than 3 months in a developing country.

Travellers should provide medical personnel with information on recent travel, including destination,. and purpose and duration of visit. Frequent travellers should give details of all journeys that have taken place in the preceding weeks and months.

Accidents, Injuries and Violence

Travellers are more likely to be killed or injured in accidents or through violence than to be struck down by an exotic infectious disease. Traffic accidents are the most frequent cause of death among travellers. Traffic accidents and violence are significant risks in many countries, particularly developing countries, where skilled medical care may not be readily available. Accidents and injuries also occur in other settings, particularly in recreational waters in association with swimming, diving, sailing and other activities. Travellers can reduce the possibility of incurring these risks through awareness of the dangers and by taking the appropriate precautions.

Traffic Accidents

Worldwide, an estimated 1.2 million people are killed each year in road crashes and as many as 50 million are injured. Projections indicate that these figures will increase by about 65% over the next 20 years unless there is new commitment to prevention. In many developing countries traffic laws are limited or are inadequately enforced. Often the traffic mix is more complex than that in developed countries and involves two- and four-wheeled vehicles, animal-drawn vehicles and other conveyances, plus pedestrians, all sharing the same road space.

The roads may be poorly constructed and maintained, road signs and lighting inadequate and driving habits poor. Travellers, both drivers and pedestrians, should be extremely attentive and careful on the roads. There are a number of practical precautions that travellers can take to reduce the risk of being involved in, or becoming the victim of, a traffic accident.

Precautions

— Have full insurance cover for medical treatment of both illness and injuries sustained in accidents.

— Carry an international driving licence as well as your national driving licence.

— Obtain information on the regulations governing traffic and vehicle maintenance, and on the state of the roads, in the countries to be visited.

— Before renting a car check the state of the tyres, safety belts, spare wheels, lights, brakes, etc.

— Know the informal rules of the road; in some countries, for example, it is customary to sound the horn or flash the headlights before overtaking.

— Be particularly vigilant in a country where the traffic drives on the opposite side of the road to that used in your country of residence.

— Do not drive on unfamiliar and unlit roads.

— Do not use a moped, motorcycle or bicycle.

— Do not drive after drinking alcohol.

— Drive within the speed limit at all times.

— Always wear a safety belt where these are available.

— Beware of wandering animals.

Recreational Waters

Recreational waters include coastal waters, freshwater lakes and rivers, swimming pools and spas. The hazards associated with recreational waters can be minimized by safe behaviour and simple precautions. The most important health hazards in recreational waters are drowning and impact injuries, particularly head and spinal injuries.

It is estimated that at least half a million deaths are caused by drowning every year. In addition, many more cases of "near-drowning" occur, often with life-long effects on health. Drowning may occur when a person is caught in a tide or rip current, is trapped by rising tides, falls overboard from a boat, becomes caught in submerged obstacles, or falls asleep on an inflatable mattress and is carried out to sea.

In swimming pools and spas, drowning or near-drowning and other injuries may occur close to outlets where suction is strong enough to catch body parts or hair so that the head is trapped under water. Drowning in swimming pools may be related to slip-trip-fall accidents leading to loss of consciousness on impact. If the water is not clear it may be difficult to see submerged swimmers or obstacles, increasing the chances of an accident in the water. Children can drown in a very short time and in relatively small amounts of water.

The factor that contributes most frequently to children drowning is lack of adult supervision. Children in or near water should be constantly supervised by adults. Drowning is also a hazard for those wading and fishing. Falling in cold water, particularly when wearing heavy clothing, may result in drowning as swimming ability is hampered. Impact injuries are usually the result of diving accidents, particularly diving into shallow water and/or hitting underwater obstructions. Water may appear to be deeper than it is. Impact of the head on a hard surface may cause head and/or spinal injuries.

Spinal injuries may result in various degrees of paraplegia or quadriplegia. Head injuries may cause concussion and loss of memory and/or motor skills. Drowning and impact injuries in adults are frequently associated with alcohol consumption, which impairs judgement and the ability to react effectively. A detached retina, which can result in blindness or near-blindness, may be caused by jumping into water or jumping onto other people in the water.

— Adopt safe behaviour in all recreational waters: use life jackets where appropriate, pay attention to tides and currents, and avoid outlets in spas and swimming pools.

— Ensure constant adult supervision of children in or near recreational waters, including small volumes of water.

— Avoid consumption of alcohol before any activity in or near water.

— Check the depth of the water carefully before diving, and avoid diving or jumping into murky water as submerged swimmers or objects may not be visible.

— Do not jump into water or jump onto others in the water.

Violence

Violence is a significant risk in many developing countries. Criminals often target tourists and business travellers, particularly in countries where crime levels are high. However, some sensible precautions may reduce this risk.

Precautions

— Be alert to muggings during the day as well as at night.

— Keep jewellery, cameras and other items of value out of sight and do not carry large sums of money on your person.

— Avoid isolated beaches and other remote areas.

— Avoid overcrowded trains, buses and minibus taxis.

— Use taxis from authorized ranks only.

— Avoid driving at night and never travel alone.

— Keep car doors locked and windows shut.

— Be particularly alert when waiting at traffic lights.

— Park in well-lit areas and do not pick up strangers.

— Employ the services of a local guide/interpreter or local driver when travelling to remote areas.

— Vehicle hijacking is a recognized risk in a number of countries. If stopped by armed robbers, make no attempt to resist and keep hands where the attackers can see them at all times.

Infectious Diseases of Potential Risk

Depending on the travel destination, travellers may be exposed to a number of infectious diseases; exposure depends on the presence of infectious agents in the area to be visited. The risk of becoming infected will vary according to the purpose of the trip and the itinerary within the area, the standards of accommodation, hygiene and sanitation, as well as the behaviour of the traveller.

In some instances, disease can be prevented by vaccination, but there are some infectious diseases, including some of the most important and most dangerous, for which no vaccines exist. General precautions can greatly reduce the risk of exposure to infectious agents and should always be taken for visits to any destination where there is a significant risk of exposure. These precautions should be taken regardless of whether any vaccinations or medication have been administered.

Modes of Transmission

The modes of transmission for different infectious diseases and the corresponding general precautions are outlined in the following paragraphs.

Food and waterborne diseases

Food- and waterborne diseases are transmitted by consumption of contaminated food and drink. The risk of infection is reduced by taking hygienic precautions with all food, drink and drinking-water consumed when travelling and by avoiding direct contact with polluted recreational waters. Examples of diseases transmitted by food and water are hepatitis A, typhoid fever and cholera.

Vector-borne diseases

A number of particularly serious infections are transmitted by insects and other vectors such as ticks. The risk of infection can be reduced by taking precautions to avoid insect bites and contact with other vectors in places where infection is likely to be present. Examples of vector-borne diseases are malaria, yellow fever, dengue and tick-borne encephalitis. Zoonoses (diseases transmitted from animals)

Zoonoses include many infections that can be transmitted to humans through animal bites or contact with contaminated body fluids or faeces from animals, or by consumption of foods of animal origin, particularly meat and milk products. The risk of infection can be reduced by avoiding close contact with any animals-including wild, captive and domestic animals-in places where infection is likely to be present. Particular care should be taken to prevent children from approaching and handling animals. Examples of zoonoses are rabies, brucellosis, leptospirosis and certain viral haemorrhagic fevers.

Sexually transmitted diseases

Sexually transmitted diseases are passed from person to person through unsafe sexual practices. The risk of infection can be reduced by avoiding casual and unprotected sexual intercourse, and by use of condoms. Examples of sexually transmitted diseases are hepatitis B, HIV/AIDS and syphilis.

Bloodborne diseases

Bloodborne diseases are transmitted by direct contact with infected blood or other body fluids. The risk of infection can be reduced by avoiding direct contact with blood and body fluids, by avoiding the use of potentially contaminated needles and syringes for injection or any other medical or cosmetic procedure that penetrates the skin (including acupuncture, piercing and tattooing), and by avoiding transfusion of unsafe blood. Examples of bloodborne diseases are hepatitis B and C, HIV/AIDS and malaria.

Airborne diseases

Airborne diseases are transmitted from person to person by aerosol and droplets from the nose and mouth. The risk of infection can be reduced by avoiding close contact with people in crowded and enclosed places. Examples of airborne diseases are influenza, meningococcal disease and tuberculosis.

Soil-transmitted diseases

Soil-transmitted diseases include those caused by dormant forms (spores) of infectious agents, which can cause infection by contact with broken skin (minor cuts, scratches, etc.). The risk of infection can be reduced by protecting the skin from direct contact with soil in places where soil-transmitted infections are likely to be present. Examples of bacterial diseases transmitted from soil are anthrax and tetanus. Certain intestinal parasitic infections, such as ascariasis and trichuriasis, are transmitted via soil and infection may result from consumption of soil-contaminated vegetables.

Specific Infectious Diseases

The main infectious diseases to which travellers may be exposed, and precautions for each, are detailed on the following pages. Information on malaria, the most important infectious disease threat for travellers. Above reffered infectious diseases described on the basis of the following criteria:

— diseases that have a sufficiently high global or regional prevalence to constitute a significant risk for travellers;

— diseases that are severe and life-threatening, even though the risk of exposure may be low for most travellers;

— diseases for which the perceived risk may be much greater than the real risk, and which may therefore cause anxiety to travellers;

— diseases that involve a public health risk due to transmission of infection to others by the infected traveller.

Advice concerning the diseases for which vaccination is routinely administered in childhood, i.e. diphtheria, measles, mumps and rubella, pertussis, poliomyelitis and tetanus, and the use of the corresponding vaccines later in life and for travel.

The most common infectious illness to affect travellers, namely travellers' diarrhoea. Because travellers' diarrhoea can be caused by many different foodborne and waterborne infectious agents, for which treatment and precautions are essentially the same, the illness is not included with the specific infectious diseases.

8

Air Travelling: Health Considerations

Air travel, in particular over long distances, exposes passengers to a number of factors that may have an effect on their health and well-being. Passengers with pre-existing health problems are more likely to be affected and should consult their doctor or a travel medicine clinic in good time before travelling. Those receiving medical care and intending to travel by air in the near future should tell their medical adviser.

Health risks associated with air travel can be minimized if the traveller plans carefully and takes some simple precautions before, during, and after the flight. An explanation of the various factors that may affect the health and well-being of air travellers follows.

Cabin Air Pressure

Although aircraft cabins are pressurized, cabin air pressure at cruising altitude is lower than air pressure at sea level. At typical cruising altitudes in the range 11 000-12 200 metres (36 000-40 000 feet) air pressure in the cabin is equivalent to the outside air pressure at 1800-2400 metres (6000-8000 feet) above sea level. As a consequence, less oxygen is taken up by the blood (hypoxia) and gases within the body expand. The effects of reduced cabin air pressure are usually well tolerated by healthy passengers.

Cabin air contains ample oxygen for healthy passengers and crew. However, because cabin air pressure is relatively low, the amount of oxygen carried in the blood is reduced compared to sea level. Passengers with certain medical conditions, in particular heart and lung disease, and blood disorders such as anaemia, may not tolerate this reduced oxygen level (hypoxia) very well. Such passengers are usually able to travel safely if arrangements are made with the airline for the provision of an additional oxygen supply during flight.

As the aircraft climbs, the decreasing cabin air pressure causes gases to expand. Similarly, as the aircraft descends, the increasing pressure in the cabin causes gases to contract. These changes may have effects where gas is trapped in the body. Gas expansion during the climb causes air to escape from the middle ear and the sinuses, usually without causing problems. This airflow can sometimes be perceived as a "popping" sensation in the ears.

As the aircraft descends, air must flow back into the middle ear and sinuses in order to equalize pressure differences. If this does not take place, the ears or sinuses may feel as if they were blocked and, if the pressure is not relieved, pain can result. Swallowing, chewing, or yawning ('clearing the ears') will usually relieve any discomfort. If the problem persists, a short forceful expiration against a pinched nose and closed mouth (Valsalva manœuvre) will usually help.

For infants, feeding or giving a pacifier (dummy) to stimulate swallowing may reduce the symptoms. Individuals with ear, nose, and sinus infections should avoid flying because pain and injury may result from the inability to equalize pressure differences. If travel cannot be avoided, the use of decongestant nasal drops shortly before the flight and again before descent may be helpful. As the aircraft climbs, expansion of gas in the abdomen can cause discomfort, although this is usually mild. Some forms of surgery, other medical treatments, or diagnostic tests, may introduce air or other gas into a body cavity.

Examples include abdominal surgery or eye treatment for a detached retina. Passengers who have recently undergone such a procedure should ask a travel medicine physician or their treating physician how long they should wait before undertaking air travel.

Cabin Humidity and Dehydration: The humidity in aircraft cabins is low, usually less than 20% (humidity in the home is normally over 30%). Low humidity may cause skin dryness and discomfort of the eyes, mouth, nose and exposed skin but presents no risk to health. Using a skin moisturizing lotion, saline nasal spray to moisturize the nasal passages, and wearing spectacles rather than contact lenses can relieve or prevent discomfort. The low humidity does not cause dehydration and there is no need to drink extra water.

Ozone

Ozone is a form of oxygen (with three, rather than two, atoms to the molecule) that occurs in the upper atmosphere and may enter the aircraft cabin together with the fresh air supply. In older aircraft, it was found that the levels of ozone in cabin air could sometimes lead to irritation of the lungs, eyes and nasal tissues.

Ozone is broken down by heat and most ozone is removed by the compressors (in the aircraft engines) that provide pressurized air for the cabin. In addition, most modern long-haul jet aircraft are fitted with equipment (catalytic converters) that breaks down any remaining ozone.

Cosmic Radiation

Cosmic radiation is made up of radiation that comes from the sun and from outer space. The earth's atmosphere and magnetic field are natural shields and therefore cosmic radiation levels are lower at lower altitudes. Cosmic radiation is more intense over polar regions than over the equator because of the shape of the earth's magnetic field and the "flattening" of the atmosphere over the poles.

The population is continually exposed to natural background radiation from soil, rock and building materials as well as from cosmic radiation that reaches the earth's surface. Although cosmic radiation levels are higher at aircraft cruising altitudes than at sea level, research so far has not shown any significant health effects for either passengers or crew.

Except in the case of severe turbulence, travellers by air rarely suffer from motion (travel) sickness. Those who do suffer should request a seat in the mid-section of the cabin where movements are less pronounced, and keep the motion sickness bag, provided at each seat, readily accessible. They should also consult their doctor or travel medicine physician about medication that can be taken before flight to help prevent problems.

Deep Vein Thrombosis and Circulatory Problems

Contraction of muscles is an important factor in helping to keep blood flowing through the veins, particularly in the legs. Prolonged immobility, especially when seated, can lead to pooling of blood in the legs, which in turn may cause swelling, stiffness, and discomfort. It is known that immobility is one of the factors that may lead to the development of a blood clot in a deep vein, so-called "deep vein thrombosis", or DVT. Research has shown that DVT can occur as a result of prolonged immobility, for instance during long distance travel, whether by car, bus, train or air.

The World Health Organization (WHO) has set up a major research study to find out if there are any factors that might lead to the risk of DVT being higher for air travel than for other causes of immobility. In most cases of DVT, the clots are small and do not cause any symptoms. The body is able to gradually break down the clot and there are no long-term effects. Larger clots may cause symptoms such as swelling of the leg, tenderness, soreness and pain.

Occasionally a piece of the clot may break off and travel with the bloodstream to become lodged in the lungs. This is known as pulmonary embolism and may cause chest pain, shortness of breath and, in severe cases, sudden death. This can occur many hours or even days after the formation of the clot. The risk of developing Deep Vein Thrombosis (DVT) when travelling is very small unless one or more other risk factors are present. These include:

— Previous DVT or pulmonary embolism

— History of DVT or pulmonary embolism in a close family member

— Use of oestrogen therapy-oral contraceptives ("the Pill") or hormone replacement therapy (HRT)

— Pregnancy

— Recent surgery or trauma, particularly to the abdomen, pelvic region or legs

— Cancer

— Some inherited blood-clotting abnormalities.

It is advisable for people with one or more of these risk factors to seek specific medical advice from their doctor or a travel medicine clinic in good time before embarking on a flight of three or more hours. DVT occurs more commonly in older people. Some researchers have suggested that there may be a risk from smoking, obesity and varicose veins.

The risk of a passenger who does not have any of the risk factors above developing DVT as a consequence of flying is small and the benefits of most precautionary measures in such passengers are unproven and some might even result in harm. Some common-sense advice for such passengers is given below:

Moving around the cabin during long flights will help to reduce any period of prolonged immobility. However, this may not always be possible and any potential health benefits must be balanced against the risk of injury that could occur if the aircraft encounters sudden and unexpected turbulence. A sensible compromise is to walk around in the cabin, e.g. go to the bathroom, once every 2-3 hours.

Many airlines also provide helpful advice on exercises that can be carried out in the seat during flight. It is thought that exercise of the calf muscles can stimulate the circulation, reduce discomfort, fatigue and stiffness, and it may reduce the risk of developing DVT. Hand luggage should not be placed where it restricts movement of the legs and feet, and clothing should be loose and comfortable. Wearing properly fitted graduated compression stockings may be helpful. These compress the calf muscles and improve the flow of blood in the deep veins. They may also help prevent the swollen ankles that are quite common on long flights.

However, they need to be the correct size to be effective and passengers should therefore ask their doctor or a travel medicine clinic which type would be appropriate for them. In view of the clear risk of significant side effects and absence of clear evidence of benefit, passengers are advised not to use aspirin just for the prevention of travel-related DVT. Those travellers who are at most risk of developing DVT may be prescribed specific treatments, such as injections of heparin. Cabin crew are not trained to give injections and travellers who have been prescribed these must either be taught to give the injections themselves or make other arrangements to have them given by a qualified person.

Diving: Divers should not fly too soon after diving because of the risk that the reduced cabin pressure may lead to decompression sickness (the bends). It is recommended that they do not fly until at least 12 hours after their last dive and this period should be extended to 24 hours after multiple dives or after diving that requires decompression stops during ascent to the surface. Passengers undertaking recreational diving before flying should seek specialist advice from diving schools.

Jet lag: Jet lag is the term used for the symptoms caused by the disruption of the body's internal clock and the approximate 24-hour (circadian) rhythms it controls. Disruption occurs when crossing multiple time zones i.e. when flying east to west or west to east.

Jet lag may lead to indigestion and disturbance of bowel function, general malaise, daytime sleepiness, difficulty in sleeping at night, and reduced physical and mental performance. Its effects are often combined with tiredness due to the journey itself. Jet lag symptoms gradually wear off as the body adapts to the new time zone. Jet lag cannot be prevented but there are some ways to reduce its effects.

Travellers who take medication according to a strict timetable (e.g. insulin, oral contraceptives) should seek medical advice from their doctor or a travel medicine clinic before their journey. General measures to reduce the effects of jet lag are given the following:

— Be as well rested as possible before departure, and rest during the flight. Short naps can be helpful.

— Eat light meals and limit consumption of alcohol. Alcohol increases urine output which can result in disturbed sleep by causing awakenings in order to urinate. Whilst it can accelerate sleep onset, it reduces sleep quality, making sleep less recuperative. The after effects of alcohol (hangover) can exacerbate the effects of jet lag and travel fatigue. Alcohol should therefore be consumed in moderation, if at all, before and during flight. Caffeine should be limited to normal amounts and avoided within a few hours of an anticipated period of sleep.

— Try to create the right conditions when preparing for sleep. When taking a nap during the day, eyeshades and earplugs may help. Regular exercise during the day may help to promote sleep, but avoid strenuous exercise immediately before sleep.

— At the destination, try to get as much sleep in every 24 hours as normal. A minimum block of 4 hours sleep during the local night - known as "anchor sleep" - is thought to be necessary to allow the body's internal clock to adapt to the new time zone. If possible, make up the total sleep time by taking naps at times when feeling sleepy during the day.

— The cycle of light and dark is one of the most important factors in setting the body's internal clock. Exposure to daylight at the destination will usually help adaptation.

— Short-acting sleeping pills may be helpful. They should be used only in accordance with medical advice and should not normally be taken during the flight, as they may increase immobility and therefore the risk of developing DVT.

— Melatonin is available in some countries and can be used to help resynchronize the body's internal clock. It is normally sold as a food supplement and therefore is not subject to the same strict control as medications (for example, it has not been approved for use as a medication in the United States, but can be sold as a food supplement). The timing and effective dosage of melatonin have not been fully evaluated and its side effects, particularly if used long term, are unknown.In addition, manufacturing methods are not standardised and therefore the dose in each tablet can be very variable and some harmful compounds may be present. For these reasons, melatonin cannot be recommended.

— It is not always appropriate to adjust to local time for short trips of 2-3 days or less. If in doubt, seek specialist travel medicine advice.

— Individuals react in different ways to time zone changes. Frequent flyers should learn how their own body responds and adopt habits accordingly. Advice from a travel medicine clinic may be beneficial in determining an effective coping strategy.

Psychological Aspects in Air Travelling

Travel by air is not a natural activity for humans and many people experience some degree of psychological difficulty when flying. The main problems encountered are stress and fear of flying. These may occur together or separately at different times before and during the period of travel.

Stress: All forms of travel generate stress. Flying can be particularly stressful because it often involves a long journey to the airport, curtailed sleep and the need to walk long distances in the terminal building. Most passengers find their own ways of coping, but passengers who find air travel particularly stressful should seek medical advice in good time. Good planning (passports, tickets, medication, etc) and allowing plenty of time to get to the airport helps relieve stress.

Flight phobia (fear of flying): Fear of flying may range from feeling slightly anxious to being unable to travel by air at all. It can lead to problems at work and leisure. Travellers who want to travel by air but are unable to do so because of their fear of flying should seek medical advice before the journey. Medication may be useful in some cases but the use of alcohol "to steady the nerves" is not helpful and may be dangerous if combined with some medicines.

For a longer-term solution, travellers should seek specialized treatment to reduce the psychological difficulties associated with air travel. There are many courses available that aim to reduce or cure, fear of flying. These typically include advice on how to cope with the symptoms of fear, information about how an aircraft flies, how controls are operated during a flight and, in most cases, a short flight.

Air rage: In recent years, air rage has been recognized as a form of disruptive behaviour associated with air travel. It appears to be linked to high levels of general stress but not specifically to flight phobia. It is frequently preceded by excessive consumption of alcohol.

Medical Conditions for Travellers

Airlines have the right to refuse to carry passengers with conditions that may worsen, or have serious consequences, during the flight. Airlines may require medical clearance from their medical department/adviser if there is an indication that a passenger could be suffering from any disease or physical or mental condition that:

— May be considered a potential hazard to the safety of the aircraft

— Adversely affects the welfare and comfort of the other passengers and/or crew members

— Requires medical attention and/or special equipment during the flight •œ May be aggravated by the flight.

If cabin crew suspect before departure that a passenger may be ill, the aircraft's captain will be informed and a decision taken as to whether the passenger is fit to travel, needs medical attention, or presents a danger to other passengers and crew or to the safety of the aircraft.

Infants

Air travel is not recommended for infants less than seven days old. If travel is absolutely necessary for babies who are over seven days, but were born prematurely, medical advice should be sought in each case. Changes in cabin air pressure may upset infants; this can be helped by feeding or giving a pacifier to stimulate swallowing.

Pregnant women

Pregnant women can normally travel safely by air, but most airlines restrict travel in late pregnancy. Typical guidelines for those who have an uncomplicated pregnancy are:

— after the 28th week of pregnancy a letter from a doctor or midwife should be carried, confirming the expected date of delivery and that the pregnancy is normal

— for single pregnancies, flying is permitted up to the end of the 36th week

— for multiple pregnancies, flying is permitted up to the end of the 32nd week.

Pre-existing Illness

Most people with medical conditions are able to travel safely by air, provided that necessary precautions, such as the need for additional oxygen supply, are considered in advance. Those who have underlying health problems such as cancer, heart or lung disease, anaemia, diabetes, are on any form of regular medication or treatment, have recently had surgery or have been in hospital, or who are concerned about their fitness to travel for any other reason, should consult their doctor or a travel medicine clinic before deciding to travel by air.

Medication that may be required during the journey, or soon after arrival, should be carried in the hand luggage. It is also advisable to carry a copy of the prescription in case the medication is lost, additional supplies are needed or security checks require proof of purpose.

Frequent travellers who have a permanent and stable underlying health problem may obtain a frequent traveller's medical card from the medical or reservation department of many airlines. This card is accepted, under specified conditions, as proof of medical clearance and for identification of the holder's medical condition.

Security Issues

Security checks can cause concerns for travellers who have been fitted with metal devices such as artificial joints, pacemakers or internal automatic defibrillators. Some pacemakers may be affected by modern security screening equipment and travellers with these should carry a letter from their doctor. Travellers who need to carry other medical equipment in their hand luggage, particularly sharp items such as hypodermic needles, should also carry a letter from their doctor.

Smokers

Almost all airlines now ban smoking on board. Some smokers may find this stressful, particularly during long flights, and should discuss this with their doctor before travelling. Nicotine replacement patches or chewing gum containing nicotine may be helpful during the flight and the use of other medication or techniques may also be considered.

Travellers with disabilities: A physical disability is not usually a contraindication for travel. Passengers who are unable to look after their own needs during the flight (including use of the toilet and transfer from wheelchair to seat and vice versa) will need to be accompanied by an escort able to provide all necessary assistance. The cabin crew are generally not permitted to provide such assistance and a traveller who requires it and does not have a suitable escort may not be permitted to travel.

Travellers confined to wheelchairs should be advised against deliberately restricting their fluid intake before or during travel as a means of avoiding use of toilets during flights as this might detrimentally affect their general health. Airlines have regulations on conditions of travel for passengers with disabilities. Disabled passengers should contact the airline in advance of their travel for guidance (the airline's own web site often gives useful information).

Communicable Diseases

Research has shown that there is very little risk of any infectious disease being transmitted on board the aircraft. The quality of aircraft cabin air is carefully controlled. Ventilation rates provide a total change of air 20-30 times per hour. Most modern aircraft have recirculation systems, which recycle up to 50% of cabin air. The recirculated air is usually passed through HEPA (high-efficiency particulate air) filters, of the type used in hospital operating theatres and intensive care units, which trap particles, bacteria, fungi and viruses.

Transmission of infection may occur between passengers who are seated in the same area of an aircraft, usually as a result of the infected person coughing or sneezing or by touch (direct contact or contact with the same parts of the aircraft cabin and furnishings that other passengers touch). This is no different from any other situation where people are close to each other, such as on a train, bus or at a theatre. Highly infectious conditions, such as influenza, are more likely to be spread to other passengers in situations when the aircraft ventilation system is not operating.

A small auxiliary power unit is normally used to provide ventilation when the aircraft is on the ground, before the main engines are started, but occasionally this is not operated for environmental (noise) or technical reasons.In such cases, when associated with a prolonged delay, passengers may be temporarily disembarked. In order to minimise the risk of passing on infections, passengers who are unwell, particularly if they have a fever, should delay their journey until they have recovered. Airlines may deny boarding to passengers who appear to be infected with a communicable disease.

Aircraft Disinsection

Many countries require disinsection of aircraft (to kill insects) arriving from countries where diseases that are spread by insects, such as malaria and yellow fever, occur. There have been a number of cases of malaria affecting individuals who live or work in the vicinity of airports in countries where malaria is not present, thought to be due to the escape of malaria-carrying mosquitoes transported on aircraft.

Some countries, e.g. Australia and New Zealand, routinely require disinsection be carried out in order to prevent inadvertent introduction of species that may harm their agriculture. Disinsection is a public health measure that is mandated by the current International Health Regulations. It involves treatment of the interior of the aircraft with insecticides specified by WHO. The different procedures currently in use are as follows:

— treatment of the interior of the aircraft using a quick-acting insecticide spray immediately before take-off, with the passengers on board;

— treatment of the interior of the aircraft on the ground before passengers come on board, using a residual insecticide aerosol, plus additional inflight treatment with a quick-acting spray shortly before landing;

— regular application of a residual insecticide to all internal surfaces of the aircraft, except those in food preparation areas. Travellers are sometimes concerned about their exposure to insecticide sprays while travelling by air. Some people have reported that they feel unwell after spraying of aircraft for disinsection. However, WHO has found no evidence that the specified insecticide sprays are harmful to human health when used as prescribed.

Airlines are required to provide minimum levels of medical equipment on aircraft and to train all cabin crew in first aid. The equipment carried varies, with many airlines carrying more than the minimum level of equipment required by the regulations. Equipment carried on a typical international flight would include:

— one or more first-aid kits, to be used by the crew;

— a medical kit, normally to be used by a doctor or other qualified person, to treat in-flight medical emergencies;

— an automated external defibrillator (AED) to be used by the crew in case of cardiac arrest.

Cabin crew are trained in the use of first-aid equipment and in carrying out first-aid and resuscitation procedures. They are usually also trained to recognize a range of medical conditions that may cause emergencies on board and to act appropriately to manage these. In addition, many airlines have facilities to enable crew to contact a medical expert at a ground-based response centre for advice on how to manage in-flight medical emergencies.

Travel by air is normally contraindicated in the following cases:

— Infants less than 7 days old;

— Women after the 36th week of pregnancy (after 32nd week for multiple pregnancies) and until seven days after delivery;

— Those suffering from:

  — angina pectoris or chest pain at rest

  — any serious or acute infectious disease

  — decompression sickness after diving

  — increased intracranial pressure due to haemorrhage, trauma or infection

  — infections of the sinuses or infections of the ear and nose, particularly if the Eustachian tube is blocked

  — recent myocardial infarction and stroke (time period depending on severity of illness and duration of travel)

  — recent surgery or injury where trapped air or gas may be present, especially abdominal trauma and gastrointestinal surgery, cranio-facial and ocular injuries, brain operations, and eye operations involving penetration of the eyeball

— severe chronic respiratory disease, breathlessness at rest, or unresolved pneumothorax

— sickle-cell disease

— psychotic illness, except when fully controlled.

9

Careers in Travel and Tourism

World's largest foreign exchange earner is travel and tourism among all industries, provides employment directly to millions of people worldwide and indirectly through many associated service industries.

Very wide industry, it includes Government tourism departments, Immigration and customs services, travel agencies, airlines, tour operators, hotels etc and many associated service industries such as airline catering or laundry services, Guides, Interpreters, Tourism promotion and sales etc.

Travel and Tourism enterprises include major internationals with a workforce of thousands, to the small private travel agent with a handful of employees. Work in the travel and tourism industry is essentially concerned with providing services for people who are away from home, on business or holiday. Travel can be leisure travel involving package tours, pilgrim travel, adventure travel etc or purely business. Work at every functional level in the industry involves dealing directly with people.

Travel agents assess the needs of tourists and businessmen and help them make the best possible travel arrangements from the many travel options available. Also, many major cruise lines, resorts, and specialty travel groups use travel agents to promote travel packages to the millions of people who travel every year.

Travel company personnel must be up-to-date on current rules and regulations and documentation required, in areas like cargo, ticketing and passports, visas etc. so as to correctly advise their clients, and to take care of the paperwork when necessary. Besides this, all tourism staff in marketing, counter sales, or guide services, should be knowledgeable about the places their clients visit, in terms of general background, how to get there connections by air, rail and road and the facilities available.

In India, Travel and tourism, as an industry, has been somewhat slower to take off than in many other places. However, with increasing worldwide interest in travel, and with the Government's encouragement of its activities, it is undergoing massive expansion and improvement. This forecasts a bright future for all those who choose to make a career of travel and tourism. Young people with drive and a capacity for hard work can rise to top positions very quickly in travel and tourism or even head their own agencies. A job in the industry gives good returns as well as perks including opportunity to see many locales at low prices.

Job prospectus both in public and private sector's, are bright. However, the best prospectus for qualified tourism professionals are in the private sector with travel agencies, tour operators, airlines, hotels, transport and cargo companies etc. Jobs in the travel and tourism industry offer good remuneration and perquisites, which include free travel for employees and their families. Salaries can vary somewhat within the industry and are higher in foreign airlines and agencies.

Travel and tourism is a major industry in this country and is at the top of the league of invisible earners of foreign currency. Travel and tourism can be thought of as a manufacturing industry. Components, e. g. hotel rooms, meals, coach or airline seats, are bought and put together by a tour operator to produce holidays. These are sold to the public by retail travel agents, with representatives of the tour operator providing the after sales service to the consumer.

Large tour operators may own the companies that produce the component, e. g. Britannia Airways are owned by Thomson Holidays, and travel agents may also sell the components separately, e. g. air rail and theatre tickets or hotel rooms. Another aspect of the travel and tourism industry is the work of the tourist authorities and boards, set up to promote the counties and regions of the UK. Some of the areas where careers can be made are described here:

Tour Operators

There are many companies operating tours for the domestic as well as the international tourist. Some may be for the usual destinations like hill stations but others are for unusual activities like river rafting, hang gliding, rock climbing and camping. Tour operators need people for selling the concept and then to accompany the groups to the destinations.

For foreign groups, the agencies prefer girls, who are friendly and helpful. For domestic groups, males are preferred. Again, the qualities required are a pleasing and outgoing personality, knowledge of the activities and often participatin in them with the tourists. A person hoping to work with a tour operator must be able to travel with the groups and know people at the destinations to make the tours pleasant for the client. Though one may do a course of tourist guide for this purpose, people with a knowledge of the activities can easily join tour operators. The jobs could be seasonal in some cases.

Although the holidays which are 'manufactured' by tour operators are usually sold by travel agents, some companies have their own retail outlets or sell direct to the public by telephone or post. Thus the work of a large operator may encompass all the stages in the production and sale of a holiday. The larger the company, the more specialised each employee's role becomes, e. g. there are those concerned with negotiating the various components of a holiday with carriers and hotel owners etc. , those who produce the brochure or 'label' of the product, those involved with the research and development of new ideas or marketing them, and those dealing with reservations,

They also have separate finance, personnel and other administrative departments. Several of the large companies run graduate recruitment schemes and operate 'in-house' training programmes for employees. Representatives/ couriers are employed by tour operators to look after the holidaymakers and escort parties of tourists. They work very long hours and are always on call. Besides supervising arrivals, departures, excursions and answering questions, representatives have to deal with any complaints, accidents or illnesses (even deaths) that occur within their group of tourists.

Employment is usually on a seasonal basis, e. g. from April to September. Most companies stipulate a minimum age of 20/21. Good conversational ability in one or more languages, besides native English, is needed. The work involves close personal contact with people and requires the ability to communicate effectively, patiently and tactfully; sometimes in very difficult circumstances.

Travel Agents

Facilitating travel and related services are travel agencies. They require people to deal with customers, guide them as they plan holidays and finally offer tickets for the best routes or offers. They also help in foreign exchange and visas. To join a travel agency, one can do a diploma in travel and ticketing from a polytechnic or an institute. This is usually a short-term course (3-6 months) and will help gain entry into an agency.

Some travel agencies and airlines offer this course. Short-term courses are also offered by Delhi Tourism. Freshers without a diploma can also join and learn on the job. The requirements are a pleasing personality and the ability to deal with customers. Of course a knowledge of destinations and procedures help a great deal.

A travel agency may either be one of a chain of retail outlets or a single operation. The work of the larger agencies is often divided between different divisions, e. g. counter service, business travel and foreign exchange. In smaller concerns each member of the staff will have to handle many aspects of the agency's business. Some agencies limit their activities to arranging travel and/or holidays to a specific area, but most cater for a very much wider demand and fulfil all the functions associated with acting as intermediary between the providers of holidays, transport, accommodation etc. , and the client.

Companies that deal only with business travel are called Business Travel Houses. They may also be responsible for dealing with the planning, publicity and bookings for trade fairs and conferences. Travel agency sales clerks take bookings on behalf of tour operators, sell tickets for travel, make hotel bookings, take payments from the public and give advice, on types of holidays, methods of travel, passports, visas, travellers cheques, foreign currency etc. , They need to have a good knowledge of the products and destinations offered by the tour operating and travel companies.

Managers and assistant managers are responsible for the day-to-day operation of branch offices. This includes staffing, marketing, accountancy, complaints etc. Travel managers should have professional qualifications and experience. In a small agency training will probably be on-the-job. Large companies may offer a training programme.

Tourist Guides

The Ministry of Tourism grants licenses to three categories of tourist guides: regional, state level and monument guides. This is a three-month course followed by a test, after which the license is granted. For 12 years after 1984, no licenses were granted as the license holders had taken a stay. People have thus been working even eithout a license. A guide gets about Rs 1,600 per day for outstation tours but they also get tips from clients and commission from hotels, restaurants and shops. The best guides and those who are in demand are those who offer clean deals and are able to get the maximum advantage for the tourists. Guides must be in touch with foreign agencies who send groups to India.

A fixed itinerary is offered and guides take the groups to those areas which they are familiar with. Apart from the activities mentioned above, wildlife safaris are also becoming increasingly popular. During the season, a guide can hope to earn a six-figure sum but a person has to be good and understand the foreign tourist and his needs. The job is exciting and satisfying and the earnings during the season are enough to see one through the off season as well. The age limit for a guide is 50 years but young and energetic persons are preferred.

Holiday Consultants

This is a new concept, the idea being that the tourist gets all the details of travel and itineraries from one source.

The holiday consultant will sell the holidays, plan out the itineraries, help in travel plans and arrange for ticketing and other details as well. A knowledge of the destinations and the activities available is a pre-requisite. With people having little time, these consultants will make all the arrangements required to have an enjoyable holiday.

Jobs in Airlines

Airlines require people for ground as well as flight duties. On the ground, the duties are in offices, at the airline desks in airports and for checking and managing flights. A course in travel or a qualification on hotel management helps to get in. Airlines also require air hostesses and stewards for flights.

The jobs are glamorous and afford the possibility of traveling to exciting destinations. Free tickets for the family offered by some airlines are an added advantage. To become an air hostess, you should be unmarried, below 25, a graduate or have training in hotel management and catering. A pleasing personality, physical fitness and lots of stamina are required.

Your height should be between 154 and 170 cm, normal eyesight and familiarity of a foreign language. There are a number of institutes offering training to become an air hostess. Indian Airlines has its own institute in Hyderabad to train cabin crew. Airlines advertise for vacancies in the newspaper and impart their own training.

Apart from a test to check your general awareness and proficiency in language, there may be a flight observation test to see if the applicant gests air sick. The flight career of air hostesses is only 10 years or shorter in the case of private airlines. Salaries range in the range of Rs 6,000 for domestic to Rs 40,000 in international airlines. If you want to become an air hostess, make sure you participate in games and extra curricular activities and develop a good personality. With more airlines targetting India, there may be many jobs available as air hostesses.

Jobs in Banks

Foreign banks and dealers in foreign exchange require people to assist their clients in their travel requirements. The idea is to provide services under one roof. Usually, MBASs from premier institutes are preferred. The bank helps in hotel bookings, ticketing and all travel-related services. Indian banks have been laggards in providing such services and foreign banks pay very well.

The jobs expected from the person may sometimes be more than travel-related, since a personal touch is added to make the traveller feel at home. With foreign companies coming in India in a big way, such services are poised to increase. For the adventurous and the travel-minded, there are a lot of avenues that could be explored. Of course one has to very good in the job, have a thorough knowledge and have lots of stamina. For the travel buff with a knowledge of Indian culture and destinations, a career in travel and tourism offers exciting opportunities indeed.

Jobs in Tourist Boards

Tourist Boards/Authorities are public bodies which have been set up to promote the public, tour operators and travel agents, both at home and overseas, thus encouraging the development or tourism. They exist at the national level, e. g. British Tourist Authority, which has 40 overseas offices, country level, e. g. Scottish Tourist Board, and regional level, e. g. London Tourist Board and Yorkshire and Humberside Tourist Board, Their main functions are marketing of an area, research/development of new ideas to attract tourists and information provision.

The development of facilities is also a role at some levels. Careers in Travel and Tourism holidays and travel are a part of life in modern society. The annual break from work, school, college or family life is an important objective - and the very thought of holiday sustains most of us throughout our daily lives. The British alone take something in the order of 21. 5 million trips abroad each year and rather more than 50 million holidays, or short breaks, are taken within the confines of the United Kingdom.

Apart from the holiday business however, the travel and tourism industry also affects our lives in many other ways. Visiting friends and relatives; attending family events: travelling for business purposes; attending conferences; winning travel prizes in advertising campaigns or on television quiz shows are all part of modern living. It is not surprising, therefore, that a vast, complicated industry exists to provide the facilities that make these journeys possible, convenient and, very enjoyable.

Recent statistics indicate that in Great Britain alone, some 1. 5 million people (out of a working population of some 26 million) depend on the travel arid tourism industry for their livelihoods. The number of jobs in the industry are increasing at the rate of some 50,000 a year therefore tourism is slowly becoming one of the most important industries in the world.

As far as Britain's economy is concerned, did you know that after North Sea Oil, the tourism industry earns more in foreign currencies than any other industry? As our manufacturing industries have declined, our service industries are contributing more and more to the country's prosperity.

These industries contribute to the economy by means of what are called invisible exports - in addition exports -

in addition to tourism; insurance, commodity dealings, shopping and financial services fall into this category. It is easy enough to define visible exports. If we export motor vehicles, machinery or textiles overseas we can actually see the goods moving out of the country carried by ships or aircraft, and payment is received in due course from the buyer who changes his own currency into sterling in order to effect payment.

But it is equally true to say that if a resident of the USA decides to come to Britain on holiday, he changes his dollars into sterling in order to spend money here on hotel accommodation or entertainment, etc. If he travels from New York to London by British Airways, as far as our economy is concerned, Britain is exporting. In other words our friend from the USA is putting US dollars into the British economy. He is not receiving tangible goods in exchange - he is, in fact, receiving services and, of course, travel and tourism is a service industry.

The travel bug begins to bite as summer approaches and children get their holidays. Keeping this in mind, we cover careers for those inclined towards travel and adventure. With domestic and international tourism picking up, many careers can indeed be made in this sector. We describe some opportunities though many more may exist in related areas. We also talk to a company which employs young people as 'Holiday Consultants'.

If you like meeting people, love adventure and have a pleasing personality, you can look for careers in a fast growing sector. The travel and tourism industry is growing very fast. Once confined to families taking an annual LTC trip, today more people are venturing out of their homes and look for quality vacations where they can relax and also do something new and interesting. Sports like river rafting and hang gliding are slowly catching on and there are many jobs that are available for a person who can arrange good holidays for the domestic as well as the international tourist.

India earned $ 2753 million from international tourism in 1995. The total number of arrivals were 21. 22 lakhs, and the figure is increasing every year. With the growth of tourist traffic, travel-related jobs are increasing by the day. These relate to various related services facilitating travel, such as travel agencies, banking, hotels, guides, airlines and other services. Some of them may be seasonal, limited to the tourist season from September to March but others are permanent in nature.

In this sector, girls are in as much demand as males and are even preferred for certain jobs. Travel-related jobs are best suited for individuals who enjoy meeting people and make them comfortable. They are for those who love adventure and travelling. True, some are desk jobs, but even these jobs entail understanding the needs of the traveller and making the best arrangements possible for him.

Many agencies are diversifying into travel services. These include foreign banks and vacation companies which offer this as an added service to their clients. For example, American Express has its Travel-Related Services Unit to provide assistance to clients. With the travel sector opening up and foreign timeshares and vacations becoming popular, tourist traffic is expected to increase manifold. Much of the traffic depends on internal stability of the country; fortunately that has existed in India.

Careers in Tourism: Challenges of Higher Education

The tourism sector provides many opportunities for well-qualified people aiming at international careers. Career opportunities are claimed to be more accessible in tourism than in many other sectors of the economy due to both the nature of the business and the strong international affiliation of tourism enterprises. Traditionally, training to become a managing director of a major hotel chain or airline includes long periods of expatriation, if not an entire career.

Despite this, the inclusion of the international dimension in studies of educational issues in tourism has been fairly limited, and we have no solid knowledge about the extent and patterns of the phenomenon or of attitudes towards it. The myths and realities of globalisation have long influenced the philosophies and practices of tourism education. The fact that tourism is a highly international activity, and that employees are frequently likely to meet foreigners in jobs at all levels, are two obvious reasons.

In addition to this, the internationalisation of firms and the cross-border influence of business standards and concepts add to the international imperative, including in the educational system. Students' own travel experiences prior to their studies - including working abroad - are a more recent trend that the providers of tourism education cannot ignore.

Worldwide, there are many university programmes for (predominantly managerial) careers in tourism, and many universities also have international departments, which attract students to full-time programmes or shorter exchange courses. Obviously, the market for student exchange has increased, hospitality courses being among the more popular. Tertiary education in tourism in particular has grown dramatically, driven by the notion that tourism enterprises are in desperate need of qualified staff.

Compared with other western countries, Scandinavian universities have generally been late starters in the development and internationalisation of tertiary education in tourism. This reluctance is partly due to the fact that tourism has traditionally been included in the vocational training system, which has its own professionalisation logic. However, their late entry on the scene, and the fact that they are unburdened by past experience, traditions and investment, make universities ideally placed to cope with the constraints that seem to be emerging for providers of tourism education in many countries, especially with regard to supply, lack of recognition, and unsatisfactory job prospects for graduates.

In this section we are discussing about the modern career issues confronted by students of tourism and hospitality. As a case study we are taking the results of a survey of career issues involving students on the Service Management Masters programme for the Tourism and Hospitality Sector at Lund University, Sweden. The results show that students increasingly regard a career in tourism as an opportunity for a career abroad or with a transnational company. Male students tend to be more adventurous than female students, who also more frequently prefer small firms to large ones. However, students have little detailed knowledge about specific enterprises or job opportunities in areas outside the core of the tourism sector, and they seem to prefer Swedish workplace cultures.

The survey was carried out with the permission of the MSM programme manager. The Masters programme runs over four years. The first year is devoted to basic training, while in the last three years, students can specialise in either hospitality or tourism management. At the time of the survey, the programme had existed for two years, and students were therefore either in their first or second year. The questionnaire was handed out to all 192 students on the Masters programme. Most of the students chose to complete the questionnaire in the class. A total of 159 responded, giving a highly acceptable response rate of 81 per cent. The opportunities to work with people and communication are other prime motives, slightly more important for female than male students. Ross obtains similar results with an Australian student population, and other studies also support the findings to some extent. Swedish students also consider it important that the degree in service management can be used in other sectors. Interestingly, in the programme material published by the university, there is no mention of this aspect, which indicates that the students must have their own ideas about which sectors the degree can be used in.

However, the University offers many other options, including Ph. D. programmes that follow the Master's programme. Slightly less than a third of the students mention international careers as a plus, though significantly more men than women. Thus, even in a population of young people from a country with a strong tradition for equal opportunities, traditional role models seem to prevail. In order to examine students' thoughts on future prospects more closely, they were also asked what they mainly looked for in a job.

As with motivational factors, both male and female students largely agree about what is important in a job. The most critical aspects of a job are a good atmosphere and co-operation with colleagues and other employees. Management style is also quite decisive, students clearly preferring open, democratic and involved leaders. Traditional career and prestige factors, such as fast-track opportunities, bonus systems, competitive salary, fringe benefits.

Image factors, such as level of technology and general reputation, are not particularly important either. The attitudes of these students are thus not very different from other groups in the Scandinavian labour market in that there is a very strong emphasis on social factors and interpersonal relations. Female students are somewhat self-contradictory with regard to international career opportunities. All students imagine embarking on great international careers, but women obviously feel they have less freedom of movement here.

Family obligations may be a legitimate reason for this, but it is also likely that women tend to 'imprison' themselves more than men in relation to careers. Studies of choice of occupation show that women generally consider a significantly narrower range of opportunities than men.

Preferred Job

The students could be said to be somewhat pre-programmed for their future careers by their choice to register for the programme. The MSM is about management, and the majority of the students see themselves in managerial jobs within ten years, as shown in Table 1.

Table 1: Type of job expect to have in 2012.

	Percentage of students		
	All	Male	Female
Managing director (CEO)	46	57	42
Middle manager	31	22	35
Specialist function, consultant etc	16	17	16
Innovator, writer, politician	6	2	8
Researcher	1	2	0

There is a clear gender difference here: male students are more ambitious than their female colleagues, who more frequently aim at middle management. However, female students imagine themselves in non-standard roles on the fringe of the traditional tourism sector, e. g. journalism, consultancy and at headquarters, to a greater extent than their male colleagues.

Even though 38 percent of the students indicate that the programme can be used in many trades and industries, they tend to stick to the areas defined by the Master's programme, i. e. hotels, restaurants and travel businesses. Relatively few regard the media and marketing as realistic and attractive, although female students are more aware of job opportunities in these sub-sectors. Students were also asked to name enterprises they found particularly attractive.

SAS/Radisson received the highest score, followed by other well-known Scandinavian and international tourism enterprises, such as Hilton, Elite Hotel, SAS, Scandic, Fritidsresor, Wonderful Copenhagen, Choice Hotels, Copenhagen Airports, and Wing Resor. A crude calculation shows that the MSM programme will supply the large hotel chains in the region with managing directors for many decades to come. Obviously, at some point in their studies or work careers, students will have to aim more broadly.

The course providers are aware of this dilemma, however, and have started to include more general retail management issues in the programme. In Sweden, tourism is not confined to the private sector. There is substantial public involvement in destination management and marketing, policy and planning, and education/research. Opportunities to work on key tourism issues outside the core sector are also appearing, but so far students have not really discovered the potential for jobs in the public sector.

A fifth of the population of Master's programme students see themselves as entrepreneurs in ten years' time. Students are far more attracted to jobs in large enterprises and international enterprises than in small ones. This is consistent with other studies, which demonstrate that the media focus on large enterprises has a side effect on human resource issues. Employment at a well-known large employer is more likely to signal success on a job applicant's CV than the name of a relatively unknown small employer.

Another consideration is that, in most sectors of the economy, large employers offer better wages and more favourable working conditions. The students' expressed wish for a good working environment with helpful colleagues reflects the need for workplaces of a certain size. Female students are less attracted to very large enterprises, and tend more to opt for the medium-sized ones. This preference is also likely to have a negative side effect in terms of opportunities for international careers, as smaller enterprises operate more locally and are less often affiliated.

The prospects for micro enterprises being able to attract better-educated personnel seem rather bleak. While not blaming the students, this might further aggravate the polarisation between professional, growth-oriented and advanced enterprises on the one hand, and the lifestyle-based small enterprises on the other. At the same time, it must be taken into account that the latter represent not only the large majority of enterprises, but also a very considerable financial turnover and employment rate in the sector.

International Careers

The adventurous nature of male students, who are more inclined than female students to opt for international careers that lead to continual moves from country to country and from continent to continent. Quite a few of the students find it best to start their career at home, in order to gain experience, and then go abroad afterwards.

International careers seem to be attractive, and many dreams and hopes are connected to working abroad. When compared with the other findings about motivations and likely job categories, however, these dreams and hopes are less likely to be realised. A control question shows that students tend to consider that the quality of life is best at home, close to home, or in countries that are not too culturally different, i. e. , the Anglo-Saxon world.

Students are less likely to take risks if jobs involve going to Third World countries or other countries ranking low in an imaginary prestige hierarchy. Other studies confirm that the best-qualified employees do not exactly queue up for expatriate posts in what are considered risky zones. Quite a number of the students say that the quality of life is best where they are at the moment, e. g. in the Skaane region, including Malmö, Lund and Helsingborg.

It is a well-known phenomenon that the more acquainted people get with their environment, the harder it is for them to imagine that life could be better elsewhere. It is remarkable that such young people as in this survey population stress the quality of life in their home region so strongly.

Future Prospects

The rate of turnover in the tourism sector is significantly high in most countries, not least in the Nordic countries. Furthermore, employees with dedicated training in the hospitality and management sectors are likely to leave the sector within a number of years. The reasons given are often salary, unsocial working hours, and lack of career opportunities.

Students indicated that the MSM programme might be useful in industries other than tourism, although their guesses as to which are not entirely convincing. A third of the students thought that the qualifications acquired could be used elsewhere. One could say that the students are realistic in their evaluation of the human resource features of the sector, and they may also be aware that the high turnover could hamper their career in the sector.

In addition, they are preparing themselves for the 'psychological contract' they will have to make with their future employers, i. e. implicitly or explicitly to negotiate employment conditions for the duration of a job. Nevertheless the majority want to give tourism a fair chance.

In comparison, a cohort study from an Australian university shows that only 40 per cent of graduates were working in other sectors three to four years after graduation. According to Purcell and Quinn, one important reason for leaving the industry is 'overeducation' - graduates tend to quickly exhaust the learning potential in typical managerial jobs in the tourist industry and want to go on to new challenges.

The survey shows that the students are very enthusiastic about careers in tourism, and that they fully expect the degree to qualify them for attractive managerial jobs in Sweden and, to a lesser extent, abroad. Despite this, students are fairly unimaginative in their job and enterprise orientation. They seem to lack a good overview of the more intrinsic opportunities in the 'experience economy' and the 'new economy'.

Students on this programme seem to be unaware of job opportunities in the melting pot between the private and public sectors, and of jobs that bridge the gap between formerly disintegrated strands of the service sector. But these students are still young, it might be objected, and there are still two or three years to graduation. At that time they may discover opportunities that are not as obvious to them now. However, the students are unlikely to develop their imaginative capabilities and become flexible unless they are supported by the programme management and teachers.

The MSM curriculum includes many of the usual core subjects, such as marketing, business finance and service management. A strong focus on cases and individual projects will, if supervision is geared to more creative interpretations, enable students to move beyond the more standardised types of hospitality studies. The portfolio of business partners attached to the programme is an indication of the rather traditional way of thinking about tourism within the MSM: most of the business partners are hotels, restaurant chains, travel services and destination management units.

An interesting exception is IKEA. Retailing is already being taught more intensively in the course. As a result, only two years after the programme was introduced, the university is already revising its previously strong focus on the core tourism industry. But there are good reasons for a strong focus and standardisation in tourism studies, and arguments against a broader perspective. First, in an international context, it is important that skills and certificates are recognisable across borders, thus facilitating the internationalisation process for employees as well as employers.

Another argument for specialisation and standardisation is the need to upgrade qualifications and ensure that enterprises can get precisely the profiles they need, thus minimising the need for introductory and training courses for new employees. This is particularly important if skills and competencies are to be transferable across borders. Third, closer links between stakeholders and educational institutions is a step towards the professionalisation of the entire sector and to improving the knowledge base and innovative and economic capabilities.

'Normalisation' describes much of the endeavours of the educational system and their collaborating partners. However, arguments for a standard professionalisation must be confronted with the reality of the tourism business. Business practices are contradicting the endeavours of the educational system. Normalisation is far from being the objective of many - small and large - tourism enterprises.

At the end of the day, the sector is not that keen on recruiting specialised candidates, and there are voices warning of an 'overproduction'. Many enterprises, e. g. Euro-Disney, value language skills and personality traits more highly than specific tourism-related qualifications that can be acquired either in the vocational system or universities. Moreover, some large enterprises actually have their own educational facilities, where the main issues are specific corporate values and management techniques.

While corporate training does not necessarily replace graduate education, it shows that the universities are operating in a highly competitive market, and that their students will suffer most if educational programmes ignore underlying business mechanisms. Becker was stressing the importance of distinguishing between general and specific qualifications almost 40 years ago. In labour markets characterised by rapid turnover and intensive changes in business operations, employees and employers will benefit most from a focus on generalist qualifications that can be used in many enterprises both inside and outside the sector.

Such qualifications, which are increasingly in demand everywhere in the labour market, include personality traits such as flexibility, the ability to learn new things, responsibility, innovativeness, and, not least, social competencies. The Swedish students seem to be intuitively aware of the fact that tourism is a sector with considerable fluctuations, making specialised skills and very industry-specific knowledge less of a life insurance.

Through a strictly neo-classical interpretation, an extension of the labour markets in space will give more room for those with very specialised qualifications. Employment opportunities in a more global job environment can thus justify the existence of a specialised programme. Extrapolating from this, knowledge niches adopted by educational institutions will support an enhanced division of labour between countries and regions, and contribute to the creation of wealth.

The MSM programme could be seen as an effort to secure an advantage for the Swedish workforce in a broader, international labour market. Ideally, graduates will then be able to participate actively in the internationalisation process, which in turn can ultimately be expected to benefit the Swedish economy.

In practice, however, while a large proportion of the students claim to want an international career, most of them expect to stay in the home region or to return after a period abroad. The country orientation is limited and concentrated on the Anglo-Saxon world. Thus, the ideal model, based on neo-classical thinking, has some very serious drawbacks.

These drawbacks are further aggravated by the gender issue. The survey shows that prospective careers and attitudes to working life are highly influenced by traditional gender patterns. Female students tend to be less adventurous, being less keen to work in the largest enterprises, a choice that might have quite far-reaching implications for them individually, as well as for gender equality in general. However, all students agree on important job features, such as the importance of interpersonal issues and non-bureaucratic managerial styles. The cultural and social values of the Swedish school system and society influence the MSM programme.

Tourism education at the tertiary level opens up many opportunities. However, given the instability and development imperatives in the sector, there are good reasons to warn against taking specialisation too far. Normalisation is far from being prevalent in the sector. To a greater extent than in other sectors, students should be told from the start that there is no such thing as a pre-programmed 'tourism career'. They will have to enact their working life themselves, as entrepreneurs if not as salaried employees.

It is the task of universities, in collaboration with partners in the private and public sectors, to provide students with the appropriate generalist knowledge in business economics, marketing and service management to help them create opportunities for themselves - and potentially for the industry. In a global context, it is particularly important that students are made aware of the career implications of new alliances in the industry. The media, film and entertainment industries are creating types of tourist attractions and modes of service production not previously seen. Retailing is merging with tourism and vice versa.

The Internet is a 'creative destroyer' of much traditional marketing and PR. Cruising is largely detached from specific national contexts in relation to labour, regulations and supplies. NGOs, e. g. in environmental protection, are becoming operators of tourism facilities worldwide or getting involved in the travel market. Curricula need to be broader than prevailing wisdom suggests. Some teachers are beginning to suggest that, in the future, tertiary studies should be about tourism rather than for tourism, and that the vocational bias should be loosened.

10

Employment Issues

Employment in the "travel and tourism industry" includes all activities in direct contact with visitors such as airlines, hotels, car rental activities, restaurants, retail and entertainment activities. Travel and tourism economy" comprises, in addition:

— suppliers to the industry (e.g. airline caterers, laundry services, food suppliers, wholesalers, accounting firms and so on which have some involvement with the tourism sector);

— government agencies, manufacturing and construction of capital goods and exported goods used in the travel and tourism sector; and

— supplied commodities (e.g. steel products, lumber, oil products and so on which are used in the travel and tourism sector).

The contribution to the travel and tourism economy of these sectors is included on a proportionate basis as derived from input-output matrices for the economies concerned.

Contribution of Tourism to GDP

Table 1 summarises the importance of travel and tourism in the economies of several Asia-Pacific countries, in terms of the sector's contribution to GDP, as estimated by the World Travel and Tourism Council. While Macau, China, and the small island nation of Fiji rely particularly heavily on the tourism sector, tourism has an above-average importance in a number of countries, notably New Zealand, Thailand, Australia and Cambodia (in the latter case reflecting an economy yet to realise its potential in other sectors). The other countries and areas shown in Table 1 on average rely on travel and tourism for around 3.1% of their GDP.

Table 1. Share of GDP of the travel and tourism industry and the travel through Asian and Pacific countries and areas.

	T & T Industry	T & T Economy		T & T Industry	T & T Economy
Australia	5.1	12.0	Macau, China	19.0	54.8
Bangladesh	1.3	3.4	Malaysia	3.9	12.2
Cambodia	4.3	10.8	Nepal	3.4	7.8
China	2.4	10.3	New Zealand	6.1	14.2
Fiji	11.8	29.0	Pakistan	1.9	4.4
Hong Kong, China	1.9	11.0	Philippines	2.7	7.4
India	2.0	4.8	Singapore	2.7	9.8
Indonesia	3.5	9.8	Sri Lanka	3.0	8.6
Islamic Republic of Iran	3.9	13.1	Taiwan,	China	1.2 4.9
Japan	3.5	8.9	Thailand	5.2	11.8
Republic of Korea	1.8	7.5	Viet Nam	1.9	6.9

To generalise, when the indirect effects of tourism are included, the sector's importance to GDP typically rises to between two and three times the level of the direct contribution shown below, although there are some considerable variations in this relationship country-by-country.

Contribution of Tourism to Foreign Exchange Earnings

WTTC also presents an analysis of the importance of travel and tourism within each country's total merchandise and services export revenues. Note that this does not discount the "import cost" of nationals travelling abroad, and thus represents only a gross measure.

Table 2, as with the GDP measure, shows Macau, China and Fiji as relying on travel and tourism for a large proportion of their export revenues. Singapore, India, Pakistan, the Philippines and Viet Nam are least dependent on tourism for export earnings, while for countries such as Cambodia, Islamic Republic of Iran, New Zealand, Australia and Nepal, tourism remains a very important source of foreign exchange earnings.

Table 2. Travel and tourism receipts as a share of exports, 2003 (%)

Australia	14.2	Macau, China	44.7
Bangladesh	4.0	Malaysia	7.6
Cambodia	18.2	Nepal	13.7
China	7.5	New Zealand	15.2
Fiji	37.0	Pakistan	6.2
Hong Kong, China	7.3	Philippines	6.3
India	5.9	Singapore	5.2
Indonesia	10.6	Sri Lanka	10.0
Islamic Republic of Iran	17.4	Taiwan, China	3.8
Japan	7.8	Thailand	11.0
Republic of Korea	7.5	Viet Nam	6.7

Trends in International Tourism

The Asia-Pacific region has been one of the most dynamic for international tourism over the last decade and the potential for further growth over the medium and long term remains strong. It currently accounts for around one-eighth of all international tourist arrivals but a somewhat larger share - approaching one-fifth - of international tourist receipts.

Following the financial crisis of 1997, when tourism to the region temporarily collapsed, international tourism had been steadily regaining lost ground until the security incidents of September 2001. While China was the clear front-runner, almost all countries saw growth in international tourism volumes and/or receipts. Since then, the region has, in common with most other regions of the world, borne the brunt of economic slowdown in the world's main generating markets as well as a widespread unwillingness to travel far from home as a result of concerns over safety and security, including income and job security.

However, the region as a whole topped the growth rankings for 2002 - up by almost 8% - (only the Middle East recorded stronger growth) but in reality only some countries - notably China, Thailand and Islamic Republic of Iran, as well as Hong Kong, China, and Macau, China - managed to maintain strong growth trends. The impact of recent uncertainty caused by the Iraq war and the SARS outbreak makes it difficult to predict when the region will regain its former dynamism. The region's main tourism destinations, judged in terms of international tourism receipts, are China, Australia, Thailand, Republic of Korea and Singapore.

Between them these five countries account for around half of the region's total receipts - some US$44.4 bn in 2001 (out of a regional total of US$87.2 bn) - and received almost 39 million arrivals (out of a regional total of 90 million). This is not to deny the relative size and importance of the industry in many of the smaller destinations, of course, with the industry playing an increasing role in countries such as Cambodia and Viet Nam and in small island states in the Pacific region.

As the tourism market in the Asia-Pacific region matures, it also accounts for an increasing share of world outbound travel - representing around 17% of all international arrivals in 2001. Travel intensity remains low, however, at 3 trips per 100 population. The region generated almost 121 million international arrivals in 2001, three-quarters of which (77%) were to destinations within the region itself. (Europe accounted for 12% and the Americas 7%.) Japan is head and shoulders above any other outbound market in terms of both volume and expenditure, but this market has been in the doldrums over the last few years. Proving particularly strong over the last two years have been China, Hong Kong, China, India, Republic of Korea and Viet Nam.

Data on Asia-Pacific intra-regional expenditure are not readily available. However, daily expenditure per capita on outbound tourism by travellers from the region is estimated by the World Tourism Organization to be US$26 (compared with a world average of US$75), a spending figure that is likely to be much smaller for travel within the region itself.

EMPLOYMENT IN TRAVEL AND TOURISM

World Travel and Tourism Council estimates have covered employment levels in each major Asian and Pacific country on an annual basis since 1998, both for direct jobs in the sector (the "travel and tourism industry") and for direct plus indirect jobs. China and India by their very scale dominate these figures. Together these two countries have 78.2 million employed in total in the sector, of which 25.1 million are direct employees of the industry and the balance, 53.1 million, indirectly employed.

Thus all the other countries of Asia and the Pacific, excluding India and China, have 36.6 million jobs in travel and tourism, of which 13.6 million are direct and 23.0

million indirect. The decline in China and India (in particular the latter) has been less marked than in many other countries in the region, while Singapore has seen the largest decline, and Indonesia, Pakistan, Philippines, Viet Nam, Thailand and Nepal have seen falls of over 10% in the period. On the other hand, increases in direct travel and tourism employment were registered in almost half of the countries, of which those in Brunei and Malaysia were by far the most important.

These trends may be due to more than one influence. The 1997 financial crisis in Asia left behind it a legacy of economic slowdown which hit employment levels hard. There may also have been improvements in labour productivity through an application of labour-saving technologies and work organization within this period. There is some evidence to suggest that the tourism industry might be contracting more work out to suppliers, thereby diminishing direct employment but raising indirect employment, since the trends in total "travel and tourism economy" employment are different from those in the "travel and tourism industry".

There has been an increase of 3.8% in total direct plus indirect travel and tourism employment since 1998, dominated by gains in China and India (742,000 new jobs). In China, although the country has been booming as an international tourism destination, the overwhelming influence has been domestic travel. According to the China National Tourism Administration, there were 810 million domestic trips (leisure trips only) in 2002, double the number recorded in 1993; Chinese tourism is reported to be growing faster than the Chinese economy as a whole, and tourism is clearly a major source of labour demand as a consequence.

With the exception of China and India, however, total labour demand in the travel and tourism economy fell by 2.6% between 1998 and 2003, representing an absolute loss of almost 1 million jobs. In 2003, direct employment in the region's travel and tourism industry accounts for 2.3% of all employment, while direct plus indirect jobs accounts for 6.9%. By global standards, these figures remain a little below average. Worldwide in 2003, WTTC estimates that direct employment accounts for 2.8% of all jobs, and direct plus indirect for 7.8%.

The labour market in Macau, China, depends to the greatest extent on tourism, with direct employment in the industry representing 26.6% of all jobs, and direct plus indirect 68.4%. This is exceptional, given the special status of Macau, China, as a centre for leisure and gaming. Elsewhere in the region, the highest proportion of direct employment (with the exception of some of the small island destinations), is in New Zealand, Australia, Japan and Thailand. Taking indirect and direct jobs together, however, the top four are New Zealand, Australia, Islamic Republic of Iran and Japan.

EMERGING TRENDS IN LABOUR MARKET

Finding and retaining staff is a key area of concern for employers in the tourism industry. A number of trends emerging in the labour market are common to many countries throughout the region. These can be summarised under the headings listed below. Greater elaboration on these issues is provided by the subsequent country details which illustrate in more depth the general points described here.

Industry Image

Generally throughout the region, as with most other places in the world, the image of the tourism sector, and particularly hospitality, is rather low and it is not regarded as an attractive industry in which to work. Other sectors such as the financial sector or IT prove far more appealing, particularly to the younger generation. Employment in hotels and restaurants is regarded as offering low pay, unsocial hours, shift work, work over holiday periods and sometimes the necessity to work away from home in remote resorts.

For those with some training in the sector, working abroad or on a cruise ship may offer an attractive alternative. It appears that as the number of educated youth grows, they prefer to avoid the service industries. In particular, the lack of a career path acts as a deterrent. However, in a few countries such as China, there was some feeling that employment by the large international hotel companies carried a certain kudos and provided an international exposure that was appealing.

Gender

Generally the employment of females in the hospitality sector is higher than in many other industries, in part reflecting the high percentage of low skilled jobs in hotels and restaurants such as waitresses, chambermaids and so on. As a broad generalisation, the ratio between male and female employees in the Asia-Pacific region is fairly equally split. Among the Hotel Survey respondents, there was no indication that female recruitment was more difficult than male. In China mention was made of legal regulations protecting female workers.

Mobility of Labour

For the majority of the emerging economies, there is - in terms of numbers - an ample supply of local labour for all sectors of the tourism industry. Asia's financial crisis of 1997 and the ensuing economic downturn has also meant that unemployment has risen in places such as Hong Kong, China, that previously had labour shortages.

Malaysia, for example, which previously welcomed foreign labour, has now introduced severe restrictions, sent some workers home and made some jobs off-limits for foreign workers. This labour surplus means that there is a ready supply of workers for all low skills jobs although there are clearly shortages of suitably qualified personnel at the mid-range and higher skills levels.

For more skilled openings, particularly at managerial and professional level, most companies noted that there was a need to import labour from abroad. Hotel companies in China, Malaysia and Indonesia made specific mention of the lack of qualified personnel at this level. They noted that the procedure for importing labour could be time-consuming and sometimes difficult. However, in all cases, it was felt that the transfer of technology and knowledge skills was an important element in their staff development.

Countries vary in the controls they place on the importation of labour, but invariably place different caps for certain types of grades. Generally, in the more developed economies, the less skilled the opening, the more difficult it is for the foreign worker to gain an entry permit. In many cases employers need to demonstrate that it is impossible to fill a post with a suitably qualified local before the employment of a foreign worker is allowed.

Skills Shortages

Low worker commitment and a shortage of skills are the most frequently cited problems facing the industry by both the trade itself and by industry practitioners and organizers. In most countries there are skills shortages across the board ranging, at the lower skills level, from fast-food cooks to waiters and waitresses to bar attendants to chefs. In Hong Kong, China, for example, training in Chinese catering is one of six sectors specifically selected by the government for those with secondary education or below. Particular mention was made of the need to train chefs in specific cuisines in order to cater to the tastes of the increasingly cosmopolitan traveller. Skills at management level were particularly lacking in many countries and a shortage of those with leadership qualities appears to be a common problem in most destinations.

Language Training

An inadequate proficiency of foreign languages among staff and potential workers needing face-to-face contact with guests was a recurrent theme for most destinations. This was the case in most countries, and became more acute for employees working away from the capital and major gateway cities where they had less exposure to foreign languages and less opportunity for language training. First mention was made in almost all destinations of the need for workers to be able to operate in English, reflecting the universal language of tourism. However, depending on the major markets for a destination, Asian languages are becoming increasingly important. Languages mentioned included Mandarin, Japanese, and even Russian.

In the Hotel Survey, most respondents in most countries described the policy environment within which the hotel sector operates as "supportive". Nonetheless it was also common for comments to be made along the lines that governments could do more to help identify skills shortages, improve the supply of trained staff, and that governments could have a role, together with the industry, in seeking to make the hotel sector a more attractive place in which to work.

Enterprise Size

The tourism sector is characterised by a high percentage of small and medium sized businesses. Indeed in many less developed countries, there are also a considerable number of operations such as food vendors and trinket sellers that do not fall within the formal economy at all. A particularly common feature of the tourism industry is a high number of working proprietors.

Generally it is only the more up-market hotels and the tourist offices in the larger destinations that employ relatively large numbers. The majority of one-, two- and three-star hotels, restaurants, and other ancillary businesses such as car hire operations, travel agents and retail outlets are generally small businesses with low numbers of employees. Singapore exemplifies the picture in a more developed destination - which has a significant number of four- and fivestar hotels - where, despite this, over 58% of hotels and 84% of restaurants employ fewer than 25 persons. In Sri Lanka, registered hotels and restaurants employ an average of only 36 people, while tour operators and travel agents employ an average of 12, and recreational agencies and tourist shops have on average just four and five employees respectively.

EMPLOYMENT TRENDS IN VARIOUS TOURIST DESTINATIONS

Data on employment (and unemployment in particular) are generally not comparable between countries, due to different definitions and statistical concepts, as well as the different methodology of the primary sources. Where no sources are mentioned specifically, the data should therefore be taken as merely indicative. However, the profiles given below serve to illustrate tourism employment trends in a variety of destinations throughout the region.

Australia

According to the Australian Bureau of Statistics' Labour Force Survey, there were some 9.5 million people employed in Australia in June 2003, representing a participation rate of slightly under 64%. In addition, just over 600,000 people were unemployed, which implied an unemployment rate of 5.9%. Of the 12 million people in the age range of 15-69, 40% (4.8 million) have post-secondary school qualifications. Of these, 27% hold degree-level or higher qualifications, 22% have an undergraduate or associate diploma qualification, 35% hold a skilled vocational qualification and 16% a basic vocational qualification.

By and large, the Australian labour force is stable in most industries, with staff turnover not generally regarded as a problem. Australia's Tourism Satellite Account provides considerable detail about the make-up of employment within the tourism sector. For standard definitions and different possible sources of data on the economically active population, employment, unemployment and underemployment see ILO, Yearbook of Labour Statistics, 2000, p. 71 In the consultation paper for the 10-year plan which has been instituted by the Minister for Small Business & Tourism, it is pointed out that around 70% of employees in the travel agency and accommodation sectors are female, against a national average of 44%, and that part-time workers in cafes and restaurants account for 70% of all employees compared with a national average of 26%.

The tourism industry in Australia has a strong component made up of small and mediumsized businesses, as is the case in other countries. In Australia, over 88% of businesses in the accommodation, cafés and restaurant sector, and over 95% of businesses in the cultural and recreational services sector are classified as small businesses employing fewer than 20 people. In addition, there are a large number of non-employing owner-occupier businesses within the accommodation, cafés and restaurant sector. Bangladesh The results from the Hotel Survey indicate that there are few recruitment problems within the country, although a shortage of management skills does arise.

No importation of labour is necessary for most jobs within the hotel sector, and there is reported to be no particular difficulty in recruiting female staff for appropriate positions. However, it is expected that labour market issues will become increasingly difficult to solve in future, and the comment is made that employment growth may be inhibited by wages tending to be rising in the industry.

Australia has perhaps the most widely developed supporting structure for tourism in the region. The tourism portfolio comes under the Minister for Small Business and Tourism, whose department in turn is part of the Department of Industry, Tourism and Resources. The Tourism Division within the department provides civil service support.

In addition to the ministerial organisation, some of the most prominent bodies whose role it is to support, develop and promote tourism include the Australian Standing Committee on Tourism, the Tourism Forecasting Council, the Bureau of Tourism Research, Tourism Training Australia and the Australian Tourist Commission which is responsibl§§e for the global marketing and promotion of Australia as a tourism destination.

The Minister responsible for tourism matters has instituted a 10-year plan for tourism, during which period it is predicted that visitors from abroad will double in number. The 10-year plan was under consideration in the first quarter of 2003 by the government of Australia. As an example of best practice in government's approaches to the tourism sector, the plan covers forecasts and targets for tourism development, investment and infrastructure, domestic and international tourism, product development, sustainable development, risk management and implementation.

Labour supply is seen as a key issue in realising the 10-year plan, which emphasises the wide range of training programmes available in the sector and also includes the specific identification of skills shortages and training needs through the actions of Tourism Training Australia In particular, the consultation paper acknowledges that not all the required skills can be found in Australia, and that "in key occupations where skill shortages have persisted, employers have been able to sponsor, on a temporary basis, overseas workers who are issued with visas which allow them to perform their specialist work in Australia".

These young foreigners, it is claimed, provide Australia's tourism sector with access to a large pool of seasonal workers. In 2000-01, over 76,000 such visas were issued, up by 39% on the 55,000 of 1996-97. The plan points out that those young foreigners spend some A$1.3 bn annually in Australia and thus generate worthwhile economic benefits in addition to performing a useful function for the tourism industry.

China

China's labour market is estimated at well over 700 million people at the end of 2002. It is estimated by the Ministry of Labour and Social Security that the level of unemployment is 7%, caused in part by the restructuring of state-owned enterprises. The government estimates that an economic growth rate of 7% a year will be necessary merely to absorb the excess labour shed from these enterprises.

In 2000, 42.9 million Chinese were employed in the "wholesale, retail and catering" sector - a further breakdown is not available. However, in the state sector only, there were 1,158,000 employed in hotels, of which

671,000 (58%) were female, in "tourism" the total was 122,000 of which 57,000 (47%) were female, and in recreational services, the total was 66,000 of which 36,000 (55%) were female. Although these are small numbers only in the context of the total labour force, the proportions indicate that female job opportunities in the tourism sector are considerable.

For the hotel and tourism industry, a key issue is that of providing staff able to operate in a foreign language - most usually English. This is reported to be relatively straightforward in the major urban areas such as Beijing and Shanghai, where college graduates are relatively plentiful and English language capabilities exist, but it is far harder to find such staff elsewhere in the country. In general, it is in China's fastest growing regions, such as the south and the emerging cities of Tianjin, Hangzhou, Chengdu and Shouzhou that a shortage of educated and skilled labour is most marked.

A respondent to the Hotel Survey - a major global company with extensive interests in China - states that there are difficulties in recruiting food and beverage staff within China, especially at the executive chef and food and beverage management level. However, what are described as "rank and file" staff can be found because "the hotel business attracts staff generally and provides international exposure and career development opportunities" which are welcomed within the country.

A respondent from another international hotel company claims that staff recruitment in China can be a problem, especially with regard to foreign language capabilities (notably in English) for those jobs which involve face-to-face contact with guests. A third respondent broadly makes the same points, but adds that financial staff with English language abilities are in short supply, as are waiters and waitresses. Important enterprises in China used to be either state owned enterprises (SOE) or foreigninvested enterprises (FIE) forming two different labour market segments.

Nominally, employees in a state owned enterprise have to seek permission to leave their jobs, making transfers from one sector to the other difficult. However, in practice this procedure is less rigidly enforced than in the past, and it is now easier to transfer. As in addition, fringe benefits such as automatic provision of free, life-time housing which used to characterise jobs in the SOE's begin to break down, it is felt that these two labour market segments will eventually merge into one, improving labour mobility within China, Also, as Chinese workers become better educated and more proficient in language skills, FIEs are increasingly inclined to hire Chinese nationals rather than automatically to think of importing expatriates.

Tourism in China is regarded as being of national importance and is subject to detailed planning, mainly under the aegis of the China National Tourism Administration (CNTA). It is fair to say that, while tourism from abroad is important to China in terms of its contribution to foreign exchange earnings, it is domestic tourism which dominates the country.

China has a 20-year tourism development plan, and has declared its intention to transform itself from an important regional tourism destination within Asia into the world's largest tourism destination within the next 20 years. The government states that it sees tourism as an important component in the national economy, and it is seeking to develop the sector accordingly.

While much of China's tourism business is nationally owned, in acknowledgement of the country's entry into the World Trade Organisation, China has started to admit foreign-owned travel agencies. These numbered eight in 2000. The CNTA has a role in identifying training and human resource needs and promoting the training and educational support required to meet these.

Hong Kong

Towards the end of 2002, the labour force in Hong Kong, China, estimated by the Census and Statistics Department to be some 3.5 million was suffering an unemployment rate of over 7%. Approximately 43% of the labour force is female, 57% male. While the workforce is generally well-educated, there is concern about a growing shortage of highly-qualified, mainly university level, people; projections indicate a shortfall of this grade of up to 120,000 people by 2006, in response to which various educational initiatives are being taken as well as a programme to attract more, highly qualified individuals from the Chinese mainland.

Table 3. Employment in restaurants, hotels and boarding houses in Hong Kong, China, 1999-2001 (thousand)

	1999	2000	2001
Total jobs	2,180	2,209	2,209
of which			
- restaurants	191	188	193
- hotels and boarding houses	28	29	27
Sub-total	219	217	220
%	10.0	9.8	10.0

A characteristic of the employment pattern in Hong Kong, China in recent years has been an erosion of the manufacturing base, as many manufacturing jobs have moved to mainland China. At the end of 2001, for example, there were nine service sector jobs for every one manufacturing job, a trend that is expected to continue. Table 3 shows official data on the breakdown of jobs in the tourism sector.

In mid-2001, the government of Hong Kong, China, initiated the Skills Upgrading Scheme, allocating HK$400 mn to a programme aimed at raising competences for workers with secondary education or below. Among the six sectors identified as priorities is Chinese catering . Training courses in all of these began in September 2001 and in November the scheme was extended to include tourism and hotels, as well as property management and hairdressing.

Immigration for work purposes is generally easier for managerial, professional and entrepreneurial skills than for less skilled occupations. Nonetheless, the Supplementary Labour Scheme allows for the immigration of workers who fall outside the general policy on entry for employment. Companies may be able to import workers provided they can show that they have given priority to locals and that they are genuinely unable to recruit from the local market.

They must also have advertised the posts locally, undertaken four weeks of potential job matching with the Hong Kong, China Labour Department and sought staff via the tailormade retraining courses for workers who are available. By the end of 2001, under this scheme 8,750 people had been admitted to Hong Kong, China, since the scheme's inauguration in February 1996. A respondent in the Hotel Survey indicated that the overall standard of English language ability gives some cause for concern, and also that the company had found a shortage of experienced cooks for their hotels' operations.

India

According to the Department of Tourism, Government of India, there were some 12 million people employed directly in the tourism sector at the beginning of this decade. The point was made that tourism has a very positive capital to labour ratio, with 89 jobs being created in the hotel and restaurant industry per 1 million rupees of investment, compared with 45 jobs in agriculture and 13 jobs in manufacturing.

By 2010, the Government of India has identified that as many as 6 million additional jobs in the tourism sector may be created, most of which will be generated by domestic tourism demand (which, very much along the same lines as in China, far outweighs the importance of international tourism; in 2001 some 190 million domestic trips were made in comparison to international tourist arrivals of 2.5 million). Thus the need for tourism training and education could become a key issue in the expansion of the sector.

Indonesia

Indonesia in common with a number of other countries, that finding suitable staff for the hotel sector is difficult. There is a view that school education provides inadequate "business orientation" for the industry, whereby it is claimed that employees in the sector often do not seem to be equipped to take the initiative but require constant and close direction. On the positive side, recruiting female staff appears not to present a major problem.

One respondent stated that there is a shortage of staff in the following skills areas: - food and beverage management, culinary staff, and engineering staff. Another respondent to the Hotel Survey provided an extensive list of employment policy issues which indicates, in this respondent's opinion, that the Indonesian labour market suffers from some strong disincentives to the recruitment of permanent (established) staff.

The respondent claims that there is too much job protection which makes shedding labour in the current difficult circumstances very hard, and thus encourages fixed term contract recruitment rather than the conclusion of permanent contracts. Among the concerns cited are "regulations regarding termination pay, even when employees have been dismissed for unacceptable conduct such as theft; the fact that pay is related to length of service rather than productivity, that an established job is regarded as permanent to the incumbent until retirement; and that severance pay rules are so high that employers cannot afford to reduce the size of their labour force even in hard times."

Japan

The labour market in Japan is changing in the face of a decline in manufacturing activity, economic stagnation and industrial restructuring. Although traditions are hard to shake, the expectation that a new recruit would have a job with the same employer for life has been changing for some time now. There is a greater degree of flexibility in the labour force, partly reflecting jobs that are increasingly subject to globalization tendencies or characterized by technological developments, and partly reflecting economic weaknesses.

Although foreign companies report some difficulty finding experienced engineers and middle managers, there is no indication of any shortage of labour within the tourism industry. In broad terms, Japan encourages the recruitment of labour from abroad where foreigners possess technological skills and knowledge, while unskilled foreign workers are generally unwelcome.

The effects of this approach are seen in an analysis of the 670,000 foreign workers who were in Japan in 1999. 252,000 were classified as "overstayers"; workers of Japanese descent, most numerously from South America, accounted for a further 221,000, part-time students for 47,000 and "others" for 25,000. The balance of approximately 125,000 comprised "professors, artists, religious activity, journalists, investors/manages, legal/ accountancy, medical, researchers, instructors, engineers, specialists in humanities, inter-corporate transferees and skilled labour". In other words, Japan only seeks highly qualified people from abroad.

Macau, China

Total employment in "hotels, restaurants and similar establishments" according to Macau, China, government data rose from 21,700 in 1999 to 22,900 in 2001, having declined slightly in the intervening year. These levels exclude many of the other sectors of activity, such as transport, which are included in the preceding WTTC data.

Macau, China, government data for 2002 show the distribution of employment in the travel and tourism sector by gender. Government statistics indicate that, in the accommodation sector, small businesses are reserved mainly for the lower grade hotels and for guesthouse types of accommodation. Higher-grade hotels follow international practice by having relatively large units - the higher the grade, the greater the number of employees per unit.

Table 4. Employment by gender in the tourism industry, Macau, China, 2002

	Number employed		Percentage	
	Male	Female	Male	Female
Hotels and similar activities	2,803	2,604	51.8	48.2
Restaurants, bars, canteens and similar	8,307	9,433	46.8	53.2
Community, social and other personal services	4,458	4,792	48.2	51.8
Gaming	7,766	5,989	56.5	43.5
Total of above	23,334	22,727	50.7	49.3

Labour migration into Macau, China, is permitted under strictly controlled procedures covering skilled and unskilled labour under separate government decrees from 1988. The Chief Executive of Macau, China, ultimately authorises the importation of foreign labour where the appropriate skills cannot be found locally. The importing company must have a contract with an officially recognised labour agent.

The two parties sign an agreement which states that the employing company is responsible for the provision of proper accommodation for the workers concerned. In the event that a worker loses his/her job, repatriation is also the responsibility of the employer. The procedure for obtaining authorisation is clearly set out. The importing employer is required to complete a standard petition addressed to the Labour and Employment Bureau.

If approved, the application is submitted to other divisions of government, such as Economic Services, on which basis the Secretary of Economics and Finance will make a decision. On approval, the Migration Service is involved in the granting of permission for temporary immigration, and the Public Security Police will issue the appropriate identification papers. At the end of 2002, there were 4,619 skilled foreigners working in Macau, China - representing some 2.3% of the employed workforce.

In hotels and similar activities, 93 foreign workers accounted for 2.0% of the sector's employment, travel agencies had 46 foreign staff accounting for 1.0%, and the gaming industry had 172 foreigners, accounting for 3.7% of the total. All these foreign workers are described as "skilled imported labour."

The Macau Government Tourism Office (MGTO) is funded directly by the government under the Secretary for Social Affairs and Culture. The MGTO has a wide range of responsibilities, including the formulation and implementation of tourism policy, improving the quality of service through tourism industry training programmes, and the protection and enhancement of the value of local tourism resources.

MGTO also encourages and promotes activities beneficial to tourism, promotes inbound Macau tours in relevant origin markets, and has the responsibility for building relationships with international organisations. It suggests legislation related to tourism to the government and monitors the activities of operators to ensure their compliance with the relevant tourism laws; it also licenses tourist venues and activities.

The MGTO in addition has licensing and inspection powers for accommodation, ranging across all the hotel grades and three of the five grades of non-hotel accommodation (such as pensions), the remaining two grades coming under the control of another organ of the state.

Malaysia

In 1998, there were 8.6 million people employed in Malaysia, of which 1.6 million (some 19%) were employed in "wholesale, retail, hotels and restaurants". By 2002, the working population had risen to 9.6 million, with an official unemployment rate of 3.1% - about 300,000 people.

Economic slowdown and the emergence of unemployment have caused Malaysia to reverse its traditional policy of welcoming unskilled foreign workers to fill national shortages.A large number of specific skilled and semi-skilled activities have been listed as jobs for which foreigners may no longer be recruited. However, commentators believe that, in the longer term, Malaysia will continue to suffer from skill shortages which may have to be met from abroad.

Respondents to the Hotel Survey provided extensive information about employment and labour market conditions across the country's hotel sector. It should be pointed out that some of the issues raised may reflect local rather than national conditions. No hotel reported any difficulty in recruiting staff in general, but there is also a clear indication of skills shortages within the sector. Mention was made of:

— room staff (e.g. chambermaids, stewards);

— food and beverage staff (notably, waiters and waitresses);

— cooks (mention was made of Chinese cooks and bakery staff); and

— housekeeping and laundry operations staff.

Generally, skills shortages within the Malaysian hotel sector are ascribed to factors such as:

— the unpopularity of hotel work due to long and unsocial hours compared to, for example, factory work;

— high staff turnover due to many new hotels opening and inducing employees to "job hop" and

— a lack of suitably trained and competitive candidates, which is blamed by employers on inadequate standards within government education and training services .

There was some indication that the recruitme nt of female staff was not easy, although the majority of respondents did not regard this as a problem. The majority of responding hotels did find it necessary to import labour, noting that the number of foreign workers is limited by the government. Several also reported that procedures to obtain imported labour could be difficult and time-consuming. Permission needs to be obtained from local government representatives and it is said to be often easier to obtain such permission for "resorts" as opposed to hotels, and that permission is often only granted for clearly specialised skills (e.g. Japanese cooking) that may not be available locally.

New Zealand

According to Statistics New Zealand's Household Labour Force Survey, migration (long term or permanent) contributed to an increase of the working population in New Zealand by around 2% in 2002. The unemployment rate, which has been steadily declining in recent years, fell to 4.9%. The labour force is highly mobile and there is no statutory retirement age.

Tourism is reported by New Zealand's Ministry of Tourism to support more than one job in ten in the economy. There are currently an estimated 94,000 full-time equivalent (FTE) jobs and 69,000 indirect jobs in the sector. The industry is reported to be made up of ten major publicly listed companies and close to 18,000 SME's.

The government's Tourism Satellite Account for 1997-99 provides a breakdown of employment within the industry. In the year ending March 1999 there were 86,000 full-time equivalent jobs (FTEs) in the tourism industry, representing 5.6% of the country's total employees. Around a third of jobs are in the accommodation, café and restaurants sub-sectors. Among the FTEs, over 17,000 are attributed to working proprietors (19%), reflecting the substantial bias of small businesses that make up the tourism sector.

In New Zealand the Ministry of Tourism was established in January 2002 from a previous agency, the Office of Tourism and Sport. It is a semi-autonomous body within the Ministry of Economic Development, with direct policy reporting to the Minister of Tourism.

The prime aim of the Ministry is to maximise the benefits to New Zealand from the sustainable development of the industry; this latter aspect is regarded as especially important in New Zealand and hence its "100% Pure New Zealand" marketing stance. The main role of the Ministry is to provide tourism policy advice to the Minister of Tourism.

It works with other government departments on policy issues and provides tourism research and statistics for the benefit of the industry and the broader investment community. It also provides advice on government investments, administers grants and assists with major events. A key role is to continue to raise awareness of the importance of tourism's contribution to the economy.

The Ministry itself has little statutory or regulatory responsibility, and as a result relies on developing relationships and educating a wide range of other government departments on their impacts on tourism. The Ministry has an annual budget of NZ$5.38 million for 2003/04 and a staff of 15 advisors and researchers to fulfil these functions.

Marketing activity undertaken by the government is carried out through Tourism New Zealand (TNZ). TNZ's international marketing activity includes tourism brand building, advertising and promotion, the international media programme, trade training, participation in trade shows, running an internet site and provision of market research. The direction for New Zealand's tourism was set out in The New Zealand Tourism Strategy 2010 launched in May 2001, hailed as a "landmark document".

It contains a comprehensive set of principles and objectives covering all facets of the industry. The aim is stated to be the maximisation of the industry's tourism potential "while ensuring cultural, social, environmental and economic sustainability".

Philippines

According to the Republic of the Philippines' National Statistics Office, the Philippines labour force was estimated to amount to around 33.6 million in October 2002; around 30.3 million were classified as employed. Some 37% are employed in agriculture, 15% in industry and the remainder in the service sector.

Unemployment in the country is high and increasing - 10.2% in 2002, compared with 9.6% two years earlier. The National Statistics Office predicts that an additional 850,000 will join the labour force annually to 2010. The Philippines economy has traditionally benefited from remittances from the substantial number of nationals working overseas; this sector, however, is facing increasing competition from other labour supplying countries. The workforce has a high literacy rate and - particularly pertinent for the tourism sector -good English language proficiency. The supply of professional, technical and skilled workers is generally adequate.

The National Statistics Office notes that employment in hotels and restaurants in the Philippines amounted to 2.4% of the country's workforce at the end of 2002. At around 712,000, this was a slight increase on the figure of a year earlier. Respondents to the Hotel Survey noted that they experienced no difficulty at all in recruiting suitably qualified staff in the Philippines. There is an abundance of local labour on which to draw, both at the skilled and unskilled levels, and as a result they found no necessity to import labour from other countries.

Generally, the regulatory environment is regarded as very supportive with a Labour Code in force which is considered rather favourable to workers. The hotels reported that it is equally easy to employ both male and female labour. The hotels did, however, express some concerns over labour issues becoming a greater problem in the future. Mention was made of the likelihood of issues such as wages and labour rights becoming challenges for outsourcing labour as the sector expands. The Philippines Department of Labour is currently working on stringent measures regarding this issue, which may affect hotels' inclination to contract outsourced services.

Singapore

Singapore's workforce is reputedly one of the most stable and productive in Asia. Adverse economic conditions in 2001 led to a slowdown in employment growth which has continued in 2002. Unemployment increased to 4.4% by the end of 2001, according to Ministry of Manpower, and remained broadly at that level throughout 2002. Older and less-educated workers have been the worst hit by rising unemployment.

Nonetheless, Singapore's workforce is ageing rapidly and there are fewer economically active people in the younger age brackets. To address this, the retirement age was raised to 62 in 1999, with the intention of raising it to 67 in due course. According to the government's Labour Force Survey, there were a total of 125,325 persons employed in the hotels and restaurants sector in Singapore in 2002, representing 6.2% of the country's total workforce.

Figures for 2000 show that over half (56%) of those were in direct service occupations, such as waiters/ waitresses, bellboys, front office staff etc., and a further quarter were in housekeeping and cleaning occupations in hotels. As a result of manpower shortages, however, there is a high degree of multi-tasking in the restaurant sector, in particular. Some 14% of workers in the sector (1999) are employed on a part-time basis (19% of all part-timers in the economy).

The hospitality sector, as elsewhere, attracts a relatively high proportion of female labour. There is an almost even ratio of females (48.5% in 2000) to males (51.5% in 2000) working in the hotels and restaurants sector which compares with a 39:61 ratio for the workforce as a whole. It is noticeable that there is a higher proportion of younger (15-19 year olds) and older (50 years and over) workers - particularly women - in the hotels and restaurants sector compared with all sectors generally.

The occupation breakdown for hotels and restaurants is as follows:

— direct service and sales workers 56%

— cleaners and related workers 25%

— clerical workers 7%

— professionals and managers 9%

— technicians and associated occupations 3%

Average earnings in Hotels and Restaurants are the lowest of any category in the formal sector. In 1999 the average monthly earnings for workers in the economy were S$2,813, while in Hotels and Restaurants they were only S$1,291. They have also been the most sluggish in terms of growth: average wages increased by 56% for all sectors in the economy, while for hotels and restaurants the growth was half that.

In 1999 there were some 3,400 establishments serving the tourists. In the hotels sector, there is a fairly wide range of sizes of enterprise, while the restaurant sector is dominated by small establishments. One-third of all hotels employed more than 100 people but two-thirds of restaurants employed fewer than ten. Hotel companies in the Hotels Survey reported that they experienced difficulties in recruiting suitably qualified staff, and the ability to attract those with leadership qualities and sufficient skills and experience - especiaily of the hotel sector - is a big problem.

For most management positions, suitably qualified managers are available locally. However, the service sector is not popular among Singaporeans and shift work is especially unpopular. This is particularly the case among the younger generation who prefer other more glamorous industries such as IT and banking. Recruitment for the private sector is not made easier by the fact that government employees are offered high salaries and incentives. Hotels also report high staff turnover rates. Because of the mis-match between jobs and staff availability in Singapore, hotel companies find it necessary to import labour from abroad.

However, there is a government-imposed quota for non-skilled workers and restrictions by sector or industry. Hotels are also faced by a set higher-salary requirement for skilled or professional workers. There is a belief in the industry that this situation is unlikely to improve and as a result, labour issues will become increasingly difficult. An added problem, they note, is the fact that the gap between young workers and old workers is not closing up because of Singapore's small workforce.

Small Island

Most of the small island states of the South Pacific are more than normally dependent on the tourism sector - particularly since the discontinuing of trade preferences on commodities such as sugar and fish, for example - and tourism is one of the few sectors that offers development potential. Across the region generally, the growth in populations, and of younger age groups in particular, together with a decline in semi-subsistence living, has led to an increase in the numbers seeking paid employment which has not been matched by an availability of jobs.

Tourism is one of the biggest sources of employment, not only in major destinations such as Fiji and Tahiti but also in smaller countries like Kiribati, Niue and Tuvalu. The South Pacific Tourism Organization (SPTO) suggests that tourism provides up to 15-20% of employment in several South Pacific countries. The industry is characterised by a predominance of SME's but the overall number of tourism enterprises is relatively small, estimated at around 1,500 in total. In the accommodation sector, if the small number of large hotels is excluded, the average number of rooms per establishment is just 15.

The South Pacific Tourism Organization, in its 2001-05 Business Plan, states that the bulk of the SME's are run by family operations. It also draws attention to the fact that in the context of the South Pacific, tourism offers opportunities to both male and female entrepreneurs, especially in the case of ecotourism, to establish businesses within their natural and cultural framework. In some cases, the report notes, "the wife and children are the main players, running small family operations. In most cases, rental cars, travel offices and booking agencies are dominated by female entrepreneurs."

Sri Lanka

In early 2002 Sri Lanka's labour force consisted of 7.3 million workers of whom some 8.7% were unemployed. Two thirds of the labour force is male but unemployment among females is double that of males (12.8% compared with 6.5%). The labour force is literate and educated, but lacking in certain technical skills. Unemployment is much higher among the better educated; for those educated to GCE (A/L) and above, the rate is 16.7%, while for those below Grade 5 it is only 2.1%.

Most permanent workers are covered by laws relating to minimum wages, hours of work, the right of association and health and safety standards. A Termination of Employment Act makes is almost impossible to fire workers who have been employed for more than six months, other than for cases involving serious disciplinary problems. Child labour is prohibited and is virtually non-existent in the organized sector. Some 35% of labour in the industry and service sector is unionized.

Table 5. Employment in Sri Lanka's tourism sector, 1998-2001

	1998	1999	2000	2001
Direct	34,780	36,560	37,943	35,443
Indirect		51,184	53,120	49,620
Total	83,472	87,744	91,063	85,063

There were nearly 38,000 people directly employed in 1,312 different establishments in the tourism sector in Sri Lanka in 2000. As a result of the poor performance of the tourism industry in 2001 following the bombing at Bandaranaike airport, direct employment reduced to 35,400. Indirect employment was also down - 49,600 compared with 53,100 in 2000.

Official figures indicate that every direct job in the tourism sector generates 1.4 indirect jobs. Nevertheless, small and medium-scale enterprises predominate, with the average number of workers per business at 29; if the airline industry is excluded, this is reduced to 26. By sector, the average number of employees per hotel is 36, while for travel agencies and tour operators it is only 12. The majority of employees working in the tourism industry - some 67% of the total - are employed in the hotels and restaurants sector.

Around 11% work in tour operators and travel agencies, and a further 12% work for airlines. Over half of all employees work in technical, clerical and supervisory jobs, although within the hotel sector, one-third of workers are unskilled. Thailand According to Thailand's Labour Force Survey, there was a total labour force of around 34.6 million at the end of 2002.

Unemployment is low, at just 1.8%, having dropped sharply, from 4.8% at the beginning of 2001. The two main problems facing the government are a shortage of skilled labour - further aggravated by the fact that recession has forced many children to leave school prematurely - and rising labour costs to levels well above those of trading rivals like China, Malaysia and Viet Nam. Employment in hotels and restaurants accounted for around 6.1% of the country's total workforce at the end of 2002. A survey conducted by the Tourism Authority of Thailand (TAT) in 1997, shows employment in the following five groups:

— unskilled and semi-skilled (37% of the total);

— basic skilled level (28%);

— technical (supervisory level) (25%);

— mid-management level (5%); and

— management level (6%).

The majority of those working in the industry were at the younger end of the age scale (21-30 years) and there was a relatively even split between male and female. Most had graduated from primary school, high school and vocational school. Despite the very low rate of unemployment in Thailand, the Hotel Survey respondents reported little difficulty in recruiting suitably qualified staff for most types of posts. Several hotels did, however, mention that there was a shortage of suitably qualified nationals who offered leadership skills to take up managerial roles.

It was also noted that recruiting employees for guest contact positions who had good English language skills could be a challenge. Due to the generally good supply of local labour, almost none of the companies had experienced a need to import labour from abroad, although it was mentioned that some positions requiring certain skills or language proficiency did necessitate this. One hotel group noted that it was sometimes not easy to obtain permits for workers from South Asia or the Middle East. For the future, it was envisaged that the recruitment of qualified staff would become more difficult, particularly as many of the good staff were attracted by working overseas in Thai restaurants or as cabin attendants on cruise ships.

Viet Nam

The labour force is growing rapidly, at around 2.5% a year, and unemployment is a problem. Around 60% of the population is of working age, with government forecasts indicating that this will rise to 70% by 2010. Half the population is aged 15-34. Although there is a large pool of workers which is generally literate and hard-working, there is a skills shortage; according to MoLISA (Ministry of Labour Invalids and Social Affairs), only 16% of the workforce were classified as "skilled" in 2000, i.e. had some form of training or tertiary education, and only 4% had university qualifications. The service sector accounts for around 20% of employment.

11

Training in Travel and Tourism Sector

While there is wide agreement on the need to improve the supply of well-educated and -trained staff for the travel and tourism industry, it is also clear that resources are lacking. Often, there is an absolute shortage of trainers, and the attraction of top quality trainers is often hampered by low public-sector pay scales within the training and education sectors.

In terms of best practice in the identification of skills needs and in the organisation of industry training schemes, Australia, China and Singapore are undertaking country-wide programmes, with Australia in particular leading the way in the design, planning and delivery of training programmes across the industry and especially at the vocational, non-academic levels.

Generally, it is at this level that skills shortages are most apparent. Since many jobs in the industry do not require academic qualifications, and also because there is generally a shortage of government and private sector vocational training schemes, in many countries the major hotel groups and travel companies tend to rely on their own in-house training abilities. This does not help the many small businesses in the industry, however, who cannot afford the luxury of in-house trainers.

The provision of suitable training programmes for SMEs is therefore a matter requiring specific attention. Some of the generally applicable issues that have emerged from many of the countries covered below include:

Quality of Training

There is concern over the quality of many of the training courses on offer; this partly reflects, in some countries, the lack of national standards (or at least of their enforcement), partly the shortage of well-qualified trainers for the reasons outline above and partly an absolute shortage of resources to fund training centres and programmes.

Relationships with the industry: In a number of countries there is concern about the lack of contact between the travel and tourism industry and the academic establishment which is responsible for higher level training and education, indicating a need for central authorities such as the relevant government ministries or the national tourist office, depending upon the distribution of responsibilities, to take the lead in improving cross-sectoral co-operation.

Career development concerns: Even where lower-level training is broadly satisfactory, there is concern over a lack of skills upgrading and opportunities for life-long learning. The point is made that it is often difficult for staff to progress through the organisation that employs them. For example, hotel staff working in rooms or food and beverage operations can find it hard to advance themselves to more senior levels. If this situation could be improved, it would create a "virtuous circle", by providing better opportunities for skills upgrading. This could help to eliminate the perception of an industry which offers poor career perspectives, thereby improving its ability to attract new recruits.

Training Programmes in Various Countries

Australia

At the end of the 1990s there were estimated to be 3,800 students engaged in tourism and hospitality studies at a variety of Registered Training Organisations. These included many from outside the country whose own countries did not offer such skills training themselves.

Tourism industry training in Australia is in the hands of Tourism Training Australia (TTA) - described as a "joint industry, government and union national training body". TTA has a major role in the definition of skills needs and shortages within the Australian tourism industry. TTA has produced a 20 year forecast of skills development needs, and has identified national skills shortages in skills such as:-

— pastrycooks (28,400 people are employed as bakers and pastrycooks where earnings are low - in the third decile);

— bar attendants (54,600 employed with earnings in the second decile);

— chefs (48,900 employed, with earnings in the fourth decile);

— cooks and fast food cooks (employing respectively 39,000 and 22,000 people with the lowest earnings of all - in the first decile); and

— food and beverage attendants (waiters and waitresses, where 98,800 are employed and earnings again are in the lowest decile).

TTA rates vacancy levels as "average" for pastrycooks, "high" for chefs and "very high" for the remainder of these skills. The current and future training programmes for the industry reflect these priorities. Overall, TTA estimates that

16,000-17,000 new cooks are required by the industry every year, against a current recruitment rate of 13,000-14,000 a year.

There is also a shortage of language skills in some of the jobs which have face-to-face contact with tourists, notably for Asian languages such as Japanese and Mandarin in areas such as tour guides and hotel staff. TTA estimates that an additional 1,200 tour guides are required annually.

Australia, under the aegis of TTA, has developed a range of National Training packages which were introduced in 1996 and which address a wide range of course requirements across all aspects of the tourism industry. As part of its long term development plans, TTA has developed a wide range of courses across the country targeted at the skills shortages and anticipated future needs which its detailed forward planning has identified. Other institutions and bodies, such as the Australian Hotels Association, Restaurant and Catering Australia and the Australian Federation of Travel Agents also conduct training programmes.

Bangladesh

In Bangladesh a respondent to the Hotel Survey stated that there is no government hotel school as such, although the National Tourism Training Centre has been used by the company to recruit some staff, nor is there any "credible" private sector source of hotel industry training. As a consequence, the company concerned undertakes most of its training on an inhouse basis.

China

In China, there is a national programme for tourism training. According to the China National Tourism

Administration (CNTA), at the end of 2000 there were 1,195 tourism colleges and schools with a total of 328,000 students (relative to 5.6 million people engaged directly in the tourism industry). Of the 1,195 colleges and schools, 252 offered tourism vocational courses which had attracted almost 74,000 students; 96 of these colleges offered courses in tourism management.

In that same year, 782,000 employees in the tourism industry participated in various training programmes, including on-the-job training for administrative personnel, professional training for technical workers, adaptation, overseas and adult schooling training. Of these 782,000, some 555,000 came from tourist hotels, 168,000 from travel agencies and 20,000 from tourist bus and shipping companies.

China has a National Association for Tourism Colleges and Universities and a National Association for Secondary Tourism Vocational Schools. These organisations co-operate on the development of curricula. CNTA also provides trainers within China, and has sent trainers to many parts of the country to help in regional and local training initiatives. National qualifications are offered at a variety of levels. In 2000, over 9,100 people took part in qualification authentication for travel agency work, of whom 6,500 received qualifying certificates. There were also examinations for:

— general manager qualification certificates for international travel services (with over 950 passes);

— department manager certificates in the same area (over 1,360 passes);

— general manager and department manager courses for domestic travel services over 2,400 and 1,780 certificates respectively);

— over 100,000 people succeeded in the national guide qualification certificate for tourist guides; and

— CNTA's system for hotel vocational English language training attracted 4,500 students and a pass rate of just over 50%.

Respondents to the Hotel Survey, among others, identify difficulties in recruiting staff offering reasonable competence in the English language. A recent example of a new approach is the joint venture that has been established under the name of "Tourism Training Institute at Tsinghua Science Park", between the Tsinghua University, located in the city of Zhuhai adjacent to Macau, China, and the Tourism Training Institute of Canada. The latter is a division of Global Education in Tourism Ltd., a company based in Vancouver on Canada's west coast. Courses will be offered from the second half of 2003, which are part of the American Hotel & Lodging Association's Educational Institute Programme and will offer opportunities for work experience overseas.

Macau, China

Tourism industry training in Macau, China is led by the publicly owned Institute for Tourism Studies (IFT). This was established in 1995 and had the distinction of being the first educational institution to be granted the Themis TedQual (Tourism Education Quality) attestation by the World Tourism Organization. It is the only higher educational establishment operated by the Macau government specifically for the tourism and hospitality industries. The IFT is also the authorised training centre in Macau for the International Air Transport Association (IATA) which certifies IATA-standard staff in travel agencies.

The Institute for Tourism Studies delivers its services though two institutions - the Tourism College of Macau

(TCM) and the Professional and Continuing Education School (PACES). The TCM provides higher diploma and bachelor courses in hotel and tourism business management, while PACES focuses on entry and supervisory level training in five areas - Travel, Hospitality and Catering, Management, Customer Service Development, and Languages and Communication.

The authorities in Macau, China expect demand for employment in the travel and tourism sector to grow rapidly, by between 7,000 and 10,000 jobs in the next two years - due to the liberalisation of the gaming industry and to the opening of new hotels. In order to provide the labour required for this expansion, the Institute for Tourism Studies has combined forces with the Polytechnic Institute of Macau to establish the Macau Tourism and Casino Career Centre.

This body will commence operations in the second semester of 2003, and has as its objective the provision of additional training opportunities to those wishing to join the industry. Part of the Macau, China government's approach to tourism development is the imposition of quality standards. For example, tour guides are requested to attend a 180 hour training programme run by the IFT, all travel agencies in Macau are required to have a technical director with related qualifications or 3 years' relevant experience (in both cases these requirements are subject to approval by representatives of the IFT and the Macau Government Tourist Office), and all taxi drivers must pass a special examination set by the Macau Civil and Municipal Institute in order to obtain their licenses.

Malaysia

The training experience and practice from five hotels within one company in Malaysia, as revealed in the Hotel Survey, shows that the same company can adopt a variety of approaches according to local needs and standards. Two out of five undertook only in-house training, only one used government schemes, and four out of five used the private sector.

It is noticeable in these responses that Malaysia offers a wide range of training institutes and organisations for the hotel sector, including schemes operated by the Ministry of Tourism, public bodies such as the Human Resources Development Council and associations such as the Association of Hotel Employers, together with a wide range of private training organisations and companies. These latter address both general and specific skills, such as information technology, and include national companies as well as foreign companies which have branches within the country.

New Zealand

There are reported to be in excess of 750 providers of tourism training courses, including secondary schools, in New Zealand. There are also three industry training organisations serving the tourism sector - Sports, Fitness, Recreation Industry Training Organisation (SFRITO), Aviation Tourism and Travel Training Organisation (ATTTO) and Hospitality and Service Industry Training Organisation (HIS).

In the view of the Tourism Strategy Group, set out in New Zealand Tourism Strategy, 2010, rationalisation is required. The large number of training organisations results in fragmented training provision and makes it difficult to communicate the needs of the sector to training providers. The current delivery of training, it notes, does not suit either SMEs or their employees.

In addition, the training content does not focus sufficiently on planning, establishing and managing businesses effectively and it is not provided in a way that makes it accessible to SMEs. The Strategy Group also draws attention to the fact that the nature of much tourism-related employment can exacerbate capability issues for the sector. Tourism generally is not regarded as an attractive long-term prospect for employment and the loss of experienced staff and low recognition of tourism's value to local communities and to the country has a negative impact on sector capability.

The Group recommends that better learning opportunities and more portability of skills within the sector should be provided. The image of the industry also needs to be raised and awareness increased of its role and importance. Other recommendations include the establishment of a process to enable the identification of sector-wide skill requirements and effective workforce planning, the need to make the development of SME and Maori tourism participants' capability a top priority, and the need to co-ordinate training opportunities and build capability at a regional level.

The Strategy paper also notes that Skill New Zealand's funding for tourism training is disproportionately low when compared to the sector's contribution to the economy. In 2000 Skill New Zealand allocated only 1.1% of total funding for industry training to aviation, tourism, travel and hospitality. This compared to 10.1% to agricultural training and 9.1% to forestry.

Philippines

The premier training establishment in the Philippines is the Asian Institute of Tourism (AIT), part of the University of the Philippines, which offers four-year degree courses in tourism. There are, in addition, around 120 other schools offering degree courses, as well as numerous others offering degrees in Hotel and Restaurant Administration and Management.

There are also many vocational and technical schools and other institutions providing training, which is supplemented by in-house training programmes offered by hotels, resorts, restaurants and tour and travel agents in specific sectoral skills. It is reported that in general the manpower supply for the industry in terms of quantity is adequate. More of a problem is the quality of courses provided. In 1999 it was noted by the University of the Philippines, Asian Institute of Tourism, that out of the 120 schools offering a four-year degree course nationwide, only 31 were accredited by the Commission on Higher Education, the office which grants state recognition to schools of higher education.

Part of the problem lies in the training provided. There is a severe shortage of qualified teaching staff and generally a lack of resources for tourism training and facilities. In addition, there is a need to forge links between the industry and academia in order to match the training of students with the requirements of the industry.

A number of other training programmes require mention:

— The Technical Education and Skills Development Authority (TESDA), a government agency involved in human skills development, has linked up with the Department of Tourism and the private sector to develop skills training, curriculum development, accreditation, standardisation and certification. The TESDA also provides scholarships for skills training.

— The Department of Tourism offers a range of tourism programmes, including housekeeping, food handling, tour guiding, tourism awareness, foreign languages and marketing and communications.

— The Tourism Industry Board Foundation is a tripartite body composed of representatives of government, the private sector and labour set up to promote human resource development. The TESDA has subsidised most of the training programmes and the development of occupational skills standards (OSS) and trade tests undertaken by the Board.

— Another government/private sector institution is the Hotel and Tourism Institute of the Philippines, an initiative involving the Hotel and Restaurant Association of the Philippines and the Department of Tourism.

— TESDA in co-operation with a number of selected tourism training institutions and the German Agency for Technical Co-operation has introduced a project to promote Dual Training at all levels in technical schools and training centres throughout the country.

— The Department of Tourism, supported by American Express, operates the Mabuhay Super Host Program, which aims to teach front office staff skills. Respondents among the different companies in the Hotel Survey - which, it should be stressed, were international hotels operating large establishments - indicated that almost all training took place in-house and virtually no use was made of either public or private sector training establishments. The exception to this was the necessity of sending employees such as engineers and plumbers for training in order to update their licences, as required by the law. Both government training and private/commercial training establishments were used for this purpose.

Singapore

The Singapore government is attempting to upgrade its post-secondary education facilities, with greater emphasis on technical, vocational and commercial education. The aim is to have about 40% following technical and vocational courses at polytechnics, 20% undertaking academic courses at university and 25% studying at the Institute of Education.

Currently there is a high proportion of workers in the hotel and restaurant sector with below average educational qualifications, reflecting the fact that nine out of 10 occupations in the sector are service, clerical or cleaning related activities. For such positions, in-house training of a suitable candidate is regarded as more appropriate than academic qualifications. However, there is an increasing emphasis on the need for workers to upgrade their skills to bring about a higher standard of service quality.

Singapore's Ministry of Manpower and the economic agencies conducted a national survey in 1999 to gather feedback from employers in the hospitality sector on the employment situation, including the amount of training being provided and the skills they would require in their workers in the next two years. The most frequently cited requirements were:

Degree	—Degree in Business Studies/Administration (with Hospitality Customer Service Modules)
Diploma	—Diploma in Tourism —Diploma in Business Administration
Specialised Skills	—Knowledge in Food and Beverage Operations —Knowledge in Hotel Management
Generic Skills	—Customer Service Skills —Supervisory Skills —Human Resource Management Skills —Sales Management Skills

The hotels sector tends to require higher educational qualifications than the restaurant sector for managerial, professional or technical positions. Generally a university degree is required in hotels, while a diploma is sufficient for a similar position in a restaurant.

For administrative positions in hotels, a diploma in hotel or hospitality management is often required, while for executive positions (e.g. assistant accountant, computer equipment operators etc.) secondary education is sufficient, although some hotels prefer diploma holders. In the restaurants industry such positions generally require only secondary education. For clerical and service jobs in both sectors (e.g. receptionists, cashiers, customer service clerks etc.), secondary education is the norm. Training opportunities in the sector include the following:

— *SHATEC courses*: the Singapore Hotel and Tourism Education Centre conducts short part-time programmes from one to eight days, customised hospitality programmes, and full time courses offering diplomas in tourism studies and hotel management.

— *Skills Redevelopment Programme (SRP)*: The Singapore Hotel Association (SHA) and National Trades Union Congress are jointly responsible for training courses designed to upgrade the skills of workers in the hotels industry in areas such as housekeeping, food preparation, F&B service etc. Courses vary in length from a few weeks to a few months.

— *National Skills Recognition System (NSRS)*: this programme was launched by the Singapore Tourist Board (STB) and the Singapore Productivity and Standards Board in 2000 to strengthen and enhance job competencies. Under this scheme, workplace skills standards for the hotel industry have been developed and training to meet these standards accorded recognition. About 130 competency standards for the hospitality sector have been identified. Up to the end of 2001, 788 hotel employees had been certified in 13 Units of Competence.

— *Temasek Polytechnic* and the STB are working on e-learning programmes in lodging and catering

— *A range of other educational establishments* (such as Ngee Ann Polytechnic) and training centres.

In order to attract more to join the sector and alleviate the manpower shortage problem, the STB and SHA have undertaken programmes to create awareness of career opportunities in the sector. Hotel companies approached in the Hotel Survey noted that, in addition to in-house training, they used both government training establishments and commercial training centres to train their staff.

Small Island States

In terms of human resource development, the islands of the South Pacific suffer from their small size and their isolation. A lack of local management expertise and poor service quality are frequently expressed criticisms of the regional industry. A Tourism Council of the South Pacific (TCSP) review undertaken in 1995 identified the following three key issues:

— low levels of training activity across the region, with an over-reliance on government parastatal provision; investment in people was not receiving the priority it deserved;

— limited public awareness of the current and potential benefits of tourism;

— the training provided was not always relevant to requirements.

Tourism training facilities in the region are limited. Seven countries have no institute for formal training (apart from visits of a mobile team from the South Pacific Tourism Organisation, the successor to the TCSP). Generally the quality of the training and the facilities are also not of a standard comparable to more sophisticated tourism destinations.

In addition, among those countries that do have training establishments, there is no region-wide certification and standards vary widely. There is a particular need for training aimed at small enterprises such as guesthouses and tour operators, and for community-based tourism in rural areas. A 1999 TCSP review identified the need for school-based training for clerical, management and cookery skills, and particularly noted waiting, cooking, housekeeping and bar tending.

However, it is often difficult to persuade employees to move away from their villages to attend training courses, so on-the-job training becomes of greater relevance. Hotel managers, however, are unwilling to invest in training when margins are low, which can lead to a vicious downward spiral. Human resource development is a major part of the activities of the TCSP. It has trained 14,000 travel agents in seminars and workshops, and 7,000 people in hotel and catering services, marketing, tourism awareness and management. As at mid-2001, it had three trainers, specialising in food production, food service, housekeeping and front office, as well as offering courses for tour guides. The University of the South Pacific based in Fiji and covering 12 countries in the region, also offers a basic Certificate in Tourism Studies as well as degree courses.

Sri Lanka

Sri Lanka has one public sector training institute, the Ceylon Hotel School & School of Tourism, managed by the National Tourist Office, which offers training for the hospitality and tourism sector at all levels. It has an annual output of around 1,200 students. The central school is located in Colombo, and a number of satellite schools have been opened in the provinces with the aim of training some of the educated but unemployed youth in the regions.

There are also several private sector training institutions. However, the provision of training facilities is regarded as insufficient for the industry's requirements and considerable training is undertaken in-house by the major hotel chains. No comprehensive courses are available for the training of tour operators and travel agents.

A particular problem is the fact that training institutions find it difficult to attract quality staff. The government sector is the largest training provider in Sri Lanka and government salary scales are such that high calibre staff is not attracted. At the same time, the industry does not have an attractive image and as a result other industries prove more appealing for quality employees.

Thailand

In a speech delivered at a conference on Human Resource Development in the Asia-Pacific organised by the World Tourism Organization in 1999, Mr. Suwat Jutakorn, the Director of Hotel and Tourism Training Institute of the Tourism Authority of Thailand (TAT), noted that the industry badly needed to upgrade the quality and numbers of both skilled and unskilled workers in the hospitality and tourism sector if it was to meet international standards.

This was particularly the case at the operations level. One major problem, he noted, was a lack of proficiency in foreign languages to deal with foreign guests, particularly English, Chinese, Japanese and Russian. This general lack of training was also mentioned by hotels responding to the Hotel Survey who noted that even among staff who had ostensibly received training and had hotel vocational or technical certificates, there was usually a need to train them (again) from scratch.

In the conference presentation delivered by Mr. Jutakorn, he outlined the efforts being made by the Tourism Authority of Thailand to upgrade the skills and quality of workers in the tourism sector. He noted that there were at that time 96 institutions in Thailand offering hospitality and tourism-related courses, ranging from short courses to those at degree level. TAT itself had introduced a programme to promote education in the industry and was undertaking research into a number of issues related to human resource development, such as curriculum development and the demands of the labour market.

It had also set up a network of education and training institutes in tourism in Thailand to be responsible for research, information and development. However, the industry is challenged by a shortage of experienced instructors and the fact that many teachers are of poor quality, study materials are in short supply, curricula need standardising and modifying and by the fact that educational establishments fail to co-ordinate either with each other or with the industry they represent.

In order to address some of the problems, TAT established the Hotel and Tourism Training Institute (HTTI) with the assistance of the International Labour Organization (ILO) and the United Nations Development Programme (UNDP). The HTTI has co-operated with various educational institutions both in Thailand and abroad, such as Australia, Canada and Switzerland, in order to improve and develop the quality of education standards through teacher and student exchanges and professional contact. It offers a large number of courses across many sectors of the industry and ranging from two year courses offering Higher Certificate of Hotel and Tourism to short courses from one year to a few days.

Respondents to the Hotel Survey in Thailand reported that, in addition to in-house training, they use a wide range of both public and private sector training establishments. Within the public sector mention was made of courses offered at State Universities, the Ministry of Industry, Ministry of Energy, the Thai Red Cross Society, the Metropolitan Electricity Authority and the Engineering Institute of Thailand under His Majesty the King's Patronage.

Within the private sector, training took place in a wide variety of disciplines such as human resource management, computer skills, engineering, live saving and so on. One hotel group noted that it imported outside instructors or suppliers to train its staff.

Bibliography

Adams, Kathleen M. Come to Tana Toraja, "Land of the Heavenly Kings": Travel Agents as Brokers in Ethnicity. *Annals of Tourism Research* 11:469-485, 1984.

Adams, Kathleen M. "Making-Up the Toraja? The Appropriation of Tourism, Anthropology, and Museums for Politics in Upland Sulawesi—, Indonesia, 1995.

Adler, Judith. "Origins of Sightseeing". *Annals of Tourism Research* 16:7-29, 1989.

Ahmed, S. A. "Psychological Profiles of Sri Lankans versus Tourists". *Annals of Tourism Research* 16:345-359, 1989.

Baier, S. "The Economic Impact of Travel and Tourism in a Mountain Area: The Case of Vorarlberg, Austria. *In Tourism: The State of the Art*. A. V. Seaton, ed. Pp. 141-143. Chichester, England: Wiley, 1994.

Ball, D. A. "Permanent Tourism: A New Export Diversification for Less Developed Countries". *International Development Review* 13(4)-20-23, 1971.

Butler, Richard W., "The Social Implications of Tourist Developments". *Annals of Tourism Research* 2:100-111, 1974.

Caneday, L., and J. Zeiger. "The Social, Economic, and Environmental Costs of Tourism to a Gaming Community as Perceived by Its Residents". *Journal of Travel Research* 30(2):45-48, 1991.

Carlson, Alvar W. "Geographical Research on International and Domestic Tourism". *Journal of Cultural Geography* 1(1):149-160, 1980.

Deitch, Lewis I. "The Impact of Tourism upon the Arts and Crafts of the Indians of the Southwestern United States". *In Hosts and Guests: The Anthropology of Tourism*. Valene L. Smith, ed. Pp. 173-183. Philadelphia: University of Pennsylvania Press, 1977.

Edgell, David L. *International Tourism Policy*. New York: Van Nostrand Reinhold, 1990.

Frew, E. "International Charter Travel--a New Opportunity for Australian Tourism". *In Tourism: The State of the Art*. A. V. Seaton, ed. Pp. 178-185. Chichester, England: Wiley, 1994.

Herbin, Jackie. "A Model Tourist Development: The Case of the Austrian Tirol". *Society and Leisure* 9:95-116, 1986.

Hiller, Herbert L. "Where Is Tourism Traveling?" *Journal of Interamerican Studies and World Affairs* 16:508-515.

Krippendorf, Jost. "The Holiday Makers: Understanding the Impact of Leisure and Travel". London: Heinemann, 1987.

TOURISM BUSINESS AND PRODUCTS

TRAVEL AND TOURISM MANAGEMENT

(In 4 Volumes)

TOURISM BUSINESS AND PRODUCTS

(Volume -2)

Editor
Prakash Talwar

ISHA

ISHA BOOKS

DELHI-110033

Tourism Business and Products

Rs. 2700 (Set)

ISBN: 81-8205-330-7 (Set)
ISBN : 81-8205-332-3 (Vol-2)

Published in 2006 in India by
Isha Books
D-43, Prithviraj Road,
Adarsh Nagar, Delhi-110033
e-mail : ishabooks@hotmail.com

Laser Typesetting at : Shiva Infosystem, Delhi
Printed at : Mehra Offset Press, Delhi

Preface

Tourism is a complex human activity, leading to the consumption of myriad transportation, accommodation, meal, entertainment, and other goods and services. The tourism industry is made up of business enterprises or establishments receiving a significant proportion of their sales revenue from visitor expenditures. In India, tourism has tended to be regarded as an elitist activity conducted primarily for the purpose of earning foreign exchange. Its vast potential as an engine of growth and employment generator has remained largely untapped.

Tourism in India has shown a phenomenal growth from its distant past. Today, Indian tourism offer array of tourist destination that attracts travellers from all over the world. The country is one of the most inimitable, incomparable and intoxicating travel destinations in this world. From culture to heritage to wildlife to adventure to pilgrimage to nature, India has all the perfect destinations for the visitors. Travelling in all the exotic tourism destinations in India is an experience, where each destination is a welcome break from the usual.

This book discusses various aspects of tourism business and product in the Indian context. It is hoped that the contents of the book will be immensely helpful to students, tour operators, policy makers, tourist guides and all those concerned.

Editor

Contents

	Preface	*v*
1.	Nature and Scope of Tourism	1
2.	Tourism in India: Recent Trends	18
3.	Historical Monuments of Touristic Significance	33
4.	Popular Pilgrim Centres	71
5.	Performing Arts with Tourism Importance	101
6.	Handicrafts of India as a Potential Tourist Resources	138
7.	Fairs and Festivals	168
8.	Coastal Tourism in India	183
9.	Development of Desert Tourism in India	213
10.	Tourist Resource Potential in Mountain with Special Reference to Himalayas	232
	Bibliography	276
	Index	278

1

Nature and Scope of Tourism

Tourism is a complex human activity, leading to the consumption of myriad transportation, accommodation, meal, entertainment, and other goods and services. An elaborate industry has developed to service consumers before, during and after they travel away from home. It is through this industry that the economic consequences of tourism are transmitted to nations, regions, cities, towns, communities and individuals.

As recommended by the United Nations Statistical Commission and the World Tourism Organization, "tourism" includes the activities of people traveling away from their usual environment for leisure, business and other purposes. The activities of these "visitors" include purchasing goods and services, traveling to, from and within a destination, and affecting in various ways the natural and social environment.

According to the UN/WTO recommendations, tourism comprises: the activities of persons traveling to and staying in places outside their usual environment for not more than one consecutive year for leisure, business and other purposes.

These "activities" include "tourism expenditure," defined as: the total consumption expenditure made by a visitor on behalf of a visitor for and during their trip and stay at a destination. While this concept of tourism expenditure encompasses a wide variety of items, there are certain acquisitions that should be excluded from tourism expenditure:

(a) purchases for commercial purposes, including items for resale or purchases made on behalf of a visitor's employer;

(b) capital type investments or transactions, such as land, housing, real estate, automobiles and second homes;

(c) cash given to relatives, friends or institutions (in the form of donations) that does not represent payment for tourism goods or services.

Tourism expenditure has both a domestic and an international component. The former is limited to residents traveling within their countries of residence. The latter is significant in balance of payment accounts and foreign exchange earnings:

— International tourism receipts are defined as expenditure of international inbound visitors including their payments to national carriers for transport. They should also include any other prepayment made for goods/services received in the destination country.

— International tourism expenditure is defined as expenditure of outbound visitors in other countries including their payments to foreign carriers for international transport.

Tourism Industry

The "tourism industry" is made up of business enterprises or establishments receiving a significant proportion of their sales revenue from visitor expenditures. While the quantification of "significant" will differ from country to country, the United Nations and World Tourism Organization have developed the Standard Classification of Tourism Activities (SICTA) to aid in this process. The SICTA is a classification of like industry enterprises or establishments comprising categories which are important to tourism or which are highly dependent on tourism demand.

The SICTA does not define the tourism industry, but rather provides a framework for selecting appropriate industry sectors to be included in supply-side tourism studies. It details 185 supply-side "economic activities" which have significant connections to tourism. For the most part, these activities directly provide goods and services to visitors, and include transportation, accommodations, food service, entertainment and recreation. Some activities, such as hotel construction and tourism schools, provide services to businesses which exist to serve visitors.

The value of the SICTA in classifying enterprises or establishments as tourism-related is at least threefold:

— it provides guidance in organizing firms or establishments into categories relevant tothe study of the economic impact of tourism;
— it provides a comprehensive listing of the types of firms or establishments that are likely to be related to tourism in acountry;
— it is consistent with and based upon the United Nations' International Standard Industrial Classification of All Economic Activities (ISIC) in its latest (third) revision, affording consistent comparisons with other countries' industrial classification systems.

In order to define the tourism industry in a given country, the country's NTA, with consultation with industry representatives, can review the SICTA and select those activities, such as establishments, where a significant share of sales receipts are attributable to visitor activities. This share may be set anywhere between 20 to 50 percent. Within this set of tourism establishments, further distinctions can be made: the primary tourism industry might be categories where 67 percent or more of receipts are due to visitors. Secondary tourism industry establishments may be those where 33 to 67 percent of receipts are due to visitors, while tertiary tourism establishments receive less than one-third of their receipts from visitors. It should be recognized that an individual establishment in a category may garner a substantially greater or smaller share of its receipts from visitors than the average for the category.

Economic Impact

Visitors' expenditures in a country begin a complex chain of economic events which are often called the "economic impact of tourism." The economic impact of tourism includes benefits or positive impacts of this activity, in terms of the income and wealth of the residents of a country or other area. The economic impact of tourism also includes the negative consequences of tourism, or its costs, to residents in the area under study. The net result of tourism's economic benefits and costs determines whether tourism contributes to the net economic welfare of its residents (i.e., tourism benefits exceed costs) or detracts from it (tourism costs exceed benefits).

The most comprehensive concept of "net economic welfare" adjusts the generally accepted measure of Gross Domestic Product to include only consumption and investment items that contribute directly to economic well-being. It adds items such as the value of leisure time and the so-called "underground economy," and subtracts items such as social disruption and environmental damage.

Other items that affect citizen well-being and should be included are price stability and the distribution of income, both among income classes and regions. These measures help us understand more clearly whether a people are better off or worse off when tourism activity takes place.

In practice, few countries have the resources to compute this measure accurately. Consequently, gross domestic product (GDP) can be used as a fair approximation to overall net economic welfare for most countries, and tourism's net contribution to GDP can be determined through quantitative estimation techniques such as economic models.

Tourism's contribution to a nation's GDP is the most comprehensive summary measure of its net economic contributions. However, policy makers have found other measures to be useful as well. These are:

A. Personal Income (this includes (1) labor income, such as wages and salaries, and proprietors' income in the case of small businesses where the owner and the operator are the same person or family; and (2) returns to capital, measured in terms of profits, dividends, interest and rent;

B. Employment (seeking to ensure there are enough jobs for all residents who seek them is a high priority of most governments; this may be measured in terms of jobs, either part-time and full-time or full-time equivalents, or in terms of number of individuals employed;

C. Government revenue (tourism generates revenue for the national government from direct and indirect taxes, user fees such as admission charges and departure taxes, fines and penalties, and profits of government-owned enterprises;

D. Foreign exchange (for many countries, earning foreign exchange is an important economic priority, financing needed imports and investment; this may be measured in terms of the national currency or in individual foreign currency denominations.

Generally, these measures follow a specific flow pattern. As visitor volume grows in an economy, this produces increasing expenditures. As they become business receipts, these expenditures generate jobs paying wages and salaries to new employees, and finance interest on debt and, perhaps, generate profits. At the same time, government revenue is generated by the increased level of tourism activity, business receipts, personal income and employment, and capital income. Figure 1 depicts this flow of economic benefits.

Economic Costs

In a world where resources are scarce, measuring the economic benefits of tourism in an area without measuring the associated costs risks wasting scarce investment and marketing resources. Moreover, such an approach may also produce serious damage to the environment, rapidly escalating public service costs to support visitors, and significant declines in the quality of life for residents. Indeed, sustainable development requires that the costs as well as the benefits of a program be compared.

The social cost of an activity such as tourism is made up of the private costs, which are paid directly by those generating them, and incidental costs which are imposed on others without corresponding compensation. When a visitor drives to an attraction such as a theme park and pays the entrance fee, they are undertaking a private cost: they are directly compensating the park owners for the use of the park. But their journey to and from the attraction requires the services of a road building/maintenance agency and the local police for traffic control and security.

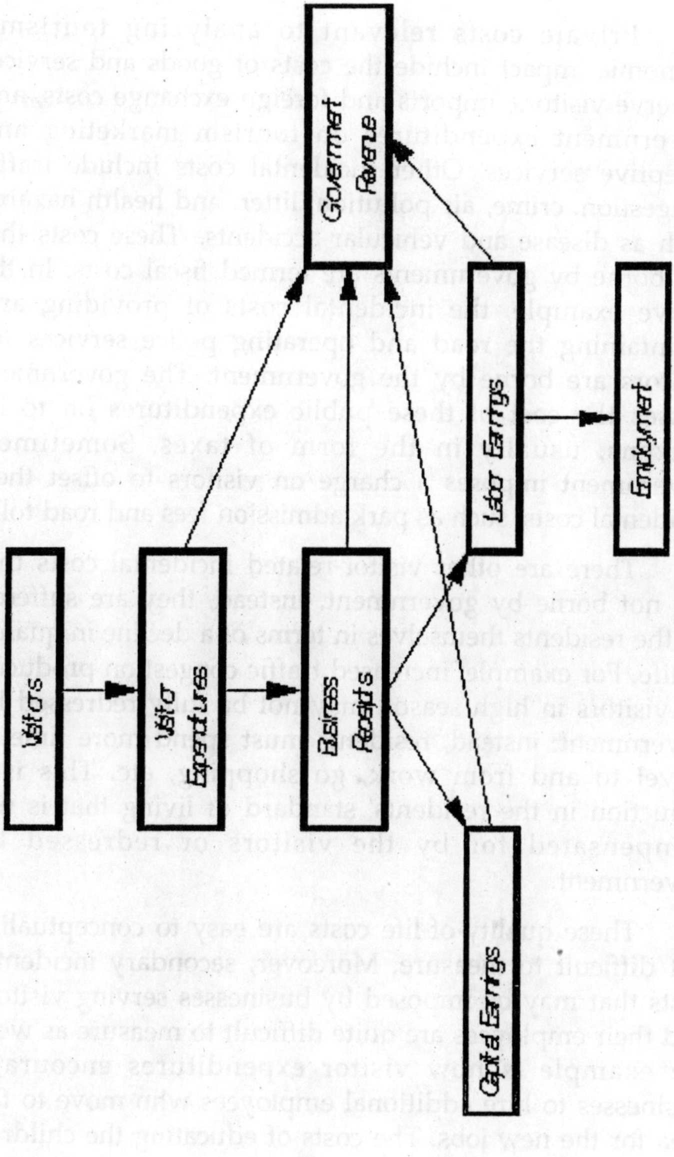

Figure 1. The chain of tourism's economic benefits

The costs of using the road and relying on police services are incidental costs: they impose them on other people without compensating them.

Private costs relevant to analyzing tourism's economic impact include the costs of goods and services to serve visitors, imports and foreign exchange costs, and government expenditures on tourism marketing and receptive services. Other incidental costs include traffic congestion, crime, air pollution, litter, and health hazards such as disease and vehicular accidents. These costs that are borne by governments are termed fiscal costs. In the above example, the incidental costs of providing and maintaining the road and operating police services for visitors are borne by the government. The government passes the cost of these public expenditures on to its citizens, usually in the form of taxes. Sometimes, government imposes a charge on visitors to offset their incidental costs, such as park admission fees and road tolls.

There are other visitor-related incidental costs that are not borne by government. Instead, they are suffered by the residents themselves in terms of a decline in quality of life. For example, increased traffic congestion produced by visitors in high season may not be fully redressed by government: instead, residents must spend more time to travel to and from work, go shopping, etc. This is a reduction in the residents' standard of living that is not compensated for by the visitors or redressed by government.

These quality-of-life costs are easy to conceptualize but difficult to measure. Moreover, secondary incidental costs that may be imposed by businesses serving visitors and their employees are quite difficult to measure as well. An example is how visitor expenditures encourage businesses to hire additional employees who move to the area for the new jobs. The costs of educating the children of these new employees is a secondary cost.

Net Economic Benefits

Once the economic benefits and economic costs of tourism have been computed, it is a simple matter to compare the two. This might be done through computing benefit/cost ratios, or simply subtracting costs from the benefits. It is particularly useful to connect benefit/cost ratios to each market segment served, such as group tours, cruise visitors, other same-day visitors, overnight visitors in commercial accommodation, overnight visitors in private accommodations, etc. Then, the productivity of each segment in terms of net contribution to wealth and income can be determined for each segment. The NTA can then determine which segments should be de-emphasized in marketing or even discouraged, and which should be pursued more aggressively.

Measuring the Economic Impact of Tourism

Measurement of the economic benefits and costs of tourism can help NTAs accomplish their missions in a variety of ways:

— inform public officials and business managers of the net benefits to a community of investing in tourism promotion and in the development of tourism facilities;

— assist tourism marketers in evaluating the effectiveness of their efforts and the effects of additional facilities on demand for current ones;

— help educate tourism-related employees about their role in economic and business development, and how their labor contributes to the economic health of their communities;

— through expressing the net returns to promotional and facility investment, these models can encourage both business and government to seek out cooperative ventures with other organizations for mutual benefit;

— by demonstrating the effects of travel development to the general public, tourism impact models help citizens rationally choose whether to encourage or resist additional tourism marketing or development;

— aid public officials in developing laws and policies that best promote sustainable economic, social and cultural benefits to their residents, and avoid decisions that would threaten this sustainability.

In short, developing measures of the economic benefits and costs of tourism activities enable NTAs to assist businesses, governments, labor unions, employees, and citizens in making efficient, effective and sustainable economic development decisions.

Measurement techniques

NTAs have employed a variety of ways to measure the economic benefits of tourism. Far less effort has been spent estimating the economic costs of tourism. On the benefits side, most research has concentrated on measuring visitor expenditures. One of the oldest methods is to use sample surveys of visitors to estimate visitor expenditures. For example, the Jamaica Tourist Board surveys departing passengers at two major airports and two major cruise ship piers.

This method can detail spending by activities, by visitor characteristic (e.g., age, gender, income, residence) and by trip characteristic (e.g., purpose, season, mode of transport, duration). Its disadvantages are that respondent difficulties in recalling expenditures accurately and the need to survey throughout the year to capture seasonal variations. Nevertheless, this remains the most popular method of measuring visitor expenditures.

The 1994 OAS study, Economic Analysis of Tourism in Jamaica, use a supply-side approach to measuring tourism's economic impact. The study estimated visitor expenditures by analyzing the receipts of the main establishments in Jamaica having direct transactions with tourists. Nearly a dozen business categories were designated as being tourism-related, and their establishments surveyed. The revenue reported, expanded to the total population of each category, was assumed to represent tourism expenditures in Jamaica.

The advantages of this method are that it can be done once a year for the previous year, employment and tax impacts can be directly inferred, and it provides substantial detail on the financial aspects of the industry. Disadvantages include lack of timely cooperation of businesses in responding to the survey, the subjective definition of whether a given establishment is tourism-related or not, and the attribution of all receipts in a category to visitors.

Economic Impact Models

It is appealing to some to use estimates of visitor expenditures as the ultimate measure of the impact of tourism. Indeed, many multi-lateral tourism reports compare visitor expenditures among nations as the only measure of economic activity derived from tourism. This habit should be avoided. The reason for this is that travel expenditures tend to obscure the impact on resident wealth and income. Although such expenditures may be substantial in an area, they often have little to do with residents' earnings and employment.

The extreme case is represented by a hotel in an underdeveloped economy, owned by non-residents, staffed with non-resident employees who send their earnings home, and serviced by imported goods and services.

Travelers may spend millions of dollars in the hotel each year, but the contribution to the wealth or income of the residents is virtually non-existent.

A similar case can be found in a developed economy. Consider a popular self-service gasoline service station in a resort area. Visitors purchase gasoline and oil provided by non-resident suppliers. The station itself is owned by an oil company headquartered elsewhere. The employees may be residents, but it takes only one to oversee the sale of several hundred thousand dollars of petroleum products a year. The dollars spent are a poor guide to the impact on resident wealth or income.

The point is that travel expenditures can be quite misleading in evaluating the economic benefits or the economic costs of travel and tourism in an area. They are best viewed as merely the initial monetary activity that stimulates the production process and initiates realistic measurement of economic impact. The flow of tourism impact initiated by visitor expenditures (Figure 1) should be embodied in a tourism economic impact model. This model abstracts the important relationships from the complexity of reality and indicates how variables interact with one another to produce economic benefits and costs through equations. Once visitor expenditures are estimated, these models require objective data on certain revenue and expenditure activities of tourism establishments. The result is estimates of the various measures of economic benefits or costs of most use to the NTA and others analyzing tourism's impact on the country.

Economic impact should be understood to include both direct or primary costs and benefits, and secondary costs and benefits. The former occur as a direct consequence of travel activity in the area. Visitor expenditures become business receipts which in turn are used to pay wages and salaries, return to capital, and taxes, the direct benefits of tourism. Visitor use of recreation areas requires expenditures on services for the visitors as well as on redressing any environmental damage: these are direct costs. These benefits and costs are directly related to the travel activity.

In addition to these primary impacts, there are secondary effects of travel activity. On the benefit side, business operators spend part of their receipts on goods and services they require to serve customers. This includes supplies as well as capital costs, such as interest on debt and profits to owners. In turn, their suppliers must purchase certain items from others. As this chain continues in a country, income and employment are produced indirectly.

The other type of secondary benefit is induced. Here we track the consumption spending of the wage, salary, and other labor income directly generated by visitor expenditures in the area. As tourism industry employees and operators purchase goods and services for personal use, they generate business receipts which, in turn, are used to purchase supplies, pay employees, and pay capital costs.

The combined effects of the direct, indirect and induced economic activities resulting from visitor spending are summarized by the "multiplier." This is the arithmetic ratio of total impact, measured in sales, personal and capital income, or employment, to the initial visitor expenditure. While difficult to estimate reliably, the sales, income, or employment multiplier is a useful tool for quickly estimating the total economic benefits generated by an increment of visitor expenditures.

Evaluating economic impact models

It is vital to judge a model used for tourism economic impact estimates as objectively as possible. One should be especially interested in the relevance, coverage, efficiency, accuracy, and transferability of the approach suggested for use.

Relevance: The approach should measure tourism's economic impact and not that of some other activity. For example, a study of the economic effects of restaurants in a country would not accurately represent tourism's impact because most of the business could be derived from local residents. Moreover, attention should be directed to ensuring an impact estimation method and the data used in it represent the country under study. Estimated economic benefits should truly accrue to the residents of the country, and these residents should truly bear any costs estimated from tourism.

Coverage: The approach should also cover all expenditures and impact related to travel away from home. On the economic benefit side, the impact of all visitor purchases in a country, as well prepaid items that accrue to establishments in the country such as package tour lodging. Direct, indirect and induced benefits should be estimated, as well as direct incidental costs.

Efficiency: Since funds available for economic impact estimation are generally limited, the approach should make maximum use of existing data commensurate with satisfying other criteria. Primary data collection is costly and difficult to do well. It should be avoided whenever possible in favor of relevant, comprehensive and accurate secondary data. Often, these data are available from governmental agencies.

Accuracy: One can also judge the approach on the basis of its accuracy. Are the input or survey data accurate measures of travel activity? Does the approach accurately reflect real relationships? Are the results reasonable? This involves investigating the techniques used to generate the primary and secondary input data. It also includes comparing the results with other, independent measures of travel impact wherever possible. Since these other measures generally do not pass these five evaluation criteria themselves, a good deal of judgment is often required to assess the accuracy of an approach and its output.

Transferability: The approach should be applicable to different geographic areas and different time periods, rather than requiring data unique to one particular case. It should also be sensitive to differences in travel patterns, industry structure and prices in different places and times. The main objective here is an approach that is feasible in different areas for different time periods, and produces consistent results in varying contexts. This permits valid comparisons across time and across countries, and provides a broader track record on which to assess the model.

Standard Tourism Definitions and Classifications recommend by the United Nations Statistics Commission and the World Tourism Organization, 1993

In June 1991, the World Tourism Organization and the Government of Canada organized an International Conference on Travel and Tourism Statistics in Ottawa, which brought together representatives of national tourism administrations, the tourism industry, national statistical offices and international and regional organizations to consider the development of reliable tourism statistics. The Conference adopted a set of resolutions that defined the statistical needs of the industry for analysis, market research, industry performance and tourism forecasts.

At its 27th Session, held in New York in February-March 1993, the United Nations Statistical Commission adopted a report prepared by the WTO and based on the Ottawa Conference resolutions: Recommendations on

Tourism Statistics. The definitions and classifications presented in this report supersede earlier work in this area and are now the new United Nations standards for defining and classifying international and domestic tourism activities.

As the United Nations (UN) and the World Tourism Organization (WTO) have pointed out, certain periodic information on tourism demand is essential to sound planning and management. This information should cover domestic, inbound and outbound tourism, and travel by all modes of transport. It should be expressed in terms of visitors, visitor-nights and visitor expenditures, and be classified in certain categories of trip and visitor characteristics. The UN and WTO have recommended a set of standard definitions and classifications to facilitate increased understanding of tourism phenomena and valid comparisons among nations and time periods.

The "visitor" is the foundational unit in the UN/WTO structure and is defined as:

> any person traveling to a place other than that of their usual environment for less than 12 months and whose main purpose of trip is other than the exercise of an activity remunerated from within the place visited.

The visitor is a subset of "traveler", defined as:

> any person on a trip between two or more countries or between two or more localities within their country of usual residence.

The critical distinction is that the visitor is away from their "usual environment," designed to designate the area where they normally live, work and conduct other day-to-day activities. The implications of these definitions are best portrayed in Figure A, which sets out the differences between the "visitor" and other "travelers."

The UN/WTO definitions and classifications further distinguish between international visitors and domestic visitors, and between overnight visitors ("tourists") and same-day visitors:

> "international visitor" describes any person who travels to a country other than that in which they have their usual residence but outside their usual environment for a period not exceeding 12 months and whose main purpose of visit is other than the exercise of an activity remunerated from within the country visited.
>
> "domestic visitor" describes any person residing in a country who travels to a place within the country, outside their usual environment for a period not exceeding 12 months and whose main purpose of visit is other than the exercise of an activity remunerated from within the place visited.
>
> "tourists" (overnight visitors): visitors who stay at least one night in a collective or private accommodation in the place visited.

In addition, the UN/WTO definitions define a "same-day visitor" as a visitor who does not spend the night in a collective or private accommodation in the place visited. This includes cruise passengers who debark in a country but spend their nights on board ship.

The WTO has published four manuals providing details on standard definitions, classifications and measurement techniques that can be of great use to countries interested in achieving consistency with international standards of tourism data collection, measurement and analysis.

The UN/WTO tourism definitions and classifications have been adopted by the Statistical Division of the European Communities (EUROSTAT). Working jointly, the national tourism authorities of Canada, the United States and Mexico are preparing for implementation, as well. It is anticipated that other multi-lateral tourism organizations will approve and begin to implement these recommendations over the next two years.

2

Tourism in India: Recent Trends

After Turkey, India is expected to achieve the fastest rate of growth of the total amount of economic activity likely to be generated by travel and tourism, at 9.7 per cent over the next 10 years. Also, the largest employment creation after China is expected to take place in India over the same period. The growth in 'visitor exports' or spending by international tourists, is likely to be the fastest in India at 14.3 per cent per annum over the next decade. On the whole, the WTTC forecast for India is promising, subject to key policy issues that affect the growth of the sector being addressed.

If India is to realise its enormous potential in tourism it must provide exclusive world-class tourism products and destinations to compete successfully for a larger share of the Asian tourism market. Today, outbound tourism from India far exceeds visitor traffic to the country partly because will have to be broadened in the Tenth Plan through the development of competitive destinations that match international standards in terms of price and quality and also satisfy the international traveller. India's international arrival figures have not been able to keep pace with neighbouring countries and have been exceeded by Thailand, Malaysia, Indonesia, Dubai and the Maldives.

Since 1995, India's share of the world market has remained virtually stagnant at 0.38 per cent, while domestic tourism has grown at a phenomenal rate and India now accounts for 4.6 per cent share of domestic tourism worldwide. In terms of tourism receipts, India has shown relative buoyancy because of the interest shown by visitors in traditional handicraft items and particularly in diamonds. The Tenth Plan visualises a mutually supportive role for tourism and handicrafts by encouraging haats and shilpgrams and recognising shopping as an integral part of the tourism experience to promote the 'Made in India' brand.

India receives the largest number of overseas tourists from the United Kingdom, which is its largest source market, followed by the United States, Sri Lanka, France, Germany, Canada, Japan, Australia and Singapore. Of the tourists coming to India, 27.5 per cent are in the age group there is a lack of world-class destinations within the country and partly because the domestic tourism policy has been largely directed towards those in the lower end of the spending spectrum.

The high spender from India prefers to visit neighbouring countries as he gets better value for money. The scope and reach of domestic tourism of 35-44 years, 23.4 per cent in the age group of 25-35 years and 20.8 per cent in the age group of 45-54 years. Women constitute only 30.5 per cent of India's total international arrivals. Repeat visitors account for 44.9 per cent of the overseas visitors.

A substantial number of these may be non-resident Indians, as hotel reservations do not correspond to the number of international arrivals in the country. The average length of stay of foreign tourists in the country in 1998 was 31.2 days. Domestic tourism, on the other hand, is largely pilgrimage-oriented and requires improvement in travel facilities and pilgrim destinations.

TENTH PLAN INITIATIVES

Tourism in India has tended to be regarded as an elitist activity conducted primarily for the purpose of earning foreign exchange. Its vast potential as an engine of growth and employment generater has remained largely untapped. Although, with 25 million jobs, India ranks second in terms of number of persons employed in travel and tourism, yet the contribution of the sector as a percentage share of all employment is amongst the lowest in the world. The Tenth Plan objective is to integrate tourism with the socio-economic objectives of the Plan by creating 3.6 million jobs a year through the promotion of domestic and international tourism and to enhance India's share of international arrivals from 0.38 per cent to at least 0.62 per cent by 2007.

Department of Tourism

Being the nodal agency for the development of tourism in the country, the department of tourism needs to make greater efforts to co-ordinate and integrate the policies of central ministries that have an impact on the development of tourism and to mobilise state governments and the private sector to develop unique and competitive tourism products and destinations. Crucial decisions affecting tourism are taken by other ministries viz. the Ministries of Finance, Home, Civil Aviation, Surface Transport, Environment and Forests, Urban Development, Rural Development, Ocean Develop-ment etc.

The Department of Tourism has tended to concentrate largely on its role as the promoter of international tourism and generator of foreign exchange earnings while paying relatively less attention to inter-sectoral policy co-ordination and the all-important development of tourism infrastructure and product quality. In the Tenth Plan, the Department will redefine and expand its role and work towards intersectoral convergence and policy integration to remove the barriers to the growth of tourism.

Barriers in Growth of Tourism

There are several factors that are respon-sible for the inadequate growth of the tourism sector in India. These are: barriers related to approach, barriers that discourage private investment, factors that affect competitiveness and factors that affect the long-term sustainability of tourism. The effective and early removal of these barriers during the Tenth Plan is an essential determinant for the success of the New Tourism Policy. The need for a national consensus on the role and level of tourism deve-lopment in the country has been voiced repeatedly but a concerted effort to achieve a consensus has not been made. Tourism should not be limited by state or regional boundaries if distortions in policies are to be avoided. It is important that a consensus among all states is evolved through the National Development Council (NDC) and the barriers to the growth of tourism removed.

Tourism has been denied the priority it deserves over successive Plan periods because its potential as an engine of economic growth has not been appreciated. This is visible in the low allocation of resources. Allocation to tourism has averaged 0.16 per cent of the total Plan outlay from the Third Plan to the Ninth Plan. In the Tenth Plan, it is likely to receive an allocation of 0.72 per cent. According to the WTTC, India is one of the lowest spenders on tourism - 153rd out of 160 countries - while its neighbouring competitors and China invest far more:

Malaysia (5.1 per cent), Nepal (5 per cent), Indonesia (8.4 per cent), Maldives (15.7 per cent), China (3.8 per cent). The growing domestic and international demand, which is set to boom, reinforces the need for higher investment. Failure to measure up to additional investment demand for domestic tourism is likely to lead to the over-exploitation of existing facilities, discouraging foreign visitors while leading to an increase in the outflow of high-spending domestic tourists from the country.

Most State Governments give scant importance to tourism even though they virtually control the tourism product located within their boundaries. They are responsible, inter alia, for local infrastructure, transport systems, sanitation and hygiene, leisure and recreation, law and order, the upkeep of local monuments and the general well-being of the tourist.

Their support and participation is essential for tourism to succeed and spread its benefits among the host population. Their lack of interest has resulted in an unprofessional ad hoc approach that acts as a deterrent to the growth of tourism. The approach of the state governments needs to be focused, highly professional and result-oriented if India is to avail of the opportunity that the currently favourable market trends have to offer.

Apart from the State Governments, the private sector plays a vital role in the growth and development of tourism. Although the Central Government and certain state governments have, from time to time, announced incentives to involve the private sector in tourism development, the results achieved have fallen short of expectations. To provide a conducive environment for private sector investment, it is important to realise that the travel and tourism sector is adversely affected by the lack of synergy in inter-sectoral policies.

The growth of the sector requires well-integrated and co-ordinated policies and stability in approach. Contradictions and arbitrary changes in policy send confused signals to the investor. Unless infirmities in policy are expeditiously removed well before the end of the Tenth Plan period, the New Tourism Policy is unlikely to succeed.

Being a long haul destination, India is more conveniently accessible by air and cannot be easily reached by rail or road. A restrictive air transport policy has a very deleterious effect on tourist traffic. There are insufficient connections to most tourism destinations. The situation could be eased if the large number of regional airports could open up as international airports. The existing international and national airports also require improvement. The price of aviation turbine fuel needs to be lowered to make air transport competitive and affordable.

Today, it is cheaper to travel by air to neighbouring countries from India than to travel to certain parts of India itself. A more liberal aviation bilaterals regime and a new aviation policy to benefit the economy of the country as a whole rather than the national carriers alone would greatly aid the development of tourism. Central and state governments need to evolve a taxation regime, which is revenue generating without being burdensome.

Accommodation and transport taxes tend to be very heavy in certain states while the excise policy in others is extremely harsh. The land policy in some states makes the setting up of a hotel a formidable exercise and as many as 48 clearances are required for the construction and running of a hotel. Such policies deter private sector investment. The importance of protecting private investment in tourism must also be appreciated and activities such as mining, unauthorised construction, encroachments and haphazard development around tourist resorts must be prevented through appropriate legislation and public support.

As tourism is a highly competitive industry; the traveller has a wide range of choices and looks for good value for money. The lack of quality infrastructure, uncompetitive rates, indifferent or poor product quality, difficulty in getting access to information on travel and tourist destinations, untrained service providers, and above all, the lack of hygiene, have an enormously negative effect on the competitiveness of the tourism product.

A world class destination requires professional planning to prevent haphazard, uncontrolled growth, spatial and land use planning, strict architectural controls, sewerage infrastructure and water treatment plants. It requires improvement of entry points and appropriate facilitation services. The lack of a visaon-arrival regime on account of security considerations places India at a disadvantage vis-à-vis its competitors. It is necessary that India strikes a balance between security considerations and the need for tourism development and reviews its visa policy to permit tourists from its major source markets to obtain visas on arrival.

Equally important is the behaviour of the host population. Training programmes are required not only for hotel managers but also for tourist guides, taxi-drivers, staff at eating places, porters etc., as the manner in which they conduct themselves affects the tourist's experience of the country. Important do's and dont's in terms of a code of ethics need to be inculcated among the service providers. During the Tenth Plan, the Department of Tourism will organise capacitybuilding programmes for service providers through mobile training units.

A major impediment to the growth of tourism in India has been the lack of awareness about the benefits that it can bestow upon the host population. Unless the host population, both in the rural and urban areas, is supportive of tourism, it cannot become a vibrant economic force. The rural sector, in particular, has been largely ignored in tourism development and has consequently been deprived of the benefits of employment and income generation accruing from tourism. The Tenth Plan will seek to rectify this, particularly in view of the world-wide interest in rural tourism.

While an awareness campaign that elicits local support for travel and tourism is essential for the long-term growth of the sector, it is also important to create awareness about the environmental impact of tourism by generating respect for the carrying capacities of tourist destinations. This is imperative as excessive exposure of ecologically fragile areas to human interference can lead to irreparable environmental degradation. As the demand for ecotourism is expected to grow enormously in the next decade, it is important to have regulations in place to prevent such damage. The local population must be convinced of the need to support such regulations in the interest of long-term sustainability.

India's hill resorts have already suffered seriously from a lack of concern for their carrying capacities and the unchecked influx of tourists during the summer months. If India's forest sanctuaries and pristine beaches are not to suffer the same fate, attention will have to be paid during the Tenth Plan to obtaining regulatory and public support for sustainability concerns.

Tenth Plan Strategy

The Tenth Plan strategy is to work towards a national consensus on the role of tourism in national development and to focus on the removal of barriers that hamper its growth. To make public sector investment more effective, it is necessary to work towards the inter-sectoral convergence of policies and programmes that could benefit tourism.

The New Tourism Policy envisages a framework, which is Government-led, private sector driven and oriented towards community welfare, with the Government creating the legislative framework and basic infrastructure for tourism development, the private sector providing the quality product and the community providing active support. The overall vision of the development of tourism embodied in the new policy will be achieved through five key strategic objectives. These are:

(i) Positioning tourism as a national priority.

(ii) Enhancing India's competitiveness as a tourist destination.

(iii) Improving and expanding product development.

(iv) Creation of world class infrastructure.

(v) Effective marketing plans and programmes.

Tourism as a National Priority

A concerted effort will be made, through the NDC, to arrive at a consensus on the role of tourism in the development agenda of the nation. Inclusion of tourism in the Concurrent List of the Constitution will provide constitutional recognition to the tourism sector and enable the central government to legislate for tourism development. A proposal to this effect has been circulated by the Department of Tourism to the state governments for comments and has also been discussed at a Chief Ministers' conference and a majority of the states have agreed to the proposal.

Other initiatives include the setting up of Tourism Advisory Council with key stakeholders functioning as a think tank and the constitution of a Group of Ministers on Tourism to improve policy integration and co-ordination. The adoption of a tourism satellite accounting system is underway to gauge more precisely the contribution of tourism to the national economy. A national awareness campaign in order to create a popular movement in favour of tourism is being planned through a professionally managed communication strategy. Most importantly, the efficiency of public investment in tourism supporting activities will be improved through effective inter-sectoral coordination and prioritisation.

Destination

As air capacity available to India is woefully short during the peak travel months, ranging from October to March, especially for the main tourism originating regions such as North America, Western Europe and South Asia, it is necessary to open India's skies to increase capacity and help enhance tourism. Additional seat capacity from the major tourism generating destinations would significantly benefit the national economy and provide a major impetus to tourism. Improvement in the standard of facilities and services at the international and national airports will need to be speeded up by employing professional manage-ment agencies and by privatising and leasing out airports.

To enhance India's competitiveness as a tourist destination, it is proposed to simplify the visa procedures and consider strategies for the speedy issue of visas including electronic visas and visas on arrival. An attempt will be made, through a consensus, to reduce the heavy and multiple taxes that reduce the competitiveness of the Indian tourism product. Special tourism police will be deployed at major tourist destinations during the Tenth Plan to provide security to travellers and promote India as a safe destination.

Product Development Strategy

Product development strategy during the Tenth Plan will be related to the special interests of tourist target markets. Cultural and heritage tourism will be expanded. India has a vast array of protected monuments with 22 world heritage sites, 16 of which are monuments. The integrated development of areas around these monuments provides an opportunity for the development of cultural tourism in India.

For the development of beach and coastal tourism, a number of sites on the west coast of India will be identified for the development as beach resorts by the private sector. The sites will be offered on long term lease at preferential terms. These sites will primarily be on the beaches of Goa, Kerala, and North Karnataka because of easier access by air.

During the Tenth Plan Kochi in Kerala and the Andaman and Nicobar Islands will be developed as international cruise destinations because of their proximity to international cruise routes and their exotic appeal. India's unmatched variety of cuisine is becoming increasingly popular in the world and will be developed as a special attraction. It is proposed to create a highly skilled workforce of culinary professionals through an innovative incentive scheme not only for India but also to promote Indian cuisine internationally.

Village tourism will be promoted as the primary tourism product of India to spread tourism and its socio-economic benefits to rural areas. India's great wildlife variety has not been developed as a tourist attraction. Wildlife sanctuaries and national parks will become an integral part of the Indian tourism product. Priority will be given to the preparation of site and visitor management plans for key parks.

The quality of tourist facilities available at the parks will be enhanced after a prioritisation of parks. Tentatively these will be: Corbett National Park, Kanha National Park, Bandhav Garh National Park, Kaziranga, Madhumali, Bharatpur, Periyar, Ranthambore, Little Rann of Kutch, Chilka, and the Sunderbans.

India has the greatest adventure tourism assets in the world in the Himalayas and its rivers. Mountain-based adventure activities will be developed and promoted. Regulations and certification for adventure tourism operators will be introduced so that the minimum standards of safety and conservation are met.

India receives only a minuscule proportion of the global meetings, conventions and exhibition market. It is important that India develops a world class international convention city not just for the sake of tourism development but also for international and domestic trade and commerce. India's most unique tourism product during the Tenth Plan will be holistic healing and rejuvenation packages. In focussing on this, it will capture the essence of Indian culture for international and Indian visitors alike.

India's fairs and festivals, some of which are already well established such as the Pushkar mela, the Desert Festival at Jaisalmer, the Kumbh Mela etc. will be promoted as unique products of India. The Festivals of India programme will be re-introduced in the top 12 future markets for India - initially with an annual event in the United Kingdom and the United States, to be followed by triennial events in the other markets.

Shopping will be recognised as an integral part of tourism. The development of dedicated shopping centres for traditional crafts designed along the lines of village haats such as Dilli Haat and Shilpgram will be encouraged and information on where to procure specific crafts made available through shopping guides.

Delhi will be positioned as the cultural capital of India supported by an ongoing and vibrant calendar of cultural events. The development of such a niche-based special interest productmix will position India as a unique and competitive destination.

World Class Infrastructure

The need for physical infrastructure for tourism ranges from ports of entry to modes of transport to destinations (airways, roadways, railways or waterways), to urban infrastructure such as access roads, power, water supply, sewerage and telecommunication. This underscores the need for inter-sectoral convergence of infrastructural schemes and programmes that could support tourist destinations.

The road network is vital for tourism as almost 70 per cent of passengers in India travel by road. Many tourist circuits are entirely dependent on roads. The current government plan for the road system in the country covering both inter-state highways and improvements to rural roads directly supports tourism development. There is urgent need to construct and improve highways linking the 22 world heritage sites and places of tourist significance. The Ministry of Road Transport and National Highways will collaborate with the Ministry of Tourism in this effort.

The Indian railway system can also become an enormous asset to the development of the tourism and hospitality industry in the country. The railways hold a special fascination for foreign tourists who wish to travel the country. For the vast majority of domestic tourists also, the railways is the most affordable means of travel linking the length and breadth of the country. Introduction of special tourist trains with pre-set itineraries and private sector participation will be encouraged.

The Indian Railways plan to establish 100 hotels at railway stations to serve specific tourist centres. The private sector will be given incentives to operate these hotels on long-term leases. These hotels will provide clean and inexpensive accommodation for budget tourists. The Indian Railways also owns a number of heritage structures, which, if effectively maintained and marketed, could serve, both as railway stations and places of tourist interest. India has five hill railways, which compare with the best hill railway systems in the world.

The enormous tourist potential of these products will be tapped during the Tenth Plan. As steam-hauled trains like the Royal Orient, Buddha Parikrama, Palace-On-Wheels and Fairy Queen are extremely popular with tourists, steam traction for special tourist segments will be continued. Trains like the Shatabdi and the Rajdhani with a special tourism and hospitality focus will be planned both for foreign and domestic tourists.

India's 7,000-km coastline and her mighty rivers will be tapped for the promotion of cruises. Care will be taken to develop world class tourism products. As the Ministry of Tourism's financial assistance to the states has not been able to have the desired impact in terms of creating of world class tourism infrastructure, the emphasis must shift to the development of specific travel circuits as internationally competitive destinations and the convergence of resources and expertise for these circuits.

The availability of trained manpower is essential to achieve excellence in the tourism sector. At present, there are 21 Institutes of Hotel Management and Catering Technology (IHM&TC) and 13 Food Craft Institutes in the country. In addition, a good number of accredited institutes also cater to the growing demand in the service sector. It is estimated that only 50 per cent of the requirement of the market is met by these institutes.

Five new Institutes of hotel management would be set up in the Tenth Plan - three in the newly created states of Uttaranchal, Jharkhand and Chhattisgarh and two in the northeast. In addition, 15 more Food Craft Institutes will be set up in the Tenth Plan, and efforts will be made to take culinary crafts and training to the rural areas through mobile training units. A new scheme on capacity building to train service providers in the unorganised sector such as small hotels, dhabas, restaurants and other eating joints is also proposed.

Effective Marketing Strategy

As there is fierce competition for tourists from India's source markets, India needs to change its traditional marketing approach to one that is more competitive and modern. It needs to develop a unique market position, image and brand, which cannot be held by any other competitor. India's positioning statement will capture the essence of its tourism product to convey an 'image' of the product to a potential customer. This image will be related not only to its ancient Vedic civilisation with a cultural heritage that continues to thrive especially in its rural areas but also to its essentially secular nature.

In the Tenth Plan, an extensive market research programme will be launched in the target source markets and tourism products developed to cater to the interests of each source market. An effective and ongoing market representation presence will be established with the travel trade in each source market and an Internet portal set up in various languages to provide information, a description of the product and the product requirements of the target market segments.

The Internet has a great impact on the marketing of travel and tourism. It has already established itself as a channel through which tourism organisations can promote their destinations and products. Indian tourism will utilise both the Internet and other emerging interactive technologies to avail of the benefits to be gained.

3

Historical Monuments of Touristic Significance

India is a land with a rich and varied history. Many different rulers, dynasties, and empires have fought over and controlled different parts of the Indian subcontinent during its eventful history. The various rulers and dynasties left behind their legacy in the form of grand monuments and buildings, in different historical places in India.

Most of India's cities have a history worth exploring, for the tales of the past are truly fascinating. The various monuments including palaces, forts, victory pillars and tombs in different historical places in India, tell glorious stories of India's fascinating history. The capital city of Delhi was originally the capital of the Tomara clan in the 11th century A.D and later it became the capital of the Mughals.

The city has some of the famous historical monuments; out of which some were built by the Mughals and the Britishers. Red Fort, Jama Masjid, Humayun's Tomb, Rashtrapati Bhawan, and Parliament House are the main monuments in Delhi, depicting its ancient history. Monuments of Prithviraj Chauhan, the Lodi Tombs, and the Siri Fort of Allauddin Khilji are some of the other monuments that you can see on your tour to Delhi.Neighboring Delhi is the city of Agra well known as the imperial capital of the Mughal Empire. City of Agra got its real grace during the reign of Shah Jahan.

In 1631,the Mughal ruler built the beautiful mausoleum of Taj Mahal, in the memory of his consort Mumtaz Mahal. The monument is still an inspiration for true lovers. The historical city of Agra also has many other Mughal monuments like the Agra Fort, the tomb of Itimad-ud-Daulah, and Akbar's fort at Sikandra.

The Royal state of Rajasthan offers many grand palaces and forts, which are part of the heritage of India. The capital city of Jaipur is one of the most visited historical places in India. The pink city was built by the astronomer King Sawaii Jai Singh in 1727 and endowed with grand palaces and magnificent forts. The Hawa Mahal, City Palace, Amber Fort and Jantar Mantar make Jaipur a must visit historical destination in India.

The city of Jaisalmer is dotted with many magnificent golden fortresses, historic carved havelis, windswept sand dunes, and desert festivals, which depict the traditional culture of Rajasthan.Udaipur is popular for its lake palaces which are historic and architectural gems of Rajasthan.The city is a popular historical place in India. The majestic Mehrangarh Fort and Umaid Bhawan Palace represent the city of Jodhpur, which is known for its magnificent palaces. The city was previously the princely state of Marwar. Jodhpur is one of the historical places in India where history can be seen even today. Another city in Rajasthan famous for its history and unequalled sacrifice is the city of Chittorgarh; this historical place in India has seen many battles and acts of heroic sacrifice.

Aurangabad, located in Maharashtra on India's west coast was known for being the capital of the Tughlaq Empire during the reign of Muhammed-bin-

Tughlaq.Devagiri Fort is a known historical monument situated in Aurangabad.The city is close to the cave temples of Ajanta and Ellora which form very important historical places in India. These Buddhist, Jain, and Hindu cave temples are marvels of Indian architecture, carved out of rock in the hills. Apart from all these historical places in Maharashtra, Mumbai city also has a rich history.

The city has some remarkable colonial architecture and monuments including the Victoria Terminus. The city was originally inhabited by Koli fishermen and was later handed over to Britishers. Hyderabad, the imperial capital of the Nizams, is one of the known India historical places including the grand monuments of Charminar, Golconda Fort, the Qutab Shahi Tombs, and the Falaknuma Palace. History and modernity coexist in this city, where a mixture of religions, cultures, and architectural styles come together to create one of the most interesting historical places in India.

Among the other historical places in India, the temples of Khajuraho in Madhya Pradesh, Konarak in Orissa and Meenakshi temples in Madurai have their own significance. The Khajuraho Temples were built during the reign of the Chandella dynasty in the years 950 and 1050 A.D. The temples are recognized worldwide for the excellence of their sculptures and for the erotic carvings on the temple walls. The Khajuraho temples are one of the most visited and studied historical places in India.

The magnificent sun temple of Konarak in Orissa was built in the 13th century. This historical monument is a UNESCO World Heritage Site and an architectural marvel, in this historical place in Eastern India. The popular Meenashi Temple is situated in Madurai, which was at one time a busy port under Chola, Pandya, and Nayaka rulers. The city continues to be an important town in Tamil Nadu and one of the most fascinating historical places in

India.Mahabalipuram is also an important historical place in South India, the city flourished as an artistic center of the Pallava dynasty.

The main highlights of the city are the five chariot shaped temples or rathas, the shore temple and the carved depictions of episodes from the Mahabharata.Varanasi, one of the oldest cities in India is famous for its ceremonial Ghats, archaeological museum, and the many temples which make it a unique city where history is very much a part of daily life.

Varanasi is one of the most important religious and historical places in India. Bodhagaya in Bihar is one of the known historical places in India, which has close association with Gautama Buddha, the founder of Buddhism. Buddhist pilgrims from around the world, travel to the historical places in India associated with Buddha's life, including Bodhagaya, the site where Buddha gained enlightenment.

Historical Monuments in India

Ancient Historical monuments of India are pieces of its heritage. Historical centres, buildings like forts, temples, palaces of India make it (India) an irresistible travel destination. Spending vacation in India, travelling the length and breadth of this vast landmass an experience unparalleled. Through the ages - passing the Vedic, the Mauryan & Gupta periods, thereafter, the Muslims followed by the Europeans, the history and culture of the vast subcontinent got enriched. Elements of all the people, races and religious were assimilated transformed and enliven. Together came their forts, temples, palaces, gardens - all providing India with some fabulous holiday destinations and making travelling in India a real joy.

India, beyond doubt, is the melting pot of various faith and creed. Given its historical and cultural richness, the whole country appears to be a Heritage site. Innumerable historical monuments, forts, palaces, churches, caves, tombs, mosques, temples gurudwaras and allied structures of various reigning powers and antiquity are spread all over the land. The masterpiece of Taj Mahal, the Fort, of Agra, Delhi, Madhya Pradesh, Rajasthan etc, palaces spread from Delhi to West Bengal and deep down the south, caves of Ajanta and Ellora caves, the temples of Khajuraho and Konark besides numerous others in northern and southern India, the gurudwaras at Delhi, Amritsar or Patna, the churches of Goa and Kerala, not to mention those in the other parts of the country - the list goes on and on.

From Rajgriha, Nalanda and Bodh Gaya in the east to the Elephanta Caves in Maharashtra and from Vaishnodevi temple in Jammu to the Jewish Synagogue at Cochin (in Kerela), the country is a 'heritage delight'. The Buddhist stupa (structure) of Sanchi and Hampi are as alluring as the Sun Temple of Konark and temples at Mamallapuram and Brihadisvara. The Goan Churches, the Sikh gurudwaras, the Jewish Synagogues - all exemplify the spirit of unity and diversity pervading the country.

Be it the Mughal forts, palaces and other structures of Fatehpur Sikri and Agra, Humayun's Tomb or a mixed effort like the old Fort at Delhi, the history and heritage is spread everywhere, providing tourism in India tremendous potential. Historical heritage is part and parcel of Indian life as much as Velha (Goa), near Victoria Memorial in Kolkatta (Calcutta), Nalanda in Bihar, Badrinath in Uttar Pradesh, Salim Chisti's Tomb at Fatehpur Sikri, India Gate at Delhi and Gateway of India in Mumbai. Given the historical heritage in the shapes of monuments, their ruins, buildings, temples, forts, palaces, churches, mosques and gurudwaras, holidays in India is virtually travelling in historical paradise - living/ witnessing so many civilizations in one life.

Lotus Temple

Located in Kalkaji in the south of Delhi, it is lotus shaped and has rightly been given the name. It is made of marble, cement, dolomite and sand. It is open to all faiths and is an ideal place for meditation and obtaining peace and tranquility. It is a very recent architectural marvel of the Bahai faith. The Bahá'í Faith is the youngest of the world's independent religions. Its founder, Bahá'u'lláh (1817-1892), is regarded by Bahá'ís as the most recent in the line of Messengers of God that stretches back beyond recorded time and that includes Abraham, Moses, Buddha, Zoroaster, Christ and Muhammad.

The central theme of Bahá'u'lláh's message is that humanity is one single race and that the day has come for its unification in one global society. God, Bahá'u'lláh said, has set in motion historical forces that are breaking down traditional barriers of race, class, creed, and nation and that will, in time, give birth to a universal civilization. The principal challenge facing the peoples of the earth is to accept the fact of their oneness and to assist the processes of unification.

Fariborz Sahba, Canadian architect of Iranian origin, spent 10 years in designing and project management, and with the help of a team of about 800 engineers, technicians, artisans and workers brought to realization one of the most complicated constructions in the world. The structure of the House is composed of three ranks of nine petals; each springing from a podium elevating the building above the surrounding plain. The first two ranks curve inward, embracing the inner dome; the third layer curves outward to form canopies over the nine entrances.

The petals, constructed of reinforced white concrete cast in place, are clad in white marble panels, performed to surface profiles and patterns related to the geometry. Nine arches that provide the main support for the superstructure ring the central hall. Nine reflecting pools surround the building on the outside, their form suggesting the green leaves of the lotus flower. Translating the geometry of the design, in which there are virtually no straight lines, into the actual structure presented particular challenges in designing and erecting the framework.

Not only was it difficult to align, so as to produce accurately the complex double-curved surfaces and their intersections, but also the closeness of the petals severely restricted workspace. Nevertheless the task was carried out entirely by the local laborers. Thanks to each one who contributed in its construction. To avoid construction joints, petals were concreted in a continuous operation for approximately 48 hours. Concrete was carried up the staging by women bearing 50-pound loads in baskets balanced on their heads. All the steel reinforcing for the shells of the lotus petals was galvanized to avoid rust stains on the white concrete in the prevailing humid conditions, guaranteeing the life of the delicate shell structure of 6 to 18 cm thick shells of the petals. India is well endowed with human resources.

The history of the Bahá'í Faith in India started with the inception of the Faith in Iran when the Báb (literally, the Gate) inaugurated a new era in the history of the human race. The Báb Himself had appointed one of the Indian believers as the 'Letter of Living' in 1844-45, the first year of His Ministry. Since then, India is spiritually connected with the Bahá'i Faith.

As foretold by the Báb, the Promised One of all ages and peoples, Bahá'u'lláh (literally the Glory of God) revealed Himself in 1863. He, Himself, dispatched one of the distinguished Bahá'í teachers, Jamal Effendi, to teach the Cause of God in the years 1874-75. Jamal Effendi (left) traveled to many States and was successful in attracting many learned people and few Navaabs (ruler of the states) including the Navaab of Rampur State (now in U.P.) to the Faith. One young man who accepted was Syed Mustafa Roumi who later became distinguished in his manifold services and was appointed as a Hand of the Cause of God.

Some of them accepted Bahá'u'lláh as the Universal Manifestation of God whose advent has been prophesied in all the Holy Scriptures. The other teachers who came to India during Bahá'u'lláh's Ministry included Mishkin Qalam, the distinguished Bahá'í Calligrapher. A series of teachers from the East and the West continued visiting India and traveling throughout the country during the time of 'Abdu'l-Bahá (literally, the Servant of Bahá), the much-loved Master of the Bahá'í Faith. Prominent among them were Mirza Mahram and Mirza Mahmud Zarqani.

Qutab Minar

In 1199, Qutub-ud-Din raised the Qutub Minar either as a victory tower or as a minaret to the adjacent mosque. From a base of 14.32m it tapers to 2.75m at a height of 72.5m and a valid reason why it took two decades to complete this monument. Its a red sandstone tower covered with beautiful and striking carvings and is inscribed with verses from the holy Quran. Qutub Minar is still the highest stone tower in India as well as one of the finest Islamic structures ever raised and Delhi's recognised landmark. The sultan's successor and son-in-law, Iltutmish, completed it.

In 1303, Ala-ud-Din established the second city of Delhi, called Siri, of which nothing remains but the embattlements. He also had dug a vast reservoir, Hauz Khas, to supply water to his city. Contemporary historians describe the Delhi of that time as being the "envy of Baghdad, the rival of Cairo and equal to Constantinople". For the sake of convenience, tourists visiting the Qutub

Complex could also see the Tomb of Adham Khan and Zafar Mahal in Mehrauli and the Tomb of Jamali-Kamali behind the Qutub Minar. These however, belong to a later date.

From the Nagari and Persian inscriptions on the minar, it appears that it was damaged twice by lightning, in 1326 and 1368. The first damage occurred during Muhammed Tughluq's reign (1325-51), and was repaired by him apparently in 1332. The second damage was attended by Feroze Tughluq (1351-88). Later in 1503, Sikandar Lodi (1489-1517) also carried out some restoration in the upper storeys.

Originally the minar had only four storeys, faced with red and buff sandstone. The uppermost storey, which was damaged in 1368 during Feroze Tughluq's reign, was replaced by him by two storeys, making free use of marble but leaving the lower portion of the fourth storey built with sandstone in its original condition. The original three storeys are each laid on a different plan, the lowest with alternate angular and circular flutings, the second with round ones and the third with angular ones only, with the same alignment of flutings, however, being carried through them all.

Its projecting balconies with stalactite pendentive type of brackets and inscriptional decorative bands on different storeys heighten its decorative effect. It has a diameter of 14.32 m at the base and about 2.75 m on the top. With a height of 72.5 m and 379 steps, it is the highest stone tower in India and a perfect example of minar known to exist anywhere.

There exists a tradition that the Qutub-Minar was built by Prithviraj, the last Chauhan king of Delhi, for enabling his daughter to behold the sacred river Yamuna, from its top as part of her daily worship. The Minar's entire architecture, however, bespeaks an Islamic origin, with two of its prototypes in brick still existing at Ghazni, although Hindu craftsmen were certainly employed for its construction, as is evident also from certain 'Devanagari' inscriptions on its surface. Sometimes sculptured stones from temples have been found utilised in it.

Originally, it was surmounted by a cupola, which fell down during an earthquake and was replaced early in the 19th century with a new cupola in the late Mughal style, by one Major Smith. It looked, however, so incongruous that it was brought down in 1848, and may now be seen on the lawns to the south east of the minar.

Quwwatu'l-Islam Masjid

Just adjacent to the tower is the mosque of Quwwatu'l-Islam Masjid, which can become a bewildering experience for those who are not familiar with its history. It was supposed to have been built using the materials and masonry of the remains of Hindu Temples and architecture. On one hand there is the beautiful, exceptional Islamic handwriting and brocaded designs. Then there are pillars with clearly pre-Islamic Hindu motifs. The reason is that the pillars were taken from the 27 temples of Qila Rai Pithora, the city of the Rajput king Prithviraj Chauhan. This in fact has been recorded by Qutub-ud-Din in his inscriptions, who call it the Jami Masjid (Friday Mosque) in his inscriptions. The mosque was started in 1192 by Qutub-ud-din Aibak, the first ruler of the Slave Dynasty and was finished four years later.

The Iron Pillar

In the courtyard of the Quwwatu'l-Islam mosque stands the famous iron pillar, which bears a Sanskrit inscription in Gupta script, palaeographically assignable to the 4th century, a date which is also confirmed by the peculiar style of its 'Amalaka'-capital. The inscription records that the pillar was set up as a standard or dhvaja of god Vishnu on the hill known as 'Vishnupada', in the memory of a mighty king, named 'Chandra', who is now regarded as identical with Chandragupta II (375-413) of the imperial Gupta dynasty. A deep hole on the top of the pillar indicates that an additional member, perhaps an image of 'Garuda', was fitted into it to answer to its description as a standard of Vishnu.

The pillar has been brought here evidently from somewhere, else, as no other relics of the 4th century are found at the site. There is a strong bardic tradition that it was brought here - wherefrom, nobody knows - by Anangpal, the Tomar king who is credited with the founding of Delhi. The base of the pillar is knobby, with small pieces of iron tying it to its foundations, and a lead sheet covers the portion concealed below the present floor-level.

The total length of this slightly tapering shaft is 7.20m, of which 93cm is buried below the ground. The metal of the pillar has been found to be almost pure malleable iron. Its portion below the ground shows some signs of rusting, but at a very slow rate. The manufacture of such a massive iron pillar, which has not deteriorated much during sixteen hundred years of its existence, is a standing testimony to the metallurgical skill of ancient Indians. A traditional belief says that any one who can encircle the entire column will have their wish granted. However, it is fenced off from tourists so as to avoid any damage.

Alai Minar

The ambitious rubble Alai Minar was started by Alauddin Khalji but the sultan lived to see it only to the height of 24.5m and no body was ready to complete his over-ambitious project. It was built to match the enlarged

Quwwatu'l-Islam Masjid. Today it is used more like an illustration, by parents, that when you get over ambitious, the plans remain unfinished.

Alai Darwaza

The southern gateway of the Quwwatu'l-Islam mosque, as extended by Ala-ud-Din Khalji, is known as the Ala-i-Darwaza and among its several inscriptions executed to form an ornamental surface, three mention the date of its erection as 710 A.H. (1311).

Alai Darwaza is the first building employing wholly the Islamic principles of accurate construction and geometric ornamentation and also betrays certain 'Saljuqian' characteristics, which had influenced the Khalji architecture. Important among these characteristics are wide and bulging dome with a central knob, pointed horse-shoe-shaped arches and squinches and lotus-bud fringes of the arches.

The celebrated gateway, built of red sandstone, is 17.2m squares with arched openings on all sides, and is surmounted by a wide but shallow dome on an octagonal base achieved through squinches with concentric series of arches. The northern arch is semicircular, while others have a pointed horseshoe shape, with radiating voussoirs laid on the principle of true arch.

The underside of the arches is fringed with lotus-bud embellishment, not merely in the openings, but also in the perforated side-windows. Its excellent proportions, profuse geometrical carvings on the interior, inscriptional bands of white marble in 'Naskh' characters and other decorative details in red stone make it a very pleasing structure. It has been rightly described as "one of the most treasured gems of Islamic architecture".

Tomb of Iltutmish

The tomb of Shamsu'd-Din Iltutmish, son-in-law and successor of Qutub-ud-Din Aibak, lies to the northwest of the Quwwatu'l Islam mosque. It was built in about 1235 by Iltutmish himself, only five years after the construction of Sultan Ghari's tomb. Yet, it is quite different from the latter and illustrates that phase in the development of Indo-Islamic architecture, when the builder had ceased to depend for material on the demolition of temples, although the arches and semi-domes below the squinches were still laid in the indigenous corbelled fashion.

Its tomb-chamber with a cenotaph in its centre, internally nearly 9m-sq and faced with red sandstone, was certainly intended to be covered with a dome, as is clear from the squinches, which appear for the first time in this building. It is believed that the original dome had fallen and was replaced by Feroze Shah Tughluq, but even this did not survive.

The interior on the west is occupied by three 'minhrabs' or prayer niches, the central one higher and ornamented with marble, to serve as a place for prayers, while the other sides are pierced by arched entrances.

The tomb is plain on the outside, but is profusely carved on the entrances and in the interior with inscriptions in 'Kufi' and 'Naskh' characters with geometrical and arabesque patterns in saracenic tradition, although several motifs among its carvings are reminiscent of Hindu decoration. To this class belong wheel, bell-and-chain, tassel, lotus and diamond. In view of its lavish ornamentation, Fergusson described it as " one of the richest examples of Hindu art applied to Muhammadan purposes".

Ala-Ud-Din's Tomb And College

To the southwest of the Quwwatu'l-Islam mosque lie some

rooms and halls in ruins making an L-shaped block. They are believed to represent Ala-ud-Din's tomb and college or madrasa, which was started by him to impart instructions in Islamic theology and scriptures. The central room in the southern wing was perhaps his tomb. The conception of a combined college and tomb appears here in India for the first time and is perhaps inspired by 'Suljuqian' traditions.

Humayun's Tomb

Humayun's tomb lies on the Mathura road near its crossing with the Lodi Road. High rubble-built walls enclose here a square garden divided initially into four large squares separated by causeways and channels, each square divided again into smaller squares by pathways ('Chaharbagh') as in a typical Mughal Garden. The lofty mausoleum is located in the centre of the enclosure and rises from a podium faced with series of cells with arched openings. The central octagonal chamber containing the cenotaph is encompassed by octagonal chambers at the diagonals and arched lobbies on the sides, their openings closed with perforated screens.

Three emphatic arches dominate each side, the central one being the highest. This plan is repeated on the second storey, and a 42.5m high double dome of marble surmounts the roof with pillared kiosks ('chhatris') placed around it. The structure is built with red sandstone, but white and black marble has been used to relieve the monotony, the latter largely in the borders.

Haveli of Hakeem Ashanullah Khan

The haveli of Hakeem Ashanullah Khan, personal physician of the emperor Bahdur Shah Zafar, was a fortress for those who were able to hide themselves here in the 'ghadar'- the Sepoy Mutiny time. The mansion almost covers 2,000-square-yards and appears to be a mohalla itself. It was because of the orders of the Hakeem that Ghalib was given the scholarship to write the history of the Mughal dynasty. Immediately after the Mutiny, British confiscated the house of the Hakeem. It was soon returned too, but not before it was stripped of the old chandeliers and lamps.

The tomb was built by Humayun's senior widow Bega Begam, popularly known as Haji Begam, nine years after his death in 1565 according to some, but fourteen years according to the manuscript of an 18th century text. It is the first substantial example of the Mughal architecture, with high arches and double dome, which occurs here for the first time in India. Although some tombs had already been sited within gardens, it is also the first mature example of the idea of garden-tomb, which culminated in the Taj-Mahal at Agra.

The enclosure is entered through two lofty double-storeyed gateways, one on the west and the other on the south, the latter now remaining closed. A 'baradari' (pavilion) occupies the centre of the eastern wall of the enclosure and a bath-chamber that of the northern wall.

Several rulers of the Mughal dynasty lie buried in the mausoleum, although it is not possible to identify their graves. Among those lying buried here are Bega Begam, Hamida Banu Begam - Humayun's junior wife, Dara Shikoh - Shah Jahan's son, and the later Mughals, Jalandar Shah, Farrukhsiyar, Rafi'u'd-Darajat, Rafi'u'd-Daula and 'Alamgir II, Bahadur Shah II, the last Mughal emperor of Delhi had taken shelter in this tomb with the three princes during the mutiny and was captured here in 1857 by Lieutenant Hodson.

India Gate

At the center of New Delhi stands the 42m high India

Gate, an "Arc-de-Triomphe" like Archway in the middle of a crossroad. Almost similar to its French counterpart war memorial. It commemorates the 70,000 Indian soldiers who lost their lives fighting for the British Army during the First World War and bears the names of more than 13,516 British and Indian soldiers killed in the Northwestern Frontier in the Afghan war of 1919.

The foundation stone was laid by His Royal Highness, the Duke of Connaught in 1921 and was designed by Edwin Lutyens. The monument was dedicated to the nation 10 years later by the then Viceroy, Lord Irwin. Another memorial, Amar Jawan Jyoti was added much later, after India got its independence. It is in the form of a flame that burns day and night under the arch to remind the nation of soldiers who laid down their lives in the Indo-Pakistan War of December 1971.

The entire arch stands on a low base of red Bharatpur stone and rises in stages to a huge molding, beneath, which are inscribed Imperial sons. Above on both sides is inscribed INDIA, flanked by MCM and to the right, XIX. The shallow domed bowl at the top was intended to be filled with burning oil on anniversaries but this is rarely done. Surrounding the imposing structure is a large expanse of lush green lawns, which is a popular picnic spot. One can see hoards of people moving about the brightly lit area and on the lawns on summer evenings.

Jantar Mantar

A unique structure raised in 1724, now lies in the heart of Delhi's commercial centre near Connaught place. This is the Jantar Mantar, one of several astronomical observatories raised by Maharaja Jai Singh II of Jaipur. The various abstract structures within the Jantar Mantar are, in fact, instruments that were used for keeping track of celestial bodies. Yet, Jantar Mantar is not only a timekeeper of celestial bodies, it also tells a lot about the technological achievements under the Rajput kings and their attempt to resolve the mysteries regarding astronomy.

The Jantar Mantar of Delhi is only one of the five observatories built by Sawai Jai Singh II, the other four being located at Jaipur, Varanasi, Ujjain and Mathura. All of these were built as far back as AD 1724-1730 during the period generally known as the dark age of Indian history, when the last great Mughal emperor Aurangzeb had died and the Mughal Empire was rapidly declining.

During this period of turmoil, Muhammad Shah ascended the throne of the Mughal Empire. As many enemies surrounded him, he sought the alliance of the Hindu rulers. Of these, the most notable was Sawai Jai Singh II of Amber, who came into limelight since the days of Aurangzeb. When Jai Singh ascended the throne of Amber in 1699, he was barely eleven, but sharp and shrewd far beyond his years.

The then Mughal emperor Aurangzeb was so impressed with the young ruler that he gave Jai Singh II the title of 'Sawai', meaning one and a quarter of an average man in worth. As Jai Singh repeatedly proved himself a worthy ally of the Mughals, Muhammad Shah, who was seeking a dependable ally, zeroed in on Jai Singh and duly raised him to the rank of governor of Agra and later, of Malwa.

Jai Singh was passionate about two things-arts and the sciences, chiefly astronomy. Once, at the court of Muhammad Shah, he found the Hindu and Muslim astrologers embroiled in a heated argument over certain planetary positions. It was imperative that the positions be known accurately to determine an auspicious hour for the emperor to set out on an expedition. Jai Singh offered to rectify the then available astronomical tables, an offer that was readily accepted by the Mughal emperor. The result was an onsite Jantar Mantar in Delhi, an astronomical observatory where the movements of sun, moon and planets could be observed.

Jai Singh's idea was to create a rebirth of practical astronomy among the Indian masses and practicing astronomers. However, the lofty ideals of the Jantar Mantar remained unfulfilled as the country at that time was in chaos and the full potential of this observatory was never realized.

In the beginning, Jai Singh tried to use brass instruments in this observatory, but soon gave them up because of several inherent flaws. They were too small, for one thing, their axes were unstable so the center often got displaced. He then decided to follow the style adopted by the renowned Arab astronomer, Prince Ulugh Beg, builder of the famous 15th century observatory at Samarkand, Uzbekistan. The massive masonry instruments at Samarkand suited Jai Singh's architectural tastes and promised to be more accurate because of sheer size. In 1730, Jai Singh sent a mission to the king of Lisbon. On its return to Jaipur, the mission brought back a telescope and the court astronomer by the name of Xavier de Silva.

City Palace

The City Palace is an imposing blend of traditional Rajasthani and Mughal art and architecture. The City Palace complex houses several palatial structures. In the heart of the old Jaipur city, the City Palace occupies a large area divided into a series of courtyards, gardens and buildings.

Jai Singh built the outer wall but other additions were made much later, some right up to the start of this century. The former Maharaja still lives in part of the palace. The City Palace sprawls over one-seventh of the area of the walled city. It houses the Chandra Mahal, Shri Govind Dev Temple and the City Palace Museum.

The first building in it, is Mubarak Mahal, built by Maharaja Madho Singh. It has a beautifully carved marble gate with heavy brass doors on either side of this gate. Beyond this gate, lies the 'Diwan-E-Khas' or the 'Hall Of Private Audience' with a marble paved gallery. Across a paved square lies the 'Diwan-E-Am' or the 'Hall Of Public Audience', with its intricate decorations and manuscripts in Persian and Sanskrit. There is also a clock tower and the newer Mubarak Mahal.

To the north-west is the stately and graceful seven-storeyed Chandra Mahal, the residence of ex-ruler. The seven-story Chandra Mahal is the centrepiece and commands fine views of the gardens and the Jaipur city. The complex contains an excellent museum, an armoury and several fine halls. The apartments are maintained in luxurious order and the museum of Maharaja Sawai Man Singh II has an extensive collection of art, carpets, enamelware and old weapons.

The paintings include miniatures in Rajasthani, Mughal and Persian schools. The armoury dating back to the 15th century and many of the ingenious and tricky weapons, which the warrior Rajputs were famous for. A section of museum also contains dresses and costumes of the former Maharajas and Maharanis of Jaipur. Each storey has a distinctive name and is a place of sheer beauty and luxury. Paintings, floral decorations, mirror walls and ceilings in the traditional style adorn the palace. The uppermost storey is called the Mukut Mahal.

Opposite the Chandra Mahal lies the Badal Mahal. The Govind Devji Temple stands in the middle of the Chandra Mahal and the Badal Mahal. A delightful system of mountains is placed in the middle of the paved path between the Chandra Mahal and the Badal Mahal. The palace has extensive and sprawling gardens.

Outside the buildings, you may see a large silver vessel which a former Maharaja used to take drinking water with him to England. Being a devout Hindu, he could not drink the English water!

Hawa Mahal

The Hawa Mahal, literally meaning, palace of the winds is an important landmark of the city of Jaipur - the Pink City of India. Travel to Jaipur is considered incomplete without a trip to the Hawa Mahal. It is an interesting building, although it is actually little more than a façade. Probably, this honeycombed building was originally built to facilitate the women of the royal household to watch the everyday life and processions of the city.

There is no definite record as to why Hawa Mahal was built, only conjecture. It certainly was not meant for residential purposes. That becomes clear if one were to view this unusual structure from the rear side. There is a total lack of ornamentation on the inner face of the building. The chambers of Hawa Mahal are plain and mere mass of pillars and passages leading to the top story. It does not seem to be part of the same building.

Built at a time when royal ladies observed very strict purdah (covering the faces), it is widely believed that this interesting palace, with its screened balconies, provided the ladies of the zenana (royal household) an opportunity to watch processions and other activities on the streets below without being observed themselves. The openings in the Hawa Mahal are almost like peepholes, partially blocked by fine latticework in lime plaster, and some with plain wooden windows. The Hawa Mahal lives up to its name as one climbs up to the balconies and is almost swept away by the cool breeze. The royal ladies not only enjoyed the view but also did so in great comfort and style.

Today, Hawa Mahal provides the travelers in Jaipur with some excellent views of the city and a bird's eye view of the Jantar Mantar (a medieval observatory and an important tourist place in Jaipur). The best time to view Hawa Mahal is sunrise when it catches the early morning sun and is bathed in its golden light making it glow like a gem. Strangely, the entrance to Hawa Mahal is from the rear side. So, the next time you travel to Jaipur, do fix up a date with Hawa Mahal.

Lake Palace

The shimmering Lake Pichola surrounds the Lake Palace with a unique mystique, all its own. The Lily pond seems to carry that very mystique inside, in the centre of the palace. Here, dining is a pleasure during the day. And magic at night. The effect is that of time coming to a standstill. Nothing intrudes your privacy, peace and tranquility. Leaving you to wonder if paradise can be this serene.

The Lake Palace Hotel is in fact a white marble palace that seems to float miraculously on the still waters of Lake Pichola. Probably the most romantic hotel in the world, this 250-year old palace offers guests a unique blend of serenity and opulence. Founded in 1568 by Maharana Udai Singh, the Lake city of Udaipur is often referred as the 'Venice of the East'. Studded with extravagant palaces, hilltop fortresses, awe-inspiring temples and romantic gardens filled with blossoming trees, this 'City of Dreams' is, not surprisingly, a favourite with travellers, both Indian and Foreign. A fantasy island palace shimmering on mirror-calm Lake Pichola, the Lake Palace is one of the most romantic hotels in the world.

Fatehpur Sikri

37 kms from Agra is built a city predominantly in Red

Sandstone and is called Fatehpur Sikri. This town was built by the Mughal Emperor, Akbar. He had planned this city as his capital but shortage of water compelled him to abandon the city. After this within 20 years, the capital of Mughals was shifted to Lahore. Fatehpur Sikri was built during 1571 and 1585. Today this ghost city has a population of about 30,000. This deserted city has retained many of the old structures, because of the efforts of the Archaeological department.

Fatehpur Sikri is one of the finest examples of Mughal architectural splendour at its height. Though the city is in ruins, it is a place to visit if one comes to Agra.But in real terms Fatehpur Sikri is a place where one should spend some time. The sunset over the ruins is sight to cherish. Fatehpur Sikri is the best example of the culmination of Hindu and Muslim architecture. Fatehpur Sikri Mosque is said to be a copy of the mosque in Mecca and has designs, derived from the Persian & Hindu architecture.

Diwan-khana-I-khaas

To the right is an apparently looking two storeyed building, with corner kiosks, known as diwan-khana-I-khaas or Hall Of Private Audience. On entering it, one finds only a single vaulted chamber. In the centre stands a profusely carved column supporting a collosal-bracketed capital. Four narrow causeways project from the centre and run to each corner of the chamber. It is believed that Akbar's throne occupied the circular space over the capital and the corners were assigned to the four ministers.

Diwan-I-Am

The journey to the royal palace begins with Diwan-I-Am or the Hall Of Public Audience. This hall was also used for celebrations and public prayers. It has cloisters on three sides of a rectangular courtyard. To the west is a pavilion with the Emperor's throne. Beautiful jali screen on either sides separated the ladies attending the court.

The Treasury

To the left of the Diwan-I-Khaas is the Treasury or Ankh Michauli, once believed to have been used for playing the game, comprising three rooms each protected by a narrow corridor which were manned by guards.

Turkish Sultana's House

To the left of the Pachisi Board is the Turkish Sultana's house. The house, as its location at the corner of Anup Talao shows, was a pavilion for repose, attached to the pool. The geometrical pattern on the ceiling is reminiscent of Central Asian carvings in wood.

Palace of Jodha Bai

To the left of the Sunehra Makan is the largest and the most important building in the royal palace, named after Akbar's Rajput wife, Jodha Bai. This spacious palace was assured of privacy and security by high walls and a 9 metre guarded gate to the east. The architecture is a blend of styles with Hindu columns and Muslim cupolas.

Daulat khana-I-khas

Located in the corner to the left is the emperor's private chamber. It has two main rooms on the ground floor. One housed Akbar's library while the larger room was his resting area. On the first floor is the Khwabgah or the bed-chamber. It was connected with the Turkish Sultana's house, the Panch Mahal, Mariam's House and the Jodha Bai's palace by corridors.

Sunehra Makan

Opposite to the Diwan-I-Khas is the palace of Akbar's Rajput wife, Mariam-Uz-Zamani. This two-storeyed building is richly adorned by gold murals in Persian style. The beams have inscriptions of verses by Akbar's brother, Faizi.

Panch Mahal

To the right of Sunehra Makan is the elegant, airy 5 storeyed pavilion, the Panch Mahal. Each floor over here is smaller than the one below and it rises to a single domed kiosk on top supported by four columns providing a magnificent view of the city and its environs.

Hawa Mahal And Nagina Masjid

To the right of Jodha Bai's palace is Hawa Mahal, the Palace of Winds. This small-screened wind tower faces the garden and is attached to the palace. The garden is laid out in the Char Bagh style with straight walls intersecting at right angles and divided by shallow channels.

Birbal's Palace

To the north west of the Jodha Bai's Palace is the 2 storeyed palace occupied by Akbar's two senior queens-ruqnayya begum and salima sultan begum. It has two storeys-four rooms and two porches with pyramidical roofs below and two rooms with cupolas and screened terraces above. The building combines hindu and muslim atyles of srchitecture.

The Jami Masjid

One of the largest mosques in India, Jami Masjid was built

in 1571 AD. Inside, there is a vast congregational coutyard. To the right, at the corner, is the Jammat Khana Hall and next ot this is the tomb of the royal ladies. To the left of the Jami Masjid is the Stone Cutters' mosque, the oldest place of worship at Fateh Pur Sikri. It is entered through the eastern entrance known as the Buland Darwaza.

Dargah Of Sheikh Salim Chisti

To the North of the Mosque is the Dargah of Shaikh Salim Chishti. This Dargah was built in 1570. Here, childless women come for blessings of the saint. Even Akbar was blessed with three sons, when he came here. The lattice work in the Dargah is among the finest to be found any where in India.

Buland Darwaza

This gate can be approached from the outside by a 13-metre flight of steps which adds to its grandeur. The gate erected in 1602 AD to commemorate Akbar's victory over Deccan is the highest and grandest gateway in India and ranks among the biggest in the world.

Taj Mahal

No word can justify the beauty of the Taj Mahal. A wonder of the world, the Taj Mahal in Agra is a monument which no other in the world can match its beauty and grandeur. Called the most beautiful temple in the world, the white marbled mausoleum at Agra has become the epitome of a man's love for a woman.

Synonymous with India, the Taj Mahal is undoubtedly the epitome of India tourism. India travel is incomplete without experiencing the Taj Mahal. This supreme temple of love, standing gracefully by the sacred

Yamuna at Agra, is set amongst the serene ambience of a well laid out garden. The massive white marble structure was built in the 17th century by the Mughal Emperor Shahjahan in memory of his beloved wife, Mumtaz Mahal. Shah Jahan was so disheartened by her death that the royal court went in mourning for two years and there was no music, no dancing, no celebrations and no feasting for two years. After such a long period when he recovered his consciousness Shah Jahan decided immortalize their love in the form of the Taj Mahal. He had selected the place for the Mahal Taj in Agra so that he could see it from his personal palace at Agra Fort.

Designed by the local Muslim architect Ustad Ahmad Lahori, the Taj Mahal is a reflection of the gardens of Paradise to which the faithful ascend. The entire complex, with gardens, gateway structures, and mosque, was completed in 1643. The mausoleum stands at one end of the garden adorned with fountains and marble pavements. The garden contains four water channels to echo the four rivers of the Islamic Paradise.

It is more than 350 years since Taj Mahal was built in Agra, but it has not lost its romantic aura, which attracts millions of visitors to India to experience it. It is because of this everlasting charm that the Taj Mahal in Agra can boast of being one of the most popular world heritage monuments on earth.

Gateway of India

Mumbai's principal landmark, the Gateway of India is a huge archway on the water's edge at Apollo Bunder. It is the starting point for most tourists who want to explore the city. This famous monument was built to commemorate the visit of the first ever British Monarch, King George V and Queen Mary in 1911. The Gateway was built by the British and designed by the architect

George Wittet. The first stone was laid by the then Governor of Bombay on March 31st, 1913. The Gate was formally opened in 1924.

It is 26m high structures, complete with four turrets and intricate latticework carved into the yellow basalt stone. Ironically, when the British Raj ended in 1947, this colonial symbol also became a sort of epitaph: the last of the British ships that set sail for England left from the Gateway.

Behind the arch, there are steps leading down to the water. Here, one can get onto one of the bobbing little motor launches, for a short cruise through Mumbai's splendid natural harbour. One can buy tickets for a short cruise on the motor launches from here. Near the Gateway of India is Taj Mahal Hotel, one of the most famous and luxurious hotels in India. Close by are the statues of the Maratha leader Shivaji astride his horse and of Swami Vivekananda, that add to the charm of this monument.

Mysore Palace

The Mysore Palace, built is Indo-Saracenic style with domes turrets, arches and colonnades, the palace is a treasure house of exquisite carvings and works of art from all over the world. The tastefully decorated and inticirately carved doors open into luxuriously decorated rooms.

The palace has now been converted into a museum, which treasures the souvenirs, paintings, jewellery, royal costumes and other items, which were once possessed by the Wodeyars. It is said that the palace displays the largest collection of gold items, quantity wise. The Durbar hall of the palace has an ornate ceiling and many sculpture pillars which are said to have been painted with gold. The walls of the palace are painted with pictures of the Dassera processions and these paintings are painted in such a manner that from any angle you can see the procession coming towards you. The royal throne of the Wodeyars is displayed during the Dassera festival. The palace was originally built of wood, which got burnt down in 1897 AD and was rebuilt in 1912 AD.

Gwalior Fort

For over 100 years this fort has been over looking the city of Gwalior. One of the most invincible forts in India, this imposing citadel has changed many hands. It is build on a hill of sandstone and towers 100 m from the plain. The outer wall of the fort is almost 2 miles in length and the width varies from one kms to 200 meters. The walls of the fort gives way onto the steep slopes. This fort has been a witness to many battles in the turbulent times as well as as festivals in the peace time. The rulers have imparted justice from the fort which has seen the imprisonment of many. The ceremonies held in the fort have been spelled out grandeur but the Jauhars have screamed distress. It was here that Tatyia tope and Rani of Jhansi fought for their freedom. Rani of Jhansi laid down her life in an assault by the British to capture the fort.

Jaisalmer Fort

Deep in the heart of the Thar Desert is Jaisalmer, one of the last princely bastions in the region. Founded on what was the cross - road of lucrative trade routes, this remote settlement came to be celebrated for the valour of its rulers, and for the aesthetic sense represented by their palaces and havelis. The rich merchants engaged stone - craftsmen who worked delicately on the sandstone mansions they built, filling up facades with sculptural filigree, screen windows, delicate pavilions and beautiful balconies. Today, these veritable art - museums are still inhabited, and their colorful celebrations and festivals have placed Jaisalmer Fort firmly on the world tourism map.

Rani Mahal (Jhansi)

The palace of Rani Laxmi Bai has now been converted into a museum. It houses a collection of archaeological remains of the period between 9th and 12th centuries AD.

Stupa Complex (Kapilavastu)

This is the main archaeological site which was discovered during excavations in 1973-74. The seals and inscriptions over the lid of the pot discovered read "Om Deoputra Vihare Kapilvastu Bhikschu Mahasanghasa" and "Om Deoputra Vihare Kapilvastu Bhikschu Sanghasa". The title Deoputra refers to Kanishka, a great patron of Buddhism who built the biggest Vihara at Kapilvastu and renovated the main stupa here.

Kushinagar

The monuments of Kushinagar are situated in three distinct groups comprising the main site of the Nirvana Temple, the central stupa and surrounding monasteries, the Mathakuar shrine to the southwest, and the Ramabhar Stupa a kilometer to the east.

Vindhyachal Places (Varanasi)

A place where the Goddess of power is said to be residing and people worship her viz- Goddess Durga,are known as Shaktipeeths and Vindhyachal is one of such peeths or abode of Shakti. The place is 90 kms from Varanasi. The temples of Vindhyavasini Devi, Asthbhuja and Kalikhoh are a must visit here.

Sikandara (Agra)

Four kilometer from Agra is the mausoleum of Akbar.

Construction of this beautiful monument was started by Akbar himself. This structure has a perfect blending of Hindu, Christian , Islamic, Buddhist, Jain motifs. The blending is much like Deen-e-Ilahi, a new religion started by Akbar. But Akbar died before his mausoleum could be completed and his son Jehangir completed it. But Jehangir made many modification in the original plan of the building.

The structure gives an idea how the Mughal art was developing. From the Humayun's tomb in Delhi to Akbar's Tomb in Sikandra which finally gave way to the Taj Mahal, all are definite stages of development of Mughal art and architecture. Sikandra is named after Sikander Lodhi. The tomb has three-storey-minarets on its corners. These minarets are built in red sandstone with stunning in lay work of marble. On the walk ways langur monkeys wait to be fed. The mausoleum is surrounded by a beautiful garden. Sikander Lodhi had built the Baradi palace in the garden. On the road from Sikandra to Agra are several tombs and also two 'Kos Minars' or mile stones.

Dhamekh Stupa (Sarnath)

Ancient Sarangnath or Sarnath also known as Mrigadava (deer park), only 8 kms. away from Varanasi in Uttar Pradesh. He set the great 'Wheel of Law' (Dharmachakra) in motion here, more than 2,500 years ago by revealing to the world his Eight fold path - the path to end sorrow, achieve inner peace, enlightenment and ultimate Nirvana.

The region once housed 3,000 monks. Remains of the Dharmarajika Stupa set up by Asoka; his Sarnath pillar edict and ruins of temples and monasteries and the spot where the Emperor meditated in seclusion; takes one back to the heydays of the Mauryan empire. The remains of an ancient monastery can still be seen here. Sarnath can be accessed via Varanasi since it is only 8 kms. away. Varanasi is well connected by Air, Rail and Road. And, accommodation is available to suit all pockets.

Jehangir Palace

This was built by Akbar for his favorite son Jehangir to provide him with the comfort and luxury inside the fort. This palace displays an excellent combination of Hindu and Muslim architecture. Inside the fort there are places like the private room for Shah Jahan, Khas Mahal. The room inlaid with mirrors called the Shish Mahal and was used as a dressing room by the harem.

The Anguri Bagh or the grape garden was a small formal Moghal garden. The Hauz-i-Jehangri is a huge bowl which is carved out of a single stone and is kept just outside the Jehangir palace. The Amar Singh gate is the place where the Maharaja of Jodhpur in a bid to escape from the fort ran his horse over the fort wall. The stone statue of the horse has immortalized the loyal horse.

Bara Immambara

Built like a fort, this huge and elegant building is also called the Asafai Imambara. This building was built in a famine relief program in 1784 by Nabab Asaf-ud-Daulla. The structure took six years to be completed. Just as we enter the building there is a hall almost fifty meters long and 17 meters wide. The architecture of this 15 meter high room is very unique and unparalleled. Here the Nawabs used to hold there ' Darbar ' or their public hearings. It is said that this hall is the worlds largest arched room without any pillars. The upper part of this building is in shape of honey bees comb and is surrounded by the famous 'Bhul Bhulliya'.

This has got numerous steps and there are 489 doorless galleries which are similar in appearance. People get lost in these galleries. The largest of these mazed rooms and galleries has a speciality that even when a paper is torn on one of the end sit is heard on the other end. In the courtyard of Bara Imambara is the Sahi Masjid which stands tall on a platform, non muslims are not allowed here. Just besides the Sahi Masjid is the bottomless well. The BaraImambara also has the tomb of Asaf-Ud-Daulla.

Chota Immambara

The third Nawab of Avadh, Muhammad Ali Shah built this imposing structure in 1840. The real name of this structure is Husainabad Imambada. The interior of this magnificent building has chandeliers from Belgium, lamp shades and other decorative pieces which might have costed a fortune in those days. The decorations inside the building are ravishingly beautiful.

Once a Prince from Russia said that this was the Kremlin of India. Inside the Imambara are the tombs of Ali Shah and his mother. Enclosed in the structure is the Royal bath or the 'Sahi Hammam'. The use of marble and arches in constructing buildings on both sides of the courtyard makes one to compare the architecture with that of Taj Mahal. The Imambara also houses silver throne of Muhamad Ali Shah.

Residency

About four kilometer from the main town is the residency which was started in 1780 by Asaf-ud-Daulla but was completed in 1800 during the rein of Saddat Ali. popularly known as Beli Gaurd, this building was occupied by the rebels during the first war of independence in 1857 but the building was soon recaptured by the British. But the rebels did not leave siege easily.

The heavy cross firing which ensued between the rebels and British had badly damaged the structure. What ever is left of the structure has been attracting tourist and visitors in great number. The lush green grass and gardens around the Residency have developed as a picnic spot. In the night the structure is floodlit which adds to the beauty of this building.

Charlieveli Hotel

This was the first hotel in Mussoorie. Charlieveli Hotel was only hotel in India which was under Queen Mary, who later became Queen of Britain. Since the last century till independence this hotel was very famous both in India and abroad. But, slowly Charlieveli Hotel lost its charm and in 1958 the hotel closed down to be lost in pages of history.

Soon Government of India took over the hotel building and converted it into the national academy for training Indian administrative service officers. This institute is today called the Lal Bahadur Shastri National Administrative Academy. This academy is pride of Mussoorie and is a very important institute in India.

Lal Tibba

This place is highest point in Mussoorie. Lal Tibba is located in Landhour area which is the oldest inhabited place in Mussoorie. Landhour still carries style of British era. It was here that Britishers first settled. The buildings, the architecture everything tells a saga of an English past.

After India gained independence many Britishers settled here. Even the name, Landhour was given by Britishers. In 1967, the municipal corporation of Mussoorie ordered a Japanese Telescope which is placed on Lal Tibba. Thorough this telescope one can have a lovely view of many peaks in Himalayan range like Badrinath, Kedarnath, Banderpunch etc. Lal Tibba is considered as most beautiful place in Mussoorie.

Sarnath

Sarnath is considered as one of the richest place to have antiques since the Ashoka period to the 12th century. The Dharmarajika stupa was also built by Ashoka and it was surmounted by the pillar. This pillar with four lions today forms the national emblem of India.

Sarnath has many more ruins of monasteries and stupas. Among these the brick temple representing the Mula-gandha kuti is very popular. The Dhamekh Stupa is the most imposing of them with intricate and delicate floral motifs on the lower part. These floral motifs/designs belong to the Gupta period. However, some of the brick work dates back to the Mauryan era. Many of the stupas were destroy by the treasure hunter of 19th century. The spot at which the stupa stands is believed to be the place from where Buddha gave his forts sermon.

The Stupa was built in 500 AD but it was rebuilt many times. The Chaukhandi stupa and Mahabodhi society's Mula-Gandha Kuti Vihar temple are also worth visiting. Sarnath has an extremely rich collection of Buddhist statues. These sculptures are the images of Buddha and Bodhisatva. These images are kept in the Archaeological museum of Sarnath.

Monuments in Karnataka

Badami Caves

The capital of the Early Chalukyas, Badami is picturesquely situated at the mouth of a ravine between two rocky hills, Badami is famous for its cave temples -

all hewn out of sand stone on the precipice of a hill. Badami is an interesting place to visit in Karnataka what with its artificial lake, ancient temples, Museum and Hindu and Jain caves carved in the Sandstone hills. The largest and most ornamental is the third cave temple dedicated to Vishnu.

Overlooking the cave temples is a reservoir dotted with temples dedicated to Vishnu and Shiva. Also a must are the Bhutanath temples that lend their name to the lake beneath the cave temples. The main attractions of Badami are the caves found there. The caves found here are :

Cave 1 - The first cave made of red sandstone, dates back to 578 A.D. and was probably the first to be carved. One has to climb up 40 odd steps to reach the colonnaded verandah, a hall with numerous pillars and a square shaped sanctum hollowed in the control back wall. Column shafts are masterfully crafted. On the ceiling one can see the paintings of amorous couples. Shiva and his consort Parvati, and a coiled serpent. The 18-armed lord Nataraja can be seen in 81 dancing poses.

Cave 2 - Dedicated to lord Vishnu depicted here as a dwarf or 'Trivikrama' of awesome dimensions with one foot mastering the Earth and the other the sky, the second cave is atop a sandstone hill. Vishnu here is depicted as a dwarf or. Another form of Vishnu portrayed here is as 'Varaha' or as a boar. Then there is a frieze endearingly depicting Vishnu as Lord Krishna.

Cave 3 - Still going higher up one comes across this cave antedating 578 A.D. The facade of the cave is nearly 70 feet wide, on the plinth one can see the carvings of ganas. The sheer artistry and sculptural genius makes this cave the highlight of Deccan art. It gives a virtual insight into the art and culture of the 6th century like costumes, jewelry hairstyle lifestyle etc. The other attractions to be looked carefully in this cave are the high relief of Vishnu with a serpent, Vishnu as Narasimha (Vishnu as Man-Lion) Varaha, Harihara (Shiva Vishnu) and Vishnu as Trivikrama.

Cave 4 - The only Jain cave, the construction of Cave four started in the 6th century and completed after nearly 100 years later then the earlier three caves. Here one can see the carvings of the Tirthankara Parshavnatha with a serpent at his feet; Mahavira in a sitting posture also can be seen in the shrine.

Bidar Fort

In medieval times Bidar belonged to the Chalukyan branch who established their capital in 977 A.D. at Kalyani, 57 kms away. Falling to the Yadavas of Devagiri (Daulatabad) and to the Kakatiyas of Warangal in 1322 A.D., Bidar fully rose to prominence under the sultanate regime.

The imposing fort of Bidar is a magnificent fort, the main gateway of which was originally built by Bahamani Sultan Ahmad Shah Wali in 1429 AD. Further improvements to the citadel were carried out by the Barid Shahi Sultans. Ahmad Shah Wali (1422 - 35) the ninth Bahamani Sultan decided to shift his capital from Gulbarga to Bidar for reasons of health.

Palaces, pavilions and seraglios; lush gardens, decorated fountains and perfumed baths have all the trappings of an Arabian Nights fantasy when Bidar was ruled by the Bahamanis and the Barid Shahi Sultans of the Deccan. Sprawled on a plateau 2,200 feet above sea level and overlooking the Manjira River Valley, cool and exhilarating Bidar was most certainly a part of ancient Vidharba mentioned in the Mahabharata.

Bull Temple

The Bull Temple situated in Bangalore , houses the 4.57

m high and 6.10 m long image of Nandi, Lord Shiva's bull. The temple was built by Kempe Gowda in the 16th century. The image has been carved out of single granite rock. The original colour of Nandi bull was grey which has now turned black due to the application of coconut oil by the devotees. The statue of the bull has been carved out of a The single rock statue attracts devotees from far and near. Non Hindus are not allowed in the temple. The temple is busy always with some ceremony that is on all the time at the temple premises. On weekends, musicians present their concerts at the temple.

Gulbarga Fort

Gulbarga fort, originally built by Raja Gulchand was later strengthened by Ala-ud-din Bahmani. The fort contained 15 towers and 26 guns of which one was 8 metres long. Within the ramparts of the fort, there is an imposing mosque, which resembles the great mosque of Cordova in Spain.

This mosque is the only one of its kind in the entire country. Several tombs of the Bahmani Sultans can be found in the eastern outskirts of the town. The imposing fort of Gulbarga has witnessed many a battle and suffered many an onslaught. Razed to the ground by Krishna Devaraya of Vijaynagar, it rose like a phoenix when Adil Shah undertook its repair with booty captured from Vijaynagar.

Monuments of Hyderabad

The city of Hyderabad is a relatively young city by Indian standards being only about five centuries old. Capital of the Golconda kingdom, it enjoyed a spate of monumental building activity during the reign of the Qutab Shahis. Amongst the most impressive of it's surviving monuments are the Qutab Shahi tombs - many of which were once decorated in polychrome colored tiles - though only some of the original tile work survives today.

Best known for the Charminar, the city has many other fine monuments including whimsical mosques, several palaces and the tombs of the Paigah Nobles with intricately carved stucco ornaments. Featured on this site are several images of the Paigah tombs and a glimpse of Hyderabad's natural beauty.

4

Popular Pilgrim Centres

India is a land that bridges the material world to the spiritual. A land that has given birth to religions like Hinduism, Buddhism and Sikhism. Ancient pilgrimage centers of India have been a source of enlightenment for many a soul. The temple sites in India is perfect for those seeking peace of mind and rejuvenation. These tourist places in India are renowned for its religious shrines and a must-see when you travel to India.

Vaishno Devi Shrine

The Vaishno Devi shrine forms one of the most popular pilgrimage sites in India. The shrine is located in a cave towards the top of the Trikuta Mountains in Jammu-Kashmir.Vaishno Devi is mostly identified with Mahalakshmi although She is the combined Shakti's of all three. This is believed to be the only place where these three Devi's are found in one temple as natural pindies.

Over 4.5 million Indians from all parts of the country respond this way to the call of the Mother every year to one of the holiest shrines in northern India. Youngsters hope to fare well in examinations; newlyweds look for conjugal bliss. Some hope to win property cases; others look forward to the blessing of an heir. And some visit Vaishno Devi for no other reason than their wish to see Mata.

Devotees aver that the revered Mata calls out to her followers, and only then can one go to her sublime shrine. An arduous journey up the Trikuta Mountain range and the final darshan (audience) of the Goddess leaves one with staunch faith in Her. It is believed that one can ask the great Mother of any needful thing and promise to visit her when the wish is fulfilled. Lakhs of people vouch for the deity's graciousness and visit the shrine in the form of thanksgiving.

The holy cave shrine of Vaishno Devi is said to have been built by the five Pandavas. The length of the cave is about 98 ft. The symbols of a large number of gods and goddesses of the Hindu pantheon can be seen here. At the mouth of the original tunnel to the holy cave can be seen the symbols of Vakra Tunda Ganesha, Surya Dev and Chandra Dev. When one crawls into the cave through the tunnel, he/she crosses over the Dhadh of Bhairon Nath. The symbol of Lord Hanuman, called Launkra Beer, can also be seen and the pilgrims have to wade through water beyond the Launkra Beer point. Twenty-three feet beyond Launkra Beer, on the upper left-hand side, the roof of the cave flares out and the weight of this overhang appears to be resting on the innumerable heads of Shesh Nag. Immediately below Shesh Nag can be seen the symbols of Shankh, Chakra, Gada and Padam. Higher up, almost touching the ceiling of the cave, are the symbols of the five Pandavas, the Sapt Rishi, the udders of the divine cow, Kamadhenu, Brahma, Vishnu, Shiva and Parvati.

There are several places to see and visit near Vaishno Devi too. The Deva Mai temple is about three miles short of Katra town. Many devotees treat it as a very holy site and go there to perform paeans. The Holy Cave of Shiv

Khori is the abode of Lord Shiva, situated at a distance of 70 km from Katra. The cave is a real wonder to be seen and measures nearly a kilometer in length with a four-feet-high naturally formed Shiv-lingam at the heart of the sanctum sanctorum.

Vaishno Devi Temple can be reached after making a steep 13-km trek from the road head at Katra, the town at the foot of the Trikuta hills. The Indian shrine of Vaishno Devi is easily accessible through air, road and rail from the other major Indian cities and states. Touristplacesinindia can arrange for you all types of transport for your comfortable journey to and in Vaishno Devi and throughout the Indian state of Jammu and Kashmir.

In order to make the travel tour to Vaishno Devi even more joyful you need to choose just the right kind of accommodation for you and your family or friends in Vaishno Devi. The various hotels packages in Vaishno Devi offer the best of facilities. You may take your pick from a range of luxury and budget hotels in Vaishno Devi besides the star categorized accommodation hotels around the landmarks of Vaishno Devi offer excellent view of the landmarks through their suites. Most of the places to stay in Vaishno Devi are strategically located in the pilgrim centers.

Golden Temple

The Golden Temple or Darbar Sahib, situated in Amritsar, Punjab, is the most sacred temple for Sikhs. It is a symbol of the magnificence and strength of the Sikh people all over the world. In the evolution of the Darbar Sahib, is entwined the history and ideology of Sikhism. The Golden Temple is the ultimate Sikh pilgrimage. The Harmandir Sahib, as it is traditionally known, actually means the temple of Hari or the Supreme God. Also known as the Darbar Sahib, the stupendous, architectural phenomena is located at the city of Amritsar. The temple's exterior is gold-plated and the structure stands in the middle of a square tank.

There is a causeway across the Pool of Nectar to reach the Temple. The shrine is symbolical of the doctrines of Sikhism. It also represents the magnificent strength of all the Sikhs. The amazing thing about Harmandir Sahib is that it has doorways on all four sides, meant to be open for the people of the all four castes. All over the, the Sikhs always look forward to visit to the magnificent temple and offer prayers at the Harmandir Sahib.

The study of the art and architecture of the Golden Temple has, unfortunately, remained a subject of unconcern for art historians and critics. Even scholars of Indian temple architecture have bypassed it and references, whenever made, were mere courtesies. Fergusson considered the Golden Temple an example of the forms, which Hindu temple architecture assumed in the nineteenth century. According to the official list of buildings of interest, published by the Punjab Government in 1875, the design of the temple, as reconstructed by Ranjit Singh, was borrowed from the shrine of Saint Mian Mir, near Lahore. Louis Rousselet, writing in 1882, regarded it as a "handsome style of architecture". Major Cole described it as an adaptation of Mohammadan styles, flavoured with a good deal of Hindu tradition. Percy Brown considered it to be a product of the synthesis of Hindu and Muslim influences, combined with elaborations that imparted it an appearance of its own.

Guru Arjan Dev thought of building a central place of worship for the Sikh community. In 1588, after finalizing the design of the Darbar Sahib, he laid down the foundation of the temple himself. His followers started living in the adjacent area and the town of Ramdaspur came up. The town of Ramdaspur later came to be known as Amritsar, deriving its name from the holy pond that beautifies the area surrounding Hari Mandir. The planning to dig the holy tank or Amrit Sarovar was made by Guru Amar Das. However, the construction of the tank took place under the supervision of Baba Budha ji. The land for the site was acquired free of cost from the zamindars (landlords) of native villages. The first Sikh Maharaja Ranjit Singh made Amritsar his spiritual capital. He developed the temple further including the gilding of the embossed plates, renewing of the pietra dura and the embellishment of the ceilings with the mirror and floral designs.

Amritsar is an institution by itself. And the Golden Temple is the cradle of Amritsar with the city growing around it nurtured by its divine sanctity. The Golden Temple stands there in simple majesty, the gilded splendor of its paneling, dome and minarets shining in the morning light, silhouetted softly in the water and etched gently across the city escape. For the Sikh community the Harmandir Sahib Gurdwara Golden Temple is the final spiritual "vision," journey's end or beginning and, for every other community too, it is a shrine to be visited.

Besides the Golden Temple there are several other Gurudwaras in India that are of great importance to the pilgrims. Another important pilgrimage site is Anandpur Sahib, where Guru Gobind Singh, the tenth Guru created the 'Khalsa' or the pure ones by baptizing them. Anandpur Sahib (in Ropar District) is one of the five Sikh takhts or thrones. Sikhs from all over India visit this holy site especially on the occasion of Holla Mohalla which coincides with the last day of Holi and marks the festival's finale. On this day, the Gurudwara Keshgarh is filled with people and colour as men in bright turbans and women in gaily-colored salwar kameezs try to live up to Guru Gobind Singh Ji's vision of Holi.

HEMKUND SAHIB

Hemkund is the World`s highest shrine, situated at an altitude of 4329 mts, and is on the bank of a glacier lake surrounded by several towering pinnacles of snow, reflected in its clear water. It is believed that Guru Govind Singh , the tenth Guru of the Sikh faith had mediated on the bank of this lake. There is a Sikh Gurudwara & a Laxman Temple on the bank of the lake.

BODHGAYA

Bodhgaya is the most important Buddhist pilgrimage site in the world. Apart from being a significant archaeological site, it is also a vital Buddhist centre. Devout Buddhists and tourists from all over the world visit Bodhgaya, to study Buddhism and the art of meditation, or to simply absorb the aura of solemn grandeur that surrounds the place.

The life of Gautam Buddha, the founder of Buddhism, is associated with the small town of Bodhgaya. It is one of the four holiest cities of Buddhist faith. The Mahabodhi temple is the main attraction of this town and is located near the spot where Lord Buddha attained spiritual enlightenment. Bodhgaya is not only an important Buddhist pilgrim center, but it is also an important center for the study of Buddhism.

Mahabodhi Temple and other monasteries are the major attractions in Bodhgaya. Places associated with the life and times of Lord Buddha are located inside the Mahabodhi complex including the Bodhi Tree and a pond where according to legends, Lord Buddha mediated for few days.

DHARAMSALA

Dharamsala is another important Buddhist pilrimage site.

It overlooks the plains and is surrounded by dense pine trees and Deodar forests. A nearby snowline with numerous streams and cool healthy atmosphere makes the surroundings very attractive. Dharamsala is better known as Dalai Lama's abode and Tibet's Government-in-exile after the Chinese invasion of Lhasa in October 1959. A visit to Dharamsala would be considered irreverent without a peek into the various monasteries dotting the hillsides.

There are several places to visit and see around Dharamsala that make excellent weekend trip and excursion options. Three km east of McLeod Ganj is the village of Bhagsu, or Bhagsunath an excellent weekend excursion place from Dharamsala. Its main claim to fame is the Bhagsunath Temple, a quiet temple that lies beside several pools where devout Hindus and monks congregate to bathe.

Head for the murky Dal Lake that is connected to Dharamkot by a path down wooded slopes. It is the scene of an animal fair and Shaivite festival each year in September. Though Dharamsala does not have an airport or railway station of its own it is easily accessible throughout the year. In order to make the travel tour to Dharamsala even more joyful you need to choose just the right kind of accommodation for you and your family or friends in Dharamsala. The various hotels packages in Dharamsala offer the best of facilities.

RISHIKESH

Rishikesh is just 24 Kms from Haridwar. Located in the laps of lower Himalayas, this place is considered to be the access point of three other pilgrim places of Badrinath - Kedarnath, Gangotri and Yamunotri the four great places which combine to make Chardham . Rishikesh is surrounded by scenic beauty of the hills on three sides with Holy Ganga flowing through it. Situated in the Indian state of Uttaranchal, Rishikesh is a very important Hindu pilgrimage site. This is also a cluster of a number of Ashrams and temples giving the entire place a spiritual feeling. The ceaseless flow of the river, regarded as Goddess Ganga adds to the beauty and the purity of the place. Along the river, the area is filled with thick green forests in the all-mountainous region. The entire area falls on the Garhwal region of Northern India. Hordes of sadhus (sages) come to this place every year in search of salvation.

Rishikesh is famous for its yoga sessions that are taught here by many yoga experts. Besides the sadhus and saints, a mass of tourists too visits this place every year to have a look at this much heard about place. Besides the Indian travelers, one can see here a number of foreign tourists roaming about while curiously clicking the cameras to catch the wonderful scenic spots all around. As if the wonderful scenery and the numerous pilgrimage sites were not enough, Rishikesh also makes some of the most popular adventure sport destinations of India. River rafting, trekking, rock climbing, hiking etc are some of the activities one can easily opt for here. Easily accessible from almost all the nearby towns and cities of India, Rishikesh is a hill station with a number of provisions for the tourist's boarding and lodging.

Rishikesh abounds in temples. Most of the pilgrims who pass through Rishikesh on their way to the Himalayan shrines of the Char Dham pause for a holy dip and puja at Triveni Ghat, in the central part of the town. The river here looks especially spectacular during aarti (evening worship) when diyas or oil lamps float on the water. Nearby is the Bharat Mandir, Rishikesh's oldest temple, dedicated to Lord Vishnu.

There are a lot of pilgrimage sites around Rishikesh. The Mansa Devi temple (10 km) is famous for its Navratri festival, Uttar Kashi (154 km) and many other such temples are within convenient distances. For more information and travel services you may contact touristplacesinindia. Besides celebrating all the general Hindu festivals, there is a special festival celebrated in this area. The International Yoga Week usually celebrated from February 2-7 every year. This festival is the ideal place and time to learn some real yoga postures to keep oneself fit and fine.

The Indian city of Rishikesh is easily accessible through air, road and rail from the other major Indian cities and states. touristplacesinindia can arrange for you all types of transport for your comfortable journey to and in Rishikesh and throughout the Indian state of Uttaranchal.

HARIDWAR

Haridwar or 'the Gateway to the Gods' is one of the seven holiest places according to Hindu mythology, as the Gods are believed to have left their footprints in Haridwar. Due to its geographical location too, Haridwar stands as the gateway to the other three important pilgrimages of Uttrakhand namely, Rishikesh, Badrinath and Kedarnath. Referred to as Mayapuri, Gangadwar, and Mokshadwar in the ancient scriptures and epics, Haridwar has always remained a major pilgrimage for the Hindus.

The list of attractions in Haridwar is endless. Har-Ki-Pauri, the sacred ghat was constructed by King Vikramaditya in the memory of his brother Bhartrihari. The golden reflection of floral diyas in the river Ganges is the most enchanting sight in the twilight during the Ganga aarti ceremony at the ghat. Haridwar has a number of interesting sites that you can include in your excursion. Rishikesh, around 28 km off Haridwar, is at the base of the Himalayas and it is where the Ganges comes down to the plains from the hills. A breathtaking experience of natural beauty and undiscovered wildlife awaits here. Not to mention the peace and tranquility of a landscape associated with sages and meditation.

Several festivals are celebrated in Haridwar. Haridwar, one of the oldest and holiest pilgrim centers of India, is also the place that plays host to around eight to ten million devotees during the Kumbh melas. The history of the Kumbh Mela dates back to the creation of the Universe and as a show of their faith, Hindus from all over the country assemble to take a holy dip in the Ganges. The Indian city of Haridwar is easily accessible through air, road and rail from the other major Indian cities and states. TouristplacesinIndia can arrange for you all types of transport for your comfortable journey to and in Haridwar and throughout the Indian state of Uttaranchal.

In order to make the travel tour to Haridwar even more joyful you need to choose just the right kind of accommodation for you and your family or friends in Haridwar. The various hotels packages in Haridwar offer the best of facilities. The well-furnished rooms make excellent place to stay in Haridwar, with most of the comforts at your feet.

Varanasi

Varanasi, or Benaras, is one of the oldest living cities in the world. Varanasi's prominence in Hindu mythology is virtually unrivalled. One of the earliest descriptions of Varanasi is found in the Buddhist scriptures as also in the epic, 'Mahabharat'. The 'Pali' version of Varanasi was 'Baranasi' which ultimately gave birth to the name 'Banaras'.

The city of Varanasi is situated along the west bank of the Ganges in the north Indian state of Uttar Pradesh. Called Benaras by the British, Varanasi is an important pilgrimage centre for the Hindus. The city finds mention in the great epics of Mahabharata and Ramayana. It was a flourishing trade center when Buddha came to Sarnath, about 10 kilometres away, to preach his first sermon in 500 BC. The renowned American novelist Mark Twain once wrote, "Benaras is older than history, older than tradition, older even than legend and looks twice as old as all of them put together."

Right from the ancient times, Varanasi has stood as a symbol of Hindu renaissance and preserved the rituals and traditions of Hindu philosophy. Down the ages, pilgrims from distant lands have come to Varanasi in search of divine blessings. Temples form the major source of attraction in this ancient city. The banks of the Ganges, considered to be a sacred river by the Hindus, are the centre of much of the religious activity that occurs in the city. The ghats built along the banks of the river for such religious activity also form a major source of attraction here.

The Alamgir Mosque is a blend of the Hindu and Mughal styles of the architecture. The Durga Temple is built in the North Indian style with an ornate shikhara, consisting of five segments symbolizing the elements and supported by finely carved columns. The Vishwanath Temple, built by the Birlas, was planned by Pandit Madan Mohan Malaviya. The Bharat Mata Temple houses, instead of gods and goddesses, a huge relief map in marble of the whole of Indian subcontinent and Tibetan plateau. The Tulsi Manas Temple, built in 1964, is dedicated to Lord Rama. The Banaras Hindu University, built in 1917, is one of the oldest educational centres in India. The Archaeological Museum, located at Sarnath, houses the capitol from the Ashokan pillar besides the figures and the sculptures from the Mauryan, Kushana and Gupta periods.

Excursions around Varanasi get you further acquainted with the mystic religion of Hinduism besides presenting an insight into the Buddhism. Sarnath is a major Buddhist centre about 10 kilometres north east of Varanasi. It was here that Buddha preached his message of the 'middle way' in order to achieve nirvana. Bodhgaya, located in Bihar, is the place where Buddha is supposed to have attained enlightenment under a Bodhi tree. Allahabad is one of India's holiest cities and the site of the Kumbh Mela held every 12 years. Kushinagar is a place famous for the Mahaparinirvana (death) of Lord Buddha. The 17th-century Ramnagar Fort was the home of the former Maharaja of Benaras.

The festive magic never ends in Varanasi. If Poornima cleanses, Maha Shivratri blesses. If Holika-Dahan is a celebration, Dhrupad Mela is a revelation.... One does not require making his itinerary according to the dates and months of the festivals. One can come and enjoy the festive season anytime of the year here. The Indian city of Varanasi is easily accessible through air, road and rail from the other major Indian cities and states. Touristplacesinindia can arrange for you all types of transport for your comfortable journey to and in Varanasi and throughout the Indian state of Uttar Pradesh.

In order to make the travel tour to Varanasi even more joyful you need to choose just the right kind of accommodation for you and your family or friends in Varanasi. The various hotels packages in Varanasi offer the best of facilities. You may enjoy the luxuries of life on your stay at the Varanasi hotels. You may take your pick from a range of luxury and budget hotels in Varanasi besides the star categorized accommodation hotels around the landmarks of Varanasi offer excellent view of the landmarks through their suites. Most of the places to stay in Varanasi are strategically located in the pilgrim centers or near the railway station

Mathura

Mathura is an important place of pilgrimage. The city stretches along the Right Bank of the Yamuna and the continuous line of ghats (riverbanks) along the river makes a splendid spectacle when viewed from the opposite bank. These picturesque ghats are of great architectural, cultural and ritual interest, for devotees from far and wide. With their steps leading to the water's edge, arched gateways and temple spires they emphasize the sacred character of the town.

The town of Mathura (Brajbhoomi) is located in the western part of the state of Uttar Pradesh in the northern region of India. It is a part of the great northern plains and is situated on the western bank of the river Yamuna. It is famous as the birthplace of Lord Krishna, an important deity in the Hindu religious pantheon. It is an important pilgrim place of the Hindus and one of the seven most sacred cities in India. The main pilgrim centre in Mathura is the Shri Krishna Janmbhoomi temple. Mathura is also an important crafts centre. Mathura belongs to the Agra Sub circuit of the Golden Triangle of India i.e. Agra-Delhi-Jaipur circuit.

It is worthwhile to visit the Mathura region for the sheer pleasure of tracing the early years of the life of Lord Krishna. The Shri Krishna Janmbhoomi (birthplace of Lord Krishna) is the main attraction of Mathura and an important pilgrimage for the Hindus. A stone slab marks the original spot of the birth of Lord Krishna. The earlier Kesava Deo temple had the room where Lord Krishna was born. According to legends, Lord Krishna was born in a small prison room where the tyrant ruler Kansa held his parents captive.

Vrindavan is 10 km from Mathura and it is associated with the childhood exploits of Lord Krishna. Like Mathura, Vrindavan is also famous for its temples. There are about

4,000 temples in Vrindavan. The main temples are Govind Dev Temple, Rangaji temple, Bankey Bihari temple, Radha Ballabh temple, Madan Mohan temple, Pagal Baba temple and the Nidhi Van temple. Hindus celebrates Lord Krishna's birthday as Janmashtami on the eighth day of the darker half of the month in July/August. For Mathura, Janmashtami is the biggest festival and it is held on a grand scale.

The Indian town of Mathura is easily accessible through air, road and rail from the other major Indian cities and states. touristplacesinindia can arrange for you all types of transport for your comfortable journey to and in Mathura and throughout the Indian state of Uttar Pradesh. In order to make the travel tour to Mathura even more joyful you need to choose just the right kind of accommodation for you and your family or friends in Mathura. The various hotels packages in Mathura offer the best of facilities. You may enjoy the luxuries of life on your stay at the Mathura hotels. You may take your pick from a range of luxury and budget hotels in Mathura besides the star categorized accommodation hotels around the landmarks of Mathura offer excellent view of the landmarks through their suites. Most of the places to stay in Mathura are strategically located in the pilgrim centers or near the railway station.

SHIRDI

Shirdi, 260 kms from Mumbai, 130 kms from Aurangabad is holy city of Sai Baba. The saga of Sai Baba of Shirdi started in the middle of last century when as a boy of about 16 years of age, he first appeared here under a neem tree absorbed in a hard penance. The most important festivals and events that are celebrated in Shirdi are Guru Poornima, Dusshera, and Ram Navami. These are the only days when the Samadhi Mandir of Shirdi opens for the whole night. Every Thursday, a palakhi bearing a photograph of the sage is taken out from the temple.

Shirdi is a small town located in the state of Maharashtra in western India. The place is around 296 km (around 6 hours drive) from Mumbai. Shirdi extends latitude 19°45¢ N and longitude 74°25¢ E. Shirdi is basically a religious tourist center. Thousands of pilgrims flock to Shirdi. There are several places of tourist attractions in Shirdi, but it is the shrine of Sai Baba that is the hub of activity.

Samadhi Mandir of Shri Sai Baba was actually owned by a millionaire from Nagpur and a famous Sai devotee Shreemant Gopalrao. He wanted to keep an idol of Murlidhar here. However, according to the legends, Baba himself became Murlidhar and the temple became the Samadhi Mandir of Baba. The Samadhi of Baba is built with white marble stones. The railings around it are full of ornamental decorations.

The idol of Baba is a marvelous statue made up of Italian marble built by Late Balaji Vasant in 1954. The temple has an assembly hall for about 600 devotees. The assembly hall also houses a showcase having various items used by the sage. The first floor of the temple has the pictures depicting the life of the saint. The temple opens on 5 am with morning prayers and close down at 10 pm with night prayers.

There are several places to see and visit near Shirdi too. Situated around 5 km from Shirdi is Sakori. The place is home to the Upasini Maharaj.

Shanisinghnapur is 70 km from Shirdi. A temple devoted to Shani is located here. The most important festivals and events that are celebrated in Shirdi are Guru Poornima, Dusshera, and Ram Navami. These are the only days when the Samadhi Mandir of Shirdi opens for the whole night. Every Thursday, a palakhi bearing a photograph of the sage is taken out from the temple.

The Indian town of Shirdi is easily accessible through air, road and rail from the other major Indian cities and states. touristplacesinindia can arrange for you all types of transport for your comfortable journey to and in Shirdi and throughout the Indian state of Maharashtra.

In order to make the travel tour to Shirdi even more joyful you need to choose just the right kind of accommodation for you and your family or friends in Shirdi. The various hotels packages in Shirdi offer the best of facilities. The well-furnished rooms make excellent place to stay in Shirdi, with most of the comforts at your feet. You may enjoy the luxuries of life on your stay at the Shirdi hotels. You may take your pick from a range of luxury and budget hotels in Shirdi besides the star categorized accommodation hotels of Shirdi. Most of the places to stay in Shirdi are strategically located in the pilgrim centers.

Puri

Puri as known to the Hindus all over the world is a holy town located on the eastern coast of India. Besides being a religious center, Puri is also known for the good stretch of the white sand beaches on the banks of Bay of Bengal. The easy accessibility from almost all the major towns and cities of India, wide beaches, the fishing farms and the superb resorts make it an important tourist destination and a major base point to visit the nearby important sites.

The famous temple of Lord Jagannath and the annual Rath yatra festival here attract a large number of tourists every year. The Jagannath Temple is one of the four most important Hindu pilgrimage sites or the chardham, the other three being Dwarka, Badrinath, and Rameshwaram. Moreover, the scenic spots all over this small town with the beaches that offer breathtaking view of sunrise and sunset and the traditional methods of fishing used by the local fishermen are some of the other aspects for which Puri has always attracted the attention of the people.

Puri, the name itself attracts the attention of all those who are aware of its importance. This shows that Puri has a lot to offer to the tourists here. Starting from the Jagannath temple, a massive temple structure made in the style of Kalinga architecture, to the much talked about white sand beaches on the Bay of Bengal, the list of attractions here is endless. Moreover, the Gundicha ghar, the home of lord Krishna's dear aunt, also attracts attention of the tourists especially during the time of Rath yatra. Temple of Child Krishna at Indradyumna Tank attracts tourists in hordes because of its close relation with Lord Krishna. Atharnala bridge was built over Mandupur stream in the 13th century. Overall the calm and cool nature of the locals here makes Puri a peaceful getaway.

A number of interesting places exist around the city of Puri where you can go out for the excursions. The sites being natural wonders, architectural marvels and local delight, definitely make themselves worth a visit. Some of such sites would include the Raghurajpur village, a village where work is worship and fine craftsmanship runs in the local people's blood. The excursion also includes a visit to the famous Konark Temple also called the black pagoda, an angle in the golden triangle of Bhubaneswar, Puri and Konark. The inviting beaches of Konark and the exotic aquatic experience in the Chilika lake is a once in a lifetime opportunity to be close to nature in her best. Moreover, the interesting legends and a life size image of Lord Krishna at Sakhi Gopal make this spot a must visit site in your excursion.

Apart from the regular Hindu festivals celebrated according to the solar calendar, Puri is famous for its Rath Yatra festival held once a year. In June-July every year,

Lord Jagannath's legendary return to his kingdom on earth is he occasion for the famous Rath Yatra or car festival at Puri. From all over the country thousands of pilgrims flock to participate in this stately event. The proceedings commence with the installation of Lord Jagannath, his sister Subhadra, and brother Balabhadra in massive, lavishly decorated chariots. Frenzied devotees pull the three gigantic chariots through the streets of Puri.

The Indian city of Puri is easily accessible through air, road and rail from the other major Indian cities and states. touristplacesinindia can arrange for you all types of transport for your comfortable journey to and in Puri and throughout the Indian state of Orissa. In order to make the travel tour to Puri even more joyful you need to choose just the right kind of accommodation for you and your family or friends in Puri. The various hotels packages in Puri offer the best of facilities. You may take your pick from a range of luxury and budget hotels in Puri besides the star categorized accommodation hotels around the landmarks of Puri offer excellent view of the landmarks through their suites. Most of the places to stay in Puri are strategically located in the pilgrim centers or near the railway station.

PUSHKAR

Pushkar is famous for its biggest cattle fair which falls in the month of Kartik. It commences two days before the full moon of the month and ends a day after it. Men and women congregate from all over Rajasthan and other nearby places with their horses, camels and cattle to buy and sell. In addition to its commercial importance, the fair is also a window to the cultural richness of Rajasthan. Days before it begins, tradesmen, craftsmen, troupes of dancers and singers, all gather here. more...

Ranakpur

Ranakpur in the state of Rajasthan is one of the five most important pilgrimage sites of Jainism. It is home to an exceptionally beautiful temple complex in the Aravali ranges and a must visit for the tourists coming to this region. Ranakpur is tucked away in a remote valley in the Aravali range. It is situated around 60 km north of Udaipur in Pali district and boasts of one of the largest and most important Jain Temples in the country. The place is well connected through a road network to other places in the region.

There are several places of tourist attractions in Ranakpur, but it is the Jain temples that are the hub of activity. The Ranakpur Jain Temple was built during the reign of the liberal and gifted monarch Rana Kumbha in the 15th century. The basement is of 48, 000 sq. feet area that covers the whole complex. There are four subsidiary shrines, twenty-four pillared halls and eligibly domes supported by over four hundred columns.

The total number of columns is 1,444 all of which are intricately carved with no two being alike. The artistically carved nymphs playing the flute in various dance postures at a height of 45 feet are an engrossing sight. In the assembly hall, there are two big bells weighing 108 kg whose sound echoes in the entire complex. The main temple is of Chaumukh or four-faces temple dedicated to Adinath.

There are several places to see and visit near Ranakpur too. Kumbhalgarh is a historical site around 30 km north east of Ranakpur. It is an important fort in the Mewar region after Chittorgarh. Other important place to visit in Kumbhalgarh is Wildlife Sanctuary known for its wolves. The Indian temple town of Ranakpur are easily accessible through air, road and rail from the other major Indian cities and states. touristplacesinindia can arrange for you all types of transport for your comfortable journey to and in Ranakpur and throughout the Indian state of Rajasthan.

In order to make the travel tour to Ranakpur even more joyful you need to choose just the right kind of accommodation for you and your family or friends in Ranakpur. The various hotels packages around Ranakpur offer the best of facilities. The well-furnished rooms make excellent place to stay around Ranakpur, with most of the comforts at your feet. You may enjoy the luxuries of life on your stay at the hotels around Ranakpur. You may take your pick from a range of luxury and budget hotels around Ranakpur besides the heritage hotels around the destination of Ranakpur. Most of the places to stay around Ranakpur are easily accessible.

Churches of Goa

Churches of Goa are of permanent interest to the historians, the archaeologists, and the student of art and architecture, the tourist and indeed to every curious intellect. To begin with, the most visible legacy of the Portuguese is their churches, not only imposing monuments of old Goa but also more typically white-washed facades nestling among palm trees elsewhere. Most of the churches in Goa display a tiered frontispiece and are framed with columns and pilasters and were built in the late 16th and early 17th centuries.

The beach capital of India, Goa has more to offer beyond the beautiful nature. Amongst the other must visits landmarks in Goa are its many churches. The entire Indian state of Goa is dotted with churches that reveal the rich religious heritage of Goa. Amongst the most popular churches in Goa is the Basilica Of Bom Jesus. Visitors from India and overseas flock to the Basilica of Bom Jesus in Old Goa, built in 1605, and now declared a World Heritage

Monument. The church houses the sacred relics of St. Francis Xavier, patron saint of Goa, who died while on a sea voyage to China on December 2, 1552. The following year, while transferring his remains to Goa, in accordance with his wishes, it was found that the saint's body was as fresh as the day it was buried. This miraculous phenomenon continues to attract the devout from all lands, and an Exposition or public viewing of his body every ten years attracts lakhs of pilgrims.

The churches of Goa are monuments of stone. They are of permanent interest to the historian, the archaeologist, the student of art and architecture, the tourist and indeed to every curious intellect. Churches glistening in the distance and soaring upwards as white objects on the most commanding spots and pointing their crosses towards heaven is a common sight in the landscape of Goa. These are the fruits of centuries of evangelisation, which bears eloquent testimony to the energy, and enthusiasm of various monastic orders established in the Old City of Goa - the first chunk of Indian Territory to fall into the hands of the new colonizers after the discovery of the sea-route to India. The alliance between the 'sword' and the 'cross' was a close one.

In order to make the travel tour to the churches of Goa even more joyful you need to choose just the right kind of accommodation for you and your family or friends in the various cities of Goa. The various hotels packages in Goa offer the best of facilities. You may take your pick from a range of luxury and budget hotels in Goa besides the star categorized accommodation hotels around the landmark churches of Goa.

GANGA(GANGES)

The history of Ganga-Ganges is as long as the history of Indian civilization. Barring, the period of Harappan civilization, it is Ganga-Ganges basin, which has been the spectator to all the actions that shaped Indian mythology, history, and people. It was in this plain that the great kingdoms of Magadha, Gupta, and Mughals found their home. It is also the region that created one of the most homogenous cultures of all times in the civilizations of the world. It was also the place which created the essence of Hinduism, Buddhism, Jainism, and Sikhism. And for this alone Ganga-Ganges is not like any other river in the world.

Gangotri, the name brings an image of solitude, tranquillity, mystery, adventure, and reverence all at one time in any Indian's heart. Gangotri is an ideal location for whatever you wish. It can be your urge to placate the Gods above, your thirst for adventure, or just seeking the tranquillity of Himalayas, Gangotri is an ultimate destination. Gangotri, more than anything else, is known as the origin of the sacred river Ganges and attracts tourists in large numbers every year.

The legend of Ganges says that the Ganges came down on earth after long penance of King Bhagirathi to Lord Shiva. However, due to the fact that the earth would be devastated if Ganges came down in her full force and her pride, Lord Shiva caught her in his locks. It was proclaimed that Shiva's consort Goddess Uma or Parvati would bathe in Ganges daily. The confrontation with the daunting rivers and attempts to unravel the mysteries of the supernatural world are ubiquitous sights here. Along with the thrill of conquering nature, what one experiences here is the mystical aura that India is so famous for.

Haridwar is considered as one of the seven holiest places according to Hindu mythology. According to the legends, when the Gods left their footprints on the land of Haridwar, metaphorically they also left an indelible mark on the spiritual ethos of every Hindu - more so, the devout, who would later follow their holy paths all across this blessed land. Haridwar, due to its geographical location stands as the gateway to the four pilgrimages of Uttrakhand. Mentioned as Mayapuri, Gangadwar, and Mokshadwar in the ancient scriptures and epics, Haridwar has always remained as a major Shaktipeeth for the devotees. Of such significance is Haridwar in the thought of India's traditional Hindus that it has earned its sobriquet of honor,`the gateway to the Gods'.

Planning to take a pilgrimage this vacation? How about the holy city of Varanasi? The virtuous Varanasi on the banks of Ganga-Ganges is one of the most important pilgrimages for Hindus and Buddhists in India. The two steams flowing through the city namely, Varuna and Assi lend their name to Varanasi. The city of spiritual light, Varanasi was earlier called the ancient living city of Benaras. Varanasi has been the center of education, religion, art of culture since ages. Varanasi indeed offers the incredible India at its religious and cultural zenith.

South India Temples

The temples of south India are famous for their architecture and design. There is a mention of the temples of south India in many known legends of south India. Every temple in south India has its own significance. Visit the famous Krishna Temple at Guruvayoor, the oldest Shiva temple of Vishwanatha Swamy at Kalpathy,temples at Mahabalipuram, Meenakshi, Somnath and Tirupati. Southern India is dotted with places of religious interest. There are several towns that are referred to as the temple towns owing to the grandeur of the temples they are home to.

Rameshwaram

Rameshwaram is an island- of Lord Rama's temple at

Tamil Nadu is a terrific destination. Along with being a major pilgrimage for the Hindus, Rameshwaram is a happening holiday spot too. Rameshwaram is significant for the Hindus as a pilgrimage to Benaras is incomplete without a Pilgrimage to Rameshwaram. The presiding deity is the Linga Of Sri Ranganatha, which happens to be one of the twelve Jyotirlingas of India. Rameshwaram is also popularly referred to as the 'Benaras of the south'. In order to attain Moksha it is believed that the visit to Rameshwaram is mandatory.

The Ramanatha Swamy Temple occupies major area of Rameshwaram. The masterpiece of Dravidian architecture boasts of the largest temple corridor in India. Different rulers built the Ramanatha Swamy Temple over a period of time starting from the 12th century. The temple comprises of twenty-two wells where the taste of the water of each well is different from the other. The waters of the wells are believed to possess medicinal properties. You may join the various festivities at the Ramanatha Swamy Temple of Rameshwaram like Thai Amavasai, Masi Sivarathiri, Thirukalyanam and Mahalaya Amavasai.

Mahabalipuram

Mahabalipuram is a temple town situated along the shores of the Bay of Bengal in the southern state of Tamil Nadu. The sheer sculptural extravaganza of the rock-cut temples is not only reflective of the artistic tastes of the erstwhile Pallava rulers: the temples are also regarded as the birthplace of an entirely new style of architecture, which came to be known as the South Indian temple architecture. South Indian temple architecture has its origins on the sandy beaches of Mahabalipuram. The style, which started here, went on to reach incredible heights in the temples in Kanchipuram, Thanjavur (Tanjore), and Madurai. The sculptural extravaganza of Mahabalipuram is a living testament of the artistic temperament of the Pallavas who were the trendsetters in South Indian art.

Tirupati

Situated in the Chittoor district in southern Andhra Pradesh, Tirumala-Tirupati is the abode of the legendary Lord of the Seven Hills. Tirupati is one of the most famous shrines in the country where an uninterrupted worship of the Lord has been carried out for over thirteen centuries. Even today, Tirupati draws enormous crowds throughout the year. The view of the deity profusely ornamented from tip to toe is in itself awe-inspiring. The idol of Sri Venkateswara has attributes of both Vishnu the Preserver and Shiva the Destroyer-two of the three aspects of the Hindu Trinity.

Madurai

The great temple town of South India, Madurai, is synonymous with the celebrated Meenakshi Temple. It is situated on the banks of river Vaigai. Madurai has a rich cultural heritage, which is more than 2500 years old. The city is believed to have been built by the Pandyan King, Kulasekara in the 6th century BC. It is also known as the Athens of the East and is the second largest city in Tamil Nadu.

The highpoint of visits to temple cities is Madurai. Spread along the rocky banks of the river Vaigai in the state of Tamil Nadu, the modern industrial city's main claim to fame is as a temple town. Whether you come by air, train or road, the first glimpse of the city that greets you are the magnificent gopurams of the Meenakshi Temple. The temple, spread across six hectares, is at the hub of all the activities in the city. The festivities, processions and grandeur of the temples attract tourist in the thousands every year.

There are several places of tourist attractions in Madurai, but it is the Meenakshi Temple that is the hub of activity. Located at the heart of the city, the Meenakshi-Sundareswarar temple has long been the focus of both Indian and international tourist attraction as well as one of the most important places of Hindu pilgrimage. It is the hub of the religious and cultural life of the city. There are several places to see and visit near Madurai too. At a distance of 69 km, on the way to Thekkady, you will come across the Vaigai Dam. It is a beautiful picnic spot and is very popular with the tourists and locals alike.

The city of Madurai, especially the Meenakshi Temple, has an elaborate cycle of festivals. However, the most important and spectacular-the only ones to involve processions and rituals outside the temples-are associated with the annual cycle. The times and dates vary and are determined by the temple authorities. The most interesting feature of the festivals is the processions that are carried out along the routes. Elephants and musicians lead the processions, especially those for the major festivals.

The south Indian city of Madurai is easily accessible through air, road and rail from the other major Indian cities and states. touristplacesinindia can arrange for you all types of transport for your comfortable journey to and in Madurai and throughout the Indian state of Tamil Nadu. In order to make the travel tour to Madurai even more joyful you need to choose just the right kind of accommodation for you and your family or friends in Madurai. The various hotels packages in Madurai offer the best of facilities. The well-furnished rooms make excellent place to stay in Madurai, with most of the comforts at your feet.

Hampi

Hampi is located in the central part of the state of

Karnataka, in the southern part of India. It is 353 km from Bangalore, and 13 km from Hospet.The temples of Hampi, its monolithic sculptures and monuments, attract the traveler because of their excellent workmanship. The Hindu style of architecture found at Hampi reflects the splendor of the Vijaynagar Empire. The rugged landscape adds to the historic ambience of this site.

Hampi is located in the central part of the state of Karnataka, in the southern part of India. It is 353 km from Bangalore, and 13 km from Hospet. It is located on top of a rugged terrain and is 467 m above sea level. Tungabhadra River flows through Hampi. It has a tropical climate with hot summers (April-June), and cool winters (October-February). It experiences the southwestern monsoon rains from June to August.

Hampi is famous for its ruins belonging to the erstwhile medieval Hindu kingdom of Vijaynagar and it is declared a World Heritage site. The main tourist spots in Hampi can be divided into two broad areas: the Hampi Bazaar area and the Royal center near Kamalapuram. The 15th-century Virupaksha Temple is located in the Hampi Bazaar area. It is one of the oldest monuments of the town. The top of the temple rises about 50 m from the ground and the main shrine is dedicated to Virupaksha, a form of Lord Shiva. Hemakuta Hill, south of the Virupaksha temple, contains early ruins, Jain temples and a monolithic sculpture of Lord Narasimha, a form of Lord Vishnu.

Kanyakumari

At the southernmost tip of India, where the Arabian Sea, the Indian Ocean, and the Bay of Bengal meet, lies Kanyakumari, an important south India pilgrimage site. Kanyakumari is also known as Cape Comorin.Pilgrims visit the place to bathe in the sacred waters and to worship the goddess Devi Kanya, an incarnation of Shiva's wife, who conquered demons and secured freedom for the world. The Kumari Amman temple, here, is dedicated to Parvati, the virgin goddess who did penance to obtain the hand of Lord Shiva.

Kanyakumari is the southernmost point of peninsular India and the meeting point of three oceans-the Bay of Bengal, the Arabian Sea and the Indian Ocean. Besides its importance as a Hindu pilgrim center, it is famous for its beautiful views of sunrise and sunset over the waters. The multicolored sand is a unique feature of the beach here.

The list of attractions in Kanyakumari is endless. The tourist destination itself is a beautiful place to move around. The Kumari Amman or the Kanyakumari Temple, located on the shore, is dedicated to a manifestation of Parvati, the virgin goddess who did penance to obtain Lord Shiva's hand in marriage. The temple and the adjoining ghat, picturesquely situated overlooking the shore, attract tourist from all over the world. The diamond nose-ring of the deity is famous for its sparkling splendor said to be visible even from the sea.

Vattakottai (literally, circular fort) is an 18th-century fort overlooking the sea, located six km from Kanyakumari. The Indian city of Kanyakumari is easily accessible through air, road and rail from the other major Indian cities and states. touristplacesinindia can arrange for you all types of transport for your comfortable journey to and in Kanyakumari and throughout the Indian state of Tamil Nadu.

Puttaparthi

Located in the south-western part of Andhra Pradesh, Puttaparthi is surrounded by the arid and rocky hills bordering Karnataka. Famous for its Sathya Sai Baba Mandir, it is one of the famous religious tourist destinations of the world. A number of domestic as well as foreign tourists visit this place every year just to have a glimpse of the legendary Sathya Sai Baba and also to see his most talked about ashram. It is believed that the present Sai Baba is the reincarnation of the former Sai Baba of Maharashtra popularly known as Sai Baba of Shirdi. The income of the ashram has been used for the establishment of a number of public utility services.

Although there is not much to see in Puttaparthi, the ashram itself keeps the attention of the visitor with its varied attractions. Puttaparthi belongs to the Bangalore Circuit of South India. The other destinations that come under the circuit are Bangalore, Kolar, and Nellur. Being at Puttaparthi, the best thing one can do is to visit the ashram and pay reverence to Sai Baba. The nearby areas like Lepakshi are also worth visiting.

The Sai baba ashram itself is a huge complex with room for thousands, with canteens, shops, a museum and library, and a vast assembly hall where Sai Baba gives darshan twice daily (6.45-7.00 AM and 3.45-4.00 PM). Queues start more than an hour before the appointed time, and a lottery decides who gets to sit near the front. On the way between Bangalore and Puttaparthi, one can find the Veerbhadra temple at Lepakshi. At the entrance of the town, there is a huge, monolithic Nandi, the sacred bull of Lord Shiva. The temple is about 500 meters away.

On November 23, the birthday of Sai Baba is celebrated in the ashram. On this day Sai Baba delivers a message to his devotees. The devotees of Sai Baba regard this day as a holy day. The Indian city of Puttaparthi is easily accessible through air, road and rail from the other major Indian cities and states. touristplacesinindia can arrange for you all types of transport for your comfortable journey to and in Puttaparthi and throughout the Indian state of Andhra Pradesh.

Puttaparthi is basically a religious tourist center. There are several accommodation options available at Puttaparthi. Most visitors stay at the ashram in large bare sheds or smaller rooms, if available. Except in the case of families, accommodation is strictly demarcated by sex. Costs are minimal, and though one cannot reserve in advance, one can enquire about availability of accommodation.

5

Performing Arts with Tourism Importance

Dance is the primeval expression of joy and wonder in any part of the world, transcending barriers of culture and development. Ancient humans were probably mimicking the movements of birds and animals in an attempt to acquire or depict their unconscious grace and freedom of form and motion. Dance as a structured entity was essentially part of the devotional process. When combined with song and story-telling, dance metamorphosed into theatre. One aspect or the other predominates in theatre and the performing arts as we recognize them today.

The Natyashastra, the earliest Indian text on the subject, speaks of ekaharya (solo dance) and the anekaharya (dance as performed by more than one person). Written between 200 BC - AD 200 by Bharatmuni, the work divides dance into Nritta i.e. pure dance and Nritya i.e. expressional dance or pantomime. While the former is an act of beauty, not seeking to convey any meaning, the latter depicts emotions through facial expressions, movements of the eyes, and stylized gestures of the hands (mudras, less commonly known as hastas).

Kuchipudi

Kuchipudi, one of the art forms of the South had its origin in Andhra Pradesh. It presents scenes from Hindu Epics and mythological tales through dance-dramas combining music, dance and acting. The lyrics used in Kuchipudi are usually in Telugu, though Sanskrit verses are also not uncommon. While Kuchipudi, like Bharata Natyam comprises pure dance, mime and histrionics, it is the use of speech as well that distinguishes its presentation as dance drama.

Kuchipudi dance-dramas, each present a particular episode or a series of episodes. A solo recital, on the other hand, typically consists of such items as the 'Sabdam', 'Bhama kalapam' which is the main item, 'Padams' and 'Tarangams'. In 'Bhama kalapam', the dancer has enormous scope for the dramatisation of characters. The main character is Satyabhama, a beautiful but arrogant queen who goes through the process of discovering the path of true love and devotion. In the 'Tarangam', the dancer frequently perform a balancing feat, her feet poised on the edge of a brass plate as she moves around.

Kuchipudi, a representation of a fine combination of Natya, Nritta and Nritya was earlier never a solo affair and required a number of actors. It was presented in the open air on an improvised stage by men and boys who were given a vigorous training in abhinaya, music, dancing and singing. Earlier the female roles were played by boys and young men of comely appearance. The Sutradhar or the director of the stage played the key role. He was the conductor, dancer, singer, musician, comedian, all rolled into one.

The play began with the orchestral music which included Mridanga, Madala and a pair of cymbals, followed by an invocation to a deity and appearance of Ganesha, the elephant headed god to bless the performance. Then came the dancers offering worship to the Flagstaff or Flag of Indra. The Sutradhara then announced the theme of the play, introduced the characters in his sing-song voice and appealed the audience to witness the show with attention. This marked the end of the prelude and the beginning of the play proper.

Today Kuchipudi is considerably a different style of dance form than it originally used to be. In most of the cases it is now a solo performance done by female dancers. The Sutradhara has become a phenomenon of the past and the Vachika abhinaya, that is, expressional numbers are sung by the danseuses herself instead by the vocalists in the background on the stage as was the traditional practice. The element of devotion to gods has also been done away with and it has become purely a secular affair with predominance of 'sringar' or erotic flavour.

Besides the drama component has also been totally reduced. The main expressional number is from Jaideva's Ashtapadi, the Ramayana, the Puranas, Tirtha Narayana's Krishna Lila Tarangini or Tyagaraja's compositions, but now the dancer combines into herself the roles of the singer who sings the 'daruvu', the actor who speaks the lines and the dancer who mimes and dances to interpret the text. Elements not indigenous to the dance drama such as sculpture like stances and freezes based on perfect iconographic forms motifs and shapes have also been incorporated into Kuchipudi dance recitals to make it more competitive with other dance forms.

Peacock Dance

The Khonds, also called Samanlas are the most backward hill men dwelling in the inaccessible hilly region of Visakhapatnam and Srikakulam districts. During weddings and festival which falls in the month of April, the Khonds perform the peacock dance. Pirodi, a kind of flute and the tinkling bells around the ankles are the only musical accompaniments.

All the dancers put on white dhotis, tie anklets called Muyyangam, wear turbans, made of locally growing grass and tugged with colourful rags and fasten bunches of peacock feathers behind at their waists which look like peacock tails whenever they bend forward. All the dancers stand in two rows in the beginning and imitate the cry of peacock. They form a circle and bend forward from their knees so as to look like a dancing peacock. After paying obeisance to mother earth and the Sun god they commence dancing.

Putting their palms to their right legs move their left legs rhythmically, the anklets produce jingling sounds. They step forward and backward while the pirodi produces sonorous motes sitting, circling, stepping, bending and waving kerchiefs in their right hands, they look like dozens of peacocks dancing joyously in a circle. This includes gestures of the bridegroom going to the bride's house.

Mango Dance

The Hill Reddis or Konda Reddis also called the Reddis of the Bison hills dwell in Khamman, East Godavari and West Godavari districts. These parts are famous for mangoes. Before plucking the mangoes, the Konda Reddis have a ceremonial festival with a community Dance. They neither decorate nor paint their body like the Gusadis. As an act of worship to Mutyalamma and Konda devata, they dance rhythmically to the accompaniment of drums. This dance commences during the night, with a gentle beat of drums.

Three to four women hand in hand with the castanet like sound of dry nuts join the dance. The men and women both join the dance but they form separate groups. Leaning towards the left they circumambulate around the place. The women, while tapping the ground with the foot, take four steps forward. This is done in a particular manner.

Stepping forward with the right foot four times, leaning towards one side, they come back with one step in the same manner. The circle of men and women moving rhythmically to the centre and retreating with waving arms and the clatter of nuts provide a fascinating pattern for the dance. Keeping the feet apart and jumping with the right and left foot alternately with the other foot forward is another feature of this dance.

The dance steps of the men are different from those of the women. The men while stepping forward, put the right foot first and bring the left foot up to the heel of right foot. This facilitates stepping forward again with the right foot. The drummers and other instrumentalists stand in the centre in the beginning, later they join in the dances and step accordingly forward and backward along with the whole group. The two types of drums used as accompaniment provide regular rhythm to this foot work. When drum beats quicker, the dance also gets momentum and vigour.

After feasting about midnight; men, women and children again begin to dance. They also sing songs invoking Mutyalamma and the hill gods and goddesses. This singing has some religious significance. The song comes to an end by the time the ritual dance reaches its climax. The groups break up and dancing, circling and jumping in frenzy, again form into groups. This dance continues till the next morning and concludes when fatigue overtakes them.

Dimsa Dance

The Araku valley is the most charming hilly region in Visakhapatnam district. Valmiki, Bagata, Khond and Rotia tribes inhabit this valley and other areas of this district. The favourite dance of these tribes is Dimsa which is performed by old and young men and women, during the month of chaitra i.e. in March/April, during weddings and other festivals. During festivals people go from one village to another to participate in the dance and are honoured with community feasts. People of different villages enjoy such festivities and dances called 'Sankidi Kelbar'.

Dimsa Dance not only provides amusement to the dancers and spectators but also develops friendship and fraternity between people of different villages. The instruments accompanying Dimsa are mori Kiridi, tudumu, duppu and jodukommulu.

Gusadi Dance

Deepavali is the biggest festival for the Raj Gonds of Adilabad district. As the harvest is over and the season is cool and congenial the Gonds dressed in colourful costumes and decorated with ornaments go to neighbouring villages in troupes, singing and dancing. Such troupes are called Dandari dance troupes. Each troupe consist of twenty to forty members. 'Gusadi' is a part of Dandari and consists of two to five members. This starts on the full moon day and goes on till the fourteenth day of the dark fortnight of Deepavali. Each member puts on a turban of peacock feathers and horns of the deer, artificial beard and moustaches and goatskin to cover the body. Dappu, tudumu, pipri and kalikom are the accompaniments. The Dandari troupe dance accompanied by beats of gumela reaches its climax with regulated steps and rhythm in a circular form.

The Dandari dance starts with stepping slowly towards the left side and swinging the right foot on to the left foot at every step. Every dancer has two small sticks in his hands. First everyone strikes the two sticks in his own hands, then strike at the sticks of the person on the right side then strike his own sticks and then the sticks of the person on the left side. In this way, with steps and striking together of sticks held in hands they play kolattam and come back to the original position. Then they bend down and touch the ground with their sticks and step on to the four sides. This is paying obeisance to the gods. After this they put into order their circular form and lay down the sticks. Then they sing and clap their hands. They sing a group song in duet, one group singing the first line and the second group singing the second line of the song.

While this is going on, the Gusadi troupe intrudes into the circle with peacock feathered turbans, artificial beards and moustaches, goat skins as covers, strings of cowries and beads around the neck, tinkling bells on wrists, white stripes and dots on the bodies, with modesty pieces around the waists and poles in their hands they enter the circle. After the scattering of the Dandaris, the former raising their hands, and swaying and jerking to the accompanying sounds of the bells and cowries on their bodies. It present a dreadful scene to the on lookers. They jump hither and thither and they utter war cries and with vehement motion and frenzied laughter they frighten the boys and come up on the spectators. They also touch the waists of the spectators with the poles in their hands and tickle them. After some time they dance rhythmically, stepping forward and backward and hither and thither and also zigzag to the accompaniment of instruments. Lastly, the hosting villagers invite them and wash their feet.

Lambadi Dances

Lambadi is the semi - nomadic tribe that is spread all over Andhra. They are also known as Banjaras or Sugalis. Their dances are inspired by the movements associated with daily tasks like harvesting, planting and sowing. The costumes, embroidered with glass-beads and shining discs are picturesque; matched by the abundance of ornate jewellery worn by them. The jingling brass anklets, the hanging cowry bunches and the ivory bangles from wrists to elbows provide a natural rhythm to their dances.

Dussehra, Deepavali and Holi are the festive occasions when the Banjaras go from house to house dancing and receiving alms. Twenty to thirty Banjara women dressed in colourful costumes with shining brass vessels filled with water either on heads or waists present a group dance. The graceful movements of their waving hands and supple waists provide a feast to the onlookers.

Siddi Dance

The Siddis present tribal dances during marriages and other festive occasions. Their dances depict the tribal warfare of their home land in all its ferocity. Armed with shining sword and matchlock and dressed in their exotic primitive costumes, they dance with vigour and force.In rural Andhra some folk dance forms are confined to certain regions, some dance forms are common to all the regions.

Tappeta Gundlu

Tappeta gundlu is a folk dance confined to the coastal districts of Srikakulam, Vijayanagaram and Vishakhapatnam. This was originally performed by cowherds and shepherds as a ritualistic dance propitiating the rain god and their favourite deity Gangamma. While dancing they sing devotional songs on Sri Krishna, Dasavataras and on goddess Gangamma besides other folk songs and narratives.

Tappeta or gundlu is a small percussion instrument in the shape of a drum hanging on the chest and tied to the sides and neck of the players. A troupe consisting of eight to sixteen artistes sing and dance in circles beating with their hands the drums tied to their chests. The players tie jingling bells to their ankles. They put on tight knickers stitched with jingling bells all over. They tie colourful clothes around their waists and long loin clothes hanging up to their feet in front as well as at the back resembling two tails.

This dance requires skill and muscle power. The artistes exhibit rare skills in acrobatics while dancing. The drum beats, the sounds of jingling bells tied to their ankles and the sounds of the bells stitched to their shorts blend harmoniously with the different gaits and steps of the artistes. Their repertoire constitutes twenty to thirty gatibhedas. The dance, styles along with a variety of songs composed in consonance with the dance styles. All dancers sing pallavi of a song or a narrative following their troupe leader.

While dancing, the artistes, eight in a group, stand one above the other on the thighs and shoulders in the shape of a gopuram or a tree with its branches hanging. They lie down and move like the hands of a clock. They stand one above the other on an earthen pot with tumblers full of water on their heads. They whirl fast and fall down with a heavy thud. They come out of their dancing circle and exhibit shoulder and limb movements as in the Bhangra dance of Punjab. The beating of drums, dancing and singing always goes on.

Urumulu or Thunder Dance

Urumulu or thunder dance is found only in Anantapuram district. The instrument employed in this dance is called urumu. It is a percussion instrument which sounds like thunder. The instrument is made out of brass or bell metal - a hollow round pipe. Both sides are covered with goat skin fixed on to iron rings and tightened with ropes at the top of the drum. It hangs from the left shoulder on the belly of the artiste and it is tied to the right side of the waist. The left side of the instrument is rubbed with a thin stick and the right side is beaten with a thick stick.

The urumu dancers belong to the scheduled caste. They are a pious and virtuous group of people who observe religious austerity and worship goddess Akkamma. They abstain from drinking and eating meat. They present urumu dance to please their deity. It is a ceremonial dance. They move in circles adopting different styles and foot steps and play on urumu. They put on big turbans and strings of beads or coins like metal pieces around their necks. They smear their faces with turmeric and also put on Namam on their foreheads. They wear long shirts covering from neck to feet and an upper garment hanging from both shoulders. While dancing they sing devotional songs on Lord Kadiri Narasimhaswami, Dasavataras and goddess Akkamma.

Butta Bommalata

Marionette play is the oldest surviving art form in India. The marionette's or puppets are made of different materials. Butta Bommalu are made of bamboo, tamarind seed paste, paper, cattle dung or husk and hay. The figures are coloured according to the tradition and used for plays.

It is made up to waist only and hollow inside. The dolls are three to four times bigger than the human figures. A coloured cloth is tied around the doll at the waist that covers the player who enter into it. There is a hole in the doll at the navel through which the artiste can see the outside world. Figures of Siva and Parvati,Vishnu and Lakshmi, Garuda and Hanuman, Radha and Krishna are very common in Butta Bommalata. It is presented at festive gatherings, car festivals, marriage ceremonies, Navaratri celebrations, Ganesh immersion festivals and recently in election campaigns. These puppets are large enough to serve as full masks for men and women who dance to the rhythm of a Dappu or Mridangam. Band, Dhole, Sonnayi are used as accompaniments in the Butta Bommalata.

The troupe consist of at least ten members four of whom are in the puppets and dance, four who play instruments, one instructor and the troupe leader. This is only a dumb dance, accompanied only by the sounds of instruments.

GORAVAYYALU

Gorava or Kuruba or Kuruma is a sub caste of shepherds who tend sheep and weave wool blankets. The priests among Kurubas are known as Goravas. They dedicate one male member to the god Srisaila Mallikarjuna when he grows up he is initiated into the Moilara cult by a Ganachari and trained in the lore ritualistic music and dance by a senior Gorava. During the festivals and Kalyanotsavas of their family deities Goravayyalu present their ritualistic dance with great fanfare. During the other days they move from one place to another singing the ballads of Mallanna and other Saiva panegyrics, beg alms and bless the devotees.

They put on a long black coat made out of sheep wool with white strips, a big triangular jar cap made out of bear's skin. One upper cloth hanging from both shoulders, another cloth serving as a waist band. A bag made of deer skin containing the sacred turmeric called Bandaru to be offered to the devotees, a brass cup tied to the waist for drinking milk or pancamritam. They wear strings of cowries around their necks, tie jingling bells to their ankles. They hold a damaru in the right hand and a flute in the left hand.

They play these instruments when they dance. While dancing they move in circles and jump forward and backward like fighting rams. They bark at each other like fighting dogs. They call themselves faithful dogs of god. Mallari or Mailaru. They drink milk or Pancamritam contained in the brass cups placed on the ground like dogs kneeling on the ground without holding the cups with their hands. The remnants are shared by devotees as prasadam when they perform this ritual dance in the temple precincts they pierce their cheeks, calf wrist with iron pikes and blued as offering to the deity and beat themselves with big hunters called veratallu. This dance is purely ritualistic performed during religious occasions.

Garaga Dance

Garaga means a pot or vessel. The dance performed with a vessel on the head is known as Garaganrityam. This is very popular in Karnataka and Tamil Nadu. This dance was performed as a ritual by Asadis during propitiating ceremonies of village goddesses. In Andhra this is popular in the coastal districts and the border districts of Karnataka and Tamil Nadu. In olden days the priest in trance known as Ganachary used to dance without any make up for himself, with a decorated earthen pot on his head in-front of the temple of a village goddess or along with her retinue in procession to the beats of Dappu. It is a strong percussion instruments.

In course of time the Garaga dance has acquired many attractive adjuncts in make up and dance styles. Brass vessels covered with colourful cloths, decorated with vermilion and turmeric are held on the heads by the artistes when they dance. The mouth of the brass vessel is covered with a five hooded serpent made in brass or bronze. The dancers put on colourful clothes and hold a bunch of margosa leaves symbolic of Shakti worship. The adept Dappu players produce varying beats in Trisara, caturasra and other gatis and the garaga dancers dance and produce the same sounds with the jingling bells tied to their ankles. The artistes maintain the balance of the vessels on their heads by without moving their heads though their bodies and limbs move very fast. They have introduced many nuances and acrobatics in their dance styles for attracting the spectators. They lie down on their bellies and pick up coins and sticks with their lips. They stand facing each other on one leg and make a knot with each others leg and dance to the drum beats. They also play kolatam striking at each others stick. All these while maintaining the balance of the vessels on their heads.

VIRANATYAM

Viranatyam also known as Virabhadra natyam is a community or the traditional ceremonial dance that used to be presented in the Siva and Virabhadra temples when Virasaivism was at its Zenith. Veerabhadra, the destroyer of Daksha's sacrifice is said to be the originator of this dance. Holding a sword in one hand and a shield in another hand the devotee dances and plays steps according to the beat of Viramam. It is a big percussion instrument which produces sharp and piercing sounds. Viramam sounds resembles the sounds of war drums and trumpets and Viranatyam resembles Tandavanrityam in its force and vigour. Dhole, Tashamarpa and Sonmayi are also played during the Viranatyam. At the time of Lingodbhava on the sacred day of Sivaratri, these artistes present Urdhava Tandavam, a special type of dance.

Viranatyam is performed by Viramushti, Jangam, Balija and Devanga communities of Virasaiva cult. In Telangana, Viranatyam is presented by Viramushti and Jangam communities during the festivals in Virabhadreswara temple at Kovari and Kottakonda while offering Virabhadra palleram to the deity. A big plate with burning oil or camphor flames is held in both the hands from palms up to elbows and shown before the deity as an offering.

The dancers also recite poems called Khadgalu in praise of Virabhadra and his exploits. The artistes wield swords while singing these panegyrics. It is a vigorous and awful dance with long steps and upward movements of legs and hands. In devotional frenzy and fervor, the artistes also pierce their tongues, cheeks, eyelids, throats and lips with spears and spikes of different denominations called Ekanarasam, Kantimarasam, Kanthanarasam and Sulanarasam. They bleed and dance in frenzy. This ceremonial dance has now gained wide popularity as a folk art due to the many nuances introduced in the dance styles.

Dappu Dance

Dappu is a percussion instrument. It is a counterpart of Dandora of North India. It is also called Tappeta in coastal Andhra. It is made out of calf hide fixed to the margosa wooden structure in a circular shape. It is beaten with two sticks one thin and the other thicker. The form belongs exclusively to Harijans. Dappu dance is a vigorous type of dance as the Dappu is a powerful percussion instrument.

A troupe consisting of ten to twenty artistes presents Dappu dance during marriage processions, car festivals of deities and village fairs and festivals. Tiger steps, bird steps, horse steps are some of the styles of dance movements presented in the Dappu dance. Sometimes the songs sung verge on obscenity as in Lella Patalu to settle old scores.

The beat of the Dappu and the foot work of the dancers synchronise with each other so perfectly that from a slow moving, low-beating rhythm, it reaches its climax with the frantic drums keeping pace with the dazzling foot work by the dancers. They play several kinds of rhythms like Trisra, Chaturasa, Mirsa, Khandagati, Sankeerna, jatis, comprising seven type of beats. They follow different kinds of dance, leaping from one side to another with complicated foot work. They tie jingling bells to their ankles. Spectators throw coins on a Dappu placed on the ground. when the players around that Dappu beat their drums vigorously, the Dappu placed on the ground responds to the sound vibrations and the coins over it dance and slide down to be picked up as a reward by the artistes.

Gobbi Dance

This is a popular dance in coastal Andhra during the Samkranti festival. The courtyards of all houses are cleaned and decorated with different kinds of rangavallis. Gobbillu i.e. balls of cow dung are placed in the middle of these designs and worshipped with flowers, kumkum and turmeric. During evenings young girl's gather around these gobbillu to dance and sing. This dance is a derived form of Garba described in dance treatises.

Horse Dance

Horse dancers are popular in Guntur district. Life size horse puppets are prepared with cattle-dung, hay and husk and coloured to look like real horses. These puppets are hollow in the middle, where the dancers -men and women- stand resembling riders on horse back.

In Guntur district, real horses are trained to dance according to the rhythm of the drums. Tinkling bells are tied to the fetlocks of the horse. During marriage processions and fairs the horse dance is a popular pass time in this district.

Karuva Dance

Karuva dance is popular in East Godavari district. Eight men dressed as Gopika's and eight dressed as Krishna's stand in a circle alternately. In the middle of the circle stand two more dancers dressed as Radha and Krishna. They dance to different rhymes. The movements in this dance are the most important. The gatis generally employed are chaturasara, Trisara and Misra.

The classical dance forms of Andhra Pradesh are mainly Kuchipudi and Bhamakalapam. They belong to the ancient school of Bharatnatyam. The temple dances and the court dances too have their own styles in Andhra.

Folk Dances in Arunachal Pradesh

The Wancho Dances

The Wancho tribes perform dances during appropriate occasions like festivals, ceremonies etc. Ozele festival of Wanchos is celebrated in February-March after the sowing of millet. It lasts for four days and was observed in Longkhau village. The dance is performed from about 9 p.m. to 11 p.m. inside the chief's house. Among the male-folk, boys, youths and adults take part while among women, only girls and those young married women who have not joined the husband's family, take part in the dance.

The dancers, dressed in their fineries, stand in a circle surrounding a bonfire. The girls stand on one side of the circle holding each other's hands. The male dancers hold a sword in the right hand and most of them place the left hand over the shoulder of the dancer to the left. The male dancers start singing when all take a short step with the right foot to the right, flex the knees with an accompanying forward swing of the sword and gently bring the left foot up to the heel of the right one.

They repeat this sequence of movements. When the singing of the male-dancers, end, which is generally on the eighth or ninth step, all stamp their right foot twice on the ground. The female dancers take up the singing in reply. They stamp the right foot twice on the ground during their turn of singing, once generally in the fourth step and the next at the end of the singing which generally falls on the ninth step. Again the male dancers take up the singing and thus the dance continues.

All the male dancers have a cane basket hanging at the waist over the buttocks. The basket is decorated with coloured straw tassels, monkey skulls or wild boar's tushes. The straw tassels of the baskets are decorated with coloured beads. The straps of some of the baskets are decorated with white conch-shell discs. Each basket has a bell fitted at its bottom.

The tinkling of so many bells is the only musical sound. All have anklets of straw and girdles of one or two loops of red cane or of bands of cowries or beads just below the knee. The boys and a few youths are naked but others wear a loin-cloth which is white or light blue in colour with two red stripes at the ends decorated with small beads of different colours. This loin-cloth is tucked in position with a cane waist-band which is about six inches broad. The armlets are either of ivory, brass or red cane loops.

The handle of the sword is decorated with coloured goat's hair. All wear some bead necklaces. Some wear necklaces of coins. The ear decorations are tufts of red woolen threads or ear-plugs decorated with the red seeds. Some have head-dresses made of bamboo, silver-shaped in a cone and decorated with horn-bill feathers. Some have red cane head-dresses decorated with wild boar's tushes. The hair up to the middle of the crown is brought forward and cut so that the fringe reaches just up to the top of the fore-head while the hair of the back is kept long and tucked round a red or yellow coloured rectangular piece of wood, called the Kahpak.

Some of these kahpak's are studded with small pieces of glass while some are decorated with carvings of the human figure or human skull or with a tuft of coloured goat's hair. The side of the head are shaven.

The Idu Mishmi Ritual Dance

The Idu Mishmis have a ritual-dance and a fertility-dance. The ritual-dance is performed by the priest or priestess in the ceremonies of Ai-ah, Ai-him, Mesalah and Rren. The fertility-dance is performed on the last day of the Rren ceremony.

There is no definite myth about the origin of this dance. According to local tradition, the first priest who officiated in a funeral ceremony was Chineuhu and his brother, Ahihiuh, was the first priest who officiated in the other three ceremonies in which this dance forms a part. This dance is associated with the priestly office.

Besides the priest, there are three or four other dancers who are selected from amongst the spectators. In addition it is the usual dress which consists of a loin-cloth, a short-sleeved coat, and a sword slung on the right side, a leather bag slung on the left side and a few bead-necklaces, the priest wears a few other articles.

These articles are an apron with particular designs, a head-band decorated with two or three rows of cowries, a necklace studded with the teeth of tiger and bear and a few metal bells. A priestess wears these special articles in addition to the usual Mishmi woman's dress of a skirt, a long sleeved coat and bead-necklaces. The priestess is generally accompanied by female dancers. The accompanying dancers wear the usual dress.

The dancers stand in a line, the priest is second either from the right or left. During the dance, one dancer standing at one end of the line plays a small drum slung from his neck. The priest and the other two dancers play a very small semi-globular single-membrane drum, striking it with a bamboo-stick which is kept tied to the drum with a string.

The fifth dancer, if any, plays a horn bugle. When there are five dancers, the priest stands in the middle of the line. He sings a line of invocatory song while all the others play the musical instruments, flex the knees bobbing up and down and alternately raise the right and left heels and stamp these on the ground in time to the drum-beats. When the priest finishes singing the line, others repeat it in chorus. Again the priest sings another line of the song which the others repeat in chorus and thus it goes on.

After a prelude of flexing of knees and stamping of heels, they place one foot forward and immediately bring the other up beside it. If in the first step, the right foot is taken forward, then in the next step it is the left one. After each step, they flex the knees. Thus, they dance forward to the accompaniment of drumbeats and invocatory song. When they have danced forward for some distance, they dance backward with the same movement. Thus they dance moving forward and backward.

Sometimes they break away from the line formation and the four dancers standing in the four corners sing an invocatory song, play the musical instruments and dance flexing the knees and raising the right and left heel alternately and stamping these on the ground. Now and then they change positions dancing all the time but facing inward. Sometimes they dance in a circle following one another with tripping steps.

In another movement, they dance sideways either in a clockwise or anti-clockwise direction. They stand in a semi-circle and in the anti-clockwise movement, they take one step with the right foot to the right and immediately bring the left foot beside the right one. Thus they dance in a circle, flexing the knees after each step.

The priest does not demand any money for his priestly services, but the performer usually remunerates him according to his ability. The remuneration may also be paid in kind, e.g. with handloom coat, brass utensils or pigs.

Digaru Mishmi Buiya Dance

The Digaru Mishmis have two types of dances called Buiya and Nuiya. The Buiya dance has two types of movements and it is performed for entertainment while the Nuiya is a ritual-dance performed by a priest.

Buiya dance is performed on any festive occasion like the Duiya, Tazampu and Tanuya festivals which are performed for the prosperity and good health of the performer and his household. This dance may also performed after a feast arranged by a family to entertain the fellow villagers who co-operate with it opening a new field.

The dance is performed in the passage which runs along one side of the house from the front to the rear. Men and women take part in this dance. There is no limit to the age of the dancers although generally children and old persons do not take active part in the dance itself but merely sit by, as spectators.

There is no special costume for this dance, so they perform this dance wearing their usual dress. The male dancer wears a loin-cloth a sleeveless jacket, a turban and ear-rings. The female dancer wears a blouse, a long skirt reaching down to the ankle with a short one wrapped over it and a side-bag on the left side. They wear necklaces, large silver-ear-plugs and a silver fillet with its strap studded with coins or cowries.

The dancers stand in a line, one behind the other, in the passage. One of the dancers plays a drum while another plays a gong. Cymbals are played, if available, by another dancer. Keeping time to the beats of the drum, gong and cymbals, the dancers take one step forward with the right foot, then gently bring the left foot up to the heel of the left one flexing the knees as before.

They dance forward repeating this sequence of movements till they reach the rear of the passage with the same sequence of movements. Thus they dance up and down the passage of the house. They may or may not sing to the accompaniment of the dance. When they sing a song, it may be solo or in chorus.

There is another movement when they dance with skipping steps but with no accompanying song. The skipping steps of the female-dancers are lower and graceful while those of the male-dancers are higher and more vigorous. The dancers get no remuneration. There is no formal training but they learn the dance movements by imitating those of the elders.

The Khampti Dances

The Kamptis, who are Buddhists, have many dance-dramas through which they unfold some stories or depict mythical events bearing ethical lessons. These dramas are generally staged during the religious festivals of Potwah, Sankian or Khamsang, constituting the entertainment part of the festivals.

The dance is called ka and the dance-drama is called kapung (ka-dance; pung-story) and actually means a story depicted through the dance. The rehearsal of a drama starts about one month before a festival. This may be done in the monastery or in any house of their choice. The well-to-do-villagers invite the drama-party when the drama is staged in the front courtyard or in some suitable open space near their house.

Women do not take part in the drama. The female role, if any, is played by a man in woman's costume. After the performances, the party is given a remuneration of seven, fourteen, twenty-eight or forty-two rupees-always an amount divisible by seven. They purchase with this money the costumes and masks used in the dramas. The surpluses, if any, is shared by the members of the drama party.

Ponung Dance (Adis)

Adi village has a rich cultural life. The tribal people are famous for their Ponung that is dancing with the accompaniment of songs. A group of girls dance in a circle holding each other by stretching their hands over each others shoulders while the leader-usually a man called the Miri-dances and sings in the centre-holding aloft and shaking a sword like musical instrument called 'Yoksha'. First he sings a line and then it is repeated in chorus by the maidens rhythmically in circle at a low pace. On all important occasions ponung is arranged.

Sadinuktso (Akas)

The Akas have a number of dances and songs for the different socio-religious festivities. One of the well known dance among the Akas is the Sadinuktso. A member from the boy's group comes forward, gives his performance for a short while and recedes. A girl then comes and she also dances all alone. This relation goes on till all the boys and girls of the group have danced. No song is sung with this dance. It is generally performed in marriages, guest, entertainments or on the construction of a new house.

Dance Styles in North-east India

Husari and Bihunas

The two main forms of dancing are Husari and Bihunas in Assam. Husari is carol singing. Batches of boys and young men led by older men go from house to house, sing and dance in the front or back courtyard and collect subscriptions to be spent on repairing the village Namghar (community centre) and on feasting. The dance commences with singing of hymns led by a comparatively elder person.

The music is staccato. Each dance lasts only a minute or two. Husari is more religious than festive and gives clear indications of the origin of the Bihu festival in some ancient fertility cult. Bihu songs and dances invariably follow the main item of Husari singing which consists of specially composed songs of religious themes sung by members of the party moving in a circle. These songs have a wide range of folk-tunes and are sung in praise of the great festival with the music of accompanying drums and various bamboo instruments. It is a dance of youth and of the spirit of spring, it expresses an exuberant spirit, like a Bihu song, it tends to express the erotic sentiment more than anything else. The Bihu drummer, often utters his bols and follows their reproduction on his drum, and then dances in such a way that he appears to have no bones in his body at all.

Dhuliya and Bhawariya

Generally accompanying bhawuas, i.e. theatrical performances of the type of miracle plays of Europe in the middle ages. These dances verging on acrobatics are performed to tunes of vigorous music provided with drums and cymbals. Masks are sometimes used. Deodhani This dance form is associated with the worship of the snake goddess Manasa. A Deodhani girl, in a trance like inspired state, goes on dancing to the accompaniment of Kham (drum) and Ciphung (flute) propitiating many a deity beginning with Siva and ending with Lakshmi, she at one stage takes a sword and a shield and performs a virile war-dance.

Zikirs Zikirs are songs sung by Assamese Muslims to the accompaniment of dancing in circles and clapping of hands. Mohauhau or Mahkheda It is also considered as a festival. In Kamrup district on a full moon night in Nov-Dec, boys in groups go from house to house and sing and dance, striking the ground with bamboo sticks and taking leaps and turns. The ceremony is believed to be helpful in driving away mosquitoes. Apsara-Sabah This is a ceremony in which the nymphs of the air are invoked during calamities and lean times, women with flowing hair dance in circles. The rhythm is provided by striking bamboo sticks on conch-shells or bangles.

Classical Dance

Heritage of Classical dance in Assam is of remote origin. In Assamese dances, Hastas (hand gestures), Shirokarma (movement of the head), Padachari (foot work), Karana (posture), etc are performed after the manner of Natya Shastra or Sanskrit treatises on dance. The foot-work in an Assamese classical dance is extremely intricate and is called "Gati" or "Belan". It always reflects the theme of the dance in its infinite variation, speed and pattern.

There are "Hasti Bulan", i.e. the slow majestic steps of the elephant, "Ghora Bulan", i.e. the swift galloping steps of the horse, "Maira Bulan", i.e. the majestic steps of a peacock and so on. There are several kinds of "Karanas" or "Bhanges", i.e. poses of the body in an Assamese dance. They are expressive of meaning and require to be mastered by long practice. Those postures of the body accompany the movements of the head, neck, eyes and feet. The mastery of the movements is a matter of long practice under expert guidance.

The hand gestures is called "Hasta", commonly known as Mudras. They are performed either with a single hand (Asanguta Hasta) or with both the hands (Sanjuta Hasta). Those gestures that are expressive of meaning are called "Shree Hastas" and those performed only for the sake of beauty and rhythm are called "Nritta Hastas". The combination of all the Hastas will be nearly one hundred.

The indigenous classical dance forms of Assam or Asamiya Margi Nritya has been classified into (i) Bhaona, (ii) Temple dances, and (iii) Oja-Pali. Bhaona is a theatrical performance of a Vaishnava Ankiya Nat, a one-act play, initiated by Sankardeva. It is chiefly aimed at propagating Vaihnava tents and performed in village Namghars and Satra premises. The Sutradhara of an Ankiya Nat, though not a character of the play, is an integral part of it; he recites slokas, sings, dances and explains in prose what is what at every stage of Bhaona.

The Natuwa or Cali dance is perhaps modeled on some temple dance, although it is included in the Bhaona. There are two kind of Natuwa dances, Pakha Jiya and Hajowaliya. Hajowaliya is a woman's dance and both tandava and lasya have been combined to make it. The hair style of a knot tied as the crest, small karamanis (beads) over a lahanga (mekhala) and an orna over the face constitute the dress. Oja-Pali is a group of chorus singers and dancers. The Oja is the leader of the chorus, the Palis are his assistants and the Daina Pali is the principal assistant. The number of assistants may be three, four or more.

They dance, play small cymbals and sing stories from the Epics and the Puranas. Their dance bears clear evidence of many aspects of Indian classical dances like hasta, gati, bhramari, utplavana, asana etc. The Oja wears pag-jama or ghuri, bangles, unti, ring and nupur, and ties a tangali . The classification of Svaras by Oja-Palis into ghora, mantra and tara corresponds to the Indian classification of udara, mudra and tara. The songs sung by Ojas: malaci or malanci geets and jagar are Sanskritic language; they also sing a kind of mixed song, Patsha geet. They are written under Muslim influence.

Tribal Dances

Garai-dabrai-nai, a fighting dance on horses. Gan-daula-ban-nai, an insect catching dance. Nenlai-gela-nai, mongoose dance. San-galao-banai, a dance depicting a skirmish between two parties over a boundary. Lakharu-li, sword dance performed by women carrying two swords each. Khaijama-Phanai, sword dance performed by men.

Performing Arts in Kerala

Kathakali

Kathakali, is an efflorescent art form of Kerala. It has been described as a true representation of the artistic traditions of India and one of the most magnificent theatres of the imagination. It is a highly stylised dance-drama which serves to present story themes derived from the Ramayana, the Mahabharata and other Hindu epics, myths and legends. The dance aspect consists of pure dance (nritya) as well as mime (abhinaya).

Mohiniyattam

The Devadasi dance tradition which developed through the temple danseuses is an important type among the dance patterns of India. Mohiniyattam in Kerala took shape in the tradition of Devadasi dance and grew and developed a classical status.

The word 'Mohini' literally means a maiden who excites desire or steals the heart of the on looker. It is a solo female dance in which the striking features is the musical melody and rhythmical swaying of the dancer from side to side and the smooth and unbroken flow of the body movement. The dance is focused essentially on feminine moods and emotions.

Folk Dances

Traditional folk dances are of great variety. One of the most charming is the *Kummi,* where the rhythm of the song and steps begins in slow beats and gets exciting acceleration as well as complication.

Tiruvathira

Another favourite form is the *Tiruvathira* dance by maidens in a circle which revolves with steps alternating with the palms of each maiden meet those of a girl next her in rhythmic claps. A narrative song is also sung by the dancers as they go round. The cultural level has always been fairly high in the middle and upper classes and women fully participate in it.

Margamkali

Among the performing arts of Christians, Margamkali deserves special mention. It is a group dance developed by the Syrian Christians of Kerala. The word 'Margam' means path, way, religion or creed. The real source of inspiration for Margamkali was Kalaripayattu which was very popular when the Christian community had developed the form.

Kolkali

Muslim Kolkali is similar to the Kolkali practiced by the

Christians and Harijans. It is a group dance in a circle with short sticks in the hands of the dancers with which they make the rhythm by beating them. The vibrant steps are accompanied by the vocal music consisting of meaningless syllables followed by songs. The dance goes from slow to a fast tempo creating an interesting climax. There are diverse choreographic patterns in the dance. Males only participate in this dance and they require basic martial training.

Oppana

Oppana and Aravanmuttu are the popular forms of entertainment among Muslims. Oppana is a form accompanied by clapping of hands. Both men and women participate in it. In marriages, the women move in a circle and receive the bride while men stand aside singing songs and receive the bridegroom. Aravana is a dance, which the Muslims of Kerala had learned from the Arabs. Being an Arabic dance, the music that accompanies it also Arabic. The rhythm is played on an instrument called daf or tap, a round percussion instrument with one side covered with hide.

Chavittunatakam

Chavittunatakam is a Christian dramatic form which was introduced during the time of the Portuguese in Kerala in the16th century A.D. 'Chavittu' means the rhythmic steps which accompanied the recitation of lines.

Krishnattam

Manavedan, a great scholar and patron of art was considered as the creator of Krishnattam. He wrote a drama based on Krishna's life and choreographed it into an elegant art form called the Krishnattam (the play of Krishna). He also gave it a dance base.

Ramanattam

Ramanattam was introduced by the Raja of Kottarakkara. As the name indicates, this play was based on Ramayana. Ramanattam was in Manipravala style and performed by the Raja himself and his Nayar soldiers. Actually, this was brought into being as a challenge to another form, the Krishnattam, which then held sway. It continued for eight days.

Semi Classical Dance

Thullal

The Thullal emerged in the eighteenth century. Thullal literally means dance. This art form is the cumulative product of all traditional theatrical arts of Kerala, both folk and classical. Kunchan Nambiar was the creator of Thullal, was vigorously earthy.

The art of Thullal was evolved as a system out of the various singing and dancing art forms of the people incorporating apt features of classical styles so that by the harmonious blend of the folk and classical forms of art it represented the accumulated aesthetic experience of all sections of the people high and low. The themes were drawn from the never failing myths and epics of India.

Based on different styles of narrative singing, rhythms of dancing, foot work and make-up of the dancer, three varieties of Thullal were evolved in course of time. They are: Ottan Thullal, Seethankan, Thullal, Parayan Thullal.

Koodiyattom

The Koodiyattam which emerged by the ninth century was a full-fledged dramatic presentation in Sanskrit, the repertoire including plays by Bhasa, Harsha, Mahendra Pallava and Sanskrit plays by Kerala writers like

Saktibhadra and Kulasekhara. Koodiyattom is a temple art performed traditionally by a specific community. It belongs to the genre of drama. Koodiyattom is probably the only surviving form of the traditional presentation of Sanskrit drama. Koodiyattom embraces elements of music and dance.

Nanniar Koothu

Nanniar Koothu is a dance form conducted in some prominent Kerala temples purely as a ceremonial ritual, presented by women only. The Nanniars, who are the womenfolk of the Nambiar community, stage the Nanniar Koothu in a hereditary tradition.

Calssical Dances and Dance Styles in Tamil Nadu

Bharathanatyam

Bharathanatyam, the most famous classical dance of India originated in Tamil Nadu.

Kolattam

Kolattam, derived from Kol (a small stick), and Attam (play) is the name of a charming Tamil dance practiced by groups of young girls. A festival connected with this art has both a cultural and a religious significance. According to legends, once there lived an Asura called Basavasura who could not be controlled by anybody. Some girls joined together in a group, went to this Asura and played Kolattam with charming music. The Asura was so pleased with the divine music and grace of the girls, that he gave up all his evil designs. This has since been celebrated as Kolatta Jothrai in a number of places in Tamil Nadu.

'Basava' - the bull, the personification of Shiva is the centre of the Kolattam festival, commencing every year on the new moon day of the October-November and ending on the full moon day. Daily, girls take their bath early in the morning in the holy rivers and they pick up a handful of grass and water in a small container and return to the place where they have installed the clay idol of Basava. The girls then offer the grass to lord Basava, place the water near the bull and worship. While playing Kolattam the girls visit some houses in the village to play Kolattam in each house. On the purnima day, scheduled for the immersion of Basava, the girls dressed in new clothes placing the Basava in a decorated palanquin ultimately immerse it in a river. In every stage of the festival, each girl has one stick in each of her hands and the stick in the hand of each girl is struck against those of the other girls in rotation, producing beautiful music.

Kavadi

Lord Muruga or Subrahmanya, the son of Lord Shiva, has annihilated all the evil forces of demons. He is said to be reside in six embattled field-camps called Padaiveedus. Palani and Thirupparakundram in Madurai district are two such holy places. They are hillocks described in mythology as carried by a giant called Idumban slung on the two ends of a pole placed on his shoulder. This Idumban became one of the principal devotees of Lord Subrahmanya. He has a shrine half-way up the Palani hill and receives the first honours from all devotees proceeding to worship Subrahmanya. Actually the worship of Lord Subrahmanya without paying homage to Idumban is considered ineffective. The carrying of Kavadi by pilgrims is symbolic of Idumban carrying the hillocks, the abodes of the Lord slung on a pole.

There are several kinds of Kavadis- the milk and rose-water Kavadi being the principal ones. The central shaft of the semi-circular wooden structure is placed on the shoulders and the pilgrims dressed in yellow costume and decorated with garlands, undergoing many privations to fulfill vows. They dance their way through the streets and up the hillock under the hypnotic music provided by the drum, the pipes and the tom-tom.

It is a Tandava as opposed to the Lasya form of dance. Extreme devotion prompts some Kavadi dancers to disfigure their lips. The lower lip is pierced through for the insertion of a copper or brass ring, often with a view to maintain silence. The dancers subject themselves to rigorous austerities and try to get rid of their ego, anger, lust and other vices. They dance to the tunes of Kavadi-c-cindu, sung by admiring groups of devotees who follow the dancers. The divine songs are rendered in charming music by a trained singer and repeated by others in chorus and the emotion-chocked dancer goes into raptures hearing them. Sometimes they react by shifting the Kavadi over their shoulder, head, nose etc. in see-saw position displaying great artistry with many a pose and movement in rhythm, unaided by hands.

Kavadi-c-cindu, a peculiar folk art of Tamil genius has blossomed into a literary and technically brilliant form. It gives a lilting tune and inspiration to listeners and relieves the bearer of the Avid of physical pain. It is also called Vazhinadai-cindu. It is sung by pilgrims while trekking long distances, to forget the tedium.

Karakam Dance

Karakam is a folk art developed along with the cult of Mariamman. It is of two varieties- the religious and the professional.

The religious type is called Sakti Karakam. A small pot is filled with water and sealed with a coconut. Flower wreaths decorate it and a lime fruit is placed at the top of the Karakam. The temple priest or his nominee carries it with great ceremony and sentimental attachment since this is one of their hereditary privileges.

The professional type is known as Attak Karakam and is performed anywhere by anyone with necessary practice and skill. It is one of the Tamil Nadu's regular showpieces at the republic day floats in New Delhi every year.

The Attak Karakam or balancing of the pot on the head is accompanied by peculiar musical instruments called Pampadi, Urumi, Thavil, Nadaswaram and Thamukku which are among the distinctive components of Tamil music. The Karakam dancers wear a close fitting dress and look like warriors. They remind one of the Kudak-Koothu dancers described in the literary work, Chilappadikaram.

The word Karakam denotes a pot or kumbham filled with sacred water for purificatory purposes. During ordinary rituals all the seas of Varuna, the Lord of rains and the seven sacred rivers are supposed to be attracted and confined in the Karakam and released only when the final ablution is performed and the water is poured or sprinkled over the heads of the worshippers.

Puravai Attam

Puravai Attam also known as Poikkal Kuthirai, is a dummy horse show. The dummy horse is made of jute, cardboard, paper, and glass. The show is performed by men as well as women.

The main attraction is the richly decorated cardboard horse. The dancer uses this as his dress. He gets into it through the holes made therein and looks as if he is riding on horse back. Wooden stilts are tied to the dancers feet and these can be successfully used only after months of experience. The purpose of using the stilts is to prevent the dancer from being harmed by snakes or scorpions. This dance is performed by a pair of dancers impersonating a king and queen. Sometimes, they indulge in acrobatics and they entertain the folk for hours together. The dummy-horse show is one of the chief attractions in the republic day festivities at New Delhi and folk artists are sent from Tamil Nadu every year to perform this show.

Arayar Natanam

Arayar Natanam is enacted in December-January in Shrirangam and other Shri Vaishnava temples by groups of musicians and a dancer who are engaged to recite the sacred hymns called the Thiruvaimozhi. This class of choirists called Arayar or Chanters are on the temple staff receiving allowances and perquisites. They wear a uniform which includes a Kireetam or special conical cap as their badge during the chanting. While chanting the hymns, they also use a pair of cymbals made of bell-metal. One of them assumes the postures. In between their recitations, they utter the glory of the presiding deity by singing Kondattam.

Podikazhi Attam

Podikazhi Attam is a popular dance among the fishermen of the coastal villages near Pondichery during the festival of their favourite deity Muruga. Eight to sixteen men in their traditional costumes perform the dance to the accompaniment of drums, and music is performed mostly by women.

Navasandhi

Navasandhi meaning nine directions is a dance performed to the accompaniment of music at the flag-hoisting ceremony, which heralds the annual festival of the temple at Tiruchendur. Several other dance traditions have been noticed in a number of temples in Tamil Nadu. The dances performed by the Palanquin-bearers of the Lord are other variations of the drama tradition combining music and dance.

Kuravaik-Koothu

This is a type of dance in which seven girls form a circle clapping one other's hand. This dance is referred to as Aichiyar Kuravai or the dance of the cowherd women in Chilappadikaram.

This dance has a peculiar musical significance. The seven notes of the musical scale are arranged in a circle and the seven girls are called by the names of the seven musical notes viz Kural, Tattam, Kalikkilae. The Achoponga Folk dance is a remnant of this defunct dance. In this dance, a number of girls form a circle and do simple rhythmic movements, singing and clapping their hands according to the rhythm.

Kazhaikoothu

This is a dance performed by standing on bamboo poles. A specimen of this occurs in bas-relief sculptured in the Sri Andal Temple at Srivilliputhur. The dancer balances himself standing on two poles, each two meters long, dancing to the accompaniment of a two-faced drum played by his wife.

Kummi

In Kummi, girls sing several songs. Kummi consist of common Kummi and the Oyil Kummi. In the common Kummi, the dancers are rhythmical and the girls dance in different postures. The rhythm of both dance and music delights the audience. The word Kummi is said to be derived from Kommai and means to 'dance with clapping of hands' to time and singing poems in a metre adopted to Kummi dance.

Oyil Kummi

Oyil Kummi or Oyil Attam is performed by large groups of men wearing bells on their feet and narrating mythological stories. The invocation song prays to gods and also instructs the participants to give adequate space for the movement of the neighbours legs and prevent their coming into physical contact.

Bhagavatha Mela

Bhagavatha Mela, one popular throughout the Tamil Nadu, is now confined to a single village, Melatur in Thanjavur district. It is held as a part of the annual Nara-Simha Jayanthi festival in May-June. A large flat thatched canopy and a small stage are put up in the streets in front of the temple and the dramas are enacted to dedicate the deity installed in the front hall of the temple.

Bhagavatha Mela dance-drama is subdued and graceful with, mellifluous vocal and instrumental music. Dialogue of high diction and suggestive strained abhinaya and other symbolical action are its hall-marks. Violent scenes of war and killing are not enacted but only narrated. The Bhagavatha Mela dance-drama has dramatic interest, aided by classical music and dance. Every actor is well trained in Bharatha Natya.

The performance commences with the appearance of the Konangi or buffoon. He dances for a few minutes and requests the audience to witness the play patiently. A group of musicians then sing the Todaya-mangalam or invocation song followed by the introduction to the drama that is to be enacted. Lord Ganesa then appears to bless the play. A young boy is usually made to wear the mask of Ganesa and dance to the accompaniment of background music. Each actor or character is then introduced. After this elaborate introduction, the drama begins.

Harikatha Kalakshepam

This is the art of extempore story telling for three to four hours. It is introduced into Tamil Nadu from Maharashtra by the Mahratta rulers of Thanjavur. The exponent of this art commands a stage and audience by his knowledge of many languages, by his scholarships in the epics and by handling of Chappalakkattai (a pair of wooden planks) in one hand controlling the movement and tempo.

The themes are drawn from the epics Meenakshi Kalyanam, Sita Kalyanam and Rukmini Kalyanam are popular subjects. The dialogue is forcefully mono-acted in a modulated voice to give the effect of light and shade. The words and music roll as Krishna's chariot wheels at a terrific speed in a high lilting rhythm to carry Rukmini away. In this act music plays a very important role and unless it is carefully fitted and woven into the very texture of the story the artist cannot produce the desired effect.

6

Handicrafts of India as a Potential Tourist Resources

The history of Indian crafts is as old as its origin. The first references to Indian crafts can be found from the Indus Valley Civilization (3000 B.C.-1700 B.C.). The craft tradition in India has revolved around religious beliefs, local needs of the commoners, as well as the special needs of the patrons, royalty and trade. These craft traditions have withstood the ravages of time and continue to flourish owing to the assimilative nature of Indian culture.

Andhra Pradesh has the distinction of having all important categories of handicrafts practiced in their traditional locations spread over different parts of the state. The skills of artisans can be seen in caskets, vases and trays.While places like Nagarjunakonda and Amaravathi have influenced the growth of stone-carving in places like Durgi, wood-carving received its impetus from the temple sculptures. This has made possible the creation of a variety of products in the shape of both figurines and panels that depict them from temple chariots and Gopuram (typical Hindu temple domes).

Metalware has found a new expression in the context of Andhra Pradesh with exquisite pieces of sheet-metal art deriving its motifs from the historic monuments of the

Kakatiya sculpture. At the same time, the art has successfully adapted itself to imbibing the use of Persian and other motifs. This has resulted in the evolution of a whole range of utility-cum-decorative items like plant pots, vases, wall decorations and stationery items. Cast art metalware, including icons and temple sculptures depicting various themes, is also produced in certain parts of the state.

Nirmal painting, unique for reproducing motifs from the well-known art schools, has greatly expanded its market by evolving a number of household items which include large-size furniture for drawing, dining and bedrooms. Leather puppet-making is yet another speciality which has made its way into Andhra Pradesh and developed its roots in different parts of the state. Originally conceived to meet the needs of the shadow puppet troupes, this technique is being increasingly adapted to evolve articles of home decoration.,

Andhra Pradesh has created a niche for itself in the wooden toy industry, combining both carving and painting to present interesting themes, such as village occupations, models of mythological figures, and animals in both stylised and natural forms. Andhra Pradesh has its claim on some of the most distinguished crafts like the Kalamkari work with its origins traced back to antiquity. Kalamkari, with its resist process and application of vegetable dyes has made an impact in various parts of the world. The Kalamkari craft, as it has recently evolved in Srikalahasti, offers themes in the form of small and large decorative panels ideal for household and office decoration.

Andhra Pradesh has a rich tradition of handloom textile which has attracted attention from both within and outside the country. By carefully assimilating some of the best features of weaving styles and techniques without sacrificing on the originality, and showing a high degree of flexibility to change, the artistic handloom weaving industry of Andhra Pradesh has emerged as a potent source of some of the most unique products made in the country. The world-famous Tie and Dye cloth with its more recent innovation in furnishing fabrics, the well-known brocade and silk saris of kothakota and Gadwal, the famous Narayanpet saris and superfine Venkatagiri saris, besides Pondur Khadi are among the better known handloom textiles from the state.

The mirror embroidery of the style practised by the tribal women Banjaras, nomenclatured "Banjara Embroidery" is another important craft. It offers possibilities for the profitable use of embroidery skills of this economically backward community in the state. Andhra Pradesh has a place of pride in floor coverings too. Carpets of Eluru and Warangal have long been known not only within the country but also in many parts of the world. All natural-wool pile carpets produced in these places are a speciality. The artistic Durry industry evolved in and around Warangal. Durries with floral and figurative motifs have contributed significantly to exports.

EMPROIDERY

The embroidery of Kashmir, called kasida, is world-famous. Varied, rich in colour, elaborate in detail and exquisite in execution, the kasida patterns are freely drawn by the naqqash mostly from memory. The finest kasida work, particularly embroidered on shawls or saris, has no 'wrong' side.

The chain-stitch is also used for the making of a large number of miscellaneous articles such as bags, screens and cushion covers.

Banjara Embroidery

It is from this that the Banjaras in Andhra Pradesh seem

to have captured their exuberant clothes. Nomads in the past, the Banjaras today aggregate in groups called 'tandas'. Staying in communes, they still strive to preserve the fascinating and unpredictable traditions of their ancestors. Tattooed women with hands weighed down by ivory bangles create the memorable mirror work which the Banjaras are famous for.

Banjara Needle Crafts(Embroidary)

Banjara Needle work is a local tribal craft practised by the 'Banjaras' (tribals) of Telangana Region. It differs from the embroidery of Gujarati and Kutch Banjara. It has a style of its own, the originality and brightness are accentuated by its matchless quality. Needlework is an integral part of this craft and patterns are basic geometric combinations, squares, triangles and diamonds.

The Banjaras produce exuberant embroideries using colourful threads. All they need is a piece of cloth and a needle and their imagination gets going. Intricate stitches in vibrant colours and the use of beads, shells and mirrors conjure a magic created by nimble fingers.

The distinctive feature of their work is the extensive use of mirrors. A rich appearance is created by filling the background with simple chain stitch, herringbone, long and short stitch. Typical items include cushion covers, bags, skirts, 'kurtas', dress sets for girls and women, blouse pieces, bedspreads and other household furnishings.

The Crafts Council of Andhra Pradesh with its sustained market promotion is revitalising the art by improving the quality and standard of work by assisting them in procuring better raw material.

BIDRI CRAFT

Bidriware is the most well known of Andhra's handicrafts

- a metal craft that derives its name from 'Bidar', the hometown of this exquisite craft. It is an art of inlaying silver on black metal and it is believed that this ancient and eye-catching craft entered India more than 4000 years ago from the culture-rich Persians, Syrians and Iranians.

Bidri craftsmen were patronised in the Mughlai courts and settled down to practice their craft in the fortress town of Bidar in Karnataka, giving the craft it's name. It originated with the ornamentation of royal swords and other weapons, and was later applied to domestic use in items like cigars and cigarette boxes. Typical Bidri items include plates, bowls, vases, ashtrays, trinket boxes, huqqa bases, jewellery etc. Glass and studded bangles of Bidri are a favourite with women.

Behind the breathtaking beauty of Bidri, lies hours of meticulous effort by the artisans. The original technique involved the inlaying of gold or silver on a steel or copper base. This method had its origins in Persia. However, the metal used for the base today is an alloy of zinc and copper. The black colour is the result of the heating the zinc and copper surface gently and applying sal ammoniac with old fort earth. It is engraved or overlaid with silver or brass.

Crochet Lace

Introduced in the middle of the 19th Century to provide employment to the poverty-striken women of the area, lace work was, to start with, sent to friends and relatives abroad as gifts which were highly appreciated. Starting with a mere dozen designs, the local skills were used to evolve as many as 300 designs over the years which speaks of the high artistic sense of the artisans. The raw materials and implements required for this industry are simple, consisting of only a hooked needle and cotton thread. The thread used is twisted mercerised cotton yarn made out of superior grade cotton. The craft is carried on by thousands of women working part time at their homes in Narsapur and Palakol areas of West Godavari District and Razole Taluka of East Godavri District. Articles produced include those that are wholly lace, as well as those in which lace work is used as decorative insertions in cloth.

Dokra Metal Craft

Tribal in origin, the Dokra metal craft is common to the tribal belts of Madhya Pradesh, Orissa, Bengal and Andhra Pradesh. In Andhra Pradesh this craft is found in Chittalbori and Ushegaon in Adilabad District. What makes Dokra unique is that no two pieces are alike. Deftly created by hand, the objects have an individualistic touch. Figurines, horses, drummers, peculiar shaped spoons and hauntingly original tribal Gods can be seen in Dokra. Primarily made from brass scrap, the objects also have a core of clay preserved within the metal casting, unlike other metal work.

Filigree

"Standardisation is alien to them." So say admirers of the silversmiths of Karimnagar - the creators of silver Filigree. Because, the most fascinating aspect of silver Filigree is the element of newness and surprise. Every piece looks different, delicate and unique. In Filigree work, twisted silver wire is the material, and the articles have the trellis-like appearance of 'jali' (net) which endows them with a rare charm.

The silversmith crimps thin strips of fine silver into zigzag patterns and loops using it to fill up the ground of designs formed by thicker silver strips. The- strips and fine silver are then deftly soldered, carefully avoiding the trellis-like Filigree pattern. Leaves, flowers, trees, animals, and birds in the area of origin seem to be predominant. However, the versatility of the art is not restricted by tradition. The art has been extended from jewellery to other household articles like tea-trays, ornament containers, key chains and even cigarette boxes.

Folk Paintings

There is a very picturesque origin to the art of painting. "Narayan", the Supreme Being was engaged in meditation when celestial dancing girls, called apsaras, tried to disturb him with a display of coquetry and blandishments. The God conceived of a plan to cure the maidens of their vanity. He extracted the juice of a mango tree, and using that as his paint, he drew an imaginary portrait of a nymph, large eyed and delicate, with a form so filled with grace that no Goddess or woman, could vie with her in all the three worlds. The apsaras were put to shame when they saw this painted maiden, Urvashi, and crept away silently from God's presence. And the picture, into which Divine skill had infused the golden breath of life, became the ideal form of feminine beauty. Vishwakarma, the architect of heaven, was then instructed in the art and science of painting so that he might transmit his knowledge to the people of the earth.

So in Telangana, in the tradition of the venerable Vishwakarma, the artists created innumerable scroll paintings. Originally used by bards who went about reciting verses describing episodes from religious texts, the artists evolved a method of painting individual situations taken from Indian mythological sources as well as a whole range of village deities in limited sizes. These types of paintings are ideal wall hangings, but if you are lucky you can acquire a scroll running into several metres. Cherial in Warangal District is the traditionall centre of this art.

Another unique item is the peak of playing cards known as ganjifa, a speciality of the craftsmen of Nirmal. They are circular in shape and richly decorated. The method of making these is rather intriguing. They are made from pieces of thin cloth pasted in three layers with a gum-like substance, then coated with liquid chalk to give it a white surface. The pieces are then turned into a round shape, polished with stone and painted like a miniature. The rear sides are then coated with lacquer.

Ikat

Ikat, the technique by which the warp or weft or both can be tie-dyed in such a way that when woven, the 'programmed' pattern appears in the finished fabric. Of resist-dye techniques, the use of clay or wax-resist has long been known to Indian textile printers and painters, who would stamp or delineate the fabric with resist and then immerse and re-immerse in dye. To reserve areas of the warp or weft or both, before the process of weaving with tied threads, and then to dye the yarn, is a more interesting process that requires greater skill. And this seems to be more closely aligned to processes of tie-resist and warp-resist after weaving, than to the application of impression of a resist to the surface of a fabric.

Kalamkari and Block Printed Fabrics

Kalamkari is the craft of painted and printed fabrics. It derives its name from Kalam or pen with which the patterns are traced. It is an art form that developed both for decoration and religious ornamentation. The discovery of a resist-dyed piece of cloth on a silver vase at the ancient site of Haarappa confirms that the tradition of Kalamkari is very old. Even the ancient Buddhist Chaitya Viharas were decorated with Kalamkari cloth. The great

Alexander is also supposed to have acquired this Kalamkari cloth.

In Andhra Pradesh, Kalamkari is done in Machilipatnam and Srikalahasti. With their roots in temple rituals, Kalamkari cloth also followed the old tradition of religious mural paintings.Craftsmen painted the narratives of religious legends from which people learnt the stories of their Gods. Bards recited verses describing these episodes, using these paintings as illustrations.

Lacquer craft

Lacquer craft is the application of lacquer on wood in pleasing shades to create a distinctive appeal. Etikoppaka in Andhra Pradesh is one of the most important centres of this craft. Lacquering is done on a lathe, hand- or machine-operated. For turning slender and delicate items, the hand-lathe is preferred. Lac is applied in a dry state. That is, the lacstick is pressed against the woodenware to be lacquered. As the latter keeps revolving the heat from friction softens the lac, enabling the colour to stick. Designs are painted with a brush on figures, objects and toys. Among the most popular lacquerware are the lac bangles. Hitherto studded with gold and precious stones, today they are also available with beads, glass, stones, mirrors and more.

Sari

Andhra has the bright Venkatagiri saris which are woven with the help of a fly-shuttle loom, thrown from side to side. Venkatagiri saris have pleasant colours with gold dots, coins, leaves, parrots, or simple geometrical patterns. Narayanpet saris, in cotton and silk, come from a place with the same name. The cotton saris woven in dark earthy colours are particularly eye-catching. The pallav in these saris is characterised by a unique pattern of alternating red and white bands. The border is usually a flat expanse of deep maroon red or chocolate red thinly separated by white or coloured lines. These saris follow the Irkal style which has its roots in a place called Irkal in the state of Karnataka. The Gadwal cotton, and Kothakota saris from Vanaparti have rich gold borders and heavy panels like pallavs. Siddipet and Armoor also produce cotton saris with rich designs

Stone Carvings

In classic Sanskrit treatises, the sculptor has been given various names. He is known as the Sadhak (Admirer), the Mantrin (Wizard), and the Yogi (Visionary). This is perhaps explained by the ultimate aim of the sculptor to be primarily spiritual and only secondarily aesthetic. The sculptor was not endeavouring to portray the mere perfection of the physical structure, as with the Greeks. He believed that even the perfect human figure could not fully manifest the higher spiritual values of life, nor contain within itself the attributes and qualities of the divinity. Therefore, to give expression to such abstract conceptions , the sculptor consciously set for himself an ideal, which was not based on the contemplation of the natural form, but upon meditation of the divine form. Consequently, you would notice a distinctive power of suggestiveness in the sculpted forms. Perhaps their supreme function, the idols and forms suggest attributes and possibilities beyond the range of mortals.

But every time the chisel carved a shape, it was based on Shilpashastras (axioms of sculpture). Drawing inspiration from the mind, mythology and experiences, the sculptor has left behind an impression that cannot be ravaged even by time itself. Durgi, Allagadda and Tirupati are among the stone-carving centres in Andhra Pradesh.

Wood Carving

Wood carving is a tradition with some of the tribes of Arunachal Pradesh. The Monpas, Khamtis, Wanchos, Phom, Konyak tribes occupy significant place in this art. Wood carving like in the case of Nagaland finds expression mainly under three categories; firstly, with head hunting, secondly with the decoration of the morungs or men`s youth dormitory and thirdly, the funerary images erected for warriors and other important person.

In carving of the human figure, special attention is paid to the head. The features are carved in low relief and are fairly realistic. Usually the image depicting a warrior is decorated with special cowerie belt and several other artefacts. The top of the head is rounded and usually has some indication of haircut. Tattoo marks are carefully represented, and most figures are dressed up with little bits of cloth and even ornaments with tufts on head or beads in the ear.

Wancho woodcarvers have deep sense of proportion, despite their preoccupation with the head. Of late departure from the traditional fixed form is noticed in many carved figures. Symmetrical postures are replaced by asymmetrical ones, relief works are experimented in various themes.

The Monpa wood carver make beautiful cups, dishes, fruit bowls and carve magnificent masks for ceremonial dance and pantomimes. The Sherdukpen The Khampa and the Monpa make masks which appear almost like real faces, while other represent birds and animals and some represent apes and men twisted mouths, women with goire to drive away the evil spirit.

The masks are made of a single block of wood hollowed inside; holes are usually but not always, made for eyes and mouths; most masks are painted, but the older ones are generally found dark and discoloured. Women never wear the mask which are used only by men and boys.

Kerala has one of the richest traditions in wood carving. Temples and palaces are the best preservers of the wood-carving styles of Kerala. Doors, windows and ceilings of most of the ancient houses are testimonial of the high level of craftsmanship and tradition of wood carving. Carvings are made on rosewood, sandalwood, cedar wood and teak. Life-size wood carved figures which are highly stylised with exaggerated features, gestures and postures like the characters of Kathakali dance drama, mythological and religious figures were produced. Now items also include intricately carved Elephants in different postures, other animal figures, paper weights, lamp stands, Jewellery Boxes like Nettoor jewellery boxes in its unique conical shape, with brass edgings at the corners, decorative furniture etc. Kerala style of work on sandalwood and rosewood is quite distinct from that prevalent elsewhere.

The main centre for the craft is Ernakulam district in Kerala. Rose wood and white wood pieces are cut into required sizes and pasted on a plywood base according to the particular design and polished. The brass metal pieces are fixed in different designs to make the final product. The product include Dancing Lady, Peacock, Candle Stand, Star Wheel, Kathakali Heads, Key Stand and Butterflies etc.

Screw pine mat weaving is an ancient craft and one of the major cottage industries in Kerala. Three types of mats are woven with Screw pine leaves. The main centres of this craft in Kerala are Karunagapalli Taluk of Kollam Dist, Mavelikkara and Karthikapalli Taluks of Alappuzha dist. Thazava, Vachrai and Vallikunnam Panchayaths, some villages in Thiruvananthapuram and Kottayam Districts. Screw pine leaves are also woven, hand embroidered and shaped into products like household linen, straw hats, and carry bags.

Walnut and chinar wood, abundant in Kashmir, provides material for the wood-carving, which is among the best known cottage industries of Kashmir.

To make excellent furniture and toilet articles such as chairs, cabinets, writing-or dining- tables, jewellery boxes and ornamental caskets, which are greatly appreciated. Some of the walnut wood products-cigar boxes and trays, table-tops, handkerchief and collar boxes-are delicately carved. Floral designs of almost every conceivable variety are made with great accuracy of detail in chased or raise work.

Weaving

Weaving is the occupation of the womenfolk throughout the territory. They have an excellent sense of colour. The basic colours that dominates the weaves are black, yellow dark blue, green and scarlet - all put together in the most fascinating combinations. Originally natural dyes were used which today have given away to synthetic dyes.

Pottery

Dafla women are skilled in this craft. The legend is that Abo Takam was the first Dafla potter and from him the art passed on to the women. The process involves pounding a specific kind of earth called dekam on a big stone with a wooden hammer. When it turns into powder, water is mixed and it is hammered till it gains the required softness. Clay lumps are taken home. The woman sits with a piece of gunny bag, or old fibre blanket spread over her thigh. She takes a lump and shapes it with her finger into a crude pot with a shallow opening at the top and rim round it. When several such crude pots have been shaped they are kept in the top-most tray over the hearth to dry.

Making of Sudhum

The Apatani smoking pipe is called sudhum. The bowl is made from a cane called tarre while the stem is made from the reed bamboo called pepu. The hollow of the bowl is created by burning, to remove the soft pulpy centre of the cane. A similar pipe is made by the Apatanis where the bowl is made from bamboo. The Nishi tribe of Subansiri District in Arunachal makes a pipe similar to the Apatani one, and is called hutusilli.

Making of Yatee

The Yatee, the Apatani rain shield from Arunachal, is made in two parts, held together by long loops of twisted bamboo rope. The top part is rectangular. The second part is a flat rectangular piece that shields the back. Both parts have braided bamboo straps that rest on the forehead.

When the top part is not required, it is pushed back to hang suspended from the back shield by two long loops of twisted bamboo rope. Both parts are made with two layers of an open-hexagonal weave, sandwiching a layer of leaves between them. All the edges are held between two half splits of cane tightly bound together.

Making of Monpa Hat

The Monpa tribe of Arunachal Pradesh uses a shallow conical hat to protect them from the sun and rain. The hat is made in two layers. The outer layer is woven in close diagonal twill, while the inner layer is made in an open-hexagonal weave. To make the hat waterproof, a layer from the stem of a banana tree is dried and sandwiched between the layers.

The layers are held together around the edge which is sandwiched between two strips of cane, tightly bound together. A braided bamboo headband is fitted inside the hat, which is held on to the head by a strap looped below the chin.

Making of Bopa

The Apatani and Nishi tribes of Arunachal use coiled hats that fit close on to the head like a skull cap. The bopa is slightly conical in shape. These hats are decorated with twisted cane ropes, and a hornbill beak that is dyed red.

Making of Bolup

The bolup is a hat used by the Adi Gallong tribe of Arunachal. It is made by coiling lengths of cane to obtain a semi-elliptical bowl with a horizontal boat-shaped rim. The hat is extremely sturdy. A similar construction is used in hats made by other tribes of Arunachal. The form and decorative elements vary, but the basic structure is similar. In some cases, there are thick strips of cane that are tied onto the head as extra protection. In other hats, dyed wool or feathers are used as decorative elements

Ornaments Making

Ornaments making is a craft widely practised in Arunachal Pradesh. The work of a silver smith is more intricate and artistic. The first stage in the manufacture of the traditional ornaments he makes, is to make a wax mould of the ornament. This is done by warming the wax sticks or coils and then placing them on the standard moulds made of wax and wood. Where design are essential, they are made with thin wax coils and cut with a knife where necessary.

Once the wax mould is ready, the next stage is to make the earthen container for mould and metal. For this purpose, a wet mixture of clay and charcoal dust called takam is used. A lump is placed on a bamboo frame and shaped flat with a knife and spittle. The mould is first covered inside with charcoal dust and then placed on it. A small plug of wax is stuck to it, joining it at the other end to the bottom opening of a small banana-leaf funnel. The mould and the funnel are finally covered with charcoal dust, shaped to smoothness, and allowed to dry near a fire.

After sometime the banana funnel is removed and the empty place is filled with metal pieces. The mouth is covered with a potsherd, and sealed with charcoal dust. It is dried again. A hole is made almost in the centre of the funnel and the earthen container is ready for the next operation which is burning. The hard and dry wood of the taja tree is used for melting metal. The earthen container, with its mouth downwards is supported on the hearth-stones. It is covered with fire wood and set to fire.

After about twenty minutes the metal is tested by inserting an iron rod in the hole. When it turns into liquid and discharges a turquoise flame, the earthen container is removed with the help of two pairs of strong bamboo tongs and slowly turned upside down. The wax in the mould is burnt by then and the plug has disappeared, leaving a passage for the molten metal to pass into the mould.

The molten metal fills the empty space created by the wax mould. This is what is technically known as the cire perdue process, and is prevalent in Mexico and other parts of the world. The ornaments thus cast is taken out by breaking the earthen container. It is scraped with a knife and rubbed with stones to make it clean and bright.

Besides beads of various colours and sizes blue feathered wings of birds and green wings of beetle are used in decoration. The Noctes and Wanchos tribals weave the beads in their own unique and distinct patterns. Wanchos make ear-ornaments from glass beads, wild seeds, cane, bamboo and reed.

The gallong women wear ear-plugs and the earring. Plugs are generally of leaf, wood or bamboo, while the rings are heavy for they are made of iron. The rings are coiled in several turns and specially used by the Karka Gallong women. Very often women have their ear-lobes slashed due to the heavy weight of the ornaments. Yet, the women never give up wearing them. In such cases, the rings are not worn in the lobes but are suspended with the help of a string below the ear- lobes. Bead necklaces are worn by both men and women alike.

Every bead has its own value, according to its colour and lustre. Sometimes, the bead necklaces are so numerous and heavy that if there is no cloth over the breasts, these bead necklaces can easily cover them. Brass wristlets are common and three to eight wrislets with increasing circumference from wrist to elbow are worn by the women. Around the waist, men wear several cane strips, which with constant use attain a shine and smoothness.

Iron discs, varying in number and fastened together with a cane string or thread are worn by women around their waist. The larger disc is in the middle, hanging in front and the succeeding ones gradually diminish in size and are on both sides of the largest one towards the thighs. Women generally wear cane anklets. A thin strip of cane work is woven on the legs between the ankle and the knee. Necklaces made of metal coins are much favoured by the Gallong women. Such necklaces generally contain one - rupee, eight-anna and four anna coin. Hooks are made on the coins and these are suspended with thread. Waist band of leather, studded with stones is another ornament. The stone are bigger in front and smaller towards the end. One such band generally contains from 100 to 150 stones.

The Aka women wear number of ornaments of silver. The common silver ornaments are melu- a flat-shaped ornament worn over the chest, rombin- the big ear bulbs, gichli- the ear- rings and gejjui-the wristlets. Well-to-do women specially wear a fillet of silver chain work called lenchhi. Along with these ornaments, women also put on around the neck a number of coloured bead-necklaces.

Ancestral necklace called aesheri, is worn invariably by women and often by men. It forms a necessary part of a girl's dowry to be given to the groom at the time of marriage. It is regarded as sacred and more valuable than other ornaments since it is a part of the ancestral property of the house.

The ornaments of the idu mishmis are few and simple. The men and women wear necklaces of various kinds of beads. The most common necklace is the arulaya, which consists of forty to sixty white beads strung together. Another kind of necklace is the lekapon made of small white beads in twenty strands. Usually both men and women wear a cylindrical piece of bamboo in the extended lobe of the ear: some wear silver rings adorned with either silver coins or beads of red and blue. Akakhre are earring made of thin silver-plate and worn by women.

Mithila Arts

Bihar boasts of an enviable wealth of rural handicrafts comprising of hand—painted wall hangings,wooden stools, miniatures in paper and leaves, stone pottery, bamboo and leather goods, and applique work. But Bihar's most famous and fascinating indigenous art forms, by far, are its Madhubani Paintings.

This art is a strict monopoly of the women of Mithila. Done in primary colours of natural origin on paper and cloth, they narrate mythological and religious events.

North of the river Ganges, in the state of Bihar lies a land called Mithila, shaded by old mango groves and watered by melt water rivers of Nepal and the Himalayas.

The men of the community have been famous as priests and scholars. The women largely illiterate, find cultural expression through exquisite paintings created for ritual occasions. They cover their courtyard walls in abstract images in brilliant colour, resembling in form and function the sand paintings of the Navahos.

In the 1960s some local officials realised that if the women would only put some of their paintings on paper there might be a worldwide market for their creations. They proved to be correct and it is a mild irony in Mithila that the fame of the women has surpassed that of the men, because Mithila Art, otherwise known as Madhubani Paintings also, is now recognised throughout the world.

The art of Mithila is linked to religious ceremonies, particularly marriage and its consequence, procreation. Interspersed with the Vedic marital rites, with the Sanskrit chanting by the Brahmins, is a tradition controlled by the women and devoted to female deities Durga, Kali and Gauri.

The bride and groom are pulled away by the women for their own ceremonies devoted to Gauri in which men other than the groom are forbidden. Gauri is the goddess to whom the bride has prayed since childhood to bring her a good husband. These ceremonies are performed in courtyards before painted images of the goddesses. The function of the paintings being ritualistic the art is very symbolic.

The primordial energy of the universe is embodied in various female forms, both living women and Goddesses. Some common themes include one of the Snake goddess, a form in which snakes are worshipped at Nag Panchmi during the monsoons, a time when snakes abound. Durga astride her tiger is another common representation. Probably the most powerful symbolism is the one associated with Duragoman Puren.

A single seed that is dropped in the pond produces many lotus flowers, an appropriate thought for the bride and the groom at the time of their wedding. Lakshmi, the Hindu Goddess of wealth, is a newer and common addition to the repertoire of Mithila symbolism. Among the male deities Ganesha, Krishna and Shiva are more commonly depicted.

Trees, birds and animals are extensively used in combination with other ritual and religious paintings. Sometimes, rarely, one will see these alone without religious implication.

Wall Paintings

The paintings on wall have deeper themes, also narratives, for they are the stories being told sometimes in a series of panels. Apart from their decorative purpose, they also constitute a form of visual education like picture books, from which ones learns of ones heritage. Some outstanding ones are done in the Madhubani area. They have a naivete and simplicity which perhaps is their attraction, that both soothes and pleases the eyes.

The multiarmed *DURGA* riding the lion flanked by serpents, with their upraised hoods, is awesome. The subject matter varies according to the occassion. The Gods and Goddess are normally there to bless. Their most elaborate picture is in the nuptial chamber the "Kohbar Ghar" designed to bless the couple. Here there will be divine couples like *SHIV-PARVATI, RADHA-KRISHNA*, then the signs of fertility and prosperity for good luck like elephants, fishes, parrot, turtoil, the Sun, the Moon, bamboo, shrubs in bloom and trees laden with giant flower.

The women with very limited resources use indigenous colours that they can make themselves and find bamboo sticks wrapped in cotton for painting. Painting on the wall is communal act done by all the women of a family or group.

The palace at Chamba, the Akhan Chandi palace, the Laxmi Narayan temple, the living rooms of old houses in Durga Mangnu and the palaces of Bilaspur have beautiful wall paintings. The Kangra fort, the Narvadeshwar temple, the palaces at Sujanpur and the temples and palaces at Vijapur and Alampur also have wall paintings. In Kulu the tradition of decorating the palace walls with wall-painting began during the reign of king Preetam Singh.

The wall paintings in the Sheesh Mahal show the influence of the Kangra school. Connubial paintings (Dehre) and ornamental door hangings are examples of this art. These are usually made in houses of the rich by women from poorer families. Their subjects deal with traditional and mythological figures like Ganesh, birds, flowers, vedika scenes, Kahars carrying Palanquins, the bride and the groom, the barber and his wife ,the *Shehnai* players and women folk all dressed in local finery. The wall paintings done by women on the occasion of fasts and festivals describe the stories connected with the occasion.

Sikki Works

The sikki grass articles made by the women of North Bihar are entirely different from anything else you see in any other part of the country. Sikki seems to grow almost anywhere in this region, even by the road side , tall and rush with a lovely golden shade, it is most attractive. It is out only once after the rain and the cut pieces are stored for use throughout the year. As it is intimatily connected with important ceremonies and rituals, it has evidently come down from very ancient times.

The coiling technique, which is the oldest, used in sikki. The common long grass is wired and stitched together with the pasikki, dyes in several different shades, using a thick needle called takua. Espacially in constructing the sclespturelque a forms, the whole build up is made by the coils. There are human figures, animals, birds.

Tasels are used for extra embellishment and brilliantly hoed wings of the betle or coloured buttons to emphasise eyes and ears. Every functional item such as a box for keeping cloths,spices toilet articles are all wrought out of sikki in multitude of shapes in dazzling colours.

Tikuli Art

This art originated from the gold foiled Tikuli, bindis with a glass base, adoring the forehead of the Queens and Aristocrats ladies of yore. Today hard board, enamel paints and Madhubani motils are used to create produce for interior decorations and utility items like tablemats and coaster. Making of the hard board plates follows a Japanese technique. In 1982, the then Indian Prime Minister Mrs. Indira Gandhi, chose Tikuli as official gift for the International athletes participating in the Delhi Asiad. These art pieces are heat proof and water proof.

Tapper Mats

Tapper mats are made on a large scale in Palamau district, Bihar. Tapper is rather like jute, taken out of the sun hemp plant. The usual method of soaking and using pressure is used to extract the fibre which is then spun into yarn and used for making tapper. This is said do be more durable than jute fibre. The yarn is dyed generally in indigenous colours which used to transport grain on any heavy stuff.

Today a number of article, of modern use are made like travel kit and hand bags, some of them quite; stylish looking. Hazaribagh and Purnea also produce tapper.

Metalware

The metalware in India may be roughly divided into the religious images, ritualistic items and objects of utility. The metal used are brass, copper and bell metal. The raw materiai is obtained either through smelting minerals or more often by melting old scrap and how more often through sheet metal.

The shopping of an object is done either by beating with a hammer the ingot or sheet metal to the approximate shape while heating, or by pouring the malted metal into a mould made of eleey for ordinary ware, wox for more delicate objects. Polishing is done by vigorous rubbing either by hard or if it is a plate by feet, using a rag or by machine where power is used.

Mask Making

Mask making is an exciting craft, for it calls for something more than more workmanship. The dance in Bihar is highly sophisticated and uses masks. The mask one may say mirrors the essence of the dance, for the totality of the emotions is crystallized in it.

Among the paper mask of Bihar, apart from the figures, there are others of quite distinctive variety. As mask is an essential item in certain presentations, mask making has been a heredity vocation. But the various thing is that traditionally only those who were dancers were permitted to make their masks. Originally, they were made of wood, later of bamboo, then pumpkin shells and now of papier mask.

Bronze Sculptures

Studios in Chatarahadi, Bharmaur and Bojora have produced several beautiful bronze sculptures in the past.

The statues of Ardha Vishnu are beautiful examples of the art of metal casting. Some statue forms found in the state are those of *Shiva* and his wife *Parvati, Ganesh, Vishnu* in Baikunth, Uma-Maheshwar, Mahishasur Mardini (Durga), Kartikeya and Durga as Shakti. Their shapes and postures follow the strict classical patterns. The Shimla and Nirmand areas produced good artists.

The traditional metal (brass and bronze) pots produced locally have a beautiful finish. The Mangath region in Kangra district is well-known for brass utensils. Many of these Musarabbas (brass pots for storing water), tumblers, platters and charotis (large pots used for feasts), boxes and articles used for puja, bells, stools and tables display beautifully rendered floral motifs and miniatures.

Stone Sculpture

The temples and Madhis in the Himachal area are full of stone statues of deities. The tribal areas have their own kind of statues which reflect the religious beliefs of the tribals.

In the Googa Madhis in the villages, the Googa and his Googadi, his horse and soldiers are carved out in great details. Many walls display beautiful relief work. The Shiva temple at Baijnath and the Krishna temples at Masroor are carved out of a single rock. The temples at Chamba, Mandi, Kulu and Bilaspur areas display feats of architectural skill by local artisans much before the advancement of science.

The stone masons are known as 'Batai Hadai'. Large buildings and small articles of daily use in the houses like pounding stones, moohras, pots and basins also display the skill of local masons amply. Many houses have statues of lord Ganesha near the door. These and the divine animal statues in the local temples are all carved locally.

Stone masons can be found in each area and locality in Himachal.

Pahadi Handkerchiefs

The Pahadi handkerchiefs enjoys a special place among the handicrafts of the area. These handkerchiefs are produced in the Chamba, Kangra, Mandi, Bilaspur and and Kulu areas. Originally the art came to Chamba from Basohli and the king Samarchand of kangra helped it grow and spread all over the region.The Handkerchief has come to be known as the Chamba handkerchief and it is said that this art was patronised by King Rajsingh and his queen Sharda of Chamba.

These handkerchiefs are made of square or oblong pieces of cloth and are embroidered all over with silken threads. The embroidery depicts scenes from the life of the Lord Krishna and the Puranas. Some of them depict the classical Ragas and Raginis of India. Some times little round pieces of mirror are incorporated beautifully into the embroidery pattern .

Thapada (a large embroidered shawl), Kohana (a wall hanging), pillow covers, blouses and caps are also embellished with fine embroidery. The caps in the Kulu, Sirmair, Kinnair and Lahaul regions are also embroidered. The shawls from Kulu, woolen rugs and carpets from Lahual all depict the traditional Pahadi designs. Beautiful patch work quilts, rag dolls and elephants are also made in the area. These dolls and elephants are necessary parts of bride's trousseau.

Dyeing and printing of fabrics has been a traditional craft in the area. This work is done traditionally by the Farahada and the Chhiba people. The long knee length gown worn by he Gaddi women known as Juan chadiyan and their Chola (a white woolen garment) are good examples of this art. Fine gold ornaments are also crafted by the local gold-smiths. The jewellery by the woman of Kulu, Sirmaur, Kinnaur, Pangwati and Bharmor region is very attractive.

The Dom tribe in the area is well-known for producing fine house hold articles made of bamboo which are painted in brilliant colours. They produce boxes, sofas, chairs, baskets, racks and several articles of daily use. Leather craft is highly developed and the slippers and shoes made in Chamba are in great demand. Presenting the bride and the groom with gold embroidered slippers at the time of a wedding signifies good taste. But now people are using shoes, mass produced in factories and so this art is slowly dying out.

The custom of embellishing the body with tattoo patterns is common in the Himachal. The figures made by tattooing range from one's name to birds and flowers and figures of gods and goddesses. This is usually done during fairs and festivals. The tribal women under go the tortuous operation quite cheerfully. Henna is also used for embellishing palms and soles of the feet. The Kinnaur and Kulu areas produce beautiful masks.

The Himachal folk are adept at the art of making pots and figurines with clay. These pots are crafted in many shapes and sizes and include pitchers, bowls, platters, cups, lamps and small and large pots. These are decorated with white patterns drawn with Golu clay. Toys and figures of gods and goddesses are made during festivals .One such festivals is Rali, when the figures of lord Shiva and his wife Parvati are made. Culinary arts have also developed in the area. Cooks from Kinnaur and Kulu are invited to faraway palaces to prepare feasts at which they serve traditional delicacies.

Shawl Making

A unique position among Kashmir textiles is held by the

celebrated shawl. The process of shawl-making is fascinating from the start. Assiduously, women sort out of the lustrous, rough substance from the smooth fleecy wool of the Kel goat, and they ply it over a charkha (handloom) of the indigenous type, while chanting folk-songs. This fabric, called pashimina, takes two forms of the loom: the loom shawl (entirely woven on the loom) and the embroidered shawl, which is woven with an embroidered pattern. The celebrated 'ring shawl' has been given in the popular name, because it can actually pass through a ring. Rare and different from the others is the Jamavar shawl. In this case, the threads of the warp and weft are dyed before weaving. The peculiar charm of this famous shawl is derived from the symphony of colour schemes depicting architectural and mythological figures interwoven with landscape designs.

A high-class shawl is expected to have the designs worked evenly on both sides. The price of a pashmina shawl may range anywhere from a few hundred rupees to thousands of rupees, depending upon the craftsmanship and the time factor involved in its creation.

Carpets

The namda, felt rug, made from beaten wool, which is then embroidered over, is an important branch of the kasida industry of Kashmir.

The gabba- a unique type of floor covering, prepared from old woolens in a variety of forms and designs- come next to the namda industry, and its manufacture is localised at Anantnag (Islamabad). Baramulla specialises in printed gabbas. The chain-stitch rung, which resembles the gabba carpet, is also manufactured economically, as the base is Hessian cloth and coarse wool, over which floral and other motifs are worked.

The carpet industry, introduced into the Valley by Sultan Zain-ul-Abidin, justly renowned. From the point of weaving, carpets are broadly divided into two classes: smooth-faced carpets and pile carpets. Pile carpets (kalins), made in Kashmir since the Muslim rule, attained great perfection. Worked with floral and other designs, the hand-woven pile carpet became the national craft of Kashmir.

Coconut Shell Craft

Coconut shell craft is a popular craft in Kerala as coconut trees are found in abundance here. A high degree of skill is required for carving coconut shell as it is hard. The main centre for coconut shell craft is Calicut district in Kerala. The common products are cups, flower vases, snuff boxes, sugar basins, nut bowls, powder boxes and spoons etc and also products decorated with brass, which are in great demand.

Coir Products

Making of coir and its products one of the main village industry of Kerala. Coir is extracted from the protective husk of the Coconut. Coir is used to make a range of floor coverings, door mats, floor Mattings and rugs, crush-proof pile carpets, Flowered Mourzouks etc. The mats come in a range of colours and intricate designs. Besides that rubberised coir, a blend of coir and latex, is also used to make mattresses and cushioning. The husks separated from the nuts, are retted in lagoons upto ten months. The retted husks are then beaten with wooden mallets manually to produce the golden fibre. The fibre is later spun into yarn on traditional spinning wheels called "Ratts", ready for dyeing and weaving into myriad shades of floor coverings. Some of the main centres for coir products are Alleppey, Kollam and Calicut.

Horn carving

Horn carving is an ancient craft practiced mainly by artisans belonging to Viswakarma Community in Thiruvananthapuram. A wide range of products like flower set, birds, animals, combs, cigarette cases, lamps etc. are made out of horn.

Bamboo Mat Paintings

Bamboo mat painting is one of the major craft in Kerala. The artisans initially make mats of required size as canvas and paint on it. Painting on the mat requires more concentration than ordinary painting. Most of the paintings are human and religious figures, animals, birds, scenery etc. in different size and in attractive colours. The products looks beautiful with bamboo reed frames at the top and bottom.

Bihar is greatly noted for its bamboo work. Bamboo sends itself to multifarious uses. The use of cut bamboo as a containers to drink water is an ancient practsice; as also simple scoops for kitchen use. Large containers far storing grain are a comman sight. In fact the rural people in remote, bamboo graving are as still keep their precious possessions in bamboo basket with side.

Against this tradition, commendable experimentes work has been done in Patna to adopt these very objecte to modern use, In fact a whole house can very neatly be filled up through bamboo articles. Finely shaped lamps and lanterns, elegant furniture, complete tableware, travel kit, almost anything seems possible to get from the bamboo.

Metalwork

Metal work is an ancient art of Kerala. The production of

Temple bells and lamps have been in existence from very early times. Kerala is a home of bell-metals. Gleaming bell metal alloyed from a mixture of brass, tin and copper provide the raw substance for making tower-like lamps. Different types of cooking vessels, like the magnificent 'Varpu', tumblers for drinking etc are some of the other bell metal items. Trivandrum, Irinjalakuda and Kasargod are the main centers of bell-metal.

The religious icons from Kerala has a wonderful directness, devotion and serenity associated with them like the unusual icon of the tandava dance, known as gaja tandava or gajasamhara, where Shiva is crushing the demon in an elephant form. The chief centres in Kerala for icons are Trivandrum, Payyanur is Cannanore district, and Angadipuram in Palghat district. A special and famed product of Aramula, a village near Chengannur in Kerala is the metal mirror made out of an alloy of copper and tin and its polished face resembling glass because of its wonderful reflecting quality.

7

Fairs and Festivals

India is a land of myriad festivals, in rhythm with the cycle of the seasons, with sowings and harvesting. and around them have grown legends, most depicting the victory of good over evil. These fairs and festivals lend color and gaiety to life and Indian calendar is marked by plethora of such big and small occasions. Some festivals are of religious nature, others are related more to, change of season and harvesting. They have a long past and many have undergone major modifications.

Though the enthusiasm for some also seems to be fading, nevertheless they do bring about a change in the lifestyle of the people. Some festivals and fasts are religion specific protocols aiming towards communication with the divine. The liveliness of the people is reflected in the colorful vibrancy of the fairs and festivals. Processions, prayers, new attires, dance, music etc. are elements related to any such celebration.

Adi Festival

The 'Solung' is the main festival of 'Adis' and is a manifestation of the Adis festival cult in Arunachal Pradesh. There are various stories about its origin, but the most commonly accepted one is that the Adis were asked by Kine-nane, the Goddesses of wealth and prosperity to perform the Solung Puja. The story goes like this. One 'Doying-Bote' (god of heaven) came in contact with Kine-nane and become sexually excited.

When he was about to copulate with her two monsters Totel-Mone and Dubeng-Mone, intervened and snatched off his testicles to destroy it and in the process scattered the divine sperms over different places from some of which sprouted paddy plants. This was found by Kine-nane. Finding human beings starving for want of food, she sent the paddy seeds through a dog.

Since then men have been producing paddy in plenty to meet their requirement of feed. Kine-nane asked the men so helped by her to offer Puja in the name of Solung which they were only too willing to do. Kine-name also helped them to acquire Mithun, and pig, the two animals which are sacrificed at the time of Solung.

In the Solung they try to propitiate both Doying-Bote and Kine-nane and if they are pleased and satisfied the former will appear in the form of clouds and rains and latter will appear in the form of great fertility of soil. They land together on the surface of the earth where ultimately their union take place. It is believed that their successful union will lead to high yields of crops, more animals like mithun, pigs etc and ultimately wealth and prosperity for men.

Solung celebration continues for five days, first day is called, 'Solung-Gidi Dogin' or the day of preparations, second and the main day of the celebration is called Doreph-Long (the day of animal sacrifice), third day is 'Binnayat Binam' or worshipping the goddess of plenty and prosperity. Fourth day is Yaktor of Ekoph when the villagers remains busy preparing bows and arrows and other weapons of war. On the fifth day the Miri (religious leader or priest) is given a ceremonial send off when the girl's sing and dance.

During Solung festival, every evening the Miri sings 'Solung Abung' and through the song he relates the stories about the origin of man, animals and plants, ancestry of the Adis, lives and deeds of the Adi Heroes. Solung is celebrated in the month of August or September but there is no fixed date for it. Now-a-days in some places, the festival is celebrated with a three day programme. Solung is celebrated to reap a rich harvest after sowing of seeds and transplantation of paddy plants, to raise more mithuns and pigs and also to be free from natural calamities, fire, accidents, diseases etc.

Myokoh-Apatani Festival

It is the most highly solemnized community festival of the Apatani society in Arunachal. It is purely a religious ceremony which is observed for the general well being of the whole Apatani society and is participated by each and every Apatani with great enthusiasm, devotion and respect. It is celebrated every year during the month of March and lasts for the whole month. For full participation, the whole Apatani villages of the plateau have been divided into three major groups-the first group consist of villages like Hija Duta, Mudangtage, Bamin and Michi.

The second group consist of Hong village alone and the third group consists of Hari, Kalong, Tajang and Regu. The actual solemnization ceremony is conducted alternatively among the three major groups and then the other groups take full participation with the villages who actually perform the ceremonies.

Dree—Apatani Festival

The Apatanis observe a series of agriculture rites and festival by sacrificing domestic fowls, animals and eggs in different times, starting from the sowing to the harvesting periods for ensuring of bumper yield of crops in the year such as Dree, Tamu, Metri, Chandii and Yahung etc. Chandii Tamu rite is performed during the sowing period, Dree during every growing periods of crops and Yahung just before the harvest.

The literary meaning of 'Dree' is one who borrows or purchases food grains from others in order to meet out the shortage by addition to one's old and new stock of food grains. During Dree festival, a few rites are performed to worship and appease Gods and Goddesses, who protect the crops, and ensure well-being of man. These divinities include Tamu God, Metii God, Sky God and Danyi Pilo (sun and moon).

They are worshipped by offering sacrifices of fowls, dogs, pigs, chickens, eggs, mithuns and cows. The divinities associated with Dree are collectively knows as 'Dree or Dri Wuhi' (Gods). For conduction of ritual of Dree, one or two persons are appointed permanently or temporarily from each clan of the village. These persons are known as Dree Kholi or Dree Gora.

They collect small quantity of rice or millet from each individual in order to meet the expenditure of the ceremony. The collected rice is kept by these persons. When the time of festival approaches, they prepare rice beer and collect the sacrificial animals, fowls, chicken and eggs for sacrifices. After completion of these preparation they inform the people about the date of performance so that they could store the required food grains and fire woods etc for the taboo period observed after the festival.

On the appointed day, the priest, his assistant and other Dree Kholi or Gora sit on the oldest clan 'lapang' of the village after being dressed up as warriors. They recite incantations called Dree Barni for a day. For instance, Hong village priest sits on the lapang of Nami clan, which is one of the oldest clans of the Hong village. After the completion of the recital of incantation, they go round all the clans lapang of their village along with sacrificial animals, fowls and eggs and sacrificial structure (Yuygyang).

All these things are taken to the place of sacrifice. The sacrifice-place is generally located near the river of Apatani valley. The sacrificial structure or Yuygyang is cut into pieces and thrown into the river and it implies that the pests and insects are to be flooded out from the agricultural fields.

The Yuygyang for Dree is constructed from a particular plant called 'pemupello'. Only two pieces are required for the construction of sacrificial structure for Dree. The Yuygyang for Tammu God and Metii are constructed from bamboo decorating it nicely with bamboo shaves and basket (Byodungchukha). The children and women are not allowed to take the meat of sacrificed animals and fowls.

On the festive occasion of Dree, every individual prepares rice beer and women present a vessel of rice beer to their elderly bothers, sisters, son-in-law etc, as a symbol of love and affection. They reciprocate by presenting a piece of bacon or roasted meat of mithun-cow to them. On the same day, the woman and children are involved in rejoicing and merry making singing traditional songs called 'Damingda' which is associated with Dree festival. This song basically welcomes man and god on this occasion, describing the greatness of Apatanis of the past and present, sketches the geographical location 'Khallo Sanii' of the Apatanis and their neighbouring tribes, and recalls beautiful memories of love affairs of man and woman exemplifying their ancestors Loder-Byai and Umi-Ubyang etc.

After observing Dree, seven days taboo period is strictly observed in every village with effect from the date of festival. During this period, people are not allowed to work in the field or garden nor they can bring green vegetables and fire woods. It is believed that if the observance of these taboos is violated the performance at the time of festival may not be successful.

Dree festival has been modernised with increasing popularity all over the state as well as outside. The joint celebration at a central place was started in 1967 at Nenchaya near the old Ziro town by the initiation of intellectual group of Apatanis. Since then the date of celebration of the festival was fixed from 4 to 7th July for every year. They not only introduced folk-song and dance competition, but also introduced various games and sports.

On the appointed day, mithun, cow, goat, fowls and eggs are sacrificed at altar of Dree. In olden days, these were not sacrificed except fowls and eggs. The meat of these animals are cooked and offered to the guest along with rice, cucumber and beer. One of the most important change of the Dree celebration is, singing of 'Dree Flag song' in the inaugural function at altar of Dree and modern songs, dance, games and sports introduced which gives great gaiety of enthusiasm. Now-a-days, they do not strictly follow the religious taboos of Dree. It is celebrated as a seasonal festival of joy and glee when plantations of all crops are over, for the well being of the seasonal crops like paddy, millet etc.

This celebration is done to appease the gods and goddess to ensure better crops and prosperity to mankind. The season is marked by maturity of strawberries and cucumber which are the only two fruits utilised in the celebration of Dree. In this community festival the children normally takes maximum part.

Murang

It is a festival of abundance and richness of wealth and is generally celebrated in the month of January every year. Although this is an individual family festival, the entire Apatani as well as others are also openly invited to take part with a liberty to eat and drink and enjoy freely. It is being celebrated for the well being of the individual family members alone, specially with a hope to be blessed with more wealth and prosperity for that individual family members.

Reh Festival—Idu Festival

Reh is one of the most important festivals of the Idus in Arunachal. The Idus believe that they are the sons and daughters of the divine mother 'Nanyi Inyitaya'. But none can get her blessings and keep alive bond of brotherhood and social feeling strong, unless one performs the puja or celebrate the Reh festival. But it is so expensive that only a few people can afford to celebrate the festival for propitiation of the supreme creator, the great mother 'Nanyi Inyitaya'

The festival is celebrated during February-August. The people who inhabit snow fall areas viz. Talo, Amru, and Dri villages of the Dibang valley celebrate it during summer and monsoon i.e. during June-August, when the climate is moderate and shoal of fishes are available in streams and rivers. The Idus in the other parts celebrate the same during February to May.

The festival requires a number of sacrificial buffaloes for offering to the great mother 'Nanyi Inyitaya'. Presents such as money in cash and pigs are given to the relatives. The festival being very expensive, all arrangements and preparations for the festival have to be made four or five years before the actual celebration of the festival. As such a person wanting to celebrate this festival has to take resort to the system locally called 'Ada' which is nothing but collection of mithuns, pigs, cash, money etc., even by way of loan from others. When 'Ada' is completed a tentative year is fixed about one year ahead of the actual celebration. The preparation of rice beer in large scale locally called 'Yunyiphri' is under taken, three to four months before the actual celebration.

After all necessary arrangements and preparations are made, 'Tayi' a form of calendar is served to all kith and kin as an invitation to come to the celebration on scheduled dates. The 'Tayi' is counted by knots on a string and each knot is cut off as a night passes on, one after another. The invited kith and kin arrive at the place of celebration when two knots remain on the string.

The Reh festival is celebrated for 6 days. The first day is called 'Andropu'. It is observed by offering prayers so that the festival may pass off smoothly. The mithuns are brought and tied near the house. The 'Naya' dance is held during the night. Eyanli is the second day and may be termed as killing day of animals such as mithuns and buffaloes. The guests are entertained with rice, meat and rice beer. The third day is called 'Iyili' and on this day heavy feast is arranged and everybody is entertained. Presents of meal-rice are also supplied to the neighbouring villagers who fail to come to the festival.

Ilyiromunyi is the fourth day of the festival. There is not much feasting on this day. The priest only performs the rituals in favour of worshiper for bestowing upon him wealth, all round prosperity and for general well-being. Omen is observed by pouring 'Yu' rice beer into the ears of a pig, bound and laid on the ground. If the pig does not fidget, it is considered evil and result in bad crops, epidemic etc otherwise it is good.

The fifth day is called Aru-Go. On this day the remaining food stuff and other drinks are prepared for the feast and taken with co-villagers. The sixth day is the concluding day of the festival is known as 'Etoanu'. On this day the blood smeared seeds are sown in the fields and rice beer is poured at the trunk of the stump for the goddess of the house hold.

Tagin Festival

It is the most significant festival of the Tagins and is celebrated in January. Si signifies the earth and Doni is the sun. They believe that, the sun, the moon, the earth and the natural elements around them play a vital part in their day to day functions. It is with these factors in back ground that their important festivals are performed. During the festival 'Etting', rice powder mixed with Apeng (rice-beer) is made to a paste and everyone liberally applied with it.

Everybody contributes in kind and cash. Si-Doni festival being conducted on a large scale cannot be performed individually due to huge expenditure involved. Hence it is celebrated collectively. The local youths work day and night for about a month in preparation of the festival. The elderly person who form the members of the Si-Doni committee direct the operations and the selected Nibu (priest) guides and performs the Si-Doni festival like 1) Sune-Rabo, 2) Takar, 3) Gene Koni Bakar and Hoye Penam. It is understood that by celebrating the Si-Doni festival the creators Si and Doni would not only be satisfied but also bless the people with good crops and prevent diseases. In fact Si-Doni festival is the festival for prosperity, plenty and success. During this festival boys and girls in colourful dresses and split bamboo head gears (Donger) sing and dance.

The major festivals celebrated in assam are Bihu-Bhogali or Magh Bihu (January), Rongali or Bohag Bihu (April), and Kongali or Kati Bihu (May) celebrated by people irrespective of caste, creed and religion throughout Assam. Other festivals are- Baishagu (celebrated by Bodo Kacharis during mid April), Ali-Ai-Ligang (festival of the Mishing tribe, February-March), Baikho (Rabha tribe, spring season), Rongker (important festival of the Karbis, April), Rajini Gabra and Harni Gabra (Dimasa tribe), Bohaggiyo Bishu (spring festival of the Deoris), Ambubashi Mela (most important festival of the Kamakhya Temple is celebrated during mid June every year. It is a ritual of austerities celebrated with "tantric" rites) and Jonbill Mela (spectacular fair held every year during winter at Jonbeel of Jagiroad, near Guwahati) and so on.

The people of assam also celebrate Janmastmi (August), Durga Puja (October), Diwali, Idd, Muharram, Me-Dam-Me-Phi, the birth and death anniversaries of the Vaishnavite saints Shrimanta Sankardev and Shri Madhabdev.

The Maharashtrians are a vibrant, earthy people for whom life itself is a celebration. Small wonder then that all festivals in Maharashtra are celebrated with abundant fervor. These times provide a unique opportunity to absorb Maharashtrian culture, with all its colorful customs, rituals and traditions. The song, music and dance that accompany almost every festive occasion add joy and excitement to the lives of the people from every walk of life.

These festivals attract world-renowned artistes - musicians, dancers, painters, sculptors, weavers - who come together to pay tribute to Maharashtra's rich culture and legacy.

The Maharashtrians are a hearty, festive people. The love for celebration is deeply ingrained in their culture and it finds expression through the various occasions on the Maharashtrian calendar. There is festivity all round the year and people cherish the good times with music, dance and delectable food.

The Most Important festivals are :

— Kumbh Mela

— Nag Panchami

— Narali Pournima

— Gokul Ashtmi

— Ganesh Chaturthi

— Gudhi Padwa

— Pola

— Dussehra

— Diwali

— Makar Sankranti

— Holi

— Modern Festivals

— Pune Festival

— Banganga Festival

— Elephanta Festival

— Ellora Festival

— Kalidas Festival at Nagpur

Maharashtra festivals, are a tribute to its rich culture and legacy. Ganesh Festival, Gokul Ashtami, Diwali, Holi, Dussehra, Padwa etc. provide a common platform for people from all walks of life to interact with one another. In all. Maharashtra signifies culture and a modern cosmopolitan outlook.

Maharashtra celebrates many festivals of deverse hues and colours. The more significant of these are the Kumbha Mela, the Pandharpur yatra etc.

In early January people celebrate Makar Sankranti, the passing of the sun from Dhanu (Sagittarius) to Makar (Capricorn). The sky is ablaze with colourful kites. Sweets flavoured with sesame seed is an important item during this festival. In March, the festival of Holi is celebrated which is a winter harvest and the advent of spring. People throw coloured water over each other and have great fun on this occasion. This is an important festival celebrated all over north India.

Gudhi Padwa is the new year for the Maharashtrians. On this day people offer rituals, prayers, prasad of neem leaves, gram pulse and jagerry and they buy new clothes. Families erect a gudhi or bamboo staff, with a coloured silk cloth and a bright garlanded goblet is hung on top of it.

Kumbh Mela

Situated on the banks of the Godavari, Nasik is an important pilgrimage center specially during the Simbastha Mela held every 12 years. According to Pauranik lore when amrit (nectar) was being distributed, a dispute arose between the gods and demons over the possession of the kumbh. In the tussle, the nectar was spilled at Haridwar, Ujjain, Prayag and Nasik.

Mahavir Jayanti

During April, Mahavir Jayanti is celebrated when thousands of Jains make pilgrimages to Bahubali, where two Jain temples have been constructed one for the Swetambara sect and another for the Digambara.

Christians observe Good Friday and Easter Sunday around the same time.

Buddha Purnima

Buddha Purnima is celebrated in May. Muslims celebrate Bakrid in the same month and Muharram is witnessed in June in remembrance of the Prophet Mohammed on his death anniversary.

The full moon of Shravana is celebrated around August as Shravani Purnima, Rakhi Purnima and Raksha Bandhan. In the coastal areas it is celebrated as Narli Purnima to appease the sea gods. Fisher folk worship the sea and decorate their boats, sing and dance, and make offerings of coconut. Raksha Bandhan is celebrated on the same day in different parts of the state.

Ganesh Chaturthi

The most important Mahrashtrian festival is Ganesh Chaturthi, in honour of Lord Ganesh. It is the birthday of Ganesh - the elephant headed son of Shiva and Parvathi. Ganesh is believed to be the harbinger of good luck who removes all obstacles to success. He brings prosperity and keeps natural calamities at bay in the lives of those who worship him. This ten day festival begins with the installation of the deity, who is then worshipped daily till the immersion on the final day.

Small Ganesh idols are installed in homes. Idols can tower 10m high and weigh several tonnes. On the tenth day, serpentine processions fill the streets and with the accompaniment of drumbeats and music the image of Ganesh is immersed in the water. Devotees chant 'Ganapati Bappa Morya' which means Ganesh, Daddy, please come back soon next year.

Nag Panchami

Nag Panchami, the snake festival, is observed at the village called Battis Shitale in the Sangli district towards the end of August or early September. The devotees collect hundreds of cobras, place them in earthen pots and worship them to the accompaniment of folk dances and song. Later they are carried in processions of bullock carts and chariots. On the following day they are released into the fields from where they were captured.

Dussehra and Diwali

Dussehra and Diwali are celebrated in October and November. Dussehra which is the celebration of good over evil is an auspicious day for new ventures. Tools of trade, vehicles and machinery are worshipped on this day. Diwali which is the festival of lights marks the end of one commercial year and the beginning of another. Homes are decorated with oil lamps. A unique Maharashtrian touch is seen in the akash kandeels or lanterns that are hung outside homes. Bhaubij, the last day of Diwali, is similar to Raksha Bandan and deals with the relationship between brother and sister

Gokul Ashtami

Gokul Ashtami is celebrated in August. Young men form human pyramids to break pots of curds strung high up from buildings. In the villages, the Pola or the harvest festival is celebrated in which bullocks are bathed, decorated and taken out in a procession to the accompaniment of beating drums.

Onam

Onam is the national festival of the people of Kerala. It is the festival of flowers, which falls in 'Chingam' or

Bhadrapada usually in August or September. It is a harvest festival and goes for 4 colourful days with song and Kathakali dances, feasting and boat races.

VISHU

Vishu is one of the important festivals of Kerala. It comes in the month of April. According to the old traditional Malayalam calendar it is the 1st day of the New Year. 'Kani-Kanal' is the main event of the day. The night before Vishu, the mistress of the house prepare the Kani. In big pots, coconuts, fruits, cereals and Konna flower is kept. Behind the pot a mirror and the garlanded deity of Krishna is kept. Around the deity, lighted lamps will be arranged. Early morning on the Vishnu day, the master of the house sees the Kani and then the rest of the family follows. Children's are brought blind folded from their beds to where the Kani is kept. The elder in the family give money to the youngsters and bless them. It is believed that the Kani we see and its good tidings will stay with you till the year ends.

TRIKARTIKA

It is celebrated in honour of Bhagvati. It falls on the day of 3rd lunar asterism. It is the birthday of Bhagvati. The houses are all well lighted and lights are also left burning in the Verandah, front yard and at the gates. There is general illumination through out. Offering are made at the temple of the goddess and women turn out in the evening for worshipping the goddess.

THIRUVATHIRA

Thiruvatira is the women's festival of Kerala. It is celebrated in the Malayalam month of Dhanu. The popular conception of this festival is that it is the commemoration of the death of Kamadevan; the cupid of our national mythology.

8

Coastal Tourism in India

India has almost a 6,000 km long coastline, which is home to some of the finest beaches in the world. More and more holidaymakers are beginning to realize the numerous activities that the Indian beaches can offer together with their beautiful surrounding, and making them their preferred destination. For the unique quality of the beaches in India is that they have something for everyone.

Every beach in India is an experience unto itself, for each beach has an exclusive atmosphere, facilities, level of development and popularity that makes it distinctly different from the others. For instance, some of the more developed beaches of Goa have all the tourist facilities are popular tourist destinations. These beaches are almost always teeming with activity and are full of holidaymakers. The other lesser-developed beaches, on the other hand, are quieter places, which are suitable for those who are looking for some undisturbed peace and quiet.

The beaches of Andaman and Nicobar or the Lakshadweep are perfect for scuba diving and snorkeling, and exploring the rich treasures of the under water world. They are also among the untouched beaches of India that have managed to retain their pristine charm, and are an ideal getaway for nature lovers. Gopalpur-on-Sea, which lies south of Puri is another surviving quiet hamlet with white beaches, picturesque swaying palms, colonial ruins and a few tourists that delights the heart.

Most Indian beaches enjoy a pleasant climate that the Europeans can specially be seen relishing! They also have increasingly modern tourist facilities coming up such as luxury resorts and five star hotels with every modern facility imaginable. The best and the latest water sport facilities are most easily available in the beach capital of India, Goa.

Some of the famous beaches of Goa are - the Anjuna Beach, which is popularly known as the freak capital of the world, and is the perfect place for lazing holidaymakers. Besides the calm waters of the Arabian Sea lapping softly on the Indian shore, Anjuna comes is famous for its full-moon trance and rave parties! Calangute and Baga lie in north Goa, and Calangute is also known as the Queen of Beaches.

Calangute was the first hippie beach resort in India during the hippie era. It is one of the most popular beaches in Goa with a host of facilities to cater to visitors, including beach and water sports like surfing, snorkeling, jet-skiing, boogie boarding, scuba diving, water-skiing, parasailing, windsurfing, and deep sea fishing.

The Palolem Beach is one of the most beautiful and untouched beaches with white sands, coconut palms and a gentle ocean breeze. However, it is hardly developed and travelers will not find the facilities available on the other beaches.

Indian beaches are just the right place for fun and frolic, and either a family holiday or a lone excursion. The hospitality of the people adds to the charm of the beautiful surrounding, as does the all-pervasive holiday mood. While, some of the beaches are well prepared for tourists and appointed with every facility, be it hotels and resorts, beach shacks and small restaurants serving delicious but affordable food, or beach bazaars with colorful balloons, the others are sandy and isolated retreats perfect for unwinding and relaxing.

And what makes matters even better is the fact that should you decide that you have spent enough time at a particular beach, there are numerous others that you can chose from as your next stop. So the next time you are planning a vacation, think of the lovely, languid, and golden beaches of India. Just the thought of all the relaxation and fun that is available here is sure to make up your mind for you!

India beaches have been the perfect destination for the sun-starved traveler from around the world for decades now. The beaches in India offer intoxicating combination of sun, sand and surf with a dose of Indian hospitality. Though beaches all over world are about the three S i.e. Sun, Surf and Sand but beaches in India promise to take you beyond the three S. Ayurveda and Yoga are added attractions on the beaches of India. Relax, rejuvenate and discover a new you on the beaches of India.

BEACHES IN GOA

Anjuna Beach

The Anjuna Beach is rightly referred to as the Freak Capital of the World and happens to be one of the most popular beaches in the Beach Capital of India Goa. The swaying coconut palms and the soft white sand add to the holiday mood on the shore of the Arabian Sea. The hippy hang out of the sixties is still a major draw. Tourists from the younger generations as well as the flower generations flock to Anjuna Beach. Thus, even if you seek nirvana or just want to enjoy the magic of the nature you must head to the Anjuna beach. Take a plunge into swimming the most relaxing water activity that can be pursued at the Anjuna Beach. It is safe as the sea is calm. Sun bathing is the most favored activity of the sun starved European tourists. The more adventurous of you may even try out bungee jumping.

Besides enjoying the natural at its best at the Anjuna beach you may even check out the monumental Mascarenhas Mansion. The Mansion is a must visit owing to its woodwork and the finest floral etchings on glass. Anjuna beach the spot for hippies, parties and techno also boasts of the amazing Albuquerque Mansion. The structure was built way back in 1920. The structure has a beautiful border made up of the octagonal towers. Even the Mangalore tile-roof of the mansion is marvelous.

At Anjuna you may shake a leg at the Acid house parties. The parties that are held on the full-moon nights are a major draw for the tourists. There is trance and then there is of course dance! The fun and frolic around the fire are fantabulous. Anjuna is all for hip-hop! There are amphitheatres, dance clubs, restaurants and bars. All you need to do is just relax and rejuvenate yourself.

For those of you whose holiday is incomplete without shopping Anjuna Beach has the perfect offer- the weekly Flea Market. Every Wednesday it's time for shopping and bargaining at Anjuna Beach. You may take your pick from the Tibetan, Kashmiri and Gujarati trinkets and handicrafts. The beach market offers everything that your heart may desire. The Wednesday Flea Market is a must visit for every tourist.

You may plan your trip to Anjuna Beach any time of the year but the months from June to October may be avoided owing to the heavy rainfall. Rests of the months are pleasant and it's a pleasure to be at Anjuna. There are plenty of hotels and guesthouses that take care of accommodation at Anjuna. There are even some of the houses that may be hired.

Anjuna village that houses the beautiful beach is well connected with the rest of the places. The Dabolim airport is the nearest at a distance of 47 kms. The Karmali railway station takes care of the tourists who travel by train. For road transport there are plenty of bus services besides motorcycles and taxis that may be easily hired.

In order to make the most of your holiday at the Anjuna beach keep away from drugs and nudity. Even though swimming is considered safe you must check out with the lifeguards for the strength of the undercurrents.

Bogmalo Beach

The Bogmalo Beach is one of the most popular beaches in the Beach Capital of India Goa. The swaying coconut palms and the soft sand add to the holiday mood on the shore of the Arabian Sea. Take a plunge into swimming the most relaxing water activity that can be pursued at the Bogmalo Beach. It is safe as the sea is calm.

In fact the blue waters are so clean that is hard to keep away from it for long. The Sun bathing is the most favored activity of the sun starved tourists especially Europeans. The beach unlike the other beaches in Goa is not very crowded. The red brick huts add color to the green coconut canopies. The most picture perfect spot at the Bogmalo beach is at the end of the cove.

The not so long coastal stretch of Bogmalo beach is dotted with several eating joints. You must check out these shacks for some excellent seafood. Besides a lot of food Bogmalo beach offers a wide variety of fun and frolic too. You may indulge into the amazing array of the water sports that are offered at the Bogmalo beach. Surfing and parasailing are amongst the must checkouts any way is to just relax and rejuvenate you.

Near the Bogmalo beach is the must visit tourist destination of the Naval Aviation Museum. This museum will give you a better insight into the Indian Navy. While on the Bogmalo beach you may pay a visit to the captivating café bars or take a pick from the range of Kashmiri handicrafts items.

In order to make the most of your holiday at the Bogmalo beach keep away from drugs and nudity. Even though swimming is considered safe you must check out with the lifeguards for the strength of the undercurrents. There are a lot of hotels and budget accommodations available at the Bogmalo beach to take care of your shelter needs. The beautiful beach is well connected with the rest of the places. The Dabolim airport is the nearest at a distance of 4 kms. For road transport there are plenty of taxis that may be easily hired though there bus services are also available.

Benaulim Beach

Beaches in general don't have a mythological tale attached to them. But Benaulim in Goa is exception to this; it is the place where arrow of the warrior saint Parasurama landed when he ordered the sea to recede. Dolphin cruises are what attract many to this beach. The white powdery sand and cool blue waters are another added attraction. The beach gets crowded during weekends, when local visitors throng the beach.

The Colva and the Benaulim Beaches happen to be amongst the most popular beaches in the Beach Capital of India Goa. The white powdery sand on the shores of the Arabian Sea along with the swaying palms and the sensuous sun creates the picture perfect holiday spot. The beaches are at a mere distance of two kilometers and make excellent holiday destinations.

Besides enjoying the nature at its best at the Colva beach you may even check out the Nossa Senhora de Merces (Our Lady of Mercy) Church. The captivating church is a major tourist attraction. The Landmark hosts the annual religious feast of Fama of Menino Jesuse (Child Jesus). The Catholics have been celebrating the feast in a big way on the third Monday of October every year since the 17th century. The bullfight at the Benaulim beach is a major draw from early October till late May in the evenings. In the old rice fields with the Konkani music in the background the bullfights are a must watch. The Beach Bonanza fair is another must check out for all the tourists. The live music, dance, and other entertainment add to the holiday mood. It is time for more and more merry making. You can participate in the Beach Bonanza on successive Sundays from mid-April onwards.

At the Calangute beach you must check out the local market for some good bargains. The market offers a wide range of items from daily food items to souvenirs. There are artifacts, antiques, and other trinkets that make excellent gift options. In terms of food do check out the Portuguese delicacies that are available in abundance at the seashore. Its time to treat all your senses at the Colva and the Benaulim beaches.

You may plan your trip to the Colva and Benaulim Beaches any time of the year but the months from June to October may be avoided owing to the heavy rainfall. Rests of the months are pleasant and it's a pleasure to be at Colva and Benaulim. There are plenty of hotels and resorts that take care of budget accommodation at Colva and Benaulim. There are even some of the local houses that may be hired. The beautiful beaches of Colva and Benaulim are well connected with the rest of the places. The Dabolim airport is the nearest. The Karmali railway station takes care of the tourists who travel by train. For road transport there are plenty of bus services available.

In order to make the most of your holiday at the Colva and the Benaulim beaches keep away from drugs and nudity. Even though swimming is considered safe you must check out with the lifeguards for the strength of the undercurrents. Get ready to get bewitched by the beauty of the Colva and the Benaulim beaches!

Calangute Beach

The Calangute Beach is aptly referred to as the queen of the beaches and happens to be one of the most popular beaches in the Beach Capital of India Goa. The swaying palm tress and the picturesque saltpans add to the beauty of nature on the shores of the Arabian Sea.

Besides enjoying the nature at its best at the Calangute beach you may even check out the Church of St Alex. The captivating parish church is a major tourist attraction. The Landmark comprises of terrific towers, dome and ornate altars. The style of architecture of the church will sweep you off your feet. Then for the art lovers the Calangute Beach offers the unparallel Kerkar Art Complex. While at Calangute you must check out the complex that treasures exhibits arts and crafts of local artistes. The complex also hosts the concerts for the benefit of the enthusiasts of Indian classical music and dance.

At the Calangute beach you must check out the Saturday bazaar for some good bargains. The market offers a wide range of items from daily food items to souvenirs. Then there is the Tibetan market that offers gems and silverwork, wooden statues of the Buddha's besides Hindu deities. You may pick up the Kashmiri carpets, embroidery, and papier-mâché boxes from the Calangute beach that makes excellent gift items. For some exclusive art pieces pay a visit to the Cocoon Art Gallery.

You may plan your trip to Calangute Beach any time of the year but the months from June to October may be avoided owing to the heavy rainfall. Rests of the months are pleasant and it's a pleasure to be at Calangute. There are plenty of hotels and guesthouses that take care of accommodation at Calangute. There are even some of the local houses that may be hired. The delightful beach of Calangute is well connected with the rest of the places.

The Dabolim airport is the nearest. The Karmali railway station takes care of the tourists who travel by train. For road transport there are plenty of bus services besides motorcycles that may be easily hired. In order to make the most of your holiday at the Calangute beach keep away from drugs and nudity. Even though swimming is considered safe you must check out with the lifeguards for the strength of the undercurrents.

Vagator & Chapora Beaches

The Vagator and the Chapora Beaches happen to be amongst the most popular beaches in the Beach Capital of India Goa. The beauty of Vagator and Chapora lies in their beaches, the wondrous white sands, black lava rocks, swaying palms and the gorgeous greens.

Besides enjoying the nature at its best at the Chapora beach you may even check out the Chapora Fort. The Portuguese fort that was built 500 years ago is now a landmark. The investment of climbing the lava-bedecked black rock stepping-stones returns the soothing sights of the sea and hills covered with coconut trees and rice fields to the tourists. The rural life along the beaches is worth watching, the hurried pace of the urban life is best forgotten in Vagator and Chapora. The picture perfect beaches are just for relaxation and rejuvenation. For colorful nightlife Vagator and Chapora offer several night bars and dance floors.

At the Vagator and the Chapora beaches you must check out the local market for some good bargains. The market offers a wide range of items from daily food items to souvenirs. There are artifacts, antiques, and other trinkets that make excellent gift options. In terms of food do check out the Goan delicacies of 'Bebinca' that are available in abundance at the seashore. Its time to treat all your senses at the Vagator and the Chapora beaches

You may plan your trip to the Vagator and Chapora Beaches any time of the year but the months from June to October may be avoided owing to the heavy rainfall. Rests of the months are pleasant and it's a pleasure to be at Vagator and Chapora. There are guesthouses that take care of budget accommodation at Vagator and Chapora. There are even some of the local houses that may be hired. The beautiful beaches of Vagator and Chapora are well connected with the rest of the places. The Dabolim airport is the nearest. The Karmali railway station takes care of the tourists who travel by train. For road transport there are plenty of bus services available.

Colva & Benaulim Beaches

The Colva and the Benaulim Beaches happen to be amongst the most popular beaches in the Beach Capital of India Goa. The white powdery sand on the shores of the Arabian Sea along with the swaying palms and the sensuous sun creates the picture perfect holiday spot. The beaches are at a mere distance of two kilometers and make excellent holiday destinations.

Besides enjoying the nature at its best at the Colva beach you may even check out the Nossa Senhora de Merces (Our Lady of Mercy) Church. The captivating church is a major tourist attraction. The Landmark hosts the annual religious feast of Fama of Menino Jesuse (Child Jesus). The Catholics have been celebrating the feast in a big way on the third Monday of October every year since the 17th century. The bullfight at the Benaulim beach is a major draw from early October till late May in the evenings. In the old rice fields with the Konkani music in the background the bullfights are a must watch. The Beach Bonanza fair is another must check out for all the tourists. The live music, dance, and other entertainment add to the holiday mood. It is time for more and more merry making. You can participate in the Beach Bonanza on successive Sundays from mid-April onwards.

At the Calangute beach you must check out the local market for some good bargains. The market offers a wide range of items from daily food items to souvenirs. There are artifacts, antiques, and other trinkets that make excellent gift options. In terms of food do check out the Portuguese delicacies that are available in abundance at the seashore. Its time to treat all your senses at the Colva and the Benaulim beaches.

You may plan your trip to the Colva and Benaulim Beaches any time of the year but the months from June to October may be avoided owing to the heavy rainfall. Rests of the months are pleasant and it's a pleasure to be at Colva and Benaulim. There are plenty of hotels and resorts that take care of budget accommodation at Colva and Benaulim. There are even some of the local houses that may be hired. The beautiful beaches of Colva and Benaulim are well connected with the rest of the places. The Dabolim airport is the nearest. The Karmali railway station takes care of the tourists who travel by train. For road transport there are plenty of bus services available. In order to make the most of your holiday at the Colva and the Benaulim beaches keep away from drugs and nudity.

Cavelossim Beach

The Cavelossim Beach is one of the most famous tourist destinations in the Beach Capital of India Goa. The

Cavelossim is considered the most beautiful beach in south Goa. The charming Cavelossim lies between the Arabian Sea and the Sal River.

While at the Cavelossim beach let your hair down and enjoy the quaint natural surroundings. The amalgamation picture perfect paddy fields, the scintillating Sal River and the soft sands create the ambience for the unforgettable beach bonanza. Along with the usual relaxing and rejuvenating activities like sun bathing you may indulge in Dolphin trips and sunset cruises on the River Sal. It is time to enjoy the nature at its best at the Cavelossim beach.

The Cavelossim beach offers a complete holiday with attractive shopping opportunities. Besides the items of daily needs an amazing array of Indian crafts and gifts are also available. Many accommodation facilities are also available on the Cavelossim beach itself. A variety of hotels and beach resorts offer the best of facilities for a luxuries stay at the beach. Though there is ample shelter for the budget tourists too. Food goes hand in hand with at the Cavelossim beach with ample choices.

The charming Cavelossim beach is well connected with the rest of the places. The Dabolim airport provides the connectivity through air. For rail transport there is the Margao Railway Station. Though you may plan your visit of the Cavelossim beach any time of the year though the months from November to March are the best in all respects. In order to make the most of your holiday at the Cavelossim beach keep away from drugs and nudity. Even though swimming is considered safe you must check out with the lifeguards for the strength of the undercurrents.

Candolim Beach

The Candolim Beach is one tourist destination that is far from the madding crowds of the other beaches in the

Beach Capital of India Goa. The quiet resort is charming with the bountiful beauty of nature. The white sandy beach is a major draw now though earlier it used to be the hangout of the few travelers. The scrub-covered dunes enhance the beauty of the straight and sandy Candolim beach.

While at the Candolim beach do not miss out the Aguada Fort. The fort was built by the Portuguese way back in 1912 for defense against the Dutch and the Maratha invaders. Along with the fort the church, lighthouse and the barracks of the Aguada Jail have become tourist attractions.

Take a plunge into swimming or just sun bathe. For the more adventurous amongst you there is option of indulging in water sports like parasailing and jet skiing. The Candolim is the place to be in to spend the evenings in the best possible manner. You must check out the makeshift bars and restaurants made from wood and palm leaves on the beachside.

Besides the fun for food there are several restaurants that offer excellent seafood though the continental dishes are also available. There are many eating joints in the hotels. Many accommodation facilities are also available at the Candolim beach. A variety of hotels and boarding houses dot the beach. The captivating Candolim beach is well connected with the rest of the places. The Dabolim airport provides the connectivity through air.

For road transport there are plenty of buses that ply between Panaji, Calangute via Sinquerim. In order to make the most of your holiday at the Candolim beach keep away from drugs and nudity. Even though swimming is considered safe you must check out with the lifeguards for the strength of the undercurrents.

Dona Paula Beach

The Dona Paula Beach is aptly referred to as Lover's Paradise and happens to be one of the most popular beaches in the Beach Capital of India Goa. The swaying palm tress and the casuarinas groves add to the holiday mood on the shore of the Arabian Sea.

Besides enjoying the nature at its best at the Dona Paula beach you may even check out the National Oceanography Institute. The institute is a must visit owing to the explorations made in marine biology and coastal and marine oceanography. The Marine Biology Museum and Taxonomy Reference Center of the institute is a major draw. The Dona Paula beach has been a used as a backdrop for various film shootings too.

While at Dona Paula you make indulge in sports like windsurfing, parasailing, water-skiing, toboggan ski-biscuit, skibob, sports fishing, snorkeling, harpoon fishing, kayaking, and yachting on the beach. Though water-scooter, cycle, and motorboat rides are also available. The Dona Paula beach hosts the famous annual water sports festival every November. Water scooter and cycle races along with the surfing competitions are held and participated in with much fun and frolic.

At the beach you must check out the local items like straw hats, lace handkerchiefs, and spices. The liquors Feni and port wine that are must buys are easily available. In order to enjoy the natural beauty that is present in bounty at the Dona Paula beach you may take a river cruises on the Mandovi river. You may avail the ferry or the bus services to reach the river from Dona Paula, The sensuous sunrise, sundown, and full-moon cruises are so soothing and unique.

You may plan your trip to Dona Paula Beach any time of the year but the months from June to September may be avoided owing to the heavy rainfall. Rests of the months are pleasant and it's a pleasure to be at Dona Paula. There are plenty of hotels and guesthouses that take care of accommodation at Dona Paula. There are even some of the beachside huts that may be tried.

The delightful beach of Dona Paula is well connected with the rest of the places. The Dabolim airport is the nearest. The Karmali railway station takes care of the tourists who travel by train. For road transport there are plenty of bus services provided by Kadamba Transport Corporation besides motorcycles, auto rickshaws and taxis that may be easily hired.

Majorda Beach

The Majorda Beach is one of the most marvelous tourist destinations in the Beach Capital of India-Goa. The soft white sands will not fail to sweep you off your feet. The gorgeous greens are clubbed well with the wondrous whites! The Majorda Beach has been mystical since ages. It is believed as per the Ramayana in Goa that when Lord Rama was a child he was kidnapped and brought to Majorda! Later, again in life while in quest of His consort Sita He came to the Cabo-de-Rama, which lies at the southern end of the Majorda beach.

The history of Majorda is noteworthy for its bakery and toddy. The sap of the coconut palm i.e. toddy was used to leaven the bread. Till date the art of baking European bread remains unsurpassed anywhere else but at Majorda. Thus bakery and Majorda go hand in hand as Pizza and Italy. Today the Majorda beach has become a major tourist attraction with the amalgamation of nature and surroundings.

Majorda is the treasure of fun and food. You name it and Majorda has it from fresh seafood to the schezhuan specialties and steaks. In terms of accommodation there is a wide variety of luxury hotels and budget shelters. The Majorda Beach Resort is the most renowned with world-class comforts and facilities amongst the many resorts. The marvelous Majorda beach is well connected with the rest of the places. The Dabolim airport provides the connectivity through air. For rail transport there is the Margao Railway Station. Then there are the bus services, motorcycles and the taxis.

Palolem Beach

The Palolem Beach is one of the most popular beaches in the Beach Capital of India Goa and is often referred to as the 'Tiny Bay of Goa'. The swaying palms, the soft white sand along with the gorgeous green mountains add to the holiday mood on the shore of the Arabian Sea. The beauty of the beach makes Palolem the 'Paradise Beach'.

Take a plunge into swimming the most relaxing water activity that can be pursued at the Palolem Beach. It is safe as the sea is calm and the water is shallow. In fact the waters are warm and have very little surf. The water is so clean that is hard to keep away from it for long. The Sun bathing is the most favored activity of the sun starved tourists especially Europeans. The beach unlike the other beaches in Goa is not very crowded in fact it had been amongst the virgin beaches of Goa till now.

In case you know swimming then wait for the low tide and dive into the fresh water stream that flows at the northern end of the beach to explore the tiny island. The high tides are considered unsafe and must be avoided. Dolphin cruises and fishing trips are other exciting options that you may take up.

In order to make the most of your holiday at the Palolem beach keep away from drugs and nudity. Even though swimming is considered safe you must check out with the lifeguards for the strength of the undercurrents. There are a lot of cheap accommodation options available at the Palolem beach to take care of your shelter needs. The Palolem beach is heaven on Earth for the budget tourists. There are the souvenir stalls and the boat parties that add spice to the holiday at Palolem Beach.

The pulsating Palolem beach is well connected with the rest of the places. The Canacona railway station is the nearest at a distance of 4 kms. For road transport there are plenty of buses that ply. Cycles may be hired though there Taxi services are also easily available.

Varca Beach

The Varca Beach is one tourist destination that is not so famous in the Beach Capital of India Goa. The quiet resort is charming with the bountiful beauty of nature. The soft white sandy beach is a major draw for several tourists. The Varca beach is quieter and cleaner when compared with the other renowned beaches in Goa. The palm-thatched long houses dot the sandy Varca beach.

Along with the usual relaxing and rejuvenating activities like sun bathing you may indulge in Dolphin watching and boat trips. It is time to enjoy the nature at its best at the Varca beach. Besides the fun for food there are several restaurants that offer excellent seafood at reasonable prices and good service. There are many eating joints in the hotels. Many accommodation facilities are also available on the Varca beach itself.

A variety of hotels and beach resorts dot Varca. Though there is ample shelter for the budget tourists too in the form of houses that may be rented in the village. The latter offers an excellent first hand experience of the true Goan lifestyle. Though you may plan your visit of the Varca beach any time of the year though the months from November to March are the best in all respects.

The vivacious Varca beach is well connected with the rest of the places. The Dabolim airport provides the connectivity through air. For road transport there are plenty of buses and auto rickshaws. For local transport also scooters and cycles are easily available on hire basis.

In order to make the most of your holiday at the Varca beach keep away from drugs and nudity. Even though swimming is considered safe you must check out with the lifeguards for the strength of the undercurrents.

Velsao Beach

The Velsao Beach is one of the most vivacious tourist destinations in the Beach Capital of India-Goa. This small stretch of sandy beach lies on the southern coast of Goa. With the Bogmalo beach on the north and the Majorda and the Colva Beach on the south the Velsao Beach is easily accessible and makes an excellent day trip from the other beaches of Goa too.

Velsao is a storehouse of natural treasures. The sands seem to beckon the tourists for a walk. The pure air, the cool breezes on the beach, warm waters create the perfect backdrop for a picture. The ambience that is developed is ideal for an unparallel holiday. Away from the madding crowd in the lap of nature you can unwind, relax and rejuvenate yourself. In true sense you can enjoy nature at its best at the Velsao beach. The first hand experience with the rural life will make you relish the sweetness of simplicity in each aspect of life.

Thus, in case you are planning to holiday at a beach consider Velsao. The broad beach that stretches for 20 kms from Mobor to Betul happens to be the most splendid and breathtakingly beautiful. The vivacious Velsao beach is well connected with the rest of the places. In terms of road transport there are regular bus services from Margao, Colva and Vasco-da-Gama. For rail transport the Majorda and the Verna stations. In fact the Velsao beach is just 25 kilometers away from the capital city of Goa - Panjim. You may even ride a cycle from Vasco to the Velsao beach.

Beaches in Tamil Nadu

Mahabalipuram Beach

Though Tamil Nadu is famous for its temples, there are beaches in the state that are equally captivating. Mahabalipuram Beach is one such beautiful beach that attracts tourists from all over India and abroad. Shore Temple is another highlight of the beach.

The magical land of Mahabalipuram is probably one of the finest un-spoilt beaches in India on the coastline of Tamil Nadu. Tourists from across the globe come to Mahabalipuram. On the shores of the breathtakingly beautiful Bay of Bengal Mahabalipuram is truly mesmerizing.

The port town of Mahabalipuram along with its beaches will sweep you off your feet. The beach of Mahabalipuram attracts thousands of tourists throughout the year though the best time to check out the beach at Mahabalipuram is from November to February. While at the beach you may sun bathe, relax, unwind et al.

While at Mahabalipuram you may check out the magnificent monuments besides the beautiful beaches. The rock cut art is amazingly attractive. For the more religious tourists there are the shore temple, rathas, arjuna's penance that are worth visiting. Then there is the captivating crocodile farm, the snake venom-extracting center besides the schools of art and sculpture, which form the prime attractions for tourists. You may plan your trip around the Dance Festival that is held at Mahabalipuram and is hosted by the Department of Tourism of the Government of Tamil Nadu. The classical music, Bharathanatyam, Kuchipudi, Kathakali, Odissi and folk dances will not fail to charm you. Accommodation is easily available with the options from the beach resorts, deluxe hotels and budget hotels.

Mahabalipuram may be easily accessed. Mahabalipuram is well connected through air, rail and road networks. The nearest airport of Chennai connects Mahabalipuram with other major cities of India and the world through frequent flights and trains. In terms of the road transport buses to and from Pondicherry, Kanchipuram, Chengalpattu and Chennai et al ply to Mahabalipuram.

Beaches in Maharashtra

Ganapatipule Beach

The gorgeous beach village of Ganapatipule in the Ratnagiri district of Maharashtra is amongst the virgin beaches on the Konkan coast. The pristine air, the blue waters, the golden sands and the emerald pastures add to the beauty of the holy land of Ganapatipule.

The beach village of Ganapatipule derives its name from Ganapati and Pule. The former is an alias for the elephant headed God Ganesha and the latter means sand dunes. Thus, your trip to Ganapatipule will be considered incomplete without a visit to the Ganapatipule temple. The temple is set at the foothills of the lush green Konkan hills and adjacent to the amazingly beautiful Arabian Sea. It is dedicated to Lord Ganesha and is built on the sand dunes.

Since the 16th century Ganapatipule receives thousands of pilgrims and tourists. People have encircled the sacred hill n number of times. The encircling or pradhikshina is a sacred ritual. Besides the temple you may check out the Malgund, the birthplace of the famous Marathi Poet Keshavsoot or pay a visit to Pawas renowned for the ashram of Swami Swaroopanand.

Ganapatipule provides ample accommodation options. There are the luxury beach resorts and cottages on one hand. For the budget tourists the dormitories and the lodging in the local village houses are possible. The holy land of Ganapatipule offers excellent vegetarian food. The Maharashtrian meals are simple and savored by all. The local flavors are available at nominal prices.

The gorgeous beach of Ganapatipule is well connected with the other cities. In terms of air transport the Ratnagiri airport is the nearest as a distance of 50 kms. Similarly, the railway station on the Konkan Railway Network caters to the needs of the rail travel. Ganapatipule boasts of excellent bus services too. In fact there are luxury buses that ply between Mumbai and Ganapatipule, they cover a distance of 375 kms in an overnight journey.

Beaches in Kerala

Kovalam Beach

Owing to its natural beauty the beach resort of Kovalam is often referred to as the "Paradise of the South". The amazing Arabian Sea, the golden glowing sands and the coconut canopies all come together as a package for the picture perfect holiday. Tourists from across the globe throng the dream destination of Kovalam. Just laze around on a moonlit night! Swim or bath for rejuvenation and relaxation. Feel the cool breeze of the wondrous waves on your face! Better still try out the various Ayurvedic massages. Catamaran cruising is a not to be missed. You may even snorkel and catch some unparallel underwater views. The colorful corals are so captivating!

Life on the Kovalam beach starts late in the day and the fun continues till late in the night. Kovalam offers you some of the best seafood specialties. Do not miss out the lobsters, king prawns and kalamari. Though Kovalam has enough eating joints for the European food too. There are several hotels and budget accommodation options available at Kovalam.

Holiday sans shopping, of course not, Kovalam beach offers hot and happening handicraft items from Kerala as well as Kashmir. These items are excellent options for souvenirs and gifts. Since Kovalam is just 16 kms away from the capital city of Kerala- Thiruvananthapuram, reaching your holiday destination is hassle-free. Thiruvananthapuram happens to be the nearest railway station as well as the airport. Though Kovalam is pleasant throughout the year the best time to visit Kovalam is from September to May.

Beaches Shanghumugham Beach : It is situated about 8km from the city and is a popular city beach adjacent to the Thiruvananthapuram airport. An indoor recreation club, the children's traffic training park, the matsya kanyaka, a gigantic 35mt long sculpture of a mermaid and a restaurant shaped like a star fish are some of the attractions here.

Beaches in Gujarat

Ahmedpur Mandvi Beach

One of the finest beaches in Gujarat, Ahmedpur Mandvi is an ideal spot for water sports lovers. You can enjoy skiing, surfing, Para sailing and water scooting. For the less adventurous one, a quiet stroll along the beach is a wonderful thing to do. One can also enjoy the scenic beauty or explore the fishing hamlets near by. Ahmedpur

Mandvi is probably one of the finest beaches in India on the coastline of Gujarat. Ahmedpur Mandvi is a renowned historic port town of the Maharao of Kachchh.

While on the Ahmedpur Mandvi beach check out the beautiful blue waters, bubbly birds, soft sands and the captivating colorful fishing hamlets. The beach at Ahmedpur Mandvi is heaven for the water sports freaks. There is water scooting, skiing, surfing, Para sailing, and speed boat trips. The less adventurous of you may just laze around or take a stroll on the beach. The picture perfect setting has complimentary water for swimming.

Ahmedpur Mandvi a part of the Junagarh district is easy to reach. Ahmedpur Mandvi is at a distance of 298 kms from the capital city of Ahmedabad and is well connected through air, rail and road networks. The nearest airport of Keshod is approximately 145 kms away; it connects Ahmedpur Mandvi with Mumbai through frequent flights. The Delwada railway station caters to the need of the rail transport to Ahmedpur Mandvi. In terms of the road transport buses from most of major cities of Gujarat ply to Ahmedpur Mandvi.

Porbandar Beach

Amongst the many un-spoilt beaches of Gujarat is the beach of Porbandar on the southeast coast in between Veraval and Dwarka. As a seaport on the Arabian Sea Porbandar is picture prefect with the many beautiful beaches and beach villas.

Besides the beach Porbandar's claim to fame lies in the fact that it is the birthplace of the father of the nation Mahatma Gandhi. Thus, the old residence of the Mahatma Kirti Mandir is a must visit at Porbandar. The residence has been converted into a memorial museum with exhibits providing a deeper insight into the life and times of the Mahatma.

You may get a bewitching view of the beach from the chowpaty where several modern villas have mushroomed. At the beaches of Porbandar you may spot the flamingoes and other shore birds and just unwind yourself by strolling in the lap of nature. There is a fusion of the nature with history. Porbandar lies amidst the hills, overlooks the lake and is on the shore of the Arabian Sea with many monuments that are worth visiting. At the other tourist attraction of Bharat Mandir illustrations of the great Indian men and the religious preceptors are incredible.

The ancient maritime city of Porbandar is now a major center for industries of cement and chemical units. Though dhow making and fish drying still remain important activities. While on a shopping spree you will never run short of items at Porbandar the renowned center for gold and silver trinkets, fine quality silk and cotton.

You can easily access Porbandar. In terms of the air transport domestic airlines connects Porbandar with Mumbai. The western railway connects Porbandar with Ahmedabad. All the major cities of Gujarat are well connected with Porbandar through the State transport buses.

Beaches in Orissa

Puri Beach

Looking forward for an amazingly wonderful holiday? Welcome to the beach of Puri. The pious land of Puri is probably one of the finest beaches in India on the coastline of Orissa. Situated on the shores of the breathtakingly beautiful Bay of Bengal.

Though the pulsating beach of Puri attracts thousands of tourists throughout the year the best time to check out the beautiful beach at the pious Puri is early November when you may participate in the annual Puri Beach Festival. The combination of the crafts, cuisines and cultural of Orissa will not fail to charm you. The catamarans the cane hats will get embossed in your mind.

While at the Puri beach you may take a holy dip or swim in one of the finest beaches in India. Water lovers and pilgrims alike throng the pleasant and pious Puri. The golden memories of the golden glowing sands, the scintillating surf and the beauty of the beach all are unparallel. With time at hand you may move another 8 kms from Puri to the Balighai Beach whose natural beauty has made it a popular picnic spot.

Accommodation is easily available with the options from the excellent guesthouses, star hotels and budget hotels. You just cannot miss the superb sunrise and the sunset at the beach! Shopping at the Bada Danda will complete your trip to Puri. The traditional items that are typical to Orissa and Puri may be picked up easily as gifts and souvenirs.

Puri may be easily accessed. Puri is at a distance of 60 kms from the capital city of Orissa, Bhubaneshwar and is well connected through air, rail and road networks. The nearest airport of Bhubaneshwar connects Puri with other major cities of India through frequent flights. The Puri railway station caters to the need of the rail transport. In terms of the road transport buses to and from Calcutta, Vishakhapatnum, Guwahati, Chennai et al ply to Puri.

Andaman and Nicobar Beaches

Andaman and Nicobar beaches are not only about sun and sand but the beaches here also offer an exciting opportunity to enjoy an exotic marine life. Crystal clear waters and soft white sands are what punctuate the beautiful beaches in the Andaman and Nicobar islands.

Andaman and Nicobar is an archipelago of about 572 emerald islands.

Radhnagar Beach and Vijaynagar Beach

Radhanagar and Vijaynagar Beach in Havelock are real exposures of unpolluted nature for an environment lover. Vijaynagar beach is just infront of Dolphin Yatri Niwas and Radhanagar beach is 7km away from Dolphin Yatri Niwas.

Harminder Bay Beach

These beautiful beaches are situated at Hut Bay island at a distance of 100kms from Port Blair and are connected by Inter Islands shipping services.

Karmatang Beach

Karmatang beach, at turtle nesting ground is being developed as tourist complex. Situated at Mayabunder, northern part of Middle Andaman, 240 kms by road and 136 kms by boat from Port Blair.

Ramnagar Beach

A sandy beach situated at Diglipur Island. It is connected by two daily boat services from Mayabunder and from Port Blair twice a week.

DAMAN & DIU BEACHES

The tranquillity is what symbolises the beaches of Daman and Diu Islands. The twin islands are a perfect example of a place where history and nature meet. Daman was the Portuguese colony for over four centuries and joined the Indian Union in 1961. These twin islands of Daman and

Diu attract tourists from all over the world and offer peace and solitude to city-jaded souls.

Devka Beach

Devka Beach located about 3km from Nani Daman has a long shoreline. There is an Amusement Park here containing landscaped walkways, fountains and children's playground.

Jampore Beach

Jampore Beach located about 3km south of Moti Daman is a pleasant spot. The beach line is broad and even and the solitude and serenity is seldom disturbed. This beach is most suited to swimming. During low tide, one can walk on the soft wet sand right into the sea.

Nagoa Beach

A 20min refreshing drive from the town through the open arid land and dense coconut groves brings you to the Nagoa Beach. It is located in the Nagoa hamlet of the village of Bucharwada. The beach stretching about 2km from one end to the other is exceptionally beautiful and quiet and its horse-shoe shape is unique. It is safe for swimming.

Ghoghla Beach

Ghoghla Beach is among the six beautiful beaches in Diu District. It also has facilities for water sports like parasailing, water scooters etc.

Chakratirtha Beach

Chakratirtha Beach is centrally located and contiguous to

the town at Diu. It is said to be the place where Lord Vishnu left his sudarshan chakra (disc) after killing the demon Jallandhar. The hill and the surrounding areas and landscape has been beautifully illuminated.

Gomtimata Beach

Gomtimata Beach is one of the best beaches of the region. Secluded and spread with natural white sand, it is located at the western corner of the island.

Lakshadweep Beaches

If you are looking for a beach destination, which is different from the rest, Lakshadweep is the place to visit. Lakshadweep is surrounded by water on all the four sides and is made of 36 islands. The turquoise blue and a rich marine life is what attract tourists to the beaches in Lakshadweep.

Kavaratti

Fifty two mosques are spread out over the island, the most beautiful being the Ujra mosque.

A well within its precincts is believed to contain water of curative powers. The Ujra mosque has an ornately carved ceiling, said to have been carved from a piece of driftwood. The aquarium with tropical fish and corals, the lake nearby and the tombs are the other sights.

Kadamat

A particularly fine lagoon, of even depth, and an endless shoreline, perfect for swimming, makes Kadamat a haven of solitude. The tourist huts are situated some distance away from habitation. Water sports facilities are available and a water sports institute has been set up.

Kalpeni

Kalpeni has three uninhabited, satellite islands, all surrounded by an immense lagoon of spectacular beauty. Sunlight on the water causes it to sparkle and flash like a million aquamarines. Koomel, the gently curving bay where the tourist facilities are located, directly overlooks Pitti and Tialkam, two of the islands. This lagoon is particularly rich in coral life.

Minicoy

Farthest from Kavaratti island, 200 km away to the south and also nearest to the Maldives. Minicoy has a lighthouse built by the British approximately a hundred years ago. Visitors are allowed up, right to the very top. One of the largest in Lakshadweep, Minicoy has a culture very different from any of the other islands- dress, language, food differs, for Minicoy has a cluster of 9 villages, which are called Athinis.

Bangaram

Bangaram, in the Lakshadweep, is a breathtakingly beautiful island quite out of this world. Tear drop shaped, it is encircled by a continuous halo of creamy sand. There are three uninhabited islands in the same atoll consisting of Tirmakara, Parali-I, Parali- II. Bangaram is surrounded by one of the largest and safest lagoons with its calms, unimaginable blue-green waters. The exquisite coral formations, including the black coral formations and the large variety of coral fish: the angel, the clown, the butterfly, the surgeon, the sweetlip, the snappers, the groupers, not to mention the abundance of the awesome, but harmless sharks, manta rays, sting rays, moray eels (morena) and turtles, make diving here an addictive experience. There is a diving school in Bangaram. The Bangaram Island Resort is fast becoming a by word among the island hoppers of the world. The Island of Bangaram has recently been opened up for international tourists.

Water Sports

Water sports facilities like kayaking, sailing, paddle boats, inflatable motor boats, glass bottom boats and water skiing are available in the islands of Kavaratti, Kalpeni, Kadamat and Minicoy.

9

Development of Desert Tourism in India

The Thar Desert (also known as the Great Indian Desert) is a desert mainly located in the state of Rajasthan in northwest India. It continues into Pakistan as the Cholistan Desert. It is a region of constantly shifting sand dunes, with sparse vegetation in some areas. Thar Desert is spread over northwestern India and eastern Pakistan covering an area of about 4,46,000 square kilometres. The Thar desert is about 805 km (about 500 mi) long and about 485 km (about 300 mi) wide. It covers four states of India and two states of Pakistan.

The Thar Desert is bounded on the northwest by the Sutlej River, on the east by the Aravalli Range, on the south by the salt marsh known as the Rann of Kutch, and on the west by the Indus Valley. NASA has prepared a satellite map of the Thar Desert. The Indian Desert is the eastern part of the Thar Desert. It is spread over four states in India, namely Punjab, Haryana, Rajasthan, and Gujarat covering an area of 2,08,110 square kilometres. The maximum area is covered in Rajasthan, about 3/5th of the total geographical area of the state. Of the total desert in India 61% falls in Rajasthan, 20% in Gujarat and 9% in Punjab and Haryana combined.

The Indian Desert is said to be extending at a rate of ½ km per year towards Punjab, Haryana, Uttar Pradesh and Madhya Pradesh. Indian Desert is mainly inhabited by Hindus but Muslim population is also there in minority. The Thar Desert also extends to the southeast of Pakistan. Within south Pakistan it is inhabited by Sindhi and Kolhis.

Origin of Thar Desert

The origin of the Thar Desert is a controversial subject. Some consider it to be 4000 to 10,000 years old, whereas others state that aridity started in this region much earlier. Another theory states that area turned to desert relatively recently: perhaps around 2000 - 1500 BCE. Around this time the Ghaggar ceased to be a major river and now terminates in the desert. It has been observed through remote sensing techniques that Late Quaternary climatic changes and neotectonics have played a significant role in modifying the drainage courses in this part and a large number of palaeochannels exist.

Most of the studies have the same opinion with the palaeochannels of the Sarasvati coinciding with the bed of present day Ghaggar and believe that the Sutlej along with the Yamuna once flowed into the present Ghaggar riverbed. It is postulated that the Sutlej is the main tributary of the Ghaggar and that subsequently the tectonic movements might have forced the Sutlej westwards, the Yamuna eastwards and the Ghaggar dried.

Remote sensing is widely useful for revealing the palaeochannels in the desert areas using various digital image processing techniques of satellite images. The present disorganized state of many streams in the Thar desert of Western Rajasthan has been attributed by many investigators to change in climate during Quaternary, and in the particular Holocene.

Climate of desert

The climate of the desert region is characterized by extremes of temperatures ranging from even below freezing point in winters to as high as 52 °C in summers. Rainfall is precarious and erratic, ranging from below 120 mm in the extreme west to 375 mm eastward. These rains are of the monsoon type (July to September) and are generally of thundershowers. Mean wind velocity varies from about 3 km per hour during December and January to about 32 km per hour during May and June.

Dust storms are also a normal feature during summers. The velocity of dust storms may reach as high as 130 km per hour, and may deposit as much as 7cm of dust on the floor of residential buildings. Frosts are severe during winters in the sandy areas and tree saplings up to 2 m height some times succumb to such frosts.

There are three principal landforms in the desert region i.e.

— The predominantly sand covered Thar

— Plains with hills including the central dune free country

— Hills

It is a desolate country where sand is piled up into huge wind blown dunes. The sand dunes are of three types viz., longitudinal parabolic, transverse and barchans. The first type, running NNE-SSW, i.e. parallel to the prevailing winds, occurs to the south and west of the Thar. The transverse dunes, aligned across the wind direction, to the east and north of Thar and barchans, with the conclave sides facing the wind in the interior, predominant in Central Thar. On the whole the Thar Desert slopes imperceptibly towards the Indus Plain and surface unevenness is mainly due to sand dunes. The dunes in the south are higher, rising sometimes to 152 m whereas in the north they are lower and rise to 16 m above the ground level. The Aravalli ranges form the main landmark to the south-east of Thar Desert. The more humid conditions that prevail near the Aravallis prevent the extension of Thar Desert towards the east and the Ganges Valley. In the heart of the sand covered area, the bare, dune free country of Barmer, Jaisalmer and Bikaner present an anomaly.

Desert Soils

The soils of the Arid Zone are generally sandy to sandy-loam in texture. The consistency and depth vary according to the topographical features. The low-lying loams are heavier and may have a hard pan of clay, calcium carbonate or gypsum. The pH varies between 7 and 9.5. The soils improve in fertility from W & N.W. to E & N.E. Desert soils are Regosols of wind blown sand and sandy fluiratile deposits, derived from the disintegration of rock in the subjacent areas and blown in from the coastal region and the Indus valley.

The desert soils occupy the districts of Jodhpur, Bikaner, Churu, Ganganagar, Barmer, Jaisalmer and Jalore. The Thar consists mainly of the wind-blown sand. The area is covered not only by sheet of sand but also of rockey projections of low elevations which constitute the older rocks of the country. Water is scarce and occurs at great depths, from 30 to 120 m from the ground level.

Some of these soils contain a high percentage of soluble salts in the lower horizons, turning water in the wells into poisonous. Being poor in organic matter they show a low loss on ignition. They contain varying amount of $CaC0_3$.

Biodiversity of Desert

Stretches of sand in the desert are interspersed by hillocks and sandy and gravel plains. Due to the diversified habitat, the vegetation and animal life in this arid region is very rich. About 23 species of lizard and 25 species of snakes are found here and several of them are endemic to the region.

Some wildlife species, which are fast vanishing in other parts of India, are found in the desert in large numbers such as the great Indian bustard, the black buck, the Indian gazelle, and the wild ass in the Rann of Kutch. How these animals and insects survive in these harsh conditions, under such high temperature and without drinking water and green vegetation are amazing. They have evolved excellent survival strategies, their size is smaller than other similar animals living in different conditions, and they are mainly nocturnal.

There are certain other factors responsible for the survival of these animals in the desert. Due to the lack of water in this region, transformation of the grasslands into cropland has been very slow. The protection provided to them by a local community, the Bishnois, is also a factor.

The Desert National Park, Jodhpur, spread over an area of 3162 sq.km, is an excellent example of the ecosystem of the Thar Desert, and its diverse fauna. Great Indian bustard, black buck, chinkara, desert fox, Bengal fox, wolf, desert cat etc. can be easily seen here. Seashells and massive fossilized tree trunks in this park record the geological history of the desert. The region is a haven for migratory and resident birds of the desert. One can see many eagles, harriers, falcons, buzzards, kestrel and vultures. Short- toed eagles, tawny eagles, spotted eagles, lagger falcons and kestrels are the commonest of these.

Tal Chhapar Sanctuary is a very small sanctuary in district Churu, 210 km from Jaipur, in the Shekhawati region. This sanctuary is home to a large population of graceful black buck. Desert fox and desert cat can also be spotted along with typical avifauna such as partridge and sand grouse.

Natural Vegetation of Desert

The natural vegetation is classed as Northern Desert Thorn Forest. These occur in small clumps scattered in a more or less open forms. Density and size of patches increase from West to East following the increase in rainfall. Natural vegetation of Thar Desert is composed of following tree, shrub and herb species.

The people of Thar Desert are simple and brave. The main occupation of the people in desert is Agriculture and animal husbandry. In past years there has been a tremendous increase in human population as well as animal population. This has led to improper control of grazing and extensive cultivation resulting into the deterioration of vegetation resources. The increase of human and livestock population in the desert has lead to deterioration in the ecosystem resulting in degradation of soil fertility also. The living standard of the people in the desert is low.

A large irrigation and power project has reclaimed areas of the northern and western desert for agriculture. The small population is mostly pastoral, and hide and wool industries are prominent. There are around 50% Muslims and 50% Hindus in the Pakistani part of the Thar Desert. The desert turns into a green meadow after rain and is worth a visit. A colorful culture rich in tradition prevails in the desert. The people have a great passion for music and poetry.

The Thar or the Great Indian Desert, as it is generally known, is a fascinating area. It has taken its name from the word Tahl that in local dialect is the term for the sandy ridges of the dunes. The Thar Desert in spite of the inhospitable climate is not an endless stretch of sand, devoid of life and vegetarian. It is a living and dynamic eco-system. It is actually one of the most populous deserts of the world. In order to preserve its geo-morphological features, fauna and flora and to continuously study and understand their ecology under undisturbed desert conditions, an area of about 3,126 sq. kilometers.

Species of wild animals and plants that can adapt to these harsh climatic and environmental conditions flourish in the area. Amongst the mammals, chinkara (Gazella gazella), Indian fox, desert fox, jackal, desert cat, jungle cat and nilgai are common in the Desert National Park. The area provides suitable conditions for survival of a number of species of lizards, gerbils and snakes. The spiny tailed lizards with their prehistoric looks are quite common in many areas of the Park.

Among the snakes the saw scaled viper, the large rat snake and sand boa are noteworthy. Most of these animals survive the scarcity of water by adopting special mechanism so that life can go on without water. They reduce their physical activity considerably and avoid exposure to hot winds by keeping in shade of shrubs or by burrowing down in the sand. Earth has an admirable insulator against heat and aridity, and an animal burrowing a few centimeters below the surface will comfortably survive the hottest day and coolest night. In the Desert National Park the foxes, cats, lizards and snakes all enter the burrows to avoid the hot and desiccating air outside. Most of the sunset animals are active in early morning or after the sun set, when the temperatures are much lower.

The chinkaras, which cannot enter a burrow, go under the shade of bushes. They can tolerate a rise in body temperature up to seven degrees above normal without serious injury to any vital organ. These animals can withstand considerable haemo-concentrations or blood thickening, which takes plated. Chinkaras for example can go without water for a number of days by feeding on green plants like Aak (Calotropics procera) and obtaining water from its leaves. Similarly, the gerbils, which serve as staple food for the desert fox and the desert cats, provide much of the water to these carnivores.

The plants in the desert also have to adopt various strategies to endure the intense heat, bitter cold and long dry spells. To reduce the water by evaporation the leaves of these plants are reduced in size, as is the case of khejri (Prosopis cinerara) with relatively few stomataon them. Some species like kair (Cappairs dedicua) and phog (Calligonum polkygonides) do away with the leaves altogether and develop stomata on the green stems which perform the work of photosynthesis. Sevan is one of the hardiest plants to grow in the Thar Desert. This perennial grass can stand long periods of drought.

The lesser bustard, locally called tilore is a winter visitor to the Desert. This bird is also extremely shy. Tilore has not been observed drinking water on the water hole so far. Foxes are generally shy of human beings but during the winter months they are visible throughout the day looking for the gerbils or just basking in the winter sun.

The Thar's geological history; based on the study of fossils found in the area is interesting. The area has been in and out of sea at least four times during the last two hundred and eighty million years. It appears that this area was under sea in the early Triassic period. The sea withdrew after twenty five million years and the sediments were uplifted animal fossils of that period are found in the rocks in many areas.

Again, after about twenty five million years this area came under the sea. The limestone and the sandstone of Jaisalmer with their fossils of ammonites were deposited during this period. During the lower Cretaceous period, between a hundred and thirty five million years and sixty three million years, the area became a land mass with forests. It is believed that the plant fossils of Paliwal village around Jaisalmer belong to this period. This was followed by yet another invasion of the sea when the rocks containing marine fossils were deposited. At the end of the Cretaceous period and in the beginning of Cenozoic, sixty three million years ago, the sea took over again and was inhabited by for aminifera or tiny unicellular, shelled organisms.

Accumulation of their dead bodies at the bottom of the sea and their slow decomposition is believed to be responsible for the formation of oil and natural gas in the Thar Desert. The sea finally withdrew from the area about thirty five million years ago. Wood fossils found in Akal near Jaisalmer are the remains of the forests of cycades and ferns that flourished in the region during the early Jurassic period, that is about one hundred and eighty million years ago.

At present about twenty five fossilized tree trunks are lying exposed on the grounds in the Akal wood fossil park. The largest is about seven meters long and one and half meter in girth. There are more wood fossils lying deep under the surface. Evidences of similar fossils are surfacing in other areas of Jaisalmer region. The whole area is now preserved as a natural wonder in the Desert.

Desert Safari

Safaris are the best way to explore a region, its culture, tradition, to experience its geographical and topographical features and almost everything that a place can offer to us. The insight you gain through the safaris that can be at best explained as a treasure that will with throughout your life and after. India with its varied culture and tradition provides excellent opportunities for someone who has seen them all and want to see more. Whether it is Jeep safari, camel safari, horse safari, and motor biking or cycling options are great, views are out of this world, and the experience can be out of this world.

Jeep safaris can be quite an experience in Thar Desert, the region, which is part of Rajasthan, the state where royalty can still be seen in its forts, havelis, and the colors that the place has on offer. Desert jeep safari can prove to be most adventurous and rewarding of all the safaris that you have undertaken. After all, going through a rugged terrain on a desert is not the kind of experience that you can have every other day in your life.

Camel safaris across the Thar Desert in the open country of Jaisalmer and Bikaner listening to the folk music and enjoying folk dances in the nights are an experience that you can never forget. Sleeping in the night under the stars with sand dunes all around is an added attraction that you will cherish.

Take a chance to explore India as the way it should be, in its true colors with all its chaos and confusions all around. This is real adventure or to say adventure of life. Various levels of difficulties can be experienced and they are different according to the nature of Safari expedition you are venturing into. Camel, horse, and jeep safaris in the Thar Desert and other parts of the country are more about the cultural and social adventure rather than physical adventure. Camel safaris deep into the deserts may require some advance preparations if you are not very much familiar with the geography of the region. Take a desert safari in is India for your next holiday.

Rajasthan's Thar is the only desert in world, which is rich in color and culture (in most other deserts, for example, the people wear only white), and warm with the hospitality of courtly traditions. These find a reflection in the desert safari too. And the splendor of the desert combined with the experience of camping and riding in it, truly makes one of the most impressive activities for travelers. It also brings alive an era when this was the way elements to create romantic kingdoms in the desert.

However, since the desert is the best for the sport, the regions of Mewar (Udaipur and its surroundings which, however, are ideal for horse safaris) and around Kota should be avoided. For many, the best areas constitute what forms the golden triangle for the desert safari: Jaisalmer, Jodhpur, Bikaner. In these three former royal kingdom, the fortified cities are surrounded by vistas of sand.

Those adventurous can take an entire trail combining these three cities, and including in it parts of the Shekhawati region (which can be used as a starting or concluding point because of its proximity to Delhi). Jaisalmer is the heart of the desert with a beautiful fort which is inhabited, and which is known for its carved, sandstone mansions. Bikaner has a camel farm, the only one of its kind in the country, and along with Jodhpur, forms two ends of a route, which has several other interesting settlements along its route. These include Khimsar and Nagaur. From Bikaner, one can head for Shekhawati where the attraction is a number of fierce castles with a bristling history, and the painted mansions of the merchants who once lived here.

However, those who would prefer a smaller safari (a night or two in the desert), should plan a journey so that they move out of the town into the desert, and choose a route devoid of sightseeing options. This way, they can feel the essence of the desert, and the loneliness of the landscape, while being in close distance to modern conveniences.

Shorter safaris still would merely be in the nature of rides, stretching to a full day for those so inclined, or merely a few hours with a meal thrown in. However, to be able to spend at lest one night in the desert would be a unique experience, and should be built in if at all it is possible.

Camal Safari

The camel safaris in the deserts of India are fast catching up with the masses and have become the fastest selling adventure holidays. The theme of the adventure attracts all the daredevils who have a passion to experience India as it is. The hardships in the course of the safari go hand-in-hand with the novel manner of seeing the dry desert areas. The nature is at its hardest in the safari without unending stretches of wilderness that are in abundance in the deserts of Sahara and Namibia. In India the camel safari offers a lot more of fun and adventure. The area is a lot more accessible than its counterparts owing to the airports and railway stations that are close at hands to most of the popular sand dunes.

The variety of safaris offered by the Great Indian Desert is simply dazzling. You may take your pick from the short treks around the joyous town of Jaisalmer or take on an extensive trip on the terrific Thar. The journey is bound to remind you of the Lawrence of Arabia on his epic journey across the Sahara, or probably of Marco Polo, on the historic silk route or even a medieval trader leading his caravan through the hostile spice route or a royal caravanserai heading for one of the medieval kingdoms.

The desert safaris in India are centered on the princely kingdoms in the desert belt of India namely Jaisalmer, Jodhpur, and Bikaner, all of which are integral to the royal state of Rajasthan. Besides offering the awesome view of the open desert sands the camel safari is a great way to get introduced to the villages and the wildlife. The architectural heritage of Rajasthan is best covered in the camel safari. It is owing to the trade caravans across the desert of India that the trade prospered. The nobility invested the gains in the construction of the mansions, citadels, forts and palaces. Sandstone formed the basic material used in the making these masterpieces of art that are today nothing more than the ruins.

A typical safari will take you to the architectural ruins of Lodurva that are close to Jaisalmer. The oasis at Anasagar, the sand dunes of the Samm and the water source of Moolsagar are exquisite examples of the lives of the villagers. After the sailing safari through the day the nights are meant for entertainment and rest. The halts in the en-route villages amidst the desert scrubs for camels are out of the world adventures.

If the adventure in the sand along with the sun beckons you take care of the extreme temperatures likely to be experienced during the safari. The afternoons are as hot as 30 degrees though later at night the temperature may drop down to as low as zero degrees. Thus you should be adequately equipped with the cotton and the woolen clothing. The clothes should be comfortable for the journey sans the luxuries but at the same time should consider the values of the rural habitants who will be visited in the villages.

The regular use of the large rimmed sun hats is mandatory. These may be replaced with the cotton caps, which are dipped in water when it gets too hot around midday. The ways and the means to beat the heat will be invented throughout the course of the day in the desert. For the protection of the skin the scarves or balaclava may be worn around the neck and the forehead. The camel safari friendly umbrellas are easily available at Jodhpur.

While on the dry desert safari the adventure will be enjoyable if the water bottle is kept close at hand. The mineral water may be collected from Jodhpur or Jaisalmer. Basic medicines and suitable medication against the swaying gait of the camel but be carried. Do not forget to take A torch and a knife along. These will prove to be useful when handy. After the adventure in the Great Indian Desert all of you will start believing in the age-old adage that it's the slow and steady that wins the race. Happy safari, hope the caravanserai will be as charming as the camel.

If the idea of a camel safari in India does not appeal to you, then we have an alternative. Contrary to the swaying moments of camel you may enjoy a desert safari in India on a jeep. Discover the royal land of Rajasthan in a jeep. The travel destination of the Thar Desert in Rajasthan beckons all adventure seekers to the jeep safari. Check out the stretches of sand dunes. The jeep safari in Indian desert will captivate you in the charming culture of the Rajasthan.

Jeep Safari

Most jeep safari operators route journeys through the desert so you are close to villages, but remain hidden from them. In the afternoons, trips to the villages can be planned. An advance group moves ahead to set the evening's camp-usually self-sustained, with its own kitchen (food is cooked over wood fire), and tented accommodation. Baths are prepared for the travelers, and kerosene lamps used for lighting. A bonfire is organized around which evening cocktails and dinner is served. Here, in this enchanted setting with the stars looming large under the dark sky, village balladeers and minstrels are invited to sing, dance, play a musical instrument or two.

Most meals will be Rajasthani cuisine with vegetables and, usually, chicken and mutton cooked in fiery spices (after a while you get addicted to the chillies). Buttermilk and yogurt accompaniments are best to cool (and calm) the palate. However, on request and with advance notice, simple Western pasta and salads can be prepared. Don't ask for sandwiches, however, for bread is an unknown factor in the villages, and you'll have to get by on the more-than-sufficient Indian varieties that will be served before you.

It goes without saying that winter is the season for such jeep safaris (October to March) and to attempt it in summer would be impossible. In the cold months, the dry climate and the reflection of the sun's heats on the sand can make the day under the sun warm, and the nights bitterly cold. It is advisable, therefore, to carry a mix of woolens and lighter clothing, and to have suntan lotions and moisturizers for the skin.

Horse Safari

What makes Shekhawati Brigade Horse safari tours memorable is the experience of riding pure bred Indian horses like the Marwaris, Kathiawadis and the Sindhis cross country, in unspoilt terrain where you also interact with nomads many a times, the comfortable luxurious camps and cultural scenario with accompanying and invited folk musicians. This way you get to see the real India, the experience becomes even more memorable when shared with like-minded people having love for horses, nature and the environment.

The horse/camel safaris are organized with the base at Roop Niwas Palace, in Nawalgarh, Shekhawati, Rajasthan. In the stables at Roop Niwas there are several bred horses and camels. Various routes and itineraries have been surveyed thoroughly and worked out. Special care was taken to make these routes as varied and interesting as possible.

The planned itineraries are meant to give the guest an interesting experience with horses/camel along with a complete insight into the desert life style. To view the flora and fauna of Rajasthan and to interact with the local population by way of village visits. The Lunch halts and camping sights are in unique settings. Unlike routes of mountain trails, the routes pass semi desertic terrain, forests, salt lake, marshes and flat grasslands. This offers opportunities for the riders to trot canter and may be gallop.

The camel routes move northwest from Shekhawati in unspoilt desert terrain unexploited by any body as yet. The team has been carefully put together, and there is a well experienced, out rider, an Ex-Army cook and camp incharge, folk musicians, people trained to erect and wind up camps, cross country jeep and truck drivers.

Desert Tourism in Jaislmer

The golden city of Jaisalmer, which lies courageously as the western sentinel of India, is a place worth visiting. The golden ray of the setting sun draws a heavenly picture on the sands of Jaisalmer. The magnificent wood- and stone-carved mansions and buildings display the love of the Rajputs towards the fine arts.

Jaisalmer is situated in the westernmost part of the state of Rajasthan, the heart of the great Thar Desert. It has neighboring Pakistan on its western side. On its south, there is the beautiful city of Bikaner. The eastern part of the place is bordered by Jodhpur, another city of color and tradition. The climate of this city is of typical desert character. Population of this city is quite low compared to the other parts of the state. The best time to visit this desert city is the winter season (November to February) when the heat becomes comparatively low. The desert festival held during the last winter months of January and February is the most opportune time for the people to visit Jaisalmer.

The city Jaisalmer was founded by Bhatti Rajput Rawal Jaisal in 1156. The history of Jaisalmer also reveals the courage and determination of the Rajputs. The city used to be a major trade center as it was the trade route of the western countries to India.

Tourist Destinations

— Visiting Jaisalmer itself means a visit to the Jaisalmer Fort. Built over the Trikuta hill, this fort is the biggest and the most beautiful landmark of the city. The fort is occupied by shops, stalls, and a number of other business concerns. This fort accommodates quarter of the city's population.

— Just outside the fort is the Manakchowk, the famous marketplace of Jaisalmer. It is a good place for bargaining the local products.

— The Jain temple, a place worth visiting, is also situated inside the fort itself. The temple, made between 12th and 15th century, bears testimony to Rajasthan's unique artistry.

— Havelis are the mansions built by the wealthy merchants, which are still in very good condition. The intricate craftsmanship is beyond parallel. The havelis like the Patwon-ki-Haveli and Salim-Singh-ki-Haveli are remarkable for their exclusive cutwork, yellow and red stone treatment and the bracket-shaped decoration of peacocks.

— Gadsisar Sagar Tank is a famous place for an outing. Earlier it used to be the source of water for the entire city. A number of migratory birds flock this place during the winter season.

— Desert Culture Center and Museum is another place that would give the visitor a clear insight of the place. The museum has a number of old coins, different kinds of textile, traditional Rajasthani instruments, and some fossils that were found in the desert.

— Baba Bagh is an oasis at the bank of a man-made dam. It has greenery all around to give a much-needed relief to the local people.

— The Jain temple of Lodhruva, which reminds of the glory of the former capital city Lodhruva, is a place worth visiting.

— Sam Sand Dunes, situated at the edge of the Thar Desert, is a place gaining tremendous tourist attraction these days. This sandy place is famous for watching sunset and taking a camel ride.

— Khuri, another place in this glittering golden sand, impresses the tourists with its mud houses and straw roofs.

— Desert National Park is another place that preserves the natural ecosystem of the desert land. Cactus, thorny trees and shrubs could be seen growing easily without being taken care of. It has some vegetation that survives in the dry and arid soil. It also has few animal species like the monitor lizard, desert foxes, porcupines and black bucks, etc.

Desert Festival

Held in the months of January-February, the Desert Festival exudes a delightful spirit. For three days, the otherwise barren land of Jaisalmer comes to life and is clustered with hordes of colourfully dressed people.

In fact during these days, Jaisalmer gets a chance to parade its exuberant charm to the world. Some chosen and cherished moments of the glorious and illustrious past and affluent culture are on display. The traditional dances backed by high pitched music take the folk dancers and the audience on an euphoric trip. The turban-tying competition and Mr. Desert Contest add a touch of excitement to the festive celebrations.

The famous Gair dancers and the traditional fire-dancers leave the crowds enchanted whenever they perform. The grand finale is a trip to the sand dunes where one can enjoy the pleasure of a camel ride and at times also view the musicians and dancers performing on the dunes. All arrangements are made by the Department of Tourism and RTDC.

Once a year in winters and on the middle of the continually rising and falling stark yellow sands of the great Thar Desert, the empty sands around Jaisalmer come alive with the brilliant colour, music and laughter of the Desert Festival. The festival is organised by the tourist authorities as tourist entertainment around January-February.

The very rich and colourful Rajasthani folk culture is on show here for a few days. Rajasthani men and tall beautiful women dressed in their brightly costumes dance and sing lingering ballads of valour, romance and tragedy. Traditional musicians attempt to outdo each other in their musical superiority

The high points of the festival are - snake charmers, puppeteers, acrobats, folk performers do rapid trade. Camels, the lifeline of the desert, play a foremost role. Proud moustached villagers, dressed in their ethnic best come astride their picturesquely caparisoned camels to join in the camel dances and competitions of camel acrobatics, camel races and décor, camel polo, tug of war and the like.

10

Tourist Resource Potential in Mountain with Special Reference to Himalayas

The Himalayan mountain system developed in a series of stages 30 to 50 million years ago. The Himalayan range was created from powerful earth movements that occurred as the Indian plate pressed against the Eurasian continental plate. The earth movements raised the deposits laid down in the ancient, shallow Tethys Sea to form the Himalayan ranges from Pakistan eastward across northern India, and from Nepal and Bhutan to the Myanmar (Burmese) border. Even today the mountains continue to develop and change, and earthquakes and tremors are frequent in the area

Physically, the Himalayas forms three parallel zones: the Great Himalayas, the Middle Himalayas (also known as the Inner or Lesser Himalayas), and the Sub-Himalayas, which includes the Siwalik Range and foothills and the Tarai and Duars piedmont (an area of land formed or lying at the foot of a mountain or mountain range). Each of these lateral divisions exhibit certain similar topographic features. The Great Himalayas, the highest zone, consists of a huge line of snowy peaks with an average height exceeding 6100 m (20,000 ft).

The width of this zone, composed largely but not entirely of gneiss and granite, is about 24 km (about 15 mi). Spurs from the Great Himalayas project southwards into the Middle Himalayas in an irregular fashion. The Nepal and Sikkim (a state of northern India) portion of the Great Himalayas contains the greatest number of high peaks. The snow line on the southern slopes of the Great Himalayas varies from 4480 m (14,700 ft) in the eastern and central Himalayas of Nepal and Sikkim to 5180 m (17,000 ft) in the western Himalayas. To the north of the Great Himalayas are several ranges such as the Zaskar, Ladakh, and the Kailas. The Karakoram Range lies on the Tibetan side of the Great Himalayas.

The Great Himalayan region is one of the few remaining isolated and inaccessible areas in the world today. Some high valleys in the Great Himalayas are occupied by small clustered settlements. Extremely cold winters and a short growing season limit the farmers to one crop per year, most commonly potatoes or barley. The formidable mountains have limited the development of large-scale trade and commerce despite the construction of highways across the mountains linking Nepal and Pakistan to China. Older trails, which cross the mountains at high passes, also have limited trade and are open only during the summer months.

The Himalayas influences the climate of the Indian subcontinent by sheltering it from the cold air mass of Central Asia. The range also exerts a major influence on monsoon and rainfall patterns. Within the Himalayas climate varies depending on elevation and location. Climate ranges from subtropical in the southern foothills, with average summer temperatures of about 30° C (about 86° F) and average winter temperatures of about 18° C (about 64° F); warm temperate conditions in the Middle Himalayan valleys, with average summer temperatures of about 25° C (about 77° F) and cooler winters; cool temperate conditions in the higher parts of the Middle Himalayas, where average summer temperatures are 15 to 18° C (59 to 64° F) and winters are below freezing; to a cold alpine climate at higher elevations, where summers are cool and winters are severe. At elevations above 4880 m (16,000 ft) the climate is very cold with below freezing temperatures and the area is permanently covered with snow and ice. The eastern part of the Himalayas receives heavy rainfall; the western part is drier.

Since 1950 tourism has emerged as a major growth industry in the Himalayas. Nearly 1 million visitors come to the Himalayas each year for mountain trekking, wildlife viewing, and pilgrimages to major Hindu and Buddhist sacred places. The number of foreign visitors has increased in recent years, as organized treks to the icy summits of the Great Himalayas have become popular. While tourism is important to the local economy, it has had an adverse impact on regions where tourist numbers exceed the capacity of recreational areas.

Historically, all transport in the Himalayas has been by porters and pack animals. Porters and pack animals are still important, but the construction of major roads and the development of air routes have changed the traditional transportation pattern. Major urban centers such as Kathmandu, Simla, and Srinagar, as well as important tourist destinations, are served by airlines. Railways link Simla and Darjiling, but in most of the Himalayas there are no railroads. The bulk of goods from the Himalayas, as well as goods destined for places within the Himalayas, generally come to Indian railheads, located in the Tarai, by road. The pack animals and porters transport goods from road heads to the interior and back.

Himalayan Destinations

For the rest of the world Himalayas is a mountain range

that encloses the Highest peaks of the world. For the thrill seekers, Himalayas is the ultimate adventure sports destination. And for the tourists they have the most exotic and picturesque holiday resorts found on earth. But for the pilgrims they are the most sacred and revered mountain ranges in the world. From ancient times these holy mountains were considered the abode of Lord Shiva. It was here in the mist shrouded crags of these mystic ranges that the legends and myths of Hinduism were born and thrive to this day.

Drive along ancient pilgrim trails, visit the remote Himalayan temples and shrines and experience the serenity and tranquillity of the Himalayas. Travel on the same trail used by pilgrims for centuries to visit sacred pilgrimage site such as Kailash Mansarovar, the Holy Mountain in Tibet and the Char Dhams Kedarnath, Badrinath, Yamunotri, and Gangotri. In the Trans-Himalayan regions the Monasteries, often built on steep slopes, still dominate social life and religious practices that continues in much the same way.

Himalayan range covers the entire northern part of India, nestling five major states of the country within it. The ancient Indian pilgrims who have travelled in these mountains since time immemorial coined a Sanskrit word for the Himalayas meaning "Abode of Snow".

Some of the reasons why people have been so fascinated by the Indian Himalayas is because of the Hindu pilgrim routes, the low valleys that abruptly rise up in high mountain ranges, the lovely trekking hikes, densely forested areas lying just a mountain range away from barren cold deserts, and the lovely people of the mountains with their unique hospitable lifestyles.

Jammu Kashmir is the first Himalayan state of India, but its not another hill land of India. Jammu and Kashmir is really three regions: the foothill plains of Jammu; the lakes and blue valleys of Kashmir rising to alpine passes, the high altitude plains and starkly beautiful mountains of Ladakh, which lies beyond those passes. It's enough to move one to poetry. Among the most attractive part that this Indian state has is the adventure oppurtunities that can be seggragated into trekking, mountaineering and Trans Himalayan Jeep Safari.

Kashmir Valley

Kashmir is one of india's most beautiful and touristically popular regions and has been since the time of the great Moghul emperors. It's probably most famous for the houseboats on picturesque Dal Lake you've not really been to Kashmir until you've not really been to Kashmir until you've stayed on one - but there's a lot more to the Kashmir Valley than just lazing on board.

Around the capital, Srinagar, there are a number of interesting mosques, temples and forts and, of course, the delightful Moghul Gardens - laid out in formal patterns hundreds of years ago and every bit as beautiful today. But you have to get away from Srinagar, up to the hill stations around the valley, to really enjoy Kashmir. Pahalgam, Gulmarg and Sonamarg are all delightful in themselves, but they also serve as the jumping off points for Kashmir's many Trekking possibilities.

Jammu

Jammu, the second largest town in the state of Jammu and Kashmir, and is situated 290-km from capital city of Srinagar on the south-eastern slopes of the Shiwalik range. In winter it becomes the headquarters of the Jammu & Kashmir administration and many Kashmiris move here for the winter because the temperature drops.

Ladakh

Ladakh's landscape has more in common with the lunar landscape than any other place on earth. Being in a complete rainshadow region, cut off from the monsoon clouds by the Great Himalaya and a host of subsidiary ranges, it is a cold high altitude desert where the wind, water from the minimal winter snows, and chemical reactions within the rocks themselves, have carved a fantastic, sometimes grotesque, landscape.

The majority are Muslims living in the Kashmir valley; culturally and ethnically, the closest links are with peoples in the northwestern highlands of the Gilgit district in the Pakistani sector. While Hindus dominate the Jammu region and Ladakh is majorly influenced by the Trans-Himalayan Buddhism.The Kashmiri language is influenced by Sanskrit and belongs to the Dardic branch of Indo-Aryan languages also spoken by the hill tribes of Gilgit. The great majority of the population resides in the lower reaches of the valley.

The ancient caves and temples of Kashmir, reveal a strong link with Indian culture at the beginning of the Christian Era. At one time the classical dances of the south are believed to have been practised. These arts survived only in folk forms and were performed principally at marriage ceremonies. The popular Hafiza dance performed by Kashmiri women to the accompaniment of Sufiana Kalam was later replaced by the Bacha Nagma, performed by young boys dressed like women. The Bhand Jashna or the "festival of clowns", a 300- to 400-year-old genre of Kashmiri folk theatre performed in village squares, satirizes social situations through dance, music and clowning.

Himachal Pradesh

Himachal Pradesh is the land of snow, lofty peaks,

cascading streams, alpine meadows & lush fruit-laden valleys. Many parts of the Himachal state have a distinctly Austrian look with conifer-clad mountains, chalet-like huts with overhanging balconies and serene blue valleys watered by snow-fed streams. Shimla the capital of Himachal Pradesh, is still very much a Raj township in appearance and atmosphere.

Himachal also store numerous wonderful hill stations, which are particularly cool in summers. Shimla, Dalhousie, Kullu, Manali and Kufri are a few of the hill Stations in Himachal Pradesh which offer breathtaking scenery and countless options of adventure sports. Dharamshala, where the Dalai Lama lives, is another important centre on the tourist map.

For sheer geographical diversity, few places in the world are as richly endowed as Himachal Pradesh. Low rolling bills, just a couple of hundred metres above sea level, climb on to touch the core of the Himalaya mountains. Here lie peaks that are several thousand metres high and never lose their perennial snows. Then, past these forbidding heights, lie the visually stunning cold deserts of the Trans Himalaya.

The State can be divided into two regions: the Southern part, which is almost as hot as the plains and the northern region having a temperate summer and a winter with extreme cold and heavy snowfall. The rainfall is around 180 cms. Best time to visit Himachal is during the months Mid-May to Mid-October.

Hill resorts of Himachal Pradesh

Himachal also store numerous wonderful hill stations, which are particularly cool in summers. Shimla, Dalhousie, Kullu, Manali and Kufri are a few of the hill Stations in Himachal Pradesh which offer breathtaking scenery and countless options of adventure sports. Dharamshala, where the Dalai Lama lives, is another important centre on the tourist map.

Shimla

Built in the mid-eighteenth century, Shimla was highly popular among the British royalty after it was named the 'Summer Capital of India'. The Parliament used to move up to the hills to get a break from the hot Indian summers. The town is a picturesque place dotted with charming bungalows and shops made of stone. A perfect setting for romance or to go on a idle holiday. The best way to see Shimla is to pick up a tour book, which tells a small history of the buildings and churches.

Uttaranchal

Lying in the north of the vast and bountiful expanse of India and cradled in the awesome beauty and calm serenity of the stately Himalayas, Uttaranchal - the "Devbhumi" that has attracted tourists and pilgrims from world over since time immemorial. Comprising of eight hill districts and an area and population that equals the state of Himachal Pardesh,, Uttaranchal is an expression of divinity, austerity, meditation, penance and attainment.

Nanda Devi is the highest mountain situated completely in India, and forms part of the main axis of the Great Himalayan Range. To the North of the Himalayas, the Zanskar range forms a formidable divide between India and Tibet. To the south of the Himalayan range the main tributaries of the Ganges and the Kali River form rugged gorge country before cutting though the Shivalik range, where the peaks rarely exceed 3,000m.

The Peak Regions

The Great Himalayan Range forms the backbone of the Garhwal and Kumaon regions of Uttaranchal. In Eestern Garhwal, it includes the Swargarohini range with Swargarohini I (6,252m) at the head of the Tons River, and the Bandarpunch range, including Bandarpunch (6,316m) forming the main divide between the headwaters of the Yamuna and the Bhagirathi Rivers.

The main Himalayas extends to the Gangotri region, where a huge concentration of peaks almost encloses the Gangotri glacier. The peaks include Yogeshwar (6,678m), Sri Kailash (6,932m) and Mana Parbat (6,794m) to the North; and Kedarnath (6,490), Kedar Dome (8,831m) and Bhirigupanth I (6,772m) to the south. Up at the head of the glacier, the Chaukhamba range, including Chaukhamba I (7,068m), provides an impressive divide between the headwaters of the Bhagirathi and Alaknanda Rivers.

To the east of Badrinath, the peaks of Nilgiri Parbat (6,474m), Ghori Parbat (6,708m) and Hathi Parbat (6,727m) are the highest of the Himalayan peaks, while to the North, Kamet (7,756m), Mana Peak (7,272m), Abl Gamin (7,355m), and Mukut (7,242m) are some of the 7,000m peaks forming the main axis of the Zanskar range.

Pilgrimage Centres in Uttaranchal

Sacred pilgrimages of different religions including the world famous "Char Dham" or the four Hindu pilgrimage destinations of Shri Badrinath - Kedarnath - Gangotri - Yamunotri; the sacred Sikh pilgrimage of Hemkund - Lokpal, Nanakmatta and Meetha - Reetha Sahib and Piran Kaliyar have drawn pilgrims and seekers for spiritual fulfillment to Uttaranchal. Kailash Mansarovar, Tholingmath are all in the Chinese occupied Tibet, but for the people of yesteryears, these were some of the most important landmarks in Uttaranchal.

Garhwal & Kumaon

Uttaranchal is undoubtedly India's most beautiful canvas. Studded with green strokes, wild splashes and quaint highlights. What makes Uttaranchal a holidayer's delight are the sketches of Kumaon and Garhwal. Enchanting, captivating in their own ways. Mesmerising, spellbinding to the last kilometre. Unspoilt, untouched and unbelievable. If Kumaon is a green table spread, Garhwal is a challenger's delight. If Kumaon plays host to clear lakes, chirpy forests, floral rainbows, garhwal flaunts its snow-clad peaks, quaint retreats and infinite mountain rivers.

Uttaranchal is undoubtedly India's most beautiful canvas. Studded with green strokes, wild splashes and quaint highlights. What makes Uttaranchal a holidayer's delight are the sketches of Kumaon and Garhwal. Enchanting, captivating in their own ways. Mesmerising, spellbinding to the last kilometre. Unspoilt, untouched and unbelievable. If Kumaon is a green table spread, Garhwal is a challenger's delight. If Kumaon plays host to clear lakes, chirpy forests, floral rainbows, garhwal flaunts its snow-clad peaks, quaint retreats and infinite mountain rivers.

Sikkim

Shrouded In Heavy Mist, the guardian deity Kangchenjunga both protects and terrifies the inhabitants of the magical kingdom of Sikkim . An awe-inspiring mass of rock clothed in dazzling white snow, this Himalayan giant in the world's third highest peak at 8,590m (28,199ft). The name itself means 'House of Five Treasures' represented by its five soaring summits. These treasures are the gold lacquered on it by the rising and setting sun, the silver from its mantle of virgin snow, and the jewels of the scriptures containing the teachings of the Gods and enlightened reincarnates.

Omnipresent and mystical , Kanchenjunga finally yields to nature's power and sheds ite monsoon veil in Autumn. Sikkim's inhabitants celebrate this re-awakening with great pomp and ceremony during the Pang Lhabsol Festival. It then becomes easy to believe the myth that a great God created, from beneath the slopes of this sacred mountain, the original man and women from whom all Sikkimese are descended.

The climate varies with elevation and ranges from tropical in the low valley bottoms to Arctic-like conditions of perpetual snow and ice in the higher reaches. The annual rainfall varies from 50-200 inches, mostly during May-October months, and snow in the upper levels often accumulates to a thickness of 30m. The best time to visit this state is during the months of March to late May and from October to December.

The state's cultural life is related to Tibetan religious and aesthetic traditions. The cultural climax of the year comes with the 2-day Phanglhapsol festival, when masked dances are performed in honour of Kanchenjunga, presiding deity and the mountain. There are also many secular folk dances. The Namgyal Institute of Tibetology has one of the largest collection of Tibetan books in the world. Many Buddhist monasteries are repositories of artistic treasures, including wall paintings, Tankas or Thangkas, and bronze images.

The North Eastern States

The reason has so much to see, so much to experience and so much to write about that it would take volumes. The region of northeastern India will whet the appetite of the traveller, the tourist, the anthropologist, the observer. It is impossible to describe the nuances that make this area unique, challenging and interesting. Get to any one place and the result will be that you will return for more.

he seven sisters comprise of Assam, Arunachal Pradesh, Nagaland, Manipur, Tripura, Meghalaya and Mizoram. While the seven sisters are unique in their own way, the major Himalayan destination over here is Arunachal Pradesh. The state provides abundant scope for angling, boating, rafting, trekking and hiking. Besides, there are a number of wild life sanctuaries and national parks where rare animals, birds and plants will fascinate the visitor.

Travel across the Brahmaputra and reach the land where myth meets magic and wishes are horses! The land where nature endows man and is yet to be trimmed and pruned to represent a synthetic civilisation. This land is better known to the worth as the North-Eastern region of India, that comprise of seven states called the "Seven Sisters" - Assam, Nagaland, Tripura, Meghalaya, Manipur, Mizoram and Arunachal Pradesh.

The region of northeastern India will whet the appetite of the traveller, the tourist, the anthropologist, the observer. It is impossible to describe the nuances that make this area unique, challenging and interesting. Get to any one place and the result will be that you will return for more.

Assam

Assam possibly has more folklore and tradition than any other place in India. There are archaeological ruins all over Assam but the ones around Sibsagar simply must be seen. The largest river island of the world, Manjuli, is a must too along with Kaziranga wildlife sanctuary. Crossing the magnificent Brahmaputra so deeply linked to life in

Assam, one reaches Guwahati, the capital where the famous Kamakahya temple is located on a hilltop. Guwahati has evolved into a major business centre and most of the travel linkages pass through it.

Travelling in the northeast will take one criss-crossing Assam so one gets to see many places. If one is travelling at the time of any of the festivals like Rongali Bihu, then the charm of Assamese culture will permeate your very being with its rhythm, colour and bonhomie. The dark green tea gardens blend beautifully with the pastel green of paddy. Digboi, Duliajan and areas around have oil wells.

Arunachal Pradesh

Because of the remoteness, the state of Arunachal has not been overtaken by urban ethos. Yet the fine balance between advancement and keeping in touch with ones roots is nowhere as clearly manifest as in this state. Most of Arunachal Pradesh has primary jungles, deep gorges and villages in really remote places. The changing colours provide a constant reminder of diversity and cheerful spirits. Cane bridges, swaying precariously over roaring white waters we often the only means of moving from one place to another. Itanagar is the capital of Arunachal Pradesh. One can travel along National Highway 52 and keep branching off to visit places like Ziro, Daporijo, Along and Pasighat.

Nagaland

Inhabited by swarthy tribes, Nagaland has its own distinct culture and ethos. Happy and cheerful, the people have an innate sense of music and colour. All the land here is basically owned by villages and individuals and this is true of many areas of the North-East and, therefore, one rarely hears of land disputes and clashes. Gateways to villages and houses are really something to see. Nagaland grows a fair amount of oranges and pineapples. The all-prevalent green continues and the scenic beauty of the state overwhelms us. Christianity has had a profound influence on the region, and one sees well-maintained churches all over.

Tripura

Tripura is steeped in history with linkages established from the legendaiy Limar dynasty. Recorded history dates back to almost 3,000 years. Even Samudra Gupta's pillars mention the existence of this state. This is yet another state like Manipur where Christian influence is negligible. It is the unique continuous history that has to be absorbed here. In geographical terms, Tripura is a small state and the second smallest state of India.

The architecture of the temple of Lord Jagannath is interesting and worth studying. It rises from an octagonal base. The Ujjayant Palace, dating back to Bir Bikram, is equally interesting with its Indo-Saracenic architecture. Old buildings and ruins worth exploring are in plenty like the lake palace called Neer Mahal on Rudrasagar Lake in Udaipur, the ancient capital. Sipahijala is an interesting area to spend the day. There is a comfortable guesthouse in the complex surrounded by forests and overlooking a large lake where one can go boating.

Meghalaya

Unlike the others of the seven sisters, Meghalaya's terrain consists more of rolling hills and less of steep climbs. There are beautiful meadows with fringes of pine forests everywhere. As if to complete the picture, there are breathtaking waterfalls with the waters plunging down hundreds of feet's. Meghalaya is a unique mixture of the traditional and the modern. People are fiercely proud of their roots and yet British influence is quite pronounced. Shillong is the busy hub centre of Meghalaya. The Idew Market or Burra Bazar is one of the most interesting markets one can ever see over here. For hours, one can explore the different levels and myriad alleys with shops displaying a mind-boggling array of items.

Mizoram

Over the years, Mizoram has managed to maintain its special touch with Aizawl being the hub centre. Pollution is low and despite "Jhuming" - a slash and burn type of cultivation - the greenery is intact. The hills rise towards the centre of Mizoram therefore Aizawl is pleasant throughout the year. Lunglei, Champhai and Saiha are the other centres. Driving along the road, if it is the right season, one comes across plenty of orchids. If one ventures into the forests, the rewards in terms of varieties of orchids would be great. The beauty of Mizoram lies in its unique harmony between man and nature. The clouds come to rest in the valleys, rainbows abound, small waterfalls gurgle past, greenery is all encompassing handicrafts are in plenty, the shawls are colourful, the markets exude cheer. Wherever one turns, a separate type of beauty unfolds and cheerful and innocent laughter is all pervasive.

Leh

Leh is breathtaking. Towering over the city is the tall nine storeyed palace built by Ladakh's ruler Sengge Namgyal in the early 17th century. It is said to have served as the model for the Potala palace in Lhasa. Another palace in Lhasa. Another palace built by King Tashi Namgyal in the 16th century stands above it on the Namgyal Tsemo peak. Down below, the town is a maze of little box like buildings bristling with brushwood stored on the roof for winter, set in an oasis of green fields.

Within the town of Leh itself there is plenty to see and do. An easy walk away through the interesting coppersmith's quarter, past the Moravian Church, the Ladakh Ecological Centre and across the fields, is the Sankar Gompa. Another interesting walk to the Ladakh Shanti Stupa goes through the picturesque village of Changspa. In the colourful bazaar are fascinating little shops with everything from semi precious stones - Lapiz, Coral, Turquoise and Pearls to fine curios and artefacts. It is a marvellous shopping experience. Skara another pretty village and the ramparts of the old Earthern Fort of Zorawar Singh makes another little expedition. Eating out is fun at open air garden and sidewalk restaurants that offer Tibetan, Indian and even Continental cuisine.

Buddhism & Monasteries in Leh

Though Leh has been capital of this region since the 17th century, strewn around it along the Indus valley are earlier capitals of he region. From Leh one can wander off on marvellous day expeditions to get a glimpse of some of the treasures of Ladakh.

Not far from Leh, Shey is the oldest capital of Ladakh from where its earliest Tibetan kings ruled. Perched on top of a huge rock are the royal palace and temples adorned with brilliantly coloured murals and a 7.5 metre gold statue of the Buddha. Basgo and Tingmosgang with their forts and palaces were also capitals of Ladakh. Stok Palace across the river from Leh is the home of the erstwhile royal family. The Palace Museum here has collections of beautiful royal costumes and jewellery, exquisite Thangkas, porcelain, jade, weapons and armour.

Within easy reach of Leh is the Spituk Monastery with its commanding view of he indus. It has fine Thangkas and a collection of ancient masks. Thikse Monastery one of the most impressive in the area is spectacularly located and is noted for its beautiful murals. Hemis is of course the biggest gompa in Ladakh and the best known for its magnificent summer festival that celebrates the birth anniversary of Guru Padmasambhava. The largest thangka in Ladakh is to be found here. It is unfolded only once every 12 years.

Other magnificent gompas located in the vicinity include the splendid Lamayuru, Likir, Phyang, Rizdong, Stakna, Matho and Chemrey Gompas, all easily accessible from Leh. Alchi no longer an active religious centre, is among Ladakh's most beautiful monasteries. Over a thousand years old, its wall paintings like those of Tabo in Spiti are reminiscent of the Ajanta style of painting. Around Leh in the upper Indus valley is the cultural heartland of Ladakh, where the old capitals of the area are located and where many of the splendid palaces and Gompas are also to be found.

The people of Ladakh are predominantly Buddhist and practise 'Mahayana' Buddhism tempered with the old Bon animistic faith and Tantric Hinduism. It was brought Buddhism to Tibet and Ladakh during his travels in the 7th century AD. In the 11th century the Buddhist scholar Rinchen Tsangpo established 108 monasteries in the region. The Gompas at Lamayuru and Alchi are said to date from that time.

The living Buddhist heritage is manifest in the villages where 'Mani' walls are engraved with the mantra 'Om Mani Padme Hum' and stones are piled into commemorative mounds known as 'Chorten'. The Gompas precariously perched on steep hillsides or rock faces seem an integral part of the rugged landscape. In Western Ladakh, in Drass, Kargil and the Suru valley where the Muslim Shia faith prevails there are mosques and imposing Imambaras in the Islamic style, surmounted with domes.

The flight into Leh, the capital of Ladakh, is an unforgettable experience - over the dramatic expanse of the Himalayas - for Ladakh straddles four main ranges - the great Himalayan, Zanskar, Ladakh and the Karakoram. This is the highest inhabited region in India and the River Indus with its tributaries, slice their way through the ranges.

Remote though it is, Ladakh has never been totally isolated. Over the centuries the trade route from India to central Asia passed through this area undeterred by its high passes and desert landscape. Caravans carrying spices, brocades, pearls, carpets and more mundane merchandise like salt and tea took just two months to cover the distance from Amritsar in the Punjab to the central Asian towns of Varkand and Khotan! Leh and Kargil on this ancient route developed then into centres of trade.

Travelling into Ladakh by road is exciting. It takes two days from Srinagar to Leh with a mid way halt at Kargil, which gives the visitor a marvellous introduction to this spectacular destination, while easing the acclimatisation process to the high altitude low oxygen atmosphere of Ladakh. The road leaves behind the verdant beauty of the Kashmir valley at Zoji-la, the pass in the Great Himalayan wall that is the gateway into Ladakh. Densely forested slopes give way to bare mountains in shades of russets and brown as the road descends to the alpine meadows of Minamarg on to Drass, the first village after the pass. It is reputed to be the second coldest habitation in the world after Siberia! The people here are different. They are of Dard origin and believed to be an Aryan people who migrated from the Central Asian steppes.

Onward the road traverses a narrowing gorge on to the little trading town of Kargil, the mid point of the journey. Located on the river Suru, at 9,000 feet, Kargil is the base for visits to the spectacular Suru and Zanskar valleys and for a variety of adventure activities in the region. 40-km ahead of Kargil is Mulbekh noted for its immense figure of Maitreya, the future Buddha, carved in deep relief into a rock face high above the village.

The road climbs its breathless way to more passes Namika la and Fotu la a truly top of the world feeling. It sweeps past the amazing Lamayuru monastery spilling spectacularly over a mountain side down the incredible Langroo loops to meet the river Indus at Khalatse - a descent of 4,000 ft. /1,219 m in about 32-km. A panoramic view of the amazing russets, yellows and greys of the Ladakh range unfolds as the road follows the river. Gompas and forts can be glimpsed in the distance. At the Spituk monastery the visitor gets a first dramatic glimpse of Leh, floating like a mirage in the distance.

Though Leh has been capital of this region since the 17th century, strewn around it along the Indus valley are earlier capitals of he region. From Leh one can wander off on marvellous day expeditions to get a glimpse of some of the treasures of Ladakh.

Not far from Leh, Shey is the oldest capital of Ladakh from where its earliest Tibetan kings ruled. Perched on top of a huge rock are the royal palace and temples adorned with brilliantly coloured murals and a 7.5 metre gold statue of the Buddha. Basgo and Tingmosgang with their forts and palaces were also capitals of Ladakh. Stok Palace across the river from Leh is the home of the erstwhile royal family. The Palace Museum here has collections of beautiful royal costumes and jewellery, exquisite Thangkas, porcelain, jade, weapons and armour.

Within easy reach of Leh is the Spituk Monastery with its commanding view of he indus. It has fine Thangkas and a collection of ancient masks. Thikse Monastery one of the most impressive in the area is spectacularly located and is noted for its beautiful murals. Hemis is of course the biggest gompa in Ladakh and the best known for its magnificent summer festival that celebrates the birth anniversary of Guru Padmasambhava. The largest thangka in Ladakh is to be found here. It is unfolded only once every 12 years.

Other magnificent gompas located in the vicinity include the splendid Lamayuru, Likir, Phyang, Rizdong, Stakna, Matho and Chemrey Gompas, all easily accessible from Leh. Alchi no longer an active religious centre, is among Ladakh's most beautiful monasteries. Over a thousand years old, its wall paintings like those of Tabo in Spiti are reminiscent of the Ajanta style of painting. Around Leh in the upper Indus valley is the cultural heartland of Ladakh, where the old capitals of the area are located and where many of the splendid palaces and Gompas are also to be found.

The people of Ladakh are predominantly Buddhist and practise 'Mahayana' Buddhism tempered with the old Bon animistic faith and Tantric Hinduism. It was brought Buddhism to Tibet and Ladakh during his travels in the 7th century AD. In the 11th century the Buddhist scholar Rinchen Tsangpo established 108 monasteries in the region. The Gompas at Lamayuru and Alchi are said to date from that time.

The living Buddhist heritage is manifest in the villages where 'Mani' walls are engraved with the mantra ' Om Mani Padme Hum' and stones are piled into commemorative mounds known as 'Chorten'. The Gompas precariously perched on steep hillsides or rock faces seem an integral part of the rugged landscape. In Western Ladakh, in Drass, Kargil and the Suru valley where the Muslim Shia faith prevails there are mosques and imposing Imambaras in the Islamic style, surmounted with domes.

The second largest town in Ladakh marks the mid point of the journey from Srinagar to Leh. Kargil is also the take off point for excursions into the Suru valley and the remote Zanskar Valley with their exciting opportunities for mountaineering, camping, river rafting and trekking trails into Himachal Pradesh, Jammu and the Indus valley.

Kargil was once at the cross roads of a network of trade routes that led to kashmir, Baltistan, Afghanistan, Central Asia and Tibet and an air of romance still lingers around its narrow cobbled streets and bazaars spilling over with locally crafted curios. The town retains its conservative Balti Shia Muslim culture and has two fine mosques built in the Turkish style.

Nestling in the Suru valley, Kargil is set amidst green, richly cultivated hill sides. The two tributaries of the river suru the Drass and Wakha meet there. There are pretty walks around the town breathtaking views of the mountains. A day long excursion into the Suru valley goes past the picturesque Imambara of Trespone.

The Suru Valley one of the prettiest areas of Ladakh, runs for 140-km beyond Kargil to the Penzi La pass, the point of entry into the Zanskar valley. Its verdant hills are intensively cultivated. Enough snow and water during the year sustain two crops annually. The valleys are especially picturesque in spring when they are the Sankoo-Panikhar tract is magnificent. The open valley adorned with undulating alpine meadows strewn with wild flowers, groves of poplars and willows are set against the majestic backdrop of the Himalayan peaks dusted with snow.

At Thangbu, a little village, the traveller gets a first glimpse of the spectacular Nun - Kun massif. Panikhar 12-km beyond this is the base for treks to Kashmir and Kishtwar. The road goes past the glaciers of the Nun - Kun massif to descend to Rangdum set in wild and beautiful surroundings. It is located at the furthest end of the suru valley before the Penzi La pass. Set high on a central hillock the Rangdum gompa with a little stream forming a moat around it, looks like an ancient fort protecting the valley.

The altitude of this region ranges between 4877-m.-8848 m. it includes 8 of the highest 14 summits in the world, which exceed altitude of 8,000m including Annapurna, Dhaulagiri and others. This region accounts for about 64% of total land area. It is formed by the Mahabharat range that soars up to 4,877m and the lower Churia range.

Nepal - a country with a long historical tradition is an amalgamation of a number of medieval principalities. Before the campaign of national integration launched by King Prithivi Narayan Shah the Kathmandu valley was ruled by the Malla kings, whose contributions to art and culture are indeed great and unique. In 1768 A.D. the Shah dynasty ascended the throne of the unified kingdom. His majesty king Birendra Bir Bikram Shah Dev, was tenth king in the Shah dynasty. The new democratic constitution of the kingdom was promulgated on November 9, 1990. Nepal is one of the founder members of South Asian association for Regional Cooperation or SAARC, of which the third summit was held in Kathmandu in November 1987

Hinduism and Buddhism constitute two major religions of Nepal. A remarkable feature of Nepal is the religious homogeneity what exists, particularly between the Hindu and Buddhist communities. Apart from the Hindus and Buddhists, Muslim from the third largest religious group.

Tibet, one of the extra ordinary destinations where indeed adventure lurks around every corner. Its name the "Roof of the world" is not a mere statement. The valley bottoms of tibet are highter than the highest mountains elsewhere. Adventure on the road is never short on the beautiful Trans-Himalaya drive of over 970-kms, through four mountain passes, promising a panorama of a cultural and scenic diversity unsurpassable anywhere. The Buddhist monasteries of Drepung, once the largest; the Jokhang- a spirtual centre, and the awesome palaces of the dalai lama. Norbulingka or the Summer Palace and the Potala - the Traditional Seat are some of the highlights of visit.

Adventure on the road is never short on the beautiful Trans-Himalayan drive of over 970-kms, through four mountain passes, promising a panorama of a cultural and scenic diversity unsurpassable anywhere. The Buddhist monasteries of Drepung, once the largest; the Jokhang- a spirtual centre, and the awesome palaces of the dalai lama. Norbulingka or the Summer Palace and the Potala - the Traditional Seat are some of the highlights of visit. Tibet has got the harshest climate in the world. It is cool in summer but freezingly cold in winter. The average temperature in north Tibet is subzero and winter hits in October till the coming May or June, July and August are the best time to visit the area, enjoying warm temperature, intense sunshine, beautiful scene and festive events.

Bhutan often reversed as the 'Land of the peaceful Dragon' is still regarded as one of the last "Shangri-La" in the Himalayan region because of its remoteness, it's spectacular mountain terrain, varied flora and fauna and it's unique ancient Buddhist monasteries. It is relatively unexplored pockets of Asia, which allows only limited number of discerning travelers to enter the country with special travel visa permits.

Bhutan's isolation has resulted its culture and traditions remaining much the same for many hundreds of years. Our weekly departure allows you to experience the stunning beautiful alpine valley flanked by step slopes and terraced pastures dotted with temple. Festival (Tsechus) are held in Bhutan through out the year at difffrent locations. These festivals are celebrations of faith, legends, mythsand history of Bhutan in ancient rituals of colorful dance and music. To coincide a visit to Bhutan during the festive season will be even better way to observe the uniqude culture.

Adventure Activities and Sports

So you are planning a adventure holiday within the Himalayan range, but are you aware about the adventure options that Himalayas have got instored for you. The first in the list of adventure activities over here is Trekking. Whether its the harsh and rough climate of the cold deserts of Ladakh, Zanskar, Lahaul and Spiti or the green pastures of Uttaranchal and Kumaon Hills or the high mountain zones of Nepal, the Himalayas is a trekker's paradise.

When there are mountains and glaciers, there's bound to be numerous rivers and untamed rivers such as the Ganges make the experience of white water rafting all the more exciting. Another adventure sport that has really caught the attention of adventurers is skiing. Mountaineering and skiing on the high slopes of Himalayas is undoubtly a dream every skier would love to fulfill. Other adventure options include Heli skiing, Rock climbing, Para gliding and Jeep and Jungle Safari. But to get the adrenalin pumping you have to visit the Himalayas first.

Camping

Camping is perhaps the best way of enjoying the wonders of nature given to Himalayan regions and sharing the warmth of its people. Wildlife camping is not very different from normal camping, except the wild camping doesn't get restricted to season or any adventure activity.

It works as a recreational program and there isn't any age limit in this. Any one who likes to explore nature and want to learn the facts about what nature has given to us and what we can give in return, can take up this camping expedition.

Take along your camping gear and opt for any of the several camps that are pitched in various parts of the state of Himachal Pradesh. These camps offer accommodation, catering and a variety of activities like hikes, fishing, nature-tours and rafting. Himachal Tourism has camps organised at Sarchu in Lahaul, and in addition to built-accommodation, tents are available at Sangla and Kalpa in Kinnaur, and at Kaza in Spiti.

Among the Indian wilds and forest regions there are various places where one can enjoy wildlife camping. Among the northern regions is Chitrauli, situated near to the hill station of Nainital in Uttaranchal and is considered to be a prime trekking paradise in this region, where nature lovers can witness panoramic views of the Himalayas and the Ratighat Valley with the Ghuna River in between.

Surroundings of Chitrauli is abound with beautiful flora and fauna offering ample opportunities to Naturalists, Trekkers, Painters and Bird watchers to try out their favourite adventure activity over here. The wild camps of Chitrauli take one to a little off beaten natural treks midst of Oaks, Deodars and Pine trees. This camp provides a pleasant escape from the pollution and grime of the cities to terraced fields, small villages, shimmering water streams and the complete range of the snow clad Himalayas.

The Himalayas are not just for mountaineers and very experienced ice climbers and trekkers. They offer a range of treks to suit all aptitudes and abilities, from a modest hike in the foothills to more challenging high altitude treks. Anyone who lives an active life and is in good health will enjoy a trekking within the Himalayas.

Nepal is singularly blessed with marvelous and impressive trekking & camping country. It is home to eight of the world's ten highest peaks. Only by hiking the ancient foot trails that link the remote village communities can one gain access to these Himalayan giant peaks. The range of scenery, from sub-tropical jungle to glacier, is as varied as the many ethnic groups cultural heritage. It is not only the mountains that cast their spell. The people, the flora and fauna and the immense landscape combine in a kaleidoscope of sights and sensations that make a camping trip among the Himalayas a unique experience.

Canoeing & Kayaking

Whether it is the challenge of taming the white waters or the pleasure of gliding over calm waters on a lake, canoeing or kayaking can be thrilling and exciting adventure to any sports enthusiast.. Kayaking is just like backpacking on an off beaten path, except that this time your adventure is on the sea. This sport provide the best opportunity for sports lovers to come close to nature. While canoeing presents quiet a unique combination of exploration.

Besides keep a person fit, canoeing and Kayaking are eco-friendly water sports. Canoes and kayaks are boats tapered at their ends so that they may cut through water easily. This unique feature makes them highly efficient on trying on most kind of water bodies. Canoes can accommodate atleast two people with their gear and is usually practiced on lakes and rivers, which have flat and still water.

On the other hand, Kayaks look like small fishing boat and are not a new thing in the Indian coastal sites, but they are fastly picking up as a favourite water sport in India. A Kayak can accommodate more than two people and can be done of both flat and white water. Ofcourse, the beach is one of the best option to try out these kind of sports, but second best in the lines are the lakes and rivers of India. Gliding through the untamed waters of rivers such as Teesta is something that you won't experince any where else in this world.

Check out the state of Uttaranchal where whitewater canoeing can be combined with moderate hiking and a naturalist holiday in the forest. For whitewater kayaking, the suitable areas are Rishikesh, Dakpathar and the Ramganga in Corbett National Park. For the ones who seek a little more adventure, kayaking can be a good option. The degree of difficulty while Kayaking would depend on the river gradient and its rapids.

A recently introduced Kayaking and Canoeing tournament in the state of Jammu & Kashmir is another event that will definitely attract the sports lovers. Organised by the J&K Kayaking and Canoeing Association in collaboration of the J&K Sports Council and the Departments of Youth Services and Sports and Tourism, this event takes place in Srinagar and works as a platform for the popularising water sports athletics. The winners of the tournaments are then selected as contestants for the National Kayaking and Canoeing tournament.

White Water Rafting and Canoeing are Adventure Hill Sports, which are relatively new in the Darjeeling Hills having introduced in 1991. Since then these sports have gained tremendous popularity compelling DGHC Tourism to take up the sport in a very big way. Graded on the international scale at Grade IV, the icy cold waters of the rugged Teesta with a series of rapids with varying intensity and character, extend a challenging invitation to one of the finest rafting stretches in the world. The turbulent waters of the Rangeet with its multidimensional rapids provide rafters with a variation meant for professionals. The spectacular scenery confronting a rafter while one snakes down the mountain rivers make this experience a must for all lovers of adventure.

Angling

Angling could become a very enjoyable sport that is if you've got planty of time in hand and loads of patience. This eco friendl;y sport is not for those who run out of patience every time they lose a fish or get tired for waiting for their catch! Hardly any anglers round the world have any idea that India makes a wonderful paradise for anglers.

With the so many rivers, streams there are numerous oppurtunites available for anglers to opt for sport fishing and angling in India. Beside the coastal areas, the foothill region of the Himalayas in northern states of India and the southern region of Nepal offer numerous oppurtunites to catch fish especially trout and Mahseer. Whether you're the type who likes to string a worm onto a makeshift line and catch your own dinner or a thoroughbred professional angler with the latest in fishing tackle- India's waters, both fresh and salt, can be a pleasant surprise.

Another kind of fishing related activity is Angling that has important methods of conservation. A good, healthy stock of fish is not the only product of the conservation efforts of anglers, waterside plants, insects, birds, mammals and reptiles also get benefit of Eco friendly sport. More of all angling or sport fishing is quiet an easy sport for even a beginner because most of major Indian cities lie along rivers, that's why these cities become a favourite fishing spot for most of the anglers.

Most of the states in India have also organised Fishing hatcheries, the breeding centres of bothy local and exotic fishes. Fish sanctuaries and hatcheries in Jammu and Kashmir, Himachal Pradesh, Uttaranachal have major flow, and maintain a vast stock of fish, which are specially bred for re-stocking rivers.

The high altitude rivers and high altitude lakes of the state of Jammu & Kashmir such as Tso Moriri abound in brown and rainbow Trout. Areas of Himachal and Garhwal region in Uttranchal too are excellent for Trout fishing and the best sport season is from May to September.

The Kullu valley has numerous places for trout fishing. These include Katrain, Raison, Kasol and Naggar, then along the river Tirthan near Lad, in the Sainj Valley and in the Hurla kund. The river Beas offers excellent opportunities for white water rafting.

Angling is also among the favourite sport of Assam. The major fishing point in the state is River Brahmaputra, yet one can also check out Jia Bhoroli River, Kapili, Manas, and Bhalukpung too for a better game of angling. Brahmaputra is one of the most fascinating rivers - full of joy and life - which leaves the adventure loving tourists, anglers and naturalists in utter awe. It is also the home of the Golden Mahseer known as the "Tiger of Indian rivers" and the "Dread of every Angler".

The state of Arunachal Pradesh, Pasighat have a lot of places like Yingkiong, Bodak, Siom, etc., that provide good spots for Fishing and Angling. The Mahseer being a favourite among angles, getting a 20-30 kg over here is not uncommon. The colder waters of the higher reaches of Arunachal have the golden and the rainbow trout and anglers can easily enjoy the traditional but effective methods of fishing while trekking in the jungles of Arunchal.

Maybe the regions of Nepal are not that known when it comes to angling and sportfishing, but if you hget a chance do bring your fishing rod with your travel gear to Nepal. Some of the popular fishing trips in Nepal are done in Karnali, Babai valley in the Bardiya National Park. Chitwan also hosts a number of places like the confluence of Seti and Trisuli rivers on the Tribhuvan Highway and also in the confluence of Kaligandaki and Trisuli river.

Anglers can try their luck in the clear waters of Pokhara's lakes as well. While Phewa Tal offers some good sport, there is considerable activity and is not the ideal place for a quiet day's fishing. Begnas Tal and Rupa Tal are a better bet. Get out there on any of several local buses that start plying early morning or bike your way there. You can hire a boat and go out to some of the good spots in the lake.

Hang Gliding

Hang gliding is usually performed by using air current without an engine power. The pilot is suspended in a swing harness from the centre of the keel and maintains control wholly by weight shift arrangement with the help of airframe. To take off, the pilot runs on a down hill approximately 40-degree slope and is airborne the moment he crosses the gliders stalling speed, which vary from 15-km to 30-km per hour. Soaring can be done by using ridge lifts created by wind striking the hill face or by hot air columns known as "thermals" that keep rising upward from the sun heated surface. One can fly as long as one wishes once he has acquired good experience.

Hang gliding is an outdoor sport and Mother Nature is unpredictable—weather is always a big consideration. The primary safety factors are personal judgment and attitude. You must be willing to learn gradually and use good judgement and have an appropriate attitude. If you don't, then you can get injured or killed; if you do, then you can hang glide until you're 90.

If you want to touch the skies ans sky is the limit for you, then hang gliding is the sport for you. You jog down a slope and glide away from the mountain. You do not free-fall or jump off of a cliff. Your launches and landings are deliberate and, once in the air, you will probably be surprised by how peaceful the experience is. Even if you are afraid of heights, it will rarely be a factor, since there is no sensation of falling. Your solo lesson will require more effort physical as well as mental, than your tandem lesson, but it lays the basic groundwork necessary to becoming your own pilot.

Hang Gliding, comparatively a new sport in India, is gaining popularity. India has got thermal soaring effects in the summer months and hill soaring almost year-round. The monsoons are the only months when this sport is not possible in India, otherwise even the winter months are also ideal for it.

Most Indian hang gliding sites have been highly rated and those in the lower regions of the Himalaya are among the best the world has. Hang gliding clubs in India are located at Pune, Delhi, Mumbai, Chandigarh, Shimla, Devlali and Bangalore.

Hang Gliding is a new sport practised at Billing, 14-km from Bir and is said to be among the finest sites for hanggliding in the world. An annual hanggliding tournament is also held over here. Situated in Dharamsala, Dharamkot is situated at 11, 800 ft and requires a 2-km trek from the nearest roadhead.

Motor Ralleying

Motor ralleying is a one of a kind extreme sport of driving to the limits and beyond that. And while there are rules on the road, in motor rallying expecially in the mountain regions the rules are set by the nature. Its upto the rallyists discretion to whether to go by nature or to to go by his own instincts. Basically your driving instincts help a lot and in motor rallying especially on the off beaten tracks of the Himalayan regions, it tottally depends on you tackle the driving challenges. One of the major coverage areas of motors rallying are mountainous zones and the countryside areas.

The countryside towns are extremely variable and offer exciting opportunities for motor rallying. The popular ones include safari rallying in the forestsed regions and its a test for both the driver and the vehicles as the route takes them over mountanous terrain and bush and grassland areas, which is not even included in a jeep safari expedition.

Himalayan Car Rally

Himalayan Car Rally is one of the most important and challenging of all the rallies, which attracts rallyists from India as well as abroad. New Delhi is both its beginning and the concluding point. Usually, the rally is divided into four legs totalling over 3,200-kms, concentrating on the mountain terrains of Himachal Pradesh and Uttaranchal.

Himalayan Wildlife Travel

The Himalayan region displays great variety in flora and fauna. It is also where rare medicinal herbs are said to grow. In the Terai - the Himalayan foothills.

Blossoming Blooms

Where the tree-line ends, the 'Buggyals' or alpine meadows begin to unfold like a green, velvet carpet. Himalayan flowers of rare beauty are seen here in abundance, their soft petals adorned with raindrops reflecting the delicate hues of sunrise and sunset. These meadows have been aptly described as the "Eden of Flowers". In the upper hills of Garhwal region Lilies and Potentillas change the landscape dramatically from a weird barren wasteland to a heavenly pasture within a short distance. It is difficult to imagine today that these Himalayan slopes were densely wooded less than a century ago. While Himalayan forests are not as lush as the rain-fed South Indian forests, they do attain an impressive magnificence in the unspoilt upper regions.

Wildlife

Wildlife in the Terai comprises Tigers, Elephants, Deer, Wild Boar, Crocodiles and Pythons. At greater heights dwell more exotic species like the elusive Snow Leopard, the sure-footed Blue Sheep and the famous Musk Deer.

Avifauna

Birds with colourful plumage like the Monal Pheasant are common to the eastern central and the western segments. It is surprising that many of these species have survived, despite the ruthless destructions of their habitat.

Jungle Safari

Jungle Safari can be called a little different because you are basically exploring the wilds in this activity. Whether you are riding on an elephant's back or inside a jeep, this safari trip is a must if you like the wilds. Jungle Safari can be defined as a forest trail, except that beside the options of walking, hiking and trekking, you can also explore the jungle via a jeep or a Elephant.

Jungle safari not just involves exploring the jungles of a particular region. The options can involve national parks and wildlife sanctuaries as well as protective reserves. And you can also opt for wild camping as well as nature walks too. All in all saying hello to Mother Nature in the best possible ways. Staying in the jungle lodges provided by the various forests departments within the sanctuary areas is also the part of this safari deal and the best way you can enjoy your holiday to hang out in the Jungle area, relax and do nothing!

Corbett National Park

Aptly called the land of roar, trumpet, and songs, Corbett national park is a legend come alive. The park embraces the picturesque patladiun, a broad flat valley consisting of the vast savannas and surrounded by hills. The Corbett National Park of Uttaranchal enable the wild life enthusiasts to view the wild in their natural habitat. A safari on the Elephant back affords a splendid view of the flora and fauna of the region.

Great Himalayan National Park

Decorated with stunning beauty and conserved with care, the Great Himalayan National Park is a virtual treasure for the researcher, the sensitive nature lover and the adventure seeker. The months of September and October are the best visiting months in this park, when the weather is generally good, to observe the Bharal and the Musk Deer. Between November to early March, when the higher reaches are under snow, the high altitude species descend towards the valleys for sustenance. Though difficult, wildlife observers could undertake field studies in these months.

Namdapha National Park

Namdapha Tiger reserve in Changlang district of Arunachal Pradesh is spread in an area of 1,850-sq-kms rugged terrain. Perhaps no other national park in the world has a wider altitudinal variation than the Namdapha national park that rises from 200m to 4,500m in the snow-capped mountain. This variation has given rise to the growth of diverse habitats of flora and fauna. And because this region is the most unexplored wild reserve of India, makes it all the more attractive jungle safari option for any wildlife lover.

Royal Chitwan National Park

The park is one of the richest and well known game sanctuaries of Asia and so offers one of the finest wildlife experience. From the pickup point, upon arrival at the fringe of the National Park, the visitors are transported to the jungle lodge or the camp site by Elephant, Safari Jeeps or dugout -canoes or a combination of them.

Royal Bardia National Park

The Royal Bardia National Park is the largest and most undisturbed wild area of the Terai region of the Nepal Himalayas. Similar to Chitwan park, but with a drier climate and a more remote location, Bardia encompasses 1,000-sq-kms of riverine grassland and sal forests. While on a jungle safari the best activity you can try out is Bird watching as this sanctuary is a natural habitata of 350 bird species.

Mountaineering

The lure of Himalayas is irresistible for the mountaineers, as the Himalayas are the greatest range of mountains on earth, their beauty, vastness, fascination and mystery will always have an everlasting appeal for those who venture in this region.

The Himalayas, by humbling those that come to them with its magnitude and power, gratifying them with its splendour and beauty, testing their determination by glaciers and peaks, defying their spirit with their inviolate mysteries-enables man to acquire the qualities which only danger and nature in the raw can sharpen. Mountaineering accentuates and exercises the quality of self-reliance, leadership and discipline amongst adventure sports lovers.

The conquest of Everest acted as a stimulus to Indian mountaineering and in 1954, the Himalayan Mountaineering Institute at Darjeeling was established with the late major N.D. Jayal (Nandu) as its first principal. Since then other institutes have been set up at Uttarkashi in Uttaranchal and at Manali in Himachal Pradesh.

In addition to these three institutes, there are a number of small institutions and clubs all over India where short courses on rock climbing etc are available. Basic courses in mountaineering are devoted to theoretical training-consisting of lectures on high altitude physiology, history of mountaineering, mountain fauna and flora, geomorphology, geology, map reading and glaciology.

The Suru and Zanskar valleys provide some of the more spectacular and difficult climbing in Ladakh. The Nun Kun Massif is one of the most frequent climbing areas of the region and is booked out for months ahead, sometimes years, by climbing expeditions. The approach to the twin peaks is from the Kargil-Padum Road, about 70-km south of Kargil. The main approach is either from Tangole or Gulmadong. Some expeditions have also approached from Parkutse along the Kangri Glacier. To reach the base camp for Kun it is for the climbers necessary to cross the Suru River.

Pir Panjal mountaineering range is situated south of the Himalayas. The vale of Kashmir is sandwiched between the Pir Panjals and the Himalayas. Similarly the Lahaul valley, north of Manali and south of Ladakh, is sandwiched between the two ranges.

The area around Manali presently forms the core of mountaineering in Himachal. The Beas Kund region and lower reaches of the Hanuman Tibba (5,930m), the Manali and Shitidhar peaks around the source of the river Beas, and the Deo Tibba (6,001m) area, are suggested for beginners with some experience.

The Garhwal and Kumon region in the state of Uttaranchal not only constitutes a large part of the Himalayas, but also contains some of the most challenging peaks - Nanda Devi, Trisul, Dunagiri, Kamet, Chaukhamba, Nilkanth, Bandarpoonch, etc.

The Sikkim Himalayas, the epitome of the world's mountains, encompass a wonderland, which for sheer beauty and magnificence remains unbeaten elsewhere in the globe. In the southwestern part of Sikkim, in the main Himalayan range, lies the majestic Kanchendzonga or Kanchenjunga, rising to a staggering height of 8,585 m (28,169 ft) above sea level. Beside this third largest peaks, other famous mountaineering peaks in Sikkim include - Kabru, Kirat Chulior Tent Peak (7,365 m) and Sinolchu (6,887 m).

The Everest or Khumbu region is justifiably the most famous of all trekking and mountaineering regions of Nepal. Populated by Sherpas, the attractions of this area are the majestic mountains, the high mountain villages, the isolated monasteries, and the local peoples. This area includes the highest mountain in the world, Everest at 8,848m, and many of the world's 8,000m peaks such as Lhotse, Cho Oyu, and Makal.

Even if Tibet is new to the mountaineering and adventure sport circuit, still if you like to explore the unexplored visit this cold desert land. Tibetan mountaineering associations have been issuing permits to foreign climbers for mount Everest and twenty other summits. The majority of these mountains are part of the high Himalayas between Everest and Shishapangma, though several other interesting 7,000m and 6,000 peaks have been opened on other regions of Tibet.

Just like Tibet, mountaineering in the Bhutanese Himalayas is a recent development . Bhutan is one of the most exclusive and rare destinations for any tourist. The unique culture, architecture, lofty snowcapped peaks, fortress like "Dzongs", Lamaist Buddhist traditions and its friendly people leave an everlasting impression on the visitor. Almost all the trekking and mountaineering expeditions in Bhutan range above 3,000m.

Paragliding

Ever since man first looked up at the sky, he was yearned to glide and soar like an eagle in the sky. Parasailing and Paragliding are indeed, experiences that combine the wonder of smooth sailing in the air and the thrill of soaring high above the ground. Once in the air, one may experience the ethereal serenity of the sport. It is an experience that is surprisingly, thrilling as well as becalming. Para gliding uses "thermals' as the driving force, and is the closest one can get, to being a bird. In perfect weather conditions one can stay aloft for over three hours and can soar to heights more than 3,000m.

River Rafting

The magic behind River Rafting also referred, as Whitewater River Rafting is the extreme and never-ending thrills in the untamed rivers. The rivers in the upper Himalayas are among the best in the world for river rafting sports, with many staircase rapids that challenge the body and spirit of the river runner. The river cuts against the rocky banks, crash into rocks, crevices and breaking into white water rapids, foaming, swirling, and falling in a thunderous din. India and Nepal has a wide range of river rafting regions, which suits both amateurs and professionals.

The rafting trip can be started off from the options available on the Indus River and its major tributaries. The best stretch for professionally guided runs in whitewater is on the Indus between Spituk and Saspol. Beyond Saspol, the river becomes difficult and running it requires technically skilled participants and careful organization.

The most difficult and exciting whitewater rafting option is on the Zanskar River, along its spectacular course through the gorge in the Zanskar mountains, between Padum and Nimo regions. This river course is suitable only for well-organized whitewater expeditions, prepared for several days for river running and camping in the absolute wilds of Zanskar region.

Himachal Pradesh's snow-fed rivers offer tremendous opportunities for the challenging sport of rafting. The rivers Chandrabhaga (Chenab) in Lahaul, the Satluj near Shimla, the Ravi near Chamba and the Beas near Kullu offer immense whitewater rafting possibilities. There are tremendous river running expedition oppurtunities between Shamshi and Aut on the Beas. The 20-km stretch has exciting and extreme whitewater rapids.

In Garhwal, the sacred river Ganga offers the professional as well as the amateur the exhilaration of whitewater river rafting. The rivers Alakananda & Bhagirathi are the main tributaries of the Ganga and meet Devprayag, frothing from their racy descent. Their waters are grade IV to V, challenging the expert to survive the thrill.

Down river from Devprayag, the Ganga changes into a pool drop river. This stretch of almost 70-kms is a perfect for the amateur and the novice, for here the river offers some fine grade III rapids and two grade IV rapids, the 'WALL' at Bysi and the 'Golf Course' 4-kms. Below Shivpuri village; each followed by deep and placid pools. Sandy beaches line the river at intervals, allowing river rafters to pull up alongside. The slopes on either side are covered with oak, pine, spruce and fir, with the occasional village and its terraced fields dotting the landscape. Wildlife can be sighted at a distance, especially spotted Deer, Monkeys, Leopard, while multi hued butterflies flit among flowering.

Ganges River has always remains a mystery for explorers and full of surprises for the rafters. Ganga near Rishikesh in Uttaranchal is a popular spot for white water river rafting. The whitewater river rafting stretch of the Ganges is from Kaudiyala to Rishikesh where the river has 12 major rapids over 36-kms long, most of which are easily negotiable and some require our expertise.

GMVN conducts river rafting courses at Kaudiyala. They provide rafts, equipment, river side camping items besides all safety precautions and trained guides who make the sport a pleasure. Nestled amongst the dense forest on the Rishikesh-Badrinath highway at an altitude of 480 mts., Here the mighty waters of ganga are ideal for whitewater river rafting. There is ample opportunity to view wildlife in its natural habitat. Nature walks along the river are a real treat and for adventure lovers rock climbing can also be arranged.

Uttaranchal tourism has recently developed a water sports resort at Asan Barrage, Dakpathar in the Dehradun district, which is located at the foothills of the Shiwaliks and on the banks of river Uamuna. The resort is only 40-kms drive from Dehradun on the Dehradun-Chandigarh highway. GMVN also offers water skiing, speed boating, paddle boating, rowing, sailing, Canoeing and Kayaking.

River Teesta of Sikkim extends the most challenging invitation to the rafters in the eastern Himalayan region. Teesta provides a series of whitewater rapids with various intensities at regular intervals. Meandering down the rough and rugged mountain river, one can savour a blend of nature and adventure.

The mighty Brahmaputra cascading down the heights of immense beauty across Tibet into the north-eastern state of Arunachal Pradesh is an exciting experience for the rafters. Though inaccessible, the region is the ultimate destination a rafter can look for.

There are numeorus fine rivers in Nepal, which offer excellent rafting or canoeing. You can glide on calm jade water with magnificent of scenery all bout of rush through roaring whitewater rapids, in the care of expert rivermen employed by government authorised agencies. One can opt for a day of river running or more. A rafting trip in one of the rivers here in Nepal gives you a chance to get the real fragrance of Nepal while you raft through beautiful countryside enjoying the sight of traditional Nepali houses perched on the hillsides and slopes, terraced paddy fields where the people sow their dreams with hopes of growing better future for themselves and for their offspring.

Skiing

Skiing is one sport that has gained immense popularity all over the world and in the past decade have become quiet attention grabbing sport because of the Himalayas.. The vast open spaces above the snowline have flung open to the skiing enthusiasts. A plethora of ski locales in Jammu and Kashmir, the hills of Kumaon, Himachal Pradesh and the North eastern states of India have become the favourite ski hideouts of adventure lovers.

The awesome height and spread of the snow clad mountains, with the added advantage of powdered snow are tempting enough to magnetize the adventurous spirits of the avid skier, providing all the thrill and excitement attached to the game. Realizing the immense prospect for tourism, India has developed some of the most modern and also the resonable ski resorts in the whole world.

In winter, Gulmarg acquires a new persona - that of the country's premier skiing resorts. Skiing, to many who watch it on TV, seems like a very elitist sport, requiring a high level of training and expensive equipment. They are surprised, when they visit Gulmarg for a day's expedition to see the snow, that others with the same level of physical fitness and training are skiing down slopes. Gulmarg is the ultimate beginner's skiing resort. One doesn't requite a heavy woolen wardrobe - slacks or a Salwar Kameez will do fine. In Gulmarg one will also be able to drift to one of the many Ski shops and hire skis, sticks and goggles. Just find yourself a ski instructor and set off down a slope.

Neither does one need to exert oneself climbing up slopes. The gentlest slope of 200m is linked with a ski lift, which helps one to go up. When one graduates to intermediate level - which will happen after the first few days of practice, there are other slopes, longer and steeper, which are connected by chair lift. The longest ski run in Gulmarg is provided by the Gondola cable car, which allows a ski run of 2,213m.

Snow capped slopes of Auli are flanked by all, dense deodar forest which cuts wind velocity to the minimum 16-kms from Joshimath on the Badrinath route, Auli offers a 180 panoramic view of Himalayan peaks like the Nanda Devi (7,817m) Kamet (7,756m) Mana Parvat (7,273) and Dunagiri (7,066m) seemingly only a snow ball thrown away. Seasonal skiers have a clean stretch of 10.20-kms of absolutely virgin slopes to sport on. These slopes provide excellent opportunities for cross country and downhill skiing events.

During winter Dayara Bugyal provides excellent ski slopes over an area of 28 sq. kms. Dayara bugyal affords a panoramic view of the breathtakingly beautiful Himalayas. There is a small lake in the area that provides an excellent camping site.

Mundali offers an unforgettable panoramic view of the snow-capped Himalayas. This place has vast ski slopes on which professions can enjoy skiing.

Munsyari is situated at a distance of 66 kms. from Jauljibi and 127 kms. from Pithoragarh via Thal. Munsyari is the center as well as the gateway of the Johar region. Munsyari is the base of treks to Milam, Namik and Ralam glaciers. Khalia Top and Betulidhar are two high altitude places that offer excellent condirions for skiing.

Who can forget the ultimate destinations such as Kufri, Narkanda, Manali in Himachal. The Manali Region in Himachal Pradesh also offers scope for winters as well as summer skiing. It has excellent natural slopes and in the summer months has limited skiing possibilities at Narkanda. Last but not the least is Kufri, which has always been a favourite among ski lovers who visit Shimla in winters. So prepare your skies and zoom through the snow.

Skiing & Heli Skiing is a new sport in Nepalese Himalayas. Being the home of eight of the highest mountains in the world, Nepal brings out the best of skiing and mountaineering expeditions. The Everest region, Annapurna, Dhauligiri, Makalu, Cho Oyu, Kangchenjunga, the Dolpo regions, and more are all ready and waiting for your on-snow signature. It would take a lifetime of skiing each and every area before you skied the same run twice.

Trekking

While a powerful motorbike is the best mode of transport for covering vast stretches of mountains, paved roads restrict one. This is where trekking blended with rock climbing skills take you far in your quest for discovering the mountains at their pristine best. Most important thing while trekking in the Himalayas is to appreciate the scale and match one's destination with one's ability, for after all its about conquering the highest mountain ranges in the world! The best seasons to trek are the pre-monsoons and post monsoons.

Bibliography

Boniface, Priscilla. *Managing Quality Cultural Tourism.* London: Routledge, 1995.

Bosselman, Fred P., Craig A. Peterson, and Claire McCarthy. *Managing Tourism Growth: Issues and Applications.* Washington, D.C.: Island Press, 1999.

Chambers, Erve (ed.). *Tourism and Culture: An Applied Perspective.* Albany: State University Press of New York, 1997.

Drummond, Siobhan and Ian Yeoman (eds.). *Quality Issues in Heritage Visitor Attractions.* Oxford: Butterworth / Heinemann, 2001.

Harris, Rob, Tony Griffin and Peter Williams. *Sustainable Tourism: A Global Perspective.* Oxford: Butterworth-Heinemann, 2002.

Honey, Martha. *Ecotourism and Sustainable Development: Who Owns Paradise?* Washington, D.C.: Island Bress, 1999.

Judd, Dennis R. and Susan S. Fainstein (eds.). *The Tourist City.* New Haven: Yale University Press, 1999.

Kirchenblatt-Gimblett, Barbara. *Destination Culture: Tourism, Museums, and Heritage.* Berkeley: University of California Press, 1998.

Lippard, Lucy R. *On the Beaten Track: Tourism, Art, and Place.* New York: The New Press, 1999.

MacCannell, Dean. *The Tourist: A New Theory of the Leisure Class, 3rd Ed.* Berkeley: University of California Press, 1999.

McKercher, Bob and Hilary du Cros. *Cultural Tourism: The Partnership Between Tourism and Cultural Heritage*

Management. New York: Hayworth Hospitality Press, 2002.

Mowforth, Martin and Ian Munt. *Tourism and Sustainability: New Tourism in the Third World*. London: Routledge, 1998.

Rothman, Hal (ed.). *The Culture of Tourism, the Tourism of Culture: Selling the Past to the Present in the American Southwest*. University of New Mexico Press, 2003.

Rothman, Hal. *Devil's Bargains: Tourism in the Twentieth-Century American West*. Lawrence: University Press of Kansas, 1998.

Rojek, Chris and John Urry, eds. *Touring Cultures: Transformations of Travel and Theory*. London: Routledge, 1997.

Rypkema, Donovan. *The Economics of Historic Preservation: A Community Leader's Guide*. Washington, D.C.: The National Trust for Historic Preservation, 1994.

Shackley, Myra. *Managing Sacred Sites: Service Provision and Visitor Experience*. London: Continuum, 2001

Smith, Melanie K. *Issues in Cultural Tourism Studies*. London: Routledge, 2003.

Index

Ala-ud-Din 40
Anjuna beach 185

Bangaram 211
Banjara embroidery 140
Banjara needle crafts 141
Benaulim beach 188
Bodhgaya 76
Bogmalo beach 187
Bronze sculptures 160
Buddhism 71, 247

Calangute beach 190
Camal safari 224
Cavelossim beach 193
City palace 50
Coastal tourism 183

Dharamsala 76
Dimsa dance 105
Domestic tourism 19

Emproidery 140

Fatehpur sikri 53

Garaga dance 112
Gateway of India 58
Golden temple 73
Gross Domestic Product (GDP) 5
Gusadi dance 106
Gwalior fort 60

Haridwar 79

Himalayan car rally 263
Hinduism 71
Humayun's tomb 46

Ikat 145
India gate 47
Indus valley civilization 138
Institutes of Hotel Management (IHM) 31
Iron pillar 42

Jaisalmer fort 60
Jami masjid 56
Jantar mantar 48
Jeep safari 226
Jehangir Palace 63

Kasida 140
Kathakali 126
Kavadi 131
Kolattam 130
Kolkali 127
Kuchipudi 102

Lacquer craft 146

Lake palace 53
Lal tibba 65
Lambadi dances 107
Leh 246
Lotus temple 38

Mahabalipuram beach 201
Mango dance 104
Metalware 160
Mohiniyattam 126
Motor ralleying 262
Mysore palace 59

National Development Council (NDC) 21
Natural vegetation 218
Peacock dance 103
Porbandar beach 205
Qutab minar 40
Quwwatu'l-islam masjid 42

Rishikesh 77

Shirdi 84
Sikhism 71
Sikkim 241
Skiing 272
Stone Sculpture 161

Taj mahal 57
Thar desert 213
Tourism industry 2

United Nations Statistical Commission 1

Varanasi 80

Wall paintings 157
World Tourism Organization (WTO) 1, 16

TOURISM AND TOUR OPERATOR'S BUSINESS

TRAVEL AND TOURISM MANAGEMENT

(In 4 Volumes)

TOURISM AND TOUR OPERATOR'S BUSINESS

(Volume-4)

Editor
Prakash Talwar

ISHA

ISHA BOOKS

DELHI-110033

Tourism and Tour Operator's Business

Rs. 2700 (Set)

ISBN: 81-8205-330-7 (Set)
ISBN : 81-8205+349-8 (Vol.4)

Published in 2006 in India by
Isha Books
D-43, Prithviraj Road,
Adarsh Nagar, Delhi-110033
e-mail : ishabooks@hotmail.com

Laser Typesetting at : Shiva Infosystem, Delhi
Printed at : Mehra Offset Press, Delhi

Preface

Tourism is one of the world's largest industries. The World Travel and Tourism Council (WTTC) estimates that tourism generates some 12 per cent of the world total GNP. Tour operators, tour agencies, and ground operators are on the front line of the industry. Tour operators are companies that sell tours to customers, either directly or indirectly through travel agents. They can play a vital role in the management of a site by making financial contributions, aiding monitoring efforts, or instructing their clients in responsible tourism. They provide travel agents with marketing support, for example by offering familiarisation visits for staff members. They can help to bridge low travel seasons by providing a steadier market, develop new destinations and can help to define service and infrastructure needs at local level.

This book explains the functions of tour operators in the tourism business. It provides a set of management practices intended to help tour operators to solve tourism problems. It also offers a set of tools applicable to monitoring policy and management implementation, promoting sites and communicating with stakeholders. The needs of tour operators and site managers are also addressed. The contents of the book will be highly beneficial to tourism professionals and students of tourism and hospitality.

Editor

Contents

Preface v

1. International Tourism Markets 1
2. Impacts of Tourism 18
3. Functions of Tour Operators 30
4. Tourism Marketing 49
5. Tourism Planning 74
6. Tourism Management Objectives 101
7. Tourism Management Strategies 116
8. Accommodating Tourists 142
9. Involving Public Participation 154
10. Tourism and Promotion of Destination 165
11. Tour Operators and Sustainable Tourism 172
12. Managing Environmental and Social Issues 182
13. Social Leadership in Travel and Tourism 203
14. Supply Chain Engagement 221

Bibliography 251

Index 253

1

International Tourism Markets

Tourism is one of the world's largest industries. The World Travel and Tourism Council (WTTC) estimates that tourism generates some 12% of the world total GNP. With studies predicting continued growth, tourism is an increasingly important factor in the planning and management at UNESCO World Heritage sites. While no formal data have been collected, a site's inscription on the World Heritage List often coincides with a boost in visitation rates. Even at current rates, tourism is an important issue at World Heritage sites.

Tourism offers well-known advantages. Visitor fees, concessions and donations provide funds for restoration and protection efforts. Visitors may be recruited as friends of a site and can help generate international support. Tour operators and hotel chains can play a role in the management of a site by making financial contributions, aiding monitoring efforts, or instructing their clients in responsible tourism. Tourism can also promote cultural values by supporting local handicrafts or by offering alternative economic activities.

On the downside, tourism spawns well-known problems. Managing rapid tourism growth is a time-consuming process demanding clear policies, ongoing dialogue with stakeholders, and constant monitoring.

Tourism activities require environmental impact assessments (EIAs) and procedures for minimising impacts. At sites with limited budgets and staff, growing tourism can stretch scarce resources and take managers away from protection efforts.

While tourism can contribute to protection and restoration efforts, the right balance between economic gain and undesirable impacts can be elusive. Managers know that a tourist attraction must be periodically renewed to remain competitive. They are also aware that they are under an international obligation to maintain or restore the site's original values. This responsibility poses difficult questions regarding the degree of change that should be permitted to accommodate tourism growth. Another problem is ensuring that a portion of tourism revenue remains in the community as a means of fostering local protection, conservation and restoration efforts.

Structure of the Tourism Industry

The tourism industry is multi-tiered, from those responsible for promotion to those who serve the consumer directly. The industry comprises the following organisational structures:

National Tourism Offices

The main responsibility for promotion of a country's tourism attractions lies with government-funded tourist organisations such as national tourism offices. National tourism offices collaborate with hotels and air carriers to raise finance for destination promotion programmes. They devote much of their overseas efforts to establishing relationships with tour operators and travel agencies. They support new developments or new tours by providing introductions and influencing development plans affecting destinations, as well as legislative or financial policies. They provide support for familiarisation trips, hold promotional events and produce research data.

Tour Operators

Tour operators (outbound providers), tour agencies, and ground operators (in-country or inbound providers) are on the front line of the industry. Tour operators are companies that sell tours to customers, either directly or indirectly through travel agents. Tour operators vary in size. Many of the smaller firms handle specialised markets such as eco-tourism and adventure travel. They provide travel agents with marketing support, for example by offering familiarisation visits for staff members. Tour operators often go to the same locations, and promotional materials and brochures tend to look alike. Tour companies try to differentiate their destinations with gradations of challenge or price, for example at ski resorts, where accommodations may be more or less luxurious and the skiing may be more or less difficult.Although Tour Operators respond for only about 12 % of global tourism flows, they can help bridge low travel seasons by providing a steadier market, develop new destinations and can help define service and infrastructure needs at local level.

Travel Agencies

In contrast, travel agencies handle a wide variety of travel packages available from tour operators and airlines. In Europe and in North America, a high percentage of tours are marketed to the public through travel agencies. In Europe, travel agencies dominate the supply of holidays and largely determine the information on which most clients base their holiday decisions. Large tour operators select travel agents to represent them on the basis of the agency's productivity. Local individuals, national groups, international enterprises or any combination of the three may own travel agencies.

Although website sales to individual consumers are on the rise, generally, travel agencies sell tours from brochures and the computerised reservation systems of major tour operators. Therefore, brochures are pivotal to the business. However, so many brochures are available, that travel agencies simply cannot stock the full range. What winds up on their display cases is a function of the commissions paid by tour operators, the efficiency of their reservation systems, and the strength of the business relationship.

In general, travel agencies are not prepared to offer information from outside the core package tours that they sell. Related to tour operators are ground operators, or in-country operators who handle logistics or ground operations. They handle tourist groups from the moment of arrival off the plane or boat, until departure. They can also sell tours in the countries in which they are operating. Ground operators are mostly based in capital cities and are usually welleducated host nationals who can speak several languages.

In some countries a key to increasing a site's popularity is to have reliable ground operators working with tour operators in Europe or North America. A scarcity of ground operators, while unlikely to deter independent travellers, may discourage consumers of organised tours who depend on their services.

Tourism markets

The tourism market comprises three general classifications:

— the independent travel market,

— the speciality activity market, and

— the general package-holiday market.

Independent travellers are not part of organised groups but travel alone or in small groups of friends. They travel either out of a general interest or because they want to practise a certain activity in a new and different environment. Most independent travellers are young, adventurous, willing to use rustic accommodations, eat traditional foods, and take public transport.

Independent travellers get much of their information on a tourist destination either from friends who have visited the area or through guidebooks, newspaper and magazine articles, or, increasingly, from the Internet. Many in the tourism industry discount these tourists because they tend to travel cheaply, falling into the category of the budget-conscious "backpacking crowd". In reality, independent travellers are "explorers" who are often responsible for popularising a destination.

Their financial input is often enough to enable local businesses to expand and improve rustic accommodations for more demanding tourist groups. Such travellers, often young, are more willing to use local goods and services, and interact more with the community outside the supervision of an organised tour, which unfortunately may cause negative social impacts.

Speciality tourism firms organise trips for clients wishing to participate in a specific activity such as bird-watching, wildlife viewing, photography or archaeological, historical and cultural tours. Also in this category are adventure travel firms offering activities such as backpacking/ trekking, white water rafting, kayaking, canoeing, rock climbing and sport fishing. Other speciality firms organise field research trips for scientists. These firms attract groups of paying volunteers who sign up to work as field assistants on projects such as archaeological digs and wildlife monitoring programmes. In addition, this market includes organisations and universities with special interest travel programmes. For example, the World-wide Fund for Nature and many museums organise tours for their members. These tours generally help to raise funds for a particular cause or project. These groups generally sub-contract to other tour operators to handle the travel arrangements.

Speciality tour operators commonly use host-country ground operators for in-country logistics. These national firms, based in the country in which the tour is operating, provide all services (transportation, hotel accommodations, guides, etc.) from arrival to departure. Some speciality firms in North America and Europe handle ground operations in a foreign country for themselves, but they tend to be exceptions to the rule. Managers should be aware that many speciality companies are small and go in and out of business rapidly.

The general package-holiday market attracts groups wishing to see an area and its culture but without a specific interest in a defined activity or subject matter. These tourists tend to be interested in general sightseeing and shopping, and may be interested in cultural attractions such as museums, ruins or other well-known or documented historical sites. Tourists in this market tend to want the standard services and amenities offered by most general tours. They will probably not be satisfied with the services that a rural community can offer; more often than not, general international tour groups want comfort, ease of access, security and more upscale accommodations and food.

Speciality of Tourism Markets

Tourism is more than ever before divided into market

segments defining different types of experiences. Specialised holidays cater to people's particular interests, such as sailing, bird-watching, photography or archaeology. Markets or market segments have been developed around the different activities. Specialised holidays have become so popular that whole new categories of travel have emerged, including ecotourism, adventure travel, heritage tourism and cultural tourism. A trek in the Himalayas is now likely to be considered adventure travel, and a week visiting cultural sites in India as cultural tourism.

Eco-tourism is one of the most frequently cited categories of the "new" tourism: It is defined by the International Ecotourism Society as, "responsible travel to natural areas that conserves the environment and sustains the well being of local people." A number of activities have been labelled eco-tourism, including bird- and whale-watching, helping scientists conduct conservation research, snorkelling off coral reefs, game viewing and nature photography. Eco-tourism is linked to and overlaps with heritage tourism and cultural tourism. Surveys show that eco-tourists tend to be young and highly educated, with professional and managerial occupations.

Eco-tourism trips tend to be longer, with fewer people in the typical tour group. Researchers report that eco-tourists are more likely to use small independent hotels, as opposed to mass tourists, who tend to stay at chain hotels. As would be expected, the eco-tourist is interested in a more natural environment, preferring less crowded destinations that are off the beaten track and that offer challenging experiences.

At the site level, the demands of eco-tourists and mainstream tourists may overlap and be difficult to differentiate. Some eco-tourists, for example, may demand condominiums, not campgrounds, for lodging. People on a bird-watching cruise to Patagonia could be considered eco-tourists but may have demands similar to those of tourists on an expensive Caribbean islands cruise. In practice, eco-tourism connotes a travel ethic, promoting conservation behaviours and certain economic policies. Examples are, an emphasis on low-impact techniques for viewing wildlife and a preference for hiring local guides.

Adventure tourism includes a wide range of outdoor activities: Adventure tourists engage in activities that are physically challenging and sometimes dangerous, or perceived to be so. Examples are sports such as trekking, mountaineering, white-water rafting and scuba diving. Adventure tourism does not necessarily require expensive facilities and infrastructure, but it does require good organisation, guides, transportation services, basic accommodation in the field, and opportunities for more comfortable accommodation at the end of the tour. Adventure travel is a rapidly growing sector of the speciality tourism market.

Cultural tourism is frequently used to describe certain segments of the travel market: It may be associated with visits to historical, artistic and scientific or heritage attractions. The World Tourism Organisation (WTO) has two definitions of cultural tourism. In the narrow sense, cultural tourism includes "movements of persons for essentially cultural motivations such as study tours, performing arts and cultural tours, travel to festivals and other cultural events, visits to sites and monuments, travel to study nature, folklore or art, and pilgrimages."

In the broader sense it is defined as "all movements of persons, because they satisfy the human need for diversity, tending to raise the cultural level of the individual and giving rise to new knowledge, experience and encounters." Because culture is subjective, definitions of cultural tourism tend to be either too wide or too narrow, limiting their practical use in the field.

Heritage tourism is a broad category that embraces both eco-tourism and cultural tourism, with an emphasis on conserving natural and cultural heritage: It is a category or market segment that includes visits to historic sites, museums and art galleries, and exploring national and forest parks. Heritage tourism, because of the large number of activities it covers, is difficult to define and measure. In recent years city planners interested in urban regeneration have adopted the term to describe many tourism programmes, a strategy that has received support from business and banks.

Many other tourism terms reflect environmental ethics and local interests. Environmental preservation concerns have given rise to what is known as green tourism, conservation-supporting tourism, and environmentally aware or environmentally sound tourism. Generally, such tourism favours minimal environmental impact and emphasises concern over environmental issues. Urban and rural tourism categories have also been created. However, since few countries have made the distinction, quantification has been difficult.

SUSTAINABLE TOURISM

The idea of sustainability is found in all the market segments and definitions of the "new" tourism. All the definitions address preservation of the resource for future generations; the use of tourism to contribute to environmental protection; limiting negative socio-economic impacts, and benefiting local people economically and socially.

The WTO defines sustainable tourism as: "Tourism development that meets the needs of the present tourists and host regions while protecting and enhancing opportunity for the future. The desired outcome is that resources will be managed in such a way that economic, social and aesthetic needs can be fulfilled while maintaining cultural integrity, essential ecological processes, biological diversity and life support systems."

The term "sustainable tourism" is frequently used in project proposals seeking international assistance. In practice, sustainable tourism programmes are an opportunity that also demands hard work. They require clearly defined goals and objectives that highlight the essential features of sustainability within the local context, an ongoing process of addressing stakeholder needs within the framework of these goals and objectives, and constant monitoring.

As with all sustainable development projects, this process is labour intensive, takes time and usually involves many interest groups, making programmes difficult to design, implement and maintain. Sustainable tourism programmes have highlighted the need for an environmental and social focus and led to the standardisation of some environmental practices as well as new ideas about how the industry should function. Discussion has produced policy goals and guidelines for planners and an impetus for self-regulation by the industry.

Tourist Types

Seeking definitions that would be more useful in practice, researchers have concentrated on tourists' behaviours and preferences. Definitions and their related market segments, such as adventure travel or cultural tourism, tend to group people into broad categories based on a range of activities. These definitions and activities necessarily overlap, making it difficult at the site level to differentiate between types of tourism.

For example, eco-tourism and heritage tourism combine aspects of both culture and nature, as do most speciality tours. So for instance, trekking in the Himalayas is considered an adventure travel activity, but most trekkers visit Buddhist or Hindu cultural sites at the same time. Bird-watchers visit archaeology sites and frequently engage in trekking.

The broad definitions of the international markets are too comprehensive to be used for site-specific decisionmaking. An effective way of addressing this overlap for research, policy and site management purposes is to classify tourists according to their motivations, behaviours and desired experiences. Researchers have developed several categories of tourist behaviours and preferences. For example, tourists may be classified according to the intensity of experiences they are seeking or the ruggedness of the conditions they desire or will accept, including the kind of accommodations expected. Thus:

— Hard-core tourists join tours or groups travelling specifically for educational purposes and/or to take part in environmental or cultural projects, such as wildlife monitoring.

— Dedicated tourists want to visit protected or cultural areas and understand local natural and cultural history.

— Casual tourists consider natural and cultural travel as an incidental component of a broader trip.

Another system that is useful for classifying preferences differentiates between "hard-class" and "soft-class" travel. This classification relates to the ruggedness factor, mostly concerning the degree of challenge involved and the comfort level of accommodations. These categories include:

— A hard-class experience that is physically difficult with an element of danger. For example, it may require walking miles into the back country, climbing a technically difficult mountain, or sleeping in rudimentary shelters.
— A soft-class experience means lower risk and more luxurious accommodations. For example, a tented safari may involve physically challenging conditions while offering amenities such as gourmet meals and comfortable transport.

Tourism Trends

Consumers are increasingly considering environmental quality as well as the quality of services as factors in their selection of tourist destinations. More and more consumers want a high standard of environmental conservation coupled with simple, efficient and pleasant service. It appears that many tourists now prefer unspoiled and uncrowded destinations. A related trend is that, before they travel, many tourists inform themselves about environmental problems at individual sites.

They want destinations to be clean and environmentally sound. Tourists will avoid places that are perceived to fall short of this image. More than ever this information is obtained through the internet. Environmental degradation can lead not only to declining tourism rates but also to changes in the types of tourists that travel to a site. Examples of this cycle are found in the Mediterranean, where the pattern has led to continued degradation and urbanisation of beach resorts.

Interest in cultural tourism seems to be expanding, but the rate of growth is unclear: More quantitative data is needed to verify the trend. For example, attendance at cultural attractions in Britain and the Netherlands over the last five years indicates that cultural tourism has kept pace with the overall tourism market. Because the cultural tourism market is difficult to quantify, experts suggest that more research would help to identify broad groupings of cultural tourists based on their motivations. Establishing categories such as arts, archaeology, language learning and so on may be the most practical way to address this issue.

Tourists increasingly want "real" experiences with other cultures and lifestyles: A study of massmarket tourists and eco-tourists found that both groups felt that knowledge of folk arts and handicrafts, as well as knowledge about the destination's history, was important.

Consumers are seeking more active and educational holidays: Specialised markets are experiencing a trend towards energetic, environment-oriented tourism, with healthy menus and plenty of opportunities for exercise. Although mass-market tourists are less active and adventuresome, and less focused on one activity, active holidays at a lower level of intensity are also a growing trend in this market segment.

Visits to protected areas are on the rise: In developed countries, tourists tend to travel in smaller groups for shorter time periods. For example, visits to Australian national parks have increased substantially in the last ten years, but often for shorter periods. The two trends together-smaller group sizes and shorter stays- have created a need for greater individual space and more facilities designed to accommodate intense use, with extra services added during certain times of the year.

The tourism industry is expected to take more responsibility for sustainable development: Professionals working in conservation are beginning to ask the industry to be more involved in site management activities. Often this involves assuming a degree of financial responsibility for the long-term maintenance of the resources they profit from.

Financial support can be in the form of direct or voluntary subsidies to management agencies or NGOs. Involvement may also mean accepting practices that limit the negative impacts of tourism.

An example is at the Great Barrier Reef Marine Park in Australia where operators have become increasingly selfregulating and accountable through the establishment of codes of conduct and guidelines for minimal impact practices. Operators at the Great Barrier Reef are also involved in the monitoring of their sites. The fact that operators are prohibited from relocating their facilities and activities once an existing site is affected by natural or unnatural environmental degradation has reinforced these actions.

— Tourism definitions can give direction to broad policy guidelines used in the development of goals and objectives for site management. For example, the International Eco-tourism Society's definition of eco-tourism states that tourism should maintain the integrity of an ecosystem and generate economic opportunities that make conservation beneficial to local people. This type of a statement can be incorporated into a policy statement defining the type of tourism a site will promote.

— Tourism definitions, such as that of eco-tourism, can be used in reports or proposals seeking funding for future projects. They can give documents a positive image and strengthen their attractiveness. Overall development concepts and definitions should match the audience for whom the proposal is being written.

For example, the term eco-tourism should be used in place of tourism when writing to nature conservation organisations; cultural tourism when writing to organisations concerned with the restoration of monuments, and so on. Market definitions can then be used in promotional materials. For example, a brochure may mention that eco-tourism is encouraged at a particular natural or mixed site.

— Operators' promotional materials give clues as to whether their products are compatible with site objectives. Tour operator literature can also help managers determine whether operators contribute locally to protec-tion efforts such as educating clients in low-impact practices.

Promotional literature will also reveal the types of clients they are targeting, what kind of experiences they value and their particular needs. For example, an operator may specialise in tours geared to a serious, single-minded bird-watching group or an amateur archaeology group.

— While knowledge of tourism definitions and speciality tourist markets can help managers set policy guidelines and understand visitor interests, the categories are general and tend to overlap. For management purposes it is useful to classify and analyse tourists according to their preferences and behaviours.

Categories such as "hard" and "soft" class provide a helpful start. These categories, which focus on visitor needs and expectations, are important for elaborating management plans and setting objectives including infrastructure development.

— Knowledge of the different market segments and the general behaviours and preferences of tourists can help managers decide which segments to promote. Different tourists present different management opportunities and requirements. For example, tourists seeking more demanding or "harder" experiences are more likely to be content with a minimal infrastructure than those seeking a "softer" experience.

Tour operators such as those working with keen bird-watchers or clients interested in archaeology may have special market demands. These specialised operators may want strict regulation of tourist numbers and noise to permit them to practise their activities undisturbed by other groups. In view of the range of preferences among nature-oriented people, the market should offer a range of accommodation.

— An analysis of the structure of the tourism industry surrounding a site can reveal opportunities for involving stakeholders in management. NTO officials could be involved in future promotional efforts. Tour operators and hoteliers who may also help with monitoring activities or establishing codes of conduct and minimal impact practices. They may also make direct financial contributions for on-site projects. Interviews with tour operators and hotel directors could determine what mechanisms, administrative and financial, would facilitate their contributions to conservation and protection efforts.

— A proactive approach will yield benefits if market trends are addressed. Continued growth in international tourism is predicted, particularly in special interest tourism. The growing concern over environmental and socio-cultural issues suggests the existence of a large potential source of support for the site.

Socio-economic profiles suggest that more and more tourists will have the means to contribute financially towards protection of the site. Consequently, if a site is planned and managed well, within defined limits, an increase in arrivals can potentially bring new financial rewards.

— Because tourists are more conscious of, and interested in, the protection of the natural, historical, cultural and social environment, it will be increasingly important to inform tourists and tour operators, through site interpretation and promotional activities, of the efforts that management is making to maintain the site.

— A preference for protected areas is a growing trend in tourism. Managers must be increasingly cognizant of these visitors' profiles and of visitation trends specific to each site.

2

Impacts of Tourism

Development impacts, usually related to infrastructure, can be widely felt and can be severe, for example, during the construction phase, and through pollution generated by hotels. Impacts caused by tourists within sites are often quite sensitive but can usually be avoided. It is important to understand the inter-relationships that cause tourism impacts which might, for example, lead one community to welcome tourists while another community develops strong opposition to a tourist presence.

The relationship between amount of use and environmental impacts is often not linear but curvilinear. That is, initial light use may cause the most damage, while subsequent use has progressively less impact. For resources such as soils and vegetation, most damage tends to occur at low use levels. An example is the relationship between the amount of trampling and soil compaction.

The first walkers to use a piece of terrain will compact most of the soil, and additional use will have proportionally less impact on the area. A similar relationship exists with vegetation impacts: initial light trampling can lead to high levels of damage, with relatively minor change thereafter. Two main impact factors are resistance and resilience.

Resistance is the ability to absorb use without being disturbed, and resilience is the ability to return to an undisturbed state after a disturbance. In practical terms, resistance is a measure of the ability of different environments and different cultures to resist change. Sherpas in Nepal have been able to absorb the presence of tourists while maintaining their culture for several generations, whereas the hill tribes in northern Thailand have seen progressively greater cultural change affecting their core family structure.

At natural sites, fertile soils are better able to withstand use and maintain vegetation; thin soils have little chance to withstand heavy use. Lichens are consistently found to have low resistance to trampling. Coral communities in windward reef crest zones, which withstand the pounding of ocean surf, are more resistant to damage caused by divers than coral communities in more protected flat zones.

Resilience can also vary. The recovery rates of damaged vegetation depend on the fragility of a given ecosystem. Species of coral vary in the time it takes for them to recover after being damaged. Communities and the people within them adjust their life styles at different paces to accommodate visitors. They may also readjust their use of natural resources if these resources become restricted when an area goes under protection.

Resistant plants include the grasses and sedges. Plants susceptible to trampling impacts include those with slow growth rates, thorns and prickles, flexible stems and leaves, and small thick leaves that fold under pressure. Plant species found in open grassy habitats are generally more tolerant of trampling, while forest floor plants are less resistant.

Tourism often leads to soil compaction, usually an unavoidable aspect of recreation activities. Compaction packs soil particles together and reduces pore space, leading to a reduction in aeration and water infiltration. This increases water runoff from rain and melting snow, causing reduced water absorption, a loss of vegetation cover and erosion. Soil compaction, while unavoidable, can be limited to certain areas.

Erosion, on the other hand, is more serious and tends to spread. Soils most prone to compaction are fine-textured homogeneous soils such as clay and silt. Wet soils are more prone to compaction and more readily churned. Meadow soil and vegetation can be rapidly disturbed when trampled during rainy periods, increasing erosion and lowering the water table.

Water turbidity from soil erosion is a frequent result of tourism infrastructure and recreation. Where soils are more prone to erosion, tourist activities and development are more likely to alter water quality to the detriment of aquatic flora and fauna. Among water pollutants, pathogens are the most dangerous. Common examples are faecal coliforms (human) and faecal streptococci (animal).

High faecal counts are associated with a lack of or malfunctioning of sewage and septic tank systems in hotels, and run-off from tourist enclaves. Organic waste such as raw or insufficiently treated sewage also affects water quality by encouraging algae and weeds. These plants can wash up on shorelines, then decay and form a breeding ground for insects. In general, chemical contamination is most severe in shallow water sheltered from wind, especially in areas such as marinas. Lakes and streams at lower elevations tend to be less vulnerable to alteration than alpine lakes.

Some species habituate, that is, after the initial impact, which may be serious, they develop a tolerance for disturbance. Habituation is often mistakenly seen as positive because it brings visitors closer to the wildlife.

Tour operators sometimes put food out to attract animals to places where visitors can see them. Attraction can be a negative response, however: habituated wildlife may become aggressive while begging for food, and can injure and even kill the unwary visitor.

Wildlife responses are variable, even within a single species or population. For example, some animals can tolerate occasional disturbances but not frequent disturbances. Nesting birds may tolerate the first few encounters with humans, but once their level of tolerance is exceeded they may abandon their nests.

Some animals develop a tolerance for predictable disturbances, noise from passing cars for example, but cannot tolerate random disturbances. Larger game species tend to be more affected by direct contact with people, while smaller wildlife are more susceptible to indirect impacts on their habitat.

More timid and sensitive species of animals become permanently displaced from recreation areas when confronted by humans, while other animals such as deer become habituated over time. Some animals frighten more easily than others, a factor that affects feeding and reproductive patterns. Maine turtles and some bird species in the Galapagos National Park withdraw from habitats visited by tourists and move to other places less suitable for survival and reproduction. Deer, which like other ungulates are relatively unafraid of humans, often graze along roadsides.

Wolves are more sensitive to tourists, whose encroachment can restrict their opportunities for hunting. Habitat is an important factor. Wildlife disturbance is much less significant on tourist trails in wooded areas where animals have more cover. Animals, like people, have accumulated experiences that guide their behaviour, and as a result there is no ideal distance from a sensitive wildlife site such as a rookery or a feeding area for infrastructure or trails. Many experts say simply that if visitors elicit a negative response from wildlife they are too close.

Common Impacts

Visitors exhibit predictable patterns: People tend to travel along established routes and be attracted to certain locations. Consequently, impacts are usually confined to these areas. However, tourism areas tend to expand over time. A related phenomenon is that once an area is opened to tourism and recreation, impacts will occur rapidly. Overall, environmental impacts have a tendency to be curvilinear.

Group size plays a role in the development of impacts: Large parties tend to expand the areas they visit. This has management ramifications for groups such as mountaineering expeditions where large parties can create small cities during the length of their stay. Large parties also can create a heavy amount of use in a short time. As a result, large parties are of particular concern in pristine natural areas and at delicate cultural sites. At cultural sites large parties can cause bottlenecks at an interpretative display.

At monuments they can overwhelm certain exhibitions, blocking the view of smaller groups or individuals. Large groups can block the flow of visitor traffic, for example, through a cathedral. There are exceptions to this pattern. Along a trail or cathedral walkway, for example, large parties probably have no more impact than small parties as long as they remain on the trail or walkway. With wildlife, large parties may have less impact than several small parties if the frequency of disturbance is a factor, as in the situation with many species of birds.

Various activities are associated with certain types of impacts: For example, rock climbing and nature photography can disturb nesting birds. Scuba diving and cruising can cause damage to coral reefs. Horseback riding, hiking and camping cause vegetation and soil disturbance. Visitors to monuments can cause abrasion through touching. Activities involving motor vehicles have negative impacts on many fragile environments. Noisy motorboats and water scooters disrupt the feeding and breeding patterns of birds, and can injure other aquatic wildlife.

Motorboat propellers repeatedly kill and maim docile freshwater manatees. Motorboats are also highly polluting; one powerboat emits 70 times more hydrocarbons than an average car does. Beach vehicles disrupt the accumulation of seaweed that provides mulch for colonising dune vegetation. Soil compacted by vehicles in the Mojave Desert in the United States would need about a century to be restored.

Because of these impacts, managers often recommend banning motorised vehicles from fragile areas such as sand dunes and deserts. Impacts vary according to how tourists practise different activities. Well-trained divers with good buoyancy control are less likely to damage coral than inexperienced divers. Mountaineers trained in low-impact camping cause far less damage than those without such training. Some conscientious tour operators adopt certain viewing policies to limit impacts on wildlife.

Many operators of whale-watching tours have their drivers maintain set distances from the whales, avoid chasing the animals, and switch off the boat engines during close-up viewing so as not to produce undue stress. At a cultural site, for example a sacred rock art site or a church, visitors can be asked to show respect by covering their heads or maintaining silence. Impacts caused by tourists are usually unintentional and can frequently be reduced through sensitivity training.

Crowding is a negative impact when it interferes with tourists' expectations. Early research found that increases in visitor numbers led to decreases in satisfaction levels. As a result, managers sought to determine the point at which visitation numbers would cause a feeling of crowding. However, it turns out that the relationship between numbers of people and visitor satisfaction is more complicated.

While large numbers of people at a site can certainly decrease aesthetic enjoyment and diminish opportunities for solitude, sheer numbers do not necessarily diminish visitor satisfaction. Instead, negative reactions tend to occur when tourists feel that fellow visitors are interfering with their desired experience.

A further complication is that the negative effects of crowding vary with the characteristics of different visitors, their experience with the area, fellow visitors' behaviour, and the characteristics and peculiarities of the setting. For example, people viewing wildlife in Maasai Mara, a nature reserve, may be annoyed by the presence of only a few other vehicles, while at a game park other vehicles are more expected. Visitors may also change their expectations associated with an activity in order to tolerate crowded conditions.

Communities and Culture

Models fail to capture the complexity of the tourism cycle because they assume a homogeneous community, a rarity in real life. For example, in the later stages of the tourism cycle, models fail to show whether the whole community is hostile to tourism or whether only certain sections of the population suffer from and complain about the social impacts. The fact that host community members adapt to tourism in various ways adds complexity to the problem.

Another factor is that tourism growth may occur alongside other changes, and the hosts' behaviour may be a response to these changes more than to the changes brought by tourism. Also, while many studies have investigated general attitudes towards tourism in particular communities, few have looked into attitudes towards specific community tourism products and services.

A major research problem has been that few studies have been designed on the advice of those being affected. Only a few researchers have asked respondents to rate or assess the importance of impacts cited by local people.

Interaction between tourism development and a community has been shown to be difficult to predict, with few consistent relationships or patterns. Following is an overview of findings on this complicated issue. High tourism concentrations can be viewed as positive by some communities and negative by others. While negative attitudes are usually associated with high levels of development, some communities support tourism despite high resident-to-tourist ratios.

Visitation to Shark Bay, Western Australia, grew from 10,000 in 1984 to 150,000 in 1990, boosting the resident-to-visitor ratio from 1:10 to 1:150 in just six years. Despite the rapid growth rate and the emergence of serious environmental problems, residents remain positive about tourism and support its continued growth. Similarly, at Nadi, Fiji, where tourism development and contact with tourists is also high, the hosts remain positive in their reactions and attitudes.

Some studies have found that residents are more likely to support tourism if they stand to benefit from it through employment for themselves or family members. Or they believe the benefits of tourism outweigh the negative impacts. Some studies show that people who do not benefit from tourism support the industry regardless.

Some research has reported local concern over the impact of tourism development on property prices, access to recreation, traffic congestion, quality of life, salaries and higher prices.

Other research shows little relationship between tourism development and indicators such as the quality of life. Residents in the Austrian Alps reported that while tourism had brought higher prices for basic necessities, higher taxes and competition over the distribution of benefits, as well as decreased participation in community projects, the overall influence of tourism on the communities was positive.

Some cultures can adapt positively to external influences while others cannot. Cultures and communities with a history of interacting with other cultures and a gradual exposure to outside groups incorporate new practices intc their lives, safeguard their own cultures, and have fewer difficulties with tourism. Groups that have had little contact with outsiders have greater difficulty. An extreme case is when Australian aborigines paid absolutely no attention to Captain Cook's ship the Endeavor in 1770, finding it unclassifiable and too bizarre to contend with.

External influences can change some cultures in one or two generations. New patterns in a culture's social structure, for example women working outside the traditional family system, can weaken interest in cultural traditions such as storytelling. With new employment opportunities, young people may no longer want or need to learn traditional skills. While in some cases tourists' interest in local art, music and language may foster a cultural renaissance, most often researchers report traditional cultures veering towards commodification.

Cultural commodification is the erosion of cultural practices until they become meaningless: In a tourism setting this develops as people and their cultural symbols are treated as commodities that can be bought, changed or sold. As this occurs people begin to perform exclusively for the tourists' benefit, and events may lose their value as a cultural and spiritual manifestation. As a defensive mechanism some communities try to limit tourists' intrusion by keeping separate cultural manifestations closed to tourists, and offering "staged authenticity" performances to visitors, including appropriate interpretation and explanations.

Community acceptance of tourism depends greatly on the extent to which the attraction reflects the needs and desires of local people and their integration into the industry: Negative cultural change can be minimised if local people are able to participate in tourist-related businesses and have a role in making decisions about the numbers and types of tourists entering their communities, and at what frequency. Cultural and economic impacts are reduced where local groups have had some autonomy over their land, where they have been integrated into the tourism industry.

Access for locals to an attraction, and the perception that the attraction brings economic benefits through the creation of jobs or additional income into the local economy are other factors contributing to community acceptance. Free access for locals is often seen as a positive development. Locals will tend to resent visitors if protected area authorities appear to be managing a site more for foreign and national visitors than for local people.

Conflicts arise when the economic benefits of tourism are unevenly distributed, especially when resulting disparities in wealth are great. In the main settlement and administrative area of Taman Negara National Park, Malaysia, about 60 percent of the local people hold jobs in the tourist sector, earning much higher salaries than the rest of the population. In neighbouring villages some 70 percent of the population live off the land, making about one-third of what the locals in the main settlement make. Tourism has created social tensions as locals resent higher boat fares and rising costs of everyday goods; conflicts arise over the use of park resources such as fish, fruit and rattan; and illegal hunting and fishing are on the increase.

Distributing economic benefits to support local populations has been difficult for a number of reasons. In a study of protected areas with tourism programmes, few generated substantial benefits for local people. Even in highly successful areas, few direct benefits went to local communities. For example, while tourists generate about $5 million annually at Khao Yai National Park in Thailand, little of the revenue benefits the surrounding communities. Tourism development in the Everest area of Nepal tends to be concentrated along strips, with little room for economic benefits to spread. Studies in some areas of Nepal showed that only the village elite were able to capture tourism benefits.

Economic development from tourism does not readily translate into community participation in conservation and protection actions. The reasons for this include the following:

— Economic benefits from tourism often create insufficient incentives for local communities to support conservation and protection.

— Strategies for creating ownership of an economic development conservation programme are difficult to develop. Often, no mechanisms exist for providing incentives for conservation activities. Donors will often provide infrastructure, schools, clinics, wells, etc., in areas outside protected zones without consulting or engaging local communities. Since these initiatives are seen as grants, people feel little responsibility for their future maintenance. Clearly they are unsustainable.

— The link between tourism benefits and conservation activities may be unclear or nonexistent. For tourism to promote conservation, local people must benefit economically and see a clear link between the benefits and the need to protect the resource. If benefits do not stay in local areas or are narrowly distributed, there is little chance of making these important links.

3

Functions of Tour Operators

Travel and tourism industry operates both in the public and the private sector. The trend, in the last few years, has been gradually shifting towards the private, corporate sector with the government role getting confined to monitoring and facilitation of tourism-related activities. The promotion of tourism in the country is now the focus of the public sector.

The public sector organisations connected with tourism not only run a network of hotels, information centres and other facilities, but are also involved in development projects aimed at improving the infrastructure and expanding the industry. But now, most of the ITDC-run hotels are gradually being sold to private parties. The Department of Tourism is responsible for formulating and initiating plans for improvement of the industry.

The India Tourism Development Corporation (ITDC), an autonomous body, looks after the publication and distribution of promotional literature on India, information brochures for tourists, organising cultural programmes, and running a network of hotels and restaurants and duty-free shops among other things. The State Tourism Development Corporations facilitate travel and promote tourism at the state level. Their functions are similar to the ITDC, albeit confined to the state. In the private sector, tourism activity is divided into two different sections.

The Indian tourism industry has been expressing much concern over the five million Indian outbound tourists that are amounting to a revenue outflow of about Rs 25000 crore annually. In an endeavour to divert some of this revenue toward domestic tourism, the industry is all geared up to develop this segment further to give it a much needed thrust.

Tour operators have awakened to the fact that domestic tourism is the foundation of strong tourist inflow. With an intent to focus on inter-regional tourism promotion and to boost the potent domestic tourism segment, Indian travel agents and tour operators have for the first time joined hands to aggressively tap this lucrative sector. Until a few years back, India's domestic tourism was limited to only pilgrim tours.

However, today the movement of the domestic market has increased tremendously. This is evident from the fact that even time-share, which till recently was one of the most infamous segments of the industry is now gaining popularity as an easy vacation option. To attract customers, travel agents are now exploring new territories and are sprucing up their itineraries and products. According to the latest travel surveys, there has been a phenomenal rise of ten per cent annual growth in the domestic tourism segment.

The explosion of domestic tourism is an inevitable by-product of economic development in the country. As there is an increase of disposable income, the demand for travel has grown exponentially, diverting most of the traffic toward the outbound segment., putting domestic tourism on the back burner. Where as Indian tourism has been equated with foreign visitors alone or the inbound tourism segment which has been sluggish over the last few years. It is time that India starts equating domestic tourists at par with the foreign tourists to boost its domestic tourism.

Experts believe that Indian tourism has no foundation and lacks projection and awareness. In addition, whenever India has tried to pep up the scenario, several uncalled for events like 9/11, attacks on the parliament and other natural calamities have become major deterrents in the movement of travellers internationally. Weighing the socio-political scenario globally and its adverse impacts on the international movement of both the business and leisure traffic it is only natural that all tour operators have turned focus on domestic tourism, which is both a profitable and feasible proposition in the given scenario. Tour operators are now diverting outbound tourists by enticing them with attractive domestic packages. The industry is now working with various airlines and state tourism departments to work out incentives for the domestic travellers.

To promote domestic tourism, the biggest hurdle has been the inadequate infrastructure. Now the Ministry of Tourism is becoming aggressive as far as infrastructure development is concerned, development of the tourism circuits is has received a big impetus by the same. While infrastructure development is a continuous process, many agents believe that it is not a burning issue. Tourism experts observe that infrastructure development will take place automatically once there is aggressive movement of tourists.

To strengthen the country's tourism, the geographical diversity can be fruitfully marketed nationally and internationally. This exercise has a lot of significance even regionally. For people in the South, Snow holidays and Himalayas are new attractions and similarly, the beaches and temples of the South can be promoted to the people of North. These products are to be co-ordinated to compete with the attractive packages available for the outbound tourists. Moreover, domestic tourist movement is not limited by seasons, but each season has its own unique selling proposition (USP).

Initiatives like re-introduction of Leave Travel Concession (LTC) are much required to boost domestic tourism. The government's decision to restore the LTC facility to its employees with the hope that the consequential additional outgoing from the exchequer on this account, will at least benefit the tourism industry, has been a welcome decision. Two years ago, the ban on LTC came as a serious blow to the domestic travel agents (since ticket bookings for the employees for the leisure travel generated a good business), depriving them from booking travel tickets for government employees willing to go for leisure tours. LTC has been termed as a good tool to offer a fillip to the leisure travel. The withdrawal of LTC for last two years was counted as an obstacle to the growth of the domestic tourism and was criticised by prominent tour operators. The government employees with the allowance as a disposable income would now be prominent travellers.

In order to create adequate awareness, tourism practitioners point out that media can create the desired hype amongst the populace. Besides, state tourism offices should carry out extensive marketing campaigns jointly with the help of media, tour operators and travel agents, finance companies, hotels and airlines by offering attractive holiday packages to lure the consumers. Due to the lack of publicity, public is unaware of the destinations within the State and outside which are worth seeing and comes under one's budget to spend holidays.

States should organise inter-state Travel Marts/ Exhibitions to expose the tourism potential in their areas. Development of integrated tourist circuits as envisaged in the National Tourism Policy need to be aggressively promoted by the travel trade. This will enable the tourist to visit more than one destination at a given time while planning holidays. Indian Railways can play a major role in this regard by developing special holiday packages for domestic tourists.

Role of Tour Operators

These people are solely into marketing the concept of travel. They plan and `sell' trips to individuals and groups. They book tickets - for air, rail, sea or road travel, arrange hotel reservations or guest houses, hire taxis etc. Besides domestic, all travel agents undertake international bookings and special business tours or conferences.

Tour operators are mostly into travel management. They organise and put together package trips and holidays. These could be for incoming tourists from abroad or outbound tours or even domestic travellers. They can offer special packages, which could include such diverse attractions as deep-sea diving, snorkelling, Himalayan trekking or even camel safaris in the Thar Desert.

Working in this field means dealing with people directly on a daily basis. Helping people plan their itinerary, providing ticketing services to company executives, co-ordinating with the airlines, railways or transport company staff, arranging passports and visas, booking hotels - all these require not only a great deal of mobility but also regular contact with representatives of the various services. One must be up-to-date on rules and regulations governing foreign travel, documents required, hindrances if any; so as to correctly advise the clients.

All the staff, be it in marketing, counter sales or guide services must be knowledgeable about the places their clients intend to visit - the best way to reach your destination, places to visit, facilities available etc. Major areas of work in a travel agency include counter work, marketing and management. Counter work involves helping clients with their itineraries, chalking out travel routes, procuring tickets, arranging for passports and visas, making hotel reservations, organising cargo transport and the like.

Counter clerks must be able to have easy access to timetable information and be extremely accurate with the information provided to clients. A small slip on their part could result in embarrassing or even disastrous consequences. Marketing area includes advertising and an aggressive promotion of the agency to potential customers. Procuring steady business for the company is their major job.

The management staff deals with the administration of the agency. The managers co- ordinate and streamline the work of the clerks and select brochures of the various tours and packages available with them, among other things.

Major Functions

— *Planning*: The planning of the tours is done by the tour directors or once-in-a-while by experienced counter clerks. Planning involves chalking out the tour programme, working out the cost, confirmation of accommodation and other facilities like food and entertainment, and consulting tourist officials.

— *Sales and Reservations*: The staff has to ensure that travel brochures are on display at agencies. They also take bookings from travel agents or individuals.

— *Representatives/guides*: These are freelancers mostly whose job involves accompanying tourists to their destination and looking after their needs while travelling. A smattering knowledge of different languages can be useful as well as a general awareness and history of the place visited. This job can be easily done by students or even office workers and others who are interested in travelling. Tour operators or local tourism departments often employ professional guides who have a thorough knowledge of the history and cultural significance of a place. Many tour operators, nowadays specialise in areas such as adventure tourism, beach tourism, mountain holidays etc.

— *Entry*: A basic diploma in travel and tourism management can be advantageous to a person seeking to work in this field. Advertisements appear from time to time for jobs available in travel agencies and tour operating companies or for a position in a government department or corporation. In general, the minimum requirement for entry into this industry are: (i) 10+2 and fluency in the spoken language up to tourist guide level. (ii) for higher positions, a graduate degree in any discipline with a specialisation in history and architecture or geography and archaeology can be a great asset as is the knowledge of one or more foreign languages. If one is applying for a government post, he/she has to clear a written test, a personal interview and a medical examination. On-the-job training is provided to all new entrants.

— *Training*: With the demand for trained people increasing by the day, it is wise to gain some insights into the field through professional training. There are a number of institutions in the country which offer training courses on different aspects of the industry. There are equally good correspondence courses too.

— *Career prospects*: A career in travel and tourism can be exciting and full of fun. Not only is it flexible, but certain jobs in the field can provide excellent travelling opportunities. Job prospects include working in: travel agencies as tour operators, in airlines (domestic and foreign) transport and cargo companies, travel consultancy services and in the government run tourism departments. With enough experience and capital, one can even start one's own travel consultancy.

The tourism industry is thus a high-growth industry which can only expand with time, what with more and more people finding the means and the inclination to discover new places and seek new adventures. At the rate the industry is growing, it is certain to be the industry of the 21st century, providing ample job opportunities to all kinds of people at all levels.

Tour Operators and Air Carriers

Tour operators enter into long term contracts with air carriers, hotels and other suppliers for the provision of bulk travel services. Discrete travel services are then assembled into a package tour featuring round trip transportation, seven nights accommodations, ground transportation and tours of local sites. The package tour is marketed to the general public through travel agents. Tour operators are principals and responsible to consumers for the provision of the component travel services of each tour package.

Liability Shifting

Each of these ruined vacations involve a complex marketing system which includes suppliers, both domestic and foreign, wholesalers and tour operators, travel agents and informal travel promoters. Often the negligence of a foreign supplier, i.e., hotel, para-sailing operator, horse or camel stable, tour bus company, air carrier or cruise ship, will be the primary cause of the consumer's injury.

Unfortunately such a potential defendant may be irresponsible, insolvent, uninsured or unavailable because of a lack of jurisdiction or the U.S. forum selected is deemed inconvenient. Assuming availability the potential defendant may be insulated from liability, in whole or in part, because of the application of foreign law, enforceable disclaimers and releases, the Warsaw Convention, U.S. federal and state statutes limiting the liability of cruise ships and hotels and tariffs limiting the liability of carriers. Successful travel litigation depends upon the selection of viable defendants and the application of modern liability theories.

Cooperating Air Carriers

Cooperating air carriers may function as tour operators and be subject to the same theories of liability. For example, an air carrier may own and/or control a captive tour operator. Or the air carrier may be a partner or joint venturer and help finance, organize, operate or market tours to the general public.

Air carriers may, however, function as independent contractors entering into arm's length transactions with tour operators. Under these circumstances a cooperating air carrier may be held vicariously liable because of an assumed duty, breach of warranty, apparent authority or third party beneficiary theory. Lastly, the duties and obligations of both tour operators and air carriers may be governed by DOT Public Charter regulations or State travel seller regulations.

As a general rule tour operators may be able to disclaim liability, in the absence of their own negligence, for a consumer's physical injures caused, primarily, by the negligence of a foreign supplier. The traditional theory being that a principal should not be liable for the torts of independent contractors. This general rule can be circumvented by applying one or more of the following theories of liability.

Safety And Assumed Duty

A tour operator may be held liable for the consumer's physical injuries if the tour operator promised, either expressly or implicitly, that the tour would be delivered in a safe and careful manner. Brochure language such as "safe and enjoyable cycling area", "Marenco's administration and staff work together to make your stay comfortable, safe", "suitable for handicapped individuals", "perfectly safe" canoeing conditions and "safe buses" may generate liability under a breach of warranty theory. Alternatively, the tour operator may assume a duty to deliver safe travel services. Assumed duties may more readily overcome written disclaimers than a warranty.

Supervision of Tour Guides

Escorted tours feature close supervision and tour coordination provided by professional tour guides. Older consumers and the parents of students purchase escorted tours. Some sports' tours provide instructors to train and supervise the activities of the participants. In their brochures tour operators will promise that " every tour will be escorted by a qualified professional tour director...carefully selected and trained...informative, they know precisely what you will be seeing and doing...they've been there before "and their " tour escort was a professional and qualified to serve travelers in all matters".

Consumers, especially the parents of students, rely upon promises of close supervision in purchasing such a tour. Consumer injuries caused by the negligence of the tour guide may support claims against the tour operator for negligent selection and supervision of tour guides and misrepresentation of their training, expertise and knowledge of the tour locale.

Ownership And Control

Tour operators and air carriers may lend their names to promotional brochures giving consumers the impression of ownership and control. When Trans World Airlines describes tours as TWA Getaway tours it is reasonable for consumers to believe that TWA owns, operates, controls and is responsible for the delivery of such tours. When Delta Airlines gives the impression that it is "connected" to Skywest it is reasonable for consumers to believe it is so.

When hotel and rental car franchisors fail to distinguish between themselves and foreign franchisees the former may be held liable for the torts of the latter. Describing foreign bus companies, taxi services and ground service providers in possessory terms can generate liability.

Tour operators select the suppliers that will provide the component travel services which make up the package tour. Tour operators should investigate the reliability and willingness of suppliers to deliver safe travel services. Such an investigation should reveal the supplier's financial solvency, prior accident and safety history, the existence of insurance and compliance with all applicable licensing and safety regulations, both domestic and foreign. A failure to conduct such an investigation may generate liability for the negligent selection of suppliers.

Tour operators should design itineraries which maximize safety and minimize the consumer's exposure to risk. Of course, calculated exposure to risk may be a strong selling point in marketing "adventure" tours featuring challenging terrain or white water rafting. Tour operators may be held liable for unnecessarily exposing consumers to risk or designing itineraries in a negligent manner.

If tour operators hold themselves out as owning or controlling a foreign service provider then they may be estopped from denying liability for the torts of foreign air carriers, resorts, rental car companies, tour bus companies and other independent contractors. Consumers reasonably rely upon the appearance of ownership and control in purchasing the tour package.

Medical Malpractice

Typically, the injured consumer will be given assistance by the medical staff of the foreign hotel, resort or tour operator. If such medical services are unavailable the consumer may be transported to a recommended foreign doctor, infirmary or hospital. The quality of medical care rendered in foreign locales can exacerbate existing injuries and expose the tour operator to even greater liability.

Certainly, domestic carriers have a common law duty to seek proper medical assistance and maintain adequate medical equipment for emergencies. Under an assumed duty theory the tour operator may be obligated to investigate the availability of proper medical care before recommending foreign health care providers.

Identification of the entities involved in marketing and delivering the component elements of the tour is important. Once identified then appropriate legal theories may be developed and applied to each potential defendant. There are situations, however, where the connection between the accident and a viable U.S. defendant is too tenuous to support litigation in a U.S. forum. Under these circumstances it may be necessary to recast the defendants and redefine their marketing function.

Most tour operators recognise that a clean and safe environment is critical to their success. Fewer have the management tools or experience to design and conduct tours that minimise their negative environmental, social and economic impacts while optimising their benefits. To develop and implement these tools in their own operations, and encourage other tour operators to do the same, a group of tour operators from different parts of the world have joined forces to create the Tour Operators' Initiative for Sustainable Tourism Development.

The Initiative is voluntary, non-profit, and open to all tour operators, regardless of their size and geographical location. With this Initiative, tour operators are moving towards sustainable tourism by committing themselves to the concepts of sustainable development as the core of their business activity and to work together through common activities to promote and disseminate methods and practices compatible with sustainable development.

The Initiative has been developed by tour operators for tour operators with the support of the United Nations Environment Programme (UNEP), the United Nations Educational, Scientific and Cultural Organization (UNESCO) and the World Tourism Organization (WTO/OMT), who are also full members of the Initiative. Under this international umbrella, tour operators who are members of the Initiative will be able to respond to international agendas while creating a platform to develop ideas and projects to address the environmental, social, economic and cultural aspects of sustainable development within the tourism sector.

In particular, the members of the Initiative have formed Working Groups in four key areas of action:

— Sustainability Reporting

— Cooperation with destinations

— Supply Chain Management
— Communication

Tour Operators' Performance Indicators

The Tour Operators' Initiative, in cooperation with the Global Reporting Initiative (GRI), has developed a Sector Supplement to the GRI 2002 Sustainability Reporting Guidelines providing Tour Operators' performance indicators. Forty-seven indicators have been developed to measure tour operators' performance in addressing the environmental, economic and social impacts of their business operations.

The tour operators' supplement adds to, but does not replace, the 2002 GRI Sustainability Reporting Guidelines' section on performance indicators. The tour operator's sector supplement applies only to businesses dedicated to organizing holiday packages, that is a pre-arranged combination of accommodation, transport and other tourism services not ancillary to transport or accommodation and accounting for a significant proportion of the package, when the service covers a period of more than twenty-four hours or includes overnight accommodation.

The supplement was not designed to capture sector-specific aspects of the various service industries associated with a package, such as transport, accommodation, and other tourism services. The tour operator's performance indicators are divided into categories that reflect the life cycle of the holiday product: from the planning stage, to the development and delivery of the product. The indicators have been grouped under five categories:

— Product management and development (PMD) includes actions related to the choice of the destination as well as the type of services to be included (e.g., the use of train vs. plane).

— Internal management (IM) reflects all the operations and activities that take place in the headquarters or country offices (e.g., use of office supplies, production of brochures, direct employment).

— Supply chain management (SCM) addresses actions related to the selection and contracting of service providers.

— Customer relations (CR) summarises the actions taken to deal with customers, not only with regards to the responsibility to serve them and reply to their comments, but also the opportunity to provide information and raise consumer awareness regarding sustainability.

— Cooperation with destination (D) includes all activities and decisions related to destinations that tour operators make beyond the production and delivery of their holiday package. This mainly includes efforts made by tour operators to engage in dialogues with destination operators about the impacts of tour packages, and philanthropic activities.

During the process of developing the supplement, the participants began to develop 'guidance notes' listing recommended best practices, as well as more specific instructions on the sustainability issues to be taken into account for three specific indicators. The guidance notes have not been officially reviewed and approved as part of the GRI framework and represent the experience and recommendations of the TOI and the members of the Multi Stakeholders Working Group.

The Tour Operators' Initiative (TOI) entered, in Summer 2001, an official agreement with the Global Reporting Initiative (GRI), to produce the tour operator's specific supplement to the GRI 2002 Sustainability Reporting Guidelines.

A key element of the agreement was the recognition that the tour operator specific supplement will be developed in full consultation with all the relevant stakeholders. Key stakeholders' representatives were then selected in consultation with relevant experts, and a Multi-Stakeholder Working Group (MSWG) was established.

The Multi Stakeholder Working Group included twelve tour operators members of the Tour Operators' Initiative, as well as representatives from Non Governmental Organizations, trade unions, tourism board, local authorities, tour operators' suppliers, consumers' associations, from various regions of the world.

The tour operator's sustainability reporting performance indicators were developed according to the following work plan:

— *Step 1*: preparation - by the members of the MSWG - of First Draft of the sustainability reporting performance indicators for the selected areas of activity/impact.

— *Step 2*: First Draft of the Tour Operators' Sustainability Reporting Performance Indicators - addressing internal and supply chain management and customers' awareness - posted on the web for public comments, and sent to key stakeholders and organizations for targeted comments.

— *Step 3*: Second Draft of the Tour Operators' Sustainability Reporting Performance Indicators prepared by the MSWG, accounting also for external comments received in Step 2. This Second draft prepared during the second Multi Stakeholder Working Group Meeting will also include an additional set of indicators addressing tour operators' impacts and influence on destinations.

— *Step 4*: Second Draft of the Tour Operators' Sustainability Reporting Performance Indicators - addressing internal and supply chain management, customers' awareness and activities at destinations - posted on the web for public comments, and sent to key stakeholders and organizations for targeted comments.

— *Step 5*: Third and Final Draft (PDF 40kb) of the Tour Operators' Sustainability Reporting Performance Indicators finalised by the MSWG, accounting also for external comments received in Step 4.

— *Step 6*: preparation by the MSWG of the vision paper: how the performance indicators will be further developed in the following years.

— *Step 7*: submission of the final draft of the Tour Operator's sector performance indicators to the GRI Board of Directors for approval.

— *Step 8*: Approval by the GRI Board in September 2002 and publication of the Tour Operator's as a supplement to the updated GRI 2002 Sustainability Reporting Guidelines by mid-2002.

Pilot phase

The members of the Tour Operators' Initiative will participate in a pilot phase in 2003, the main objectives of which are to build awareness and know-how on reporting principles and practices, and to facilitate the revisions and improvement of the indicators, through the generation of the following outputs:

— A user's manual containing guidance notes to a number of indicators based on collected best practices, as well as measuring protocols.

— Recommendations on most effective reporting formats for the sector.

— A proposed model suitable to the tour operators' sector for organising the internal flow of information to support reporting efforts.

— Recommendations of the links between the core 2002 Guidelines and tour operator-specific indicators.

— A proposed classification of core and advanced indicators for the tour operators' sector.

The pilot will not only provide the structure for tour operators to learn about Sustainability Reporting and the Tour Operators' Performance Indicators, but also the platform to revise the indicators based on a better understanding of their business and sustainability relevance. Most participants indicated that the tour operator's sector supplement should be reviewed in two- to three years' time.

Integrating sustainability into tour operators' business practices: Effectively integrating sustainability into the tour operators' business means considering environmental, social and economic aspects throughout the process of developing a holiday package. The key operating areas where tour operators can integrate sustainability practices are:

— Internal management, by taking into account sustainability principles in the management of human resources, office supplies and production of printed materials;

— Product development and management, by planning tours and selecting holiday package components that minimise environmental, economic and social impacts;

— Contracting with suppliers, by integrating sustainability principles into the selection criteria and service agreements of suppliers;

— Customer relations, by guaranteeing privacy, health and safety standards, and providing customers with information on responsible behaviour and sustainability issues at their destinations; and

— Relations with destinations, by supporting destination stakeholders' efforts to address sustainability issues and proactively contributing to conservation and development projects.

Moreover, to ensure that activities targeted toward sustainability are comprehensive, credible and lead to long-term positive changes, it is important to integrate sustainability principles into corporate policy and management systems, and to monitor and report on performance.

Responses by individual tour operators in each of these areas vary considerably, influenced by their size, type of holiday packages offered and destinations served. Since the launch of the Tour Operators' Initiative in 2000, the TOI Secretariat has been collecting from the individual members 'good' examples of how a tour operator can effectively integrate the principles of sustainability into its various areas of operations. This effort has been very successful, not only because it demonstrates that the members of the TOI actually take action, but, most importantly, because it helps spread awareness that tour operators can actually do something about sustainability.

4

Tourism Marketing

Marketing is an art and a science. Marketing involves much more, including product/service development, place (location and distribution), and pricing. It requires information about people, especially those interested in what you have to offer, such as what they like, where they buy and how much they spend. Its role is to match the right product or service with the right market or audience.

Marketing is the process of planning and executing the conception, pricing, promotion, and distribution of ideas, goods, and services to create exchanges that satisfy individual and organizational objectives. It is creating and promoting a product (ideas, goods or services) that satisfies a customer's need or desire and is available at a desirable price and place. Modern marketing is a way of doing business, heavily based on the marketing concept which holds that businesses and organizations should:

— design their products/services to meet customer needs and wants;

— focus on those people most likely to buy their product rather than the entire mass market; and

— develop marketing efforts that fit into their overall business objectives.

Rrecreation Tourism

Earlier it was mentioned that a product can be "ideas, goods, or services." Since tourism is primarily a service based industry, the principal products provided by recreation/tourism (R/T) businesses are recreational experiences and hospitality. These are intangible products and more difficult to market than tangible products such as automobiles. The intangible nature of services makes quality control difficult but crucial. It also makes it more difficult for potential customers to evaluate and compare service offerings.

In addition, instead of moving the product to the customer, the customer must travel to the product (area/community). Travel is a significant portion of the time and money spent in association with recreational and tourism experiences and is a major factor in people's decisions on whether or not to visit your business or community. As an industry, tourism has many components comprising the overall "travel experience."

Along with transportation, it includes such things as accommodations, food and beverage services, shops, entertainment, aesthetics and special events. It is rare for one business to provide the variety of activities or facilities tourists need or desire. This adds to the difficulty of maintaining and controlling the quality of the experience. To overcome this hurdle, tourism related businesses, agencies, and organizations need to work together to package and promote tourism opportunities in their areas and align their efforts to assure consistency in product quality.

Marketing Plan

One of the most important steps a business or community can take to improve the effectiveness and efficiency of their marketing efforts is to develop a written marketing plan. This plan will guide their marketing decisions and assist them in allocating marketing resources such as money and personnel time. The plan should include:

— the overall business objectives-what you want to accomplish;

— an assessment of the market environment-what factors may affect your marketing efforts;

— a business/community profile-what resources are available,

— market identification (segmentation)--the specific groups or clientele most interested in your product;

— the marketing objectives for each segment;

— the marketing strategies (or mixes) for different markets you target-the best combination of the 4 Ps (product, price, place, promotion) for each segment;

— an implementation plan-how to "make it work;"

— the marketing budget-how much you have to spend; and

— a method for evaluation and change.

Business Objectives

Businesses, agencies, and communities should develop overall objectives and regularly monitor their progress. The objectives should provide guidance for all decisions including finances, personnel and marketing. They should be quantitative and measurable statements of what the business or community wants to accomplish over a specified period of time.

Business objectives are often stated in terms of sales, profits, market shares and/or occupancy rates. Communities frequently establish objectives relating to such things as increasing the number of tourists, developing or changing their image, facility and activity development, cooperation among tourism related businesses and increasing length of stay and local expenditures. It is important that the objectives be reasonable given the market conditions and the firm's or organization's resources. Establish a few reasonable objectives instead of a long, unrealistic "wish list." This is especially true for new businesses or communities which do not have much experience in tourism development and/or marketing.

Market Environment Analysis

The next step in developing a marketing plan is to assess the impact of environmental factors (such as economic, social and political) on present and future markets. Changes in these factors can create marketing opportunities as well as problems.

Demographic and lifestyle trends

Changing demographics and lifestyles are having a major impact on R/T participation. An assessment of these trends is important to understand how they will likely affect your business or community. Some of the important trends that bear watching:

— population growth and movement;

— rural community growth compared to metropolitan areas;

— number of adult women employed outside the home;

— the number of households is growing, especially non family and single parent households, but family size is decreasing;

— the impact of two wage earner households on real family income;
— the number of retired persons with the financial ability to travel;
— better health to an older age; and
— continued aging of the population (we are becoming a middle aged society).

Economic conditions

Overall economic conditions can have significant impacts on recreation and tourism markets. A marketing strategy that is effective during periods of low unemployment rates may have to be significantly adjusted if unemployment increases. Businesses and communities should monitor and assess the likely impact of factors such as unemployment rates, real family income, rate of inflation, credit availability, terms and interest rates. Consideration should also be given to the prices of complementary products, such as lodging, gasoline and recreation equipment.

Laws and government actions

As a complex industry, tourism is significantly affected both positively and negatively by laws and by actions of governmental agencies. For instance, rulings on such things as liability issues or decisions regarding building and health codes may change or possibly prevent the construction of a proposed facility. If a public facility changes the prices of its services, this could affect the service offerings of associated private businesses. These actions may have both positive and negative effects on the marketing efforts of the business and community. To avoid wasting valuable resources it is important that R/T businesses, agencies, and communities continually monitor and evaluate governmental actions.

Technology

Technological developments are increasing rapidly. New recreation products, such as all-terrain vehicles and wind surfers, provide new ways for people to satisfy their recreational preferences. New production technologies and materials offer recreation and tourism businesses ways to reduce costs and improve the quality of their products/services. Advances in telecommunications have and will continue to create new promotional opportunities. Technological innovations, in relation to jobs and the home, have resulted in increased leisure time for many people.

Competition

Businesses and communities must identify and analyze existing and potential competitors. The objective of the analysis is to determine the strengths and weaknesses of the competition's marketing strategies. The analysis should include the competition's:

— product/service features and quality;

— location relative to different geographic markets;

— promotional themes and messages;

— prices; and

— type of customer they are attracting.

Community Profiles

Too many communities attempt to market themselves as tourist destinations without accurate information about their resources (facilities, services, staff), image, and how well their customers are satisfied. Without this information, it is difficult to make other decisions in the planning process. Included should be such things as recreational and entertainment facilities, cultural and historic sites, overnight accommodations, restaurants, shopping opportunities, special events and activities, staff size, and transportation. Each item of the "inventory" should also be assessed in terms of quality and availability.

Market Segmentation

Recreation and tourism businesses and communities often make the mistake of attempting to be all things to all people. It is difficult, and risky, to develop marketing strategies for the mass market. Strategies designed for the "average" customer often result in unappealing products, prices, and promotional messages. For example, it would be difficult to develop a campground that would be equally attractive to recreational vehicle campers and backpackers or promote a property to serve both snowmobilers and nature oriented cross country skiers. Marketing is strongly based on market segmentation and target marketing. Market segmentation is the process of:

— taking existing and/or potential customers/visitors (market) and categorizing them into groups with similar preferences referred to as "market segments;"
— selecting the most promising segments as "target markets;" and
— designing "marketing mixes," or strategies (combination of the 4 Ps), which satisfy the special needs, desires and behavior of the target markets.

There is no unique or best way to segment markets, but ways in which customers can be grouped are:

— location of residence---instate, out-of-state, local;

— demographics---age, income, family status, education;

— equipment ownership/use---RV's, sailboats, canoes, tents, snowmobiles;

— important product attributes---price, quality, quantity; and

— lifestyle attributes---activities, interests, opinions.

To be useful, the segment identification process should result in segments that suggest marketing efforts that will be effective in attracting them and at least one segment large enough to justify specialized marketing efforts. After segments have been identified, the business or community must select the "target markets," those segments which offer them the greatest opportunity. When determining target markets, consideration should be given to:

— existing and future sales potential of each segment;

— the amount and strength of competition for each segment;

— the ability to offer a marketing mix which will be successful in attracting each segment;

— the cost of servicing each segment; and

— each segment's contribution to accomplishing overall business/community objectives.

It is often wiser to target smaller segments that are presently not being served, or served inadequately, than to go after larger segments for which there is a great deal of competition. Marketing objectives which contribute to the accomplishment of the overall business objectives should be established for each target market. Objectives serve a number of functions including:

— guidance for developing marketing mixes for different target markets;

— information for allocating the marketing budget between target markets;

— a basis for objectively evaluating the effectiveness of the marketing mixes (setting standards); and

— a framework for integrating the different marketing mixes into the overall marketing plan.

The target market objectives should:

— be expressed in quantitative terms;

— be measurable;

— specify the target market; and

— indicate the time period in which the objective is to be accomplished.

For example, increase the number of overnight stays by people from the Chicago market over the next two years by five percent. Remember, rank objectives by priority and carefully evaluate them to ensure that they are reasonable given the strength of the competition and resources available for marketing.

Marketing Strategy

The marketing strategy, or mix, should be viewed as a package of offerings designed to attract and serve the customer or visitor. Recreation and tourism businesses and communities should develop both external and internal marketing mixes for different target markets.

External Mix

The external marketing mix includes product/service, price, place/location, and promotion.

Product: Earlier we said the principal products that recreation and tourism businesses provide are recreational experiences and hospitality. The factors that create a quality recreational experience often differ among people. A quality experience for one skier might include an uncrowded, steep slope. To another it might be a good restaurant and a chance to socialize.

Decisions on what facilities, programs and services to provide should be based on the needs and desires of the target market(s). They should not be based on the preferences of the owner/manager or necessarily on what the competition is providing. Recognize that a recreational/tourism experience includes five elements: trip planning and anticipation; travel to the site/area; the experience at the site; travel back home; and recollection. Businesses should look for ways to enhance the quality of the overall experience during all phases of the trip. This could be accomplished by providing trip planning packages which include maps, attractions en route and on site, and information regarding lodging, food and quality souvenirs and mementos.

Recreation and tourism businesses should also view their service/product in generic terms. Thinking of products/services in this manner helps focus more attention on the experiences desired by customers and also the facilities, programs and services that will produce those experiences. For example, campgrounds are the business of providing recreational "lodging" not just campsites to park an RV or set up a tent. Marinas should provide recreational "boating" experiences, not just slippage.

Location and Accessibility/Place: Too many tourism businesses and communities fail to recognize their role in improving travel to and from their areas. They focus instead on servicing the customer once they arrive at the site/community. A bad experience getting to or leaving an R/T site can adversely affect a person's travel experience. Ways to help prevent this include:

— providing directions and maps;

— providing estimates of travel time and distances from different market areas;

— recommending direct and scenic travel routes;

— identifying attractions and support facilities along different travel routes; and

— informing potential customers of alternative travel methods to the area such as airlines and railroads.

Potential businesses should also carefully assess alternative locations for:

— distance and accessibility to target markets;

— location of competitors with respect to target markets;

— modes of travel serving the area; and

— other attractions and activities that might induce travel to the area.

Pricing: Price is one of the most important and visible elements of the marketing mix. When setting prices it is important to take into consideration all of the following:

— business and target market objectives;

— the full cost of producing, delivering and promoting the product;

— the willingness of the target market to pay for the product or service you provide;

— prices charged by competitors offering a similar product/service to the same target market(s);

— the availability and prices of substitute products/services (for example, campgrounds, motels, and bed and breakfast are all substitutes for lodging);

— the economic climate (local and national); and

— the possibility of stimulating high profit products/services (such as boats) by offering related services (such as maintenance) at or below cost.

When establishing prices, R/T businesses should give attention to pricing strategies which may encourage off season and non-peak period sales, longer stays, group business, and the sale of package plans (combination of room, meals, and recreational facilities).

Promotion: Promotion provides target audiences with accurate and timely information to help them decide whether to visit your community or business. The information should be of importance and practical use to the potential or existing visitor and also accurate. Misrepresentation often leads to dissatisfied customers and poor recommendations. Don't make claims you cannot live up to.

Developing a promotional campaign is not a science with hard and fast rules. Making decisions regarding which type or combination of promotion types to use (personal selling, advertising, sales promotions, or publicity) is not always easy. If, however, you follow a logical process and do the necessary research, chances for success will be improved. It will be necessary to make decisions regarding:

— Target audience—the group you are aiming at;

— Image—that which your community or business wants to create or reinforce;

— Objectives–those of the promotional campaign;

— Budget—the amount of money available for your promotion;

— Timing—when and how often should your promotions appear;

— Media—which methods (television, radio, newspaper, magazine) will most effectively and efficiently communicate your message to the target audience; and

— Evaluation—how can the effectiveness of the promotional campaign be determined.

Internal Mix

As stated, marketing services such as recreation and tourism differ from marketing tangible products. Recreation and tourism businesses must direct as much attention at marketing to customers on site as they do to attracting them. In this respect, internal marketing is important because dissatisfied customers can effectively cancel out an otherwise effective marketing strategy.

The success of internal marketing is dependent on creating an atmosphere in which employees desire to give good service and sell the business/community to visitors. To create such an atmosphere requires the following four important elements:

— *Hospitality and Guest Relations*—An organization wide emphasis on hospitality and guest relations, including a customer oriented attitude on the part of the owners and managers as well as the employees. If the owner/manager is not customer sensitive, it is unlikely the lower paid employees will be.

— *Quality Control*—A program which focuses on improving both the technical quality (the standards associated with what the customer receives) and the functional quality (the standards associated with how the customer receives the service). All employees who come into contact with customers should receive hospitality training.

— *Personal Selling*—Training the staff in the selling aspects of the property (business) or community. This also includes rewarding them for their efforts. By being informed about the marketing objectives, and their role in accomplishing those objectives, they can help increase sales.

— *Employee Morale*—Programs and incentives aimed at maintaining employee morale. The incentives can be both monetary and non-monetary.

A customer oriented atmosphere usually results in customers that are more satisfied, do less complaining and are more pleasant to serve. This helps build employee morale, their desire to provide good service and their efficiency.

Marketing Budget

Successful marketing requires that sufficient money and personnel time be made available to implement activities comprising the marketing strategy. A marketing budget is a financial plan which shows the total amount to be spent on marketing during different times of the year and how it is to be allocated among alternative activities. Separate marketing budgets should be developed for each marketing mix strategy. The separate budgets should then be aggregated to develop an overall marketing budget.

If the total amount is too great it will be necessary to modify the overall objectives and the target market objectives, narrow down or drop target markets, or adjust marketing mixes. The final budget should be realistic given your objectives. When deciding on a marketing budget, consideration should be given to the job that needs to be done as defined by the objectives.

Basing marketing budgets on some percent of sales or what the competition spends usually leads to over spending or under spending. Decisions should also be based on the costs, projected revenues, and desired profitability of different activities, not just costs alone. Successful marketing activities will generate additional revenues which can be projected based on the marketing objectives (such as increase off season stay by 5%).

Although budgets should be viewed as flexible plans, every effort should be made to adhere to them. Revisions in the budget should only be made after careful consideration of the likely impact of the change on the marketing mix and accomplishment of your objectives.

Implimentation

Many well designed marketing plans fail because they are poorly executed. Businesses, agencies, and communities can increase the likelihood of successful implementation if they:

— identify specific tasks which must be accomplished;

— assign people or departments specific responsibility for different tasks;

— provide employees with information on the marketing plan (rationale, objectives, strategies);

— develop time lines and deadlines;

— adhere as much as possible to the budget; and

— regularly monitor and evaluate progress.

Evaluation

It is important that marketing efforts be continually evaluated. This will improve the effectiveness of marketing strategies by quickly identifying differences between actual results and expected performance and determining likely reasons for the success or failure to realize objectives. A framework for evaluation would include:

— *determining which elements of the different marketing mixes are most important to evaluate.* It is rarely possible or cost effective to evaluate all elements;

— *establishing performance standards to compare against actual results.* Marketing objectives, if properly formulated, should serve as performance standards;

— *development of formal and informal methods for collecting data on actual results.* There are many ways different elements of the marketing mix can be evaluated. For example, promotions can be evaluated with money off coupons. Special information request forms, telephone numbers to call or post office box numbers to write to can identify the area the request is coming from. Also, formal (written) and informal (face-to-face) surveys can be used to determine the promotional material the customer used in planning the trip;

— comparison of results with objectives;

— determination of needed change(s).

Effective Tourism Marketing Program

Step-by-step instructions describe how to inventory attractions, assess current marketing efforts, find existing market research, determine target markets, determine tourist motivators, develop promotional goals, determine campaign themes, find an advertising media, develop public relations and gather the correct data for an evaluation.

Inventory of Attractions and Accommodations

The first step in developing effective marketing plans is to inventory the attractions a community has to offer tourists. A community must know what it has to offer or sell before plans can be laid for marketing the product. These can include natural, manmade, historical, cultural or ethnic, festivals, special events and recreational attractions.

Assessing Current Marketing Efforts

Listing current advertising efforts for all attractions is

necessary to assess the present promotional campaign's successfulness, and to develop new campaigns.

Market Research

Market research is an important part of developing a market plan. Several important pieces of information are needed to develop a market plan. These include:

— An inventory of tourist attractions in the area, region, or destination

— Market trends

— Tourist motivations

— Tourist profiles, including expenditures

It helps to review other successful marketing plans, remembering that a marketing plan should meet the individual needs of the area, region or destination for which it was developed. Learning from previous mistakes is a key to developing better programs.

There are two types of research data that can provide this information. The first is primary research gathered through phone calls, surveys, or other interviewing techniques. Secondary data has been compiled by outside organizations. Be careful when using secondary data; confirm the reliability of the source.

Target Market

Trying to appeal to everyone is a common mistake made in marketing. Not everyone looks for the same thing in a destination, and every destination cannot be all things to all people. Target marketing, focusing on a particular segment or segments of the market,allows for a more effective marketing plan. Market research will define the market segments, which will find those tourists most interested in what a community has to offer. Data on past visitors can indicate the type of tourist or the geographic region on which to focus. A target market can be a geographic region, a type of tourist, a combination of the two or any grouping that makes sense.

Determine Tourist Motivators

The fifth step is detemine tourist motivetors. Tourist motivators should be studied once a target market has been defined. Discovering where and why tourists travel is important when focusing advertising. Enticing the tourist to chose a historical destination because of its mystique, or choosing a full-service resort where every need can be catered to requires different motivational factors.

Developing Promotional Goals

Establishing goals provides the basis to determine what a community wants its marketing and promotion program to accomplish. Goals should be well thought out and be measurable, and can also serve as controls. Writing down goals provides directional guidelines. It can be difficult to get feedback on promotional goals, but with specific goals set, an evaluation and feedback plan can be implemented. This will gather the necessary data for the evaluation process, which can determine the successfulness of a community's plans and program.

Determining a Campaign Theme

A campaign theme should emphasize the image aimed at tourists in a given area. Remember, always capitalize on the positive aspects in the area, region or destination. Campaign themes should be developed for a clearly defined target market. For example, New Mexico's promotion, "More to Explore... New Mexico USA," targets nonresidents, and capitalizes on the fact that New Mexico is a part of the United States, although many tourists think it is a part of Mexico.

A campaign focusing on New Mexico residents, on the other hand, would emphasize what their home state has to offer. It could incorporate a theme of "Travel Close to Home."

Advertising Media

Determining which advertising media to use should not be done until after the target market is identified. Once the market has been determined, the tourist profile of the target market can be matched to the audience profile of specific advertising media. Most advertising media can provide an accurate profile of their audience. Some advantages and disadvantages of various forms of advertising media are listed below.

Newspapers

Advantages	Disadvantages
High reach	High waste factor and inability to target
High geographic concentration	Limitations on creative format
Good frequency	Relatively poor reproduction quality
Tangibility	Clutter
Short lead times	Short life span
Relatively low cost	High cost of national coverage
Ability to communicate detailed information	
Ability to place in most appropriate location	

Magazines

Advantage	Disadvantages
Tangibility	Limitations on creative format
High audience selectivity	Clutter
Good reproduction quality	Low reach
Long life span and good pass-along rate	Low frequency
Prestige and credibility	Low frequency
Ablity to communicate detailed information	Long lead times
	Relatively expensive
	Difficulties in geographic targeting

Radio

Advantages	Disadvantages
Relatively low cost	No visual communications
Audience selectivity	Inability to transmit complex messages or detailed information
High frequency	Short life span
Short lead times	Shared attention

Television

Advantages	Disadvantages
Potentially high reach	High total cost
High persuasive impact	Short life span
Availability of uniform national coverage	Inability to transmit detailed information
Some geographic and demographic selectivity	

Direct Mail	
Advantages	Disadvantages
Audience selectivity	Junk mail syndrome and high discard rate
Highly flexible	Relatively high total cost
High level of personalization	Limitations on creative format
Ability to measure responses	
Low Cost	
Tangibility	
Short lead times	

Outdoor/Transit (Billboards, posters, painted bulletins)	
Advantages	Disadvantages
High reach and good frequency	High waste factor and inability to target
Geographic selectivity	Relatively long lead times
Long life span	Inability to transmit complex or detailed messages
Large size	Not prestigious
	Limitations on creative format

Public Relations

Public relations can be an excellent way to promote a community or attraction. Public relations activities are uniquely different from advertising. Advertising is paid, but public relations uses free public exposure to ensure goodwill. Public relations can use radio,television or newspapers. Public relations efforts not only can be used to promote the destination to tourists, but also to promote the community itself. It can help create a feeling of pride in the community by educating the local community about what it has to offer tourists. This can develop a feeling of pride for the residents when they are asked to describe their community to tourists. Instead of seeing tourists as invaders, they will be seen as an economic boost to the local economy.

Developing an Evaluation Plan

This is the 10th step. An evaluation plan requires detailed planning during the initial stages of a marketing plan. Establishing measurable goals in a marketing plan is the first step in this evaluation. From this step, decide what information is needed to prove or disprove the accomplishment of the goal. If methods to gather the information are established at the beginning, all needed information for evaluation will be available at the end.

One of the most difficult parts of an evaluation is uncovering all the information that is needed, especially if an organized system is not included at the beginning. The second most difficult part is convincing everyone of the importance of such an evaluation. It is the key to the entire marketing plan that says, "Yes, it worked" or "No, it didn't work." An evaluation can show if the wrong audience was targeted or the plan conveyed the wrong message. Evaluation also provides the information needed to improve marketing. Great care should be taken to incorporate an evaluation plan into the marketing plan.

Another important part of an evaluation is the conversion study, which compares the number of inquiries to the number of people who actually visit. The conversion study is conducted by using the list of inquiries generated over the specified time frame, randomly choosing a sample, then performing a follow-up telephone or mail survey. Other information that can be collected along with a conversion study, when it is determined that the inquiring person has actually visited, is:

— Place of residence

— What time of year visited

— Transportation

— Estimated expenditures during trip

— Purpose of trip

— Would you visit again

These questions help establish a tourist profile. Information that needs to be collected for a proper evaluation of a marketing plan is:

— Advertisement cost

— Advertisement dates

— Number of times an advertisement was run

— Advertisement agency costs (if any)

— Media in which advertisement was placed

— Number of inquiries received from each advertisement

— Request fulfillment costs (mailing costs, envelopes, mailing brochures)

— Follow up information

Gathering this kind of data provides information to determine the effectiveness of advertising. When follow-up information on actual visitation and expenditures is obtained, advertising effectiveness can be further evaluated.

— *Number of Inquiries*—The number of people who requested information through the advertisement.

— *Ad Costs*—The cost of placing an advertisement in the advertising media.

— *Ad Cost Per Inquiry*—Ad cost divided by number of inquiries.

— *Request Fulfillment Cost Per Inquiry*—Request fulfillment cost divided by number of inquiries: includes mailing, brochure, and envelope costs.

— *Ad Agency Fixed Cost Per Inquiry*—Ad agency fixed cost divided by number of inquiries.

— *Total Cost Per Inquiry*—Total costs divided by number of inquiries.

Data collection methods should be decided on and in place before any advertising is done. Thus, all needed information will be available when evaluation procedures start. Suggested advertisement monitoring methods include:

— A phone answering script that determines the caller's name, address, phone and type of information requested.

— Coding advertisements so inquiries received are easily tracked to a specific advertisement.

— Monitoring guest registrations for visitor's points of origin.

Funding

Once the marketing plan has been developed, there must be funding to support the implementation of the plan. Learning to budget the expenses that will be incurred with the marketing plan is the first step. Funding sources want to know from the beginning how the money will be spent.

Determining how much money to spend is not the hard part; determining where to get the money is. Non-profit organizations such as Convention and Visitors bureaus and Chambers of Commerce may have access to the Cooperative Advertising Program offered through the State Travel and Tourism Department, which provides matching funds. Lodgers' taxes are another source of funding. This money is usually administered by local government. Other funding sources at the local level are member fees, banks and utilities.

5

Tourism Planning

Tourism is one of many activities in a community or region that requires planning and coordination. Planning is the process of identifying objectives and defining and evaluating methods of achieving them. By comprehensive planning, planning which considers all of the tourism resources, organizations, markets, and programs within a region. Comprehensive planning also considers economic, environmental, social, and institutional aspects of tourism development.

Successful tourism planning and development means serving both tourists and local residents. This market orientation must be balanced with a clear view of how tourism serves the broader community interest and an understanding of the positive and negative impacts of tourism development.

Tourism should serve the community first and the tourist second. Tourism development must be compatible with other activities in the area and be supported by the local population. Therefore, the tourism plan should be closely coordinated with other local and regional planning efforts, if not an integral part of them.

In quantitative terms, a tourist, and thus tourism, is usually defined as a person who travels for non-business reasons more than 50 miles from and overnights away from her usual place of residence. It is around this definition, or ones like it, that most travel statistics-departures, expenditures-are compiled and computed.

From among a multitude of other definitions of tourism, there are two important views on what tourism is that have ramifications for successful tourism planning. First, there is the view that tourism is an individual human experience which some anthropologists theorize is really ritual human cultural experience. The second view is that tourism is an export economic activity.

Individual experiences of the tourist are key to the success of any tourism strategy. It is often that dream of a future experience at some place other than at home or at the office which motivates people to travel and become tourists. It is the guaranteed repeat of pleasant experiences that brings a tourist back a second time or inspires one to "spread the word" about this wonderful destination to others.

A successful tourism strategy must therefore, provided desired experiences or people will not come the first time or will not come back for a second. There is one anthropological theory which proposes that tourism is ritual experience akin to religious experience. Because a tourism experience is limited in time for most people, and it occurs for them in an out-of-the-ordinary place, there can be feelings of extraordinary reality associated with a destination.

When one takes a trip, one leaves one's ordinary life through a transition, like an airplane flight; one has heightened liminal, some would say spiritual, experiences at this extraordinary, mystical place, and then one returns to ordinary life through another transition, a coming down. Grieving the loss of the mystical place and the intense relationships that were experienced there frequently accompany this last transition. When people are in the time and space of their extraordinary, mystical place, the rules of their ordinary lives are usually suspended or may be totally reversed.

They are susceptible to seeing fate in chance occurrences, they experience déja vu, they use only first names, they get drunk in public, and they have amorous, sometimes sexual, encounters with strangers whom they will never see again. In short, they have high intensity, deeply moving experiences.

Tourism As an Economic Activity

Tourism can also be viewed as a special case of export economic activity. It is a special case because rather than shipping goods and service products out to the purchaser, the purchaser comes to the point of origin of the goods and services in order to procure-experience-them. This is the phenomena that can lead to the many undesirable externalities-congestion, pollution, crime-that occur in tourism development. This is the root of the tourism paradox and what brings ruin to the goose that lays the golden eggs of tourism's economic benefit.

Classification Of Tourism

Several tourism classification systems have been devised to help describe tourists and modes of tourism consistently. One nominal classification focuses on the primary type of attraction(s) that is being emphasized in the tourism product which is being marketed and delivered. Examples include:

— Ecotourism

— Nature Tourism

— Adventure Tourism

— Getaway & Stay

— Cultural Tourism

Another is an ordinal classification that is based on tourist party volumes. This measure ranges from mass tourism for large numbers of tourists to explorer for the single tourist traveling by herself. Images along this scale range from droves of people disgorging themselves from 47 passenger stinking diesel buses into crowed plazas before Notre Dame Cathedral (not the case anymore) to the solitary lean dirty backpacker hitch hiking her way across the Tibetan Plateau on the back side of Mount Everest.

The importance of these scales is that they begin to define segments in the whole of what constitutes the tourist population. These segments have differing tourism product experience expectations, travel service needs and demographics. This means they can be targeted for marketing purposes and specifically focused on in promotional campaigns and tourism product development.

Two Sides of Tourism Planning

Tourism planning has evolved from two related but distinct sets of planning philosophies and methods. On the one hand, tourism is one of many activities in an area that must be considered as part of physical, environmental, social, and economic planning. Therefore, it is common to find tourism addressed, at least partially, in a regional land use, transportation, recreation, economic development, or comprehensive plan.

The degree to which tourism is addressed in such plans depends upon the relative importance of tourism to the community or region and how sensitive the planning authority is to tourism activities. Tourism may also be viewed as a business in which a community or region chooses to engage. Individual tourism businesses conduct a variety of planning activities including feasibility, marketing, product development, promotion, forecasting, and strategic planning.

If tourism is a significant component of an area's economy or development plans, regional or community-wide marketing plans are needed to coordinate the development and marketing activities of different tourism interests in the community.

A comprehensive approach integrates a strategic marketing plan with more traditional public planning activities. This ensures a balance between serving the needs and wants of the tourists versus the needs and wants of local residents. A formal tourism plan provides a vehicle for the various interests within a community to coordinate their activities and work toward common goals. It also is a means of coordinating tourism with other community activities.

Steps in Planning Process

Like any planning, tourism planning is goal-oriented, striving to achieve certain objectives by matching available resources and programs with the needs and wants of people. Comprehensive planning requires a systematic approach, usually involving a series of steps. The process is best viewed as an iterative and on-going one, with each step subject to modification and refinement at any stage of the planning process. There are six steps in the planning process:

- Define goals and objectives.
- Identify the tourism system.
    - Resources
    - Organizations
    - Markets

— Generate alternatives.

— Evaluate alternatives.

— Select and implement.

— Monitor and evaluate.

Defining Goals and Objectives

Obtaining clear statements of goals and objectives is difficult, but important. Ideally, tourism development goals should flow from more general community goals and objectives. It is important to understand how a tourism plan serves these broader purposes. If tourism is identified as a means of serving broader community goals, it makes sense to develop plans with more specific tourism development objectives. These are generally defined through a continuing process in which various groups and organizations in a community work together toward common goals.

A local planning authority, chamber of commerce, visitors bureau, or similar group should assume a leadership role to develop an initial plan and obtain broad involvement of tourism interests in the community. Public support for the planning process and plan is also important. Having a good understanding of tourism and the tourism system in your community is the first step toward defining goals and objectives for tourism development.

The types of goals that are appropriate and the precision with which you are able to define them will depend upon how long your community has been involved in tourism and tourism planning. In the early stages of tourism development, goals may involve establishing organizational structures and collecting information to better identify the tourism system in the community. Later, more precise objectives can be formulated and more specific development and marketing strategies evaluated.

Identifying Tourism System

When planning for any type of activity, it is important to first define its scope and characteristics. Tourism is defined in many ways. Generally, tourism involves people traveling outside of their community for pleasure. Definitions differ on the specifics of how far people must travel, whether or not they must stay overnight, for how long, and what exactly is included under traveling for "pleasure".

Do you want your tourism plan to include day visitors, conventioneers, business travelers, people visiting friends and relatives, people passing through, or seasonal residents? Which community resources and organizations serve tourists or could serve tourists? Generally, tourists share community resources with local residents and businesses.

Many organizations serve both tourists and locals. This complicates tourism planning and argues for a clear idea of what your tourism plan entails. You can begin to clarify the tourism system by breaking it down into three subsystems:

— tourism resources,

— tourism organizations, and

— tourism markets.

An initial task in developing a tourism plan is to identify, inventory, and classify the objects within each of these subsystems.

Tourism resources

Tourism resources are any (1) natural, (2) cultural, (3) human, or (4) capital resources that either are used or can be used to attract or serve tourists. A tourism resource inventory identifies and classifies the resources available that provide opportunities for tourism development. Conduct an objective and realistic assessment of the quality and quantity of resources you have to work with. Important Tourism Resources are the following:

— Natural Resources
  — Climate-seasons
  — Water resources-lakes, streams, waterfalls
  — Flora-forests, flowers, shrubs, wild edibles
  — Fauna-fish & wildlife
  — Geological resources-topography, soils, sand dunes, beaches, caves, rocks & minerals, fossils
  — Scenery-combinations of all of the above

— Cultural Resources
  — Historic buildings, sites
  — Monuments, shrines
  — Cuisine
  — Ethnic cultures
  — Industry, government, religion, etc.
  — Anthropological resources
  — Local celebrities

— Human Resources
  — Hospitality skills
  — Management skills

- — Seasonal labor force
- — Performing artists-music, drama, art, storytellers, etc.
- — Craftsman and artisans
- — Other labor skills from chefs to lawyers to researchers
- — Local populations

— Capital

- — Availability of capital, financing
- — Infrastructure-transportation roads, airports, railroads, harbors & marinas, trails & walkways
- — Infrastructure: utilities water, power, waste treatment, communications

Tourism organization

Tourism organization combine resources in various proportions to provide products and services for the tourist. It is important to recognize the diverse array of public and private organizations involved with tourism. The most difficult part of tourism planning is to get these groups to work toward common goals. Setting up appropriate communication systems and institutional arrangements is a key part of community tourism planning.

Tourism Management Organisation and Services

Coordination, planning, technical assistance, research, regulation:

— Federal & state departments of commerce, transportation, & natural resources

— Federal, state, regional, & local tourism associations

— Educational organizations & consultants, e.g., Travel & Tourism Research Association; U.S.

— Travel information & reservation services

Development, promotion and management, of tourism resources:

— Federal agencies, NB. departments of commerce, transportation, & land management agencies

— State agencies, NB. departments of commerce, transportation, & land/facility management agencies

— Local government organizations, e.g., visitor information, chamber of commerce, convention & visitor's bureaus, parks

— Businesses:

— Accommodations: Hotels, motels, Lodges, resorts, bed & breakfast cabins & cottages, Condominiums, second homes, Campgrounds

— Food & Beverage: Restaurants, Grocery, Bars, nightclubs,

Fast food, Catering services

— *Transportation*: Air, rail, bus; Local transportation: taxi, limo, Auto, bicycle, boat rental; Local tour services

— Information: Travel agencies, Information and reservation services, Automobile clubs

— *Recreation Facilities and Services*: Winter sports: ski, skating, snowmobile areas; Golf courses, miniature golf; Swimming pools, water slides, beaches; tennis, handball, racquetball courts, bowling alleys; Athletic clubs, health spas; Marinas, boat rentals and charters; hunting & fishing guides; Horseback enterprises; Sporting goods sales & rentals

— *Entertainment*: Nightclubs, amusement parks, spectator sport facilities; Gambling facilities: casinos, horse racing, bingo; video arcades; art galleries and studios, craft shops, studios, demonstrations; performing arts: theater, dance, music, film; historic & prehistoric sites; museums: art, history, science, technology; arboreta, zoos, nature centers,

— Special festivals and events

— *Support services*: Auto repair, gasoline service stations; boat & recreation vehicle dealers and service; retail shops: sporting goods, specialties, souvenirs, clothing; health services: hospitals, clinics, pharmacies; laundry and dry cleaning; beauty & barber shops; babysitting services; pet care; communications: newspaper, telephone; banking and financial services

Tourism markets

Tourists makeup the third, and perhaps most important subsystem. Successful tourism programs require a strong market orientation. The needs and wants of the tourists you choose to attract and serve must be the focus of much of your marketing and development activity. Therefore, it is important to clearly understand which tourism market segments you wish to attract and serve. Tourists fall into a very diverse set of categories with quite distinct needs and wants. A visitor survey identifies the size and nature of the existing market and asks the following questions:

— What are the primary market segments you presently attract?

— Where do they come from?

— What local businesses and facilities do they use?

— What attracted them to the community?

— How did they find out about your community?

— How satisfied are they with your offerings?

A market survey (usually a telephone survey) also can be conducted among households in regions from which you wish to attract tourists. This type of study helps identify potential markets, and means of attracting tourists to your area.

Tourism market segments: In a general tourism plan, some clear target tourism market segments should be identified. You might begin by defining the market area from which you will draw most of your visitors. The size of your market area depends upon the uniqueness and quality of your "product", transportation systems, tastes and preferences of surrounding populations, and your competition.

Identifying the market area will help target information and promotion and define transportation routes and modes, competition, and characteristics of the market. Next, divide the travel market into the following trip length categories:

— day trips from a 50 mile radius,

— day trips from 50 to 200 miles away,

— pass-through travelers,

— overnight trips of 1 or 2 nights (most likely weekends), and

— extended overnight vacation trips.

After have an idea of your market area and kinds of trips you will be serving, begin defining more specific market segments like vehicle campers, downhill skiers, sightseers, family vacationers, single weekenders, and the like. These segments can be more clearly tied to particular resources, businesses, and facilities in your community. Tourism market segments are given the following:

I. Geographic market areas

II. Trip categories

— Day Trips:

  — short-within 50 miles

  — long-up to 200 miles

— Pass through traffic:

  — day visitors

  — overnight stays

— Overnight Trips:

  — weekend

  — vacation

III. Activity or trip purpose

— Outdoor Recreation:

  — Water-based Activity:

  — Boating: sail, power, cruise, row, canoe, water ski

  — Swimming: pool, beach, sunbathing, scuba

  — Fishing: charter, sport, from pier, boat, shore, ice

  — Land-based Activity:

  — Camping: backpacking, primitive, developed

  — Hiking: climbing, beachcombing, spelunking

  — Hunting

  — Skiing: downhill, cross country

  — Snowmobiling

  — Bicycling

  — Horseback riding

  — Picnicking

— Air-based Activity:

— Airplane rides, hang gliding, ballooning, parachuting

— General:

— Nature study

— Photography or landscape painting

— Viewing natural scenery

Sightseeing & Entertainment:

— Visiting particular sites or areas:

— historic or pre-historic

— cultural

— amusements

— scenic

— Attending particular events, shows, or demonstrations:

— ethnic festivals

— sporting events

— performances

— agricultural fair or festival

— boat show

— shopping

— Other Primary Purpose for Trip:

— Visiting Friends & Relatives

— Convention & Business/Pleasure

Tourist needs as well as their impact on the local community are quite different for day tourists versus overnight tourists. Areas catering primarily to weekend traffic will experience large fluctuations in use. In deciding the relative importance of these different segments, communities need to assess both their ability to provide required services, as well as the demand for different types of trips relative to the supply and your competition.

Environment: A tourism plan is significantly affected by many factors in the broader environment. Indeed, one of the complexities of tourism planning is the number of variables that are outside of the control of an individual tourism business or community. These include such things as tourism offerings and prices at competing destinations, federal and state policy and legislation, currency exchange rates, the state of the economy, and weather.

Local populations also must be considered in tourism planning. As they compete with tourists for resources, they can be significantly affected by tourism activity, and they are an important source of support in getting tourism plans implemented. A survey of local residents can be conducted to assess community attitudes toward tourism development, identify impacts of tourism on the community, and obtain local input into tourism plans. Public hearings, workshops, and advisory boards are other ways to obtain public involvement in tourism planning. Local support and cooperation is important to the success of tourism programs and should not be overlooked.

Generating Alternatives

Generating alternative development and marketing options to meet your goals requires some creative thinking and brainstorming. The errors made at this stage are usually thinking too narrowly or screening out alternatives prematurely. It is wise to solicit a wide range of options from a diverse group of people.

If tourism expertise is lacking in your community, seek help and advice outside the community. Tourism planning involves a wide range of interrelated development and marketing decisions. The following development questions will get you started:

— How much importance should be assigned to tourism within a community or region?

— Which general community goals is tourism development designed to serve?

— Which organization(s) will provide the leadership and coordination necessary for community tourism planning? What are the relative roles of public and private sectors?

Tourism marketing decision questions include:

— Segments: Which market segments should be pursued; geographic markets, trip types, activity or demographic subgroups?

— Product: What kinds of tourism products and services should be provided? Who should provide what?

— Place: Where should tourism facilities be located?

— Promotion: What kinds of promotion should be used, by whom, in which media, how much, when? What community tourism theme or image should be established?

— Price: What prices should be charged for which products and services. Who should capture the revenue?

Evaluating Alternatives

Tourism development and marketing options are evaluated by assessing the degree to which each option will be able to meet the stated goals and objectives. There are usually two parts to a systematic evaluation of tourism development and marketing alternatives:

(1) Feasibility analysis, and

(2) Impact assessment.

These two tasks are interrelated, but think of them as trying to answer two basic questions: (1) Can it be done?, and (2) What are the consequences? A decision to take a specific action must be based both on feasibility and desirability.

Feasibility Analysis: First, screen alternatives and eliminate those that are not feasible due to economic, environmental, political, legal, or other factors. Evaluate the remaining set of alternatives in more detail, paying particular attention to the market potential and financial plan. Make a realistic assessment of your community's ability to attract and serve a market segment or segments.

This requires a clear understanding of the tourism market in your area and how this market is changing. Also carefully identify your competition and evaluate your advantages and disadvantages compared to the competition. Plan toward the future because it takes time to implement decisions and for your actions to take effect. Therefore, look at the likely market and competition for several years to come. Review forecasts for the travel market in your area, if available. Careful tracking of tourism trends in your own community can help identify changes in the market that you will have to adapt to.

When evaluating alternative development and marketing strategies it is important to understand the impacts, both positive and negative, of proposed actions. The types of impacts and their importance vary across different communities and proposed actions. Generally, the size, extent, and nature of tourism impacts depend upon:

— volume of tourist activity relative to local activity

— length and nature of tourist contacts with the community

— degree of concentration/dispersal of tourist activity in the area

— similarities or differences between local populations and tourists

— stability/sensitivity of local economy, environment, and social structure

— how well tourism is planned, controlled, and managed.

Look at both the benefits and costs of any proposed actions. While tourism development can increase income, revenues, and employment, it also involves costs. Evaluate benefits and costs of tourism development from the perspectives of local government, businesses, and residents.

Economic Impacts:

— Sales, revenue, and income

— Employment

— Fiscal impact-taxes, infrastructure costs

— Prices

— Economic base & structure

Environmental Impacts:

— Lands

— Waters

— Air

— Infrastructure

— Flora & fauna

Social Impacts:

— Population structure & distribution

— Values & attitudes

— Education

— Occupations

— Safety & security

— Congestion & crowding

— Community spirit & cohesion

— Quality of life

Impacts on Local Government: Local government provides most of the infrastructure and many of the services essential to tourism development, including highways, public parks, law enforcement, water and sewer, garbage collection and disposal.

Evaluate tourism decisions with a clear understanding of the capacity of the local infrastructure and services relative to anticipated needs, and take into account both the needs of local populations and tourists. A fiscal impact analysis evaluates the impact of tourism on the community's tax base and local government costs. It entails predicting the additional infrastructure and service requirements of tourism development, estimating their costs, deciding who will pay for/provide them, and how.

Impacts on Business and Industry: Businesses that are directly serving tourists benefit from sales to tourists. Through secondary impacts, tourism activity also benefits a wide range of businesses in a community. For example, a local textile industry may sell to a linen supply firm that serves hotels and motels catering primarily to tourists.

A local forest products industry sells to a lumberyard where local woodcarvers or furniture makers buy their supplies. They in turn sell to tourists through various retail outlets. All of these businesses benefit from tourism. If most products and services for tourists are bought outside of the local area, much of the tourist spending "leaks" out of the local economy. The more a community is "self-sufficient" in serving tourists, the larger the local impact.

Impacts on Residents: Local residents may experience a broad range of both positive and negative impacts from tourism development. Tourism development may provide increased employment and income for the community. Although tourism jobs are primarily in the service sectors and are often seasonal, part time, and low-paying, these characteristics, are neither universal nor always undesirable. Residents may value opportunities for part time and seasonal work.

In particular, employment opportunities and work experiences for students or retirees may be desired. Residents may also benefit from local services that otherwise would not be available. Tourism development may mean a wider variety of retailers and restaurants, or a better community library. It may also mean more traffic, higher prices, and increases in property values and local taxes. The general quality of the environment and life in the community may go up or down due to tourism development. This depends on the nature of tourism development, the preferences and desires of local residents, and how well tourism is planned and managed.

Implementation, and Monitoring and Evaluation.

A set of specific actions should be prescribed with clearly defined responsibilities and timetables. Monitor progress in implementing the plan and evaluate the success of the plan in meeting its goals and objectives on a regular basis. Plans generally need to be adjusted over time due to changing goals, changing market conditions, and unanticipated impacts. It is a good idea to build monitoring and evaluation systems into your planning efforts.

Tourism Plan and its Structural Components

Structure of tourism in terms of the economic concepts of demand and supply. The importance of his analysis of tourism structure is that it points out that successful tourism depends on planning in two economic arenas, not just the one. There must be balance in creating both demand and supply or projects and plans will fail.

Demand

Demand in Gunn's model is population. The first cut of population into a tourist market occurs with the availability of two discretionary resources-time and money; this cut probably produces a potent'al global tourist market of certainly less than 10 percent of world's population. Refinement of the potential tourist population into specific market segments toward whom marketing campaigns and promotions are geared is a cash cow for many marketing and advertising consultants. The work involves survey research and sophisticated multi-variate statistical analysis of the results.

Supply

Gunn viewed supply as composed of four components: transportation, attractions, services and information and promotion. Transportation has to be considered on two levels. First is the linkage between the tourists' place of origin and their destination; the second is the destination region's transportation network. A complete planning process should consider provision of all aspects of physical infrastructure: transportation, water, sewer, energy and communications in this structural component. Attractions, and Gunn's attractions component should be explicitly expanded to include events, function in two ways in successful tourism planning. One is they are the magnets that often entice a person to travel to a particular destination, that dreamed experience, and second they are part of the real tourism experience of a destination region.

Service is the other significant experience generating component of tourism. The focus of this component is accommodation, and food and beverage establishments and their personnel. Here appropriate design, good taste and well-trained staff are often the key ingredients to successful experiences. Not always though, the Elbow Room in Vancouver, BC thrived on mild doses of tourist abuse.

When regulars would show up behind tourists waiting in line to be seated, they were likely to be told, "You can wait, these boys have to go to work!" The tourists would step aside wondering what hit them and let the regulars be seated. Gunn's last structural component is information and promotion. It is important to provide each tourist market segment with information and promotional materials that create the experience expectation and bring tourists to a destination. Unfortunately it is this component which has been so badly out of balance in traditional tourism planning to such an extent that resources that should go into training, destination design and physical development have often fallen short. This is less the case now than it was ten to twenty years ago. Another aspect of this component is providing good signage in the destination region to ease and direct movement of people.

Environmental Design Elements

There are three fundamental elements and a series of principles that should figure into a tourism plan. The elements are: local residents, visitors and visitor domain. Too often tourism planners have ignored local residents in their work. Local residents are part of the experience. Their culture contributes to a sense of place, but local residents need privacy as well; they cannot be on show all the time.

Another planning point is that tourism development should occur so that it is accessible to local residents as well as to visitors, that is, development should be affordable and unsegregated. About the visitor, Winterbottom remarks: "The truly successful visitor destination is one that is concerned more with visitor quality than quantity. The quality visitor is the one that is most likely to repeat the visit and to respect the visitor environment-both natural and man made." This statement stands as justification to actively target certain market segments in tourism planning in order to attract desirable visitors and thus conserve advertising dollars for other components of tourism development. The visitor domain is simply an area where attractions and services are clustered so that the tourist experience is aggregated and enhanced.

Tourism Planning and Development Principles

Most fundamental design principle is creating the visitor domain with a sense of place that is unique and authentic, and that contains a diversity of potential experience. Reid and Smith encourage development of gateways in designing tourist spaces. The gateway is a physical symbol of entrance to the tourist domain. The gateway also marks the transition from ordinary into extraordinary places and experience. Clustering and concentrating attractions and services is the technique of creating the visitor domain.

Use of these principles leads ultimately to a critical mass of tourist products which establishes a place as a tourist destination in the tourist market. With a critical mass, tourists become aware of the place and will purposely begin to choose to go to that place. The application of the market research technique of product/market match is the means to achieve a supply of the right tourism products, particularly attractions and services, for the targeted quality tourists of a tourism destination plan. Targeted tourists are statistically defined; the products suitable to their tastes are what should be developed at the destination.

Statistically defined tourist segments usually come from defined geographic areas, fall into specified age and gender groups, have specified education and income levels and have specific preferences for what they like to do, see and eat. Well signed transportation linkages are necessary to ease the movement of people in the tourist domain. Where large crowds of people are concentrated during the tourist season, such as now at the Grand Canyon with four to five million visitors per year, mass transit interventions are rapidly replacing automobile use.

Protecting the environment-natural, cultural and social-is now an accepted mainstay of successful tourism planning. This can be achieved by attracting quality tourists and by managing tourist flows and access while they are in the visitor domain. The Grand Canyon intervention of mass transit is a direct result of the Park Service's goal to protect the environment and preserve the visitor experience. This year Park Service introduced use of a quiet helicopter and will require commercial areal sightseeing operators to use noise-reduced equipment starting next year.

There already are restricted air space regulations. Grand Canyon will be a quieter place soon. The seasons-high, low and shoulder-can be the bane of a tourism planner's life and a test of her skills. In most cases, tourism flows are seasonal but with heavy investment in service and attraction facilities, there is generally a desire by the operators of these facilities to generate year round tourists and thus cash flow. The flip side of this principle is that the seasons with low tourist volumes give local residents periods of reduced stress and rest.

Partnership is another principle to incorporate into successful tourism planning. Because of the pluralistic nature of tourism, there needs to be destination partnerships created or formed which can more effectively take advantage of the product offerings of each member of the partnership. It is the idea of "synergy" where the total is more than the sum of the parts.

Another principle to consider in tourism planning is product life cycle. Tourism products, like many others, grow in popularity and after a while fall off in popularity. The key is to be prepared when popularity begins to wane and have plans prepared to breathe new life into the attraction or service.

A final principle for successful tourism planning is the planner should insure there is ample opportunity for economic benefits to be captured. Tourists are generally willing to spend money, but as in the Hopi situation, there may be little planned opportunity for them to spend it. For example, most tourists to Hopi are day visitors; they spend money for accommodation in the border towns of Flagstaff, Winslow and Holbrook. There are only a few places to buy food and gas.

Planners are experts, but it takes community vision and community involvement to create a successful tourism plan that reflects the willingness of local residents to go the cost necessary to support tourism in their living space. Murphy provides a comprehensive model for community-based tourism planning. Implementation and action plans are a must in tourism planning because these are the vehicles that create coordination among people and organizations in a destination area. Without coordination-who is going to do what when with what resources-specified in written or chart form people will forget to do what needs to be done. Monitoring and evaluation are important to measure the success of the plan and to modify it if it is not working out. Successful monitoring depends on establishing a baseline of data from which to measure change. It is unnecessary to measure everything about a plan; select several key indicators and work with those over time.

Scales of Tourism Planning

The range of scale in tourism planning is from site specific physical plans to intermediary community and regional destination plans to national policy plans. No matter at what scale of tourism a planner is working, it is important to incorporate and account for all the components of structure, element, principle and process that have been described. In this way balanced, sustainable tourism development has a chance of being achieved.

Promotion is not Tourism Planning & Development - This misconception has been mentioned several times before, but it is worth reiterating that promotion is only part of successful tourism structure and is only one of four vital components of tourism supply.

Tourism is not an Industry - Tourism is made up of several different indus-tries-aviation, accommodation, food and beverage, attractions-and modes of business enterprise range from a few transnational companies to numerous local small businesses. Government, the public sector, is another major player in tourism development. Governments provide numerous "public good" attractions and conduct or subsidize promotional campaigns of their regions. The nonprofit, volunteer sector also operates attractions of various kinds; most common are county historical museums.

Tourism is not a Smokeless Industry - Tourism can and unfortunately does bring pollution, overcrowding, congestion, destruction of natural and cultural resources, contamination of water supplies, decay of landscapes and vistas with oversized and insensitive physical development and cross cultural clashes in customs and values. Tourism planning must be sensitive to these issues and attempt to anticipate and mitigate the more dire impacts before they develop.

Tourism is the Salvation of Rural & Small Town Economies - Not necessarily! Rural and small towns must have reasonable access to tourist markets and be a special enough place to appeal in order to become successful tourist destinations. Clever rural and small towns see their large urban neighbors, a half hour to an hour driving time away, as their tourist market and they develop attractions and products which interest these people.

For some places, all the boosterism in the world will not overcome an intrinsic lack of natural and cultural resources on which to build a tourism attractions strategy. In other places, there is no distinct sense of place or the authentic and unique have been replaced by homogenized commercial development. In yet other places, local residents do not want tourism development; without local support successful development will be difficult at best.

6

Tourism Management Objectives

A tourism marketing process may fail to focus on a site's true cultural traditions or historical interpretation and instead package it using an imagined sense of character. World Heritage cultural sites, many incapable of accommodating large volumes of tourists, may use inappropriate modern materials and styles when trying to increase capacity.

For example, the Archaeological Survey of India ruled out lighting the grounds of the Taj Mahal. Lights would have made it easier for evening visitors but would have taken away from the experience of seeing the monument by moonlight. A historic town in the United States was practically deserted, raising the question of whether to let the cultural resource continue its natural decline or intervene to restore the site for more intensive tourism.

Unfortunately, no old photographs remained from the town's heyday, and experts feared a misrepresentation of the past if restoration was carried out. The state historical society recommended managing the site to permit the town's natural deterioration. Major restorations were rejected in favour of simple shoring and bracing. To accommodate tourism needs, minimal construction activities were recommended including parking, footpaths and signage.

The local historical society, however, recommended that the town be completely restored. It favoured more intensive tourism and was not concerned with philosophical issues and the consequences of intervention. In the end, the town was restored but with doubts remaining over whether the quality, character and authenticity of the site was compromised. Practically, policy decisions are often heavily influenced by economic considerations. A decision on maintaining the values of ancient ruins in relation to the extent to which stabilisation and conservation is carried out may be a function of the funds and personnel available.

Allowing visitors to view a ruin from a distance may be more practical and preferable than the more expensive option of structurally stabilising the site to permit visitor access. In some cases all that may be needed is vegetation control to reduce deterioration.

When developing tourism policies at World Heritage sites, the overriding priority is to maintain the form and fabric of the resource. The nomination dossier of a World Heritage site can give guidance to the process of balancing policy and management objectives against tourism needs. These dossiers usually describe a site's features and previous changes in detail and may set out necessary preservation actions. Dossiers are available through each country's State Party and/or through the World Heritage Centre.

Policy Goals

Policy goals are broad statements that set out a vision of how a site will be managed on the basis of its environmental and social conditions. Policies guide a variety of actions including building infrastructure and developing social programmes such as promoting local educational and economic development through tourism.

Where this policy development process is a joint exercise, a policy statement can unite people with different viewpoints and give direction to public and private tourism management.

The general nature of policy goals is reflected in a policy statement from the Australia Wet Tropics Management Authority. It says the Authority's purpose is to "provide for the implementation of Australia's international duty for the protection, conservation, presentation, rehabilitation and transmission to future generations of the Wet Tropics of Queensland World Heritage Area, within the meaning of the World Heritage Convention."

While policy goals are general, management objectives set out in detail how a site will be managed. Within the framework of the general policy goals, the objectives spell out desired conditions, reflecting what management wants to maintain and the experiences a visitor would ideally encounter at a site. For example, if a policy goal is to provide local employment opportunities, then a management objective may be to encourage the use of local guides.

If a goal is to maintain a sacred site in a manner ensuring respect and tranquillity, then objectives may include limiting visitation and noise levels. Objectives should be subject to evaluation. They should therefore be specific, quantifiable, have time limits and be stated in clear language so that they can be understood by all those responsible for implementation.

They should be the basis for a standard by which to gauge the performance of site management. For example, at a historical monument, a policy goal may be to support local educational activities, while a management objective could be to increase the number of local schoolchildren who attend the site's educational programme. In this case a quantifiable measure could be the number of school groups that visit the site during the year.

Clearly stated policy goals and objectives provide direction in decision making and responding to change. Constructing a tramway through a wilderness park, building a high-rise modern hotel near a low-lying archaeological site, installing artificial lights at a monument, and increasing helicopter traffic in a national park are all examples of tourism initiatives that World Heritage site managers have had to face.

Clearly documented goals and objectives give direction and provide a historical context for addressing tourism initiatives in a consistent manner. Any new initiative can change a site. Examining initiatives within the context of policies and objectives can help managers determine whether they are within acceptable parameters. If goals and objectives are based on stakeholder needs, and fall within the law and the World Heritage Convention, they can form a solid basis for management decision making.

In addition, activities such as interpretation, promotion, carrying capacity control and monitoring all depend on the direction given by policy goals and objectives. A project in the Carpathian Mountains in Eastern Europe illustrates the need for clearly defined tourism policy goals. An international funding agency assigned a team of experts to write a regional tourism development plan to aid small businesses. Market research suggested a comparative advantage for small-scale accommodations, emphasising natural and cultural attractions.

Some members of the government and business community, however, favoured the rebuilding of large-scale tourism infrastructure from the Soviet era. At the time, no unified national or regional policies for tourism development existed to give direction to and clarify these efforts. The disparity of goals persisted throughout the life of the project.

When the time came to present a final report, the team found it impossible to present strategy and cost recommendations that met the needs of both groups. A forest reserve in Costa Rica whose operational budget is largely based on visitor fees had no clear-cut policies on tourism development until several years ago. A project to build a larger visitor centre met with opposition from some in the administration because they saw the site more as a nature reserve than as a tourist destination.

Others liked the idea and wanted to attract more tourists. While members of the community were against it, people in other nearby communities were in favour of increasing tourism because of the economic benefits it would bring. After months of controversy, the issue was resolved with a consultant's study and dialogue among the different stakeholder groups. With an established process within the reserve's administration to discuss policies and define goals, these conflicts would have been minimised and no doubt resolved without outside help.

Stakeholder Concerns

Stakeholder concerns should make up the list of management issues from which policy goals and objectives are developed: Stakeholders' involvement in setting goals and objectives links a tourism strategy with those who will have an impact on a site now and in the future. Stakeholders can be consulted on a number of management concerns such as infrastructure development and monitoring programmes. Stakeholders usually include government officials, members of the environmental and conservation community, scientists, historic preservation organisations, hotel and tour agency owners, visitors, guides and residents.

Following is a list of stakeholders with suggestions on how they may contribute to developing tourism goals and objectives.

— Park, forestry or archaeological department officials may provide information on past management and visitor issues.

— Guides can offer information on the social and environmental conditions of the site, and their input can bring to light important interpretation issues.

— Guides working for tourist agencies can give advice on their employers' concerns and input on site monitoring needs.

— Community leaders often have concerns and ideas about how tourism will affect local social values and economic development. For example, local leaders may think it necessary to avoid tourism impacts on the main population centre.

— Hotel owners can have a direct influence on tourism development and community interactions. They may be concerned about potential crowding, or coordinating visitor arrivals between the hotel and site management personnel through a reservation system. Hotel owners can also help in the development of interpretation and promotional materials.

— Tour operators will have concerns about visitor comfort and security. They stay apprised of changes in the international travel market and usually have information on user preferences and demand. The value of contacting tour operators to discuss their concerns, potential demand for a site, and possible cooperation on activities such as marketing should not be underestimated.

— Scientists can spell out concerns about significant flora and fauna or historical or archaeological remains. They can suggest ways to protect resources from impacts and offer advice on attracting research grants. Field assistants working directly with scientists can share practical concerns and complementary information.

Background information should supplement the list of stakeholder concerns: When developing goals and objectives, libraries and department archives are useful sources of valuable supplemental information, for example on endemic or endangered species of fauna or flora, or on visitor use and impacts on wildlife or archaeological ruins. National tourism and protected area laws and policies including the legal requirements for licensing and taxation can help in setting government policies and in understanding current conditions of tourism development.

Old master plans and the recommendations contained in them are also useful. At Copan, a Mayan World Heritage archaeological site in Honduras, a major international hotel was built even though many had suggested that smaller existing hotels in a nearby town would have been adequate with some minor upgrading. Many unattended ruins were destroyed just because they lay near a new access road to the Copan ruins.

Common Interests with Stakeholders

Conflicts with the local community may prevent cooperation in tourism development: For this reason consultation with community members during planning is essential. They may voice concerns that development will bring increased pollution or crime; that tourist traffic may endanger their children; or that tourists will have a negative impact on social conditions, for example by wearing inappropriate dress. They also may fear that the development will not benefit local people, for example that jobs as guides will be given to outsiders.

Consultations may result in actions such as the creation of a tourism development committee or a system for training local guides. Tour operators may be asked to educate their clients to respect community values. A visitor centre may be built some distance away from the village to avoid encroaching on everyday village life.

Environmentalists and conservationists have important concerns over the potential negative impacts of tourism development on natural and cultural sites: Environmentalists involved in the protection of flora and fauna may fear that opening an area for tourism could also invite hunters, or they may voice concern over potential disturbances to nesting birds, for example. Archaeologists might warn against vandalism and other potential damage to ruins and monuments.

Both groups may complain about increased litter, particularly if existing funds are insufficient for garbage collection. Both are likely to press for conditions in which visitors do not feel rushed or crowded, or spend too much time waiting to enter a site. Members of this stakeholder group often complain of a lack of communication with the tourism sector, including both the ministry and private operators.

They may also complain that staff members value tourism development more than educational activities and scientific research. This stakeholder group might wish to persuade site managers to implement an efficient reservation system, to limit access to areas with pristine, fragile ecosystems or to vulnerable archaeological sites, and to mount an education campaign to minimise impacts. They might insist on strict supervision of visitors, especially student science groups. Researchers often advocate the appointment of a science adviser at the site who could promote and manage research. Agreement could be reached on specific targets for tourism promotion and development.

Tour guides are a valuable source of information and advice concerning conditions affecting the environment as well as the visitor experience: They will point out unsafe trail sections and help ensure that trails are maintained for comfortable walking, as well as alert management to problems of crowding and noise. Guides can inform management when local people use the site for hunting and killing birds and other wildlife. Like the environmentalists and conservationists, guides are usually concerned about the quality of their clients' experience, and will insist that the time it takes to purchase a ticket be kept to a minimum, that congestion on the access road to the site be eliminated, and so on.

They may suggest maintaining limits on the numbers of visitors permitted at a site through use of an effective reservation system, and measures such as staggering visits by promoting afternoon tours. A direct telephone or radio connection between site management staff and guides would ensure consistent and effective communication.

Hotel owners and managers usually want a site to provide a broad base of opportunities for different types of visitors: They are also concerned about crowding and littering, the amount of parking at the site entrance, and the presence of persistent beggars and/or souvenir hawkers. As with independent guides, hotels appreciate consistent and reliable communication with site management, perhaps by a specially installed direct phone line. Members of this stakeholder group might ask staff management to develop a reservation system for tours. They would also advocate formation of a tourism advisory committee to meet with the local community about development issues and the needs and preferences of tourists.

Overseas tour operators and ground operators are especially concerned about logistical questions: Will their tour groups have to wait in line behind other tours scheduled at the same time? Will their groups meet up with noisy or inconsiderate groups? Is there enough parking? And, as with other shareholder groups, operators are anxious for a site to be well maintained and safe for visitors, and in the case of natural sites that the wildlife are adequately protected. These stakeholders often advocate efficient reservation systems, good communications and regular maintenance.

A stakeholder advisory group can facilitate the development of policy goals and management objectives: Such a panel provides a mechanism for exchanging ideas and information. The group should draft a written policy or vision statement that can be developed and publicly endorsed. The group could also help to set management objectives, including standards for desired conditions and actions. Practically, stakeholder groups can be engaged in the management process and serve as forums for exchanging views and reaching agreement on tourism issues. If an advisory group is not feasible, some mechanism for exchanging ideas is needed.

This can be as simple as a regular exchange of memos between site management staff and stakeholder groups, to solicit opinions and describe current activities. The process of developing goals and objectives should also take into account the site's uniqueness in relation to other sites with which it competes. Tour operators and other tourism professionals who may be members of the advisory group can be a valuable source of information about a site's comparative advantage over others in the area.

Demand and Preferences of Visitors

Data about visitors' preferences and demand for a site is essential for establishing objectives: Information on the number of visitors and their likes, dislikes, motivations and expectations will help the planner divide visitors into subgroups of people with similar characteristics, needs and spending behaviours. This information is useful in setting objectives for infrastructure, personnel needs and education and interpretation programmes. Combined with data on tourism markets, the information can be used to develop objectives for attracting certain types of tourists to a site. For example, managers with a policy of boosting local community development might set a goal of attracting tour operators who use local guides.

Numbers of visitors also affect management objectives and infrastructure and facility design: The experience at Liffey Falls in Tasmania illustrates the usefulness of information about visitor preferences when setting management objectives. The Forestry Commission discovered that visitors wanted to see the falls and were not interested in the other available recreation facilities. Knowing this, officials were able to concentrate their efforts and save a considerable amount of money and staff time. At Uluru National Park in Australia, a survey found that most tourists mainly wanted to see and to climb Ayers Rock. Fewer cited experiencing the outback and seeing wildlife as prime reasons for visiting. This information helped park staff to focus their attention on Ayers Rock.

Existing sources can be used to start the process of assessing visitor preferences and demand: Information and statistics from the tourism ministry, protected area staff and tour operators can help provide an idea of current and future demand and the mix of market segments. National tourism officials have information on tourism development and studies or statistics on tourism markets. Statistics and reports from the site staff and tour operators can provide an idea of visitor preferences and demand.

Existing studies from national tourism officials can provide information on the kinds of tourists the government is attempting to attract and the type of tourist expected to visit a site in the future. Interviews with retired parks, forestry or archaeological survey officials may shed light on past management plans and visitation records. Records may include statistics on the number of park visitors, their country of origin and the number of days they spend in the area. Through discussions, officials can help managers identify changes in visitor interests, activities and travel patterns.

A look at tourism development in neighbouring communities can indicate a site's potential demand and show how tourism has affected the economies and social conditions of the community. Local guides and hotel and pen sion owners can provide information on visitor preferences and demand cycles. Also, because they are in constant touch with changes in the international travel markets, they can help in identifying and tracking user preferences and demand, for example, whether visitors travel in tours or organised groups or travel independently. They can provide helpful information for developing infrastructure and interpretation material. Scientists and archaeologists can also share information about visitor preferences and patterns.

Observations, surveys and interviews provide more detailed visitor profiles: Such information on visitors and their interests may be needed to fine-tune management objectives, for example, on crowding preferences or tourists' spending patterns. Observations are qualitative and less exact than surveys and interviews, but they are quick, inexpensive and useful for indicating trends or suggesting targets for an eventual survey or interview.

Observations may include: organisation (group size), forms of transportation, type and amount of equipment, uses of time, maps of where people go and behaviour including languages used and noise levels. Since most people have difficulty analysing their own behaviour and motivations, observations can be a quick and useful technique for monitoring what people actually do.

Surveys are less expensive than face-to-face interviews, can reach a broad range of visitors and can provide valuable quantitative data, which is useful for reinforcing management decisions. However, with surveys communication is only one-way, and they require skills in questionnaire design and data management. They are also less effective than interviews in educating visitors.

Ideally, a combination of methods should be used to determine preferences and construct accurate visitor profiles. Categorising tourists according to preferences and behaviours can contribute to the realisation of a site's goals and objectives. For example, if income generation is a key goal, information should be compiled on variations in spending by visitors. If education of schoolchildren is a priority, they should figure in a survey.

Sites Offering Multiple Activities

At large sites, whether cultural, natural or mixed, management objectives may vary from one area to another within the site: People visit attractions with different expectations. Serious bird-watchers may come to a site to see an endangered species in a seldom visited, quiet environment. At the same time, local tourists may come to the site to see an archaeological ruin and to picnic or socialise with family members, and they may be not be particularly bothered by noise levels.

The Recreation Opportunity Spectrum (ROS) has proven a useful tool for setting objectives for these different visitor experiences. The ROS is a means of describing how tourism and recreation will be managed for different areas within a site. It works under the assumption that certain activities fit best in certain physical areas, for example, wilderness trekking fits better in relatively untouched forests than in farming areas.

It also assumes that activities should provide visitors with certain experiences or opportunities, such as solitude or adventure. For example, on Tanzania's Mt. Kilimanjaro, planners created a hiking zone where numbers were restricted and visitors could expect infrequent contact with other walkers. An even more restricted wilderness zone allowed only very minimal use. All huts and other permanent facilities were removed, only tent camping was permitted and the highest degree of solitude was provided, the area being free of permanent human presence.

To separate different activities, the ROS system uses preestablished categories called opportunity classes that match the site's physical resources with the activities best suited to them. For example at a mixed site, one area may be managed for archaeological tourism and another for bird-watching. Opportunity classes set out the desired conditions for the different areas and provide guidelines for management objectives.

These include guidelines on tourism/recreation activities and infrastructure development. In the United States, parks and forest services use a set of predetermined opportunity classifications including primitive, semi-primitive non-motorised, semi-primitive motorised, rural and modern urban.

Other countries have designed their own categories to fit the physical realities of their particular region. Each classification entails management standards and desired conditions that fall within a site's policy goals. The information needed to identify and establish opportunity class areas is drawn from background information on policy goals, existing legislation and stakeholder concerns. Each opportunity class encompasses a set of experiences and activities for the visitor.

Each has guidelines for ecological, social and management conditions. For example, an area classified as primitive might be maintained as a wild stretch of terrain where vehicles are not permitted and where visitors are highly likely to experience physical challenge and solitude. Because such areas appeal to tourists seeking a wilderness experience, appropriate activities may include sports such as backpacking and canoeing.

Moving across the spectrum, rural areas within a site, for example farmland, can have varying degrees of human impacts and contact with other people is to be expected. Here activities such as wilderness backpacking would probably not be appropriate. On the other hand, birdwatching along rural roads may be an appropriate tourist activity. Infrastructure development for different activities is closely related to an area's opportunity class.

The ROS system matches infrastructure objectives with the experiences on offer. For example, if an objective is to provide an isolated wilderness experience, only basic infrastructure would be needed. In populated rural areas, infrastructure may be more sophisticated, with accommodations that fit visitors' expectations.

7

Tourism Management Strategies

Direct management actions confront problems of human behaviour through regulations that may entail enforcement, restricting activities or rationing use. Indirect methods seek to affect behaviour through education, information and persuasion. Visitors can be informed about the impacts connected with a certain activity, or given information that encourages the use of certain areas over threatened areas.

Other indirect actions include physical alterations, such as the redirection of a trail to a more resilient area of a forest, that influence the movement of visitors. In general, indirect actions are more successful in remote areas, where visitors' freedom to explore is usually a primary goal. Direct approaches are often used to prohibit visitors from entering fragile or dangerous areas, for example at an archaeological site where they might damage a priceless fresco.

Experts say regulations succeed when they have strong public support, are carefully explained, and when visitors have some say in how they are implemented. Visitors must understand why a behaviour change is desirable. Once implemented, of course, regulations must be enforced.

In practice, a combination of methods is generally used. For example, both direct and indirect actions can be used to minimise visitors' impact on a coral reef. Site staff can design an extensive public information campaign that can include printed materials, direct advertising and school programmes. Tour operators can be managed through permits, regulations and enforcement actions aimed at concentrating recreation activities at resistant reefs.

A combination of methods is also recommended for controlling vandalism, including physical protection of the resource as well as education, making a site inaccessible to vehicles, increasing admission fees and protecting sites by not promoting them. Management strategies should be in line with objectives. For example, if a management objective at a Himalayan site is to offer visitors the freedom to explore, then a softer management approach may be appropriate.

Here staff may wish to emphasise educating trekkers on low-impact expedition behaviour. On the other hand, if a site's objective is to protect a priceless mosaic at an ancient monument, a more direct approach may be appropriate such as the deployment of guards to protect the site from looters or vandals and to regulate tourism activity near the work of art. Actions should have a high probability of achieving the desired outcome.

Before taking actions that may face resistance, it is important to ensure that norms and regulations give managers the legal mandate to act, and that appropriate enforcement systems will support its application. Awareness of the visitor profile helps to ensure success. For example, a large group of foreign visitors may be strongly motivated towards the protection of an endangered species but unaware that they are disturbing the animal during feeding times.

In this case, educational materials explaining low-impact viewing techniques may be the best method for minimising impacts. Actions should be relatively easy and inexpensive to implement. In general, direct methods are considered more time-consuming and costly, while indirect actions are thought to be cheaper in the long run.

The most effective but least restrictive management actions should be implemented first. The results should be monitored, and more restrictive actions may be implemented if necessary until conditions improve. For example, to deal with uncontrolled dumping of garbage, an educational campaign may be launched describing the problem and inviting voluntary compliance with a regulation against dumping at the site.

If voluntary methods fail, a fine can be imposed. If this doesn't work, the area may have to be closed. At some sites, human and financial resource limitations may necessitate more direct approaches in the short term. Experts in both the North and the South stress the need to develop visitor education programmes and other indirect methods. However, managers often opt for direct methods when faced with problems such as proximity to high population centres and limited staff and finances.

In these situations, the cost and time involved in implementing indirect methods is weighed against immediate problems, such as the need to prevent the rapid degradation of an archaeological site by visitors buying objects stolen from the site.

Reducing Visitation in High Use Areas

Reducing visitation in high use areas is a justifiable means of avoiding social impacts such as crowding, but may not by itself substantially reduce some ecological impacts. Reducing the number of people in an area can effectively reduce crowding or congestion, for example at a historical monument. Also, where light use causes considerable environmental damage, decreases in traffic in the area may not have correspondingly positive effects. In such cases reducing visitor traffic may do little to boost recovery rates for soil and vegetation and an area may need to be closed for recovery to occur.

On sites that have already suffered degradation to vegetation, practically all use may have to be curtailed before recovery can occur. Impacts to water and wildlife resources are more varied and in some cases can respond to a reduction in use levels. For example, bears in the Yellowstone National Park World Heritage site pose a greater problem in high-use areas, and reducing visitation may reduce incidents between bears and campers.

In some areas, even if limits are imposed, measures to concentrate and control visitors are needed to reduce ecological impacts: People have a tendency to go to the same places and follow the same routes. However, once people arrive at an established site such as a camping ground, they tend to disperse within the limits of the camping area. Limiting use-for example by reducing the number of campsites around a lake-would reduce the number of visitors but not necessarily reduce their ecological impact as they spread out over all the campsites.

Actions would be needed to both reduce the number of people and ensure the permanent closing of selected campsites. On the other hand, in lightly used areas, visitor reductions can minimise ecological impacts as long as use levels are kept low, visitors are instructed in low-impact techniques and they avoid fragile areas. Even one uneducated party of visitors can inflict serious damage.

Limiting the length of stay at a site can reduce numbers and alleviate crowding problems but may not necessarily reduce environmental impacts: Limits can be placed on time spent anywhere at the site or at specific areas, a measure that helps reduce crowding. Length-of-stay limits at heavily used natural areas are unlikely to have any effect on ecological impacts unless the limits are very restrictive and targeted to reduce measurable indicators. Ecological impacts are best reduced by imposing length-of-stay limits in lightly used areas; in fragile areas, a long stay in any one place could cause unacceptable impacts.

Closing an area can be an effective way to protect or restore environmental quality: The measure encourages the recovery of vegetation and reduces wildlife impacts. For example, visitors to Big Bend National Park in Texas, USA, are excluded during the breeding season of peregrine falcons to protect their nesting sites. Closure of an area, however, is a direct action that can be controversial and have economic and social ramifications. Any closure should be explained to the local community, not just to would-be visitors.

Reducing numbers by limiting the size of parties can also help control ecological and social impacts: Large parties can cause overcrowding as well as visitor conflicts. In more popular areas, limits on party size and an educational campaign may be needed to reduce impacts and to ensure more privacy for each group of visitors.

In such cases educational programmes should stress the importance of using existing areas and keeping them pleasant for the next visitors. Big groups are likely to create wider disturbed areas than smaller groups because they tend to spread out over a larger area. They can also disturb an area more rapidly than a small party. However in an area that is already heavily affected, it makes little difference if a group size is 10 or 50.

Quotas can be used to reduce visitor levels but raise several issues: A point to consider is the financial cost of implementing and administering the quota system. If staffing is insufficient, a quota system probably cannot be maintained over the long term. Also, quotas favour people who can book in advance, excluding other categories of potential visitors. Any sort of limitation may annoy visitors who cherish their freedom. Quota systems may especially irk those who consider themselves traditional users of a site. As a result they may choose to go elsewhere, and other sites may not be able to cope with increased use. Thus, for a quota system to be successful, access should be limited to alternative sites and user groups need to understand and accept the rationing technique being implemented.

Increasing visitor fees and other charges can reduce visitor numbers: The laws of supply and demand dictate that higher fees at a site will reduce visitation. A factor to consider when raising fees is the elasticity of demand, or how sensitive visitors are to a change in the cost of entering an area. This information can be gleaned from surveys. Another factor to consider is that visitors want pricing schemes to be easy and straightforward. They tend to prefer an all-inclusive fee over a main fee plus separate charges such as for parking or taking photographs. Setting visitor fees may also involve setting different entrance fees for local people and foreigners.

Not providing facilities can reduce visitor numbers: Limiting infrastructure such as camping areas or parking spaces can reduce visitor numbers just as adding infrastructure can increase numbers. Simply making access more difficult, for instance, by locating parking farther away from entrances, can also slow visitation. In Costa Rica, community pressure to limit tourism at a Reserve put a stop to a plan to pave the access road to the community and the reserve.

On the other hand, increasing infrastructure such as adding signs and informational plaques can increase the popularity of a site and its resources, for example, an underwater shipwreck. This strategy raises several issues including safety concerns. At a rain forest park, for example, management may want to provide a system of signs, boardwalks and bridges to direct visitors safely back to the entrance rather than run the risk of having to carry out expensive searchand-rescue operations.

The elasticity of demand related to infrastructure development may vary from one site to another. Many World Heritage sites, because they are unique, can attract significant numbers of people even if infrastructure development is limited. For example, Mount Everest would probably continue to attract substantial numbers of expeditions with or without infrastructure and facilities.

The Inca archaeological site at Machu Picchu would continue to attract large numbers of tourists without the addition of a cable car. This type of policy requires managers to keep a record of visitor demand to track changes with different levels of infrastructure. Even more important are on-site interviews with tourists and tour operators to help staff to determine the effects of infrastructure policy.

By maintaining ongoing dialogue with stakeholders such as tour operators who are members of the site's tourism advisory board and who have an intimate knowledge of visitor preferences and movements, site managers can obtain practical advice on the effects of these policies.

Disperse or Concentrate Visitors

Concentrating people can limit social and environmental impacts: The strategy offers a high level of control and protection for sensitive resources: By limiting use to a few selected areas within a site, particularly areas that are resistant to impacts or at least not as sensitive to impacts, the policy confines disturbance to a smaller area. So at sites with sensitive resources, a concentration strategy can be used to direct visitors to areas where resources are more resilient and resistant.

For example, some corals are more resistant to impacts than others, so visitors may be concentrated at more resistant areas. At Stonehenge, except for certain religious groups who are free to enter at certain times, visitors are not permitted to cross the site's outer perimeter. Besides limiting impacts to certain areas, concentrating use may open up new opportunities. For example, the policy may provide a rare opportunity to experience an area in relative isolation, perhaps at an archaeological site.

The chance to be part of a small group visiting an isolated, highly protected site may be unique, and one that people may also be willing to pay more for. A policy of concentrating may help avert possible impacts on naturally fragile areas resulting from the tendency of tourism enterprises such as hotel chains and theme parks to grow and expand.

In sites that are already heavily impacted, there may be no other alternative but to encourage or restrict visitors to existing use patterns. Since people tend to use the same areas and the same routes, implementing this measure is usually not difficult and can be accomplished through regulation or through indirect methods such as persuading visitors to use a certain area or providing infrastructure in specific areas.

Concentrating tourists may produce a positive social outcome by allowing local people to escape the pressures associated with tourism. For example, in community rural village encampments developed for tourists in Senegal, tourist accommodations are situated well away from the village centre. In Ujung Kulon National Park in West Java in Indonesia, tourism activities are restricted to a zone that is managed by a private company that provides accommodation and services.

A possible disadvantage of concentrating use is that it changes the social climate of an environment for the visitors. At many sites, when tourists are clustered together, for example in an enclave of small hotels, they lose the feeling of solitude. This may be contrary to the visitor experience that was originally planned and/or what originally attracted people to the site.

Dispersing visitors is seldom simple and may not mitigate impacts: Limiting environmental impacts in natural areas by dispersing use to different areas can be effective in areas where use levels are low and visitors are conscientious about their behaviour. A dispersal policy should be supported with programmes designed to control where people go and how they engage in recreational activities. The policy may not be feasible at natural sites with limited resources for educating or controlling visitors. In addition, careful monitoring of a dispersal programme is needed because of the high potential for spreading problems.

Dispersing visitors by extending the tourist season is an option that may have ecological consequences. For example, using quotas and visitor permits can reduce crowding but may concentrate use in a season during which vegetation and wildlife are more fragile. Wildlife is especially vulnerable during the reproductive months and when animals feed for winter. During periods of higher rainfall and snowmelt, the ground may be more susceptible to compaction and breaking. Plants are more vulnerable during growth seasons.

At cultural sites, such as monuments with well-developed and protective infrastructure where there is little risk of environmental impacts, dispersing visitors is an effective way to relieve crowding. Dispersing visitors to different areas of a site can be accomplished through regulations or through information and persuasion. It can also be accomplished through the strategic placement of infrastructure. If staffing levels allow, direct actions such as issuing permits may also be effective. A permit system increases the distance between parties and supports a management objective of providing an experience in which human encounters are infrequent.

The decision to concentrate or disperse tourism should reflect policy goals and management objectives. A frequent policy goal is to assure that the benefits of tourism flow to the communities around a site. This may lead to pressure to open up new areas of a site to visitors. Tourism has a tendency to spread, and can lead in turn to the spread of social and ecological impacts.

If on the other hand local economic development is a key goal, and there is sufficient revenue-generating potential to replace current economic activities in a given area, then expanding tourism to the area may be appropriate. But if the main policy goal is protection of an endangered species and promoting visits by biologists, expanding tourism within a park may limit opportunities for research because of increased tourism impacts in sensitive areas.

Physical Environment

Increasing a site's resistance to visitor impacts by installing or modifying infrastructure is generally referred to as site-hardening: Adding infrastructure, or "hardening" a site, strengthens its physical durability. This may involve surfacing access routes and trails, or building shelters for trekkers, or barriers to prevent people from touching priceless mosaics such as at the Taj Mahal. An example of extensive hardening of a cultural site is at the Great Temple of Abu Simbel, in Egypt, where the daily influx of 2,000 tourists was causing traffic jams.

Inside the temple, their respiration increased the humidity and carbon dioxide in the air, causing salt deposits to form on the walls. To address the traffic problems, management implemented a one-way road system. A ventilation system was installed to reduce the humidity and the temperature in the burial chamber. Another way to avoid impacts is simply to move infrastructure away from sensitive areas.

Hardening has both costs and benefits because it changes the nature of the visitors' experience: Hardening can lead to a change in visitor profile. The Milford track in New Zealand and the Overland track in Tasmania, both popular backpacking routes, saw an increase in use during the 1980s. Management responded to the resulting impacts by rationing use and hardening the tracks surfaces. Consequently, some visitors considered the tracks too easy and stopped using them.

Making experiences easier by hardening a site can also increase the level of crowding. In Tasmania, a boardwalk was built to restrict access to parts of the Gorden River. For business reasons, tour group sizes were not reduced, and groups could number more than 50. Crowding onto the boardwalk, the visitors had difficulty photographing one of the site's star attractions, a famous 2,000-year-old Huon pine tree.

Another effect of site hardening is that added materials may not blend in with the surrounding environment, compromising the original values of the site. One solution is to use natural materials instead of intrusive man-made materials. For example, fast-growing plants can be used to block a trail leading to a fragile or restricted area, or an entrance may be filled in with natural debris and rocks.

Visitor's Behaviour Changing

Interpretation and education programmes can mitigate environmental and social impacts: Educational programmes instruct people on how best to behave at a site.

Interpretation programmes inform and explain the site's resources and significance to the visitor. Visitors can be taught low-impact techniques at both cultural and natural sites.

In the United States, a "Save the Manatee Campaign" involved distributing guidelines to tourists and resulted in a decline in manatee mortality and injury. At the Luxor site, in Egypt, authorities reported that by explaining management problems to visitors they succeeded in distributing visitor movements more evenly. Interpretation and education programmes, although they may take time to succeed, may be preferable to infrastructure development because they are less likely to change the visitor experience and displace original target groups.

Certain impacts can be almost eliminated by teaching visitors minimum-impact techniques. In Tasmania, on the Overland track in the Cradle Mountain-Lake St. Clair National Park, trekkers came down with gastroenteritis because they were burying their waste too close to camping huts, contaminating water and food supplies. At one point up to half of the users were reporting falling ill. To correct the situation, park management mailed materials to walking clubs, environmental groups and camping stores outlining the problem and the solution that walkers bury their waste at least 100 metres from huts, campsites and streams.

The following summer, only eight to 10 percent of the users reported contracting gastroenteritis. Similar results have been achieved with education campaigns promoting low-impact wildlife viewing and other ecologically sound practices such as using stoves instead of fires, packing out garbage and not feeding animals. Most experts in the protection of monuments also advocate visitor education as part of the strategy for combatting problems such as vandalism.

Interpretation and education campaigns need not be overly costly: Goals should be critically evaluated to determine whether they could be met just as effectively through modest means. Instead of allocating huge sums to large infrastructure projects such as sophisticated visitor centres, cheaper approaches may be more effective, for example, a programme involving personal contact between visitors and management staff.

In some situations a team could travel from site to site to update and improve interpretation facilities and materials, and to train local managers and rangers. Educational and interpretation campaigns are possible at minimal expense. For example on a short nature walk, small signs giving the common and scientific names of the flora can suffice, while larger signs can be made on more general themes.

Changing visitor behaviour is not a simple process. Interpretation and education campaigns stem from a desire to change visitor behaviour, a simple principle in theory but complex in practice. Many factors have been found to influence visitor behaviour, including the following: Visitors want to know why they should do something. A simple statement that an area is a low-use area does not provide enough information.

The interpretation programme must match the current reality, or confusion will result. For example, photographs and descriptions in promotional publications may not correspond to the visitor experience. A case in point was when the Tasmanian Forestry Commission, in educational and promotional materials, emphasised the recreational attractions of its forests.

Feedback from visitors revealed that they had not expected to be able to see clearcutting from trails and picnic areas. One solution was to include images of forest production activities in the promotional literature. The behaviour of staff including maintenance personnel must uphold the values reflected in educational and interpretation materials.

A visitor's experience and prior knowledge may influence the effectiveness of educational materials. Research has indicated that educational materials are more effective for visitors with limited experience of a site or advance information about it. Special care must be taken with the content and delivery of interpretation materials for repeat visitors. Experts recommend that if two versions of the materials are not feasible it may be better to ignore the more experienced audience.

Visitors must believe that a given issue is real and serious, that a given action is necessary, and that they can make a difference. Materials should present an issue along with information on how to address it, linking visitors' experience with future actions. The materials could include information on environmentalists' clubs, other places to visit and learn about a subject, or other additional information. A person has to believe that he or she is capable of contributing to a solution, such as by planting a seedling in a reforestation project or helping out at an archaeological dig. Individual rewards can be financial but "psychic rewards" the gratification deriving from altruistic motives are often more meaningful.

Several other factors figure in the effective presentation of interpretation and educational programmes: Clear goals and objectives are needed to determine what is to be interpreted, for whom and how, and who will develop interpretation strategies. The crucial step of identifying fundamental messages and target audiences is reportedly the weakest link in the process of developing interpretation concepts and themes. Materials should focus on the type of visitor whose behaviour is considered most in need of change. The message should clearly describe the critical problems and recommended behaviours.

The most effective educational campaigns use a combination of methods tailored for particular user groups and messages. They are based on specific visitor profiles cataloguing age, background, interests, origin (foreign or local), degree of skill in the activities the site offers, special needs, form of access to the site (road or waterway, public or private). Profiles also take into account whether visitors are on their own, in couples or families, or part of an organised group.

Interpretation criteria may change with societal changes such as shifts in ethnicity or local education levels. Such shifts may necessitate new messages, perhaps in different languages. An exhibit should satisfy the expectations of occasional tourists as well as those of local residents and repeat visitors. Layered signs offer detailed information in smaller print intended to pique the interest of repeat visitors.

Studies show the need for careful analysis of visitor interests. Many people visit World Heritage sites out of a general interest in heritage. Most visitors to World Heritage sites have little specialist knowledge or interest; the particulars of a castle or other historical site are of secondary importance. Interpretative programmes should be evaluated in terms of whether they are meeting management goals and objectives.

If not, they are a poor investment of scarce resources, at the expense of other programmes and the management's reputation. Experts warn against a tendency to produce new programmes rather than re-examine existing ones, leaving no arguments in favour of one or the other. The easiest and most common way to evaluate the effectiveness of an interpretation programme such as an exhibit is to assess its ability to attract and hold visitors' attention.

In this case an exhibit is judged on how many people stop and how much time they spend looking and/or reading the exhibit material. Staff intuition concerning attitude change is generally reliable and can contribute to assessment studies. The target audience may be reached in various ways, depending on the type of materials used. In general, visitors who must rely on public transport or a service provided by the site management for access to an area is a captive audience.

Staff can inform visitors of park regulations and provide safety advice and orientation pointers. To encourage return visits, exhibits should be changed regularly, or special exhibitions should be staged on occasion. The Royal British Columbia Museum in Vancouver saw a decline in annual visitation because the exhibits remained unchanged through lack of funds. Revenues declined as a result, compounding the problem.

Guides can be invaluable in imparting educational information to visitors. In large tropical rain forests, for example, tourists unaccompanied by an excellent guide may spend long periods without seeing any wildlife. Eighty to 95 percent of travellers to rain forest lodges in one region of Peru reported being unsatisfied with wildlife viewing.

Involving guides in the planning stages when developing educational and interpretation programmes helps to ensure consistency in visitor information. Guides and site staff should liaise closely so that guides do not compete with the aims of the site, and so that their information is correct and consistent.

Methods of presentation vary in their ability to attract visitors and change behaviour: The following materials have been found to be effective. The Tasmania Parks Department found that the most effective presentation materials were fun as well as easy and quick to read. Videos were the most popular and the most effective. Because videos bring information to life and show how techniques work in practice, they are popular for use in schools and with inexperienced groups.

Comic posters, audio-visual materials and multimedia presentations have also proven effective. Once materials raise visitors' attention, the most effective method for changing behaviours is to add personal contact. For example, walkers are more readily convinced not to use stoves when rangers inform them face to face about regulations, reinforcing a strong educational campaign. Simply erecting signs saying "fuel stoves only" is far less effective.

In the absence of rangers, guides can be trained to present interpretation information. Workshops for commercial tour guides could cover low-impact techniques and other management issues. Local guides at Nan Madol, a South Pacific island with an important archaeological site, are crucial in educating tourists and controlling graffiti and other forms of vandalism.

Interactive interpretive programmes show great promise. Participatory exhibits are more popular than static displays and are highly effective in changing visitor behaviour. Active participation seems to foster a positive attitude, especially when combined with a rewarding experience. Interactive techniques giving opportunities for feedback include despatching roving staff or placing them at fixed points to provide information; holding conferences or discussions; offering entertainment events such as puppet shows, plays or musicals, or organising activities such as making and measuring things, games and re-enactments of historical events.

Publications, signs, self-guided activities, visitor centres, audio-visual devices, indoor and outdoor exhibitions such as walks, drives and snorkelling trails in marine parks are less interactive-but less timeconsuming for staff. Hands-on workshops may be coupled with field trips and observational tours. One scientist-teacher from Puerto Rico recommended that coastal ecosystems are best understood through field trips during which participants can question and interact with the expert. The Tropen Museum in Amsterdam offers a programme in which people can seek advice from experienced travellers about current events in a particular country and various cultural do's and don'ts.

Authentic displays based on economic activities using real artefacts and materials are increasingly popular. At the National Fishing Centre in Grimsby, England, for example, former trawler hands recount their experiences to the public and encourage participation by instructing visitors in knotting fishing line. Heritage centres increasingly offer authentic experiences through imaginative interpretations of local history. Since the 1980s, old established museums, thanks to new technologies, have been offering entertainment as well as education, blurring the distinction between the theme park and museum experience.

Oral history is a particularly useful research asset and an important source of interpretative material. The process gets local people involved and makes them feel represented, which may be especially important if it turns out that the local interpretation is at variance with that of site materials. Including the voices of local people in interpretative programmes gives them a central role, encouraging popular support.

OFFERING INCENTIVES

Visitors may be redirected through scheduling: For example, a site may be opened early for bird-watchers or closed early to limit other types of visitors. The Monteverde Cloud Forest Reserve in Costa Rica opens early so that bird-watchers can enjoy their activity in relative calm.

Extending a site's opening hours may depend on whether resources are sufficient to pay staff for the extra time. The extra expense could be offset through higher visitor fees or increased publicity.

Providing or not providing infrastructure for certain activities can influence the type of activity practised: Strategic construction and siting of infrastructure can encourage the use of certain areas over others. Signs can promote one site over another, while removing signs can discourage use. In areas where there may be conflict between different user groups or where separating the groups could enhance the visitor experience, lowcost infrastructure development could encourage separation. For example, signs could direct campers away from areas used by day visitors.

Regulation and Changing Types of Activity

Regulations limiting activities and/or the way they are practised can radically affect ecological and social impacts: Some recreation activities produce more impacts than others. The types of visitor activities can be limited. For example, banning off-road vehicles and motorcycles reduces soil erosion, as does the use of horses. To limit traffic and pollution problems, Bermuda has adopted a policy of not recognising foreign drivers' licences, making car rental impossible.

Similarly, non-resident cars have been banned on the Italian islands of Capri, Ischia and Procida. To minimise negative impacts due to encounters between tourists and whales at Glacier Bay, Alaska, authorities have set limits on the number of cruise ships entering the bay and issued regulations for maintaining a minimum distance of 400 metres between ships and whales. Whalewatching regulations are also in place for local guides at Viscaino Bay in Baja, California.

Once again, such regulatory measures require sufficient resources to implement. Complementary indirect actions can provide support to direct actions. For example, at some game parks in Africa, drivers often fail to observe regulations for maintaining acceptable distances from the wildlife. To address this problem, culverts can be dug alongside roads to prevent vehicles from leaving them.

Social Environment by Reducing Visitor Conflicts

Separating conflicting activities reduces conflict: Allocating specific activities to certain areas helps reduce conflict between different types of visitors. For example, groups such as snorkellers and sports fishermen would conflict if they tried to use the same areas. The concept of separating user groups is related to the Recreational Opportunity Spectrum.

A key issue when using this technique is to ensure that the different areas for different activities remain in good environmental condition for the long term. Visitors and tour operators could be informed that if an area allocated to them is damaged, they won't be offered an alternative area.

Developing interpretation and education programmes in close cooperation with the community can help to avoid alienating local people who may otherwise feel their cultural identity is being misrepresented: The feeling of sense of place and the strong spirituality and identity which traditional people have for their land is not easily conveyed to visitors. For the local community, memory, attachment and symbolism are often of primary importance.

In contrast, visitors may seem to diminish local values by being attracted to the unfamiliar, exotic and picturesque. Interpretation and education programmes, when developed in close cooperation with the community, can help prevent a devaluation of traditional local values.

Locals are more likely to participate in conservation when it is associated with an improvement in their standard of living: Managers at Ujung Kulon National Park in West Java in Indonesia report that local income-generating activities in tourism, resource management and protection encourage local support for park protection and conservation efforts. Environmental conservation and education programmes alone will not achieve results. In Gambia, West Africa, the local community's acceptance of the new Kiang West National Park was based entirely on the expectation that they would receive a portion of the economic benefits of tourism.

However, increasing local benefits-for example, by providing training for local guides-does not necessarily draw people into conservation and protection activities. Experience has shown that conservation and economic development should be linked. Thus guides should be recruited who have an ongoing interest in conservation or community participation. Evaluations of local guide training in Costa Rica indicated a need for a comprehensive selection process, in search of both talent and environmental and community consciousness.

Experience has determined that community tourism projects are sustainable when people invest their labour and savings in them: Projects succeed when people have a stake in them. When people can see the project's benefits they willingly contribute their labour or money. In Nepal's Annapurna Conservation Area Project, people are expected to contribute cash or labour to community development projects. Lodge owners who upgrade their facilities are provided with technical assistance and training including help in the development of their standards.

Community tourism programmes may be more effective if introduced gradually and in conjunction with other economic development programmes: Gradual introduction is recommended in view of potential negative social and economic impacts. Communities may need time to adapt to the realities of the industry, to manage problems stemming from the influx of visitors, and to plan efficient ways to capture and retain economic benefits from tourism. A community's expectations of economic benefits are often disappointed because of inadequate local conditions. For example, foreign tourists may demand standards of accommodations and food beyond what the local community can immediately provide.

Thus, locals may not begin to see direct economic benefits until certain basic problems are addressed. Gradual implementation can exacerbate the problem, as people become impatient for the economic benefits. Such problems may be mitigated when other incomegenerating programmes are carried out concurrently and the community is not oriented solely towards tourism. For example, many projects at protected areas include agroforestry and other resource development programmes that can produce economic benefits such as crops and wood lots for firewood. Such options can lessen the need for more rapid tourism development.

Tourism's potential for benefiting locals is a function of the existing resources and skills that can be used to generate income: Community tourism programmes should start with an evaluation of local resources and skills with which activities can be matched. For example, in many instances local transportation support is needed for tourism activities, or local knowledge is in demand because of difficult terrain, such as at Corcovado National Park in Costa Rica, where ground transportation to the park is difficult, and flying is more expensive.

Other activities that may need local guiding and transportation skills include mountaineering, trekking, sport fishing, skin diving, and horseback riding. More specialised activities such as bird-watching and river rafting usually require more education and training.

Opportunities for these activities often depend on the existence of government or NGO training programmes, and tour operators who are interested in involving local people.

Labour costs should be realistically evaluated when analysing community potential: If little or no capital is required to develop a guesthouse, for example, where rooms formerly occupied by children are converted into rooms for guests, the project may be attractive. Also, if the time spent on tourism enterprises could not be better spent on other pursuits, for example, if few work opportunities exist other than in tourism, then a community tourism project may be worthwhile even if the pay is low.

Experience has shown that tourism often fails to generate local economic benefits when local guides are under-utilised: Tour companies and hotels tend not to use local guides. In some countries and in specific protected areas, they are required to use under-skilled local guides, which they often see as a financial drain. This problem may be mitigated through intensive training of local guides in language and interpretation skills.

Guides with better skills are more readily accepted by tourist businesses. As tour operators and governments realise that site protection and the health of the tourist trade depend on local support, they begin to see that it is in their interests to support the hiring and training of local people.

Raising site revenue to produce local benefits: The costs and benefits of infrastructure and high-tech solutions should be reviewed in light of the goal of producing local benefits. Planners at the Copan Maya Ruins in the Honduras realised that luxury hotels tend to be located away from population centres, limiting opportunities for locals. Noting that most domestic visitors have modest financial resources and prefer local accommodations, they recommended upgrading existing infrastructure and related services.

They also deemed that concentrated, modest, but good quality tourist facilities could provide many more benefits to local communities than high-class, high-cost hotels, restaurants and guide services. Such services often use outside labour, are controlled by outside capital, and are intentionally located outside local communities. High-tech solutions to management problems should not be adopted without a serious review of their costs, benefits and applicability on the ground. In some countries where unemployment is already high, these measures can put even more people out of work.

It may be advisable and just as effective, for example, to use local labour to build and maintain palm thatch roofs to protect stone artefacts from deterioration instead of using chemical compounds. By the same token, power lawnmowers are obviously more efficient than manual labour for cutting grass, but lawnmowers need spare parts that may have to be imported. Visitor fees can generate benefits for both protected areas and local communities. Most studies on protected area management recommend government policies authorising the collection of fees to offset costs.

Fees can be charged for admission to parks or monuments, and for different activities such as diving and trekking, and for accommodation and rescue services. User fees are equitable because the people who use the site pay for it. Fees for public areas such as parks or museums are kept low to permit access to a greater cross-section of the population. To capture more foreign exchange and increase revenues, some sites charge a higher rate for foreign tourists than for nationals.

In countries where such a two-tier system is illegal, donations can be solicited from foreign tourists and tour companies. It should be noted that a chronic problem for many sites that collect fees is that the money is returned to a central treasury and does not go to site operations. Experts report that the tourism industry may resist visitor charges even though visitors may be willing to pay more for entrance fees. Visitors tend to accept fee increases if they know the funds will go to site protection and conservation.

They want to know where the money goes. Visitor preference data could be collected in support of a fee increase that may be opposed by certain stakeholders. Concession fees charged to individuals or groups licensed to provide services to visitors can also generate revenues both for sites and local communities. Common concessions include food, lodging, transport, guide and retail services. Concession fees and royalties can generate significant income at highly visited sites. Since concession fees are generally low relative to overall profit levels, businesses may be willing to pay higher fees.

Longer stays may raise revenue and still keep visitor numbers manageable. The availability of an array of visitor services can increase the average length of stay at a site. At Copan, setting up an interpretation programme, installing new trails and a visitor centre, developing private guide services, and offering after-dark audio-visual programmes in the nearby town all helped increase average visitor stays. At cultural sites with excellent natural resources, interpretation programmes could emphasise the natural attractions.

Tour operators may be willing to expand their itineraries to include other attractions and services and thereby raise local benefits. A base of operations such as a resort can have add-on attractions that tourists can visit within a day. Secondary attractions should offer visitors new experiences. Hiring of local staff can improve site management and bring local benefits. Experiences in Australia have shown the importance of providing employment and training to indigenous people who work as wardens, policy advisers and liaison officers.

Permitting local people to sell products can help a community's economy, but may be problematic. Tourists may feel threatened by aggressive hawkers, or locals who cannot afford to pay for concession privileges may use unauthorised areas at a site. At Grand Canyon National Park in the United States, Native Americans formerly sold handicrafts near the entrance and at other strategic places; an Native American marketplace was set up as an alternative.

8

Accommodating Tourists

The concept of carrying capacity has evolved completely with a better understanding of the relationship between the number of visitors and the impacts they cause. During the 1960s and 1970s, the main focus was on developing a system for setting limits to the number of visitors to parks, monuments and protected areas as a means of safeguarding natural and cultural resources. The aim was to determine the point at which adverse impacts were likely to begin. Experience has shown that such a simple calculation is not feasible.

The onset of environmental deterioration or adverse social impacts may come sooner or later depending on variations in visitor behaviour or the resistance and resilience of a given ecosystem. One destructive tourist can cause more damage than 50 conscientious visitors. Some areas such as meadows can handle less use than areas with more resilient vegetation; just a handful of tourists in a community may be responsible for most of the litter; some communities may accept larger groups of tourists while others reject them, and so on.

For some individuals, a single fellow visitor at an archaeological site would be too many; for others, hundreds of fellow visitors would not diminish the quality of the experience. Setting a specific carrying capacity figure may give the false impression that a protected area is safeguarded when it is not. Visitors to a ruin site may be limited to 100 at a time, while in an isolated corner some visitors may be helping themselves to priceless souvenirs.

The carrying capacity of a nature trail may be set at 100, but that will not prevent some visitors from disturbing a colony of nesting birds as they approach to take photographs. All activities cause environmental and social impacts. Site managers must set well defined and established goals for desired conditions that will serve as a baseline for determining an acceptable level of impact.

For example, managers need to know how much litter is dropped along an interpretive trail before launching a visitor education campaign against littering, so that they can determine whether their efforts are succeeding. When visitors to a natural area desire an experience relatively free of fellow visitors, managers may establish a baseline number of people considered unsatisfactory. Clearly, there is no magic number. Current models of visitor management involve setting goals and objectives, formulating indicators and monitoring results.

Planning for visitor management should be based on the idea of limits to acceptable change. The new planning methodologies assume that all activities cause impacts and that desired conditions should serve as the baseline for planning. Managers need to know not only how many people are in an area, but also how these users are affecting the area's natural and cultural resources. The new models set limits to impacts rather than visitation. It is a matter of tracking ecological and social indicators through field studies and user surveys.

The methodology known as Limits of Acceptable Change (LAC) sets standards and monitoring indicators based on management and stakeholder concerns. When the quantifiable standards are not met, impacts have become so negative that the management is prepared to take actions such as reducing access and restricting behaviours to avoid further degradation of resources, even if such actions would be unpopular. The idea is that environmental and social conditions water and air pollution, litter, crowding and so on each have quantifiable standards based on desired conditions.

When conditions approach "limits of acceptable change", management takes specific mitigating actions. LAC programmes may set numeric visitor limits, for example 100 people at a cultural site at any one time, but the overall process provides a much more comprehensive and effective system for protecting resources. The challenge is to define how much and what kind of change is "acceptable" and set indicator limits or standards for any changes that would degrade the conditions agreed upon. LAC standards are established on the basis of stakeholder and management needs, and follow legal and Convention guidelines.

For instance, stakeholder concerns may centre on a desire to limit certain impacts by maintaining a clean, safe, uncrowded environment in a particular area of a natural site. In this case, reliable indicators may include the number of people on a site's interpretive trail at any one time, dangerous areas on the trail or the amount of litter. Management objectives should lead to measurable impact standards reflecting the desired conditions. For example, one site indicator may be the number of unstable areas found on a tourist trail.

In this case, the site manager should define what is meant by an unstable area and quantify the unstable areas along the trail. With this information, the manager, in consultation with an advisory group, can set a standard for keeping the area safe for visitors. If overcrowding is a concern, visitors can be regularly asked to report the number of fellow visitors seen on the trail, producing data which can serve as an indicator. Other indicators may be social or economic, measuring for example the revenue generated by a site and the response of the local community to visitors.

While the LAC methodology was the first of the new visitor management methodologies, all the newer planning methodologies such as the Visitor Experience and Resource Protection Process (VERP) are applicable to both natural and cultural sites and follow these basic steps:

— Determination of goals and objectives derived from the concerns of management and stakeholders and how to achieve them.

— Formulation of a set of performance indicators based on the goals and objectives.

— Monitoring to determine whether these standards are being met.

— Deciding on actions to mitigate problems if the standards are not met.

Tourism impact indicators should reflect stakeholder concerns, policy or vision statements, management objectives and the needs of stakeholders who are utilizing the information. These elements, combined with field experience, should inform meetings with the advisory group aimed at selecting indicators to track changes in the ecological, physical and social conditions. It is essential to inform those making decisions how this information will be distributed.

In general, it is not necessary to monitor all indicators; some overlap with others and some may be simply too expensive or impractical to monitor. Also, indicators should not be seen as a full measure of an impact or problem, but more an attempt to describe it. Not all problem areas and concerns are conducive to monitoring through indicators. Agreement on indicators is the single most important part of a monitoring and evaluation exercise. Experience has shown that animated and collaborative brainstorming sessions are useful for identifying and agreeing on indicators.

An inventory of existing conditions provides the baseline data needed for indicators. Inventory information determines the degree to which existing conditions vary from desired conditions. Information on current conditions is the baseline for establishing realistic standards, a step needed for all the LAC-type methodologies. So for example, if vandalism at a rock art site is an indicator, a count of all the graffiti found around the site will be necessary.

Any inventory exercise should be carried out according to established, written procedures, insuring consistent monitoring practices over the long term. An inventory will test the basic data collection techniques and provide the information needed for a monitoring manual. This involves the development of standardised monitoring surveys and evaluation forms, along with instructions for making decisions on implementing actions to correct unacceptable conditions.

Measurement standards for indicators provide targets for measuring tourism impacts to keep them within acceptable limits. The written descriptions of conditions favoured in a site's management objectives can give direction to setting quantifiable standards. For example, a trail managed to offer a more natural type of exprience may be maintained at a width of two metres, while a trail in an established tourist area having to accommodate larger groups may have a standard width of three metres. Standards are usually set to prevent degradation of current conditions. An example would be a standard for maintaining the population of a particular bird species or water quality.

In some cases, however, even while managers would never desire degradation, they may set standards permitting a deterioration of current conditions if they believe that this would be a lesser evil than, for instance, having to restrict access or impose widely unpopular rules. Meetings of the advisory group and/or stakeholders will be needed to reach consensus on setting standards.

In large natural and mixed sites, the Recreation Opportunity Spectrum (ROS) system can be used to set standards for different areas within the same site, depending on the needs of different user groups. Experience in the field indicates that users may hold a wide range of opinions, and consequently managers should consider setting wider ranges of standards.

In natural areas, priority should be assigned to users with the greatest need for an unmodified environment. Once standards are set, an inventory will determine the degree to which existing conditions vary from desired conditions. For example, if a significant amount of an area's trails are found to be wider than the agreed standard, or if abrasions or damage to a monument exceed a particular standard, actions can be taken to improve conditions. This is an ongoing process in which indicators are monitored on a regular basis to track trends and changes in conditions.

Misunderstandings persist among international organisations and government agencies regarding carrying capacity. Calls continue for studies to provide policy-makers with a technical limit, a number or range of numbers that will indicate negative change. Such studies can create the false impression that carrying capacity can be reduced to a specific number indicating a clear point at which negative impacts will start to be seen. For example, at Lake Baikal, Russia, consultants were asked to determine the number of visitors per hectare that the terrain around the lake could support. Figures were derived primarily from formulas involving soil impact and slope.

The study also made predictions of cultural impacts based on the number of tourists compared with the number of local residents. While this methodology was easy to implement within the allotted time for the project, it failed to take into account variations in tourist behaviour, travel patterns and different stakeholder interests. Additional dialogue with interest groups would have made the report's figures more relevant to the day-to-day work of site managers.

More important, such dialogue would have started a process for setting tourism goals and objectives among the stakeholders within the limits of legislation on the environment and protected areas. Managers may still feel the need to set numeric limits to control people at their sites. Visitor numbers should be set in accordance with agreed upon standards. In the field, this is not an exact science, but a matter of tracking impacts through monitoring programmes and arriving at an approximate judgement of when limits are reached.

In practice, several strategies will help managers justify decisions to limit visitation. Data on numbers of visitors and their preferences make up the best justification for actions restraining the number of people permitted to enter an area. This is especially true if an expert study can be shown to the stakeholders affected by the decision. The negative effects of crowding and the desire for solitude at an archaeological or sacred site. The staff available to carry out protection efforts in relation to the number of visitors can also be used to justify restrictions.

For example, the number of tourists admitted to an archaeological site may be a function of the number of guards available for patrolling the site to ensure its protection. Numbers may be controlled simply by reducing the size of a parking lot or visitor centre. However, such a measure may detract from visitor satisfaction if it results in crowding.

CARRYING CAPACITY ISSUES

The concept of carrying capacity addresses the question of how many people can be permitted into an area without risk of degrading the site and the visitors' experience of it. It has generally been broken down into three categories: physical, ecological and social.

— Physical carrying capacity, called "facility carrying capacity" by the World Tourism Organisation, mostly has to do with available space the number of beds available to overnight guests, how many cars would fill a parking lot, how many campers in a campground, seats in a theatre, and so on. Concomitant to such considerations is the question of fresh water and electricity supply.

— Ecological carrying capacity is the degree to which an ecosystem is able to tolerate human interference while maintaining sustainable functioning. A curvilinear relationship may exist between use and impact at a site, and wide variations in ecosystem resistance and resilience make ecological carrying capacity difficult to predict.

— Social carrying capacity is psychological and socio-cultural and refers to the limit beyond which the number of people in an available space would cause a decline in the quality of the recreational experience and the users' satisfaction. Overcrowding is a prime example of a socio-cultural carrying capacity issue. Since different user groups have different social expectations and because of complicated issues related to cultural resistance and resilience, this factor is also difficult to assess.

Monitoring Issues

The shift to LAC-type methodologies has highlighted the importance of monitoring: Managers need to know when desired conditions are being threatened, for example, with increasing water pollution in a stream or when waiting lines become too long at an entrance. A well-developed and regular monitoring programme can provide resource managers with data to justify sometimes controversial actions such as limiting the number of people allowed into a site at a time. Monitoring visitors' likes, dislikes and travel patterns, as well as their impacts, can help identify and justify needed actions in the changing tourist industry.

The most difficult aspect of monitoring is ensuring that it is carried out on a regular basis: Managers are faced with many pressing day-to-day problems and often have little time or desire to carry out monitoring exercises. However, monitoring is effective only if it is done regularly; if it cannot be sustained, its usefulness is severely limited. well as their impacts, can help identify and justify needed actions in the changing tourist industry.

Many types of monitoring procedures are possible depending on the level of accuracy desired and available resources: For example, soil erosion on a nature trail can be measured in several ways. One method is to identify eroded sections by walking the trail and counting variations in width, perhaps caused when visitors seek to avoid muddy sections. Another is to establish permanent checkpoints at problem areas along the trail to measure soil loss.

Each approach has advantages and disadvantages. Examining trail conditions in a general fashion does not give a precise measurement, but provides a good overview. On the other hand, while permanent monitoring plots will provide a more accurate measure of soil loss, the method is more expensive and time-consuming. The differences in approach can also be illustrated with bird population counts.

One inexpensive method systematically records the number of bird sightings by local guides. A more accurate but expensive method of tracking population changes involves catching specimens with nets or setting up a transect, or a fixed corridor along which species are counted on a regular basis. Fewer options exist for monitoring socio-economic conditions such as crowding and community attitudes. Most socio-economic information is obtained through questionnaires or interviews, work that is labour-intensive and time-consuming.

A monitoring procedure should be selected on the basis of what questions need to be answered and how much time and funding is available to carry out the work.At the Great Barrier Reef in Australia, travel distances made monitoring each campsite in detail prohibitively expensive. Managers decided instead on the more cost-effective tactic of sampling a cross-section of camping areas.

Finally, all monitoring programmes should be evaluated to determine how well they measure the indicators. This evaluation should also determine how large a measured change must be for management to be confident that it is the result of visitor impact and not errors in data collection.

Monitoring of historic monuments must take into account values of integrity and authenticity: Indicators of structural or engineering conditions cannot translate into an overview of the complete health of a site since they do not reflect values of integrity or authenticity. While it is important to monitor the use of a facility and visitor satisfaction, experts say more monitoring is needed to measure the effectiveness of communicating a site's historic significance.

The Canadian National Historic Sites authorities set a policy to protect "commemorative integrity", which is preserved when that which symbolises or represents a site's importance is not impaired or under threat; when the reasons for the site's national historical significance are effectively communicated to the public; and when the site's heritage values, including those not related to national significance, are respected by decisions and actions affecting the site.

To implement the policy, decision makers spell out the reasons for a site's national significance before determining objectives and standards for the purpose of monitoring. Making a statement of desired results and a list of those responsible is also part of the process.

Simple monitoring systems with built-in incentives may be the most feasible and best approach for a sustainable programme: Given the many difficulties in sustaining a monitoring programme, consideration for the practical needs of site managers, tourism officials and private operators will improve chances of success.

Monitoring can be incorporated into maintenance activities, or local guides can carry out monitoring functions. Tour operators interested in tracking visitors' preferences may be prepared to finance surveys. Government officials may also want the information because it can directly affect national tourism initiatives. Experience has shown that a simple monitoring programme is better than none at all and can be more effective than costly ones.

For example, with historic buildings and other built cultural sites, a simple report with notes and photos has been found to be far more useful than detailed, item-by-item reports on conditions. Short, simple reports covering general problems and a few specific problem areas allow staff to determine which properties require the most attention and to offer guidance to their agencies.

Site staff are given a checklist of items to monitor. The monitor notes any changes made to the property since the last visit, any problems related to general maintenance or repair, any potential problems, and any contemplated changes and repairs. Four categories are monitored: exterior, interior, the area around the building and the rest of the grounds. General photographs are taken as well as more specific problem areas.

9

Involving Public Participation

Unravelling the identity and structure of different stakeholder groups can be time consuming and the results are not obvious. For example, different agencies can be involved in the management of a site and have different goals and objectives. In many cases, several agencies control various sections of a protected World Heritage site, each with its own management strategy. While sharing a common heritage resource, visitor management strategies and issues vary from one area to the next.

Some stakeholders are unwilling to support wider participation, especially when it is seen as a threat to their authority. For example, managers may accept a policy of openness and communication but may resist supplying all pertinent information to interest groups. This situation eventually creates a climate of distrust, limiting the site manager's ability to deal with the public.

The most vocal critics can dominate the participation process. Many citizens view public participation as a means of influencing policies and decisions. Public hearings can become forums in which the most vocal critics of a plan can dominate discussions and exclude others from the process. This can happen if an organised lobby group is heavily represented. Some people with legitimate concerns may be intimidated by a venue such as a meeting hall and be afraid to speak up. Alternative venues such as community centres can facilitate a more comfortable exchange of ideas and encourage balanced communication among stakeholders.

Large numbers of people may be overlooked because they are not as vocal as other groups. Any issue that generates public interest is subject to a wide range of opinion. While most people will have an opinion, many will not feel strongly about the issue. This large majority risks being ignored. It may be felt that they are the group that can be most influenced because they are not very interested and are probably not well informed. The possibility of some event igniting the interest of this less-interested majority should however not be underestimated. Consideration of these groups is essential to ensuring long-term public support.

Hierarchical structures may inhibit stakeholder participation in decision making. In many societies the formal structure of institutions and organisations as well as cultural norms may make it difficult to elicit the opinions of certain groups making stakeholder participation in formal meetings impossible. A few powerful agencies may dominate, overwhelming other stakeholders and blocking cooperation. In some countries, the government is directly involved in the actual business of tourism, functioning as tour operators as well as making policy, which may lead to imbalances in stakeholder input.

Public participation may be more a form of appeasement than a way to solicit stakeholders' input. Offering local communities the opportunity to participate raises expectations about acceptance of their suggestions. A government may try to guide a particular choice either by representing only one opinion or by proposing a set of choices among which only one is tenable. Decisions may have already been made before public participation begins; any changes may be minor with relatively small impacts.

Before embarking on a participatory planning exercise, proponents have to be ready to change original plans according to the input received.

Overemphasis on involving stakeholder groups can lead to a failure to recognise certain effects on resources. Managers must understand how stakeholders perceive impacts and define acceptability. However, many stakeholder groups have limited knowledge about natural and cultural resources and may be unaware of potential negative impacts. Visitors adapt to deteriorating environmental conditions, accepting degradation as the inevitable result of increasing visitation. The visitors who are displeased by the degradation may not return and are not captured by surveys and public involvement efforts.

Other stakeholder groups may be concerned only with economic considerations that could outweigh the desire to protect resources. So, while public participation is necessary, over-reliance on public input can lead to inaction and a deterioration of conditions over time. With resource bases declining and the demand for recreation and tourist attractions on the rise, it is managers who must ultimately decide the parameters of how much and what kinds of tourism activity are acceptable.

Factors Promoting Participation Stakeholder Groups

Trust enhances a group's willingness to participate: Trust is the crucial element of successful public participation. Building trust and a willingness to participate depends on several factors. Positive earlier interaction builds trust. The history of the experiences with, for example, a state government agency influences the chances of fostering participation.

Rebuilding relations between conservation authorities and local people after a history of policing and exclusion can be difficult. H.S. Panwar, who taught at the Wildlife Institute of India at Dehra Dun, reported that the main criteria of success in ecologically oriented development projects were building trust and enrolling the full participation of local people in the planning and implementation process.

Honouring commitments builds trust. Amboseli National Park in Kenya, La Amistad National Park in Costa Rica and Panama, and Yellowstone National Park in the United States have all had problems with local communities after funding cuts that forced policy changes. At Amboseli, a lack of funding for maintaining pumps at watering facilities caused a gap in trust with park officials and impinged on the needs of local Maasai cattle herders.

At La Amistad and Yellowstone, personnel and budget cuts took a financial toll on the local communities. Gestures that show equality, for example, sharing information equally among stakeholders, promote trust. From its inception, the Great Barrier Reef project worked from a scientific information base, regularly issuing maps, data and carefully prepared information to the public.

Time is necessary to build trust. Many experts agree that more time and effort could be spent addressing the various agendas of interest groups. One researcher writes, "Trust-building takes time. The history of rural development initiatives is littered with enough examples to indicate that such time is a resource well spent in terms of effective policy outcomes." A non-partisan image helps build trust with stakeholders. When a particular problem arises at a site, the site manager — who is seen as a government official-may be wise to ask a popular local personality to explain the matter to the public.

If time and money permit, credible scientific information can serve as non-partisan evidence to heighten public understanding of an issue and change people's minds. Yellowstone officials published pertinent scientific information, viewed as more neutral, in the daily newspaper to advise the public about a project to reintroduce wolves into the park.

A collective approach encourages public participation: A process calling for participation and collaboration has been found to be more conducive to consensus than traditional methods involving expert planners only. Work in community extension projects has shown more progress in community relations when participatory methods are used. Experts report that no point is too early in the project cycle to begin inviting local participation. A participatory approach is beneficial in several ways:

— While issues of power and control will not disappear certain individuals will always be motivated to convert others to their position the participatory process enhances communication by showing both the common ground and the differences between the stakeholder groups. The exercise often leads to compromise and a breakdown of defensive positions.

— Evidence suggests that people are reluctant to divulge past difficulties. Informal communication systems such as surveys can help get people to reveal their interests and concerns. Reports from the North Pennines Tourism Partnership programme in England revealed that such informal communication helped to resolve issues between the different groups.

— Public involvement tends to build momentum towards collaborative implementation. As one researcher has pointed out, misunderstandings between groups, rather than a lack of information, is at the core of many social difficulties.

Communication Techniques

Participatory techniques such as rural appraisals allow local people to describe their environment: Participatory Rural Appraisals (PRAs) can facilitate the exchange of informal information between local government officials, NGO staff and local people. These methods have proven capable of overcoming the problems of listening and shaping an accurate assessment of stakeholder concerns. The techniques help map out local resources, ways people make a living, trends in resource use, and the local costs and benefits of conservation and protection.

They are practical methods of encouraging local participation, fostering communication and making a more accurate appraisal of local concerns. The utility of these methods has been demonstrated in many areas of the world, particularly in Pakistan and India. Participatory techniques, including PRAs, can be used for both natural and cultural sites.

Alternative forms of dialogue can help limit public confrontations: Public meetings can be ineffective when the parties with the most vested interests attend with the goal of pressing their particular causes. Less confrontational meeting structures can reduce such undue influence and limit the posturing of interest groups for the press.

During the controversial Yellowstone wolf reintroduction project, open houses were held where individual people could sit down in a relaxed atmosphere and talk directly with representatives of the various agencies involved. Special meetings were held to allow powerful interest groups to voice their opinions, but they were listening sessions only. These were run by female park officials, perceived as less threatening and non-partisan than male officials, and local police were hired to maintain order.

The process of developing a management plan can encourage the participation of stakeholders: The process can also be used to build consensus. However, instead of releasing draft management plans for public comment, planners should begin by identifying what is needed from the public, and what a site can offer them in return. Plans and strategies should be developed slowly, be dynamic and adaptable, and be concise rather than lengthy.

Above all, they should be inclusive of all stakeholders. Examples of successful issue-based management planning include the great Smokey Mountains National Park in the United States, where many trails were in poor condition and needed to be closed to have time to recover. Park managers realised that closing trails would generate negative sentiment.

To educate the public about the situation, management decided to involve people in the process. Meetings were held to give people an understanding of the park's mission and to provide them with an opportunity to participate in setting priorities. At the Willandra Lakes Region World Heritage site, in Australia, a five-day workshop was held at which community members helped write the first draft of a management plan.

The exercise guaranteed continued support for the plan. At the Shark Bay World Heritage site, also in Australia, participatory management plans for conservation areas are also made available for public comment for at least two months, a practice required under Western Australian law.

An advisory group or stakeholders' organisation can play a crucial role in the success of management objectives: Consultation with various interest groups through regular meetings and public workshops offers opportunities for stakeholders to comment on a preliminary management plan. This relationship enables site managers to bring local people into decision-making. Ongoing conflicts will not necessarily go away, but an advisory group provides a structure for the problem-solving process so that conflicts and solutions can be identified more clearly.

Public participation is more likely to be effective and sustained through stakeholder groups than through individual participation. At the Shark Bay World Heritage site, an advisory committee played a major role in determining appropriate and practical strategies for management of the reserves and the region's resources, including setting the boundaries of the site. As was previously mentioned, Patan, a town in the Kathmandu Valley, Nepal, has a citizens' advisory group developing a tourism programme to aid preservation of the community's historic buildings.

At Tangariro National Park in New Zealand, a Maori burial site became a popular rock-climbing area. Because this use of the site was of great concern to the Maori, meetings were held between the climbers and tribal elders with the result that the climbers agreed to practise voluntary restraint in using the area.

Local NGOs can serve as a liaison for more effective and sustained participation: Non-governmental organisations (NGOs) can play an important role in linking tourism stakeholders. NGOs can act as intermediaries between the private sector and local interests. In some countries NGOs with computers and communications equipment can serve as links between stakeholders without such resources. There is reason to believe that NGOs' prestige can bring added pressure to bear in negotiations with private tourism companies.

Stakeholders in Planning and Management

Involving stakeholders saves time and money: Conflicts between communities and conservation authorities have shown that relying solely on law enforcement is less practical and more costly than involving interest groups from the outset. Long experience in World Heritage tourism management has shown that projects with limited local input are less productive and ultimately more expensive.

Failure to understand stakeholder positions can delay or block projects: Examples abound of projects that were blocked because of a lack of effective communication with stakeholders. Construction of a cultural centre on the South Pacific Island of Truk was blocked because the project officer failed to consult with the governor. Had he done so he would have discovered a conflict between the governor and a local leader in the village where the project was planned. Early attempts at ecosystem management in Yellowstone National Park in the United States were delayed because management started formulating an overall regional plan before unifying the key stakeholders.

Learning from past problems, many sites now invest a considerable amount of time in meetings with key stakeholder groups, asking them to articulate their views and defining issues to be examined together. Through such dialogue and collaboration, site management becomes familiar with the various stakeholder positions regarding tourism issues and activities that could have an impact on the site.

Stakeholders can inform managers about easily misunderstood local cultural differences: Religious or cultural values are often of primary importance to communities and can go unnoticed if locals are not involved in the planning and management process. For example, while site staff may legitimately regard certain valleys, rock formations or archaeological sites as natural or anthropological resources, such sites may be sacred to the host communities.

Fencing, boardwalks and other structures built in such areas may be offensive to the local people and compromise the site's cultural value. Without local input such values may go unobserved, setting the stage for future conflicts. At the Great Zimbabwe World Heritage Site in Zimbabwe, the creation of a living museum to bring in more visitors met with criticism and indifference.

Local people thought that the living museum misrepresented the site, was inappropriate and reduced the site's historical and cultural importance to just another attraction with little relevance to people's real identity. Since the living museum displayed a lifestyle very similar to that of the average Zimbabwean, few local people found the village to be of interest.

Stakeholders can help identify problem areas that may have been overlooked by the experts: Experts cannot always judge the perceptions, preferences or priorities of host communities when evaluating local conditions. For example, Participatory Rural Appraisals (PRAs) carried out in Ucchali, a site in Pakistan that is classified as a protected wetland and is managed as a waterfowl sanctuary, revealed a mismatch between local views and experts' perceptions.

Experts assumed that the area's lakes were longstanding geographical features. The villagers knew that increased rains had formed the lakes over the previous 50 years, and that the water had submerged prime agricultural land that had been owned by the local villages for centuries. Local communities believed that their land rights were neglected when projects went ahead to conserve the wetland.

Another pitfall occurs when experts' views are oriented towards narrow interests. In the wetland project in Pakistan, scientists tended to focus on species of special concern for international conservation and the wetland habitat. The villagers had a wider view of the ecosystem that made the connection between the forests, the watershed, the area's land use history and their livelihoods.

Also, complex phenomena such as birds' migratory patterns, changes in water quality, sedimentation rates and groundwater levels were locally monitored and well understood. If the broader picture had been appreciated, more effective collaboration could have been fostered.

Stakeholders can provide useful input regarding desired conditions at a site: Effective visitor management involves establishing limits negotiated with the stakeholders. Through tourism advisory boards or councils, stakeholders can help managers to establish visitor conditions and set quantifiable standards for problem management and impact limitation.

Experience has shown that stakeholder input is essential for developing realistic policies and management objectives that will gain long-term support. For example, the community should be encouraged to participate in decision-making on how many and what type of tourists they would like to receive, and/or areas that would be off-limits.

10

Tourism and Promotion of Destination

The site manager should decide which type of visitors to target in a promotional campaign on the basis of the site's policy and management objectives. Certain types of tourism fit a site's goals and objectives better than others. As with any management action, promotional campaigns should reflect the site's stated policy vision statement and objectives. For example, at natural sites, if local economic development is an objective, managers may wish to promote bird-watching or trekking where local people may be hired as guides or drivers.

At an archaeological site affected by theft of objects destined for trafficking in stolen art, a promotional programme may be designed to attract better-off visitors who are willing to pay an extra fee to support an artisan cooperative making high-quality replicas of objects at the site. These can then be sold to satisfy a portion of the demand fed by trafficking.

The segmentation process requires research into the characteristics and preferences of visitors who may want to come to a site. Distinct segments of consumers might include those belonging to museum associations or organisations for the protection of wildlife. Identifying people with similar motivations and needs enables the manager to pinpoint the types of promotional materials needed. A simple example is an elderly target audience, for whom promotional materials can be in larger print and may list special services for senior citizens. To be selected for management action, a market segment must have three characteristics:

— it must be measurable,

— it should be easy to reach through promotional distribution systems, and

— it should promise increased earnings sufficient to more than repay the costs of targeting it with promotional materials.

Knowing how tourists inform themselves on a site they wish to visit will help identify where to focus promotional efforts: For example, since most "eco-tourists" wishing to see polar bears in Manitoba, Canada, seek information from travel agents, the site's managers are wise to send their promotional materials to travel agencies. However, since few travel agencies are able or willing to stock the full range of available brochures and are ill-prepared to deal with specialised inquiries, a more efficient approach may be to send agents a brochure and then contact them personally to brief them on the site's attractions and the logistics of reaching it.

Developing a theme using a site's central message for the park's promotion helps develop marketing and promotional materials: Combining a site's most attractive elements to develop slogans or "soundbites", will facilitate the design and creation of brochures and interpretation displays. For instance, a park could be "the best kept secret in the Caribbean", or the place where "billions of years of nature meet thousands of years of history".

An analysis of strengths, weaknesses, opportunities and threats (SWOT) can be used to identify gaps between a site's promotion strategy and tourism trends: A SWOT analysis is a marketing tool used to evaluate a site's promotional abilities by examining the strengths and weaknesses of its promotional organisation, financial and staff resources, and existing promotional strategy. Strengths and weaknesses are considered factors over which the site has some control; opportunities and threats are external. Strengths and weaknesses include:

— the ways in which the site is being marketed, the size of the marketing budget, performance measures and the degree and nature of the staff's involvement in marketing efforts

— the site's tourism products, including the quality of service, image and reputation

— a profile of current visitors

— suppliers and the quality of goods and services they provide

— the people who handle any marketing for the site and the image they promote, for example, the way it is presented by tour operators compared with the site's own promotional materials Opportunities and threats include:

— political factors, including government legislation

— economic factors

— social factors

— competition, identifying competitors and analysing their strengths and weaknesses

Managers without sufficient time or staff to carry out promotional tasks may consider seeking outside assistance: Tasks such as writing to guidebook publishers, magazines and newspapers to publicise attractions and present management issues are time-consuming and vie for a manager's attention. An independent promotional organisation representing the different interest groups may provide a solution. Such a group can analyse a site's tourism market and management realities. It has the further virtue of being independent, so that it can bridge gaps between competing interest groups.

A group such as an NGO with ties to the site and that knows the tourism business, or a government group with a mandate to coordinate all the stakeholders could play this role. An independent organisation set up to facilitate tourism and park promotion at Lake Baikal, Russia, produced a guidebook giving the names of local tour operators and guides, and distributed it in North America, Europe and Japan.

If an outside organisation is solicited, it must be given clear direction so that its output reflects the site's goals and objectives. For example, if a goal is to support local entrepreneurs, such as ground operators, the organisation must ensure that it promotes both smaller local operators as well as larger or regional and national companies.

Developing a site's "tourism identity" is an essential element of a promotional strategy. This identity, which is based on the site's goals, objectives and market potential, becomes associated with the site in the minds of potential visitors. It could centre on a famous fresco or an endangered animal, for example, and be used to develop a logo for future promotional activities.

Strategies for Promoting a Site

International tourist guidebooks can be a free source of promotion: Guidebooks are a popular source of information for trip planning and are available for almost every country and region of the world. Because guidebook information is constantly changing, new editions are regularly updated, and editors are usually willing to publish information free of charge. This presents an opportunity to have information on a site and local attractions and services distributed to a wide audience.

Supplying information to travel magazines, newspapers, radio and the internet is another costeffective way to promote a site: Travel magazines and newspapers publish information on tourism attractions free of charge and local radio and television stations broadcast such information as a public service. These can all be useful sources of free publicity for the site. In-flight airline magazines reach a large public, and because they are published quarterly or bimonthly, articles remain in circulation for considerable periods. Most publications can be accessed by the internet and the information transferred in this manner.

Brochures can be used to distribute site information to a wide range of audiences: They can be mailed to national tourism offices, included in promotional information sent to tour operators, newspapers, magazines, radio and television stations and distributed to hotels. However, unlike other types of promotional material, brochures are costly to produce, and should be designed to remain valid over a long period of time. Most people who receive brochures read them. However, research has found that brochures are likely to exert more influence on people who have not visited a site before and less likely to attract repeat visitors.

Contacting tour operators directly is a useful means of interesting them in a site: Tour operators are always on the lookout for new attractions to sell to their clients. Operators, particularly companies that specialise in activities offered at the site, will appreciate receiving a brochure and any information about the local community. Direct contact with tour operators bypasses travel agencies and improves the chances of a positive response.

Producing an information package to area attractions and services can help direct benefits to local residents: If one of the goals of a site's tourism programme is to benefit local communities, a multi-lingual community guide sheet may be a valuable promotional tool. It can direct visitors to neighbouring destinations and attractions, providing a detailed picture of what the area offers, including dining, shopping and accommodations. The information is especially useful for attracting the independent traveller. Such a package should be distributed to key points such as hotels in major cities and at national tourism offices or embassies abroad.

If a site has internet, it can be distributed electronically. A guide can also be used as a management tool for bringing about desired visitor behaviour, by for example discussing cultural rules and taboos and good conservation practices. Such a guide can be produced by the community with the help of site management. A local NGO may provide free computer time and translating services. Selling the guide even if it is very simple may help pay for future copying expenses.

A 10-page guide which can be easily and cheaply copied may be all that is needed initially. The copy should be stored on a computer, so that the guide booklet can be easily updated whenever necessary. If and when the attraction becomes more popular, a more sophisticated guide could be written and sold to cover the costs of publication.

National tourism offices or embassies can be a free and effective means of distributing promotional materials: Tour operators are always on the lookout for new attractions to sell to their clients. Operators, particularly companies that specialise in activities offered at the site, will appreciate receiving a brochure and any information about the local community. Direct contact with tour operators bypasses travel agencies and improves the chances of a positive response.

Holding a press day can be an effective way to introduce a site to the media: The day can be scheduled to coincide with a cultural celebration at the site, or it could be a yearly event held to mark the beginning of the tourist season. Tour operators, hotel owners and government officials who belong to the site's advisory group can be recruited to play a role.

These stakeholders usually have press contacts and may be interested in obtaining media coverage of their activities or businesses. National tourist offices sometimes organise familiarisation tours for travel writers whose expenses paid by the government or large tourist enterprises. To get a site included on a familiarisation tour is not easy, but the manager may approach the tourism ministry or perhaps a hotel chain with promotional materials.

If no outside funding is available stakeholders may be able to offer or raise financial support. If foreign press are invited, local business people are more likely to contribute time and resources to the event. Familiarisation visits for the international media are most successful if the journalists invited have special interests that match the activities of a site, such as the theatre or marine protection. One method of identifying appropriate journalists is to find their by-lines in the international press.

11

Tour Operators and Sustainable Tourism

Tourism can lead to the exclusion of local people from certain areas, particularly in protected areas that were created to conserve wildlife. Although, in most cases, the protected area designation will have preceded the development of tourism, exclusion of local people from these areas usually occurs after tourism becomes established and profitable, and thus more economically important to governments or landowners than traditional activities.

Tourism activities in and around protected areas can have both positive and negative impacts on local people and the environment. Tourism can benefit a national park or other protected area by serving as a financing mechanism, with direct revenues from user fees and taxes used to protect biological resources and maintain natural areas.

Intangible benefits can include increased awareness of and support for the purpose and role of protected areas, by both local communities and tourists. If tourism is important to the local or national economy, it may encourage authorities to manage and maintain protected areas more effectively, benefiting tourists, local communities and the environment. The negative environmental impacts of tourism can include water and soil contamination from construction or improper disposal of solid waste and wastewater, air pollution from transportation, wildlife habitat destruction, and land degradation.

Successfully addressing the challenges of tourism in protected areas requires strong co-operation among all parties, including those operating within and outside protected area boundaries, as well as those that can promote effective management of protected areas by ensuring that the appropriate planning and management tools are adopted. Although the goals of different stakeholders can be quite varied, tourism activities can only be sustainable if implemented with a common understanding and consensus-based approach to development.

Tour operators play a central role in the tourism industry. As intermediaries between tourists and tourism service suppliers, tour operators can influence the choices of consumers, the practices of suppliers and the development patterns of destinations. This unique role means that tour operators can make an important contribution to furthering the goals of sustainable tourism development and protecting the environmental and cultural resources on which the tourism industry depends for its survival and growth. The members of the Tour Operators' Initiative believe that tourism in protected areas should be:

— Developed and implemented with the consensus of, and in close co-operation with, relevant stakeholders;

— Supported by effective policies, guidelines, management strategies and technical tools; and o Focused on conserving the environment while ensuring economically, socially and culturally sound development.

Tourism Development in Protected Areas

The members of the Tour Operators' Initiative also believe that tour operators can contribute to the sustainable development of tourism in protected areas in many different ways, such as:

— Including protected areas in their itineraries and giving customers information about the natural and cultural features of visited sites and their roles in the conservation of local ecosystems;

— Limiting the size of their groups, or dividing large groups into smaller ones when visiting protected areas;

— Informing protected area managers of visits ahead of time and discussing ways to reduce visitor impacts;

— Integrating sustainability principles into the selection criteria and service agreements of their suppliers, and choosing locally owned and operated suppliers;

— Making financial contributions to conservation and development projects;

— Providing customers with opportunities to proactively support protected areas; and

— Providing customers with guidelines on how to avoid negative impacts while visiting sensitive areas, for example by maintaining appropriate distances from wildlife, staying on trails to avoid trampling plants or causing erosion, and keeping water and energy use down to avoid related impacts on the environment.

Discovery Initiatives (UK) offers Discoverer Holidays, which allow customers to get involved as field assistants in specific research projects. For example, a tour in Kalimantan, Indonesia, on the island of Borneo, allows travellers to work with the world's leading orang-utan study programme and contributes US$1,000 per client to the Orang-utan Foundation in Tanjing Putung National Park.

Dynamic Tours (Morocco) has developed a Mountain and Desert Guide's Charter for its guides, as a means to build awareness on their roles as liaisons to travellers on:

— Environmental problems;

— Economic impacts of groups in a given area;

— Financial resources generated by tourism and their role in preserving local species and heritage;

— Local social and economic development; and

— Appropriate and sustainable environmental and social practices.

Exodus (UK) has a Responsible Tourism policy that includes:

— Hiring more local guides to provide better experiences and support to local communities;

— Purchasing local products and services, where appropriate, for all trips;

— Working with local operators to implement the policy; and

— Limiting group size based on local situations.

Hapag-Lloyd Kreuzfahrten (Germany) specialises in expedition and luxury river and ocean cruises, particularly in the Arctic, Antarctica, the South Pacific Islands and the Amazon basin. To minimise the environmental impacts of its tours and improve the experience of its customers, the company has developed a handbook for travellers to Antarctica, which provides:

— Guidelines and practical information for appropriate behaviour in Antarctica;

— Historical, geological and scientific facts to accompany lectures offered on cruises; and

— Supplementary reading on Antarctica, covering topics such as the region's history, the Antarctic Treaty, native plants and animals, and environmental issues in the region.

Hotelplan (Switzerland) established an Eco-Fund in January 2001. Funds are raised through a contribution of five Swiss Francs (about US$3) per customer on any of Hotelplan's 'Holidays at the Seaside' packages, which represent 20-25 percent of sales. In 2002, the fund raised about US$750,000. The money is used for internal and external sustainable tourism projects, environmental efforts by partners at Hotelplan destinations, and emergency help in case of natural disasters or one-off projects.

Premier Tours (US), which specialises in safari tours to Southern and East Africa, selects tented camps and lodges in national parks and private game reserves that are committed to sustainable practices and apply a sensible approach to tourism, conservation and local community involvement. Premier Tours favours camps that:

— Employ full-time ecologists to ensure sustainable environmental practices in camps;

— Provide electricity through solar panels;

— Do not allow hunting, but support photographic safaris;

— Provide for direct or indirect benefits to local communities and/or conservation projects;

— Have garbage removed to appropriate places for safe disposal; and

— Have lined tanks for safe sewage processing.

TUI Nederland (the Netherlands) launched the Environmentally Aware Tourism project in Bonaire and

Curaçao in 1999, to provide customers with information on responsible travel and sustainable products. Initial information is provided in the brochures of TUI Nederland's brands Arke and Holland International. Once a client has chosen a holiday to Bonaire or Curaçao:

— TUI Nederland provides tips for environmentally sound practices in the voucher booklet that includes their air tickets;

— KLM, a project partner, shows an on-board video about the sustainable excursions and activities that are part of the project;

— Upon arrival, trained TUI Nederland hostesses introduce guests to the sustainable excursions and activities that are available; and

— The TUI Nederland resource book, available in hotel lobbies, further directs guests to sustainable excursions, activities and attractions.

Viaggi del Ventaglio (Italy) decided in 1998 to grant US$1 per bed/night to the Ministry of Tourism of the Dominican Republic, to help repair damage from Hurricane George. Contributions lasted for one year and generated about US$150,000. Part of the funds were invested in the conservation and development of Saona Island, inside the Parque Nacional del Este. The island represents a unique and beautiful, but delicate, ecosystem, and is a favourite excursion for hotels located in the area. Funds were also used to reconstruct 63 houses in the village of Manojuan, which was badly damaged by the hurricane, and to promote and develop local handicrafts, through grants to local enterprises.

Promoting Sustainable Tourism in Destinations

Tour operators is the most important factor in the tourism

industry. As intermediaries between tourists and tourism service suppliers, tour operators can make an important contribution to furthering the goals of sustainable tourism development and protecting the environmental and cultural resources on which the tourism industry depends for its survival and growth.

It is thus in the tour operators' interest to preserve the environment in destinations and establish good relationships with local communities, to improve the quality of their tourism products and increase customer satisfaction. The members of the Tour Operators' Initiative for Sustainable Tourism Development (TOI) recognise that they cannot achieve their sustainability goals without working in partnership with all stakeholders in the destinations where they operate.

Only by working together, they can create a better tourism experience that safeguards a destination's culture, economy and environment, and increases benefits for the local community. TOI members have therefore committed to establish and strengthen links and develop partnerships with local authorities, the private sector, civil society and non-governmental organisations (NGOs) in the destinations they visit. The TOI's network offers its members the opportunity to approach them together, with a common voice, and develop in a full participatory approach a shared vision on sustainable development and a common action plan, which is the base for a solid partnership between tour operators and the various destination stakeholders.

Side Partnership

Side, on the southern coast of Turkey, is the first destination in which the TOI members have forged a partnership with the local stakeholders. TOI members and their local partners bring to Side approximately 300,000 tourists each year. To prepare the grounds for the partnership, local stakeholders and TOI members were interviewed on their individual views of the key sustainability threats in Side.

These interviews were then followed by a multi-stakeholder Workshop in April 2002, organised with the support of one of the TOI members, VASCO Travel, and TUDER, the local hotel association. The meeting was attended by the Mayor of Side, representatives of WWF Turkey, and representatives of the private sector, including the Manavgat Chamber of Commerce (MATSO), individual hoteliers, excursion providers and local travel agencies. Several TOI members, along with representatives of UNEP, UNESCO and WTO/OMT, were also present.

The meeting gave the participants the opportunity to share their views on the main threats to sustainability in the Side region and ways to address these. The participants agreed on three priority actions:

— Waste management (with a focus on waste separation and recycling).

— Education and training on sustainable tourism in hotels, bars and restaurants.

— Promotion of Side's culture and cultural activities.

The participants also agreed on the benefit of a continuous dialogue between tour operators and local stakeholders. During follow up meetings with local stakeholders, a detailed plan of action was developed, and a locally based coordinator was appointed, financed by the Side administration and TUDER. Activities implemented in the two years include:

— A waste separation scheme has been designed and is now in operation in the municipality of Side. Recycling companies have been identified and pick-up times for participating hotels have been set.

— The local recycling company posts signs on its vehicles to promote the Side initiative, and hotels and restaurants post signs at their entrances.

— The Side Tourism Association (TUDER) has placed containers for collecting used batteries in every Side hotel, in the Ali Ihsan Barut elementary school and in the Tourism Hotel Vocational High School.

— Waste separation bins for organic and recyclable waste have been placed in Side for use by residents and tourists.

— Training sessions on solid waste management and waste separation techniques, organised with technical input and background material from UNEP, were held for managers and staff at hotels, apartment hotels and pensions; Side Municipality sanitation workers; sanitation manager and association presidents; members of the Garment Association and of the Bar and Restaurant Association.

Today, over 100 hotels and all local shops and restaurants participate in the waste separation scheme. Data from the last seven months of 2003 are promising: 276 tons of inorganic waste, and 11.978 batteries were collected. Moreover, the new land fill area has been identified and approved and it will be in operations in Summer 2004.

Bavaro Partnership/PuntaCana/Bayahibe

A second TOI partnership has been initiated with Bayahibe, PuntaCana and Bavaro, three of the most visited destinations in the Dominican Republic. Following informal discussions and visits, a Sustainable Tourism Round Table was convened in December 2003, in collaboration with the Bayahibe-La Romana Hotel Association and the Punta Cana Group.

The Round Table was also made possible thanks to the financial and technical contribution of the German Technical Cooperation (GTZ), and Conservation International's Center for Environmental Leadership in Business. The participants of the Round Table committed to an Agenda for Action, that include:

— Establishment of a 'Garbage free' zone,

— Improved management of the marine excursions to Isla Saona in Parque del Este,

— Process for greater community involvement,

— Support by tour operators of a promotional program for the hoteliers in Bayahibe that implement social and environmental programs.

Participants agreed also on the creation of a Co-ordinating Body that include the Bayahibe-La Romana Hotel Association, the Del Este Hotels Association, the associations of Excursion and local tour operators, the Punta Cana Ecological Foundation, the Bavaro Reef Fund, Ecoparques, the office of the Archbishop of La Altagracia, and the Tour Operators' Initiative. The Co-ordinating Body will oversee the implementation of the agenda and support the continuous communication and co-ordination of actions among all players.

12

Managing Environmental and Social Issues

In all area of the world, hoteliers are recognizing that responsible environmental and social practices translate into benefits for business, the environment and the global community. From providing cost savings and reputation benefits to ensuring the long-term appeal of a destination to travelers, good environmental and social practices make good business sense.

Good practice can result in direct cost savings by reducing energy and water bills, and sewage treatment and waste disposal costs. Conservation efforts such as hazardous waste management and water treatment will mean a safer workplace and common spaces, which, in turn, can decrease staff turnover, reduce lost work time due to injury or illness, and lower liability risks.

Publicity about poor practices may damage a hotel's reputation and lead to loss of business. On the other hand, good practice can be an effective marketing tool within the growing international market of guests seeking enviionmentally and socially responsible destinations.

Furthermore, adopting sound environmental and social practices offers an opportunity to maintain the quality of a hotel's surroundings, thereby improving the overall experience for guests and increasing support from government officials and neighboring communities. Hotels that fail to protect their environmental and cultural surroundings may contribute to the destruction of the very attractions upon which they depend for success, including clean air, safe water and beautiful, healthy surroundings.

Energy Management

Hotels use significant amounts of energy for daily operations and recreational activities. In many facilities, energy costs are the second-highest operational costs after payroll. This high demand for energy is often due to the use of energy-intensive technology to provide modern comforts and conveniences, such as air conditioning, to large numbers of guests.

The vast majority of hotels and resorts meet their energy needs by purchasing energy produced through the burning of fossil fuels (coal, oil and natural gas), which contribute to local air pollution and global climate change. The extraction, refining and transport of fossil fuels can also cause environmental damage. Improvements in housekeeping and efficiency measures and use of renewable energy can decrease dependency on energy produced through fossil fuels.

Hotel operators should give much importance to energy management because:

— Investments in more efficient energy use and improved housekeeping practices can lead to significant reductions in operating costs and energy bills, with relatively short payback periods. The average 300-room hotel spends an estimated $1.2 million per year on energy.

— Using renewable energy can reduce local air pollution, maintain destination quality and enhance the guest experience.

— Energy efficiency and conservation practices can enhance reputation among guests and others who are concerned about reducing global energy consumption and the effects of climate change.

To confront the problems they have to:

— Start by assessing existing energy use to determine where the highest energy consumption takes place within your premises and the most likely places for efficiency improvements.

— Continue to regularly monitor your energy consumption. Daily or weekly monitoring of energy use helps to identify abnormal consumption and to quantify energy savings when efficient equipment is installed or a good practice is implemented.

— Encourage guests to follow energy-saving practices, such as switching off lights and air conditioning, closing window shades before leaving their rooms and using towels or linens for more than one day.

— Work with employees to identify energy-saving practices, such as lowering heating or air conditioning to a fixed temperature when cleaning the room, or operating dryers and dishwashers only with full loads. If you have a swimming pool, turn off the pump in the evening.

— Regularly monitor and service all equipment, to ensure that it is running as efficiently as possible. Upgrade older, inefficient equipment or replace with newer technology.

— Use products that require less energy to maintain, such as colored sheets and towels or eco-labeled cotton products that can be laundered at lower temperatures.

— Use sensors and timers to turn off unnecessary lights in intermittent-use areas, such as meeting rooms, storage areas and public and staff bathrooms.

— Reduce the number of elevators and escalators running during times of low use.

— When feasible, use renewable energy sources, such as biogas, wind or solar power.

— Contact national environmental protection agencies involved in promoting renewable energy and energy-saving measures for help in implementing an energy management plan. The UNEP Energy Programme provides advanced information on available renewable energy technologies.

Water Use Management

In many areas of the world, demand for water exceeds supply and is seriously straining available water resources. Some of the most water-stressed areas in the world, such as the Mediterranean, are also home to some of the largest international tourism destinations. Guest demand for water usually far exceeds that of local residents.

In addition to the water required for each hotel room and general hotel management activities such as kitchens and laundry, features such as swimming pools, lawns and golf courses can add significantly to total usage. Excessive water use can degrade or destroy local water resources, threatening the availability of water for local needs. Problems may be made worse in areas where high tourist season corresponds with periods of low rainfall.

Hotel operators should give much importance to water use management because:

— Decreasing overall water use can lead to cost savings, especially during periods of drought, use restrictions or increasingly strict government regulations on water use.

— Reducing water use can conserve and protect local water resources upon which a hotel and the local community depend.

— Preserving the quality of local water resources can eliminate the need for costly drinking water treatment processes.

— Water conservation can enhance reputation among guests and others who are concerned about reducing water consumption and protecting local resources.

To confront the problems they have to:

— Identify the main areas of water consumption in your hotel where significant water savings may be achieved.

— Regularly monitor your water consumption for each area of the hotel (kitchen, laundry, rooms, etc.). Daily or weekly monitoring helps to identify leaks and to quantify water savings when efficient equipment is installed or a good practice is implemented.

— Encourage guests to use their towels or linens for more than one day. Provide guests with tips about watersaving measures such as turning off the taps in the sink when shaving or brushing their teeth.

— Work with employees to identify water-saving practices, such as avoiding leaving water running, or operating washing machines and dishwashers only when full.

— Engage your housekeeping and engineering departments in an active campaign to detect and repair leaking toilets, faucets and showerheads.

— Install water-saving devices such as low-flush toilets and low-flow shower heads and faucets. Low-flow fixtures in showers can reduce the flow of water by

50 percent without affecting the comfort level of the user.

— Maintain your equipment regularly. The absence of preventive maintenance generates small but regular leaks, which can correspond to an important loss of water.

— Use technologies that reduce water use through recycling.

— Avoid wasteful landscaping practices, such as hosing outdoor surfaces and watering gardens during the day.

— Use drip irrigation systems and choose drought-resistant native plant species for landscaping.

WASTE WATER MANAGEMENT

Hotels can produce significant quantities of wastewater, both graywater, which mainly comes from washing machines, sinks, showers, baths and roof runoff, and blackwater, which comes from kitchen dishwashing and toilets. In a number of destinations, little or none of this waste is treated, and pollutants such as fecal coliform bacteria and chemicals are discharged directly into the environment.

Poor sewage treatment can lead to pollution of ground and surface water, and degradation of marine resources, such as coral reefs. Among people, inadequate treatment of human waste can cause infection, gastro-intestinal disease, leptospirosis and cholera. In some coastal areas, beaches have been closed to the public because of high levels of chemical and organic pollution.

Hotel operators should give much importance to waste water management because:

— Proper wastewater treatment can reduce the chances of contamination of local drinking and agricultural water supplies, reducing the need to buy or treat drinking water and improving relations with local communities.

— Effective wastewater treatment can avoid serious illness among guests and staff members and limit the risk of litigation from guests who become infected after drinking or swimming in polluted waters.

— Treating wastewater and sewage may avoid fines and clean-up costs.

— Avoiding the discharge of untreated wastewater or sewage can protect tourism resources by conserving marine habitats and reducing coastal pollution.

— Coastal pollution can decrease business as potential guests cancel trips and seek alternative destinations.

To confront the problems they have to:

— Minimize wastewater discharge by reducing water use.

— Collect waste oil and grease for separate processing.

— Use biodegradable detergents and cleaning agents that are compatible with the wastewater treatment technologies.

— Minimize the use of chlorine, bleaches, detergents and other chemicals that end up in wastewater.

— Ensure all wastewater is properly treated before it is released into the environment.

— If a municipal system is available, check that the wastewater collection network is really going to a wastewater treatment plant and is not just discharged directly into the environment.

— If no municipal system is available, work with other businesses and organizations and the local municipality to support the development of modern municipal wastewater treatment systems.

— If no municipal system is available, identify the best options for treatment on site. If feasible, use natural wastewater treatment options that use plants and natural bacteria to purify water, rather than chemicals.

— Reuse treated graywater for washing floors, flushing toilets and irrigating gardens and golf courses.

Waste Management

Hotels produce large quantities of solid waste, from packaging to food scraps to cleaning and maintenance materials, some of which is toxic. In many cases, this waste is collected in badly designed waste dumps, discarded directly into oceans or rivers, or simply dumped in areas out of sight of guests. In addition to visually degrading a destination, improper waste disposal can lead to water and soil pollution through leaching of contaminants from waste piles.

Poorly designed waste dumps can result in fires, odors, flies and ineffective containment of wastes. Uncontrolled disposal of toxic items such as paint cans and batteries can severely contaminate water, air and soil resources, threatening the environment and human health. Even where waste is disposed of legally, land fills have limited capacity, which is a particular problem on small islands.

Hotel operators should give much importance to waste management because:

— An effective waste management program can reduce hauling and disposal fees.

— Reuse and recycling of products can cut product purchasing costs.

— Improper or illegal waste disposal may lead to significant fines and clean-up costs.

— Proper waste disposal may limit the risk of litigation from guests or area residents who become ill from hazardous wastes.

— Effective waste management can protect a hotel's image by limiting visual degradation of the area and enhancing approval from guests. The visible effects of waste disposal is the most mentioned concern by guests regarding their holiday destinations.

— Waste dumped directly into oceans or rivers can decrease the quality of tourism resources by reducing fish populations and making the water unsuitable for recreational activities.

To confront the problems they have to:

— Begin by reviewing the types and quantities of waste produced and current disposal methods and costs.

— Develop your solid waste management program around the three R's: Reduce, Reuse and Recycle.

— Reduce: Buy products in bulk and with less packaging, to reduce waste generation.

— Reuse:

  — Replace disposable items with reusable ones, such as rechargeable batteries, refillable soap and shampoo containers and cloth laundry bags.

  — Require vendors to take back pallets and crates.

— Recycle:

  — Separate waste at the source, rather than having to go through all the trash after it is collected. For example, provide containers for recyclables in guest rooms and compost bins in kitchen work areas. Hotel operators where there is a market for recyclables, recycle items such as paper, glass, metal and plastic.

— Compost organic wastes such as food scraps, leaves and tree cuttings.

— Provide waste bins for your guests in key areas, particularly by the beach and along nature trails. Hotel operators keep solid waste in a safe, sanitary holding place until it is picked up by the municipality or other disposal entities.

— Work with other businesses and organizations and the local municipality to support the development of efficient waste separation, collection, recycling and treatment systems.

Chemical Use

Excessive or improper use, storage and disposal of chemicals and other hazardous wastes in daily operations can result in pollution and contamination of local environmental resources. Use of pesticides, fertilizers and herbicides for gardening and to control insects can lead to toxic runoff into streams, coastal waters and groundwater.

Chemicals used for cleaning guest rooms or in recreational facilities such as swimming pools can contaminate local soil and water supplies and may pose a potential hazard to human health. Leakage of CFCs and HCFCs from refrigerators, air conditioners and other cooling equipment, as well as chemicals used for dry cleaning, in aerosols, fire extinguishers and foams, contribute to the depletion of the ozone layer.

Hotel operators should give much importance to chemical use because:

— Reduced use and responsible handling of chemicals and hazardous wastes can maintain the quality of tourism resources by minimizing the potential for air, water or soil pollution.

— Improper use, including overuse, of chemicals poses a real threat to the health and safety of guests and staff members.

— Effective management of chemicals and hazardous wastes can reduce water treatment costs and the quantity and cost of chemicals purchased by the hotel.

— Proper use, storage and disposal of chemicals and hazardous wastes can ensure compliance with government regulations and reduce potential fines or clean-up costs.

To confront the problems they have to:

— Limit the number of chemical products used on your property.

— Reduce contaminants by using natural products such as salt, vinegar and baking soda to clean ovens, drains, windows and floors.

— Use biodegradable and environmentally certified (e.g. Green Seal, The Nordic Swan, the EU Flower) cleaning agents, paints, solvents and other products.

— Use automatic dosing for chemicals for cleaning and swimming pools, to ensure that the appropriate amounts of chemicals are used for each task.

— Train staff in how to handle and dispose of chemicals and hazardous materials responsibly and safely.

— Dispose of hazardous materials responsibly and according to local laws and international standards.

— Regularly monitor air conditioners, heat pumps, refrigerators, freezers and kitchen cooling equipment to detect and eliminate leakage of ozone-depleting CFCs and HCFCs.

— Convert existing equipment to utilize low-Ozone Depleting Potential (ODP) or zero-ODP chemicals. This generally requires replacement of existing equipment parts and/or change of lubricating oil. When purchasing new equipment, choose those that use zero-ODP chemicals.

— When making landscaping decisions, choose native plants that require less water, pesticides, fertilizers and herbicides.

— Use compost or other organic substitutes for chemical fertilizer.

— If possible, use fish, iguanas or other animals to control insects, in place of dangerous pesticides and other chemicals.

Purchasing

Hotels purchase vast quantities of products, including cleaning and laundry supplies, food and beverages, equipment, vehicles, office supplies, furniture, bedding and toiletries for guest bathrooms. These products can have negative environmental impacts through their manufacture, distribution, use and disposal. Products can also have negative social impacts if they are produced using unfair labor practices.

By working with suppliers and service contractors, hotels and hotel associations are in a position to promote environmental and social improvements in manufacturing and production. Product purchasing decisions also impact the levels of waste produced by a hotel, as well as the potential for local air, water or soil pollution generated through the use or disposal of these products. Hotel operators should give much importance to purchasing because:

— Purchasing materials with a minimal environmental impact from manufacturing, use and disposal can maintain the quality of tourism resources by reducing the potential for air, water and soil pollution.

— Buying products made with less packaging or materials can lower waste disposal costs.

— Purchasing environmentally and socially benign products can enhance reputation among guests and others who are concerned about wasteful or harmful product use.

— Buying local, sustainable products can reduce waste and improve relationships with local communities by increasing tourism-generated income in the wider community.

To confront the problems they have to:

— When possible, purchase products that are certified for their environmental quality. Looking for products with reliable third-party environmental labels, such as Green Seal, the EU Flower or Nordic Swan, will allow you to take advantage of external expertise when making purchasing decisions.

— When possible, buy fair trade products.

— Take an active role in influencing and working with suppliers. Environmentally friendly products cannot always be identified with eco-labels. Working with suppliers will also help you to identify environmental issues and the best available products.

— Where possible, require suppliers to have and adhere to an environmental policy and fair labor practices.

— Ensure that on-site vendors use environmentally and socially sound practices.

— Provide guests with information on locally produced alternatives to imported goods, such as bottled water, as well as a list of local products and services to avoid, such as souvenirs made from endangered species.

— Buy paper products that have a high post-consumer recycled content and are not chlorine bleached.

— When feasible, buy products for which a recycling market already exists.

— Buy products in bulk and with less packaging, to reduce packaging, storage, transport and disposal costs.

— Buy local products and materials that require less transport, packaging and storage and may enhance community relationships and goodwill.

Contribution to Biodiversity and Nature Conservation

Tourism development can have significant environmental impacts on both inland and coastal areas. The previous sections have discribed some of the ways that hotels can take action to minimize and/or prevent those impacts. Beyond simply reducing negative impacts, hotels can also seek opportunities to benefit biodiversity and nature conservation by contributing to improving the state of the environment at a local, regional or national level. Such action can be particularly important in countries where capacity and resources for environmental conservation are limited. Hotel operators should give much importance to biodiversity and nature conservation because:

— In many places, the natural environment is the basis of a holiday. Contributions to conservation can help to preserve natural tourism resources.

— Support for conservation can minimize the risks of future environmental problems and preserve destination quality.

— Contributions to conservation can enhance reputation among guests and others who are concerned about global and local biodiversity loss and environmental damage.

— Promoting responsible ways to enjoy the environmental resources in a destination will improve the guest experience.

— Supporting conservation efforts can generate positive publicity and improve reputation and relationships with local people and organizations.

— Winning environmental awards for successful conservation programs can lead to positive publicity.

To confront the problems they have to:

— Work with government officials and other local groups to evaluate the local situation and identify the best strategies for benefiting conservation.

— Partner with local or national groups to promote conservation.

— Make financial contributions to local conservation efforts.

— Sponsor environmental education in surrounding communities.

— Provide in-kind support to biodiversity management.

— When possible, set aside land as a private reserve.

— Encourage staff to become involved in volunteer projects such as beach clean-ups.

— Educate guests as to how they can make a positive contribution to local biodiversity conservation efforts.

Contribution to Community Development

Tourism development can have significant impacts on local communities. Environmental damage from development may degrade or restrict access to resources, such as farmland, water or forests, upon which local people depend. In some cases, people may be displaced by hotels or other guest infrastructure. Local people who initially welcomed tourism as a source of employment, wealth, resources and infrastructure may find that development fails to provide them with the benefits they envisioned.

Although hotels do generate jobs in many service and support sectors, these jobs often do not go to the local people who are most impacted by tourism development, particularly those who lack skills or start-up capital. Much of the revenue from tourism may never make it to local communities because of foreign ownership of hotels or use of imported goods. Finally, insensitivity to local cultures, traditions and practices on the part of guests or hotel staff may lead to conflict and anti-tourist feelings among local communities.

Hotel operators should give much importance to community development because:

- Contributions to community development can help to improve relations with local communities and minimize the risk of future conflicts.
- Supporting community development can generate positive publicity and improve reputation.
- Contributions to community development can enhance approval from guests and others who are concerned about local community welfare.
- Providing benefits to local people can support conservation goals by offering alternative, relatively non-destructive sources of livelihood.

— Improving economic linkages with local communities and businesses supports the sustainability of tourism destinations.

To confront the problems they have to:

— Help to develop and actively support locally run tourism-related businesses.

— Buy locally produced goods and services. Buy from medium, small and micro-enterprises, as well as entrepreneurs from ethnic minorities and indigenous groups.

— Employ local people.

— Develop training programs covering both basic skills and those necessary for promotion, so that local people can be phased into management positions over time.

— Provide language classes for local workers who do not speak the dominant language of the guests.

— Encourage employees to volunteer in local communities and to follow environmental practices at home.

— Provide information to guests on the area's cultural and religious characteristics and offer tips on how they can ensure that their own behavior respects these characteristics. Encourage guests to purchase locally produced products and support local service providers.

— Work with local partners to support projects that increase community well-being.

— Provide support for local schools.

— Support local communities with old or unused products.

Social Issues in the Workplace

The tourism industry provides employment for 230 million people - about ten percent of the world's formal labor force. There is a growing movement to ensure that tourism develops ethically and respects human rights. The 1948 United Nations Universal Declaration of Human Rights states that all human beings have certain basic universal human rights.

These rights include the right to life, liberty and security of person, freedom from torture and slavery, protection under the law, freedom of thought, religion and travel, and the right to work, form trade unions and have an adequate standard of living and well-being. The U.N. Declaration calls upon "every individual and every organ of society" to promote and respect human rights; as parts of society, hotels and other tourism businesses all have a role to play in achieving this goal.

Most of the focus on human rights in the tourism industry has revolved around labor laws and poor working conditions (such as long hours, low pay, lack of job stability and limited career prospects), as well as the use of child labor or forced labor, child sexual exploitation and gender issues. Also included are non-discrimination issues, poverty issues, environmental and indigenous issues, including land rights, protection of human dignity and freedom of association and the rights to collective bargaining.

Hotel operators should give much importance to social issues in the workplace because:

— Respecting employees' human rights can ensure that operations comply with relevant laws and avoid fines and lawsuits.

— Ensuring that employees are treated well and are fairly compensated can minimize the risk of antagonism and anti-tourist feelings and help promote a welcoming and supportive attitude toward guests.

— Fair treatment of employees and local communities can bolster staff morale and enable a business to become an employer of choice.

— Promoting equal rights among all employees can minimize friction between local and foreign employees and management and support staff.

— Ensuring that dialogue and negotiations are conducted with freely elected workers' representatives can guarantee authentic consultations on management decisions affecting staff and their acceptance by staff, as well as a constructive long-term attitude of employees toward the goals of the hotel.

— Respecting the rights of employees and neighboring communities can help safeguard the reputation of the business.

— Respecting the rights of indigenous communities can mitigate against adverse attention from non-governmental organizations or the media.

To confront the problems they have to:

— Undertake a study into the potential human rights impacts of your business on employees, local communities and other stakeholders.

— Provide a fair living wage and benefits to all employees.

— Sign formal contracts with all employees.

— Adopt a formal position/policy on human rights that commits the business to upholding fundamental human rights.

— Establish policies and guidelines to protect employees' health and safety in the workplace.

ENVIRONMENTAL MANAGEMENT SYSTEMS

By providing a systematic method for integrating environmental and social considerations into business operations, an EMS can help a business evaluate, manage and reduce its impacts. Although the traditional name for such a scheme is an environmental management system, it can be used to guide both environmental and social activities.

The key to a successful and effective EMS is ensuring the full support, contribution and participation of all people who are involved, including employees, guests, business partners and local communities. Staff commitment and participation should come from all parts of the organization, not just top management. Guest education is also an important part of an effective EMS, as many of its components, such as turning off lights and other electrical appliances, using less water or avoiding unsustainable local products, will require active guest support.

Hotel operators should give much importance to environmental management systems because:

— An EMS can allow a hotel or company to avoid duplication of effort by integrating environmental and social practice into operations in a systematic way.

— Organizing environmental and social activities under an EMS can allow more efficient use of a company's resources.

— An EMS allows a company to monitor and assess its successes and failures related to environmental and social issues, identify problems and improve its performance based upon this information.

— Having a single, public EMS can facilitate the buy-in of staff, guests, business partners and local communities.

To confront the problems they have to:

— Appoint a task force that includes staff from all departments and levels to design, implement and evaluate the EMS.

— Conduct a thorough review of current practices at the hotel, identifying opportunities for improvement and setting priorities for action. This review should include energy use, water use, waste management, chemical use, product purchasing, community relations and potential impacts on the local environment.

— Work with your staff and other relevant parties to develop and publish an environmental and social mission statement, standards, goals and action plan.

— Designate a specific staff member or group to have responsibility for each component of your action plan and then report back to the task force. Provide these individuals with clear instructions on how to accomplish each goal.

— Educate staff about goals and activities, through orientations, briefings, memos, incentive programs, performance reviews and other methods.

— Communicate goals and activities to guests and advise them on how they can reduce their environmental impact and support local conservation and community development projects.

— Regularly assess if goals have been met and evaluate successes and failures.

— Use information collected during regular assessments to review your policy, goals and action plan, to determine what changes need to be made.

— Provide regular feedback to staff, guests and the local community on achievements and acknowledge outstanding individual performance.

13

Social Leadership in Travel and Tourism

Travel and Tourism is one of the largest sources of economic activity in the world. It can be an important force for sustainability by raising living standards in under-developed areas, promoting preservation of the natural and human environment and providing a vehicle for peaceful international exchange. Travel & Tourism can be part of the solution to the world's challenges because of these key characteristics, which are described further below:

— *As one of the world's largest and fastest growing industries,Travel & Tourism is, and will continue to be, a significant source of growth and prosperity worldwide:*Using Tourism Satellite Accounting, an accredited econometric tool, WTTC each year measures the full economic impact of Travel & Tourism in over 160 national economies. The results have shown that this impact is far greater than had previously been expected. According to WTTC research, Travel & Tourism generates economic activity worldwide representing over ten per cent of total global GDP. The industry also accounts for over 200 million jobs (direct and indirect). With 4.5 per cent growth forecast per annum for the next ten years,Travel & Tourism is not only one of the world's largest, but one of its fastest growing industries.

— *Travel & Tourism can help raise living standards and alleviate poverty in underdeveloped areas*: Present in local communities throughout the globe, Travel & Tourism is often an early investor and one of the few sources of economic activity in some of the world's least developed areas. As a consequence, it can raise incomes and contribute to poverty alleviation by:

- Stimulating the development of infrastructure that underpins the entire economy, including: transport such as airports, seaports and roads, public utilities to supply water and power and recreational facilities such as parks, stadiums and museums.
- Generating demand for a wide variety of locally supplied goods and services, providing jobs and training for local people and opportunities for entrepreneurs;
- Employing women, youth, the unskilled and people in rural and remote areas, who might otherwise have few opportunities.

Travel & Tourism is regarded as the best development option in many emerging economies, an effective way of utilizing their natural and cultural resources to create jobs and wealth. The share of international tourism arrivals to developing countries grew from 19 per cent in 1980 to 30 per cent in 2000.

— *Travel & Tourism provides powerful market incentives to protect and preserve fragile eco-systems, endangered wildlife and unique cultural heritage*. Travel & Tourism's 'product' is the places that people visit. Protecting destination communities - the people, their unique cultures and beautiful natural settings - is critical. Failure to maintain their well-being destroys the very attractions on which the industry depends directly for success. For governments, tourism can represent an alternative 'use' for natural and cultural resources that might otherwise be destroyed - by land development, by illegal activities such as wildlife poaching and the looting of ancient cultural sites, or through neglect. Tourism often provides a better economic return on these valuable assets, while rewarding their long-term preservation.

— *As a primary medium of international exchange,Travel & Tourism brings people from diverse cultures together.* In a very real way,Travel & Tourism depends on international peace and prosperity. By creating opportunities for hosts and visitors to learn about each other and share experiences, tourism can even contribute to international understanding and cooperation and, in the long term, has the potential to build bridges of peace.

For all these reasons, the Travel & Tourism industry has a vital stake and a critical role to play in helping to address the challenges now facing the world, contributing to development that is economically, environmentally and socially sustainable.

Travel & Tourism and Sustainable Development

Making Travel & Tourism work for everyone requires the active engagement of all stakeholders - governments, businesses, local communities and the travelling public. While governments have begun to understand the contribution that the industry can make to sustainable development, their record in adopting appropriate policies to encourage sustainable, economically viable tourism is mixed. For progress to be made, the Travel & Tourism private sector must play a central role. Between the 1992 Rio Earth Summit and the World Summit on Sustainable

Development in 2002, considerable advances were made towards sustainability in the Travel & Tourism industry:

— Many Travel & Tourism companies have integrated environmental protection into their operations, mitigating their impact on fragile eco-systems and scarce resources.

— Some companies are also addressing their economic, social and cultural impact on host communities, for example: working with public authorities to ensure that plans for tourism growth are compatible with development goals; actively promoting locally based tourism related businesses; training local people for employment in management positions; educating visitors about local conservation issues; and promoting culturally-sensitive tourism activities.

— A wide variety of cross-industry programmes - such as global funds and foundations, eco-labels and certification schemes, codes of conduct, and awards - have been set up to further encourage sustainable Travel & Tourism company practices. The industry as a whole has contributed proactively to the global dialogue on sustainable development, making concrete proposals for how it can help implement Agenda 21.

But, while these are important steps, they are not enough. The response of the Travel & Tourism industry is still piecemeal and change is relatively slow. One reason for this is the highly fragmented nature of the industry, the great majority of which consists of independent small and medium sized businesses scattered across the globe, often running on fragile operating margins. The real challenge is to move beyond the current ad hoc approach, to evolve new patterns of Travel & Tourism business that integrate social, economic and environmental sustainability and to encourage a vast and fragmented industry to follow suit. In short, what is required is a greater leadership in corporate social responsibility within the Travel & Tourism industry.

SOCIAL CORPORATE LEADERSHIP

Greater Corporate Social Leadership within Travel & Tourism is vital to the industry's future because it will help ensure thriving, attractive and welcoming destination communities that will draw visitors, the basis for long term growth and profitability. Creating a positive environment for tourism in the long term will require the entire industry to adopt responsible, sustainable practices. Not only is corporate social leadership important for the good of the industry as a whole, it is also becoming a competitive issue for individual companies. Those companies with a reputation for social leadership today will be the winners of tomorrow. Travel & Tourism's corporate social leaders will:

— Be favoured by a growing number of national government authorities and local communities who are prioritizing sustainable tourism that benefits destinations;

— Build brand value and win market share with the growing number of environmentally and socially conscious tourists and other travellers;

— Attract socially conscious investors, improving access to capital and building share value;

— Enhance their ability to recruit, motivate and retain employees, both in destination communities and throughout the organization;

— Be better positioned to assess and respond to risks and opportunities in the market.

A voluntary approach is crucial. To take advantage of what business has to offer - entrepreneurship, innovation, and management capability - companies must be free to choose how they respond to community needs as the competitive market dictates. Attempting to regulate social responsibility would not only be impractical, given the diverse needs of different communities, it would undermine the personal commitment and creativity that fuel it. Companies that take the lead now will find themselves at a competitive advantage in five years. Incorporating environmental and social issues into the bottom line makes business sense and doing it now will serve shareholders in the long term. WTTC encourages its Members and the key players of the industry to show corporate social leadership and integrate this social and environmental focus into its core values and operations to ensure the sustainable long term growth and development of the Travel & Tourism industry.

Abercrombie & Kent

Bringing visitors to some of the world's most remote and pristine areas, Abercrombie & Kent is committed to low-impact, sustainable tourism that protects the environment and benefits indigenous peoples. The Abercrombie & Kent Global Foundation provides long term support for the protection of natural ecosystems. It aims to achieve preservation through the sustainable unification of environmental and economic goals, linking commercial tourism to local conservation programmes. It provides assistance to reserves and parks and surrounding communities and helps to cope with the environmental consequences of man-made disasters. All Foundation projects are conducted in cooperation with local peoples and regional non-governmental organizations.

In 2001, $500,000 in support was given for projects in 20 countries on all seven continents. Guests often visit project sites, providing an opportunity for meaningful contact between travellers and residents. The company has also created a model for ecologically sensitive safari lodging at its Olonana resort in the Masai-Mara region of Kenya.The aim is to share the economic benefits from tourism with the indigenous population, to encourage the preservation of the sensitive habitat. An agreed allocation from tourism revenues is provided to the local community.

The model also includes: a wetlands project through which treated wastewater is returned to the eco-system; the Olonana Forestry Initiative, in which indigenous seedlings are used for reforestation; and a shop where artisans from the local Maasai village sell their traditional arts and crafts. Abercrombie & Kent maintains more than 45 offices on six continents, which employ more than 3,000 local citizens with an intimate knowledge of local flora and fauna. Extensive training is provided and professional advancement is encouraged.

Accor

As a global tourism company, Accor believes it has a responsibility to care for the local environment where it operates. To fulfil this commitment, Accor has integrated environmental stewardship into its corporate governance and reporting structure. An Environmental Charter and a senior-level Committee on Sustainable Development, headed by a member of the Management Board, guide environmental activities worldwide. Recently, Accor created a new position of manager for sustainable development to coordinate actions and programmes. Local initiatives are identified and carried out by the staff of individual operations, who are familiar with local issues - more than 800 projects have been initiated to date, in various fields, primarily humanitarian aid and protection of environmental and cultural heritage.

Examples include the A Tree for a Child programme in Indonesia, aimed at helping to alleviate poverty while protecting the environment, and the restoration of the Red Chapel at Karnak in Egypt. The success of each project is measured using indicators developed by outside special agencies. Assessment has shown the projects to be effective and economically viable. Accor believes that these actions, together with its overall commitment to sustainable development, have both enhanced the global reputation of the group and increased customer demand for its brands.

Avis Europe

In 2002, Avis Europe launched a major initiative aimed at actively combating global warming, taking concrete steps to ensure that its business is carbon neutral. In partnership with Future Forests,Avis Europe has launched a three-point 'green plan' to offset the carbon dioxide emissions from both its own operations and its car rentals, which has been well received by staff, customers and business partners. The plan includes:

— A Europe-wide carbon neutral initiative to offset operational emissions through Future Forests' tree planting programmes. Indigenous trees planted at sites across Europe will re-absorb an equivalent of 32,510 tonnes of carbon dioxide over their lifetime.

— The world's first carbon neutral car rentals for online customers, in which customers are encouraged to offset their car rental emissions as part of the online booking process.

— A target to reduce operational CO_2 emissions from 2003.

British Airways

British Airways has made sustainability an integral part of its business management process. A company-wide

Social and Environmental Policy was developed and is published on the company's website.A Sustainable Business Unit was created to oversee activities, provide advice and support, and monitor and measure results. A senior management level Environment and Social Council has met two to three times per year to discuss policy and strategies and review performance against targets. All activities are published in an annual Social and Environmental Report. The company uses the Global Reporting Initiative guidelines for sustainability and has introduced a code of business conduct for social and ethical accountability. With regard to charitable giving, British Airways meets the UK's Business in the Community Percent Club criteria and support is maintained irrespective of financial performance. Specific initiatives include:

— The Tourism for Tomorrow Awards, which recognize innovative sustainable tourism projects around the world, and have received wide media attention.

— The Change for Good programme in partnership with UNICEF, in which British Airways customers have given more than £14 million for children's programmes around the world.

— The Communities and Conservation programme, which donates some £1 million each year in travel awards to organizations working on youth development and education, heritage and tourism, and the environment.

Carlson Companies, Inc.

Carlson Hospitality Worldwide is committed to supporting both responsible environmental and social best business practices in hotel operations. Environmentally sustainable practices are encouraged company-wide, including water conservation, paper reduction, energy management and employee awareness training. Carlson Cruises Worldwide is a strong supporter of local charities and surpasses International Maritime Organization standards for cruise ships, employing state-of-the-art water treatment systems.

Carlson Restaurants Worldwide assists non-profit organizations that focus on diversity, hunger, children and education, through volunteering and fundraising. These activities are part of Carlson Companies' long-standing commitment to business ethics and humanitarian community involvement. For example, every year, the company gives five per cent of pre-tax profits to community causes, and it actively facilitates employee community involvement. In 2002, the Curtis L. Carlson Family Foundation co-founded the World Childhood Foundation, whose mission is to promote better living conditions for vulnerable and exploited children and give them the opportunity to become strong, secure people and good citizens.

In 2001, the Carlson Volunteer Connection was launched, an automated on-line intranet system that connects employees with hundreds of community volunteer opportunities in its home city of Minneapolis. The company has also been recognized for creating an excellent workplace for employees, and in 2001, Marilyn Carlson received the FIRST Award for Responsible Capitalism.

Diners Club International

As part of Citigroup's corporate citizenship programmes, Diners Club, in partnership with other Citigroup businesses, uses its financial expertise to help build economic competence and capacity in emerging markets around the world. All projects are initiated and conducted by local affiliates, with active participation by employees.

— Three main areas are targeted: Financial education programmes that increase people's ability to make informed financial decisions and develop assets - such as a home, small business or an education - that will contribute to family stability, good consumer habits and an increased stake in one's community.

— Preparing the next generation through teacher training programmes in low-income communities and scholarships to increase access to higher education.

— Building communities by helping local financial institutions to construct affordable housing, revitalize low-income areas, make infrastructure improvements and encourage environmentally sustainable practices.

Lusotur

In 1996, a new ownership and management team at Lusotur undertook to transform Vilamoura - one of Europe's largest tourism destinations - into an environmentally sustainable resort. The 'Vilamoura XXI' project was designed to integrate the holiday, residential and recreational facilities harmoniously with their natural environment. A company-wide environmental action programme was adopted at the site to monitor and control the environmental impact of all activities - including resource utilization, waste management, staff awareness-raising and stewardship of local natural and cultural heritage - and management structures were adapted to make environmental protection an integral part of operating policies and practices.

The model is being applied at Vilamoura to all upcoming residential developments and company operations, including real estate development, marina and golf course management. The golf course and marina are already operated under an ISO 14001 certified Environmental Management System. Lusotur's success in converting a large scale tourism destination into an eco-friendly resort, while maintaining economical viability, has received recognition from international media, government authorities and environmental groups.

Marriott International

Marriott actively supports communities around the world through its wide-ranging outreach programme, 'Spirit To Serve Our Communities'. Through this programme, Marriott encourages its hotels and employees to give resources, time and energy to activities that help solve critical needs. Staff involvement is central to all activities, and each year employees give tens of thousands of hours, and millions of dollars in cash and in-kind support, to help sick children, build houses, mentor students, assist in disaster recovery and clean up the environment. Activities are conducted in cooperation with non-profit partners such as the International Red Cross & Red Crescent Societies, Habitat for Humanity International and Children's Miracle Network.

An annual day of global service called Spirit To Serve Our Communities Day is set aside to help employees get involved. Marriott is also committed to addressing environmental issues. All operating units employ methods of waste removal, recycling, and energy and water consumption that preserve natural surroundings and resources. And all Marriott hotels are encouraged to adopt eco-friendly practices, using a framework established by the company's Environmentally Conscious Hospitality Operations (ECHO) programme.

Mövenpick

Mövenpick is dedicated to the development of local people, including employees, wherever it operates. For example, at the Mövenpick Resort Petra and the Mövenpick Nabatean Castle Hotel in Petra, Jordan, local people are encouraged to follow careers at the hotel. Four local employees are selected each year for a one-year management training programme. The hotel's Executive Assistant Manager, in charge of operations, is a local employee who began as a front office clerk, and the hotel is working with the community to employ local women.

In addition, hotel executives volunteer to regularly conduct lessons at local schools in basic hotel and other business practices, broadening the perspectives of both the executives and local students. These programmes have received praise both from members of the local community and from guests. They have also resulted in a high standard of service that has enhanced the hotel's market performance and revenues.

Noel Group

Noel Group co-founders John & Patty Noel are committed to leaving a positive legacy in communities around the world where the Group does business. With the company motto,'Where our directions are led by our values', social responsibility stands side-by-side with sales and profitability as a core business objective. The Group's focus is on social needs: helping children and the disadvantaged and promoting diversity. The Noel Compass Foundation was founded to fund these activities. One of its programmes, the Make a Mark Foundation, funds sustainable building projects such as clinics, schools and orphanages in developing countries.

In all projects, emphasis is placed on employee participation and partnership with community organizations. Time, money and other material assistance are used to encourage wider involvement at the local level and ensure that projects are self-sustaining. The company's social involvement has attracted both customers and clients, many of whom contribute their own funds and time to projects. It has also engendered a sense of pride among employees and helped to create a positive working environment.

Radisson SAS Hotels and Resorts

Radisson SAS has a long-standing commitment to environmental protection and by 1997 most of its hotels had fully adopted practices laid out in its Environmental Standards Manual. However, understanding that a hotel's impact is as much social as environmental, in 2001 Radisson SAS launched a company-wide Responsible Business programme - a systematic, integrated framework for addressing both social and environmental issues at all of its 114 hotels in operation in Europe,Middle East and Africa. Indicators were developed to measure performance and improvements against concrete objectives, on which hotels are required to report annually.

Each hotel has a part-time Responsible Business Co-ordinator who assists hotel General Managers with implementation, under the supervision of the corporate Environmental and Social Affairs Director. A Responsible Business Handbook provides a step-by-step guide for implementation and improving performance. The programme includes:

— A Responsible Business training programme for all employees, educating them about environment and social issues in the hotel business and how they can make a difference;

— Community involvement, particularly assistance for children in need;

— A rigid health and safety programme to protect guests, staff and operations;

— Procedures for reducing environmental impact through energy efficiency, use of renewable sources and waste management based on the principles of reduce, reuse and recycle.

Singapore Airlines

Singapore Airlines has long practised good corporate citizenship through support for the arts, sports and education. Recently, however, the company has shifted its focus to providing long-term support for disadvantaged people - such as the elderly, the intellectually challenged and the poor - who may get little or no support from other sources. The company has pledged $4 million to the Movement for the Intellectually Disabled of Singapore (MINDS) to help build a new headquarters and workshop, employing up to 400 intellectually disabled members. Company employees are also encouraged to volunteer to assist with other MINDS fund-raising activities. In Indonesia, where an estimated 12 million children have left school as a result of the regional economic crisis, the company has launched a seven-year scholarship programme that will benefit 4,000 school and university students.

Six Continents

Six Continents has implemented a series of strategically focused, continuously developing environmental initiatives designed to conserve energy while delivering tangible benefits to the bottom line. Across the Group, the use of external benchmarking of consumption is promoted with a view to managing energy and water use and waste controls in a more proactive way. With regard to social contributions, Six Continents uses external benchmarks — including FTSE4GOOD, the Dow Jones Sustainability Index and Business in the Community's PerCent Club guidelines - to measure achievements, identify shortcomings and take appropriate corrective action. In addition, a 'Code of

Business Conduct' guides all employees, to ensure that they act with integrity. Last year £1.5 million was contributed to charity, including contributions to partnerships with UNICEF and Victim Support, as part of a long-term commitment to return a percentage of profits back to the communities where they operate.

Tata Group of Hotels

As part of a long-standing commitment to support community development, the Tata Group, which includes the Tata Group of Hotels, has integrated corporate social responsibility into group-wide management processes. A series of charitable trusts provide financial support for development, and most Tata Companies have these trusts as significant shareholders, dividends paid by the Tata companies provide funds for charitable and development activities. Each Tata company also has a mandate to conduct its own community development programmes using company resources, and a senior-level Tata Council for Community Initiatives ensures this mandate is fulfilled.

The Group conducts regular assessments of what employees have learned from involvement in these projects and how this affects the organization. Within this framework, the Taj Group of Hotels focuses each year on one of several areas: women and development, education, health, vocational training and watershed development. For 2002-03, the focus is 'Empowering the Underprivileged Woman', which involves employees training women in skills that will help them get jobs and be economically independent. Employee involvement is strongly encouraged, to build a sense of service to the community and the underprivileged, an approach that has helped the Group build trust with local communities.

TUI

TUI has made environmental sustainability a priority for

its extensive network of tourism holdings and destination partners. All activities are coordinated by a Group Environmental Management Department, whose purpose is to ensure that environmental quality management is integrated into every link of the tourism value chain. Several thousands of TUI hotel partners are monitored in accordance with TUI's environmental quality standards - on energy and water use, waste treatment and conservation - and checked annually for compliance. Awards are used to encourage exemplary practice: the TUI Environmental Champion Award for hotels and the TUI Environmental Prize for community groups.

TUI travel agencies and brochures give customers information about environmentally friendly hotels in destinations and local TUI tour services actively participate in conservation projects, such as reforestation and endangered species protection. All work is conducted in cooperation with experts, government agencies, nature conservation associations and other competent players in the field of environmental management. Because environmental degradation carries real economic costs and risks for business as well as communities, the company is guided by the conviction that tourism can and should be a leading force for conservation and sustainable development.

Uniglobe Travel Inc.

Within the Uniglobe organization, the concept of 'franchising' is used to maximize the effectiveness of is community activities. All operating units focus their energy and resources towards a common direction, thereby delivering greater results collectively than could be achieved individually. Efforts are focused on supporting the Easter Seal Society, which helps children with physical disabilities to achieve their full potential and independence. Within this broad common direction, each region makes a local decision about the extent of its involvement. The company is guided by the philosophy that contributing to society at large is both the right thing to do and good for business because it creates a collaborative organizational culture that is key to retaining motivated employees.

Worldspan

Worldspan President & CEO, Paul Blackney, believes that corporate social responsibility should be a philosophy that permeates the organization and a process in which everyone is involved. Hence, with the CEO as a catalyst, the company focuses on direct employee participation in community initiatives. To ensure appropriate focus, a dedicated department within Worldspan reviews and decides on each request for assistance or participation. Worldspan programmes address both environmental and social needs.

In its home community of Atlanta, Georgia, the company designed the city's largest van pool programme, to help reduce air pollution and fuel consumption, and it is now helping state and local authorities to promote the practice with other companies. Worldspan also supports the arts, supplies materials, equipment and tutoring to disadvantaged youth at local elementary schools, and funds preferential house mortgages for disadvantaged people. Company employees have helped to build five 'Habitat for Humanity' homes and they participate in walks, runs and many other types of fund-raising projects, benefiting the communities where they work and live.

14

Supply Chain Engagement

Tour operators can integrate economic, environmental and social sustainability criteria into their choices of service suppliers and their contracts with those suppliers. From establishing a sustainability policy and action plan and developing a baseline assessment of tourism service suppliers to enabling suppliers to meet set targets and reviewing and reporting on progress made, the document maps out a methodology for improving the sustainability of the tour operator's supply chain.

A wide range of possible actions that tour operators can take, each company should select the actions that are most appropriate to its organization and the types of destinations and suppliers with which it works. It is not necessary to try to implement all the actions at once; indeed, it is often better to start with a few achievable actions and then build on those in the future. What is important is that a company start to take action.

As intermediaries between tourists and tourism service providers, tour operators bring together a variety of tourism-related services to form a complete holiday package, which is then marketed to customers either directly or through travel agents. Each package generally consists of accommodation (often including some food provision), transport both to and from the destination, ground transport within the destination, and events or activities such as excursions and social activities.

Because most of the goods and services included in a holiday package are provided by a supply chain of subcontracted companies, organizations and agents, tour operators are not always in direct control of the environmental and social impacts of those products. Yet, consumers increasingly expect the companies they buy from to ensure that their products provide not just quality and value-for-money, but also safeguard environmental and social sustainability.

Companies must take responsibility for ensuring the sustainability of all the inputs that go into their products. For tour operators, who offer products comprised almost entirely of contracted goods and services, this means that effectively implementing sustainability policies requires working closely with suppliers to improve sustainability performance in all the components of a holiday - throughout the life cycle of a holiday package. "Consumers are increasingly interested in the world behind the product they buy. Life cycle thinking implies that everyone in the whole chain of a product's life cycle, from cradle to grave, has a responsibility and a role to play, taking into account all the relevant external effects."

The actions presented are applicable to tour operators of any size, from the smallest to the largest. Although the way each company is organized can differ - thus affecting the staff who will need to be involved in various actions - here outlines the different roles that need to be brought together to develop and implement a sustainable supply chain policy and action plan.

Developing Sustainable Supply Chain

Working with suppliers to integrate sustainability into the supply chain can benefit tour operators, suppliers, customers and destinations. From a financial standpoint, improved sustainability can lower costs through greater operating efficiency, reduced waste generation, and reduced consumption of energy and water. Sustainability practices can also lead to increased revenue and shareholder value by generating more repeat business and attracting new business from customers who value good environmental and social performance.

A strong positive reputation as a company that cares about sustainability issues, coupled with improvements to the quality of the tourism experience provided to clients, can result in increased customer satisfaction and loyalty, strengthened brand value, enhanced publicity and marketing opportunities, and better acceptance by local communities in destinations. Good performance and a high-quality, sustainable product can also help a tour operator reduce the risk of conflict or problems with suppliers, governments, staff and local communities, and improve its status as a respected partner in destinations.

This may mean enhanced access to key business resources such as capital, the ability to develop products to meet growing market demand, improved relationships with governments, and a motivated and loyal staff. The costs and benefits of integrating sustainability criteria into the supply chain will vary for each company, depending on:

— Purchasing and contracting arrangements with suppliers;

— Availability of alternate suppliers in key destinations;

— Suppliers' current levels of sustainability performance and potential for change;

— Barriers to sustainability, such as external factors;

— A company's main sustainability and operational concerns; and

— Resources available to implement and promote sustainability throughout the supply chain.

Supply Chain Policy and Management System

For a tour operator, effectively integrating sustainability into its supply chain will require the establishment of a coherent company policy and accompanying management system that set out clear targets and actions on economic, environmental and social performance. Building this system on already existing internal processes will help keep down the costs of implementation and promote integration within a company's overall operations.

To establish this policy, a company needs to conduct a baseline assessment of its tourism service suppliers' current performance on sustainability, in order to determine priority targets and actions. The management system should include procedures for monitoring, reviewing and reporting on progress made in integrating sustainability principles into the company's supply chain. This helps to ensure transparency and allow tour operators to adapt any policies or actions that are not achieving their stated goals. Progress can be measured against the initial baseline assessment.

Create A Policy

Goal

Develop a coherent policy for improving the economic, environmental and social sustainability performance of suppliers, and for integrating it into existing company management systems.

Actions

— Build a team to develop and implement the policy

- Bring together representatives of each area or department in the company that may have a role in implementing the overall policy, or which may be affected by it.
- Create a management team to develop and implement the policy at each stage, drawing on expertise from all departments.
- Consider inviting your company's suppliers to participate in the policy and planning process.

— Assess the company's strengths and opportunities

- Assess the company's current position and policies and how they relate to sustainability issues.
- Consider trends and potential developments, including product quality, supplier performance and markets, as well as the way the company interacts with its suppliers.
- Identify opportunities to improve the sustainability performance of suppliers.

— Develop a policy

- Elaborate a common vision that can be shared by all departments in the company, based on the results of the strengths and opportunities assessment.
- Discuss the common vision with key staff, and invite their suggestions for policies and actions to implement this vision.
- Based on these discussions and the common vision, develop and agree on a policy and strategic goals for improved supply chain sustainability, and on the types of methods that could be used to meet these goals.

Baseline Assessment of Suppliers

Goal

Assess suppliers' current sustainability performance and their strengths and weaknesses, to generate data for designing a sustainability action plan, and to provide a baseline against which to measure progress over time and review and modify the sustainable supply chain policy and actions.

Actions

- Prepare an approach for assessment
  - Develop assessment tools for measuring the sustainability performance of suppliers.
  - Select a sample of suppliers to involve in the assessment.
  - Consider prioritizing certain supplier groups, based on ability to influence them and the ease of addressing any identified impacts. Trying to tackle every type of service and every supplier or contractor at the same time can be very resource intensive.
- Assess suppliers' current performance
  - Use questionnaires, personal meetings and/or workshops to assess suppliers' current sustainability performance, strengths and weaknesses, their main concerns and the key areas requiring improvement.
  - Determine suppliers' general levels of awareness, technical capacity and desire to be involved in a sustainability program. In particular, it is important to understand their motives and values, and to identify any potential challenges or barriers to sustainability.

— Identify any opportunities for additional cooperation with external stakeholders, in particular local authorities or NGOs.

— Ask suppliers for information on how they select their own suppliers. They may already implement a range of good practices, such as buying food from local producers and organic and/or fair trade suppliers.

Prepare an Action Plan

Goal

Prepare an action plan for implementation of policies for improving the economic, environmental and social sustainability performance of suppliers, taking into account suppliers' strengths and weaknesses and existing company management systems.

Actions

— Define actions and set targets

— Define and agree on actions and targets to be achieved, based on the company's sustainable supply chain policy.

— Ensure that targets are SMART (Specific, Measurable, Achievable, Realistic and Time-specific).

— Set standards by which to measure suppliers' performance.

— Ensure that standards are achievable. It is better to set standards that are achievable and can provide real satisfaction for suppliers and staff, rather than set over-ambitious standards that are unlikely to be achieved.

- Develop an action plan to implement the strategy and meet set targets
- Agree on specific responsibilities for each department and the resources they will need to implement them, such as training or technical information. Incorporate departmental action plans in regular company procedures for reviewing progress and staff appraisal.
- Prepare a timetable for implementation of the overall plan and for each individual action.

— Get the word out

- Inform suppliers about the sustainability policy and action plan, and the benefits of improved environmental, social and economic performance, through normal company communication channels, dedicated workshops and personal meetings between suppliers and company representatives.
- Inform staff about the sustainability policy and action plan through training workshops, briefings and feedback materials, and internal capacity-building on how to raise awareness of the policy and provide support to suppliers.
- Establish a system to keep staff informed of progress, for example through staff newsletters and the intranet.

— Put the plan into action

- Consider prioritizing suppliers for involvement in the first stages of the program, based on economic and managerial considerations. It may be more practical to begin with just a few destinations and/or selected suppliers, rather than trying to introduce the program everywhere at once.

- — Recognize that suppliers may have different priorities for improvements and are likely to make progress at different rates.
- — Understand that change takes time. It is important to focus on achieving continuous improvements, rather than trying to achieve everything all at once. The key is to initiate programs with all suppliers to improve their performance and see measurable improvement over time.
- — Consider working with other partners, including public authorities, NGOs and other tour operators operating in the same destination, to help encourage sustainability performance improvements amongst all suppliers, for example by developing a common approach in certain geographic or supplier areas.

Monitor and Report on Progress

Goal

Monitor and report on progress made in integrating sustainability into the company's supply chain, to ensure that goals have been achieved and to identify any potential problems.

Actions

— Create and implement a monitoring system

- — Select appropriate indicators for monitoring performance.
- — Hold regular meetings with relevant individuals, to review progress and help sort out problems as they arise. Key staff in each area often understand best where and how improvements can be made,

and involving them in the process helps to build and maintain their commitment to sustainability.

- — Ensure that monitoring is frequent enough to detect problems at an early stage, so that corrective action can be taken if needed.
- — Identify and refine the most successful approaches to improvement of sustainability performance across the company's supply chain.
- — Store information collected through monitoring in a central database.
- — Learn from successes and difficulties in implementing planned actions and modify plans accordingly; use the results of a progress review to plan for the year ahead.

— Report on performance

- — Report internally by communicating the results of monitoring back to staff, to show what has been achieved, recognize their commitment to the project and remind them of the program's objectives and targets.
- — Agree on the format for a public report on supply chain sustainability, for example as a separate report or a section of the company's annual report.
- — Consider using a third party to review the company's sustainability report before publication.
- — Disseminate regular reports on progress to demonstrate a commitment to improving overall sustainability performance in the supply chain to key stakeholder groups, including suppliers, staff, customers, media, destinations and others in the tourism industry. Reporting also helps to foster openness and discussion about problems and

successes and enables companies to more effectively prioritize future activities.

Reaching Sustainability Goals

Tour operators are well-placed to support suppliers in improving their economic, environmental and social performance. As tour operators interact directly with potential customers, they understand their clients' growing demands for high quality and sustainability. They also often have access to technology and information that smaller suppliers may have difficulty obtaining on their own. Because tour operators deal with a wide range of different suppliers, they can more easily gather information on a variety of best practices and facilitate the sharing of experiences amongst suppliers.

There are a number of ways that tour operators can enable their suppliers to improve their sustainability performance and meet set sustainability criteria and targets. Three of these measures - awareness raising, technical support and the provision of incentives. The appropriate mix of support measures for each company and supplier will depend on the results of the baseline assessment and the approach that the company has chosen to adopt for implementing its sustainable supply chain strategy.

Awareness on Sustainability Issues

Goal

Raise awareness amongst suppliers on relevant sustainability issues and demonstrate why sustainability performance is important.

Actions

— Develop awareness-raising messages on sustainability

— Take into account feedback from suppliers, existing relationships with targeted supplier groups, the level of interest amongst suppliers in participating in the program, and suppliers' current capacity and priorities for performance improvement.

— Design messages based on the dissemination channels that will be used to raise awareness, such as mailings, personal visits, workshops, etc.

— Identify potential partners and support. Local partners, such as business associations or training institutes, can help open communication channels with local suppliers, especially amongst smaller enterprises, and may be influential in reinforcing awareness-raising efforts.

— Focus on key issues that are important to the company's situation and its suppliers.

— Provide information in the awareness-raising materials on the overall strategy and time frame for the company's sustainability program.

— Communicate sustainability messages to suppliers

— Identify the characteristics of each group of suppliers, including their values and concerns, and select appropriate tools, media and styles to best reach these target groups. Tools might include workshops, bilateral meetings or dialogues, briefing materials and feedback forms for staff, checklists and questionnaires, or printed materials, such as leaflets, posters and manuals.

— If questionnaires or checklists are used, indicate clearly what the information gathered would be used for. Consider preparing a summary report on the results, for example highlighting sustainability issues identified as priorities by suppliers and illustrating the general level of performance for each of the issues addressed.

— Use personal communication wherever possible. Staff in contact with suppliers can provide up-to-date information on sustainability issues and the company's progress. Trained staff should be available to inform suppliers about environmental and social issues, provide contact phone numbers, make personal visits, etc.

— Ensure that sustainability issues are followed up and discussed regularly with suppliers. Encourage feedback from suppliers to help evaluate the effectiveness of awareness-raising activities and provide important information on the attitudes of target groups to sustainability issues. This feedback can be used to refine awareness-raising activities and plan future developments.

— Monitor the response to the awareness-raising actions. Check how suppliers and staff respond to the project, recognize and appreciate results, and support continuous improvement. A newsletter may be a good way to publicize examples of good practice and progress made by particular suppliers.

Provide Technical Support

Goal

Support suppliers in improving their sustainability performance, particularly in areas that have been identified as priorities.

Actions

— Assess where support is needed

— Determine where technical support is needed amongst suppliers and establish targets for improvement.

— Identify the most appropriate technical support and capacity-building actions to match the suppliers' and company's targets.

— Develop and deliver support

— Identify, develop and deliver the most appropriate and effective technical support tools for suppliers, including printed material, workshops, bilateral meetings or dialogues, briefing materials and feedback forms for staff, training sessions, checklists and questionnaires, and telephone and on-line information and support services.

— Provide training and practical education opportunities to suppliers' staff at all levels, including managers, engineers, hotel maids, catering staff, guides, etc., on reducing resource use and procedures for waste separation and recycling.

— Offer links to networks of local, national and international advisers on sustainability and business issues who can provide on-line and on-site assistance to suppliers - for example local experts on environmental and socio-economic issues, possibly in collaboration with local trade associations and non-governmental organizations.

— Consider promoting the use of eco-labeling schemes to support improvement and provide information on technical issues tailored to a specific destination.

— Identify external sources of information and support. Numerous technical materials on environmental management and solutions are already available through international and national hotel associations, international organizations and NGOs.

Arranging for suppliers to contact these sources directly can help such organizations disseminate their resources more widely and avoid overwhelming an internal team with requests for information and support, which might be difficult to meet with limited internal resources.

Incentives to Sustainable Suppliers

Goal

Build support for the sustainable supply chain strategy by recognizing and rewarding suppliers for improvements on key environmental, social and economic issues.

Actions

— Create an incentive scheme

- — Establish sustainability performance standards for the sustainability priorities set by the company's policy, to identify which suppliers will be offered additional promotional opportunities and/or other incentives.
- — Identify the most suitable incentive measures to reward suppliers making significant improvements, such as preferential contracting, promotional opportunities, awards and events, for example:
- — Indicate that suppliers who demonstrate improved performance will be the company's first choice when decisions are made on whom to contract in any destination or category. Preferential contracting offers a major incentive to suppliers to improve their performance.

- — Highlight good performers in catalogs and brochures with a special logo, making sure to provide clear information to customers about what the logo denotes.
- — List specific sustainability actions that each supplier has adopted in the catalogs.
- — Present certificates to suppliers who demonstrate the best sustainability performance.
- — Organize events - in a destination or at company headquarters - for groups of suppliers who are making good progress in implementing sustainability performance improvements.
- — Develop and agree on the internal procedures for providing the identified additional promotional opportunities and incentives.

— Get the word out

- — Inform suppliers about additional promotional opportunities and other incentives and the criteria that the company will use to allocate them.
- — Ensure that available recognition and reward opportunities and incentives are discussed with each supplier in personal meetings with a company representative.

— Verify supplier performance

- — Define mechanisms for collection of data on suppliers' performance in the identified action areas, such as questionnaires, personal visits, etc., and train staff to implement these procedures.
- — Create a monitoring and assessment system and procedures to verify suppliers' declared sustainability performance.

— Establish a database to record information on suppliers' sustainability performance and ensure that the database can be easily used by all staff who need to access the information it will hold. Where appropriate, integrate the database with existing systems, such as health and safety databases.

Integrate Sustainability Criteria

Full integration of sustainability issues into a tour operator's business practices will require alterations to the way purchasing choices are made and suppliers' contracts are written. Inclusion of sustainability criteria in suppliers' contracts highlights the importance of sustainability issues to the tour operator's core business and ensures that priority issues are addressed with suppliers from the start. Sustainability criteria can be incorporated into suppliers' contracts to set both minimum performance standards that all suppliers of a particular type must meet and further optional criteria that they are encouraged to achieve. Performance against sustainability criteria will need to be monitored and assessed as part of regular reviews of suppliers.

Goal

Integrate environmental, social and economic criteria into suppliers' contracts and reward performance improvements by preferentially contracting suppliers that meet those criteria.

Actions

— Set sustainability contracting standards

— Establish the minimum sustainability performance standards to be included in suppliers' contracts, and link them to the performance standards set as part of an incentive scheme.

— Set standards sufficiently high so that they represent good performance and real improvements, but also ensure that they will be realistic and achievable for suppliers.

— Allow flexibility to accommodate varying local socio-economic and environmental conditions among different destinations and different types and sizes of suppliers.

— Seek guidance on standards for different types of suppliers from relevant national or international bodies.

— For each destination, review the sustainability performance of the full range of suppliers for each service or item and identify alternate supply options.

— Set a sustainable contracting system

— Develop and agree on an internal approach and procedures for implementation of sustainability performance as a contracting criteria.

— Draft contractual clauses to reflect minimum performance requirements on key issues and consider legal matters arising from incorporation of sustainability standards into suppliers' contracts.

— Establish procedures to deal with suppliers that fail to meet minimum set standards or that have submitted false information. In serious cases and on specific issues, companies may decide to suspend contracts with suppliers who are in breach of contract conditions.

— Consider appointing an individual staff member or a small team to develop and update standards and support materials, coordinate training for suppliers and staff, manage informational databases, coordinate monitoring, auditing and verification, and provide progress reports.

— Get the word out

— Run workshops to train staff on contracting procedures for sustainability issues and procedures for monitoring and auditing suppliers' sustainability performance.

— Set up a communications program to inform suppliers about the new contract clauses and contracting policy.

— Consider developing a parallel voluntary program with additional sustainability performance standards.

— Offer assistance to help get suppliers back into compliance, for example by making suggestions for improvements and sources of technical assistance.

— Monitor and evaluate the system

— Set up assessment and monitoring procedures to evaluate supplier sustainability performance in relation to standards set in contracts. For example, arrangements could be made for sustainability performance to be audited as part of existing health and safety audits.

— Arrange for this assessment and monitoring to be conducted by the supplier, the company or a third party, using checklists, questionnaires, site visits and staff interviews as appropriate. Customer feedback through surveys or informal comments can also be an important source of information.

— Establish a database to record information on suppliers' sustainability performance and ensure that the database can be easily used by all staff who need to access the information it will hold. Where appropriate, integrate the database with existing systems, such as health and safety databases.

— Ensure the confidentiality of any sensitive or confidential data in the database.

Examples of Sustainable Supply Chain Management

There are many tour operators that are currently integrating economic, environmental and social sustainability criteria into their choice of suppliers. Here showcases the efforts of five leading tour operators to create a sustainable supply chain. From monitoring environmental performance, to training staff on sustainability issues - these examples illustrate how companies can develop a sustainable supply chain.

Aurinkomatkat

Aurinkomatkat, a Finnish outbound tour operator, began integrating sustainability measures into its supply chain system in early 2000. The company developed sustainability criteria for partner hotels, based on existing tourism literature and using expertise from academia, with priority given to good water management and energy saving. Minimum criteria were established for partner hotels, including connection to a wastewater treatment system and water- and energy-saving measures.

The sustainability program has been implemented in phases, to give existing contract partners a several-year transition period to meet the requirements of the program and understand what will be expected in the future. The first phase of the program included monitoring of environmental performance, but did not actually require accommodation providers to meet all the requirements. Most of the monitoring of the program is done by the Manager for Sustainable Tourism, together with staff and agents at the destinations.

The initial monitoring takes place through a checklist completed by a representative of the facility, which is then checked by Aurinkomatkat personnel at the destinations and verified annually in conjunction with the regular hotel check performed by destination staff. All Aurinkomatkat staff have been trained in sustainable tourism through lectures and roundtable discussions.

Training continues through discussions, an intranet site, a newsletter on sustainable tourism and an information package. Responses to the program from Aurinkomatkat agents and accommodation suppliers in the destinations have been positive, and some hotel managers have provided information on their environmental performance before being asked to do so. Aurinkomatkat informs its suppliers about the program and how to fulfill the sustainability criteria through letters and personal visits, depending on the destination.

Because many of the accommodations are family-owned enterprises, the environmental program and the criteria are translated into the language of the destination. In some destinations, the Manager of Sustainable Tourism visits and arranges meetings for hotel owners and managers with tourism and environmental authorities. To provide incentives for its partners to improve their environmental performance, Aurinkomatkat has created a sustainability classification system for its hotels and holiday apartments, which will soon be available to customers.

Currently, this information can be accessed by sales personnel, who can assist customers in booking a more sustainable accommodation option. The classification system will soon appear beside the traditional quality classification in Aurinkomatkat brochures, web pages and marketing materials. The classification system is based on a 100-point scale. By meeting the minimum criteria of connection to a wastewater treatment system, and water- and energy-saving measures, a facility can achieve the 30-point minimum required for inclusion in the sustainability program.

Additional points are awarded for having an environmental or sustainability policy, developing an effective waste management system, using renewable energy sources, implementing a sustainable purchasing policy and having a community relations program. Hotels can receive up to three stars for environmental performance, based on information provided by the contract partners and annual checks by destination staff.

In addition to company monitoring of sustainability, feedback from customers is collected through questionnaires and via the feedback option at the company web sites. If there is negative feedback from customers or if issues arise that compromise the criteria, a hotel may have its environmental classification downgraded.

By 2003, Aurinkomatkat had completed monitoring all of its existing partners and introduced environmental criteria into its partner hotels' contracts. Until December 2005, there will be no penalties for breaching the environmental criteria, because some contract partners may not fully understand what the policy and new requirements mean.

However, after that, contracts will not be renewed without evidence of improvement in those practices that do not fulfill the criteria. Concerned that integrating of environmental criteria into hotel contracts might increase the risk of losing touch with the socio-cultural and economic sides of sustainability, Aurinkomatkat has also integrated indicators for social, cultural and economic sustainability into the program. These criteria recognize that an 800-room hotel has a different scale of impact than a six-room holiday apartment hotel, and their resources are not comparable.

A five-star multinational resort with eco-certificates is not always a "better" choice than a family-owned apartment building that has no environmental program but which employs the family next door and helps the local economy by encouraging tourists to buy food and other goods from local stores.

Thus, the company has made it easier for small familyowned properties that cannot invest in environmental technology to the same extent as large hotels by giving an additional five points to small-scale locally owned accommodations. This will mean that a small family-owned hotel that uses water- and energy-saving measures and treats its sewage appropriately will meet the minimum requirements for inclusion in the sustainability program. Achieving a higher environmental classification will require more investment.

LTU Touristik

In summer 2000, LTU Touristik, a German tour operator that specializes in package tours to all continents, launched a campaign to help contracted hotels improve their environmental performance. The campaign was based on the company's experience with contracted hotels that showed that most hoteliers felt a general sense of responsibility for the environment, but needed suggestions for how they could implement good environmental practices.

To determine where assistance was most needed, LTU Touristik's Environmental Department worked with a consultant to distribute a questionnaire to contracted hotels. The department also held personal meetings with hotel managers in a number of destinations, allowing them to learn firsthand about the contracted hotels' environmental practices and environmental impacts.

As the centerpiece of the campaign, the company developed a small manual, Das Umweltfreundliche Ferienhotel (The Environmentally Friendly Holiday Hotel) to give technical assistance to contracted hotels (those that are not directly operated by LTU Touristik). Topics addressed in the manual include drinking water, outside areas, energy, purchasing, waste and communication.

Each section includes a general description of the problem and concise suggestions about how to solve it, presented in simple language and a user-friendly layout. Great importance is attached to explaining why actions should be carried out in the way described and symbols show how much time an action will take and the investment required. Many examples are given of how actions to improve the environment can save money.

The manual, which targets hotel managers and other staff members responsible for hotel operation, was launched in all destinations worldwide where LTU Touristik does business. Now in its 3rd edition, the 20-page manual is published in German, Greek, English, French, Italian and Spanish.

In 2002, about 15,000 manuals were distributed, and several large hotel companies ordered the manual to use for staff training or reprinted it on their own. Where possible, the manual was distributed personally to hotel managers. Tour guides, buyers and the head of the destination agency delivered the manuals during routine visits, explained LTU Touristik's objectives and offered initial suggestions for environmental practices.

These representatives then reported back on the first reactions of the hotel managers to LTU Touristik's

Environmental Manager. Along with the manual, hotel managers received a personally addressed letter and a one-page questionnaire about whether they were able to use some of the practices in the manual, whether they needed further information and which environmental protection measures they already implemented.

Nearly 20 percent of all contracted hoteliers have offered feedback to the company. If hoteliers need further assistance beyond these first contacts, LTU Touristik provides it through its Environmental Department's two-person technical assistance team, thus guaranteeing a continuous dialogue with hotels that want to improve their environmental performance.

Training is offered to buyers, heads of destination agencies and tour guides, and the Environmental Manager personally updates them on the campaign. Information is also provided on what type of technical assistance is expected from them and how to make an informal evaluation of the visited facilities. The company's web site provides all interested employees with more detailed information. LTU Touristik has recognized that relying solely on manuals has its limitations, principally that there are no mechanisms for enforcement of the voluntary practices nor incentive for their implementation.

The company's long-term goal is to be able to demonstrate the benefits of environmental action and to establish environmental standards for holiday hotels. As a next step, LTU Touristik plans to collect all information about environmental action introduced by the hotels and report its findings to other hotels and eventually to its clients.

Orizzonti

In 1997, Orizzonti, an Italian inbound tour operator, launched an environmental program, Attenzione per l'Ambiente (Care for the Environment), aimed at opening up a constructive dialogue on environmental issues and raising awareness among its suppliers, authorities at destinations and customers. The objective of the program is to generate interest among all stakeholders and stimulate good environmental management practices.

The program includes materials targeting customers (through an informational brochure), decision-makers at destinations and suppliers. The supplier checklist, which is specifically aimed at hotels and self-catering accommodation, was developed in cooperation with Check Soluzioni per il Turismo, an Italian tourism and environmental conservation consultant.

The checklist takes into account existing national legislation and scientific guidelines on environmental management in tourism facilities, in particular the European Union's Environmental Management and Audit Scheme (EMAS). An assessment of hotels and self-catering accommodations in seaside and mountain resorts was conducted before defining the criteria for the checklist, in order to identify and define the issues affecting the two main types of accommodation used by Orizzonti. Some suppliers were also asked to evaluate the checklist before it was used.

Water and energy saving, and pollution. Under water and energy saving, the checklist asks questions about low-energy and renewable energy equipment, variable temperature controls, water-saving faucets and toilets, re-use of gray water and rain water, and monitoring of energy and water consumption.

Under pollution, the checklist asks about the use of non-toxic and renewable materials, internal air quality, solid waste separation and recycling, use of local products and client awareness programs. Suppliers are asked to answer each question by simply ticking yes or no (only two questions ask for quantitative information). Space is provided for establishments to provide further information about their environmental activities.

The program is coordinated by Orizzonti's Environmental Monitoring Office. The checklist is sent every year to accommodation suppliers by email with a cover letter introducing the program, summarizing the results of previous years and noting that all answers will be treated confidentially. The checklist was distributed for the first time in 1997, to 700 Italian hotels and selfcatering facilities. The reply rate was about 25 percent.

In 1998, an additional 115 hotels and self-catering facilities in France were added, and the reply rate was about 26 percent. In 1999, about 900 checklists were distributed, and a total of 233 (about 26 percent) were completed. Using information collected through the supplier checklist, Orizzonti is able to inform customers about which facilities have implemented environmentally friendly practices and what these practices are, and can offer these facilities a marketing tool that recognizes their commitment to the environment.

The information is published in Orizzonti's brochures, with an introduction explaining the environmental program in detail and describing the checklist. An ECO symbol highlights the hotels that have adopted ecological initiatives. The 33 questions in the checklist are numbered, and the number appears next to the ECO symbol to indicate which actions have been implemented by each of the hotels that completed the questionnaire, allowing clients to make comparisons and informed decisions when selecting their accommodation.

Monitoring and evaluation of the effective implementation of the 33 criteria is conducted through customer feedback forms and routine visits by Orizzonti staff to the contractors. A customer feedback form (preaddressed) is included in the brochure distributed with travel documents. The forms are collected and evaluated by the Environmental Monitoring Office. When customers file negative comments, Orizzonti requests explanations directly from the hotel manager. Technical support is offered, by both Check Soluzioni per il Turismo and Orizzonti staff, for suppliers expressing an interest in improving their environmental performance.

TUI Nordic

TUI Nordic, one of the leading tour operators in Europe and part of World of TUI (TUI AG), has established a close relationship with the "Blue Village" hotels, in order to integrate sustainability practices into the Blue Village quality requirements. Blue Village hotels are quality properties in sun and beach destinations, designed for families and couples. TUI Nordic's relationship with the hotels focuses particularly on promoting environmental and social responsibility and supporting the dissemination of sustainability information to customers.

The decision to pursue this partnership was based on the recognition that Blue Village customers support environmental actions, such as recycling and water saving, and that they regard engagement in responsible tourism development as part of a hotel's quality performance. In developing the sustainability requirements, the company decided to use two widely accepted Codes of Conduct, the hotel section of the World Wide Fund for Nature's (WWF) Code of Conduct for the Travel and Tourism Industry, and the ECPAT Code of Conduct against Commercial Sexual Exploitation of Children in Travel and Tourism.

The company decided that these codes would permit a fxible approach to communication and allow different methods of implementation. This decision was supported by the fact that TUI Nordic, together with other stakeholders, had been active in the elaboration of both Codes. In a second phase of the program, UNESCO's Ten Rules for Responsible Traveling were included in the information platform. These guidelines were developed in collaboration between the Nordic UNESCO World Heritage Foundation and TUI Nordic.

All Blue Village Hotels contracted by TUI Nordic are required to have implemented both the WWF hotel code of conduct and the ECPAT code on commercial sexual exploitation of children. In addition, the hotels must have in place an Environmental Management System (EMS), appoint a staff person responsible for environmental matters, have a written environmental plan, use non-polluting products, give priority to local suppliers and goods, sort solid waste, treat wastewater and introduce water-efficient hardware.

Blue Village hotels also have to inform their customers about UNESCO's Rules for Responsible Traveling through information in the reception area and in each room and briefings bytrained tour leaders and hotel employees. The company worked with Blue Village hotel managers to create a common communication system that would allow benchmarking between hotels, support the message of sustainability to customers and become a part of the Blue Village concept. The common platform also allows tour operators to use the same information in brochures and leafets, thus reinforcing the sustainability concepts. Management in each hotel has been trained on the content of the Codes of Conduct.

Hotels monitor their own performance in implementing the Codes and report regularly to TUI Nordic's Concept Department. Each hotel also reports on performance and lessons learned at a yearly conference, giving them an excellent opportunity to exchange views and experiences. In promoting Blue Village hotels, TUI

Nordic includes information on the hotels' environmental performance in its catalogs and on its web site.

Among the benefits of this program have been reduced operational costs for hotels, through lower water and energy consumption, and enhanced reputation and increased client satisfaction and loyalty for TUI Nordic. The quality criteria and environmental requirements for each hotel are included in the Blue Village Product Agreement, which is an appendix to the ordinary agreement signed by TUI Nordic and the hotels.

Bibliography

Brown, T. and N. Connelly. "Tourism and Employment in the Adirondack Park," Annals of Tourism Research, 13, 481-489. 1986.

Brown, Tommy L. and Nancy A. Connelly. "Tourism in the Adirondack Region of New York State". *Natural Resources Research and Extension Series* No. 21, Cornell University, Human Dimensions Research Unit, Ithaca, NY, 1984.

Cook, S. and V. Azucenas. "Research in State and Provincial Travel Offices," in *Travel, Tourism, and Hospitality Research, Second Edition*, J. Ritchie and C. Goeldner eds., John Wiley & Sons, New York, pp. 165-180, 1994.

Costas, Christ. "Taking Ecotourism to the Next Level - A Look at Private Sector Involvement with Local Communities," *Ecotourism A Guide for Planners and Managers*, The Ecotourism Society, North Bennington, Vermont, 1998, 1998.

Dawson, C., K. Alberga, and M. Washburn, "Recreation and Tourism Participation and Demand in the Adirdondack Park: An Assesment of the Limited Information Available for Planning and Management", *draft report*. NY State DEC, Albany, New York, 1994.

Eagles & B. Higgins. "Ecotourism Market and Industry Strucutre" in Ecotourism A Guide for Planners and Managers Vol.2", *The Ecotourism Society*, North Bennington, Vermont, 1998.

Higgins, Bryan. "The Global Structure of the Nature Tourism Industry: Ecotourists, Tour Operators and Local Business," *Journal of Travel Research*, 35 (2), 11-18, 1996.

Elkin, R. and R. Roberts. "Evaluating the Human Resource (Employment) Requirements and Impacts of Tourism Developments," *in Travel, Tourism, and Hospitality Research, Second Edition,* J. Ritchie and C. goeldner eds., John Wiley & Sons, New York, pp. 403-412, 1994.

Mackun, P. "Tourism in the Third Italy Labor and social-business networks," in Ioannides, D. and K. Debbage eds., *The Econonic Geography of the Tourist Industry.* Routledge, New York, 1998.

McArthur, Simon. "Introducing the Undercapitalized World of Interpretation" in Ecotourism A Guide for Planners and Managers Vol.2, The Ecotourism Society, North Bennington, Vermont, 1998.

Middleton, V. and R. Hawkins. *Sustainable Tourism: A Marketing Perspective,* Butterworth and Hinemann, Oxford, 1998.

Ritchie, J. and C. Goeldner eds. *Travel, Tourism, and Hospitality Research,* John Wiley & Sons, New York, 1999.

Yaman, H. and R. Shaw. "The Conduct of Marketing Research in Tourism," *Journal of Travel Research,* 36, 25-32, 1998.

Index

Adventure tourism 76
Archaeological 5
Archaeology 7
Aurinkomatkat 240

Communication techniques 158
Cultural tourism 8
Cultural tours 5
Customer Relations (CR) 44

Domestic tourism 31

Eco-tourism 7
Environmental Impact Assessments (EIAs) 2
Environmental Management and Audit Scheme (EMAS) 246
Environmental Management System (EMS) 249
Environmentally Conscious Hospitality Operations (ECHO) 214

German Technical Cooperation (GTZ) 181
Global Reporting Initiative (GRI) 44
Global tourism 209

India Tourism Development Corporation (ITDC) 30
Informal Communication (IC)158
Internal Management (IM) 44

Leave Travel Concession (LTC) 33
Limits of Acceptable Change (LAC) 143

Managing rapid tourism growth 1
Manavgat Chamber of Commerce (MATSO) 179
Multi-Stakeholder Working Group (MSWG) 45

National tourism offices 2
Non Governmental Organizations (NGOs) 45, 161

Participatory Rural Appraisals (PRAs) 159
Photography 7
Physical Environment 125
Product management and development (PMD) 43

Recreation Opportunity Spectrum (ROS) 147

Recreation Opportunity Spectrum (ROS) 113
Rrecreation Tourism 50

Spiritual manifestation 27
Supply Chain Management (SCM) 44
Sustainable tourism 10

Taj Mahal 101
Tour operators 3
Tour Operators' Initiative (TOI) 44
Tourism industry 2
Tourism management organisation 82
Tourism markets 4

Unique Selling Proposition (USP) 33

Visitor Experience and Resource Protection Process 145

Wildlife monitoring programmes 6
World Tourism Organisation (WTO) 8
World Travel and Tourism Council (WTTC) 1
World Wide Fund (WWF) 248

EMERGING CONCEPTS OF EFFECTIVE TOURISM DEVELOPMENT

TRAVEL AND TOURISM MANAGEMENT

(In 4 Volumes)

EMERGING CONCEPTS OF EFFECTIVE TOURISM DEVELOPMENT

(Volume-3)

Editor

Prakash Talwar

ISHA

ISHA BOOKS

DELHI-110033

Emerging Concepts of Effective Tourism Development

Rs. 2700 (Set)

ISBN: 81-8205-330-7 (Set)
ISBN : 81-8205-333-1 (Vol. 3)

Published in 2006 in India by
Isha Books
D-43, Prithviraj Road,
Adarsh Nagar, Delhi-110033
e-mail : ishabooks@hotmail.com

Laser Typesetting at : Shiva Infosystem, Delhi
Printed at : Mehra Offset Press, Delhi

Preface

Tourism has long been considered as a potential strategy for economic advancement of both developed and developing countries. However, the growth of tourism industry is often affected by a variety of issues. A number of historical, political, social and economic factors are responsible for the varying levels of success and failure of countries in tapping their tourism potential. An appreciation of these factors is essential for formulating effective tourism policies, which could contribute to the sustainable development of tourism.

This book is designed to develop a critical understanding of various issues in tourism, which will lead to a more realistic approach to tourism policy making and development, an important competency for the future tourism development professionals. It gives emphasis to identifying and analysing the historical and emerging issues of development and how they influence tourism policy options. The roles of government, private sector, and international organisations are considered and the dynamics of formulating appropriate tourism policies and implementation strategies are also analysed.

Editor

Contents

	Preface	*v*
1.	Growth of Tourism in Developing Countries	1
2.	National Tourism Policy Initiatives	21
3.	National Civil Aviation Policy	60
4.	Integrated Tourism Planning	86
5.	Development of Tourism Infrastructure	100
6.	Energy for Tourism Development	124
7.	Tourism and Economic Development	170
8.	Employment in Tourism Sector	193
9.	Tourism and Sustainable Development	217
10.	Initiatives for Sustainable Tourism	237
	Bibliography	273
	Index	275

1

Growth of Tourism in Developing Countries

Tourism is a potential source of growth and development in poor countries. It is a major world industry. It is growing faster in the developing world than elsewhere. Tourism makes a substantial contribution to their GDP and is a higher share of exports there than in OECD countries. Many of the countries in which tourism is important are among the poorest and least developed in the world.

Tourism data are collected and analysed by organisations such as the World Tourism Organisation (WTO/OMT) and the World Travel and Tourism Council (WTTC), while crosssectoral data on trade flows are collected by the United Nations Conference on Trade and Development (UNCTAD) and Balance of Payments data are produced by the International Monetary Fund (IMF). The most limited definition of tourist services is that of the World Trade Organization (WTO), which includes only hotels and restaurants, travel agencies and guides. This definition, based on producing sectors, is designed to cover services provided internationally which may be regulated (and therefore which need to come under the General Agreement on Trade in Services - GATS) and which are not included in other categories.

While these are a major component of tourism, and for some purposes the question of what is regulated internationally will be important, the WTO definition clearly excludes a great many activities which are commonly purchased or used by 'tourists' and includes some (restaurant meals or hotel conference facilities for non-visitors, for example) which are not. An alternative approach is to measure the activities of particular types of people. This is the basis of the WTO/OMT definition, of spending by people away from their homes. It corresponds to the normal balance of payments definition, of spending by tourists, and to what is measured by most national surveys of tourists. National sources give more detailed data according to their different specialisations.

For some purposes, other types of data (regional data, information about particular activities or data from types of supplier) can supplement these. The international and macro-economic data allow us to compare countries and to compare tourism to other exports or other sectors. The more specific data help us to understand the details of its impact. The international tourism data are built up from information on movements of people and some country data on their spending. International balance of payments data, although some use the same surveys, are based on what is spent, not who spends it.

Since data on services tend to be less accurate than those on trade in goods, tourism and other services data in balance of payments information are often less carefully estimated and checked than in those sources that are dedicated to tourism. Balance of payments data also, of course, exclude data on domestic tourists, an increasingly important part of the sector in many developing countries. The World Tourism Organisation defines tourism as 'the activities of persons travelling to and staying in places outside their usual environment for not more than one consecutive year for leisure, business and other purposes'.

This broad definition of tourism is then broken down into six categories according to the purpose of the trip:

1. Leisure, recreation and holidays
2. Visiting friends and relatives
3. Business and professional
4. Health treatment
5. Religion/pilgrimages
6. Other

Tourists can also be divided into international tourists and domestic tourists and into overnight tourists and same-day visitors. Official statistics tend to focus on 'international visitors'. Each classification may be useful for looking at the effects of tourism or at expectations for how it will grow. Business travel, for example, will respond to some factors which are different from those driving leisure travel. Within the conventional understanding of tourism, as leisure trips of days or weeks, there are a range of possible activities, with potentially different impacts on the country by creating different demands on it.

Other distinctions possible are between 'high quality' (in the sense of high spending tourists) and low or between 'high impact' (in either the sense of integrated into the non-tourism activities of the country or in a specifically poverty or environmental sense) and low. Much of the basic infrastructure of all these (accommodation, food, and travel) are the same and therefore a high proportion of the effects, are constant, but not all. If we are studying 'spending or activity by tourists', not just 'production in the hotel and other tourism sectors', we need to know absolute numbers of tourists, not just estimates of spending, partly because for many supplier industries information on numbers will be the only firm information on which to base estimates of tourism's impact, but also because concern about the environmental and other non-economic impact is often based on the quantity of tourists, not the value of services.

We also need to know from which countries they come, because surveys show that different nationalities use different services with different impacts. The WTO/OMT has done a great deal of work on the refinement of the technical standards used to collect and report the data. However, not all countries are members of the WTO/OMT and the reliability of the data varies from country to country. The most basic statistic is international arrivals. But some countries do not report international arrivals figures and may have no effective mechanism in place for collecting them. Where the figures do exist, they have a number of limitations in assessing the potential significance of tourism for pro-poor growth:

— By definition these do not reflect the strength and significance of domestic tourism.

— National data have limited utility in assessing the importance of tourism in different localities within a country. At the local level there is no standard mechanism available for the collection of data that can inform decision making - hotel occupancy figures are sometimes used as a proxy indicator but are commercially sensitive, time-consuming to collect and under reporting can have tax advantages for accommodation owners.

— Visitor arrival figures focus on volume rather than value. It is the amount of time each tourist spends in any location and the amount of money he or she spends on accommodation, transport and other goods and services as well as the overall volume of tourists that determines the economic impact that will be felt. Even where figures on average daily spend and in-country tourism expenditure are calculated however, they do not generally provide any information about the potential for pro-poor tourism unless this is specifically analysed (e.g. by focusing on expenditure on goods that are, or could be, produced locally).

— Figures on visitor numbers often say little about the potential of the industry for pro-poor development. In West Humla, Nepal, for example very small numbers of tourists have a significant impact on local livelihoods.

— The form of tourism and the extent of access to tourists by local people as well as the volume of tourists define opportunities for pro-poor tourism. If tourists arrive in a destination or at an attraction in coaches in the evening, drive straight to the hotel and eat dinner without venturing out, and in the morning pack and depart by coach to visit a cultural monument before driving on to their next overnight stop, there are very few opportunities for poor producers to sell to tourists - what ever volumes they arrive in.

Beyond visitor arrival statistics, a Tourism Satellite Accounting (TSA) system has been developed by the World Tourism Organization and the World Travel and Tourism Council to estimate the economic value of tourism at the national level. Satellite accounts involve the 'rearrangement of existing information found in the national accounts' in order to estimate the significance of sectors such as tourism that are not accounted for separately. Including the sectors from which tourists or their suppliers buy inputs is logical in examining the nature and tourism.

But it is not legitimate then to use the data to compare the size of tourism to other sectors, because all sectors buy from others, and therefore aggregating sectoral accounts is double- (or multiple) counting. And there are limitations of this system in determining the potential of tourism for pro-poor growth. Aside from the fact that the development and reliability of satellite accounts is heavily reliant upon the quality of the data available, as with visitor arrivals statistics the analysis is generally carried out at the national level and again is not disaggregated at the destination level. Apart from the WTTC approach, other methods for assessing the impacts of tourism tend to be specific to sites, disciplines and researchers.

To fully understand the economic impacts of tourism - on poor people, on the local economy, on the national economy, on national poverty levels -would require a considerable amount of data and a strong methodology. For example, while most effects of an increase in tourism revenue lead, eventually, to an increase in national income, the direct consequences for the distribution of this among households (and within households) are not necessarily the most favourable for reducing poverty. Poverty may decrease for some and even increase for others. An increase in tourism provides a direct increase in income to those who supply the hotels, transport, and other services, and also to the host country through tax revenues and perhaps some service charges.

It then provides indirect increases in income to others through the spending of the direct income. How these changes are distributed will determine the direct impact of tourism on poverty, thus distribution needs to be assessed. A major potential impact comes from how policy makers react to the increases in income: if they have a pro-poor orientation, they can both redistribute the income (through taxes and public spending) and influence its original allocation (e.g. by regulating the types of tourism).

If a high share of the increased income is easily available to the government in taxes or easily taxable sectors, then this will increase its ability to act. Important impacts may occur through physical changes, such as development of infrastructure or use of natural resources, rather than through monetary flows. Therefore data on total tourism impact, information on where this comes from, and consideration of different types of impact, are important.

Advantages and Disadvantages of Tourism

Tourism is not a panacea for economic development. In any context decisions about whether or not tourism - domestic or international - presents viable opportunities for local economic development need to be made locally in the context of the other opportunities which exist for propoor development. As with other industrial sectors, economic growth as a result of tourism development does not necessarily result in poverty reduction. However, tourism does have some advantages over other sectors for delivering pro-poor growth:

- Tourism delivers consumers to the product rather than the other way round. This opens up huge opportunities for local access to markets for other goods and services. Development strategies can enhance potential links to local enterprises and poor producers.
- Tourism does not face tariff barriers, although taxes on air travel can have a similar effect.
- Tourism has considerable potential for linkage with other economic sectors - particularly agriculture and fisheries. Realising these linkages will increase the proportion of tourism revenue retained in the host country.
- There is a possibility of other types of linkages, for example demand for tourism may add sufficiently to another sector's demand for the combination to provide a basis for introducing local provision of goods or services, e.g. transport.

— It may create initial demand for a good or service that can then itself become a growth sector. In furniture, both Jamaica and Kenya provide examples where furniture firms whose first major market was hotels have developed to provide other consumers.

— Tourism provides opportunities for off-farm diversification. Tourists are often attracted to remote areas with few other development options because of their high cultural, wildlife and landscape values.

— Tourism provides relatively labour-intensive opportunities. It is more intensive than manufacturing and non-agricultural production, although less labour-intensive than agriculture. Its relation to the economy as a whole therefore depends on the relative weights of agriculture and manufacturing: this suggests that it is more likely to be among the most labour intensive sectors of the economy in more developed countries.

— Tourism employs a relatively high proportion of women and can contribute to gender equality. This is, however, less true in developing countries where there is higher male unemployment than in developed countries.

— Tourism can provide poor countries with a significant export opportunity where few other industries are viable. The large number of countries for which tourism receipts are important is evidence that it is a much less demanding sector in terms of initial conditions than many other commodities available to developing countries. In particular it is more widespread than most agricultural goods, which are its superior in labour intensity. It appears to be more like manufactures, where comparative advantage can be created through a combination of identifying a possible product and creating a specialised demand.

— Tourism products can be built on natural resources and culture, which are assets that some of the poor have.

— The infrastructure associated with tourism development (roads, electricity, communications, piped water) can provide essential services for rural communities which would otherwise be excluded from general infrastructure provision.

— It appears to have relatively few market distortions (either as barriers to entry or trade policy rents). It is particularly sensitive to marketing skills, and also to public sector action (or inaction).

— It has a high income elasticity, and therefore offers a relatively rapidly growing market. Tourism may be expected to perform 'better' than traditional commodities, but not necessarily better than newer exports such as manufactured products.

— It can take different forms, using different inputs, and is therefore available to a wide range of countries (and regions within a country).

At the same time, tourism operates in a market economy and it is subject to international market forces. New destinations emerge and others decline because they are undercut on price or become unfashionable. Countries dependent upon undifferentiated products like the traditional beach, sun, sand and sea holiday are particularly vulnerable. It is relatively easy for tour operators to respond to new opportunities and to switch operations when new destinations come in at a more competitive price.

Political instability and security concerns (both domestic and international) also have an impact on tourism. Countries with significant domestic and regional tourism industries tend to suffer less because these are not affected by declining numbers of air travellers in the face of terrorism fears but internal security issues can also pose a threat. Experience suggests that tourism numbers rapidly recover from terrorism and other events, although not uniformly so. Seasonality is also a notable feature of the tourism industry. Whether tourism is seasonal and whether the seasonality is compatible with agricultural work in particular are likely to affect its pro-poor potential.

Risk is reduced if countries (as well as individual households) are not overly dependent on any one economic sector and in the case of tourism, which is vulnerable to changes in consumer preferences, undercutting from new competitors and recession in originating markets, on any one market. The constraints described above are not unique to tourism but affect many other industries. There are also myths surrounding tourism and the view that tourism is not a worthwhile or 'serious' local economic development strategy is widely held.

To a large extent this view is a result of a failure to recognise the heterogeneity of the industry, but there is also a view that services, and tourism in particular, are not 'serious' development drivers, like agriculture and manufacturing. It is therefore often neglected and subject to policies and priorities designed for other sectors. It is rarely singled out as strategically important, because of either its potential effects as a pole of development for other industries, or its poverty effects. Therefore, when it comes into potential conflict with the interests of industries that are regarded as national priorities it is tourism whose interests come second. But this 'neglect' is in the context of a much greater acceptance that government has a direct interest in the outcome than would be true for most other predominantly private industries.

Most countries have a tourism ministry, even if it is 'tourism and...', not just tourism; most other sectors do not. This puts tourism in an odd, intermediate position; the government has an interest, but no clear perception of what that interest should be. In contrast to the view that linkages are an important advantage, there is a widely held view that tourism's effects are dissipated by 'leakages'.

Unusually high levels of leakage are often cited as one of the major disadvantages of tourism as an economic development sector - for example UNEP (undated) notes levels as high as 70 per cent in Thailand and 80 per cent in the Caribbean. It is clear, however, that the amount of leakage will depend greatly on the form of tourism and the nature of the economy and no standard figure can sensibly be applied across the globe. In small countries and islands (for example Mauritius), a share of spending goes on imports, but that is equally true of other industries in small countries and islands. In larger and more developed countries (for example South Africa and Jamaica), the shares are much smaller. The most important point about 'leakage' is that it can be used to identify opportunities to create economic linkages within the host country - some of which could have the potential to benefit poor producers.

Other criticisms of tourism and the answers include:

— Foreign private interests drive tourism, so it is difficult to maximise local economic benefit: There is no evidence that levels of foreign ownership are higher than for comparable sectors. It is clear that many small enterprises and individual traders sustain themselves around hotels and other tourism facilities and that these SMMEs are not foreign owned. There is often confusion about levels of foreign ownership; local ownership is often masked by franchise agreements and management contracts.

— Tourism can impose substantial non-economic costs on the poor through loss of access to resources (particularly beaches), displacement from agricultural land and social and cultural disruption and exploitation: The losses can be substantial for the poor and minimising them is an important PPT approach. However, many forms of development bring with them disadvantages of this kind.

— Tourism is vulnerable to changes in economic conditions in the originating markets, which cause major swings in the level of tourism in the destinations, and international visitor arrivals are also vulnerable to civil unrest, crime, political instability and natural disaster in the destination: It is not clear that the volatility of export markets for tourism is significantly greater than for other commodities. The destination has some control over civil unrest, crime and political instability.

Five developing countries were in the list of twenty major tourist destinations according to international visitor arrivals statistics in 2000. The volume of arrivals to the top destination in the developing world - China - was only just over 40% of the volume to the world's leading tourism destination - France. That developing countries feature within the list of the top 20 destinations is a relatively recent phenomenon. Only 15 years earlier China, for example, received only 1.3 million arrivals due to its restrictive travel policy. More established destinations like Mexico have seen very similar growth rates when compared to France, i.e. a doubling of arrivals between 1985 and 2000.

Compared to other developing country exports, this gives them exceptional prominence. While developing countries receive 42% of tourism spending they only supply 25% of traditional primary commodities. Developing countries have a surplus on tourism trade (they are net exporters). For purposes of comparison, Table 2 provides details on the 20 largest developing country destinations and illustrates the significantly lower volumes of international tourists that most of these countries receive compared to the totals in Table 1.

Table 1: Top 20 destinations in terms of international arrivals in 2000

Position	Country	Arrivals (millions)
1	France	75.5
2	United States	50.9
3	Spain	47.9
4	Italy	41.2
5	China	31.2
6	United Kingdom	25.2
7	Russian Federation	21.2
8	Mexico	20.6
9	Canada	29.7
10	Germany	19.0
11	Austria	18.0
12	Poland	17.4
13	Hungary	15.6
14	Hong Kong (China)	13.1
14	Greece	13.1
16	Portugal	12.0
17	Switzerland	11.4
18	Malaysia	10.2
19	Netherlands	10.2
20	Turkey	9.6
20	Thailand	9.6

Only China, Mexico and Malaysia attracted over 10 million arrivals in 2000 reaching levels seen in some of the newer European destinations such as Poland, Hungary and the Czech Republic. South Africa and Tunisia, which are relatively small destinations in a global context, are major players in an African context.

Table 2: Significant developing country destinations in terms of international arrivals in 2000

	Country	Arrivals (millions)
1	China	31.2
2	Mexico	20.6
3	Malaysia	10.2
4	Turkey	9.6
5	Thailand	9.6
6	South Africa	6.1
7	Croatia	5.8
8	Brazil	5.3
9	Egypt	5.1
10	Indonesia	5.0
11	Tunisia	5.1
12	Morocco	4.1
13	Argentina	3.0
14	Dominican Republic	3.0
15	India	2.6
16	Philippines	2.2
17	Vietnam	2.1
18	Bahrain	2.0
19	Uruguay	2.0
20	Zimbabwe	1.9

Economic Significance

It is very difficult to measure the scale of tourism activity within an economy and hence its contribution to GDP. This is because tourism is not traditionally measured in national accounts. To address this problem, WTTC have developed 'satellite accounts'. However, construction of satellite accounts requires detailed data - which are unlikely to be robust in poor countries. The accounts therefore are useful for providing indicative figures, for example to compare across different countries or to highlight countries with major tourism sectors. But to gain further information on the significance of tourism activity within any one country, local data and local knowledge, for example discussions with the Ministries of Finance, Tourism, and Statistics are necessary.

In terms of vulnerability to a sectoral shock, whether domestic (e.g. a hurricane) or international (e.g. security), clearly it is. But tourism has a high income elasticity and it is a many-sided product. These facts mean that it less vulnerable to the poor demand prospects which make commodity dependence so undesirable. For small countries Brau et. al. have shown that tourism dependence leads to higher growth, in sharp contrast to commodity dependence. While the effects will be smaller for larger developing countries, it is likely to be in the same direction.

Growth of Tourism

That tourism is a growing sector is thus important, and within this developing countries are increasing their share. Tourism's growth rates have been similar, in size and changes over time, to those of manufactured trade. It grew very rapidly in the 1950s and 1960s, but slowed in the 1970s to 6%, and the 1980s to 5% and the 1990s to 4%. These numbers are greater than the growth of world output, so that the share is rising, but no longer spectacularly so. Given its composition, as partly business, partly leisure, it is not surprising that it should keep pace with other types of spending, with an implied elasticity to income greater than 1, but probably now less than 2. Between 1990 and 2000 the growth of international travel to developing countries was 94.4%, compared to 29.3% to OECD countries and 38.4% for EU countries.

Table 3 shows the developing countries with the highest growth in international tourist arrivals between 1990 and 2000.

Table 3: The 20 fastest growing developing country destinations in terms of visitor arrivals between 1990 and 2000

Position	Country	Arrivals in 1990 (in '000)	Arrivals in 2000 (in '000)	Growth 1990-2000 (in %)
1	Cambodia	17	466	2641.18
2	Lao PDR	14	300	2042.86
3	Iran	154	1700	1003.90
4	Myanmar	21	208	890.48
5	Vietnam	250	2140	756.00
6	Cape Verde	24	143	495.83
7	South Africa	1029	6001	483.19
8	Cuba	327	1700	419.88
9	Chad	9	44	388.89
10	Brazil	1091	5313	386.98
11	Nicaragua	106	486	358.49
12	Nigeria	190	813	327.89
13	Micronesia Fed.	8	33	312.50
14	El Salvador	194	795	309.79
15	Zambia	141	574	307.09
16	Bhutan	2	7	250.00
17	Oman	149	502	236.91
18	Tanzania	153	501	227.45
19	Peru	317	1027	223.97
20	Zimbabwe	605	1868	208.76

The highest growth figures were shown in South East Asia although in many cases these can be explained by the very low starting points. Cambodia, Lao and Myanmar, in particular, received few tourists in 1990 and although numbers are still not high in 2000 the rate of growth appears spectacular. This table also highlights strong tourism growth in African countries. These figures are rather more significant that those for South East Asia given a higher starting point -particularly for South Africa. Their growth started later than that of other countries. In 1980, tourism was only 2% of Africa's exports (less than half the world average).

By 1995, it had caught up, and by 1998 gone ahead (both were about 7%). Africa's share in the total volume remains low, but it doubled from 1.5% in 1970s to 3% in the late 1980s, and is now 4%. The question is whether it can continue to increase its share of output and trade or whether its growth will also slow to the plateau of about 4% found in the rest of the world. In Mauritius, tourism is now a slowly growing sector, as labour is no longer abundant and cheap, and it is being devolved to neighbouring countries rather than diversified and developed within Mauritius itself.

A recent meeting of the Least Developed Countries, convened by UNCTAD and the WTO/OMT noted that although these 49 countries account for less than one per cent of total international arrivals, visitor numbers have doubled in the last decade from 2.4 million in 1988 to 5.1 million in 1998. In seven LDCs (Cambodia, Mali, Lao, Myanmar, Samoa, Uganda and Tanzania) growth was particularly strong with an increase from 0.4 million international arrivals in 1992 to 1.2 million in 1998. The international forecasts for tourism appear to be simple projections based on past performance, and can be questioned as too high or too low by taking different forms of naïve projecting.

The generally stable nature of tourism demand, however, suggests that the variations in different projections might not be as large or as sensitive to assumptions as in projections for other commodities; the probable growth rates are between 3% and 6%. The most worrying trends for developing countries could be in the long term if tourism ceases to be a 'luxury' good, with a high income elasticity, and becomes either a commodity good, with a unit elasticity, or an inferior, out of fashion, item, or if new forms of 'tourism' such as activity parks move the activity back to developed (even home) countries.

Developing countries (and particularly the Least Developed Countries or LDCs) also showed higher growth rates in terms of receipts per international arrival between 1990 and 2000 than the developed world. LDCs secured an increase of 45% while developing countries saw a growth rate of nearly 20% in international receipts. This compares with 18% for OECD countries and 7.8% for the EU countries.

Tourism in the 'Poorest' Countries

There are a number of different ways of defining 'poor' countries. Here we focus on:

1. Those countries which contain the greatest numbers of the 1.2 billion people who live on less than $1/day;
2. those with the highest proportion of their population living on less that $1/day;
3. those defined by the United Nations as the 'Least Developed Countries' (LDCs).

The first criterion identifies large countries with large numbers of poor people such as India and China, whereas the second highlights smaller countries which may have a larger proportion or poor people, but a smaller absolute number, such as Mali and Burkina Faso. Average GDP or GNI per capita is a useful way for comparing the overall economic performance of countries but can fail to identify countries with high levels of wealth inequality, where many are poor despite high 'average' income.

Tourism is significant for the vast majority of the 50 countries with the highest numbers of people living below the poverty line of US$ 1 per day:

— Of the 47 of the poorest 50 countries for which there is data, tourism is significant in all but two: in 45 it contributes over 2% of GDP, or 5% of exports, or both.

— More strikingly still, in 41 of the 50 poorest countries (out of the 47 for which there is data), tourism contributes over 5% of GDP and/or over 10% of exports.

Of the top twelve poorest countries, homes to 1.01 billion people living below the poverty line, tourism is significant in all of them (over 2% of GDP and/or 5% of exports). It is strikingly significant, at over 5% of GDP and 10% of exports in at least 11 of them.

With respect to the Least Developed Countries, WTO/OMT and UNCTAD (2001) note that 'tourism can make a substantial contribution to ... development ... and in combating poverty'. In 1998, tourism was a leading export sector for 31 LDC countries and it is the first source of export earnings in seven. Tourism receipts to LDCs more than doubled between 1992 and 1998, from $1 billion to $2.2 billion, with five countries: Cambodia, The Maldives, Nepal, Tanzania and Uganda capturing 51 per cent of the total. Apart from the petroleum exporting countries (Angola, Yemen and Equatorial Guinea) tourism is a primary source of foreign exchange earnings for all others.

Encontre argues that steady tourism development is likely to have a measurable socio-economic impact and can drive a Least Developed Country near the threshold of 'graduation' (moving out of LDC status). He argues that the five countries to graduate from LDC in recent years (Botswana, Cape Verde, Maldives, Samoa and Vanuatu) show a close association between tourism development and 'the socio-economic progress that explains the context of proximity to, or realization of graduation'. Four of these LDCs (except Botswana) were in 1999 among the top 20 tourism destinations in the developing world with high "Tourism Intensity Rates" and three were among the destinations with the highest tourism contribution to GDP or to export earnings.

Small countries (under 1 million population) dependent on tourism (tourism receipts more than 10% of GDP) grew significantly better than other small countries: for the others, smallness was associated with slower than average growth, while the tourism countries grew faster than the average. Thus the reason small countries are observed to grow faster than larger developing countries appears to be their dependence on tourism, a sharp contrast with the results for dependence on primary commodities. They offer, however, both an 'optimistic' and a 'pessimistic' explanation: the pessimistic corresponds to what we have observed in Mauritius, that tourism countries initially grow fast because they are using their supplies of labour. This cannot last indefinitely. The optimistic corresponds to what has been argued here about the income elasticity for tourism: if demand for tourism increases sufficiently faster than the average growth in demand to compensate for any decline in productivity, it can still contribute to growth.

2

National Tourism Policy Initiatives

Today tourism is the major instrument of socio-economic development. For developing countries it offers a reliable route to job creation in a faster and less expensive way, advancement of deprived sections of society, especially the youth and women, and in fact, a sure way of removing poverty. For a country of India's continental size, a billion strong population, diversity of languages, culture, cuisine and heritage, tourism has assumed a special role in national integration and conservation of its natural and man-made assets of fauna, flora, arts, crafts, architecture, customs and traditions.

According to figures released by the World Tourism Organisation (WTO), a United Nations affiliate, the number of tourists who crossed international frontiers during 2002 exceeded 715 million. Of them only 2.4 million came to India while some 80 million went to France, the world's number one destination, followed by more than 50 million each to the US and Spain. China with its 37 million arrivals now occupies the fifth place among the top destinations. Even smaller countries like Malaysia and Thailand have crossed the 10 million mark in the visitor count.

India's 0.38 per cent share of the world market has remained stagnant for decades. It needs, however, to be pointed out that in spite of the miniscule market share there are a few significant factors of the Indian scene. First, even with being at the bottom of the world tourism ladder, the sector is earning for the country the equivalent of Rs. 13,000 crore in foreign exchange with only six or seven per cent outgo. Secondly, tourism is the third largest earner of foreign exchange after handicrafts and gems and jewellery in gross terms and the second largest after handicrafts in net terms. Thirdly, the average stay of a tourist in India is estimated at 30 days, among the highest in the world.

The federal nature of our Constitution and segments constituting tourism spilling into both the Central and State Lists (and not finding a place in the Concurrent List either) also came in the way of a coordinated effort: aviation and railways are a central subject while road transport comes within the purview of the States as do hotels. Monuments are a national responsibility but law and order in their environs is cared for by the States. The Planning Commission also could not help tourism's growth. Plan after plan it persisted in distinguishing between international and domestic the tourism, reserving the international part to the Centre and the domestic for the States. This, too, came in the way of the evolution of a national approach to tourism as a whole.

While there has been a separate Tourism Ministry in place since 1967 and a few initiatives like the setting up of the India Tourism Development Corporation (ITDC) as a catalyst for infrastructural growth and promotional activities and opening up of beach and wildlife destinations, poor funding and lack of political will never gave a push to the sector. Plan allocations to tourism never crossed even one-fifth of one per cent of the total outlay. The States were content with replicating their own tourism development corporations and spending even less than the Centre on infrastructure.

Lack of unity in the industry, a malaise that continues till today, came in the way of a lobby for tourism. Until recently the media too did not include it in its own priorities. Commendable recommendations made by committees set up by the Government itself remained unimplemented. It was in this era of apathy towards tourism that success stories started wafting in from our neighbourhood. China, which was on par with India in 1978 when it decided to globalise its economy (both were hosting 750,000 tourists annually) had by mid-90s leap-frogged to 23 million arrivals; tiny Singapore was welcoming 5 million visitors and Indonesia, Thailand and Malaysia had crossed the 7 million mark.

Interestingly, the first signs of awakening to tourism's potential came in the run up to the 1996 general elections when the undaunted travel industry leaders were able to persuade the Bharatiya Janata Party (BJP) to include a reference to the sector in its election manifesto, a lead later followed by other parties. This, then, was the beginning of a process which has culminated in the Tenth Five Year Plan with a huge chapter on tourism, giving the sector a place on the national agenda, a five times higher allocation than the Ninth Plan and a target of raising India's market share to at least 0.62 per cent by the end of 2007.

Translated into arrivals if the target is achieved, it would mean 5.6 million overseas visitors, more than twice as much as the current count but still a long way behind our neighbours and other successful destinations. Interestingly, it is the Planning Commission itself, which as a part of the Government, took the first step towards salvaging tourism from the painfully slow growth it had been left to. In the mid-term appraisal it conceded that tourism had not been given its due. The Commission's diagnosis of what ailed Indian tourism is pretty close to what experts, trade bodies and even officially appointed committees have said all along. Major causes cited for the low performance are lack of professionalism, unhygienic conditions, poor infrastructure, lack of easily accessible information, lack of safety, poor visitor experience, restrictive air transport policy, inadequate facilitation services, multiplicity of taxes and the low priority accorded to tourism.

Around the same time, the World Travel and Tourism Council (WTTC), a global think tank of industry leaders, in a study presented to the Government gave a new dimension to what it called the tourism imperative. The WTTC has found that India has one of the fastest growing demands for tourism services in the world. One of the major reasons for this is a surge in domestic tourism, which has grown from 64 million tourists to 176 million in the last decade. The latest figure is 234 million.

But the extent of the demand by itself does not mean much, the study points out. This demand has to be matched by adequate supply in terms of infrastructure, accommodation and facilities. Thus, it warns that lack of supply will create grave distortions, overcrowding of the existing facilities and increased visitor exports out of India. Four million Indians go abroad against 2.4 million foreigners that come in.

The Tenth Plan focus on tourism has an interesting story behind it. In a rare appearance for a former Finance Minister, Shri Jaswant Singh spoke to a CII-organised seminar on tourism and candidly conceded that the elitist tag given to the sector in the days of socialist fervour had prevented its growth. He promised that this distortion would be corrected in the Tenth Plan in a separate chapter. So right at the outset the chapter points out that the Tenth Plan approach towards tourism "signifies a distinct shift from the earlier plans" by recognising the "vast employment generating potential of tourism and the role it can play in furthering the socio-economic objectives of the Plan".

Like the earlier appraisal, it lists five main barriers to the growth of tourism but perhaps in a more explicit way - absence of consensus on the role of tourism, lack of priority on account of unappreciated potential, relatively low levels of investment, lack of interest on the part of the States, the primary player and an unprofessional ad hoc approach. Hence, the Tenth Plan allocation of Rs. 2,900 crore is 0.72 per cent of the total outlay compared to 0.16 per cent average of the earlier Plans. Apart from raising India's market share the Tenth Plan also hopes to create 3.6 million jobs a year through tourism. The 2003-04 Budget too is an important landmark.

Abolition of the hotel expenditure tax is a major relief to the hospitality sector as is the extension of sections 72A and 10 (23G) of the Income Tax Act to hotels. But what is going to make a real difference is the outlay of an additional Rs. 60,000 crore for such infrastructure which is the lifeline of tourism - roads, railways, airports and seaports. The Golden Quadrilateral linking the four metros and the East-West and North-South corridors will considerably improve connectivity as will privatisation of airports now under process. The development of Mumbai and Kochi ports has special significance because of the potential they will offer of promoting cruise tours to and from India.

Kochi already has plans to build a modern passenger terminal along with a golf course and shopping malls on the marina. The allocation in the Budget for two international standard convention centres in public-private sector partnership is yet another initiative to promote the lucrative conference and exhibition business. Since the Government will take care of the viability of the convention centres, it will spur the industry to put its weight behind the projects. Economic reforms have already eased considerably two other hurdles in the way of tourism - telecom and automobiles. Even quality coaches have begun to be made in the country.

The only stumbling block that would need a national effort is land for hotel and other tourism projects. Archaic laws on land use and building bye-laws and the clearances regime have made hotel building a hazardous adventure. This is an issue which has to be addressed at the central, state, civic and down to the panchayat levels. The sooner an effort is made the better. Even to be able to host 5 million foreign tourists we need to double the present number of rooms estimated at a little over 80,000. Going by the average growth of rooms - about 3,500 annually - it may take us decades to achieve that target. Incidentally, China has 900,000 rooms.

. There have been suggestions to restructure the tourism set up in a way that it will be able to carry with it other segments like aviation, railways, road transport, finance and even home and external affairs. The WTTC has been urging that a cabinet committee on tourism under the Prime Minister would be a good idea. Another view is that the present arrangement of group of ministers (GoM) is more practical. Whichever route is preferred, this will only smoothen matters at the national level. About coordination with the States the National Tourism Policy suggests that this be achieved by making tourism a concurrent subject. In fact, a majority of the States have already approved the idea though some of the larger States have reservations. But a constitutional amendment of this kind is bound to take a long time.

The Tenth Plan has also addressed this subject. It speaks of the imperative of the States, which virtually control the tourism product, adopting a focused, highly professional and result-oriented approach as well as the need for a conducive environment for private sector investment. "It is important to realise", it says, "that the travel and tourism industry is adversely affected by the lack of synergy in inter-sectoral policies". It adds that "a concerted effort will be made through the National

Development Council to arrive at a consensus on the role of tourism in the development agenda of the nation".

Fortuitously, there are stirrings in the States too, albeit only in two or three so far. Kerala is the most shining example where the State is now effectively marketing itself globally as "God's Own Country". Large sums are being spent on infrastructure and promotions and, more importantly, there is a growing public-private sector partnership as exemplified in the two successful international travel marts that have been held in Kochi. Andhra Pradesh is the other state where its former Chief Minister, Shri Chandrababu Naidu, had set an example not only of priority for tourism but also being the highest in Government spending and lowest in taxes.

Rajasthan is now concerned about losing its premier position which it had acquired for being the third point of the Golden Triangle formed by Jaipur with Agra and Delhi. It is setting in motion corrective measures. Goa has already emerged as India's beach holidays destination, equally popular with domestic travellers. It augurs well for tourism that it has at its helm a man like Shri Jagmohan, whose commitment to good governance is well known. The clean-up of our great monuments like Ajanta and Ellora is an excellent beginning not only for preserving our rich heritage but also for enhancing visitor experience.

Five Year Plans and Promotion of Tourism

Tourism development in India has passed through many phases. At Government level the development of tourist facilities was taken up in a planned manner in 1956 coinciding with the Second Five Year Plan. The approach has evolved from isolated planning of single unit facilities in the Second and Third Five Year Plans. The Sixth Plan marked the beginning of a new era when tourism began to be considered a major instrument for social integration and economic development.

But it was only after the 80's that tourism activity gained momentum. The Government took several significant steps. A National Policy on tourism was announced in 1982. Later in 1988, the National Committee on Tourism formulated a comprehensive plan for achieving a sustainable growth in tourism. In July 1991, tourism was also declared as a priority sector for foreign investment.

In 1992, a National Action Plan was prepared and in 1996 the National Strategy for Promotion of Tourism was drafted. The other major development that took place were the setting up of the India Tourism Development Corporation in 1966 to promote India as a tourist destination and the Tourism Finance Corporation in 1989 to finance tourism projects. Altogether, 21 Government-run Hotel Management and Catering Technology Institutes and 14 Food Craft Institutes were also established for imparting specialised training in hoteliering and catering.

India is a country known for its lavish treatment to all visitors, no matter where they come from. Its visitor-friendly traditions, varied life styles and cultural heritage and colourful fairs and festivals held abiding attractions for the tourists. The other attractions include beautiful beaches, forests and wild life and landscapes for eco-tourism, snow, river and mountain peaks for adventure tourism, technological parks and science museums for science tourism; centres of pilgrimage for spiritual tourism; heritage trains and hotels for heritage tourism. Yoga, ayurveda and natural health resorts also attract tourists. The Indian handicrafts particularly, jewellery, carpets, leather goods, ivory and brass work are the main shopping items of foreign tourists. The estimates available through surveys indicate that nearly forty per cent of the tourist expenditure on shopping is spent on such items.

Domestic tourism is as old as the Indian society. According to available statistics, domestic tourism has grown substantially during the last one decade. It increased to 175 million in 1999 from just 83 million in 1991, thus registering a compound annual growth of 9.8 per cent. The growth of inbound tourism since Independence has been quite impressive. It was just around 17 thousand in 1951. From this level it rose to 2.48 million in 1999.

Economic Impacts

Tourism has emerged as an instrument of employment generation, poverty alleviation and sustainable human development. During 1998-99, employment generation through tourism was estimated at 14.79 million. Domestic tourist spending per year is around Rs. 24,000 crore and foreign exchange earnings from the tourism are estimated more than Rs.12,011 crore. Tourism receives have grown at a phenomenal rate of about 18 per cent since 1951. Thus Tourism has become the second largest net foreign exchange earner for the country.

In order to speed up the development of tourism in the country several thrust areas have been identified for accomplishment during the Ninth Five Year Plan. The important ones are development of infrastructure, products, trekking, winter sports, wildlife and beach resorts and streamlining of facilitation procedures at airports, human resource development and facilitating private sector participation in the growth of infrastructure.

The basic strategy during the 9th Plan is to establish effective coordination with all the relevant agencies to as to achieve synergy in the development of tourism. For the 9th Plan period (1997-2002), the Planning Commission has approved a Plan outlay of Rs. 793.75 crores for the Ministry of Tourism comprising Direct Budgetary Support of Rs. 485.75 crores and internal and external resources of Rs. 308.00 crores. Tourism development is a composite subject and does not necessarily mean the development of only the tourism facilities like hotels, restaurants, recreational activities etc.

In fact, creation of tourism infrastructure will be meaningful only if the areas has the minimum basic amenities and infrastructure like roads, water, electricity, sewerage and telecommunication facilities. This aspect has given importance in the Tourism 'Synergy' programme. The State Governments have been asked to prepare Master Plans for the development of tourism based on the same concept.

The organisations involved in the development of tourism in India are the Ministry of Tourism and Culture with its 21 field offices within the country and 18 abroad, Indian Institute of Tourism and Travel Management, National Council for Hotel Management and Catering Technology, India Tourism Development Corporation, Indian Institute of Skiing and Mountaineering and the National Institute of Water Sports for HRD development in the area of Tourism.

Accommodation Facilities

Accommodation of quality is basic infrastructure for the development of Tourism. The Ministry of Tourism approves hotels from the point of view of their suitability for international tourists. Various incentives and benefits are linked to such approvals. As on September, 1999 there were 1229 hotels with 68032 rooms and on the approved list of Ministry of Tourism. Break up of these hotels category wise is as below:

Star Category	No. of Hotels	No. of Rooms
5-Star Deluxe	55	12948

5-Star	50	6654
4-Star	79	6131
Heritage Hotels	62	1916
3-Star	316	15590
2-Star	324	11391
1-Star	146	5059
To be classified	197	8307

Boosting Tourism

Some of the recent initiatives taken by the Government to boost tourism include grant of export house status to the tourism sector and incentives for promoting private investment in the form of Income Tax exemptions, interest subsidy and reduced import duty. The hotel and tourism-related industry has been declared a high priority industry for foreign investment which entails automatic approval of direct investment up to 51 per cent of foreign equity and allowing 100 per cent non-resident Indian investment and simplifying rules regarding the grant of approval to travel agents, tour operators and tourist transport operators.

ITDC

In 1996 a public sector corporation was set up under the Ministry to pioneer the development tourism infrastructure specially hotels in the country. The present network of ITDC comprises 26 Ashok Group Hotels, 6 Joint Venture Hotels, 5 Restaurants, 11 Ashok Travel and Transport units, 29 Duty Free Shops at 6 Airports and a Down-Town Duty Free Shop in Delhi. The Government is actively considering disinvestment of ITDC to ensure private participation.

The major constraint in the expansion of international tourist traffic to India is non-availability of adequate infrastructure including adequate air seat capacity, accessibility to tourist destinations, accommodation and trained manpower in sufficient number. Much has been achieved by way of increasing air seat capacity, increasing trains and railway connectivity to important tourist destinations, four-laning of roads connecting important tourist centres and increasing availability of accommodation by adding heritage hotels to the hotel industry and encouraging paying guest accommodation. But much more remains to be done. Since tourism is a multi-dimensional activity, and basically a service industry, private sector and voluntary organisations become active partners in the endeavour to attain sustainable growth in tourism if India is to become a world player in the tourist industry

Impact of Tourism Policy

The impact assessment of the sectoral policies on the specified sector suffers from a serious methodological problem. Briefly, it may be argued that the development of a sector is not solely dependent on the factors within the sector: it is influenced by the general socio-economic environment, the political system and the overall policy framework. Thus the study integrates within itself the dynamic aspects of historical changes that are taking place at the macro-economic level. Similarly, Tourism Policy would not have evolved on its own without being influenced by the general tenor of macro-economic policy. Tourism policy thus has a socio-political grounding as much as it has a macro-economic colouring.

The 1980s witnessed the era of liberalisation initiated by the Congress Government at the Centre. The process of liberating the Indian economy from the shibboleths of 'license-permit Raj' culminated in the initiation of the structural adjustment programme in 1992. "Objectives, Thrusts and Macro-economic Dimensions of the Eighth Plan" endorsed by the National Development Council, clearly outlines the context within which the structural reforms were initiated: "The need to restructure our systems of economic management has become an imperative if India is to emerge as a vibrant and internationally competitive economy in the 90's.

Systems of control and regulation, developed for good reasons in the past have outlived their utility and some positively (sic) stand in the way of further progress. Such dysfunctional systems have to be overhauled in the light of emerging realities. "The process of structural adjustments has brought about far reaching changes in the Indian economy at a breath-taking pace. The impact of these changes over the tourism sector need to be studied in a dynamic context. Nevertheless, the above should not be taken as ignoring the fact that sectoral policy does have a direct and unambiguous impact over the concerned sector.

Tourism Policy, as a statement of intent by the Government, would form the reference point for action and criticism. Any initiative by Government in Tourism by way of legislation or direct investment is envisaged within the framework of Tourism Policy. The debates in Parliament had taken recourse to the received policy of the Union Government while making references to particular cases. The backdrop of a policy always serves as a guideline for further executive and legislative initiatives. It would be cynical to regard these policy statements as mere exercises in eloquence and additions to the already existing volumes of wishful thinking.

Furthermore, Policy statements by Government should be viewed in their evolutionary stance. It would be a negation of the democratic content of our political system to view a Policy statement as a static and rigid formulation, at a point in time, applicable for years to come. Thus, since 1982, various initiatives undertaken by the Government need to be perceived as additions or modifications to the received Policy. While it may be argued that these changes in the policy are only marginal and superficial from the viewpoint of equity and social justice, it would be an oversimplification to view the latest policy statement as nothing but the "nth" version of the Policy formulated in 1982.

Recognising the all-pervading inertia that looms large in matters governmental, one is often tempted to deny the scope for lobbying which makes possible the desired modifications in the policy corpus. In short, policy, as a body incorporating proactive intentions, is amenable to periodic reviews and possible modifications. The issues stressed in the preceding paragraphs provide the framework within which Tourism Policy needs to be considered. In brief, there is more to policy in tourism than is found in the Tourism Policy. Perhaps, the links within a macro-economic framework need no special mention.

The first ever Tourism Policy was announced by the Government of India in November 1982. It took ten long years for the Government to feel the need to come up with a possible improvement over this. Thus the National Action Plan for Tourism was announced in May 1992. Between these two policy statements, various legislative and executive measures were brought about. In particular, the report of the National Committee on Tourism, submitted in 1988 needs special mention. In addition, two five-year plans - the Seventh and the Eighth - provided the basic perspective framework for operational initiatives.

The Seventh Plan advocated a two-pronged thrust in the area of development of tourism, viz., to vigorously promote domestic tourism and to diversify overseas tourism in India. While laying stress on creation of beach resorts, conducting of conventions, conferences, winter sports and trekking, the overall intention was to diversify options available for foreign tourists. The Tourism Policy, 1982 was more an aggressive statement in marketing than a perspective plan for development. Its main thrust was aimed at presenting India to the foreigners as the ultimate holiday resort. With a view to reach this destination, the following measures were suggested by the Policy:

1. To take full advantage of the national heritage in arriving at a popular campaign for attracting tourists;
2. To promote tourist resorts and make India a destination of holiday resorts;
3. To grant the status of an export industry to tourism;
4. To adopt a selective approach to develop few tourist circuits; and,
5. To invite private sector participation into the sector.

The Planning Commission recognised tourism as an industry by June 1982. However, it took ten years to make most of the States to fall in line and accord the same status within their legislative framework. At the beginning of the Eighth Plan, 15 States and 3 Union Territories had declared tourism as an industry. Four States had declared hotels as an industry. The National Committee on Tourism was set up in July 1986 by the Planning Commission to prepare a perspective plan for the sector. Within the broad framework of the Seventh Plan, the Committee had to evolve a perspective plan for the coming years.

By September, 1987, the Central Government declared more concessions for the sector: these included tax exemption on foreign exchange earnings from tourism (a

50% reduction on rupee earnings and a 100% reduction on earnings in dollars), a drastic reduction in tariff on import of capital goods, and concessional finance at the rate of 1 to 5% per annum. The Tourism Development Finance Corporation was set up in 1987 with a corpus fund of Rs. 100 crores. Until then, the sector was financed on commercial lines by the Industrial Development Bank of India, Industrial Credit and Investment Corporation of India and other commercial banks.

The National Action Plan for Tourism, published in May 1992, and tabled in the Lok Sabha on 5 May 1992, charts 7 objectives as central concerns of the Ministry:

— socio-economic development of areas;

— increasing employment opportunities;

— developing domestic tourism for the budget category;

— preserving national heritage and environment;

— development of international tourism;

— diversification of the tourism product.,

— and, increase in India's share in world tourism (from the present 0.4% to 1% during next 5 years)

As per the Action Plan, foreign exchange earnings are estimated to increase from Rs.10,000 crores in 1992 to Rs.24,000 crores by 2000 AD. Simultaneously, the Plan aims at increasing employment in tourism to 28 million from the present 14 million. Hotel accommodation is to be increased from 44,400 rooms to 1,20,000 by 3 years. Other provisions in the Action Plan include a discontinuance of subsidies to star hotels, encouraging foreign investment in tourism and the setting up of a convention city for developing convention tourism.

The Action Plan envisages the development of Special Tourism Areas on lines of export processing zones. Special

Central assistance is to be provided for the States to improve the infrastructural facilities at pilgrimage places. It proposes to set up a National Culinary Institute, and projects a liberalised framework for recognition of travel agents and tour operators. The Eighth Plan document makes a special mention that the future expansion of tourism should be achieved mainly by private sector participation.

The thrust areas as enumerated in the Plan include development of selected tourist places, diversification from cultural related tourism to holiday and leisure tourism, development of trekking, winter sports, wildlife and beach resort tourism, exploring new source markets, restoration of national heritage projects, launching of national image building, providing inexpensive accommodation in different tourist centres, improving service efficiency in public sector corporations and streamlining of facilitation procedures at airports.

The Eighth Plan aims at luring the high spending tourists from Europe and USA. It also envisages a 'master plan' to integrate area plans with development of tourism. This is envisaged to ensure employment opportunities for the local population. In April 1993, the Government announced further measures aimed at export promotion. The existing Export Promotion of Capital Goods Scheme (EPCG) was extended to tourism and related services. Against the existing 35%, the tourism sector would now pay an excise duty of 15% only on capital goods import, subject to an export obligation of 4 times the cargo, insurance and freight (CIF) value of imports. With an obligation period of five years, this came as a boon to the hotel industry. The cost of construction had also come down by 20%.

In addition to the above policy pronouncements by the Union Government, our planners had envisaged the possibilities of developing specific regions on a zonal plank. Special area programmes like the Hill Area Development Programme and the Western Ghats Development Programme form part of the overall national plan. The Eighth Plan document stipulates that the strategy in such designated special areas is to devise suitable location-specific solutions, so as to reverse the process of degradation of natural resources and ensure sustainable development. This approach perhaps needs to be integrated into the project of special tourism areas, now being made popular by the Government.

The federal principles enshrined in the Indian Constitution require that the tourism sector be treated as a State subject. As such, the Department of Tourism (under the Ministry of Civil Aviation and Tourism at the Centre) undertakes certain promotional and developmental activities with a view to enhance the sectoral potential. The Department has certain regulatory functions to perform involving the hotel industry, travel agencies and tourist operators. Over the years, there has been considerable erosion of powers so far as State Governments are concerned. The sustained campaign for privatisation in all the policy documents has left limited space of operation for the States.

The public sector is increasingly being perceived as an agent of inertia than of change and hence the pressure for a hands-off policy. On the other hand, the Union Government has been usurping the powers of the State with some pretext or the other. Promotion schemes, designed at the Centre, are transferred for implementation at the State level. The special Central Assistance, for example, granted for the development of infrastructure at the pilgrim centres, carries with it a pre-defined scheme and mode of execution. Furthermore, there are occasions when the Centre forces the State Governments to extend certain subsidies and concessions to the sector.

The terms of such concessions would have been fixed by the Centre and the States would have no choice but to fall in line. For example, during the State tourism minister's conference in December 1991, the States were urged to freeze water and electricity rates for 10 years. They were also asked to exempt certain hotels from local and state taxes for 10 years. Seventeen circuits and destinations were identified under the National Action Plan for development through Central assistance and investment by the States and the private sector. The centres were identified by the Centre and the States were asked to do the needful. There were also times when the federal division of power resulted in operational contradictions.

For instance, by 1989, many foreign hotel chains like Hilton, Hyatt, Penta and Kempinski had applied for licenses for investing in India. However, the revenue departments of the respective States failed to locate and allocate land for the construction of hotels. The scheme, thus, fell flat. Curiously, the Union Government was not hesitant to make use of Constitutional provisions when it suited its interests.

As has been stated earlier, the Yunus Committee had suggested the creation of the Tourism Board on lines of the existing Railway Board. To begin with, the empowered committee of secretaries challenged the idea of creation of a Board. It was said that the Railway Board as an independent entity was created for historical reasons. It would be difficult for tourism to be looked after by a Board, because legally the sector would come under the Industrial (Development) Act. It was also found that such a Board would not be viable financially.

In 1991, the think-tank on tourism created by Minister Madhavarao Scindia rejected the idea of a Board in toto. It was emphasised that the Board cannot be in charge of a sector that is basically under the jurisdiction of the States!

FEDERAL INTERVENTIONS

It is common knowledge that the resource-base of the States is very narrow, making them vulnerable at the negotiating table. However, States have the freedom to resist the Centre's strong- arm tactics, provided State assemblies stand-by the interests of the States. For instance, State legislatures may refuse to freeze water and electricity rates on grounds of revenue generation. In that event, the concerned Chief Minister or the Minister of Tourism may convey the intensity of resistance that he is confronted with, and thus refuse to comply with the Centre's diktats. It is heartening to realise that the States have often exercised their power of self-determination and consequently refused to toe the line drawn by the Centre. This offers enough scope for possible interventions at the federal strata of our political system in matters of policy formulation.

Implications of Privatisation

According to the Approach Paper to the Seventh Plan, " there is a vast potential for development of tourism in the country. Tourism should be accorded the status of an industry. Private sector investment will have to be encouraged in developing tourism and public sector investments should be focused only on development of support infrastructure". Thus the seeds of private initiatives were sown during the Seventh Plan. The Government took the matter of privatising the tourism sector seriously by 1988. It was during the tenure of Mr. S.K. Mishra as Tourism Secretary that the talk of inviting private investment into the sector began.

The Government permitted foreign equity participation up to 5 1 %in tourism projects. Foreign charters were allowed to operate in the country for the first time. Foreign companies were allowed to repatriate their profits to the extent of 3%. The structural adjustment programme, initiated in June, 1992, paved the way for privatisation in almost all sectors of the economy. The Annual Plan (1992-93) document emphatically enunciated the Government's position vis-a-vis tourism: "The future growth of tourism will have to be achieved mainly through private initiative. The State will contribute to tourism by planning broad strategy of development, provision of monetary and fiscal incentives to catalyse private sector investment."

The process of privatisation brought in its wake big investments and private involvement at various levels. As an offshoot, environmental considerations were thrown to the winds and there were instances of large scale human rights violation. The self- correcting nature of policy made provisions for stricter controls in this regard. More seriously, privatisation meant alienation of the majority of our population and their deprivation. Employment generated in tourism is generally seasonal and ill paid. The private sector- induced pockets of tourism had the potential of turning into centres of pollution, drug trafficking and prostitution.

The Seventh Plan proposed that tourism be declared an industry. However, it took time for the States to implement this, even though they agreed in principle. The smokeless industry had the advantage of generating maximum value-added, because of low-cost inputs. The Tourism Policy Statement carried certain provisions in favour of the hotel industry. It stated that there should be provision for depreciation in the balance sheets of hotels. Being an export industry, hotels were to be given excise concessions. The provisions of the Monopolies and Restrictive Trade Practices (MRTP) Act were relaxed for hotels, because any hotel with 300 or more rooms would have incurred an investment of Rs. 25 crores. The document also hinted at lower tariffs for power and water and regulations for easy import of equipment.

As a follow-up, hotel and shipping were added to the list of 27 industries exempted from Section 22 A of the MRTP Act. The consequences of declaring tourism as an industry need to be studied in detail. It is not possible to capture its implications in an exploratory work like this. However, it is obvious that the private sector has primarily benefited to a great extent by this measure.

The arena of policy formulation should be self-evaluating and self-correcting. In the case of Tourism Policy, this has proved to be the plus point. As an illustration, the Policy statement of 1982 made no mention of infrastructure development. The successive governments at the Centre failed to create proper tourism infrastructure, thus resulting in loss of traffic. This lacuna was corrected in the National Action Plan. However, much of this change was due to intensive lobbying by such agencies like the Indian Association of Tour Operators (IATO), the Travel agents Association of India (TAAI) and the Indian Hotels and Restaurants Association (IHRA).

It is for the voluntary agencies and pro-people forces to exploit the avenue of lobbying at various levels. The environmental implications of tourism development did not form part of the 1982 Policy. The consequences are too obvious to be written about. However, the NAP, 1992 did carry specific provisions for environmental protection and harnessing. From Policy to Cartooning Policy statements may also lead to justifiable flights of fantasy.

Broadly, our successive policy pronouncements in the realm of tourism falls within the "liberalising" framework of the macro- economic policy environment. The Finance Bill, 1988, had assured 50% tax exemption on foreign exchange earnings in the sector, and a further 50% exemption if re-invested. In effect, it amounts to 100% tax concession. Luxury hotels enjoy exemptions of all kinds with a view to encourage tourism earnings. These tax exemptions coupled with provision of soft loans to the sector led to a boom in the tourism related private investment.

The Economic Survey 1991-92 aptly summarises the ultimate aim of such incentives for private sector participation: " The Government has tried to expand the economic space in which the people can exercise their initiative and ingenuity. It hopes to do more to expand their opportunities, to enhance their potential. But what shape the economy takes ultimately depends on what the people make of it. In that sense, the future is in their hands." We should not forget that tourism is an industry which emerges in the context of unresolved socio-economic structural issues, such as land distribution patterns or the take over of traditional occupations by modem mechanised capital.

Tourism happens to be a source of livelihood for millions in India and aggressive privatisation does not ensure social and economic safety nets. In the face of the unhindered entry of international capital and successive alienation, perhaps, it is difficult to agree that "the future is in our hands" Eco Tourism and Sustainable Development. The Draft Tourism Policy 1997 states that "in the context of economic liberalisation and globalisation being pursued by the country, the development policies of no sector can remain static." The policy further states that "the emergence of tourism as an important instrument for sustainable human development including poverty alleviation, employment generation, environmental regeneration and advancement of women and other disadvantaged groups in the country" requires support to realise these goals.

India's tourism resources have always been considered immense, in a tourism audit. The geographical features are diverse, colourful and varied. The coastline offers opportunities for developing the best beaches in the world. There are a wealth of eco-systems including biosphere reserves, mangroves, coral reefs, deserts, mountains and forests as well as an equally wide range of flora and fauna. The Policy further states that "international tourists visiting interiors of the country for reasons of purity of the environment and nature contributes to the development of these areas particularly backward regions". Thus Tourism "should also become a reason for better preservation and protection of our natural resources, environment and ecology".

The policy recognises that sustained growth of tourism can give rise to conflicts. To ensure that the growth of tourism takes place along desired lines, certain guidelines have been framed:

1. to remove the constraint of the information gap.
2. to create a tourist product that is desirable and supported by an integrated infrastructure.
3. to involve all agencies, public, private and government, in tourism development.
4. to create synergy between departments and agencies that have to deliver the composite tourist product.
5. to use both the circuit and scheme approach so that peoples participation through panchayats, local bodies, NGO's, and youth organisations will create a greater awareness of tourism. The Central Government can thus concentrate on larger investment oriented projects.
6. to create direct access for destinations off the beaten track.
7. to diversify the product with new options like beach tourism, forests, wild life, landscapes and adventure tourism, farm and health tourism.
8. to ensure that the development does not exceed sustainable levels.

9. to develop the seven north-eastern states, the Himalayan region and Islands for tourism.
10. to maintain a balance between the negative and positive impacts of tourism through planning restrictions and through education of the people for conservation and development.

The strategy for development should take into consideration the carrying capacity, local aspirations and benefits likely to accrue to the community. In particular specific policies and guidelines for eco-tourism development and adventure tourism are to be formulated, primarily through a regulatory framework.

The Draft Guidelines have been approved at a State Ministers Conference and have been circulated to various trade and industry bodies. The guidelines draw a distinction between mass or resort tourism and nature or eco tourism, as the kind of tourism that has a lower impact on the environment and requires less infrastructural development. The Ministry hopes that the environment conscious international tourist will be made aware that India is taking steps to protect its ecology and environment.

Apart from the do's and don'ts, the guidelines are governed by a tourism management plan, the key elements of which are the protection of natural resources and a positive involvement of local communities, along with an optimum number of environmentally conscious visitors. The principles of management are scientific planning, effective control and continuous monitoring, development of physical infrastructure, zoning and a Management plan for public use of natural sites. The management plan should establish standards for resort development, style and location of structures, waste disposal, treatment of sewage, control of litter, use of public spaces and fragile areas.

The operational guidelines rely on sensitisation of all the role players and this programme is based on a self-regulated environmental code. Area specific rather than universal development plans keeping in mind the unique character of the location and its economic and social environment are important. This would help the State Government to coordinate with the industry in managing visitors and their activities. NGO's working on socio-economic programmes in forest and remote areas could have a closer coordination with tourism service operators to transfer economic benefits, particularly the handicraft production and marketing sector. The guidelines are only a beginning, and it is hoped that with increasing awareness of the visitor the industry will regulate its practices.

There is an emphasis on the needs and perceptions of the international tourist running through the discussion on the guide lines although the data from the National Parks makes it evident that the domestic tourists outnumber international visitors, although they do not pay the same amount as the foreign visitor either in entry fees or for board and lodging and transport facilities. They do however demand a much higher per capita use of resources like water, fuel for heating and cooking and transport. They also make the same intensive use of time and try to maximize their stay by the number of animals and birds they can view in the 24-hour period.

It is interesting to note that no democratic participation has been called for in the policy formulation process, and all the amendments to the policy have come from trade associations and government think tanks. The tourism Advisory Committee also consists of eminent persons and community representation has been ignored. The elite nature of the policy makers is well represented in the quotations given above from the policy document.

The policy clearly recognises the debate on the tourism issue which has surfaced wherever tourism development, particularly in the case of tourism projects relating to the "gifts of nature" like beaches, rivers, mountains and forests, have already been developed. However, mere recognition of the hostility of people to tourism development is not enough to change the nature of tourism development or the resistance to tourism or what many have termed a poor tourism culture.

Perhaps to understand this in a better perspective, we should look at the issue of sustainable development in a critical way. Perhaps we can question the impact of sustainable development on the environment and sift through the jargon of development planners, international agencies, and environmental activists to see how sustainable development can be achieved without all the contradictions that are apparent as in the case of the tourism sector.

Sustainable development is change that can be sustained or continued for the time period concerned. Development we can say with some confidence is a process of directed change, but any process embodies both the objectives and the means of achieving the stated objectives. Can we set sustainable objectives (as growth in sustained consumption of) for resources that now are recognised to have ultimate limits or what we may call non-renewable resources or what we may call the balance between the use and conservation of such resources?

The concept of sustainability originated in the context of renewable resources like forests and fisheries and was subsequently adopted by the environmental movement. In most cases it is understood to mean "the existence of the ecological conditions necessary to support human life at a specific level of well being through future generations." However, in addition to ecological conditions there are social conditions that influence ecological sustainability in a nature-people interaction. The social connotations have been described by Barbier who has defined social sustainability as "the ability to maintain desired social values, traditions, institutions, cultures or other social characteristics."

The term sustainability came into usage in 1980 when the IUCN presented the World Conservation Strategy where sustainable development was linked to conservation of living resources. However, the fundamental goals have often been lost sight of because of operational goals (e.g. food, water, shelter, health are fundamental goals to be realised through self reliance, cost effectiveness, appropriate technology, people centred-ness etc.) Consequently, the WCED made its definition brief: Social Development is development that meets the needs of the present without compromising the ability of future generations to meet their own needs. They did not make any assumptions on the direction in which changes in demand would take place. (E.g. equity, social justice, self-determination, or cultural diversity).

India's tourism policy follows the mainstream SD thinking by adopting all the critical objectives: revive growth change the quality of growth meet essential needs for jobs, food, energy, water and sanitation ensure sustainable levels of population conserve and enhance the resource base reorient technology and management risk merge environment and economics in decision making reorient international economic relations make development more participatory. These objectives are responsible for building a very broad consensus on the issue of sustainable development, yet the debate at the operational level continues.

Most participants in the debate now accept that many human activities are reducing the long-term ability of the natural environment to provide goods and services, which will eventually affect human health and well being. Many also accept that poverty is devastating the lives of millions in the Third World since there is no consensus between what is environmentally necessary and what is economically and developmentally feasible. The level of inter-dependence between the two insights is yet to be incorporated in the concept of Social Development. Some problem areas are: Environmental degradation, already affecting millions in the Third World, is likely to reduce human well being across the globe. Who is responsible for this rapid degeneration? Is it the poor or the rich? The poor have no option but to exploit resources for short-term survival.

If we take the example of forests and their resources, which have been traditionally outside the market system and in the sphere of tribal or indigenous peoples rights, they are today seen as exploiters of the forests as against tourists, with all their demand for infrastructure and superstructure, who are seen to be conservationists. The inter-linked nature of the problem of sustainability is such that the impact of degradation will be quicker on the poor than on the rich. Can Sustainable Development be the metafix it claims to be in reconciling increasing industrial, agricultural and resource use productivity with environmental needs.

The weakness of the Social Development argument lies in the techno-economic approach to solutions with regard to common property resource management, through know how transfers, resource pricing, subsidy policies and building management capabilities. Deeper processes such as land reforms, industrial demands on raw materials, over consumption, changing legal and political structures are either ignored or looked at in a cursory manner. For instance how can we claim a consensus between those who are concerned for the survival of future generations with those who are concerned with the survival of wild life, or human health and subsistence?

We will also fail to understand why, even when there is a broad consensus, projects on the ground result in conflicts. Suggested refinements could be:

— a distinction between ecological and social sustainability and in the process an identification of the inter-linkages

— a distinction between renewable and non-renewable resources, between environmental processes crucial to human life and crucial to other forms of life dependent on the resources.

— a distinction between the techno-economic aspects of social sustainability (infrastructure, services, government) with political and cultural sustainability.

— a distinction between equitable development and local participation, and decentralisation, what many have called NGOisation of sustainable development.

This is because no rigorous testing of local participation leading to social equity or to sustainable resource use have been reported. Case studies reflect personal, organisational or political preferences. Tourism is one of the activities which has caused concern because of the effects of increasing human traffic on fragile environments. Countries which are looking towards Tourism as a means of economic growth, like India, have limited resources and cultural restraints and they have the greatest need to pay heed to the possible negative impacts of tourism. The environmental impact of tourism is a basic issue, whether we are looking at a developed or an underdeveloped area, region or country.

The costs of tourism for a country like India include extensive investment in fixed assets with a low rate of return for infrastructure, transportation, accommodation, cultural institutions, exhibition centres, and park facilities. To this maybe added the social and cultural costs like additional demands on infrastructure like land, water, health services; the creation of new jobs for displaced people; the cost of positive community relationships; the disparity between the lifestyle of visitors and those who serve them; the possible friction between local residents and new users of valued local resources; the perception of local residents of the spending of scarce capital resources on what they consider low priority areas like tourism; cultural cost of alterations in local ceremonial or traditional values; loss of privacy for local communities as tourists come to gape at their living conditions and rituals.

Tourism also causes increasing congestion and pollution as thousands of visitors flock to parks and sanctuaries in motorised vehicles; there are changes in accessibility, landscape and the ecological balance between man and nature; there is the cost, both monetary and human, of creating conservation zones (core/buffer) with unforeseen or undesirable side effects; which have been observed in the ecotourism movement. The benefit of revenue from tourism does not always redress these problems but goes towards the cost of administering the project. The tourism industry is generally self-centred and not given to educational, cultural or exchange programmes on a philanthropic basis.

The natural environment, with the best will in the world, cannot escape damage with the volume of visitors. As more and more tourists, both domestic and international seek the exotic and remote destinations around the world, the likelihood of the environment suffering as a result become greater. Forests can suffer from trampling, fires, tree felling for facilities and waste. Wildlife, despite the protection in national parks, has suffered a loss of habitat, hunting and poaching, viewing and photographing, leading to an interruption of feeding and breeding patterns or hunting for food undisturbed.

These are the prized moments for the viewer. The trade in wild life trophies or tourist souvenirs is the more deliberately destructive aspect of such tourism.

The building of tourist lodges in materials that are not integrated with the environment and the pressure they put on the land and water bodies is also wilfully destructive. Management techniques that include being less user friendly or control of numbers by closing access or by multiplying the number of attractions and areas or charging higher admission fees are generally not popular with the tourist or the tour operator and are also difficult to implement because of high administrative costs.

Women and Tourism

The Government of Kerala has taken a policy decision to develop tourism. The tourism programme has grown very rapidly, as the figures for tourist arrivals in the state indicate. The growth has covered both inbound and outbound international tourism as well as the arrival of domestic tourists to Kerala. The Department of Tourism at the State level has also taken up Central Government projects and following from the National Action Plan, Kerala was the first state to identify a special tourism area, Bekal, to be developed with foreign investment into a big mass tourism project, to help India achieve its 5 million arrivals and access higher returns in foreign exchange.

None of these developments have involved discussion and debate at the state or local level. These have been administrative decisions, and when the secretary, tourism was questioned on the undemocratic manner in which tourism decisions were taken, he saw the issue of tourism as beyond the comprehension of local people. On the other hand, foreign experts were invited to suggest how and what kind of tourism should be developed in Kerala, which had had very little exposure since the Kovalam

Beach Resort never realised the potential of international arrivals, being overshadowed by Goa.

Today, the tourism policy of the government visualises many new products and new players in the sphere of tourism. These include new beach resorts, hill and wildlife as the basis for adventure tourism, special tourism areas for intensive development, backwater cruising and festivals that package the culture and craft of Kerala for the benefit of the tourist. Every district now has a privately sponsored tourism festival, which often contravenes the Coastal Zone Regulation as it promotes tourism awareness. The second aspect of the tourism policy is the dependence on the private sector to develop the infrastructure and the superstructure for tourism and its related activity.

Today, the Kerala Government, Tatas and the Casino Group are the major players in tourism development and they have an understanding of tourism that does not look beyond the commercial aspect of tourism development. There is also the desire to invite foreign investment for large-scale development to increase the number of arrivals from abroad to enhance foreign exchange earnings.

An intervention-in policy making by office bearers of local self government bodies who can function in the interest of local people is essential. This can be effective only when they have an enlightened awareness on the developmental options that the government offers to the people of the state. When EQUATIONS began to acquaint itself with the Bekal development plan, it was surprising for us to learn that not a single panchayat opposed tourism development because the thrust of the government's propaganda was that tourism generated income and employment. Several studies relating to tourism development in Kerala indicate that the socio-cultural impacts of tourism have been very negative, particularly, relating to the issue of drugs and prostitution.

Tourism projects have also displaced local people and affected their traditional occupations. The environmental impacts of tourism have also been negative particularly in the coastal zone and in the hills. Tourism needs regulation rather than promotion. Not only regulation, but the issue of tourism needs to be debated so that there are people-centered objectives rather than growth-centered objectives. Unless the people of Kerala arrive at some consensus on the kind of tourism they want to develop to achieve economic objectives, the control of outsiders, multinationals, international agencies and the monopoly houses in India will not end.

One area that needs to be focussed on is the issue of gender and tourism. Women panchayat members, being leaders of their communities, have the added task of familiarising themselves with the gender issues that emerge in the developmental debate, since most planners are male and most models are male dominated. India is a gendered society, which means that human relations in economic, social and cultural life, as well as in the political framework are determined and rnediated by gendered perceptions.

To clarify further, gender does not mean only the difference between men and women biologically but on their human relations being based on the status of women in society and therefore the perceptions of their social role and function. Tourism and the industry that supports it, as well as the administration that encourages its development, growth and expansion, is an interpersonal activity which is influenced by and in turn influences local and global gender perceptions. There is a list of global perceptions that have been researched, to develop a gender framework, for analysing developmental activity particularly tourism.

1. *Tourism as a part of modern consumerism*: Consumerism embodies social practices as well as signifies social

change. As leisure time and wealth increase, tourism consumption also increases. As expansion reaches the remotest corners of the world, the marketing and consumption models between guests and hosts have indicated several possibilities for gender analysis. Power, control and equality in tourism are articulated through race, class and gender in the practice of tourism.

Men and women through interconnected economic, political, cultural, social and environmental dimension., are involved in different ways in the construction and consumption of tourism. It is the recognition of these differing realities that shape tourism marketing, tourist motivation, and resident action. This process may be called the creation of stereotypes. For example, in all Asian societies where traditional society is intersecting with global economic systems, we have seen that the major public role of women in the tourism industry is in sex tourism. The faster the process of liberalisation and globalisation, the greater the spread of sex tourism.

2. *Tourism as an aid to development*: Women activists have always seen the statistical approach to tourism as apolitical. If tourism is seen as an activity that depends on leisure time and disposable income, then the enabling conditions are hierarchical and influenced by class and global economic strengths. In tourism advertising women are seen as passive, available and dependent. Women are thus sexual and exotic markers in the tourism brochure. Destinations reinforce this stereotype not only of the resident community as a whole (poor and ready to serve) but also of the women as inferior or as objects of gratification or as playthings.

3. *Tourism and Division of Labour*: Tourism, like other activities, perpetuates the international and domestic

division of labour. This means that there are gendered employment activities (cooking, cleaning, serving, handicraft etc.) as well as control of waged work. There is also no computation of unpaid labour by women. The question that tourism raises is that women do not have leisure from certain types of work, and this compulsory, unpaid labour is extended to their working life as well as economic opportunity. Tourism encourages classifications like women's work.

4. *Tourism development and its influence on changing value systems*: Tourism is an essentially modern activity that promotes 'tradition' as a unique and authentic product. In this process of commodification, not only is it important to define the other, but to define the gendered other. These changes are reflected in identification with tourist behaviour, changes in family systems age and sex hierarchies in the struggle for economic power as well as changes in the social and political status of different sexes in different classes and different production systems.

5. *Tourism and environment*: What is our relationship to the environment, how do we use these resources, how can we regulate the consumption driven nature of tourism and how can traditional practices be documented and compared with the approach of providers of tourism services, is now being looked at. For example, it is suggested that as agriculture becomes less productive, tourism (rural, farm, beach or resort) ecomes a va ua e a ternative ecause it a ows a combination of domestic responsibilities of women, with tourism work, which is seen as an income source that can support small scale farming and thus conserve the countryside. Such an approach suggests that there is a need to change women's relationship with nature, the environment and their place in the ecological system.

Our perspective must include certain issues. For instance, the division between one who enters the business and earns an income from it and one who is displaced. The latter has to move away, adapt to a new location and find new survival strategies on how to access new resources. For example, tobacco, coconut harvesting, fish sorting and processing are women-dominated activities in Bekal. Tourism is a loss of income for them and does not use their traditional expertise. Neither does it provide them compensation or retraining or reemployment. Then there is the time element in tourism benefits trickling down.

The deterioration of traditional communities and their activities is faster and the upward mobility slower. This is because tourism is established for the high spenders and in the organised sector, rather than in the informal sector. Similarly, in the handicrafts production industry, market forces demand mechanisation, which results in the retrenchment of women workers, who are then shifted to finishing, which is lower paid. Soon this process is also mechanised and women have to look elsewhere for jobs.

At the social level, tourism has forced middle class families to send their girls (aged 9-12 years) away from Kovalam, so that they are known as the Kovalam girls whom no one wishes to marry since the reputation of the beach resort for prostitution brings dishonour to the whole community. Honour of the family and the community in gendered societies rests in the chastity of the women of the household, the village or the township. Domestic tourism is also predominantly single male tourism, which encourages prostitution. Indian women are not encouraged to travel on their own. Tourist behaviour is seen to be unsafe for women who are the repositories of the family's honour and the tourism process may bring dishonour. This need for safety and security is not met for women in Indian society although it is seen as the duty of the men in the family.

The changes that tourism introduces benefit those sections that are a part of the new land use pattern. This is generally the educated, urban middle class. Since the middle class owns land, it recognises and promotes money as an indicator of status, aspiration etc. However, the landless, the poor and the small peasants are also looking for an opportunity, therefore they look at the panchayat plan and the government policy for such openings. Rural women, though educated do not find the time or the money to attend courses or find employment in the travel trade. They have to await the establishment of the services in the organised sector and then find employment at the lowest level.

The policy and the People's Plan look at basic needs like roads, drinking water and have now included tourism, but there is no support in the policy for the informal sector in tourism. Similarly, when a district, like Wynad, is declared a tourism district by doing an audit of its resources for tourism, does the developer and the planner focus on the needs of the tribal, the migrant, the agriculturist, the plantation owner or the women who need an income supplement? Or is the focus on the tourist and the industry? What happens to the demands and needs of women and their role in development?

It is upon these questions that we need to focus on, bring in support for women's organisations and see that the tourism issue is put on their agenda and that we adopt their understanding on women's issues in our agenda. There is need, therefore, to build a data base and alliances with different sections of the government, the industry and social activists and concerned citizen groups to study the issue of tourism and debate the model being implemented in Kerala. Information and awareness is not only to be based on the motivations of the tourists and their need for services and products. It is to be based on the needs of the people and their perceptions of how tourism is to be developed and what benefits are to be derived. We must also be made aware of the negative consequences of tourism.

Finally, there is the issue of income generation as the only measure of development. Income, particularly in the case of tourism, is not stable, not under the control of the hosts, but manipulated by the trade. Secondly, income alone need not indicate growth or mobility because income is only one relation in the production-consumption process, and its impact on interconnected social issues need not be productive or liberating. As far as the issue of foreign exchange earnings is concerned, one must examine how global economy and lifestyle affects the individual and the community.

3

National Civil Aviation Policy

MISSION

To maintain a competitive civil aviation environment which ensures safety and security in accordance with international standards, promotes efficient, cost-effective and orderly growth of air transport and contributes to social and economic development of the country.

STRATEGIC OBJECTIVES

The objectives of this policy are the creation and continued facilitation of a competitive and service-oriented civil aviation environment in which:

i. the interests of the users of civil aviation are the guiding force behind all decisions, systems and arrangements,

ii. safe, efficient, reliable and widespread quality air transport services are provided at reasonable prices,

iii. there exists a well-defined regulatory framework catering to changing needs and circumstances,

iv. all players and stakeholders are assured of a level playing field;

v. private participation is encouraged and opportunities created for investors to realize adequate returns on their investments;

vi. recognizing that aviation today is an important element of infrastructure, rapid upgradation of airport infrastructure to world class with priority to the busiest airports and those handling international flights;

vii. recognizing that transportation of air cargo is vital to the economic growth of the country, creation and development of specific infrastructure for air transportation of cargo and express cargo is encouraged,

viii. "airline operations and acquisition of aircraft" is conferred "infrastructure" status for overall growth of civil aviation sector in the country

ix. domestic and international aviation in the country are encouraged to grow at par with world aviation industry;

x. inter-linkages with other modes of transport are encouraged and stimulated;

xi. trade, tourism and overall economic activity and growth is encouraged;

xii. international cooperation in aviation and development in tune with international trends and best practices, consistent with airspace sovereignty is promoted;

xiii. indigenous development of aircraft, components and aviation products is encouraged,

xiv. Security of civil aviation operations is ensured through appropriate systems, policies, and practices, and

xv. Effective systems are put in place for timely crisis and disaster management, including investigation of incidents/accidents.

Consultation with Users

1. The success of any policy depends upon the benefits it gives to the various users. A constant interaction with and amongst all categories of users is paramount for successful implementation of and constant improvement in the policy. There is an urgent need for an institutional arrangement at different levels for such interaction.
2. Therefore, Facilitation Committees consisting of representatives of various users of civil aviation sector i.e. government, passengers, tour and travel operators, aircraft-operators, airport-operators, exporters and importers, cargo handling agents, aerosports, Flying Clubs, etc. will be set up at national, regional and local levels to ensure that the interests of ultimate users are best safeguarded. There will be regular monitoring and feedback between the Facilitation Committees of national regional and local levels. There will be mandatory prior consultation with these Facilitation Committees before amendments in policy/ rules / regulations are undertaken.
3. Highest priority will be accorded to the passengers/ users and suitable mechanisms will be set up for this purpose, including publication of Citizens' Charters and effective action for, and monitoring of, grievance redressal.

Regulatory Framework

1. In the context of a multiplicity of airlines, airport operators (including private sector), and the possibility of oligopolistic practices, there is need for an autonomous regulatory authority which could work as a watchdog, as well as a facilitator for the sector, prescribe and enforce minimum standards for all

agencies, settle disputes with regard to abuse of monopoly and ensure level playing field for all agencies. Therefore, a statutory autonomous Civil Aviation Authority (CAA) will be constituted. The basic objectives of setting up of the Authority will be to ensure aviation safety, security and effective regulation of air transport in the country in the liberalised environment.

2. The functions of the CAA will be as under:

   i. set the standards for various agencies and personnel of civil aviation sector;

   ii. issue license to these agencies and personnel;

   iii. regulate tariff;

   iv. ensure that these agencies and personnel continuously fulfil the standards;

   v. take appropriate preventive/corrective/punitive action against the agencies and personnel for violations of set standards;

   vi. ensure that there are no unfair trade practices and market dominance through encouragement of entry and fostering of competition in accordance with Competition Policy of the Government;

   vii. ensure level playing field for all agencies and

   viii. study and analyse the trends in international and domestic civil aviation, project likely future scenario and publish periodical reports.

3.

   i. The agencies mentioned above include airport, airport-operators, passenger aircraft operators, cargo aircraft operators, helicopters, private aircraft operators, flying clubs, aero-sports clubs, security agency, training institute, air-travel operators or any other agency having role in civil aviation sector.

ii. The personnel mentioned above include pilots, flight engineers, navigators, cabin crew, flight despatchers, aircraft maintenance engineers/ technicians, air traffic controllers and personnel engaged in the maintenance of communication, navigation, surveillance/ air traffic management systems and other ground aids.

4. Civil Aviation Authority will conduct safety and security audit including flight inspections of the concerned agencies to ensure that they are meeting the prescribed standards.
5. Civil Aviation Authority will be required to publish Annual Report on the Air Safety and Security Environment in the country.
6. Civil Aviation Authority will also be required to make available information regarding passenger and cargo traffic including regular analysis in an appropriate consolidated format on a commercial basis.
7. A comprehensive Indian Aviation Law will be framed to replace the existing Acts relating to aviation and security which will be in tune with the present day civil aviation scenario, and would also put the proposed CAA in place.

Private Sector Participation

1. Private sector participation will be a major thrust area in the civil aviation sector for promoting investment, improving quality and efficiency and increasing competition.
2. Competitive regulatory framework with minimal controls will be created to encourage entry and operation of private airlines/ airports.

3. Private sector investment in the construction/ upgradations/ operation of new as well as existing airports including cargo related infrastructure will be encouraged.

4. Rationalization of various charges and price of ATF/ AVGas will be undertaken to render operation of smaller aircraft viable so as to encourage major investment in feeder and regional air services by the private sector.

5. Training Institutes for pilots, flight engineers, maintenance personnel, air-traffic controller, security will be encouraged in private sector.

6. Private sector investment in non-aeronautical activities like shopping complex, golf course, entertainment park, aero-sports etc. near airports will be encouraged to increase revenue, improve viability of airports and to promote tourism. CAA will ensure that this is not at the cost of primary aeronautical functions, and is consistent with the security requirements.

7. Government will gradually reduce its equity in PSUs in the sector.

8. Government will encourage employee participation through issue of shares and ESOP.

Airport Infrastructure

1. The Government will aim at ensuring adequate world class airport infrastructure capacity in accordance with demand, ensuring maximum utilization of available capacities and efficiently managing the airport infrastructure by increasing involvement of private sector.

2. Greenfield airport will be permitted by the Government where

(i) the existing airport is unable to meet the projected requirement of traffic or

(ii) a new focal point of traffic emerges with sufficient viability and

(iii) the new location is normally not within an aerial distance of 150 kilometers of an existing airport

3. Encouragement will be given to development/ construction in private sector of small airstrips/ helipads /heliports, which are smaller and cheaper to construct. These will be particularly suitable in remote hilly or island areas, large business, city centers, factory locations and at other important nodal points. This will also facilitate increase in small aircraft operations

4. Private sector participation

(i) Private sector will be free to undertake

(a) construction and operation of new airports/ airstrips/ helipads/heliports including cargo complexes, express cargo terminals, cargo satellite cities and cargo handling facilities

(b) upgradation and operation of existing airports/ airstrips/helipads/heliports in consultation with the existing operator including cargo complexes, Express cargo terminals, cargo satellite cities and cargo handling facilities

(ii) Foreign equity participation will be permitted up to 74 % with automatic approval and 100 % with special permission of government

(iii) Private sector participation will include participation of state government, urban local bodies, private companies, individuals and joint ventures on Build-Own-Operate (BOO) basis or any other pattern of ownership and management depending on the circumstances.

(iv) Restructuring of major airports of Airports Authority of India will be undertaken through long-term lease to private investors for efficient management, improvement of standards of services/ facilities and attracting private investment

(v) At privately managed airports, air traffic control (ATC) and aviation security will continue to be provided by the Airports Authority of India (AAI) and customs and immigration facilities by respective Government departments.

(vi) The equipment needed for any service would normally be provided by the agency responsible for the service and an equitable system would be established for sharing of revenue between different agencies. Keeping in view their respective investments and responsibilities.

5. All airports /airstrips /helipads /heliports used for scheduled air-transport services will be licensed by Civil Aviation Authority.

6. Airport/ airstrip/ heliport/ helipad operators will follow ICAO guidelines for levying airport/ airstrip/ heliport/ helipad charges based on cost recovery principle. The CAA would put in a place a regulatory mechanism to prevent abuse of monopolistic nature of such infrastructure.

7. An objective and well-defined transparent mechanism for allocation of slots at airports will be ensued at all times.

8. CAA will ensure fair play between different airport/ airstrip/ heliport/ helipad operators and user agencies so that no airport/ airstrip/ heliport/ helipad operator

is accused of discriminating against any particular airline or any other user. Similarly, Government will ensure that no airport-operator is discriminated against with regard to allotment as point of call, if there is demand for air services from such airport.

9. More international gateways shall be provided. It would be ensured that there is at least one international airport in every region of the country in order to give a boost to trade and tourism and adequate capacity in all the routes.

10. Major thrust will be given for increasing the share of commercial revenue from non-aeronautical sources by giving total freedom to airport/ airstrip/ heliport/ helipad operators in the matter of raising non-aeronautical revenue

11. New Ground Handling regulations with following broad particulars envisage :

    (i) At airports managed by AAI, new private investors have been allowed by AAI to undertake ground handling besides national carriers and self-handling by carriers which will increase competition resulting in improvement in services and reduction in costs.

    (ii) At private airports, at least limited competition will be mandatory.

12. A rationalized dynamic system for airport charges for AAI airports will be introduced for

    (i) optimum utilization of airport by using peak and off-peak time charges,

    (ii) increasing revenue of airport operators

    (iii) promoting airports in far-flung regions by having varying airport charges from airport to airport depending upon the facilities available at the airport.

(iv) promoting use of small aircraft

13. A new Directorate of Lands shall be established in AAI and land use guidelines will be formulated for utilizing vacant land.

(i) Vacant land at airports will be evaluated for construction of aviation related activities (e.g. cargo complexes, aircraft maintenance facilities, etc)

(ii) For optimal exploitation of airport land for civil aviation purposes, private-sector/ State Government participation would be welcome.

(iii) Land at such airports where there is no likelihood of future use for civil aviation purposes will be utilized for other commercial purposes like gold courses, tennis, etc. either by AAI itself or in joint venture.

(iv) Effective steps will be taken for removing encroachments from AAI land and if necessary, comprehensive rehabilitation package will be formulated.

14. Cargo handling

(i) Infrastructure like satellite freight cities with multi-modal transport, cargo terminals, cold storage centers, automatic storage and retrieval systems, mechanized transport of cargo, dedicated express cargo terminals with airside and city side openings, computerization and automation etc. will be set up on priority basis.

(ii) Private sector participation in cargo handling will be encouraged.

(iii) Efficient Electronic Data Interchange systems will be developed and linked amongst all stakeholders in the trade.

(iv) Air cargo complexes and dedicated express cargo terminals (with airside and city-side openings) will be integral part of all major airports.

15. Operation of airports would be in accordance with the provisions relating to prevention of air, water and noise pollution.

16. Guidelines for naming of airports will be formulated to ensure that the airports are named after the cities they are situated in as per international norms.

17. Air Traffic services

(i) Air Traffic controllers will be licensed by CAA.

(ii) AAI will continue to provide Air Traffic Services over the Indian air Space as per standards set by CAA in accordance with ICAO norms.

(iii) Approach and aerodrome control services may be provided by licensed ATCs engaged by the airport operators

(iv) New satellite based CNS/ATM systems will be introduced as per ICAO's Regional Plan

(v) India to have a significant say in the provision of new satellite based CNS/ATM services in Asia-pacific/ SAARC regional airspace

(vi) Fresh Air traffic Services and Controlling (Departure, holding and approach) procedures will be evolved for helicopters and small aircraft to exploit their inherent advantages and to reduce the cost of their operations and efficient use of airspace without compromising safety. This will also give boost to Flying Clubs.

(vii) Efforts will be made for Civil-Military co-ordination for

(a) Greater sharing of civil and military airspace for unidirectional air-corridors and straightening of air-routes to save fuel and time,

(b) Uniform air-traffic procedures,

(c) Additional slots for civilian flights at military airports,

(d) Sharing of revenues at civil enclaves

DOMESTIC PASSENGER AND CARGO AIR TRANSPORT

1. The government will encourage provision of safe passenger and cargo air transport services to every region of the country at economic prices.

2. It is necessary that both airline operations as well as airport infrastructure be treated as mutually dependent and complementary and given similar concessions to promote a balanced growth of the sector. Therefore, airline operations and acquisition of aircraft should be given the status of "infrastructure ".

3. Private sector participation in providing domestic passengers and cargo air transport services will be encouraged.

4. Permission to start scheduled passenger and cargo air transport service would be given by government on demonstration of competency, minimum capital requirement and viability of the company to provide a safe and reliable service. CAA may also fix a minimum number of aircraft for scheduled operators permit.

5. Capacity induction will be regulated with a view to ensuring safety, security and preventing unhealthy levels of capacity.

6. Government and CAA will ensure that there is no discrimination between different passenger and cargo air-operators.

7. Foreign equity up to 25% and Non-Resident Indian investment up to 100% will be permitted for domestic passenger transport services. However, participation from foreign airlines either directly or indirectly will not be permitted. Substantive ownership and effective control by Indians will be a pre-requisite.

8. Wet leasing of foreign registered aircraft by operators will be permitted only in special circumstances like grounding of aircraft, augmentation of capacity for short term, to meet the capacity requirements for handling natural calamities, etc.

9. ATF will be taken out from administered price mechanism for petroleum prices. The price of ATF for domestic airline will, therefore, be governed by market and customs duty. Airlines will also be permitted import of ATF.

10. There will be freedom to operate non-revenue and passenger charter and cargo flights to any foreign destinations. Indian passport holders will also be allowed to travel on these flights.

11. Helicopter operations will be given a new boost by a total change in outlook. At present, fixed wing norms with minor changes are broadly applied to rotary wing aircraft. Fresh guidelines will be formulated in consultation with user industry from the point of view of rotary wing aircraft. Fresh Air Traffic Services and controlling procedures, which exploit the inherent advantages of helicopter without compromising safety, will be evolved. This will also reduce the cost of operations of helicopters and efficient use of airspace. Encouragement will be given to use of helicopters in the areas of heli-tourism, adventure sports,

mountaineering/ trekking, point-to-point heli-services to bypass traffic congestion on the road, connecting remote areas and islands in Northeast, Andaman and Nicobar and Lakshdweep, religious places, sky crane for construction/ laying of transmission lines etc.

12. Flying clubs, Aerosports like hang-gliding, ballooning, heli-skiing, para-jumping etc. will be promoted by encouraging private investment and formulating liberalized guidelines in consultation with users. This will include rationalized Avgas prices and liberalized air space control.

13. Special consideration will also be given to Private operators and Corporate operators by way of rationalized Avgas prices, encouragement for construction of smaller airstrips/helipad et. in private sector.

Promotion of General Aviation and Small Aircraft Operation

1. There is need to open up the country and tap the latent demand for air services in many parts of the country currently not on the air map. However, the traffic profile in these areas does not permit viable operations of jet. Even smaller aircraft operations are not viable because of the high cost of operation and high break-even factor.

2. While Route-Dispersal Guidelines do help in providing air services in the remote and inaccessible areas, further measures are required to encourage widespread air-connectivity. Passenger and cargo air transport services to many regions will not be possible unless operation of small aircraft is made economically viable either on stand alone basis or in conjunction with major trunk routes.

3. Therefore, Aviation Turbine Fuel (ATF) for turbo prop aircraft operations will be provided at par with price for international air services, with a cap of 4% on sales tax. Operation of smaller aircraft/ charters will be further encouraged through rationalization of airport charges, Inland Air Travel Tax (IATT) and Avgas prices. For the NorthEast region, IATT has been fully exempted on all routes. Government will consider extending similar facilities to other category II areas.

4. There is a need to change the traditional concept of airport development, ownership and operations in view of the economics of small aircraft/charters operations. Participation of state Government, urban local bodies, airline/ aircraft operators, other private investors will be encouraged in development, upgradation and management of small airports/ airstrips. These airports will be distinct from traditional airport and will be bare-bone type with no frills. Such airports need not be mandatorily manned and onus of ensuring security and safety of operations will rest on the aircraft operator in conjunction with the local administration/ bodies, etc. This will encourage the operation of small aircraft/ air taxis, as operators themselves or in collaboration with State Government / Urban local bodies/ residents of a specific locality, factory, nearby factories, tourist operators will be able to manage such airports/airstrip flexibly and efficiency at reduced cost. This will boost passenger transport and tourism

5. Single engine aircraft of seating capacity upto 10 seats can be permitted for passenger charter and cargo flights. Such operations shall be in accordance with the single engine operation guidelines and over land areas having no hilly terrain or other obstructions.

INTERNATIONAL AIR TRANSPORT

1. The Government will aim at ensuring adequate capacity to fully meet the requirement of international trade and tourism.

2. Liberal bilateral rights will be given for promoting international operations to less developed regions of the country as well as to ill-connected far away countries (e.g. Latin America) to promote trade and tourism in those regions.

3. Government will ensure that traffic rights are utilized to the maximum extent possible through direct operations, creation of virtual equipment by way of joint flights, code sharing arrangements etc. by the two national carriers i.e. Air India and Indian Airlines. Other domestic carriers who fulfill the minimum criteria for designation as Indian carrier to operate international passenger flights will also be permitted to meet this objective. Initially, they may be permitted to fly to neighbouring countries against unutilised rights subject to right of first refusal by national carriers. The requirement of substantial ownership and effective control of the airlines by Indians would continue to be operative.

4. There will be freedom to international tourist Charter operation to different custom airports.

5. Government will also establish, in the long run, an objective and well-defined mechanism for sharing of international traffic rights amongst all airlines in a transparent manner.

6. Government will ensure that there will be no discrimination between different airport operators in allotting capacity to foreign carriers as per bilateral agreements if demand exists.

7. Efforts will be made by national carriers to join global alliances in their own commercial interest and in the interest of travelling passengers through code-sharing, exchange of frequent- flier programs etc.
8. There will be no restriction on international cargo flights. However, they will not be allowed to carry domestic cargo on their flights within the country.
9. Tourist charters from domestic airports to foreign destinations will also be permitted subject to safeguards for scheduled operations.
10. Air India and Indian Airlines would be guaranteed the use of traffic rights actually being utilised by them for five years following privatisation.

Information Technology Plan

1. The government will give thrust on use of Information technology in all aspects of civil aviation sector. Each organisation will have time-bound IT action plan.
2. The following information will be made available by CAA on internet
   (i) Policies/ Rules/ Regulations related to aviation sector
   (ii) Status of various pending proposal and applications
   (iii) Syllabi, schedule and results of various examinations conducted by the CAA
3. Increasing use of Intranet/ video-conferencing facilities for consultation for quick decision making and reducing administrative costs.
4. In the national carriers, revenue yield management systems will be increasingly used for flexible tariffs and maximisation of revenue

5. Internet based flight reservation, inquiry and status information system will be introduced.
6. There will be web-site for all major airports where information required by various users like passenger facilitation,transport facilities to and from city, duty free shops, car parking, cargo, guide map etc. will be available
7. Electronic data interchange (EDI) system will be introduced in cargo terminals linking all stakeholders for quick transactions and availability of latest information about the status of cargo movement.

Promotion of Aviation in North-East and Remote Areas

1. In the Northeast region and other remote areas, the management of airport infrastructure as well as air services is not economically viable because of low utilisation and low fare structures etc. However, given the topography and inaccessability of the region, the need for such infrastructure and air services is much greater. But at the same time, forcing commercial airlines and airport operators to invest in these areas, distort the functioning in other areas also and affect their efficient functioning commercially. Therefore, there is need to correct these imbalances.
2. It has been decided to exempt all the currently operated routes in the North-East from payment of Inland Air Travel Tax (IATT). The decisions to provide ATF to turbo prop aircraft operations at par with price for international air services and capping of sales tax at 4% would also encourage new air services in the North-East. Operation of smaller aircraft and helicopters for passenger and cargo flights will be further encouraged through rationalisation of airport charges and Avgas prices.

3. Airport Infrastructure will be upgraded wherever necessary keeping in mind the linkage with the aircraft type and traffic profile.
4. Adequate funds as grant-in-aid through North East Council (NEC) will be made available for the infrastructure development work needed to be carried out in the North-East region.
5. The air-links between the capitals of the States in the North-East region and between major stations on both sides of the Brahmaputra river will be encouraged.
6. Guwahati and Calcutta will be developed as hub station and main base of turbo-prop aircraft operations by the airlines
7. Regular airservices will be encouraged at convenient timings to enable onward connections to other parts of the country without involving night stop.
8. Suitable infrastructure like hotels, organised taxi-services at the airports and tourist spots in the North-East will be encouraged to help growth in tourism in the region.

Tourism and Trade Promotion

1. Tourism and trade sectors are closely linked to civil aviation sector. Therefore it is important that airport infrastructure and air services are planned keeping in view the requirement and promotion of these sectors. Multi-modal approach will be used for planning to ensure better connectivity.
2. A thrust for international tourism in India will be given by
   (i) Providing freedom to International Tourist Charters to all airports linking places of tourist interest

(ii) Declaring additional airports as international airports resulting in easy connectivity and better services,

(iii) Upgradation of airports at places of Tourist interest like Buddhist circuit, sanctuaries, beach resorts etc.

(iv) Encouraging private sector participation in building tourist infrastructure near airports like transport services from airports to nearby cities, golf courses, amusement park, business centres, duty free shopping complexes of international class, aviation recreation activities, adventure aviation, hang-gliding, microlight aircraft, parachuting etc

(v) Efforts will be made to issue visa on arrival at the airport in larger number of cases.

(vi) Improvement in passenger facilitation and sensitisation of personnel of immigration, customs, security and AAI at airport to make them more courteous and passenger friendly.

12.3. For promotion to trade and industries, following steps will be undertaken :

(i) Abolition of On-Board Courier Scheme to facilitate courier trade

(ii) Introduction of "Known Shipper " scheme for reducing dwell time in exports by doing away with "cooling off" requirement

(iii) Introduction of EDI (Electronic Data Interchange) interlinking trade agencies, customs, immigration for faster efficient trade transactions

(iv) Private sector participation in cargo handling for increasing competition and improved services.

SAFETRY

1. Standards for civil aviation safety for all agencies will be set as per international norms prescribed by ICAO and enforced by CAA
2. New Communication, Navigation Surveillance/ Air Traffic Management (CNS/ATM) system will be introduced on a priority basis as per ICAO's regional plan.
3. Safety audit of various agencies in the civil aviation sector will be carried out by CAA.
4. Installation of Airborne Collision Avoidance system (ACAS), Ground Proximity Warning System (GPWS) and transponders will be mandatory on specific categories of aircraft to enhance safety in civil aviation.
5. Regular Flight Inspections will be carried out by CAA
6. Regular and systematic monitoring of recordings of Flight Recorder shall be mandatorily carried out by the operators as part of accident/ incident prevention programme. Random monitoring by CAA shall also be carried out.
7. Minimum Safe Altitude Warning (MSAW) system shall be provided in all secondary surveillance radars in the country to prevent Controlled Flights Into Terrain (CFIT) accidents.
8. Excellence in maintenance of equipment would be accorded high priority and system will be further refined to safeguard against any malfunctioning leading to loss of life or property.
9. The personnel should be specifically trained in responding to any safety-related emergency situation and role and responsibility of every functionary should be clearly specified. Regular mock exercises

will be conducted to deal with various possible emergencies.

Security

1. A strict national civil aviation security programme to safeguard civil aviation operations against acts of unlawful interference will be established through regulations, practices and procedures, which take account of the safety, regularity and efficiency of flights.
2. Periodic review of threat perception will be carried out taking into account the international situation, internal security scenario and other relevant inputs. Security arrangements and drills will be updated and upgraded regularly on this basis.
3. Strict security standards/ security programme will be set by BCAS (Bureau of Civil Aviation Security) under CAA as per ICAO Standards and recommended Practices with periodical review and enforced by them through regular security audit of various agencies involved.
4. Airport Security will be primary responsibility of AAI in all the airports whether managed by AAI or by private operators, as per the standards set by CAA. AAI will reorient its structure and processes suitably for the purpose.
5. Aircraft security will be primary responsibility of Airline-operator as per the standards set by CAA. Suitable manpower, training and procedures will be provided and set up by the airline operators to ensure this.
6. All arrangements made and personnel engaged for security functions will have to be licensed/ cleared by BCAS.

7. Evolving technologies and equipments will be constantly scanned for identifying those more suited to our secuity needs and their use will be encouraged thereby resulting in more effective security arrangements with leaner organisations.
8. Emphasis will be given on unobtrusive, effective, passenger-friendly security.
9. Emphasis will be given for state-of-art training of personnel engaged in security functions including in the areas of use of modern technology, passenger friendliness, specific requirements of aviation security. Special training modules will be developed for all types of possible emergencies, with clear analysis of different parameters, options available with consequent implications, and tune to developing requisite mindset and skills to act effectively
10. Contingency plans will be developed, kept up-to-date and the resources will be made available to safeguard airport and ground facilities used in civil aviation against acts of unlawful interference
11. Effective measures relating to passengers and their cabin luggage, checked baggage, cargo and other goods and access control will be taken as per international standards and recommended practices to prevent weapons, explosives or any other dangerous devices which may be used to commit an act of unlawful interference, the carriage or bearing of which is not authorised from being introduced, by any means whatsoever, on-board an aircraft engaged in civil aviation.
12. The plans and procedures for management of response to acts of unlawful interference in civil aviation operations would be reviewed and suitably modified from time to time.

Aviation Support Services

1. The role of aviation support services like human resource development, maintenance facilities and manufacture of aircraft is very important, as these are the backbone of civil aviation services. These services should be available in state-of-art condition in adequate supply in accordance with demand. For this, the role of private sector needs to be emphasised.

2. Training

   (i) Standards and guidelines for training institutions will be prescribed and enforced by CAA.

   (ii) Private sector participation will be encouraged in training institution for pilots, maintenance personnel, security staff and air-traffic controllers.

   (iii) Existing training and management institutes like Indira Gandhi Rashtriya Uran Akademi (IGRUA), National Institute of Aviation Management and Research (NIAMR), Civil Aviation Training College (CATC), Central Training Establishment (CTE), Flying Clubs etc. will be strengthened by involvement of private sector.

   (iv) Emphasis will be given for training of personnel for customer service including safety aspects of various equipment at the work places.

3. Maintenance

   (i) Private sector participation will be encouraged in existing maintenance infrastructure of Indian Airlines and Air India like Jet Engine Overhaul Complex (JEOC) and new maintenance facilities including engine overhaul and repairs with up to 100 % foreign equity.

4. Manufacture of Aircraft/ Engine

(i) Indigenous design, development and manufacture of light trainer and small transport aircraft, engine, components and spares etc will be encouraged

(ii) Offset clauses for sourcing aviation products/ services from India will be incorporated in the RFQ itself for import of aircraft by national carriers.

(iii) private sector participation will be encouraged.

(iv) Co-ordination with Department of Defence Production, Defence Research and Development Organization (DRDO), Hindustan Aeronautics Limited (HAL), Bharat Heavy Electrical Limited (BHEL) and other organisations will be strengthened.

Role of Regional and International Civil Aviation

1. India will continue to take active interest in the formulation of global policies on civil aviation and promote international cooperation between member states of International Civil Aviation Organisation (ICAO) to develop global aviation and infrastructure. India will continue its efforts to strengthen cooperation in the field of civil aviation in the region.

2. India will ensure participation in International Co-operation programmes like

   (i) Co-operative development of Operational Safety and Continued Airworthiness Programme (COSCAP) for training by international experts

   (ii) European Union Project for cooperation in civil aviation sector with European countries

   (iii) Regional Co-operation with for development/ provision of satellite based CNS / ATM systems as per ICAO plan

CO-ORDINATION

1. A number of department/ agencies are involved in the development of civil aviation infrastructure and facilitating the convenience of the traveling public. Inter-linkages with other modes of transport for travel and trade need to be emphasised.

2. An Inter-Ministerial Standing Committee will be constituted for coordination with Ministries of Commerce, Tourism, Industry, Railways, Surface Transport, Defence, Home Affairs (Immigration and Security), Finance (Customs) and External Affairs.

4

Integrated Tourism Planning

Planning usually begins with an initial idea that tourism development is a desired economic development strategy for the community. Many communities view tourism as a separate layer that is simply added to a community. Engaging in tourism from this viewpoint is always disappointing because it fails to integrate tourism into the social and economic life of the community. Tourism may already be partially included in local or regional recreation, land use, or economic development plans.

Tourism touches all aspects of a community-businesses, government services, the natural environment, and residents. Efforts to involve representatives of these various elements in discussions and decisions will help create positive attitudes and a healthy tourism industry that is in harmony with community values. All residents should be invited to participate in fundamental tourism development decisions.

Residents will be more inclined to support tourism if they are involved in initial discussions and have opportunities to voice their opinions. They will also be more willing to volunteer for tourist-related activities (recreation, information sharing, interpretation) and events (festivals, celebrations, sports) later on. The community tourism planning process described below provides a forum for local involvement. It emphasizes the inclusion of a variety of residents to:

— articulate community values

— select broad tourism goals for the community

— generate local support for tourism development

— help achieve tourism goals

— help monitor and evaluate tourism's success in meeting goals.

The steps are given below, needed to successfully build and maintain community involvement:

— Decide who should be involved

 — Assess current involvement. If lagging, actively solicit participation.

 — List people and groups affected. Invite them all!

 — Make the first meeting a well-publicized community event to draw a variety of participants who may stay on as volunteers.

— Gather information

 — Locate existing materials (current tourism efforts, information on who visits your community or region, etc.)

 — Determine whether there is enough information available for both tourism and nontourism interests to make basic decisions about tourism.

 — Gather additional information as needed (seek expert advice, conduct surveys, etc.)

— Conduct community meetings

 — Hold meetings to gather information, seek input, plan, or get feedback.

  - Present proposals and opportunities in terms of both costs and benefits.
  - Use group process techniques to elicit community values and ideas about tourism.
  - Limit the agenda to one or two questions; solutions may take several meetings.
  - Work toward consensus and establish priorities for actions.
- Communicate and evaluate
  - Distribute meeting results to the public via the media.
  - Solicit ongoing citizen feedback; be open to unexpected responses.
  - Continue meetings/consensus building until there is general agreement on goals.
  - Evaluate local involvement on an ongoing basis; assess shifts in attitudes and goals that may require a new direction for tourism development.

Community Tourism Planning Process

Planning is necessary for tourism to develop in a way that is beneficial, sustainable, and not detrimental to the environment, culture, and community. Integrate tourism planning into your overall community planning.

In communities with some tourism, development efforts often begin with an existing organization such as a chamber of commerce, retail association, or economic development group. The organization may provide initial leadership to planning efforts. Leadership may also come from tourism businesses, individuals, or elected officials. Planning will help community set goals for tourism and provide guidelines for development. Steps are given below:

Identify Tourism

The first step in the tourism planning process is to identify tourism as a possible economic development strategy.

Identify Participants

After identified tourism, identify key people who should be involved in or aware of planning activities. This group should represent the entire community. Community tourism development is often left to a small group of individuals who are directly involved in tourism-related businesses. Usually, these individuals mostly favor tourism development since their businesses and livelihoods depend on it.

Many others are affected by tourism and should be included in decision making. These stakeholders are usually more cautious about tourism and more vocal about potential negative impacts. Government agencies and elected officials are important partners for several reasons.

First, government is responsible for most of the infrastructure and services upon which tourism depends: water, sewer, law enforcement, emergency services, roads, and so on. Government participation will help ensure that infrastructure development, zoning, building policies, and regulations will facilitate tourism while meeting residents' needs. Second, government helps plan and manage many tourist attractions and facilities, such as recreational areas, parks, community swimming pools, beaches, and golf courses.

Local historical societies preserve, develop, and manage sites that attract visitors; youth organizations assist at county fairs; arts and ethnic organizations coordinate events. *Nongovernment organizations* also support specific causes such as environmental protection, youth training, and ethnic awareness development that can benefit tourism. Because nearly all businesses are affected by visitors at some point, they too should have an opportunity to be involved in tourism planning.

Small business operators may not have time to be actively involved in committee work, so you will need to identify other ways to include them. You can use simple methods such as asking for input on specific topics via mail or e-mail, or asking them to handle shortterm, specific tasks. Being involved will help them more clearly see the benefits, support tourism development, and potentially lend creative new ideas to the process. Be sure to include media-local and regional newspapers, radio stations, and cable television stations. They are important in keeping the public informed, and can be key influencers of community opinion.

Table 1 shows the variety of traditional and nontraditional community members and organizations that should be invited to participate in tourism planning. They are divided into those traditionally included in tourism and nontraditional stakeholders, who might easily be overlooked.

Table 1. Potential Participants for Community Tourism Planning

TRADITIONAL	NONTRADITIONAL
City, County, Government Officials	
Mayor or Chief Executive	Fire/Police Chief
City Council	Natural Resource/ Public Land Agencies
City Manager	Local Parks & Recreation Director
County Commissioners	Planning & Zoning Department

County Extension Educators	Transportation Dept. & Public Utilities
	Other Local Political Leaders
Civic, Business, Nonprofit Organizations	
Chamber of Commerce	Historical Society/ preservation Groups
Convention and Visitor Bureau	Cultural Organizations
Hotel/Restaurant Associations	Minority Groups/ Indigenous Populations
Downtown Business/Retail Associations	Environmental/ Conservation Groups
Economic Development Officer	Rotary/Lions/Optimist/ Kiwanis Civic Clubs
Attractions Associations	American Legion/Veterans of Foreign Wars
Business/Professional Clubs	Junior Chamber
Event & Festival Organizations	Garden Clubs and Other Civic Groups
Fine & Performing Arts Councils	Sports Clubs – Ski, Snowmobile, etc.
Local Businesses	
Hotel/Motel Managers	Service Station Owners
Tourist Attraction Operators	Automotive Dealers
Restaurant/Food Service Managers	Real Estate Agents
Theater/Amusement Operators	Newspaper Editor or Columnist
Outdoor Recreation Outfitters	Radio/TV Station Managers
Retail/Shop Owners	Grocers/Pharmacists
Taxi/Car Rental Operators	Banks or Financial Institutions
Travel Agents	Hospital/Medical/Insurance

Other Community Decision Influencers	
College & University Officials	Church Leaders
Local Tourism or Business Professors	Religious Organizations
School Principals/ Superintendent/Teachers	Other Decision Influencers

Hold an Initial Meeting

Once you have identified potential participants, schedule a meeting to explore the interest and support within your community for tourism development. Publicize the meeting widely and be sure people understand that it's open to all community members. Objectivity and facilitation/moderation skills should be key criteria. A county extension educator, local college or university faculty member, or paid professional facilitator can help keep the discussion flowing and directed toward your goals. This individual can also help develop the agenda. The agenda should include:

- introduction to tourism development
  - what it is, who is involved, etc.
  - tourism as an economic diversification strategy
  - benefits and costs of tourism
  - need for planning, community involvement
- open discussion
- identification of current tourism efforts
- quick identification of local assets
- decision to proceed or not to proceed

Tourism is not appropriate for every community. If, on the other hand, there is sufficient support and interest among he key decision makers in the community to proceed, you are ready to form a planning committee.

Form a Tourism Planning Committee

Before establishing a new committee, identify entities already involved in tourism. You may choose to have an existing entity lead the tourism development process. If it is a committee within a larger organization such as a chamber, you will develop the tourism planning effort under that umbrella and it will have to fit within the organization's goals and plan of work.

At some point down the road, you may want to create a separate organization. If you establish a separate committee, include representatives of key business, government, and nongovernment interests. Also include a representative from any organizations already involved in tourism to help avoid opposition or ill feelings. The committee may be appointed by government, the community, or a local organization, or it may be a self-determined group of interested parties. If it is a self-determined group, consider developing an organization early in the process.

Planning Process

Figure1 illustrates the flow of tourism planning. Planning is an ongoing process, not a one-time effort. Each step of the process should allow for modification or response to unforeseen circumstances. Monitoring and evaluating will help to refine your approach as needed to achieve the intended outcomes.

Step 1: Define tasks and roles

The committee should begin its work by deciding who will lead it and how tasks will be assigned and completed.

You'll also need to establish a funding source for the planning process. In most communities, funding is provided through an existing organization such as the chamber of commerce or economic development group. Or, your committee may seek funds from local government or from regional or state granting resources.

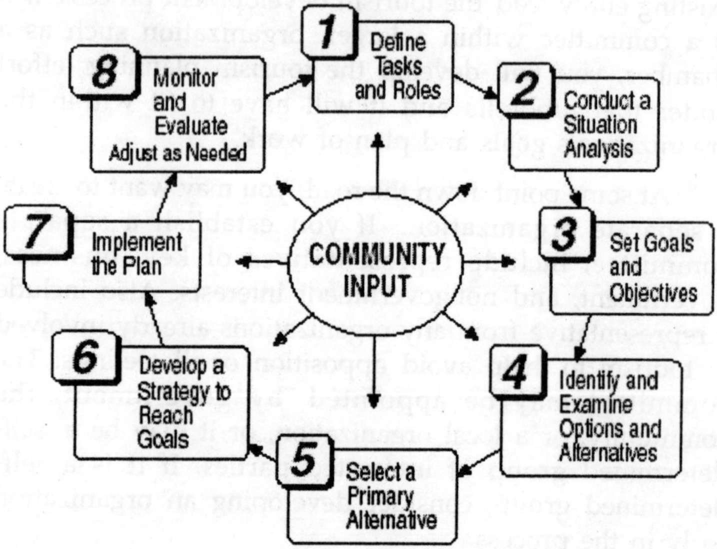

Figure 1. The Community Tourism Planning Process

Next, determine your time line. This will help you get active participation, generate community support, and show results. Communities just starting the process can expect to spend up to two years to create and begin implementing a tourism development plan. The sample time line provided in the preface can help you.

Step 2: Conduct a situation analysis

The situation analysis is the research aspect of planning. It involves gathering information about community resources, current and potential target markets, and your competition. You need to inventory and objectively assess the quantity and quality of what you have to offer in order to focus tourism development effectively. An important part of your situation analysis should be an overview of trends in external "environments" (Figure 2) that might influence your tourism development efforts.

You will also want to identify and consider tourism trends. For local tourism trends, consult regional and state tourism organizations. For international trends, consult the World Tourism Organization, World Travel and Tourism Council (WTTC) and Travel Industry Association of America (TIA). Assessments of existing attractions and services as well resident and business attitudes toward tourism is a key part of your situation analysis.

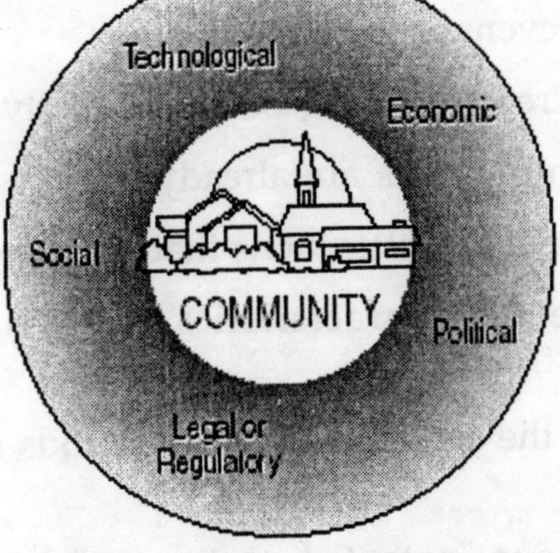

Figure2. External environments

The situation analysis should also include a profile of the current visitor market, estimated numbers of tourists visiting your community, and the economic impact. Visitor profile information includes:

— an average of the total tourist visitation (preferably by season)

— estimates of daily and total expenditures by visitors

— demographic information (age, education, income, residence)

— trip-specific information (activities, attractions visited, accom-modations, purpose of trip, satisfaction levels).

Economic profiles are useful in determining what role tourism plays in the community's overall economy (e.g., jobs, personal income, number of businesses, tax revenues). Key questions to ask at this stage include:

— How big a role does tourism currently play in our local economy?

— How does tourism compare with other sectors of the local economy in terms of jobs, income, businesses, and tax revenues generated?

— Who is already visiting our community and why?

— How many tourists are already coming per year?

— What are the key attractions that are drawing tourists?

— What are the characteristics of tourists who are coming?

— What are the current and future trends in travel and tourism?

— Who are our "potential customers," based on these trends?

The answers to these questions will provide a current snapshot of the importance of tourism to your community and a baseline to use later as you develop marketing strategies and monitor economic impacts. Finally, identify the internal strengths and weaknesses and external opportunities and threats for the community. Internal strengths are resources or capabilities that help achieve stated goals.

Internal weaknesses are deficiencies in resources or capabilities that may prevent you from achieving your goals. Opportunities are outside factors that may be beneficial, while threats are uncontrollable outside factors that may cause negative effects. Assessing these elements, frequently identified by the acronym SWOT, will help you develop effective strategies that focus on the strengths and opportunities while minimizing or overcoming weaknesses and threats.

Divide into teams or pairs. Assign each one of the four categories (strengths, weaknesses, opportunities, or threats). Allow about 20 minutes for participants to list things in their categories that may affect the community's tourism efforts. While participants are working, post a piece of newsprint for each SWOT category on the wall. At the end of the 20 minutes, ask participants to call out their responses. List them on the newsprint, consolidating similar responses as appropriate. When finished, discuss the findings and implications.

Step 3: Set goals and objectives

Setting goals and objectives means stating clearly what tourism will bring to the community. Goals are the broad statements about the community's vision for tourism. They establish long- and short-term targets you hope to achieve as a result of tourism development. Goals may relate to economic, social, or environmental needs. Some examples:

— to create long-term sustainability for natural, cultural, and social resources

— to identify and create partnerships within the region

— to create job opportunities and economic benefit

— to preserve local culture and indigenous arts.

These are then translated into objectives. Objectives explain how you will achieve the goals. They address the concerns and strengths inherent in the goals. Good objectives are clear, concise, measurable, and include a specific action within a set time frame.

Step 4: Identify and examine options and alternatives

Prioritize your goals and objectives according to the internal and external factors you identified through the situation analysis. Then, using your goals and objectives as a guide, generate a list of options and alternatives for tourism development projects and strategies. This is the time for creative thinking and brainstorming. There is no single "right" alternative.

Next weigh alternatives according to the opportunities and potential for success they offer in achieving your goals. Consider resources, time lines, market trends, and community needs. Goals and objectives will evolve and become more focused as your involvement with tourism and tourism planning grows. For example, in the early stages of tourism development, goals may involve establishing organizational structures and collecting information.

Selecting goals that produce short-term success might be an effective strategy for building community support early in your development program. There are many methods to identify and prioritize goals. The nominal group process is a method that allows everyone in a group to have input.

Step 5: Select a primary alternative: The primary alternative is simply the one(s) that you decide to move forward with. There is no "right" alternative.

Step 6: Develop a strategy to reach goals: The selected alternative will now guide the development of strategies and specific actions to fulfill the goals and objectives.

Step 7: Implement the plan: Now that you have drafted a plan, it's time to implement it. Follow through with your planned strategies.

Step 8: Monitor and Evaluate: Monitoring and evaluation of your efforts is critical. It allows you to measure how well you are meeting your goals, and to make adjustments if necessary. Evaluation will help you identify what is or isn't contributing to the progress of your tourism efforts.

Evaluation must be continual to be effective. Build evaluation measures into each effort from the beginning. Establish measures to evaluate quantity and quality of outputs, time lines, and the effectiveness of the selected alternative. Regular monitoring and evaluation enables you to identify weaknesses or problems so that corrections can be made before they become unmanageable. Regular monitoring also provides a basis for comparison, and for forecasting future trends.

5

Development of Tourism Infrastructure

The tourism industry includes establishments whose products are mainly sold to visitors, though they do not form a major share of tourist consumption. Several infrastructure sectors like power,telecommunication, water supply, roads and some production sectors like travel items, sports equipment, photographicmaterials, medicines and cosmetics are included in this category. The infrastructure for tourism thus includes basic infrastructure components like airports, railways, roads, waterways; amenities like electricity, water supply, drainage,sewerage, solid waste disposal systems and services and facilities like accommodation, restaurants, recreational facilities and shopping facilities.

Planning for sustainable development of tourism, therefore, involves the integrated development of basic infrastructure and amenities along with all the tourism facilities in a balanced manner. In India, the responsibilities of the union government and the state/union territory (U. T.) governments are elaborated in the Constitution in separate schedules. The union government is responsible for matters such as external affairs, visa regulations, foreign exchange regulations and import/export procedures, while the state/U.T. governments are responsible for law and order, land use, civic amenities, shops and establishments.

Both the union government and the state Governments have departments and specialized agencies dealing with specific subjects and regulations. For example, the Central Department of Tourism is concerned with the over-all coordination and planning of tourism development in the country, apart from undertaking tourism promotion and publicity abroad. It also provides some incentives and undertakes several developmental schemes.

The Reserve Bank of India is a specialized agency dealing with foreign exchange regulations and granting automatic approvals to foreign investment and collaborationproposals. Most of the delivery systems and infrastructure for tourism are in the hands of state/U.T. governments. They control all factors of production, including land in their territories.

Policy of Tourism

A comprehensive tourism policy highlighting the importance of tourism and the objectives of tourism development for the country was promulgated by the Government in 1982. The policy envisaged developing many attractions in India for tourism through well-planned, well-defined and fully-integrated national programmes. It specified the responsibility for tourism development as a common endeavour of all agencies vitally concerned with tourism at central and state levels, including public and private sector enterprises; airlines, railways and road transport systems; municipal and local bodies as well as cultural and educational institutions. It further provided an action plan based on a "travel circuit" concept to maximize the benefits of tourism.

The plan proposed to achieve intensive development of selected circuits, dispel the tendency of concentration in a few urban centres, encourage the diversification of tourist attractions and open economically-backward areas which have many tourist attractions. Tourism was recognized as an industry by 1986 and became eligible for incentives and facilities, including taxincentives, subsidies, priorities in the sanctioning of loans by state financial institutions and preferences in providingelectricity, water and sewerage connections.

A National Action Plan for Tourism was drawn up in 1992 and it envisaged an increase in the percentage share of tourist arrivals in India from 0.4 to 1 per cent of world arrivals within a period of five years. Employment in the tourism sector was also expected to double by the turn of the century.

The basic strategy for increasing the tourist flow includes improvement of infrastructure facilities in identified circuits and destinations, development of special tourism areas, diversification of tourism products, development of pilgrim tourism and a package of incentives for attracting private investment to the tourism sector. It is now being proposed to increase tourist arrivals to 5 million by the turn of the century. This would mean substantial expansion of tourism infrastructure facilities like hotels, restaurants, tourist coaches, cars, air taxis, entertainment facilities and so forth.

The strategy for achieving the national objective is to establish all inclusive "Special Tourism Areas" and undertake intensive infrastructure development for identified circuits and destinations.

Development Schemes

Since most infrastructure elements and the delivery systems are within the puNiew of the state Governments or private sector, tourism infrastructure is being developed mainly with financial assistance to state/U.T. governments and by providing various incentives to private entrepreneurs. Specific schemes for which financial assistance is provided to the States include the following:

- Construction schemes
  - Forest lodges
  - Tented accommodation
  - Tourist complexes/tourist lodges
  - Wayside amenities
  - Mote 1st cafet e ri as/resta u rants
  - Tourist reception centres
  - Pilgrim sheds/dormitories, etc. at pilgrimage centres
  - Public conveniences
- Tourist transport
  - Mini-buses, jeeps, elephants, etc. for wild life viewing
  - Cruise boats, ferry launchers, etc. for water transport
  - Tourist coaches in selected circuits
  - Special tourist trains

The most frequent pattern of funding which has continued over successive plan periods is known as "normalfunding". Under this pattern, the Central Department of Tourism meets almost the entire expenditure, except the cost of land and interior decoration in the case of construction projects. A new method of funding by way of grant-in-aid towards project cost was introduced during 1992-1993. In this scheme, 28 per cent of the project cost is provided by the central government and 12 per cent is provided by the state government.

The balance of 60 per cent has to be raised as a loan from financial institutions or banks. This method of funding is applicable to projects requiring large investments. It is expected that the state governments would be able to mobilize more resources from financial institutions for investment in tourism projects through this method.

Incentives to Private Entrepreneurs

Hotels and tourism-related activities have been declared as a priority sector for foreign investment. As aresult, foreign equity participation in tourism projects is automatically allowed up to 51 per cent, and higher percentages of foreign equity can be approved on a case-by-case basis.

Tourism industries are also eligible for a number of incentives, such as interest subsidy, income tax exemption, reduced customs duty, etc. There are specific incentives being provided by the Central Department of Tourism. One specific incentive is for approved hotels up to the 3-star category and heritage hotels outside the four metro-cities which are eligible for an interest subsidy for loans from the Industrial Finance Corporation of India, Tourism Finance Corporation of India and State Financial Corporations.

The rates of interest subsidy are (a) 5 per cent for 1 to 3-star category hotels in areas identified for intensive development; (b) 5 per cent for heritage hotels outside metropolitan areas; and (c) 3 per cent for all other 1 to 3-star category hotels outside metropolitan areas. In order to encourage the owners of heritage properties to convert palaces, forts, havelis, etc. of any size into heritage hotels, a capital subsidy scheme was introduced since May 1993.

Under the scheme, a capital subsidy of 10 per cent of the project cost or Rs.500,OOO, which ever is less, is available for developing any structure of 75 years or older as a heritage hotel.

Domestic travel agents and tour operators are given assistance to develop markets abroad. Assistance isgiven for market research, promotional visits abroad, and so forth. An Investment Facilitation Cell has been set up in the Department of Tourism to provide assistance to prospective entrepreneurs. The specific activities of the cell are:

— . Formulation of national investment policies related to tourism industries;

— Coordination and integration of state policies on tourism;

— Prepare investment profiles for each state in collaboration with the respective state Governments. Profiles will include information on identified priority centres for tourism development, details of existing infrastructure, expected demand, availability of land and other support services, agencies to be contacted, etc.;

— Regular interactions with prospective entrepreneurs both within the country and abroad to promote investment in tourism;

— Establishing linkages with embassies and other institutions to highlight investment opportunities in tourism;

— Process investment proposals received from both local and foreign investors and obtain approvals and clearances from various agencies;

— Assist entrepreneurs to get import licences, finance, land, etc., by coordinating with the respective agencies and the state governments; and

— Provide technical assistance wherever required.

Product Development

India has been mainly conceived as a cultural tourist destination, but it has diverse tourist attractions which need to be developed. A conscious policy has, therefore, been adopted to diversify and improve tourism products of India, including cultural tourist attractions. The schemes implemented through state governments for product development are:

- Promotion of fairs and festivals, rural craft, melas, etc.
- refurbishment of monuments and environmental planning;
- flood lighting/son et lumiere (SEL) shows;
- development of pilgrim centres;
- development of adventure sports facilities;
- designation of special tourism areas; and
- development of specific circuits through external aid.

National Sstrategy for Development Tourism

A national strategy for the development of tourism has recently been developed for synergizing the activities of different infrastructure sectors, the state governments and the private sector for tourism development. The specific components of the strategy include:

- Infrastructure development;
- Product development and diversification, including development of mega-tourism resorts;
- Entrepreneurial development and promotion of self-employment opportunities;

— Enhanced tourist facilitation;
— Human resources development;
— Research and computerization;
— Promotion and marketing;
— Environmental protection and cultural preservation;
— Provision of incentives; and
— Monitoring and evaluation and strengthening of organisations.

The word tourism encompasses all activities of persons travelling to and staying in places outside their usual environment for not more than one consecutive year for leisure, business and other purposes. These activities make demands for goods and services, and the establishments which provide such services are considered as part of the tourism industry.

Use of Mobile Technologies

Tourism is an activity of great importance both economically and in terms of the pleasure it gives to holidaymakers worldwide. Nearly all individuals in the western world take some sort of holiday away from home every year, although the number of days differs across and within different countries. Tourism is also an activity that can divide rich and poor, through a negative or parasitical effect that damages places: 'touristification' .

The cities, Edinburgh and Glasgow, are the second and third most popular cities for tourists to visit in the U.K., after London. Summer is a particularly busy time of the year for both cities, with the Edinburgh Festival a major tourist attraction. Some of the tourists are predominantly independent travellers, who had mostly arranged their own travel although some used the assistance of a travel agency.

While the package tour market is obviously a very important part of tourism, since this group suffers more acutely from problems of organisation. While a major proportion of independent travellers are 'backpackers', young people travelling for a prolonged period of time before entering paid employment, independent travellers are a diverse group with a wide age range.

One example is that tourists often need to use public transport to get between places. To do this they need to solve a number of practical problems, such as finding where bus stops are, finding out which bus to get, and so on. The most important part of tourism for the purposes of designing new tourism systems. This emphasises the decisions that tourists make and the information they use to make these decisions.

Tourist Problems and Solutions

The first, seemingly straightforward, problem which tourists face in an unfamiliar place is what to do. Unlike work, where tasks are often determined (in part) by an overall goal or by other people's plans, tourism is much more open-ended. Tourism encompasses a broad range of activities such as sightseeing, relaxing, shopping, visiting friends and visiting family.

Indeed, since tourism can be part of business travel, the boundary between work and leisure is often blurred. Yet whatever tourists do, they must at least make some sort of decision about what to do, often in advance. This decision must take into account the time it takes to get to different places, as well as balancing the attraction of different sites.

When one reaches a tourist site one has to be careful about how one acts, since behavioural norms can be different in different countries. Ignorance about local customs is an oft mocked feature of tourists. Even straightforward activities such as buying goods can be organised differently in different countries, compounded with the problems of working with a new currency, and avoiding being exploited, or just 'looking stupid'. Along with what and how, tourists have to manage when they do different activities. Tourism is usually constrained in time, because of the need to return home.

Time is also a problem in that tourists work with organisations that provide services: opening times must be co-ordinated with the times of public transport, such as trains or buses. This is compounded by the 'pre-booking problem'. Many facilities require pre-booking, so decisions need to be made before one has been to a place. In visiting a city many of the attractions are distributed around the city. There is therefore a need to minimise the times spend travelling between places, understand what one might see and do along the way, and group together attractions which are close together.

In doing so tourists must also navigate public transport, often with limited information, or unfamiliar road systems. Lastly, an important part of a holiday is sharing that holiday with others who are at home. Although the tourist fascination with taking photos or videos has been often criticised, it displays how visitors are not isolated individuals but are part of a social group. Tourists record and represent experiences in the form of photos and stories, to remind themselves of the visit and to share with others after they return home. This is a valuable part of tourism.

The most successful tourist technology is the camera, specifically designed for this 'taking the visit back home'. The popularity of Internet cafés for tourists also suggests that email sent back home is becoming a significant part of the tourist experience.

These 'problems' are not a negative part of tourism. Travelling and finding out where to go is part of the very enjoyment of tourism. Tourism transforms what might seem mundane activities into something enjoyable or even romantic. Train journeys, for example, are a common resource for the travel writer, and bus and underground travel can have their own pleasures (such as the smell of the train's tires in the Parisian metro, or the electronic sounds of the Tokyo subway).

Particularly in city visits, walking between places is an important part of being in a place, with 'street life' being one of the easiest ways to access the natural life of locals. These pleasures are a whimsical yet crucial part of the enjoyment of tourism. So, in solving these problems tourists are not simply looking for some optimal solution. Instead, solving these problems is part of the enjoyment of the experience; finding a nice café or reading a map, for example, is enjoyable in itself. Accordingly, the solutions that tourists have to these problems are often finely tuned to both the problem and the enjoyment of working through the problem.

One method that tourists use to solve their problems is sharing the visit with other tourists. Tourism is very much a social activity. A tourist generally travels with others, e.g. as part of a family group, and statistics from the US show that 79% of leisure visits involve groups of two or more. Since leisure travel is predominantly group-based, there is considerable intra-group interaction and collaboration.

The first tourist holds an "A to Z" street guide and is looking through it. While the second tourist glances around the railway station, the first tourist finds the correct page of the map. Then the second tourist takes out her glasses to look at the map, glances at the map and then points at an exit sign in the train station that names the street to which the exit leads. They then give the street guide a last look, pick up their bags and leave the station. Even in this simple excerpt one can see a division of labour between the two tourists. The second tourist looks around the station to find the exit, while the first tourist tries to find the correct page on the map. She holds the map so as to make both the map and her progress in using it available to her companion.

On finding the station, she describes the location of the station to her friend, and the friend adds the name of the street reached via the exit. With these two items of information, they now know where they are on the map, where the exit will take them and how to proceed to their destination. Reading the map is done here in such a way that it can be 'checked' by the first tourist's companion. If she makes a mistake (which is easy to do), or if they later find themselves lost, the companion can intervene. The job of remembering the route is thus shared by the two tourists. Together they use the environment to move between the map and a course of activity. The sign in the station is used to link the map with where the station exit leads.

Along with these collaborative advantages of working together, visiting with others is not without its own overheads. With the collaborative 'working out' in this clip there is also an implicit negotiation going on. The two tourists are deciding what they are going to do as well as how. Visiting with others involves considerable co-ordination in this way. The desire to visit different attractions, or simply to see different museum exhibits, means that tourist groups often split up and then need to co-ordinate getting back together. This can present considerable challenges since tourists are highly mobile. It is in these situations that mobile phones become a useful tool, in that calls can be made between individuals or sub-groups.

A more local form of this co-ordination problem also takes place in particular sites where individuals go to different rooms, or different exhibits, and they need to locate their travelling companions. This is particularly the case for tourists with children, since children sometimes run off, and must be carefully watched to see that they come to no harm. In the incidents researchers observed, mothers spent considerable time shepherding children around museums, in particular, collecting all the children together before leaving the museum. For these parents a large part of their holiday was 'managing' the group and making sure that nobody got lost.

A second way in which visits are shared is through meeting other tourists. The standard jokes about holiday romances displays something of how meeting other people is an integral part of many tourist experiences. In part, these opportunities come from the lowered barriers to social contact. Individuals are 'on holiday' from many of their home commitments. The facilities that tourists use, such as hostels, trains and buses, also can also afford social contact. One reason behind these social contacts, and certainly a common conversation topic, is the exchange of stories and advice on where to go and what to visit.

Role of Guidebooks in Tourism

A second way tourists solve their problems is the use of published information. The two most quintessential tourist publications are the guidebook and the map. These are often used in combination when tourists navigate and find out about what to do in different places and how to get between them. While both have been subject to computerisation, this has had only limited success.

In part, this limited success can be put down to a lack of knowledge about how maps and guidebooks are actually used by tourists. Studying the use of these conventional paper publications can reveal some of the advantages of paper publications and how to better design their digital equivalents. Guidebooks come in many different forms, from free handouts to Michelin and Baedeker guides. One reason why guidebooks are so useful to tourists is that they catalogue, in a structured and relatively standardised form, relevant aspects of the places that tourists visit. They list accommodation (with phone numbers), attractions (with opening times), recommended bars and restaurants, and so on. This standardisation can make strange places feel considerably safer to tourists by reducing their uncertainty.

Guidebooks also offer short 'guides to action'. highlighting differences in everyday activities that might cause embarrassment. In use, however, this information needs considerable interpretation-guidebooks need to be 'put in their place'. What the guidebook says has to be combined with other information, in particular information on maps, or advice from locals. Tourists holding a map and a guidebook, and using these in combination.

In particular, guidebooks were collaborative artefacts, conversation would take palce around the guidebook with tourists pointing at the guidebook, and then pointing either at a map or in a direction, so as to link together the establishments being discussed with their position.

The tourists go through a number of descriptions of where the house is and what it is like to help them find it with eventually the age helping them to find the house "its probably the old one". These descriptions help the tourists to find the house, along with informing them about what they are visiting. Even with a map, a guidebook, and the assistance of a local, the tourists need to work the guidebook to 'place' the old house on the street they are actually on, and overcome some of the confusions of streets which change name, the difference between how a street is named on a map and a name that locals use.

In this way, tourists take the information held in guidebooks and combine this with information they find from particular places, such as street names or train timetables in a railway station. This is how guidebooks are 'put in their place'. In designing technologies for tourism also pay attention to a second aspect of guidebooks: their physical form. Pages in guidebooks can be easily bookmarked by placing one's fingers into the pages at multiple points in the book, and opening the book on a particular page.

While this might seem a trivial operation, it supports jumping between different pages quickly so as to compare and combine information, with the fingers acting as bookmarks. This is important, since much of the work of tourists is this very comparison and combination-as in combining information on maps with descriptions.

Different publications can also be arranged so they are in the visual field at the same time. Conversations over accommodation at the TIC would often take place with the guides laid across the serving desk, with staff helping visitors through the guides to show where different sorts of accommodation in the city were. In this way, the format of the paper guide allowed both staff and visitor to interact around the guide.

Role of Maps in Tourism

Maps have of course been a well-researched artefact in fields as widespread as cognitive psychology and cultural studies. The specific topic of way-finding has been explored in depth. One finding from these studies is that map users are significantly better at tasks that involve configuration information than those without maps, sometimes better even than local people with years of knowledge of a place.

However, perhaps surprisingly, there is little work that has examined the in-situ, non-experimental use of maps. As Correll and Heth argue, there is a need for work which studies "humans navigating real world routes" since little work has looked at the 'naturalistic' use of maps: how they are used in situ without an experimental task.

Tourists using maps in situations where they did not know exactly where they are going, but only had an idea of a particular area that they were heading towards. This was usually because they believed that they would find something interesting in that area, although they had no specific attraction in mind. Alternatively, tourists used maps to go towards a specific type of attraction, such as a café, but with no specific café in mind-they would head towards a street where they thought there would be cafés.

Tourists also often only had a rough idea of where they were, and would use a map to locate or orient themselves so as to head in a 'roughly correct' direction, rather than along a specific route. So, in using a map, tourists might not know where they were, might have little idea about their orientation, might not know where they were going, and might even be unsure about what they were looking for. So, map use is often less about explicit route planning and more about wandering a city in a 'roughly correct' manner. The routes that tourists used were more directional than specific, with tourists frequently stopping en route, using the map to find the direction to walk in, and then setting off again.

A second feature of map use is their combination with guidebooks. A key aspect of this is how tourists combine characteristics and geography in an attempt to simultaneously solve the problems of where things are and what things there are. One way of doing this that researchers observed exploits the 'social zoning' of cities. As any frequent visitor will know, one of the most effective ways to find a restaurant in an unfamiliar city is to simply wander around a central area.

Although by no means a perfect way of finding particular amenities, walking around exploits the tendency of certain facilities (such as bars and restaurants) to be clustered in particular area. In this way, one can also judge establishments by their appearance and menu, as one walks past.

These 'clusters' are exploited in tourists' use of maps. When choosing where to go to, it is often safer to pick an area with more than one potential facility. Researchers observed tourists heading towards a 'restaurant zone' of a city, often with one restaurant in mind, but with the flexibility to go elsewhere should that restaurant prove to be busy or unsuitable. By combining maps and guidebooks, tourists can look for 'clusters' of facilities in particular areas and go towards these particular areas rather than (or in addition to) heading towards a specific establishment. This is not to say that maps are never used for working out how to get to specific places or attractions, but observations showed some of the problems that tourists had in doing this.

Following a route on a map involves considerable interpretation as one moves around a city. A tourist has to link between the map and what they see of streets and landmarks. When staff in the tourist information centre gave directions, they combined two different methods. One set of directions was given by drawing a line on a map-a portable and abstract version that can be used by a tourist to find their destination. Staff combined this with 'showing' in physical space where the destination was and how to get there: saying "it's behind us on Argyle Street" while using an arm movement to point in a specific direction.

A last point about maps' use concerns how they are frequently read in advance of getting to the place the map describes. This was a common use of maps researchers observed. A major aim of using a map is to learn about a place sufficiently that one can get around without using a map, learning about a place by looking at where the streets go, the names of the streets and potential landmarks.

Technologies For Tourists

Although tourism presents a number of barriers to introducing new technology - in particular the need for devices to be sufficiently mobile - tourists have already adopted many new technologies, e.g. the web, mobile phones and digital cameras. This suggests that there are opportunities for new tourist systems which fit tourist practice.

An important part of tourism is sharing the visit with others. One problem that tourists face is co-ordinating their activities while they are separated - in particular getting groups back together again. One application that would assist this is a handheld- or phone-based system that allowed tourists to communicate their location to each other. So, if a group splits into two, they could choose to 'tie' their locations together so that each subgroup would be able to see where the other was.

'Tying' in this way could support synchronous awareness without running into difficult privacy problems. In addition, technology could support tourists showing the routes they took and things they did when they meet up again. This could allow them to make recommendations to their companions and also to other tourists who they meet.

These ideas are developing in the City system, a system that supports co-visiting between PDA users in different location, along with web and VR users in other locations. This system allows a tourists' visit to be shared with others over the Internet. Each user can see where others are, communicate over an audio link, use hypermedia related to their locations in the city centre, and share information about their visit.

A second aspect of sharing visits is collaboration between tourists who do not know each other. One recommendation here is for technology to support sharing comments and reviews on different tourist attractions. However, it is important here to make this an interactive experience between tourists; exchange of information is as much about meeting other tourists as it is exchanging information. This could be supported by using public machines or message walls where tourists can meet as they exchange information.

Role of Electronic Guides and Maps

Electronic guidebooks and maps have been a popular application area for mobile technology, with existing system generally following a similar format to paper guidebooks, augmented with GPS. There are a number of limitations with this design. In particular, the rich affordances of paper guidebooks suggests that to be successful, electronic guidebooks must offer compelling advantages over their paper equivalents. Simply copying content into an eBook is unlikely to be successful if that content is much harder to use.

One innovation that electronic guidebooks could support is in making connections between where attractions are and what they are. Electronic guidebooks should expliclty support the comparison of information, allowing users to quickly move between related pieces of information. Partly due to the limited screen size, mobile systems seldom offer this feature.

Pocket internet explorer, for example, only allows the user to load one web page at a time. One solution to this could be to produce paper maps which are designed to be used with an electronic guidebook. This would remove some of the disadvantages of the small screen by allowing users to juxtapose the PDA and the map in their visual field. In addition, by using the cameras increasingly common in devices, users could point out areas of interest on the map in a way that was apparent both to the system and to one's friends, triggering on-screen display of information.

Mapping systems could also support more of the 'wandering' behaviour of tourists; for example, showing at a glance whether a tourist is going in the right direction rather than simply displaying a pre-determined route. Indicators could show close by attractions, cafés, areas or main streets to support surreptitious discovery. These sort of representations move beyond supporting wayfinding to supporting the broader range of tasks which tourists undertake when navigating.

So, such a representation would support going between one shopping district and another, while looking for a café. In cases like this it is not the exact route that is important, although walking in the right direction is, but a more general sense of learning about the city as one wanders around.

Pre- and Post-visiting

Tourists pre-visit a place by reading about it before they go there. Through arranging information and reading about a place before travelling, a tourist can do some of the organising activity for the holiday before the holiday. As with many of the other solutions outlined above, pre-visiting is not only practical; it is enjoyable. It extends the excitement of the holiday and builds anticipation as well as giving the visitor some sort of idea of what they are visiting before they get there.

Pre-visiting also happens while on the holiday itself, with tourists gathering information about places and planning what they are going to do. One important aspect of tourist planning is that it is 'satisficing', in that plans are 'good enough' rather than detailed plans of activity. Indeed, tourists' plans are often deliberately ambiguous so that they can take into account future contingencies. As Suchman argues, plans often do not determine behaviour but rather are used flexibly in deciding what to do. This acknowledges that decisions are often easier to make when one is actually in a particular place.

For example, when planning a route, planning the complete route in advance using a map is often quite difficult. An alternative approach is to plan an ambiguous route in advance, and then picking specific roads by using road signs when one is driving. In this way, tourist plans are often deliberately designed to be only as specific as necessary.

A number of the tourists talked about allocating days to particular places before they travelled. This sort of planning leaves a lot unspecified: when each day is, and what activities are done in each place, for example. Yet this sort of planning acknowledges that these sort of details are better kept flexible until closer to the time, as they will be dependent on local transport details, and can be adjusted in the face of other local contingencies, such as changing weather.

Indeed, a stereotypical bad holiday is one that is excessively planned, in that changing circumstances are not be taken into account. A second interesting aspect of tourist plans is how they follow or copy plans provided by others. A popular example of this is the package holiday, but even on package holidays not all of one's time is structured: many activities still involve some planning during the visit.

For the tourists, bus tours were frequently used to help structure the visit in this way. One group of tourists took the tour bus on the first day they visited the city, so as to obtain an 'overview' of the city that they used on later days to organise the rest of their visit. While on the bus, one passenger drew a line on his map as the bus travelled around the city, letting him record where he had been for later recollection, and helping him to link the different sights together.

In this way these bus tours had a role as an 'organising device' for a city visit, providing information about the key streets and attractions and allowing one to visit these again at leisure. The tours thus provided information and structure about the city, as much as being a strict plans or activity to follow in themselves. If pre-visiting is about planning, then post-visiting is about reminiscing and sharing.

Photographs are very important for this activity in that they provide a framework around which stories can be told and experiences shared. Talking through the visit with photographs can take place both with those who were present on holiday and those who were not; in one form it is reminiscence, in another it allows the holiday to be shared. The combination of talk and interaction around pictures supports both these activities.

Post-visiting is thus a powerful way of extending the enjoyment of a tourist visit out beyond the visit itself. It also acts as a recommendation mechanism for different places - it allowing to see 'what places are like', and outside the commercially produced views of brochures and television.

Indeed, some tourists who are on longer holidays go to the point of creating rich travelogues of their holiday, involving photographs, videos and text which are brought together to tell the story of their holiday. These travelogues usually exist in the form of photo albums, although a number of travelogues do exist on the Internet. However, there are considerable barriers to creating travelogues online-crafting web pages can take considerable time, and access to a PC and the internet can be difficult while on holiday.

Distinct from guidebooks, electronic tour guides systems attempt to offering information about a visitor's current location, and suggestions of where they might want to go next. These systems, such as the Lancaster GUIDE system, and more recently the EU funded "m-toGuide" system, have generally been based around a 'walk-up pop-up' model where information (voice, and text) is pushed at users based on their current location.

Tourists frequently used maps and guides before visiting a place—an activity is called 'pre-visiting'. In this way tourists can plan what they want to do, but also can pass the time while waiting for public transport. Presenting information to tourists while they are actually at an attraction may have limited utility, since at that point the environment is likely to contain richer sources of information that can be provided by a PDA.

Tourists often do not follow tours in a straightforward way. Tours instead act as structures through which tourists can learn about the place being visited, and use to build their own, more ad hoc plans. Systems should therefore present tours and attractions to tourists in such a way as to allow them to browse and learn from the tours rather than strictly following them, and to be aware of 'official' tourist attractions without being restricted to them.

Viewing tours in advance would allow tourists to 'pre-visit' and judge different places and make their own plans about what to do rather than necessarily following an official tour. To explicitly support pre-visiting tourist systems could also experiment with different ways of representing information about the city. Most existing systems present the positions of tourist attractions by overlaying icons representing attractions onto maps.

Mobile systems could instead support 'occasioned maps'. These are maps which are drawn for a particular purpose. For example, if a user is going shopping the system could build a shopping map, which highlights the good shopping streets, particularly popular stores, reviews of stores, cafés and so on. Systems which understanding something of the structure of places could produce maps which are specifically focused towards particular activities.

Importance of post-visiting for tourists, allowing them to communicate and discuss their visit when they got home. Travelblog' system allows tourists to build web-based travelogues describing their travels. These entries consist of pictures, videos and text captured on a Nokia 7650 camera-phone. These entries are then emailed from the phone to a server that automatically builds a web log combining the images and text.

While some travel-blogs are already on the Internet, created through increasingly popular web-logging software. Although this mechanism is very simple, it supports travellers updating their travelblog from anywhere in the world and extends the value of weblogs to the travelling tourist.

6

Energy for Tourism Development

Every business has a balance sheet expense called 'energy'. For some, the amount is only a few percent of the total operating expense, but for many businesses - particularly in the tourism sector - it is a major item that heavily influences 'bottom line' profits. Yet, many businesses do not understand the way they use -and often pay for - energy, which is often inefficient and results in both waste and unnecessary expense. But the cost of energy is not just a business expense - its generation and use can also be a significant expense to the environment and to the community, although this cost is rarely paid.

For a tourism business that relies on the fossil fuels of coal oil and gas to run their operations, this environmental expense shows up as air and water pollution, toxic waste and climate change. Although tourism businesses and their customers may not pay these costs directly, they are all impacts that can have a direct effect on a tourism business by reducing the desirability of tourism destinations. The mounting environmental debt from fossil fuel energy use is cause for great concern, which is beginning to drive actions to reduce these environmental impacts. Further, as customers become more aware of these impacts, they increasingly demand action to reduce them through their purchases of cleaner goods and services.

In the tourism sector, this awareness is driving an expanding 'ecotourism' movement, but it is also having a general impact on the sector. Governments, business and individuals are responding through a wide range of actions, beginning with energy efficiency and continuing through investments in renewable energy. In this response, many tourism businesses are discovering that it is possible to reduce their energy expenses, increase profit and meet increasing customer expectations of environmental responsibility. Renewable forms of energy thus offer an exciting opportunity to the tourism sector.

Renewable energy is abundant, clean, and inexhaustible. It is also the most cost-effective energy source for a variety of applications, meeting between 15 and 20 percent of total world energy demand and 24 percent of the world's total electricity supply.Renewable energy in the form of traditional biomass fuels, such as wood and crop residues, represents about 14 percent of the world's total energy consumption-a larger share than coal (12 percent). However, the contribution of newer renewable energy technologies is increasing rapidly. Biomass, geothermal, solar, small-scale hydropower, and wind technologies have grown proportionally faster than any other electricity supply technology, and now supply about two percent of total global energy demand.

In just two decades, the wind energy industry has grown from a producer of small machines for remote power applications into a modern, multi-billion dollar industry supplying grid-connected power. At the beginning of the 21st century, more than 30,000 megawatts (MW) of wind turbines generate clean electricity in more than 30 countries. Consequently, the cost of wind-generated electricity has dropped seven-fold, which makes windpower competitive with most fossil fuel technologies in locations with a good wind resource.

Advantage of Renewable energy

Renewable energy is generally the cleanest option for producing energy, particularly to eliminate greenhouse gas emissions. But there are many other advantages for both individual tourism businesses and their regions or nations. These include:

Energy Security

RE can diversify the energy supply, thereby promoting energy security and price stability. Renewable energy technologies can be used in conjunction with national utility grids, local "mini-grid" systems or as 'stand-alone" systems. For some applications, RE can reduce dependence on imported fuels, an issue that is particularly important for the tourism sector in developing countries where petroleum imports can account for 50 to 60% of the trade deficit. The use of RE can help countries reduce their payments for oil imports and allow scarce hard currency resources to be used for national priorities.

RE can also enhance energy security by decentralising energy supplies with smaller, modular, and rapidly deployable projects that are particularly suited to the electrification of remote communities and businesses in developing countries. For isolated groups with small power requirements, connections to national utility grids are generally expensive and often not cost-effective. Renewable energy-based "mini-grids" or "standalone" systems are, in many cases, better options to provide electric power.

Economic Security

RE is often the most economical choice because of its scale. The modular nature of many RE systems means they can be built (and paid for) as the demand for energy grows, and embedded within the existing energy network, if there is one. By contrast, large, centralised energy systems take much longer to build and are normally designed to supply a future power demand that may not eventuate. Central power plants and transmission lines are also vulnerable to power interruptions. For the tourism sector, increasing the reliability of power supplies and minimising power outages can be a key element of customer satisfaction.

Environmental Security

For most tourism businesses, maintaining environmental quality is a prerequisite for continued business. RE can offer direct environmental benefits, particularly for developing countries, by improving air quality as a result of reduced airborne emissions of pollutants compared to traditional fossil fuels. This is particularly important in cities where carbon monoxide, nitrous oxides and hydrocarbons from petroleum-fuelled transport create ground level ozone and other forms of air pollution. Many of these centres are tourism hubs and transit destinations losing business from the environmental concerns of tourists.

The 1999 European Union 'Eurobarometer' survey showed that good air quality was a key criterion for selecting holiday destinations. Burning fossil fuels also emits carbon dioxide, the key greenhouse gas linked to global climate change. The resulting impacts from increased concentration of greenhouse gases includes altered rainfall patterns, floods and droughts, an increase in the frequency and intensity of storms, shifts in climate zones, and sea level rise - all of which can dramatically affect the tourism industry. The areas most at risk - small islands, coastal zones, flatlands and wetlands - are primary tourism destinations.

A shift in climatic zones and subsequent changes to fauna and flora may mean that many countries will loose their key tourism sites. Increased flood and storm events can also destroy basic infrastructure and increase the incidence of vector borne diseases such as malaria. These impacts will continue to lower visitor numbers to the effected regions. Although tourism businesses may only be very small contributors to greenhouse gases in these areas and unable to affect the overall global emissions, their participation in efforts to reduce greenhouse gases should not be underestimated. Indeed, it is these regions that can demonstrate the effectiveness of clean energy options to other areas of the world.

Renewable energy systems can offer tourism businesses a positive community image that can be actively promoted to clients. This positive image can also be important to employees who can not only feel a sense of pride in the environmental leadership of their employer, but also benefit from a better working environment. Several studies have shown, for example, that buildings designed to heat and cool themselves using solar design are more comfortable and lower worker absenteeism.

Employment

Developing and expanding markets will create employment in areas related to the design, development, sale, application, manufacture, installation, and servicing of renewable energy-based systems. Although this may not be a direct benefit to tourism operators, it can be a useful element in government discussions that may benefit the tourism sector, such as creating policies to invest in renewable energy projects.

Other Benefits

Creating a strategy to employ energy efficiency and renewable energy can also produce other benefits if used as a basis for sustainable development. Taking a resource efficiency approach to water and sewage, for example, can multiply the benefits obtained through energy efficiency improvements. For example, using efficient shower roses can reduce water and energy use by up to 70 percent without sacrificing shower "comfort". The saved water alone can be used in other areas, while the lower hot water demand can enable the use of solar water heaters.

Limitations in Renewable Energy

The major limitation in renewable energy systems lies in the intermittent and sitespecific nature of the energy source. Solar cells, for example, generate electricity only when light is available and wind generators operate only when there is sufficient wind. However, even though such resources are intermittent, they are often highly predictable. In terms of electricity, most modern grid systems can absorb up to twenty percent of their total capacity from intermittent generating sources such as wind. Even this limitation can often be overcome with a mix of technologies. For example, wind energy and photovoltaic systems combined with another generating source such as hydropower can provide a much higher percentage of electricity in a grid system.

Crops harvested on a continuous basis can often fuel biomass energy systems and solar water heaters can store heated water in a tank for later use. RE systems can also be capital intensive as most of their cost is incurred when they are built. However, their zero or low fuel cost means the cost of energy over the life of the system (life-cycle cost) is often competitive with other energy options. Another key issue that can limit RE development is the need to establish trained support. Past experience has shown that many failures have resulted from lack of maintenance or inappropriate operation. RE technologies are also at different stages of development and therefore may have technical limitations.

Applications of Renewable Energy in Tourism Sector

There are different renewable energy technologies, but the most appropriate technology depends on both the available renewable energy resource and the particular application, such as providing electricity for lighting or heat for cooking. There are basically three types of renewable energy:

— Heat Energy

— Electrical Energy

— Transport Fuels

For many tourism businesses, the majority of energy demand - 60-70 percent - is for hot water and space heating. About 20 percent of total demand is for electricity and the rest powers transport. Of course, these percentages can vary greatly, but they illustrate that heating applications are often the first place to look for opportunities to utilise renewable energy or energy efficiency.

Heat Energy

For the tourism sector, renewable energy technologies can provide thermal (heat) energy via solar, geothermal and biomass energy resources to heat buildings, provide hot water and cook food. Buildings and water can be heated using a number of renewable energy technologies. These include:

— Passive solar design;

— Solar thermal systems, (including domestic and commercial hot water systems and pool heating);

— Geothermal systems (including ground-source heat pumps);

— Biofuel systems.

Often, several technologies can be used together. A solar hot water system, for example, can be used together with a wood-fired boiler to heat water.

Passive Solar Design

One of the simplest and most cost-effective means to heat and cool buildings is to use passive solar design. Using a few basic principles, a building can take advan-tage of the daily and seasonal variation of the sun's path across the sky. In temperate climates, the combination of south-facing windows (in the Northern Hemisphere), adequate insulation and the use of heavy materials such as bricks and concrete, can trap winter sun to heat buildings. The same buildings can be cooled in hotter months through the use of strategically planted deciduous trees and roof overhangs to shade.

These passive solar measures can reduce heating costs by 40 percent or more. In hotter climates, wider roof overhangs, verandas, insulation, light roof colours and materials/designs that do not readily absorb heat and promote cross-ventilation can avoid or reduce the need for expensive air conditioning systems. For new buildings, passive systems entail very low or no additional cost because they simply take advantage of the orientation and design of a building to capture and use solar radiation. Passive solar buildings can look like any other building, but are generally more comfortable to live in and less costly to run.

Solar Thermal Systems

Solar energy can cost-effectively provide heat or hot water for applications where temperatures of less than 100°C are needed, including small domestic applications and larger industrial systems. These systems vary in design, but are usually based on a number of solar collectors, a pump/ controller, and storage.

A solar hot water system (also called a 'solar water heater') is a mature and commercial renewable energy application. The technology is already widely used in hospitality businesses requiring a constant supply of hot water. As water heating in an average hospitality businesses accounts for approximately 12% of total energy costs (20% of energy use), solar water heaters can lower fuel and electricity bills, provide a buffer against rising energy prices and compensate for unreliable power grids. Solar water heaters can work for up to 20 years with relatively little maintenance. Consequently, they can be very cost-effective.

In temperate climates, a standard solar water heater can generally meet between 50-65 percent of domestic hot water requirements, while in subtropical climates, the percentage can be 80-100 percent. Domestic solar water heaters range in price from about $500 to $2,500,depending on their tank volumes, which have nominal capacities of 180litres and 300 litres. The cost of a commercial system will vary greatly depending on its size. In equatorial, tropical and Mediterranean regions where solar energy is plentiful throughout the year, solar water heating can be particularly cost-effective as the reduced energy costs can "pay" for any additional system costs in as little as 2 to 4 years.

In equatorial regions, 2 hours of bright sunlight on a collector panel approximately 2 square meters will maintain the water in a 225 litre tank between 40°C to 60°C when it is used at a continuous withdrawal rate of 8.8 litres a minute. Apart from the availability of solar energy, the viability of solar water heaters depends on the price of the fuel used to augment the solar heated water. Most solar water heating systems include some type of auxiliary heating to provide hot water when there is insufficient solar energy (at night or during cloudy periods) or to raise the temperature of the solar heated water. (Hot water is generally used at 45°C to 55°C and in times of low solar energy, additional heating is needed).

In many systems, the auxiliary heating can be gas or electric and incorporated directly into the hot water tank. Solar hot water systems can often be retrofitted to existing buildings with few modifications. In new buildings, integrating the design and the development stage offers several advantages, including lower pipe runs and easier plumbing access - both of which can reduce costs. Several manufacturers offer a range of products for different regions, roof types and even colours for the tank and trim. Tourism facilities with a number of residential buildings or units can often benefit from small solar hot water systems placed on individual rooftops, while larger solar hot water systems can be used as larger central hot water systems. Solar water heaters can also be used to "pre-heat" water for certain applications. Solar heated water can also be used for space heating.

In such a system, the solar heated water is circulated throughout a building via radiators or through special collectors embedded in a cement slab. Solar space heating systems generally require much larger areas of solar collectors and hot water storage, but their operating principles are the same. Solar water heating manufacturers and distributors verify their products through several methods. In the U.S., for example, the Solar Rating and Certification Corporation (SRCC) and the Florida Solar Energy Center (FSEC) offer independent performance testing and certification for solar water heating systems. SRCC is an independent, nonprofit trade organization that creates and implements solar equipment certification programs and rating standards.

FSEC is a statesupported solar energy research facility. Similar rating programs exist in Europe and other countries where solar water heating systems are widely used. A solar water heater works by collecting solar energy in solar collectors, which are usually mounted on the roof facing the sun (south in the northern hemisphere and north in the southern hemisphere). Collectors can be mounted directly on the roof at the roof angle or on a frame titled to maximise solar exposure and match hot water demand, which is often the greatest in winter. When solar energy falls on the surface of the collector it is absorbed as heat and transferred to the water or a heat transfer liquid continuously circulating through the copper tubes of the collector (in frost-prone areas, an antifreeze solution is used to prevent freezing).

The flow of water or liquid continues uninterrupted as long as the sun is shinning and the collector plate is heated. Each time the water or liquid flows through the plates, the temperature of the water or liquid increases. In passive systems, the heat transfer fluid is circulated naturally via the natural convection process called thermosiphoning,while in active systems, electric pumps, valves, and controllers are used to circulate water or other heat-transfer fluids through the collectors. In close-coupled systems, the tank is located above the panel. In a direct close-coupled system, potable water is circulated through the collector and stored in the storage tank.

For an indirect system, an antifreeze liquid is circulated through the collector, storage tank and the heat exchanger (located in the tank). Indirect systems are most used in temperate climates where water could freeze and break the pipes or where the water contains a high level of dissolved minerals that can build-up mineral deposits and block collector pipes. In a split collector and storage system, the water storage tank is located some distance from the collector panel. In 'passive' systems, the tank is located at some distance but above the collector, which then allows the heated water/liquid to circulate naturally to and from the tank. In 'active' systems, the storage tank is located below the collector and uses an electric pump to circulate water/liquid to the collector.

Some systems utilize a small low voltage solar electric panel to drive the electric pump, which negates the need for an external electricity source. Passive and active systems can be designed as direct or indirect systems. Drainback systems are a type of indirect system using pumps to circulate water through the collectors. Because the water in the collector loop drains into a reservoir tank when the pumps stop, this system is appropriate for colder climates.

Solar pool heating: Heating the water in a swimming pool is one of the most cost-effective and simplest applications of solar energy. In such a system, the pool water is pumped through a solar collector that is usually mounted on a building rooftop facing south (in the Northern Hemisphere) or north (in the Southern Hemisphere). Because solar pool-heating collectors operate just slightly warmer than the surrounding air temperature, these systems typically use inexpensive, unglazed, low-temperature collectors made from specially formulated plastic materials. Glazed (glasscovered) solar collectors usually are not used in pool-heating applications, except for indoor pools, hot tubs, or spas in colder climates. In some cases, unglazed copper or copper-aluminum solar collectors are used for solar pool heating.

A solar pool heating collector is generally much larger than a solar water heater for domestic water heating and 50% to 100% of the area of the pool, depending on local climate conditions. Such systems often incorporate an insulating plastic "blanket" placed over the pool to prevent heat loss when it is not in use. The system requires no heat exchanger as the water circulating through the tubes comes directly from the pool. However, since the system is not protected against frost it has to be drained every winter. The solar system annually displaces 120 megawatt-hours (MWh) of electricity or 12,000 mof gas; reducing annual heating costs by DKK 42,000. With a capital outlay of DKK188,000 and annual operating costs of DKK 3,000, the simple payback period was less than five years. The solar heating system also reduces nitrous oxide emissions by 65 kg and carbon dioxide emissions by 32,000 kg per year.

Other applications: Renewable energy can be used for range of additional thermal applications, though few are directly relevant to the tourism sector. Cooking with solar energy is one application that can be used, particularly in developing countries with significant solar energy potential. Solar cookers are relatively simple devices - either an insulated box with a glass lid or a parabolic dish that focuses solar energy onto a cooking surface. Solar cookers are widely used by tourist hiking camps and rural lodges in the Himalayan region in Nepal. The cookers are used to boil water for drinking and hot beverages, boil vegetables and rice, and heat dried and tinned food.

The Nepalese Alternative Energy Promotion Centre reports an increasing number of tourism businesses using these cookers and not only in the Himalayas but also in Kathmandu. They are suitable for cooking most Nepalese dishes (which the tourists want to taste) and for boiling water. In addition, ghee and oil shops are using these cookers to melt ghee. T h e cookers lower both fuel use and the need to cut trees while improving hygiene and overall sanitation. Tourists are also pleased and often find them an attraction.

Geothermal Systems

Geothermal energy - the heat of the Earth - can be recovered at temperatures ranging from 35°C to 150°C and used to heat buildings, greenhouses, aquaculture facilities and to provide industrial process heat. Higher temperature geothermal energy can also be used to generate electricity. Using geothermal energy directly is 50 to 70 percent efficient compared to the 5-20 percent efficiency when it is used indirectly to generate electricity (although the waste heat from generating electricity can also be used and thus boost the overall efficiency). Direct applications can also draw from both high and low temperature geothermal energy sources and produce useful energy for as low as US$0.02/kilowatt-hour (kWh).

Industrial quantities of geothermal energy are retrieved via wells drilled into a geothermal field as pictured above. One of the most commercially accepted geothermal technologies is the geothermal heat pump (GHP), also described as geoexchange and the ground source heat pump. A GHP takes advantage of the natural and nearly constant heat of the Earth, which can be used as a heat resource in the winter and a heat sink in the summer. GHPs can be used for heating and cooling buildings, water heating, snow melting and swimming pool heating. It is not a new technology but their use is growing in the building heating/cooling sector. Although they can have higher initial costs, when designed and installed properly a GHP system can quickly pay for itself through energy cost savings.

GHPs are one of the most energy efficient and cost effective cooling and heating systems available; using much less energy than conventional heating/cooling systems and delivering 3 to 4 times the energy they consume. This is because a GHP moves heat to or from the ground instead of generating it from heating coils or electrically operated compressors. GHP operating costs are significantly lower than conventional heating and cooling systems and they operate for 20 years or more with minimal maintenance.

Hotels using GHPs in North America report energy savings of 40%-70% in the winter and 30%-60% in the summer. GHPs are most often used for space cooling and are usually designed to meet the entire space-conditioning load of a building. When used for heating, they are usually designed to provide approximately 80% of the heating demand. A backup heating system is usually necessary for installations operating year round in temperate regions. Other advantages of GHPs for tourism businesses include:

— Silent operation;

— Improved indoor air quality, including comfortable humidity levels and reduced pollutants; and allergens from the lack of combustion;

— Absence of reliance on air from outside the building;

— Absence of aboveground equipment (such as cooling towers and air coils) that might jeopardize exterior aesthetics.

GHP design is based on soil characteristics, the type of ground material, moisture content and ground temperature. GHPs can be used in most regions except desert areas where dry and sandy soils do not efficiently transfer heat. The technology is founded on the principle that the Earth's interior temperature remains relatively constant during most of the year. When the GHP system operates in the heating mode, the heat from the groundwater is absorbed by the circulating refrigerant.

The heated refrigerant is then pumped toward a heat pump that transfers the heat from the refrigerant to water. This heated water can then be used directly as hot water or circulated through radiators for space heating. Such installations are called refrigerant (or water)-towater systems. Alternatively, air can be blown over the heated pipes and the heat delivered to interior spaces through a system of air ducts, which is referred to as a water-to-air system. When GHPs are operated in the cooling mode, the process is reversed. The refrigerant absorbs the heat from interior spaces of the building and transfers it to the ground. One of the most important aspects of heat pumps in relation to the heating/cooling of buildings is the direct relationship between the efficiency of the unit (and the energy required to operate it) and the difference in temperatures.

In heat pump terminology, the difference between the temperature where the heat is absorbed (the "source") and the temperature where the heat is delivered (the "sink") is called the "lift." T h e larger the lift, the greater the electric power input required by the heat pump. This is the basis for the efficiency advantage of the geothermal heat pumps over air-source heat pumps. An air-source heat pump must remove heat from cold outside air in the winter and deliver heat to hot outside air in the summer. By contrast, the GHP retrieves heat from relatively warm soil (or groundwater) in the winter and delivers heat to the same relatively cool soil (or groundwater) in the summer.

As a result, geothermal heat pumps are always pumping the heat over a smaller temperature difference than the air-source heat pump, regardless of the season. This leads to higher efficiency and lower energy use. The heat removed from the indoor air during the summer can also provide a low cost source of hot water. In cold weather, however, a part of the GHP's heating capacity must be diverted for water heating, which lowers the heat available for space heating. Also, water heating can only be done when the GHP is in operation. During periods of the year when neither space neither heating nor cooling is required, an alternative water heating method is required. GHP systems are most cost effective when space cooling is required for significant periods during the year.

The most cost-effective GHP depends entirely on local ground conditions. An inspection of the site and ground conditions is therefore mandatory before the best method can be selected. There are two basic types of GHP systems: ground-coupled systems and ground/surface water heat pumps.

1. *Ground-coupled systems* use vertical loops in boreholes or horizontal pipe loops installed in trenches in direct contact with the earth. There are two types of these systems, including:
   — *Vertical loops in boreholes* : Placing the loops vertically in the ground requires more expensive drilling for a borehole than digging a trench. However, as the pipes are buried deeper in the ground (46 to 152 metres), they are in a more stable thermal zone and thus more efficient. The temperature in the ground at 30 metres does not vary during seasons as much as surface soils at 1 -2 metres. Vertical systems can therefore be a better option in areas of extreme temperatures. They are also easier to install when the exterior spaces have already been landscaped and site disruptions need to be minimised.
   — *Horizontal loops in trenches* : Horizontal installations are cheaper to install than vertical designs as the loops are laid out in a trench (1 to 2 metres below the ground), and trenching is cheaper than drilling. They are also a better option when the soil includes hard rocks. On the downside, trenches need large surface areas and longer pipes, which are often coiled to maximise heat transfer capacity.
2. *Ground and Surface Water Heat Pumps* have been used since the early 1970s. Ground water and surface water systems can be used when there is an adequate supply of water either in wells, lakes or rivers. The well, lake or river water is pumped through supply pipes into the building and returned to the source through a

discharge pipe. This method of ground coupling should be considered by tourism businesses situated near lakes and large ponds, where the loops can be submerged or where the ground water supply is relatively close to the surface. As water provides a stable thermal zone, this technology can be easily installed and is highly cost effective where temperatures are not extreme.

— *Open loops* : Open loop systems can be used when there is an adequate supply of useable groundwater. The water is pumped through supply pipes into the building and returned to ground through a discharge well. An additional heat exchanger is often installed between the building water piping systems and the ground water piping system. However, when the water has a high content of dissolved minerals (>100ppm) and/or contains hydrogen sulphide (that gives the odour of rotten eggs), closed loop systems need to be used.

— *Closed loops* : For a closed loop system, a closed heat exchanger can be placed within a lake and the working fluid pumped through it and into the dwelling being heated or cooled.

Importantly for small tourism projects, GHP can often be easily retrofitted to existing buildings. All components (including compressors, heat exchangers, fans, filters and controls) are 'packaged' into a single cabinet installed in a small indoor space. As with all renewable energy choices, the scope for GSP should be considered at the onset of the building or project design process. This can facilitate better use of space and lower costs, particularly because a GHP system:

— Requires very little mechanical space;

— Eliminates the need for a boiler room;

— Lowers the size of air distribution ducts, which can allow higher ceilings that can be an asset for accommodation properties, museums, galleries and visitor centres;

— Allows for greater individual temperature control, an important requirement for accommodation business;

— Eliminates exterior equipment such as cooling towers and split systems.

Dual-fuel heating systems : These systems use GHP as the primary resource and fossil fuel boilers/furnaces as backup. Duel-fuel systems can be easily retrofitted into existing fossil fuel systems.

Heating swimming pools : As with water heating, swimming pools can be heated by GSHP systems that recover and reuse the waste heat rejected to the ground during the reverse space cooling operation.

Biomass Systems

Biomass can be used in a variety of heating applications, depending on the type and availability of the biomass resource. The main sources of sustainable biomass include:

— Industrial and agricultural wastes and residues, such as sugar cane waste (bagasse), wood waste from forestry operations, and residues from other short rotation crops;

— Organic wastes from animal husbandry, straw and husks;

— Energy crops, such as sugar cane, corn, and trees grown in short-rotation plantations;

— Domestic and municipal wastes, such as sewage and garbage.

The main processes for utilising these sources of biomass include:

— Direct combustion, usually of solids, in boilers or as a fuel in engines or turbines;

— Gasification, via a physical or chemical conversion process to a secondary gaseous fuel, followed by combustion in an engine, boiler or turbine;

— Biological conversion, via bacterial anaerobic digestion to methane-rich biogas that is used as a gaseous fuel;

— Chemical or biochemical conversion, to produce methanol, ethanol, or other liquid fuels.

Many combinations of source, processes, and technology are possible, but direct combustion is the most commercially developed process. One of the principal biomass fuels is wood. Wood burning appliances have improved notably in efficiency, cleanliness and convenience in recent years. Room heaters as well central furnaces for heating water or air are sold commercially in many regions. In many rural areas where forest degradation is not an issue, firewood is often cheaper than oil, gas, or electricity, even when labour costs for cutting, collecting and refuelling is accounted for.

Tourists also appreciate the aesthetics of a flame, especially in cabins or rooms - even though they may require refuelling every 4 to 8 hours. Some central heating units are semi-automatic and require attention only once a day and fully automated units burning woodchips or wood pellets are also available. For tourism businesses located near saw mills or other wood processing plants, the use of sawdust and other wood waste for heating and/or cooking purposes can be particularly attractive. In many cases, the low cost of wood fuel makes it well suited to water heating. Wood-based water heaters can be used in conjunction with solar water heaters; providing additional hot water in winter (and other times when solar radiation is low).

Biofuel boilers: New model boilers fuelled by biomass can automatically switch to an existing oil or gas boiler if the biofuel supply runs out. Other options include boilers that operate on biofuels as well as oil or gas, and gasification boilers where the biofuel is first converted into a burnable gas.

Biogas: A methane-rich gas called biogas can be produced in purpose built digesters ranging from 1 to 10 cubic metres from the digestion of plant and animal wastes, sludge and wastewater. The gas can be used in a combined heat and power (CHP) plant or co-generation unit to produce heat and electricity, or fuel cooking stoves as well as boilers for space and water heating. The input of wastes into the digester can be continuous or in batches, and the digestion process can take several days to several weeks, depending on the types of biomass and the local climate. Generally, each dry kilogram of input will produce 8 megajoules of energy - an amount required to boil 250 litres of water.

Electrical Energy

There are basically two applications for renewable energy electricity: as electricity fed into central power distribution facilities - also called the transmission grid or simply 'grid' - and electricity for remote areas where a grid is either weak or not available, such as small islands. In both cases, renewable energy can often (though not always) be used in conjunction with other generating options, such as diesel generators.

Grid-based Electricity

Although electricity generated for centralised power grids tends to come from larger size units, usually tens or hundreds of megawatts (one megawatt can power about 200 average homes), the trend in the last decade of the twentieth century has been to smaller units and down to the size of a one-kilowatt rooftop system of solar cells. This approach, referred to as 'distributed generation', has derived and benefited from competition and new regulations allowing access to the power grid for smaller generators. A tourism business can also decide to generate electricity from a renewable resource and sell excess power not used by the business to the local power authority, if it is allowed. This will involve the use of special equipment such as power electronics and special meters.

In this type of system, the business buys electricity from the utility when their system is not generating electricity, thus using the local power grid as a form of battery. The price that a utility will pay for this cleaner electricity varies greatly, but can often be economically advantageous. In some US states, for example, systems less than one megawatt in size can be 'net metered' - meaning the customer pays the same for the electricity fed into the power grid as the power that is taken from the grid. In essence, this means the customer is selling electricity at the retail rate and buying it at the wholesale rate.

Greenpower

One outcome of competition and new market regulations is an electricity product based on renewable energy called 'greenpower'. In Australia, Europe and the US, there is a growing market for greenpower, which has also increased demand for renewable energy systems. If available, greenpower is one of the simplest ways to power your business with renewable energy. In most greenpower programmes, customers agree to buy a certain percentage of their power from a renewable energy resource, usually (but again not always) at a rate that is usually about ten percent more than the cost of conventional power on a per unit basis.

However, it is important to remember that your business does not pay a rate for electricity, you pay a bill. Smart businesses can combine their purchase of greenpower with energy efficiency to maintain, and even lower, their existing electricity bills. Thus, running your operation on greenpower can be a valuable, cost-effective distinction for marketing purposes.

Remote Area Power Supplies (RAPS)

Although renewable energy options such as windpower are an increasingly attractive option for generating electricity into centralised power grids, renewable energy systems are particularly cost-effective in areas where there is no electricity supply or where the supply is erratic. As most forms of renewable energy are intermittent (hydropower can be an exception), they require some form of energy storage, usually batteries. A RAPS system generally consists of:

— One or more generators, including solar, wind, hydro, petrol and diesel options;

— Energy storage;

— Controllers;

— Electronic devices to convert the electricity to the voltage required for applications (such as 230 or 240 volts AC).

Some RAPS systems rely on renewable energy generators alone, while others incorporate a backup generator fuelled by petrol or diesel. Per unit of electricity generated, RAPS systems are generally more expensive to build and maintain than grid-connected systems. However, RAPS technology has advanced rapidly in the past two decades and is generally available in a wide range of configurations and from a number of international dealers. The systems generally range in size from one to 50 kilowatts.

A properly designed and maintained RAPS system can provide a reliable, safe and cost-effective electricity supply. A version of RAPS - called an uninterruptible power supply or UPS - is also frequently used in larger businesses with access to a conventional power grid but need higher power reliability. RAPS systems can also be the basis for a village power system with the use of a local electricity distribution system, which is referred to as a 'mini-grid'. One critically important design element for RAPS systems is the choice of appliances.

For systems without an auxiliary power supply, such as a diesel or petrol generator, using an appliance that draws large amounts of power, such as washing machines and power tools, is often not possible. Such systems are better at running lights and electronic equipment, such as radios and televisions. It is critically important to choose the most efficient appliances for even small systems. In a small solar photovoltaic system, for example, the same system that powers one 75-watt incandescent light bulb can power four energy efficient compact fluorescent bulbs.

In larger RAPS systems, the choice of power electronics to convert direct current into alternating current, (called an 'inverter'), is also crucial. Motor driven appliances, such as washing machines, often consume a large amount of electricity -several times the motor rating - for a fraction of a second when starting. Inverters vary in their ability to handle this peak load and also in their efficiency of converting the DC power into AC power. The best inverters on the market today have an efficiency of 90-95% and cost about $1/watt or $2000 for a 2 kW inverter.

In smaller systems, the decision on whether or not to use an inverter depends on the type and frequency of appliances to be used. An inverter allows the use of conventional (and often cheaper) appliances and wiring. In addition, the choice of using AC or DC appliances will depend on their availability (DC appliances can be more difficult to source and more expensive) and their suitability to the application. DC appliances are usually available in low voltages of 12 or 24 volts. This means that the electric cabling must carry more current and is therefore more expensive than AC wiring.

Some systems use both DC and AC circuits; the DC circuits powering lights while the AC circuits power points AC appliances. The use of a split system means that even if the inverter fails, lights (and other DC appliances) can still be run. Following is a guide to using different appliances in RAPS systems:

— *Lighting*: Lights may be powered by either low voltage direct current (DC) or conventional alternating current (AC). In a small home, tourist cottage, RV, or boat, low voltage DC lighting is usually preferable as DC wire runs can be kept short and allow the use of smaller gauge wire. System costs are lower because an inverter is not required. Although incandescent bulbs can be used, DC fluorescent lights are often preferable because they produce 3 to 4 times the light of incandescent bulbs for the same amount of energy.

Halogen bulbs are 30% more efficient and actually seem almost twice as bright as similar wattage incandescent because of the spectrum of light they produce. Tw e l v e and 24-volt replacement ballasts are available to convert AC fluorescent lights for use with DC. For large installations with many lights, the use of an inverter to supply AC power for conventional lighting may be the most cost effective approach.

— *Refrigeration*: Refrigerators are major users of electricity and should therefore be as efficient as possible for use in a RAPS system. The most efficient models use DC motor and compressors that consume 300 to 400 watt-hours of electricity per day compared to conventional AC refrigerators that use 3000 to 4000 watt hours per day (at a 70 degree F average air temperature). Although the cost of more efficient DC refrigerators can be higher, the lower energy demand can reduce the overall system cost by reducing the required number of batteries and the size of the generator(s).

— *Major Appliances*: Appliances such as washing machines, larger shop machinery, power tools and pumps normally use standard AC electric motors (250-750 watts) and require significant amounts of power, which may not be cost-effective in systems without an auxiliary petrol or diesel generator. AC motors can also be difficult to start with an inverter power and can use 50% to 75% more electricity than efficient models. A standard washing machine, for example, uses between 300 and 500 watt-hours per load. If the washing machine is used more than a few hours per week, it may be more cost-effective to purchase a high-efficiency washing machine rather than increase the size of the system to power a low-efficiency machine. For many beltdriven appliances (washers, drill press, etc.), standard electric motors may be replaced with high-efficiency motors (either AC or DC) that can be purchased as separate units or as motor-replacement kits.

— *Small Appliances*: Irons, toasters and hair dryers consume large amounts of power but are usually operated only during short or infrequent intervals. For tourist cottages, a stand alone system with a large enough inverter and battery storage will allow these appliances to be used, although such systems will be more costly. Electronic equipment, such as stereos, televisions, VCR's and computers are well suited to stand alone systems as they have relatively modest power requirements and are available in low voltage

DC as well as conventional AC models. Generally, DC models use less power than their AC counterparts and battery-powered devices, such as portable stereos that run on "D-cell" batteries, will operate on a 12-volt DC system.

Options for Generating Electricity

For businesses that would like to generate their own power, either in a standalone system or to feed into a power grid, the following section gives some guidance on different options.

Windpower

Generating electricity from the wind is a mature technology and economically competitive with most fossil fuel applications, depending on the location. Wind turbines offer an attractive energy option for tourism businesses situated in coastal areas, flat open plains and mountain passes exposed to consistent winds. Once a wind turbine is properly installed, it requires little maintenance and does not emit greenhouse gasses or other airborne pollutants. The most common wind turbines for generating electricity today use two or three blades revolving around a horizontal axis connected to a generator. They are mounted on concrete or steel towers and usually include a gearbox, generator, and other supporting mechanical and electrical equipment.

The power that can be generated from a modern wind turbine is practically related to the square of the wind speed, although theoretically it is related to the cube of the wind speed. This means that a site with twice the wind speed of another site will generate four times as much energy. Consequently, the availability of good wind speed data is critical to the feasibility of any wind project. Most commercial wind turbines operating today are placed at sites with average wind speeds greater than 6 metres/ second (m/s) or 22 km/h, although annual wind speeds over 5.5 metres per second can also be viable.

A high-quality wind site will have an annual average wind speed in excess of 7.5 m/s (27 km/h). Although the wind resource for any site is intermittent, it can be highly predictable and thus the output from wind turbines can be integrated into existing electrical grids with a high degree of confidence. Wind energy systems are available in sizes ranging from less than one kilowatt (small scale) to 100-700 kW (medium scale) and large scale (greater than 700 kW) For commercial utility-sized projects, the most common turbines sold are in the range of 750 kW-2000 kW (2.0 megawatts), although the newest commercial turbines are rated at 2.5 megawatts.

A typical 750 kW turbine has a blade diameter of 35 metres and is mounted on a 50-metre concrete or steel tower. The minimum height for a tower supporting a small-scale turbine is generally 10m. Wind projects can vary in size from a one-turbine installation to a large number of turbines erected at an individual site, which is often referred to as a windfarm. Utility-sized commercial wind projects are usually constructed as windfarms and wind projects have been successfully built to power a wide range of applications in diverse and often extreme environments.

Costs - Wind Energy	
Capital cost equipment:	\$600 - 2000/kW
Capital costs project:	\$800 - 2500/kW
Maintenance costs:	< \$0.01/ kWh
Life-cycle Cost:	\$0.04 - 0.15/kWh
Operating Life:	up to 20 years

For most tourism businesses, small and medium scale wind turbines are the most suitable. Although a large-scale turbine or windfarm is generally outside the scope of a tourism or hospitality business, directly purchasing the electricity - or even owning part or all of a turbine - can be an economically attractive option for a large organization or consortium of smaller organizations. Wind projects can be constructed as either "build-own-operate" facilities under long-term power purchase contracts or as turnkey facilities. For large grid-connected turbines, the wind energy industry is competitive and mature and there are many choices of project developer and manufacture, depending on location.

Ten major international manufacturers currently produce 97 percent of all wind turbines in power outputs ranging from a few hundred watts to several megawatts At the beginning of 2003, 25,000 MW of wind power have been installed in more than 30 countries. Since the current phase of development began in the 1980's, the price for wind-generated electricity fed into major grids has reduced by an average of 3 percent per annum. Wind turbines produce no pollution when they are operating but care must be taken in siting turbines to account for local environmental impacts, including visual amenity, noise and avian impacts. With properly designed and sited modern turbines, these impacts can be mitigated.

In areas of very high visual amenity -such as coastal national parks - wind development may not be compatible with community values. For tourism businesses in remote areas that remain open year round, a hybrid system combining windpower and solar photovoltaic (PV) or other generating option offers several advantages over a single generator system. In many areas, wind speeds are lowest when there is excess solar energy (for example in the summer), and highest when solar energy is minimal (eg, winter).

As the peak operating periods for wind and PV occur at different times of the year, hybrid systems can be designed to provide higher reliability. For those times when neither the PV modules nor the wind turbine are working (at night and during low winds), most systems include battery storage and/or a diesel or petrol generator that can recharge batteries. For hospitality businesses, wind turbines can also be used to power electric water pumps. The turbines can be placed at some distance from the well (or other water source) and often require much less maintenance. Although standard centrifugal and volumetric pumps can be used, the manner in which they are selected and installed is different from water pumping systems powered by the grid. Of course, windmills that directly drive the water pump can also be used.

The technology to convert geothermal energy into electricity is well proven, relatively uncomplicated, and involves extracting energy via conventional wells, pumps and/or heat exchangers. Steam extracted from geothermal wells is used to drive an electrical turbine and generator to produce electricity. Generally, the generating capacity of geothermal systems is in the megawatt range. As with windpower, installing a geothermal electricity system will be restricted to larger tourism operations (or a consortia of businesses) and to areas with a significant geothermal resource.

Extracting geothermal energy can have adverse environmental impacts, particularly air pollution from radon gas, hydrogen sulfide, carbon dioxide, methane, and ammonia emissions. Using geothermal resources can also create substantial thermal pollution from waste heat. Many of these impacts can be controlled with technology that re-injects waste gases or fluids back into the geothermal well. Generally, the carbon dioxide emissions of a geothermal power plant are only five percent of the emissions from equivalent fossil fuel power plants.

The area of land impacted by a geothermal development is relatively small and such developments can usually co-exist successfully with other land uses. Other drawbacks include mineral deposits on components and the need to drill new wells after a few years of use. It is also important to note that geothermal energy is renewable only if the rate of extraction is less than the recharge rate. Currently, few geothermal projects for generating electricity meet this requirement.

Small-Scale Hydro (SSH) Technology

The energy in falling water can be converted into electrical energy or into mechanical energy by hydraulic turbines. In the past, hydropower stations were often built as a part of large dam projects. Due to the size, cost, and environmental impacts of these dams (and the reservoirs they create), hydro developments today are increasingly focused on smaller-scale projects. Although the definition of small-scale varies, only projects that have less than 10 MW of generating capacity are considered here and are abbreviated by 'SSH'. This definition also includes mini-hydro) (less than1 MW), micro-hydro (less than 100 kW and pico-hydro (less than 1 kW).

Small-scale hydro technology is efficient and commercially proven. Many companies supply small-scale hydro equipment in areas of the world where hydro resources are located. Hydro potential is very site specific but can be a viable option for tourism businesses in mountainous areas where there are streams that flow with a sharp downward gradient. Any small river or large stream with a reasonably constant water flow throughout the year can be considered. Small-scale hydro systems are modular and can generally be sized to meet individual or community needs. However, the financial viability of a project is subject to the available water resource and the distance the generated electricity must be transmitted.

The two critical variables that determine the viability of a hydro site are:

— The vertical drop at which the water falls (metres), referred to as the effective head;

— The total amount of water that 'falls' (cubic metres per second), called the flow rate.

The power (P) that can be generated by falling water is approximately 7 times the product of the flow rate (Q) and the effective head (H): P(kW) = 7 x Q x H. Therefore, the greater the available head, the lower the required water flow, and vice versa. For example, to generate 1 kW of electricity, a hydro system with a head of 100 metres will require 10% of the water flow that a site with a head of 10 metres requires. Low head sites are generally less than 10 metres while high head sites are greater than 30 metres.

Sites with very low head (<3m) present technical and economic challenges. Low head hydro equipment must accommodate considerably more water flow than equivalent capacity high head equipment and must be physically larger, which requires larger civil works. Also, the turbine's output shaft speed decreases with lower head. As a result, low head schemes generally need gears to drive highspeed generators. A head of one metre and a flow rate of 54 litres per minute are considered the minimum requirements to generate electricity. Different types of turbines are commercially available and the optimum choice depends on the both the head and flow rate.

Generally, a high head site will require smaller, less expensive turbines and associated equipment. For most hydro projects, water is supplied to the turbine from some type of storage reservoir, usually created by a dam or weir. The reservoir allows water to be stored for generating electricity according to demand and particularly during periods of peak electrical demand or when the electricity can be sold for a higher price if it is connected to the grid. In these systems the amount of electrical power that can be generated is determined by the amount of water stored in the reservoir and the rate at which it is released.

The most environmentally desirable hydro system does not impact the amount or pattern of water flow that normally exists in the river or stream. This "run-of-river" system may use a special turbine placed directly in the river to capture just the energy in the water flow. A conventional SSH plant may also operate as a run-ofriver system if the natural variability of the river flow is maintained. However, this type of system may generate less power during times of low river flow. For tourism businesses, a run of river system can bring additional challenges, as the demand of power is likely to be higher when it is hot and dry which is often when the tourist season reaches its peak.

A dam or weir may still be required if the water needs to be diverted and if the diversion is to take advantage of existing downward gradients. Although SSH systems have few of the environmental impacts of large-scale hydro projects, they can still create local environmental impacts (particularly if they significantly change the amount or timing or river water flows). With careful design, particularly with any civil works that could lead to erosion, many of these impacts can be avoided.

SSH systems do not create any air or water pollution when they are operating and generally offer highly reliable power. They also have very low running or maintenance costs and can be operated and maintained by locally trained staff. Hydro systems generally have a long project life. Equipment such as turbines can last 20-30 years, while concrete civil works can last 100 years. This is often not reflected in the economic analysis of power projects, where costs are usually calculated over a shorter period of time. This is important for hydro projects, as their initial capital costs tend to be comparatively high because of the need for civil engineering works.

Although significant potential exists for further SSH development, the availability of suitable new sites for larger developments is limited, particularly if dams or other structures must be built and where local land use and planning laws may limit such development. However, tourism businesses in mountainous areas can often tap a high head water resource without using a dam or weir. There are also existing weirs and other in-stream structures that can be retrofitted with hydro equipment. About 3000 MW of these low-cost applications are esti-mated to exist globally. As the civil works already exist, the additional environmental and land use impacts of these projects are often very low.

Hydro developers wishing to construct larger systems with dams generally need to invest in de-tailed analyses before a project can proceed. Regulator authorities may require structures or systems that prevent adverse effects on flora and fauna, particularly fish. Conversely, some hydro systems may enhance local environments through, for example, the creation of wetlands. Over one hundred companies manufacture SSH systems with the most active industries in Europe and China.

Bioenergy Electricity Projects

Bioenergy electricity projects generate electricity via conventional steam combustion technology and can often be designed to co-generate both heat and electricity (called 'combined heat and power' or CHP), which can greatly increase the overall efficiency and financial viability of a project. Such projects may also create a cost-effective solution to the disposal of agricultural or industrial wastes that may otherwise become potential environment problems. Such projects can be built in a wide range of sizes from one megawatt to as large as 100 megawatt CHP power stations. The keys to an economically viable bioenergy project are the type, amount and cost of the biomass resource.

Projects are generally more cost-effective when waste products from some production process are utilized (such as sugar bagasse or sawmill residue). For many bioenergy applications, however, big is not necessarily better as transporting the biomass fuel or feedstock over larger distances can decrease the economic viability of projects. In addition, some agricultural wastes are available only during certain times of the year and may have to be stored if they are to be used as on a continuous basis. This can be difficult, expensive and require special equipment or storage facilities.

An alternative to storing biomass is to use other fuels, such as natural gas, during these periods. This may allow a more efficient, continuous and profitable operation, but will also usually increase the project's capital cost. The intermittent availability of a biomass resource can be an issue for many bagasse-fired electricity plants operating only during sugar harvesting periods. However, the liberalization of electricity markets in some countries has created an economic opportunity to invest in facilities and equipment that allows such projects to generate electricity during non-harvesting periods, thus generating higher revenues.

Issues that can influence the viability of a bioenergy project, particularly larger projects, include competition for land-use, public resistance to proposed land-use changes, and the complexity of co-ordinating a range of activities and institutions (farmers, utilities, transport companies, etc). For these reasons, an intensive planning and management process is usually required and may also need to address these issues at local, regional and national levels.

Photovoltaic (PV) Cells

Photovoltaic (PV) cells, also called "solar cells," are semiconductor devices that convert solar energy directly into electricity. In many applications, PV is a mature and commercial technology with an estimate 400,000-800,000 photovoltaic systems installed worldwide in applications ranging from large grid-connected power stations and grid-connected roof-top residential systems, to small-scale, stand-alone units for rural use and consumer products. PV is currently most economically competitive in remote sites away from electricity grids and where only relatively small amounts of power are required-typically less than 10 kW. This makes PV applications particularly attractive for tourism facilities in such areas.

However, the market for residential and commercial grid-connected systems is growing rapidly as costs continue to decline. In remote areas, PV systems offer significant advantages over petroleumbased diesel engines including:

— Silent operation;

— High reliability;

— Absence of moving parts;

— Low operating costs;

— Low maintenance;

— Modularity (can be sized to suit demand);

— Easy installation at remote sites;

— Absence of airborne pollution or COemissions;

— Reduction in electricity losses as the electricity is generated near the point of use.

Although there are about 30 different types of PV devices under development, there are three main technologies in commercial production: monocrystalline cells, polycrystalline cells, and thin-film cells. Monocrystalline, (single crystal) solar cells are manufactured from wafers of highquality silicon and are generally the most efficient cells for converting solar energy into electricity. Polycrystalline solar cells are cut from a block of lower-quality multicrystalline silicon and are less efficient, but also less expensive to produce. Thinfilm solar cells, manufactured in a process similar to tinting glass, are made of semiconductor material deposited as a thin film on glass or aluminium.

Thin-film solar cells are generally only half as efficient as mono and polycrystalline cells, but they are much cheaper to produce and widely used to power consumer devices such as watches and calculators. Solar cells are encapsulated into modules that are often combined to form an array. There is, however, a growing market of "building-integrated" PV devices manufactured as part of conventional building materials, such as roof tiles or glass panelling. A PV array is usually part of a system that may also include energy storage devices (usually batteries), support frames, and electronic controllers. These are collectively referred to as the balance-of-system (BOS) components.

The amount of power from a PV array is directly proportional to the intensity of the light hitting the array. PV panels do not need direct sun and can even generate 50-70% of their rated output under a bright overcast sky. A dark overcast day might correspond to only 5-10% of full sun intensity, so output would be diminished proportionately. As the result of differences in solar intensity between regions, the same PV module used in an equatorial or tropical region will produce almost double the annual power output than when used in a temperate country. The amount of sunlight a PV panel receives (known as irradiance) is measured in kilowatt-hours per square meter per day (kWh/m/day).

Equatorial and tropical regions receive an average daily irradiance of 4 to 6.5kWh/m/day while temperate regions receive 2 to 4kWh/m/day. However, summer solar irradiance in higher latitudes can be greater that 6 kWh/m/day, making PV a good investment for tourism facilities that operate mainly in summer months. Photovoltaic arrays produce direct-current (DC) electricity, but the power can be regulated through electronic devices to produce any required combination of voltage and current-including conventional residential alternating current (AC). PV is a modular technology that can be used in most parts of the world and integrated with diesel, wind, and hydropower systems.

The selection and proper installation of appropriately configured and sized components directly affect PV system reliability, lifetime, and initial cost. In PV system design, trade-offs are necessary to keep costs reasonable and ensure appropriate service. PV systems can be configured as "stand-alone", "grid-connected" or as part of "hybrid" installations. Stand-alone systems (also known as "remote" or "autonomous" systems) Stand-alone systems are used in areas where power grids do not exist or where the cost to connect to the grid is not cost-effective.

A stand-alone system channels surplus electricity generated during the day into batteries to be used at night or during cloudy periods and are designed to have sufficient PV and battery capacity to provide electricity during these times. In areas with long periods of no or low sunshine, a backup generator is often installed to ensure an uninterrupted supply of electricity. A Solar Home System (SHS) is a common version of a stand-alone PV system and normally composed of a PV array, batteries, and an electronic controller. The system can be constructed in a range of sizes from 30 W to several hundred watts.

Larger systems up to 50 kilowatts can provide power for an entire village or town. Generally a small SHS system costing between $500-1000 will power a few fluorescent lights and a radio/television but are not intended to run larger appliances such as refrigerators or washing machines. Stand-alone PV systems include:

— PV arrays;

— A structure to mount the array;

— Over current protection/safety disconnects;

— Charge regulator(including circuit protection and remote monitoring);

— Batteries to store energy for use when there is no sunlight, at night and during bad weather.

— An inverter to convert the stored direct current (DC) into alternative current (AC) if AC appliances are to be used;

— Electrical cables that allow electricity to be moved between cells, batteries and usage points;

— Voltage, current and state-of-charge meters;

— Optional backup power systems that operate on wind, diesel, gasoline, propane, or other energy source.

Stand-alone systems are the preferred option when:

— The power is required in an area that is far from a power grid;

— Costs of extending the power lines are higher than the capital costs of a PV system;

— Power demand levels are modest;

— The environmental impact must be minimized;

— The grid is poorly developed with regular power interruptions;

— The user would like to operate independently from the utility grid;

— There is an adequate solar resource.

Grid connected PV systems

Grid connected PV systems supply electricity to the grid when excess power is being produced by the PV panel (when the sun is shinning) and draw electricity from the grid when the PV panel is not producing sufficient electricity (i.e. at night). The interface between the PV system and the grid can be metered in two possible manners when power is being supplied by the PV system to the grid: (a) the electrical meter will turn backwards or (b) a separate electrical meter will measure the electrical energy the PV system is feeding into the grid. Grid connected PV systems include:

— PV arrays;

— A structure on which to mount the array;

— Excess current protection/safety disconnects;

— Charge regulator /system control (including circuit protection and remote monitoring);

— An inverter to convert the direct current (DC) into alternative current (AC) and which can be synchronized to the grid;

— Electrical cables that allow electricity to be moved between cells, batteries and usage points;

— Electric metering system.

Grid-connected systems are preferable when:

— Grid access is near;

— Power demand levels are higher (>1 kW);

— Grid connection costs are economic;

— Utilities allow 'net billing' or favourable power purchase agreements.

Grid-connected PV systems can be integrated into individual buildings or constructed as a central power plant. On individual buildings, PV systems can be integrated into building components, such as PV roof tiles or large PV-tinted windows.

PV hybrid systems

PV hybrid systems combine PV technology with another energy technology (i.e. wind, hydro, and biomass). When properly designed, the combined availability of a hybrid system should be sufficient to provide power for all periods and conditions. PV/wind hybrid systems may be appropriate for tourism businesses located in coastal regions or flat open plains where wind is available on a seasonal or irregular basis. Depending on climatic conditions, PV/wind hybrid systems may offer significant advantages over single systems. If peak wind periods and maximum solar periods occur at different times of the year, a hybrid system will be more reliable than either system by itself and produce electricity year round. For periods when neither sun nor wind resources are available (at night during low wind periods), battery storage and/or a diesel generator can be installed. If the batteries become discharged, the generator can be used to charge them.

Other Applications

Water pumping: PV systems can also power motors to pump water. In most PV pumping systems, batteries are not necessary as the system works only when there is sufficient solar energy. Adequate water during hot seasons is often a critical issue for the tourism industry and as most hotels have water tanks with storage capacities for at least 2 to 3 days, PV-powered water pumps can be a cost-effective application.

Street and path lighting: Pre-configured PV lighting kits are increasingly popular in theme parks, visitor centers, museums and cottages that require lighting and other small-scale energy uses. Kits may be pre-configured or designed locally and usually include one or two PV modules, mounting structure, charge controller, cabling, connectors, and light fixtures. A battery is usually added separately. If AC appliances are to be used, an inverter will be required to convert direct current from the PV module to standard A C household current. Preconfigured kits usually range from 30 - 200 Wp.

Portable PV power systems: These systems, packed in strong boxes made for travel, are of particular interest to managers of permanent and mobile campsites as they can be used to provide electricity for lighting, public address systems, etc. at outdoor events such as festivals.

Trickle chargers: These devices are used to charge batteries in motor vehicles, boats, and recreational vehicles such as caravans, snowmobiles, go-carts, golf carts, snowmobiles and lawn mowers when they are not in use. The PV panel is connected to the vehicle battery through either a cigarette lighter or accessory outlet.

Integrating PV Systems

To cost-effectively integrate PV systems into new buildings, PV options should be considered at the outset of the architectural design process when specifications are being finalised. This allows for a better building orientation, a building shell with PV-suitable surfaces and a wide choice of PV applications. In the past, PV applications have failed to win design approval in many cases because they required anaesthetic rooftop-mounting structures. Newer PV modules and systems, however, can now be integrated into roofing materials and replace both rack-mounted panels and traditional roofing materials such as asphalt shingles, standing seam metal roofing, and slate or concrete tiles. The result is a PV system that is difficult to notice on the roof but has many benefits.

Once installed, integrated PV systems produce electricity to power some or all building functions with generally low maintenance. PV roofing systems and other building integrated PV components (such as vertical glazing) are commercially available from a number of manufacturers. In North America, an unshaded southern-facing roof is best and, depending on the PV roofing product and the contractor's experience, can be installed by roofing professional, an electrician, or both. Most PV roofing products have undergone extensive testing and certification for fire, wind uplift, and electrical safety performance.

Some have obtained evaluation reports from major building material laboratories to assure their quality. In the US, PV roofing products are tested and evaluated by testing facilities such as The Underwriters Laboratory (UL). For many applications, a UL rating is essential to comply with local building codes. PV systems can also be easily retrofitted to existing buildings. A variety of support structures are available to suit different building designs, building materials, geographical features, and maximize exposure to sunlight.

Transport Energy

Renewable energy can be converted to liquid fuels to provide motive power. The most successful and most widely used technology is to convert crops such as sugar cane to ethanol that can be used directly or blended with petrol. The largest and most successful use of energy crops is the US program to produce ethanol from corn (4 billion litres in 1999) and the Brazilian industry to produce ethanol from sugar cane (14 billion litres in 1999). Crops and crop waste can also be used to create 'biodiesel' and biogas for use in transportation applications.

Bioethanol

Bioethanol is produced through the fermentation of high carbohydrate crops such as sugar cane potatoes, maize, sorghum and other grains, wood, cassava, and sweet potatoes. The fermentation process is essentially the same as that used to make alcoholic beverages - yeast and heat are used to break down complex sugars into more simple sugars, creating ethanol.

Ethanol is used as a gasoline extender for internal combustion engines including motor vehicles. In the US and other countries, a blend of ten percent ethanol and 90 percent petrol (E10) has been used for several decades. In other countries, a widely used ethanol blend, E85, contains 85% ethanol and 15% gasoline. Vehicles running on E85 blends have a good operating record and provide an 80-90% reduction in carbon dioxide and hydrocarbon emissions. Fuel economy is more than two thirds of the fuel economy mileage from similar models running on pure gasoline. In addition, ethanol models are proving to be more reliable, easier to maintain and will last longer as an E85 blend burns cleaner than pure gasoline. Most leading motor vehicle manufactures have launched several models of flexible fuel vehicles, which are able to operate on E85 and lower ethanol blends. For sugar-producing countries, bioethanol production can diversify the sugarcane industry and displace energy imports. Bioethanol can also increase the efficiency of resource use and, indirectly, improve environmental management.

Non-Motorised Options

For many tourists and tourism facilities, walking and cycling can be the most advantageous transport options and can certainly be cost-effective. Many larger resorts operate a fleet of bicycles that can travel on dedicated pathways. Non-motorised options are often the safest transport option with the lowest environmental impacts.

Biodiesel

The seeds of many plants can be crushed to yield oils, which after simple chemical processing by 'esterifying', i.e. combining with ethanol or methanol, leads to biodiesel. This can be used alone or combined with petroleum diesel, the most common blends are B20 (20% biodiesel and 80% petroleum diesel), B30 (30% biodiesel) and B50 (50% biodiesel). The plant oils used include soybean, rapeseed (the result is called rape methyl ester or RME), sunflower oil, castor oil, palm oil, and coconut oil.

Biodiesel can be used in any conventional, unmodified diesel engine including in road and marine vehicles. It extends engine life (as it is more lubricating than petroleum diesel), and delivers similar torque, horsepower and kilometres per litre as petroleum diesels. Carbon dioxide and hydrocarbons emissions can be reduced by up to 80% and exhaust odours eliminated by using biodiesel blends.

Biofuels

Pure ethanol is a viable, high-octane alternative fuel for small aircraft. Ethanol is cleaner and cooler in use than avgas, prolongs engine life, delivers more power and is likely to become a cheaper option as supplies become easily available. Although ethanol has only 2/3 the energy of avgas, it has a higher thermodynamic e fficiency which compensates for the loss of range.

For example, an aircraft such as Cessna 152 (the world's most commonly used trainer) with a modified ethanol engine uses about 13.8 litres per 100 km on avgas and 15.7 litres per 100km on ethanol. Engine modifications are often not technically difficult or expensive. For example, converting a Cessna 152 engine costs around US$3,000, a cost that includes a larger carburetor jet, fuel pump, fuel flow metre, a totaliser, and a small avgas tank to enable the engine to be primed in temperatures below 21°C. Not all engines are expected to need this level of modification.

The biggest benefit of ethanol use has been the reduction of exhaust emissions. When comparing with diesel exhaust emissions, nitrogen oxides are lowered from 9.0 to 3.8 grams per kWh, carbon monoxide from 5.0 to 0.05 grams per kWh and hydrocarbons from 1.2 to 0.16 grams m,per kWh. Aircraft using ethanol and ethyl-tertiary-butyl-ether (ETBE) have performed at air shows all over the world since 1996. Corn and Bagasse are the most common ethanol sources, but some pilots in the US are also using ethanol from potato and orange waste and waste cheese whey.

7

Tourism and Economic Development

Tourists usually demand four main goods and services in a location: accommodation, food, transportation facilities and entertainment services. In most developing countries, to satisfy this demand, the current level of production needs to increase. This provides two positive effects on the economy. On the one hand, an increase in production and income; on the other hand, since tourism sector is labour intensive, an increase in employment. Thus, the tourism sector may contribute significantly to both economic growth and employment in these regions. This is particularly relevant in the case of regions with high rates of unemployment, low levels of per capita GDP and with export products facing difficulties in competing internationally.

In the analysis of tourism, economists emphasize the economic effects of tourism on the economy. Imagine two identical regions A and B where the only difference between the two is that region A receives tourists, while region B does not. Consider a Keynesian model of an open economy. Within this model, although traditional national accounting has considered tourists' expenditure in the domestic economy as exports, we consider it as a stimulus to consumption produced by incoming visitors. Obviously this effect implies an increase in production and in income, but also an increase in market prices and exchange rate. We can analyse this process focusing on a macroeconomic variable such as per capita GDP (Gross Domestic Product) in PPP (Purchasing Power Parity) terms, which shows the real effects on the economy leaving aside nominal aspects as inflation or appreciation of the currency.

The great advantage of tourism sector is that it tends to be labour intensive, so an increase in production is normally achieved by an increase in employment. This is advantageous for those economies that need to decrease unemployment, although it also produces a shock in the job market rising wages in the service sector, inducing mobility across sectors. Thus from a macroeconomic point of view, tourism produces economic growth and employment.

Another critical feature of the tourism sector is the attractiveness of the location to be visited. Sometimes they are natural sites, such as beaches or mountains. In other cases they are cities or particular attractions within the city. We can define any of these tourism resources, as possessing a natural capital or cultural heritage. Different tourism resources have different values given by local citizens or visitors and they are heterogeneously affected by the impact produced by visitors.

Moreover, we argue that each tourism resource is associated with a different depreciation rate and regeneration rate. Both rates are non-linear functions of the number of visitors. Obviously, the regeneration rate must be greater than the depreciation rate if sustainability is pursued. Nevertheless, this last restriction is usually relaxed during some period when natural capital is high enough to support some deterioration. The sources of this deterioration are multiple and they require a strict control. Policymakers might be concerned with the number of tourists or visitors that they receive and how many more they can receive.

Meeting a growing demand from tourism poses some critical challenges. There are three main areas which policymakers need to be concerned with: infrastructures, education and safety.

The development of infrastructures is vital in any tourism project. In this area we include aspects such as: household utilities as water, electricity and telephone and transportation facilities as roads or public transport system. Furthermore, we can include other kind of tourist infrastructures that may help to promote tourism to the region.

Education is also a necessary condition for the potential employment of local people in the tourist activities. It usually requires knowledge concerning different sectors as communication (languages), catering, hospitality, transportation and management skills. An optimal tourism development might take into account the current level of knowledge of the population and the speed of its potential improvement. This is relevant in order to design an optimal tourism development plan over time.

Safety is usually a highly appreciated feature in tourism resorts. Most of the tourists look for places to spend a nice and non-problematic stay. In this sense, we can argue that most of the tourists are risk averse. This is a very important issue to take into account when assessing the competitiveness of a tourist destination. Nevertheless, it seems that safety is related to per capita GDP and how it is distributed within the population. The relationship of these three features with tourism growth seems to be non-linear. They are usually required to attain some critical threshold, above which investment becomes relatively inefficient.

Moreover, there is also a need for private investment. This comprises a set of industries and services that are generated by tourists' demand. Further this will be proportional to the number of tourists and most of the times such industries will grow without government intervention. Thus, it seems that in order to control the development process, what policymakers need to do is to control the number of tourists allowed to stay and determine limits for accommodation facilities through licensing. Therefore, it is necessary to design an optimal path for tourism development. For this purpose, it is also critical to define an objective to pursue and the timescale of the development. In practice this requires a welfare function, a planning horizon for the optimisation as well as an adequate rate of discount.

Tourism, Globalisation and World Economy

In the course of the globalisation of economies and societies, tourism is showing many indicators of development leaps and distortions: continuing growth in tourist flows as a source of environmental damage, new destinations and markets, with resulting increase in competition, risk of overcapacity, particularly in the key tourist areas of air traffic and accommodation, polarisation and increased trend towards concentration among industry providers. There is also the expectation of growth in "manmade" travel and adventure environments worldwide and major expansion in tourist offers and infrastructures (mega-events, leisure parks, transport systems) – with uncertain economic, social and ecological prospects. The growth rates predicted for tourism and its anticipated continuing expansion, with the associated potential for employment and macroeconomic welfare effects are, however, dependent on specific conditions, such as a growing world economy, low energy prices and a global decline in conflicts.

The world economy is characterised by internationalisation and globalisation. So far, the dismantling of borders to production and trade has been concentrated on the group of developed countries in the OECD. This situation has been unaffected by the emergence of a number of Asian NICs. Within the OECD, trade is highly regionalised. Besides the international trading and production networks, regional ones are also emerging. Regional integration processes of this kind will probably continue and develop into free trade zones of increasing size. However, the picture of future economic growth in many forecasts differs widely in the individual regions and groups of countries. Whereas growth in the industrialised nations will converge, only a few of the group of developing nations and NICs will make the jump to the next stage. So far there is no indication that growth in the more developed nations will change significantly. This, together with the expectation that the group of developed nations will gain new members, adds weight to the hope of further growth in tourism.

Which are the main characteristics of the tourism of today? First, its steady and continuous growth: 25 million international arrivals in 1950, 165 million in 1970, 693 million in 2001 and 1,5 billion forecast for the year 2020. Even if tourism growth appears to slow down in the very recent years, there is no evidence of saturation of demand, at least on the global level. International tourism receipts show as well a sustained growth, with annual percentage increases higher than those of the World Real Gross Domestic Product.

Globalisation is another feature of tourism: in 1950 the top fifteen destinations in the world accounted for 97 percent of foreign visitor arrivals; in 1970 it was 75 percent; in 1990, 67 percent and in 2001 it accounts for only 62 percent. Tourism is vulnerable to international crises and economic recession. The aftermath of the 11 September terrorist attacks combined with a global economic slowdown produced, for the first time in decades, a reduction of international tourists in 2001, compared with the previous year.

One year ago, WTO carried out an analysis based on two considerations: the vulnerability of tourism, a major sector of the economy, to the externalities of war and terrorism, on one hand, and on the other, its intrinsic resilience linked to the persistence of the demand for travel and leisure, which must have an outlet despite any obstacles. No matter what difficulties and risks consumers may perceive, they will still seek to travel, even if it means changing their destination or postponing their trip. This essential consideration is what allows us to remain reasonably optimistic.

The progress of the situation from the third quarter of 2001 and through the first nine months of 2002 has largely confirmed our analysis. Six observations can be made.

1. The crisis has been global. 2001 was marked by a loss of consumer confidence and by a feeling of apprehension with regard to travel, especially by air. This was the first crisis in 20 years and the deepest one in the history of international tourism. Revenues were harder hit than arrivals: in dollar terms, international tourism receipts declined by 2.6%, and amounted to 464 billion dollars. International tourist arrivals were down 0.6 per cent from 697 million in 2000 to 693 million in 2001.

2. In spite of it all, the collapse predicted by some did not take place. Indeed, it must be kept in mind that the reference year, 2000, the millennium year, was an exceptional one in all respects. There were an additional 45 million international arrivals that year (+6.9 per cent), whereas the decline from 2001 in absolute terms was just 4 million arrivals. Taking 2000 and 2001 together, puts growth in line with the average for the decade.

3. The different regions and destinations were affected to varying degrees. Four categories of destinations have particularly suffered: those that depend on the U.S. generating market, the Unites States itself as a destination, long-haul destinations in general, and finally the Arab-Muslim world, which has been the victim of image problems and unfair generalizations. The Middle East, South Asia, North Africa, North America and the Caribbean were especially affected, while Europe and Sub-Saharan Africa held steady. East Asia and the Pacific maintained its growth.
4. The impact also varied widely according to market segment. In general, nearby leisure destinations have prospered due to widespread apprehension about travelling far from home; domestic tourism has also held its own; international tourism, generally speaking, has suffered less than long-distance air transport. Air travel, business tourism and conventions, luxury hotels, and cruises during the winter season were particularly affected, while social tourism, rural tourism, rail and road travel made gains.
5. Notable changes in consumer behaviour were observed.
6. The crisis has also accelerated structural changes on the supply side

Lingering uncertainty regarding the global economic situation has led multilateral organizations to revise forecasts they made in the first quarter. The analysis shows that the slowdown in household consumption is causing a decline in growth rates.

There is a downturn in world production, affecting the main tourism generating countries and a lowered world GDP growth expectation by three-tenths of a percent from the forecast of 2.8% earlier in the year. According to

US analysts, total production could slow down due to the effect of the stock market's decline on consumption and investment. Analysis of the industry's current situation show that the state of the economy is exerting a large influence on the number of tourism trips and that the perception that the economy is not recovering as clearly as it was hoped presents a problem with regard to expectations of maintaining employment levels. The purchasing power of the national currency of the chosen destination is another variable with significant influence. The introduction of the euro is perceived in Europe as a positive factor (enhances transparencies, facilitates transactions and purchases and eliminates foreign exchange commissions). However these effects are not easy to see in the short term and some price hikes have been attributed to the introduction of the new currency.

Economic Importance of Tourism

Tourism is one of the most important sectors in the economies of develping countries. Currently, tourism is the most important sector and major source of foreign exchange earnings in Thailand, Australia, and New Zealand. It is ranked second in Hong Kong, Malaysia and the Philippines, and ranked third in Singapore and Indonesia. For example, in New Zealand, the tourism industry employs more than 200,000 people, with projections of a 14% annual growth till the year 2000. In Hong Kong, tourism employs 12% of the workforce and contributes about 7% to the economy. The tourism sector in Thailand supports over 1.5 million jobs and contributes 5% to the economy.

Tourism is also gaining importance in China. By the year 2000, China expects to receive 55 million visitors with foreign exchange earnings of US$14 billion, which will contribute 5% to China's economy, making tourism one of the most significant components of the national economy. In Singapore, the healthy overall balance of payments is attributed to the huge surplus achieved by the tourism sector which contributes about 10% to the economy. Despite Singapore's open economy, and its vulnerability to external shocks and import leakages, tourism has made a significant contribution to output, employment, and income.

Based on 1988 input-output tables, Khan et al. estimated that tourism contributed 11.9% to Singapore's GDP (Gross Domestic Product) in 1992, while employment accounted for 13.4% of the labor force. The employment effect of a million dollars in tourist expenditures would create 25 new jobs. The results ts showed that every dollar of tourist expenditure would generate S$1.97 of output and S$1.05 in income. The income multiplier for tourism was larger when compared to Hong Kong, Indonesia and Malaysia, while the tourism output multiplier was greater relative to other sectors of the Singapore economy.

Comparisons with previous studies showed an increase in the contribution of tourism over time, a strong indication of the significance of tourism in the Singapore economy. The estimated economic impact of tourism is also significant in South Korea. According to Lee and Kwon, the total impact of tourism receipts of US$4.7 billion in 1993, generated US$11.7 of output, US$2.4 billion in income, and created 350,000 full time jobs. The secondary impacts were also found to have a considerable effect on the economy. The findings suggested that tourism should be promoted as a strategic export industry.

Tourism serves as an important means to increase economic growth, raise the quality of life, create employment, and improve the overall balance of payments by helping to offset deficits in other sectors. Many Asia Pacific countries show a net surplus in their tourism balance of payment account. Japan, Taiwan, and South

Korea are major tourist generating countries in the region and this is reflected by the deficits in their respective travel balance of payments accounts. Mak and White attributed the travel account deficits for these high income countries to a higher allocation of disposable income to leisure travel. The relaxation of travel restrictions in Taiwan also had a significant impact on its travel account, due to the large increase in outbound travel. On the other hand, China, Thailand, and Singapore are major receivers of tourists, enjoying a huge surplus. As a percentage of exports, tourism contributes more than 13/n to the economies of Australia, New Zealand, and Thailand, again reflecting its ranking as the top export. Its contribution to the GDP is significantly greater in Singapore (10%) and Hong Kong (7%).

Almost all Asian nations are committing substantial manpower and resources to attract more arrivals whose expenditures represent significant contributions to national income and foreign exchange earnings. For example, Singapore has unveiled a new tourism blueprint titled "Tourism 21" that is expected to turn the nation into a world class tourism business center and the tourism capital of the East. Plans call for increasing arrivals and receipts by 6.4% and 6.6% annually to 10 million and US$11.4 billion, respectively, by the year 2000. Even Indonesia and Malaysia have raised their commitments towards developing the tourism sector. Indonesia plans to make tourism the nation's number one foreign exchange earner by the year 2004, when arrivals will hit 11 million and receipts reach US$15 billion from current levels of 4.3 million and US$5.4 billion, respectively.

In the current Seventh Malaysia Plan, which ends in the year 2000, a number of strategies were formulated to turn tourism into a top revenue earner for the country. Millions of dollars will be allocated for tourism infrastructure in an effort to increase arrivals and receipts to 12.5 million and US$6.3 billion, respectively, by the end of this decade. With increasing competition for the tourist dollar, the national tourism organizations of New Zealand, Thailand, Australia and Hong Kong, among others, have also allocated an increase in tourism funding to tap the emerging tourism markets that promise new income and employment opportunities.

The rapid growth of the tourism industry is a reflection of the region's booming and diversified economies. Economic growth has ranged between an average of 6% to 9% in the last decade, in contrast to 3% to 4% growth achieved by the rest of the world. Only the industrialized countries of Australia, Japan, and New Zealand show a lower rate of growth than the rest of the region. China, which has achieved double-digit growth over the last 5 years, is poised to become one of the world's largest economies and surpass Japan in the next decade. The region is expected to maintain its growth at a rate between 6% to 8% over the next decade.

Strong economic growth in Asia is attributed to a focus on market reforms, export oriented industries, stable currencies, diversification of the economy, and massive injection of foreign capital. Billions of dollars are being poured into the tourism infrastructure to accommodate a burgeoning Asian tourism industry. This has intensified trade, investment, and travel within the region and with the rest of the world. Asian governments have also sought to avoid extremes of inflation and unemployment, and are keeping budget deficits small or running surpluses. It is no wonder that the region has attracted much attention from the rest of the world regarding its success. The opening up of Indochina, Myanmar, and China to tourism, and given the increasing number of companies setting u p bases and new businesses in the region the volume of business travel will rise. This will provide ample marketing opportunities for travel-related businesses.

As a result of strong economic growth, disposable incomes have soared in Asian countries and along with it, the propensity to travel. Leisure consciousness has been enhanced with travel no longer seen as a luxury. In fact, it is now seen as an affordable commodity to be enjoyed by all who choose to engage in a variety of leisurely pursuits. Some Asians may see travel as a status symbol, while others see it as relief from the pressures of work. The introduction of a 5-day workweek in China will provide Chinese residents with more leisure time that will likely be devoted to travel. A number of Asian countries have recorded significant growth in real per capita income over the last Syears with Singapore (7.3%), Thailand (6.8%), China (10.3%), Korea (6.7%), and Indonesia (7.1%) showing the highest growth.

Rising incomes have created a middle class of sophisticated and affluent Asians who are better educated, have more disposable income, and who appreciate the value of leisure. Research by Mak and White has shown travel propensity and tourism spending to be positively correlated a ed with per capita income among the major Asia Pacific countries. This means that increases in income levels will enable a greater proportion of Asians to travel overseas. Unlike previous generations, this generation of primarily young travelers are intent on enjoying the fruits of their labor.

Although price conscious, they still demand high qualify products. Since Asians are more likely to travel in groups and families, more travel products and services, such as tour packages that incorporate activities, must be designed to cater to their needs. This may include travel to exotic places, soft-adventure travel, cruises, and sports related tours, among others. Disposable incomes will continue to rise, and thus fuel the demand for leisure travel. The trend among Asia Pacific countries is towards more frequent regional holidays to various destinations and resorts within the region.

Taxing the Businesses in Tourism

The tourism sector can be taxed either by taxing the businesses in the tourism sector or by taxing the tourists directly. Both methods may be implemented either via the general tax system of the economy or through special tourism taxes. The World Tourism Organisation has identified 40 different types of taxes applied to the tourism sector in both developed and developing countries. Of the 45 taxes, 30 are directly payable by the tourists and 15 are levied on tourism businesses.

Airlines and airports, hotels and other accommodation, road transportation, food and beverages and provider of tourism services, these five broad sectors are involved in tourism taxation. The practicality of taxing each of these sectors is highlighted below.

Airlines and airports: In long haul destinations, international transport occupies a major part in the total cost of holiday packages and hence taxing this sector should, in principle, be lucrative. However, although this is an option for developed countries, this is beyond the reach of most developing countries because they normally do not own an airline company or if they do own one, it is often unprofitable. Revenue may, instead, be generated from airport-related taxes.

Hotels and other accommodation: This is normally the most important revenue generator of the tourism industry and is also easier to tax. However, the practicality of taxing the accommodation sector also varies between developed and developing countries and tends to be more problematic in the latter. The hotel sector is often highly subsidised or receives investment and tax incentives from the government in developing countries, with the aim of attracting foreign and domestic investment to the sector. The motivation is twofold, first to expand the sector as a part of a policy to expand the tourism industry and second, to protect the sector because it is a relatively unstable one due to its highly seasonal nature. The contradicting implication is that the easiest and major target for tourism taxation is most likely to be freed from taxation.

Taxis, food and beverages and tourism services: These sectors are relatively easy to tax in industrialised countries but form part of fragmented small business sectors and do not normally contribute a major proportion of tourism revenue. They include such sectors as entertainments, handicrafts, jewellery and other souvenirs. In most developing countries, these activities form part of the informal sector or of the hard-to-tax formal sector and it is difficult to raise much revenue from this source.

Environment and gambling: Ecotourism tax is a relatively new form of taxation that destinations such as the Balearics levy in an attempt to counter the environmental damage caused by mass tourism. Carbon tax and landfill tax are more general environmental taxes on the level of carbon emissions and wastes respectively, but are borne by tourists as well. Although gambling (in-shop and racing) is not legal in some countries mainly due to religious opposition, casinos are socially accepted in several countries.

Tourists are involved in gambling and casinos, and hence bear the tax associated with those activities. The tax can be levied on the suppliers rather than tourists as in the case of the UK where the betting tax that was initially levied on the gamblers is now levied on the gross profit of bookmakers. Since taxing tourism businesses is not always a lucrative way of raising tax revenue, much tax revenue from tourism is generated from consumption taxes and special tourism taxes applied directly to tourists' consumption. Consumption taxes take the form of general sales taxes or value added tax (VAT).

Sales tax/VAT is levied in almost all countries, regardless of the tourism taxation policies. Therefore, in the presence of this type of sales tax, tourists are being taxed without any deliberate tourism tax policy on the part of the government. In the spirit of optimal taxation, some countries discriminate between domestic and tourism consumption, such that the latter is taxed at a higher rate or an additional tourism tax is applied to tourists' consumption. However, this entails administration problems in enforcing and monitoring such taxes.

Special tourism taxes are generally levied directly on tourists and they can take several forms. Common forms include taxes on hotels and restaurants, passenger services, tourist transport, entry/exit taxes and hotel accommodation taxes. The last tax is the most common and, as the name suggests, hotel accommodation tax is simply a tax on the tourists' expenditure on accommodation. The rate levied usually depends on hotel class and the season. It is relatively easy to collect, although discrimination across hotel classes sometimes creates administrative problems.

Entry/exit taxes include those on airport departures, which are fixed amounts that have to be paid when leaving the country, on airport embarkation, which is paid on entering the country, and the visa fee. These taxes are usually levied at a flat rate and are relatively small in amount: for example, the airport departure tax has been within the range $1-6 in Singapore, Indonesia, Malaysia, Philippines, and Thailand, and was set at $10 in Malawi, Tanzania and Zambia.

Reasons for Tourism Taxation

Most of the arguments in favour of taxing the tourism sector are based on the fact that tourism products are consumed jointly with unpriced natural amenities and public goods. Unpriced natural amenities include the sun, sea and wildlife, while public goods can include security and health services. The question of public goods, their supply and their pricing, is relatively more important in tourism than in many other industries, in part, because of the needed role of the government in asset preservation and, in part, because of the greater role of the government in the normal routine when foreigners reside temporarily within its own borders." Main reasons for tourism taxation can be considered under the following categories.

Besides providing law and order, under which contracts can be enforced and property rights protected, so ensuring that the private sector is operating efficiently, one of the main roles of the government is to provide 'public goods'. The technical definition of public goods comprises the following: indivisibility, ie. commodities are not divisible into units that can be sold individually; non-excludability, ie. no one can be excluded from benefiting from the product; the free-rider problem, where it is difficult to charge users an appropriate fee.

Common examples of public goods include national defence and street lighting. The distinctive characteristics of public goods makes it difficult to provide them via the private sector because there is no price mechanism that controls the market. They can be provided only by the government, which uses its right to tax to generate the resources necessary to supply them.

Domestic taxpayers usually finance the provision of such goods. The influx of tourists imposes an extra cost on the government relating to the provision of items such as greater security and an improved environment. As non-residents, tourists do not pay to finance these extra costs. A tourist tax will, therefore, serve to redress the balance and impose the burden on those who are responsible for them. There are often user charges for some attractions, such as parks and safaris, but in other cases, such as street lighting and public security, enforcing payment is difficult. In such circumstances, taxing the may be the only way of 'charging' them for the public goods they consume.

Higher government revenue can increase welfare by such means as financing improvements in public services. Furthermore, it may help to reduce the burden of income taxation on domestic residents, and it may also be an alternative policy for countries that want to reduce their dependency on trade taxes while, at the same time, not imposing an additional burden on domestic residents.

The WTO estimates that 'tourist countries' obtain around 10-25% of their tax revenue from the tourism sector. In some small specialised tourism countries such as the Bahamas, over 50% of government revenue is generated from the tourism sector. the net tourism earnings in the Maldives accounted for 40% of government revenue. In Mauritius, about 12-15% of tax revenue is collected directly and indirectly from the tourism sector. The tourism sector is an unusual sector for revenue generation. Developing countries tend to undertax their tourism sector, failing to exploiting fully the economic rent emerging from the sector.

Such rent results from less than perfectly elastic demand for their tourism products, due to the differentiated nature of their natural amenities. The degree of inelasticity of demand depends, in part, on the degree of differentiation of the destination and affects the ability to tax. The greater the degree of differentiation of the destination, the more inelastic demand will be and, hence, the greater the scope for taxation. Tourism product differentiation generally occurs in terms of types and quality of attractions (endowments), types and quality of goods and services sold in the country, geographical location and distance.

Examples of attractions with very inelastic demand are the pyramids of Egypt, the Taj Mahal and the Grand Canyon. However, tourism is a composite product with multiple components, and each of the components can be taxed at a different rate. Researchers examined that the effect of a hotel room tax on non-lodging consumption and find that tourists 'respond to marginal increases in price of lodging partly by reducing some of their non-lodging expenditures and partly by reducing their savings and/or spending at home'.

Taxation on tourism may be exportable in the sense that tourists bear the major burden of the taxation. Tax incidence refers to the distribution of the tax burden between the buyers and the hoteliers whereas tax exporting refers to the extent to which the burden of the tax is distributed between the residents and the non-residents. If the hotel industry is an enclave with a high proportion of foreign investment, then the distinction between tax incidence and tax exporting is minor because the incidence of the tax on the supplier is actually exported. Under a partial equilibrium framework, the incidence of a hotel room tax depends on the relative sizes of the elasticities of demand and of supply.

Hotel room tax was more readily exported than similar taxes levied on meals, drinks and entertainment and the general sales tax. Hence the exportability of tourism taxes is liable to vary between different components of the tourism product. Many developing countries under balance of payments and foreign exchange pressure have targeted tourism as a means of development. In many cases, no proper management strategies have been formulated especially at the initial stage of the tourism development.

Natural resources have been degraded to the point where environmental sustainability is threatened. Regulating the inflow of tourists and taxation are the two most popular tools used, or considered, to remedy the problem. However, regulating the inflow of tourists may not be the ideal solution because it deliberately contracts the tourism sector and this may have negative repercussions on the economy. It should also be remembered that many countries are investing resources to expand the tourism sector, and therefore it would be contradictory to pursue these two policies simultaneously.

Moreover, it is believed that unconstrained growth (not limiting tourist arrivals) is usually beneficial in the sense that it increases the level of per capita income, thus providing more funds for maintaining the environment and sustaining growth. On the other hand, regulation through taxation not only provides the government with revenue (if designed properly) but also targets only the activities and individuals involved in the environmental degradation process and is, therefore, an efficient way to tackle the problem.

Furthermore, with higher revenues, more resources will be available to sustain the development of the industry. The tourism sector does not only rely on the natural amenities in the country but also on public goods. A strong regulatory framework, such as maintaining high health and food preparation standards, is also important in the success of the tourism sector. Taxation can generate the necessary resources to provide these requirements. Of course, the tourism industry has no inherent right to have the taxes it pays ploughed back into the industry. However, appropriate earmarking of tax revenue can help to sustain the tourism industry and also help to reduce and combat the associated degradation of the environment.

The taxation issues involved in controlling environment degradation and sustaining tourism are similar. The basic method is to use the Pigouvian tax, whereby the tax rate should correct for the divergence between the market price and the social marginal cost.

Such taxes should be applied to all users, including both domestic residents and tourists, and should as far as possible be directed to the goods and services that generate the externalities so as to avoid inefficiencies.

If resources are to be exploited only to the economically desirable limit, then the social marginal cost (hence tax rate) should be set sufficiently high to include not only the opportunity costs to local residents in terms of environmental damage and congestion costs, but also the maximum possible rent extractable. On the other hand the price, hence the tax rate, should not be set so high as to hinder consumption of the product and tourist arrivals in the country.

Congestion is an important facet of sustainability. High congestion, often caused by tourists themselves, reduces the quality of tourism services, which can lead to a reduction in arrivals, especially of high class and high spending tourists. The presence of crowds may detract from the enjoyment of tourists seeking solitude and privacy. Discomfort in crowds, long queues at popular places, traffic congestion and an untidy environment will not only affect the quality of tourism services but also the quality of life of domestic residents.

Tourism taxation may be used both to reduce the inflow of tourists and to compensate the local residents. However, many tourism activities are not priced, for example, sun, sea and sand, and if some are priced, the associated transaction costs relating to monitoring and enforcement are generally very high. Thus, they are supplied at a zero fee to all users and the problem of free riders is difficult to avoid.

An entry/exit tax is an easy way of extracting economic rents from the tourism services the destination country is selling because it is often a tax included in the airfare, unnoticed by many travellers. Sometimes countries discriminate between domestic residents and tourists, so that only tourists pay the tax. However, an entry/exit tax has some disadvantages. First, by capturing rents from tourists, an entry/exit tax does not provide any incentive for tourism to reduce their demand for the specific good that is causing the externalities, as should optimally be the case. The tax will reduce the number of tourist arrivals. Hence not only the demand of the externality generating commodity will fall but demand for other tourism services will also fall because of the complementary nature of tourism demand. The economic benefits normally attached to expanding the tourism sector may then be constrained.

Second, a uniform entry/exit tax does not offer first degree price discrimination in the sense that both low and high income tourists or short and long stay tourists pay the same amount of tax. This may discourage short stay tourists. Third, since it is levied mainly on foreigners, or at a higher rate on foreigners, it may fail to take full account of the full contribution of residents to environmental degradation.

Impacts of Tourism Taxation

Taxes levied directly on the tourism sector are sometimes difficult to justify. The amount of tax collected may be small but the tax can still have a substantial negative impact on the tourism sector, with repercussions on the overall economy. This happens especially with taxes levied directly on tourists, such as visa fees. It is not only the high fees required; there is often unnecessary bureaucracy (indeed discrimination between tourists of different nationalities) that can greatly raise the compliance costs for the tax payer and act as a deterrent to visiting the country. This may contract tourist arrivals and affect other sectors related to the tourism sector. For countries where tourism comprises a major part of the economy, this can adversely affect the employment level and the balance of payments resulting in an overall contraction of the level of economic activity of the economy.

The fiscal effects are likely to differ from country to country and from time to time, for three main reasons. First, the effects depend on the policy of the government. If the government wants to maximise revenue, the tax rates will tend to be high. On the other hand, if the government wants to promote the sector, tax rates can be very low. In some case the government goes further by providing subsidies, such as subsidies for airport and parking infrastructure, and investment incentives to businesses.

Second, the effects also depend on how important tourism is to the economy. Obviously, the higher the contribution of tourism in the economy, the higher will be the effects of tourism taxes on the government budget. Thirdly, the number and types of linkages with other sectors in the economy and leakages from the economy that the tourism sector brings about are also important. As a general rule, linkages tend to increase government revenue and leakages lead to a reduction in revenue.

The amount of revenue that is obtained from tourism taxation depends, in part, upon the value of the price elasticity of demand for tourism. If the price elasticity of demand is high, the effect of an increase in tax may be to decrease revenue. In the case of tourist accommodation, researchers obtained, demand elasticities for accommodation that were significantly different from zero. They also reported a significant price elasticity of demand for the lodging industry based on a survey of the properties owned and managed by the American Hotel and Motel Association.

Taxation generates revenue but, as in the case of trade taxes, it invites retaliation by other countries if they feel that the other government is unfairly treating their citizens. For example, Kenya and Tanzania introduced visa charges for UK citizens in retaliation to the application of visa fees by the UK on their citizens. Retaliation is always a threat and in most cases the eventual outcome is lower welfare for both countries.

The country with a more inelastic demand for tourism will lose less but, compared with the case without retaliation, both countries lose. However, if a developing country imposes, say, an entry tax on tourists who are mainly from developed countries, then retaliation will tend to affect the developing country to a lesser extent. This is because the number of tourists from the developing country visiting the developed is fewer than the number of tourists from the developed countries who visit developing country.

8

Employment in Tourism Sector

The worldwide travel and tourism industry is threatened by a crisis much deeper than the slump it has suffered in 2001-2002. If the situation does not improve soon, it is estimated that by May 2003, no less than 5 million jobs may be lost in the worldwide travel and tourism industry. This represents over 6 per cent of the industry's total employment. If these losses materialize, they will add to the six and a half million jobs which were previously estimated to be lost as a result of the crisis in the travel and tourism industry in 2001-2002.

Taken together, all job losses from the crisis of the travel and tourism industry has been suffering since 2001 would represent 14 per cent of all jobs in the industry or one in seven. The travel and tourism industry represents over 4 per cent of GDP and over 3 per cent of employment worldwide. If indirect effects are calculated in, its portion rises as high as 11 and 8 per cent respectively. Direct employment in the industry's enterprises already amounts to about 80 million jobs.

In certain tourism-oriented countries, the travel and tourism industry accounts for more than ten per cent of direct jobs, such as Spain or the Caribbean. It is certainly the most important employer worldwide after agriculture and public services. The travel and tourism industry and its suppliers together are estimated to provide close to 200 million jobs globally, or one in every thirteen. As a rule of thumb, one direct job in the travel and tourism industry generates employment in up to two jobs for the industry's suppliers.

The slump comes after a strong global economy had propelled an international tourism boom in the late 1990's. In the peak year 2000 alone, the number of international trips increased by a record 4.5 per cent from the year before. In the year 2001 the industry suffered disastrous effects from the events of 11 September and declined by around 1 per cent on an annual basis. Although tourism demand has traditionally bounced back one year after any crisis motivated by security problems, it did not grow significantly, if at all, during 2002. This is measured by the performance data of the hotel industry, tour operators and airlines in spite of an increase in traveling across international borders recorded by the World Tourism Organization (WTO).

In early 2003, the travel and tourism industry developed some optimism. after it had been suffering an economic downturn which started in 2001 and worsened after the events of 11 September that year. It grew very little during 2002 and was stagnate in the last quarter due to security incidents in Djerba, Bali and Mombasa. The optimism dampened as early as March by a general reluctance to travel in view of the hostilities in the Middle East. The Asian and Pacific region experienced few effects until it was exposed to new fears coming from a new disease.

Business travel, which is suffering the most, generates far more than half of the hotel industry's profits as business travelers roughly spend twice as much money compared to leisure tourists. The sub-sector has been suffering severely since 2001 due to the general economic downturn. More and more companies are now deferring business travel and are relying on supplementary methods of communication such as video-conferencing and other electronic means.

New habits of communication are feared to eventually replace traveling even when things return to normal. This would have a devastating long-term effect on the hotel and airline industries, as video conferencing could cost airlines' between 5 and 10 per cent of their bookings over the next 18 months. The recently booming "meeting, incentive, conference and exhibition" business, known as MICE, is the main victim. Revenues from business travel in Asia represent a fifth of the $250 billion global business travel industry and will fall by about 5% this year. That compares with double-digit growth in each of the past four years.

Three categories of locations can be distinguished by the degrees of impact in accordance with either being affected directly or indirectly by SARS, or by the general economic and political insecurity and continuously weak economy. Countries significantly impacted on by SARS are China; Hong Kong, China; Singapore; Taiwan, China; and Viet Nam.

The second category includes the rest of South East Asia and the Pacific while the rest of the world with a few exceptions makes up the third. Rough estimates indicate that since March 2003 the travel and tourism business lost at least one third of its activities in the locations directly affected by SARS. These are Hong Kong, China; the Guangdong province of China; Taiwan, China; Singapore; and Viet Nam.

South East Asia and the Pacific

In other South East Asian countries, the immediate loss is about one third, but may be about 15 per cent in the long run. In most of the rest of the world the industry is estimated to lose about 5 per cent this year instead of growing at the rate of one or two per cent expected earlier. The Asian and Pacific region suffered less from the crisis in tourism of the years 2001 and 2002 than other parts of the world.

Growth was largely due to fast growing intra-regional tourism from markets such as Indonesia, Malaysia, Singapore and the booming Chinese market, which also comprises Hong Kong, China. Even after the security incident in Bali last October, the impact seemed to affect international travel to Bali only, especially from Australia. Bali partly managed to fill the gap by attracting local budget travelers from Indonesia and neighboring countries.

Amongst Indonesia's annual 5 million foreign visitors, 4 million are from the ASEAN countries, Japan, the Republic of Korea and China, leaving only 20 per cent of international arrivals to Australia, New Zealand and long haul tourism. Domestic tourism is increasing in Indonesia, but international visitors spend on average 12 times more money during a trip.

Intra-regional tourism benefited the industry with two-digit annual growth rates in January and February regardless of the delicate geopolitical situation. Prospects were good for the year, as the impact of Middle East violence on Asian and Pacific tourism was not expected to affect the region in its peak season June-September. However since March 2003, the situation has dramatically changed due to SARS. Long haul travel activities are being particularly affected. Some U.S. carriers have reported that overseas bookings have plummeted 30% to 40% in April from yearago levels.

Traffic to Asia in particular dropped by 25 per cent since December which was mainly due to SARS as it was only off about 5 percent in early March. BA carried 27 per cent fewer people on its scheduled services to the Asia-Pacific region in April than the same month last year. Some hotels and airlines serving the directly affected locations are down to no more than 30 per cent of their usual business.

A bus company in Singapore reported that business is down to ten per cent of their usual and an outbound travel agency in Taiwan, China, reported 80 per cent cancellations. Some shopkeepers in Hong Kong, China, reported not seeing a single customer for several days. In countries directly affected, not including China, the travel and tourism industry provides about one million jobs, representing between 2.0 and 3.5 per cent of the total number of jobs. Considering all employment dependent on travel and tourism, the total is about three million jobs or between 5.4 and 9.9 per cent according to the country.

China is a special case due to its size. Whilst only one province is affected directly, the travel and tourism industry of the whole country may be affected soon. Over 15 million jobs or 2.1 per cent of all jobs are provided by China's travel and tourism industry directly, and as many as 52 million or 7.2 per cent of total employment including indirect jobs. The core countries affected by SARS have been suffering from high ratios of cancellations in leisure travel as well as in business travel and congresses.

Tourist arrivals to Hong Kong, China, slumped by some 30 per cent in the last week of March alone, and likewise, 30 per cent of flights from there were cancelled in March and early April. The occupancy rate at some of the most fashionable hotels in Hong Kong, China, was down to just 14 per cent reportedly due to the fact people could not go home. In general, the hotel occupancy in Hong Kong, China, dropped to single-digit rates. It is estimated that Hong Kong, China, will continue to lose 6 per cent of GDP as long as the outbreak lasts.

According to IATA, airlines have reduced a large percentage of flights to the region as tourist bookings have fallen by about 80 per cent impacting overall air travel to areas such as Hong Kong, China, by 30 to 40 percent. Regional airlines still in the process of recovering from the 2001 slump, have been among the first to send out an SOS, reporting that up to 50 per cent of their flights have been suspended. Cathay Pacific (Hong Kong, China) warned that it may have to ground its entire fleet with passenger numbers predicted to fall to 20 percent of normal levels by May 2003.

In general, the hotel occupancy rates in the affected locations are estimated to be down by over 30 per cent and are estimated to be below the break-even point which obliges the management to cut costs drastically. In Vietnam, hotel occupation dropped from as high as 98 per cent to a level of only 40 per cent. In the longer term, hotel occupation rates in the affected locations may stabilize with a loss of 15 per cent. Hong Kong, China, and Singapore were amongst the poorest hotel performers in March as compared to the same period the year before, with revenue per available room falling 16.8 percent and 15.4 percent respectively (measured in US dollars).

Hotels across Asia experienced a 4.6 percent decline. The Singapore Tourism Board's (STB) latest weekly report showed that visitor arrivals to Singapore plunged by 61 per cent in the first thirteen days of April, as compared to the same period a year ago. Hotel occupancy rates fell to 20-30 per cent from normal levels of at least 70 per cent. The Singapore Retailers Association reported that sales could fall by as much as 75 per cent for some firms. Declines for general stores perhaps range between 20 and 40 per cent.

Singapore, which like Hong Kong, China, relies heavily on tourism and its role as a regional transport hub, has cut its economic growth target to 0.5-2.5 per cent this year from 2.0-5.0 per cent due to the impact of SARS. The late disclosure by the Chinese authorities of the SARS outbreak has created additional concern amongst travelers. The Grand Hyatt in Shanghai reports an occupancy rate of about 30 percent compared to last year in mid-April when the hotel was nearly full.

Four major hotels in China's biggest city were closing for up to three months due to a lack of guests. Prospects are that the tourism business in all of China may be affected soon. For example, Beijing and the Shanxi province came to the limelight when the World Health Organization recommended the postponement of unnecessary travel there, as the organization had done earlier for Guangdong province and Hong Kong, China, and later also for the provinces of Tianjin and Inner Mongolia.

China's inbound tourism industry brought in 20.4 billion dollars in foreign currency last year. Chinese tourism industry analysts estimate that tourist income may fall at least 40 percent this year. In other Southern and South Eastern countries the travel and tourism industry is affected by SARS because of direct flight connections to indexed locations.

These countries are also affected by the notoriously weak geographical knowledge on the world's tourism markets which has resulted in a large de-facto "quarantine area" in South East Asia and Oceania comprising important tourism countries such as Thailand, Indonesia, and the Philippines as well as neighboring Australia and New Zealand. The travel and tourism industry in Indonesia, Philippines, and Thailand alone means over 5 million direct jobs and a total of over 12 million jobs including those in other industries depending on travel and tourism. Their share in total employment is as high as 11 and 12 percent in Thailand and the Philippines respectively, i.e.

one in nine jobs is in danger when travel and tourism slumps, and 6 per cent in Indonesia.

Direct employment in the industry represents as much as 2.4 percent of total employment in Indonesia, 4.1 and 5.7 per cent in the Philippines and Thailand respectively. In Indonesia, foreign arrivals are down about 15 percent for Jakarta and 20 percent for Bali airport. Flights arriving from Singapore fell by about 30 per cent due to the outbreak of SARS in that country. Indonesian hoteliers have seen occupancy rates quickly tumble by about 10 per cent.

Mariott reported from Jakarta that its luxury hotel there now posts a mere 40-50 per cent occupancy rate, one of the city's best. Normal hotel occupancy rates are between 60 and 70 per cent. The decline therefore represents at least 15 per cent. Thailand, one of Asia's most tourist-dependent economies, earned over USD 8 billion from tourism last year. Thai Hotels are currently experiencing cancellation rates of 5 to 10 per cent.

According to the Tourism Authority of Thailand, which predicted a 40 per cent drop in foreign visitors coming to Thailand between April and June, About 50,000 visits were cancelled for the period between April and June 2003. Five-star hotels in Bangkok are expecting an occupation rate of no more than 30 per cent for April 2003. April falls in the lean season, but in April 2002, the occupancy rate was still 50 per cent.

Arrivals to Cambodia fell by 22 per cent in March and are frustrating expectations to reach the one-million line this year, which would have brought a 25 per cent increase over last year's 800,000 visitors. Cambodia had reported a 17% one-year increase in arrivals in January and 33% in February. The Philippines remained moderately affected so far, with a drop of foreign arrivals by 4 percent in the first quarter as compared to the first quarter 2002, in spite of a 13 per cent growth in January over last December.

Similar to other visitors, South East Asian finance ministers postponed their trip to Manila where their annual summit was to be held, although the ASEAN labour ministers' meeting took place in West Nusa Tenggara (Indonesia). Malaysia, on the other hand, is heavily affected, with airline bookings down by 40 per cent and hotel occupancy rates by as much as 30 per cent.

Industry officials say some hotels are seeing occupancy rates dip as low as 30 per cent after cancellations not only from tourists but also due to postponements of corporate events and shows. In Korea, arrivals of foreign air travelers dropped by almost 50 per cent last month compared to April 2002. Australia and New Zealand are affected by SARS, as far as the markets on the northern hemisphere are concerned, due to their geographical closeness to the core countries hit by SARS.

As both countries are considering closing their borders for travelers from those locations, arrivals through places like Singapore or Hong Kong, China, would also be excluded. Already at present, the Australian Hotels Association has confirmed bookings are on the decline with occupancy falling by between 20 and 30 per cent and tour operators informed bookings of foreign visitors for May are down 30 per cent and for June 20 per cent as compared to the same period last year.

In February, cancellations were highest from the United States, the United Kingdom, Italy, France, Germany and the Netherlands, but since news of the SARS virus hit the headlines, Asian tourists have also started canceling. SARS is expected to cost New Zealand about 20,000 visits by East Asian tourists and around $60 million a month at its present level. The Tourism Board predicts a 15 per cent decline in the number of Asian visitors in 2003 because of the SARS infection scare.

In other parts of the world, the 2001-02 crisis of the travel and tourism industry continues due to SARS, but hostilities in the Middle East and the state of the overall economy play the predominant role. Instead of growing by between 1 and 2 percent or more as forecasted by several sources, the worldwide travel and tourism industry is facing cancellations and a low level of reservations for the northern summer, as well as a continuous decline of business travel.

The loss of income is estimated to amount in average to 5 per cent for the world without South East Asia, China and Oceania. The average current loss of income for the whole world is estimated to amount to 7 per cent. In the United States, hotel occupancy rates have dropped to an average of 60 per cent in the first quarter 2003 from 63 per cent over the last year according to the Travel Industry Association. They are forecast to run at about 59 per cent occupancy rate this year, whilst 65 per cent is usual in good years. As the break-even point is as low as about 55 per cent, the hotel sector in general in the United States continues being profitable due to rigorous cost cuts in the recent past and a rational financial structure.

However, PricewaterhouseCoopers projects a 7 per cent drop in the sector's earnings this year to $15 billion from $16.1 billion in 2002. Hotel loan delinquencies are at their highest level since the early 1990's. The negative outlooks for 2003 follow the release of 2002 data by the United States Department of Commerce indicating that the number of international visitors declined 7 percent compared to 2001. The demand for hotel rooms in the United States has never been weaker than at present; since before the war in Iraq and the development of SARS most companies were only traveling on business trips deemed essential. This is a significant blow to the industry since at least three-quarters of the hotel sector's profits come from business travelers.

The number of business trips this spring is expected to fall 2.5 per cent from the spring of 2002 and 13 per cent from spring 2001, according to the Travel Industry Association. A quick recovery is not likely. The Mexican tourist industry reported a 17.1 per cent slide in reservations since the beginning of the war in Iraq. More than 3.5 million travelers have called off their trips to the country, which calculates into losses of up to USD 700 million in revenues or 9 per cent of the tourism sector's annual hard currency income.

International travel to France had rebounded in the past year but is currently levelling down. In Germany, the hotel federation announced that the industry might have to cut as many as 10,000 jobs. Hotel bookings in Rome, Florence and Venice, Italy, ordinarily throbbing in springtime with art lovers and business travellers, were reported to be down by half compared with last year. In Paris, occupancy rates at four-star hotels dropped 25 percent by March 25. The drop was mainly attributed to the absence of Americans, who accounted last year for 19 per cent of all foreign visitors to Paris.

Second to the Japanese at USD 652, Americans usually spend more in Paris, an average of USD 328 a day, compared to USD 133 by British tourists, and USD 78 for Germans. In Turkey, foreign tour operators cancelled between 15 and 40 per cent of reservations. Despite being 1,000 kilometers from Iraq, congresses in Istanbul are being postponed. This affects Turkey's goal to attract 15 million tourists and earn USD 11 billion from tourism this year. There is still hope for tourism to recover as Europeans typically visit Turkey in summer.

Job Losses

The present job losses come after the industry already lost an estimated six and a half million jobs before the recent events such as SARS and the hostilities in the Middle East. The compounded loss of eleven and a half million jobs over the 2001-2003 crisis relates to an estimated total of about 80 million jobs in the industry, and represents a loss of one in every 7 jobs. The capacity of the travel and tourism industry to create employment seems to be severely damaged by the recent events.

Additional factors may need to be considered if the slump continues. The longer the loss of travel and tourism activities lasts, the possibility exists that more jobs will be eliminated entirely. The reductions in working hours and manpower tend to become permanent, as the missing labour force is made up for by new working methods such as increased versatility. Remaining core staff is induced to acquire additional skills and also accept more flexible working hours.

A hotel and resort company in the United States and Canada reported having eliminated 15 percent of 38,500 jobs and having trained many of the remaining employees to handle multiple tasks. For example, a front-desk person may also take phone reservations and an administrative person in the back office will help check people in during busy times.

Modernization of working methods, working relationships and indeed enterprise structures may thus take a sudden leap forward and leave behind a number of employees with reduced or no income. The loss of employment affects the socially weaker and lesser skilled staff members, as well as part time workers including high proportions of women, migrant workers and young workers. They risk permanently losing income and jobs as long as the industry does not return to substantial growth rates. The social effect is worse as it severely impacts on those workers who have difficulty finding alternative jobs due to lower skills levels.

If indirect effects of the crisis are counted in, that is, jobs which are lost in industries that provide inputs to the travel and tourism industry, the estimated loss amounts to over 13 million jobs worldwide. This is to be added to at least the same impact of indirect effects that was already produced by the crisis since 2001. As a rule of thumb, one direct job in the travel and tourism industry generates as an indirect effect, two additional jobs in related industries. It should be considered, however, that industries providing inputs to the travel and tourism industry will suffer from downturns in this sector with some time lag only, and employment may not be reduced as quickly as in the sector concerned directly.

Companies of the travel and tourism sector report on measures aiming at rapid cost cutting and in some cases downsizing to reduce over-capacities acquired in the 1990's. In Germany, the world leader in tour operating, TUI, recently announced a USD280 million cost-cutting programme for 2004, and the possible loss of 2,000 jobs. In the course of the crisis in the travel and tourism industry, representative bodies of the industry and government authorities have been trying in many countries to develop measures to mitigate the effects, at least in the short run.

Tourism crisis plans are being developed and government relief measures such as tax breaks are being asked for, although with limited success due to high deficits in government accounts from the economic downturn since 2001. Positive examples of privatepublic partnerships have been developed to promote the tourism destination. In some cases such as Canada, Indonesia, Australia, and others, particular efforts are being made to target closer markets in view of slumping long haul international arrivals.

Tripartite approaches are chosen by government agencies, employers' organizations and trade unions in some countries in line with the recommendations made at the Informal Meeting on the Hotel and Tourism Sector: Social Impact of Events Subsequent to 11 September 2001. Tripartite social dialogue is essential to support affected companies in their efforts to implement temporary cost-cutting measures that will help them stay viable and preserve as many jobs as possible.

The measures can include taking leave, working fewer hours, reducing lay-offs to a temporary measure and arranging for workers to improve their skills through government sponsored courses. A number of companies in the countries affected in South-East Asia and Oceania are asking their workers to take their annual leave or unpaid leave, in lieu of layoffs. In Singapore, the Ministry of Manpower, the National Trades Union Congress and the Singapore National Employers Federation said in a joint statement 15 April that whatever steps necessary should be taken to save jobs in tourism-related industries hit by the SARS scare.

Crisis Management

It is well documented that any major disruption to the security or safety of any tourist destination - from natural or man-made threats - will have an immediate effect on demand for visits to that destination and a sharp impact through the loss of employment in tourism and related industries, not least because some jobs in the tourism industry are seasonal, temporary or casual, and thus staff can easily be shed when markets weaken. If the situation lasts longer, not only employment gets lost irretrievably but enterprises are threatened in their existence.

Especially small and medium-sized enterprises are threatened to disappear as they cannot rely on sufficient capital to survive longer periods of reduced demand for their services. The effects on employment and the well-being of enterprises in tourism destinations can be attenuated if the tourism authorities succeed in managing the situation well. Experiences made in different countries recently are too fresh to be assessed comprehensively. Certain highlights are presented below:

Bali

The Asia-Pacific region has had its share of man-made disasters that have had an adverse impact on tourism. Most recently, the security incident of 12 October 2002 in Bali overnight turned one of the region's most successful destinations, and one which was especially popular with Japanese and Australian tourists, into a place from which most tourists had fled.

Prior to the incident and despite economic weaknesses and a loss of confidence in international travel occasioned by the events in the United States on 11 September 2001, tourism in Bali was booming. In the four month period May-August inclusive, during which approximately 43% of annual international arrivals come to the island, there were 538,000 arrivals in 2000, 551,000 in 2001 and 592,000 in 2002, an increase of 10% in two years.

Tourism is the mainstay of the Balinese economy and its success created large numbers of tourism-dependent employment on the island as well as elsewhere in Indonesia. Arrivals in Bali in the early years of the current decade were around 1.4 million a year, some 27% of all international arrivals in Indonesia. In employment terms, Bali had around 50,000 hotel workers and 18,500 restaurant workers prior to the security incident, in addition to 33,000 people working in the wholesale trades and 314,000 in the retail trades.

The proportion of the Balinese employed labour force working in these four sectors was 24.2%; in Indonesia as a whole, these sectors accounted for 18.2% of all jobs, indicating how important tourism is for the island's economy. Informal estimates suggest that 40% of the island's jobs depend on the tourism sector; others that 80% of households depend on tourism.

Few data are available on the aftermath of the security incident in October 2002 specifically in terms of employment, but it is clear that demand for tourism to the island remains very depressed. As an indication of its effect on demand, however, in January 2003 there were only 60,000 arrivals compared with 110,000 in the same month of the previous year. In the immediate aftermath of the Bali incident, hotels found occupancy levels falling to negligible levels.

Employees were required to take all unused leave, to take "leave in advance" and to reduce their working days, all of which were seen as "preludes to the seemingly inevitable staff reductions" which would arise if the crisis of confidence were to continue, according to the Executive Chairman of Indonesia's Culture and Tourism Board. The Minister of Manpower announced that "up to 130,000 hotel and tourism workers were likely to be laid off" within a month of the attack. It was also made clear that the impact of the incident would not be confined to Bali. Other regions of the country with strong migration, labour market or supply linkages to Bali in regions such as Central and East Java, and Lombok, would also be affected.

It was expected that international tourists would also stay away from attractions in other parts of the country, such as Yogyakarta and Lombok. The Minister of Finance estimated that at least 10 sub-sectors - including hotels, land and maritime transport, restaurants, entertainment, tours and sightseeing, souvenirs, health and beauty services, and tourist guides - would suffer. The World

Bank Country Officer for Indonesia stated that, as a direct consequence of the incident, "...by the end of 2003 there could be 2-3 million more Indonesians living below the poverty line than would have been the case without the attack".

The small beginnings of a recovery in the first quarter of 2003 have now been damaged further by the SARS outbreak in Asia, the continuing uncertainty over peace in the Middle East and by a new warning from abroad of a further terrorist threat on the island. Before those new threats arose, the Balinese and Indonesian tourist authorities had undertaken a variety of tasks intended to assist the country's recovery as a tourism destination.

At the same time, the region had rallied to do what it could to assist in the tragedy in its midst. Immediately following the bombing, the Pacific Asia Tourism Association (PATA) sent in a senior member of staff to lend practical assistance to managing the situation. An emergency task force of regional experts encompassing a variety of tourism sectors was assembled by PATA to assist the Indonesians. The PATA Bali Recovery Task Force was charged with giving practical advice on how Bali could accelerate the healing process and move the tourism sector onto a path of recovery.

Based on the experience of past events and the team's individual areas of expertise, a list of recommendationswas assembled on how the recovery could be stimulated over the short and medium term. In the immediate aftermath of the bomb, the government provided a safety net through block grants to ensure that Balinese residents received subsidised rice, and additional school and healthcare programmes. In terms of dealing with the tourism crisis itself, the authorities quickly announced a range of actions which followed international experience from previous tourism disasters.

Included in these were four steps, described as comprising the four stages of rescue, rehabilitate, normalise and expand. Under the rescue heading was included a rapid switch of marketing emphasis to domestic tourism markets and regional markets within the ASEAN group of countries. Experience has shown that a key requirement in these circumstances is to keep up a flow of accurate, factual information to tourism markets and tourism companies. This information should present a consistent picture from a single source - confusion and contradiction add to the difficulties.

The message distributed should also, wherever possible, provide a positive indication of how the problem is being tackled and what steps are being taken by the authorities to rectify matters. The Indonesia Culture and Tourism Board (ICTB) immediately (the day after the bomb) set up a Media Centre in Bali and Jakarta to act as the communication and information centre for the press, tourism industry and the public. The ICTB also held meetings with seven of Europe's largest tour operators to keep them informed and discuss possible solutions to the crisis.

Plans for the rehabilitation phase included marketing initiatives, fiscal incentives, a media campaign, familiarisation trips for journalists and travel trade representatives, a programme to raise standards across the board, making use of the time available during the drop in activity, reductions in the costs of electricity in Bali's tourism sector, in the cost of the airport departure tax, in parking and handling fees for airlines at the airport and various other tax and fiscal incentives aimed at stimulating the market.

In the short term, unfortunately, the events of March and April 2003 have inevitably set back the cause of Bali's rehabilitation. Nonetheless, the steps taken by the authorities reflect many aspects of best practice in crisis management. It may be necessary to continue these countermeasures for longer than originally intended, but the approach is well-founded in international experience.

Sri Lanka

Sri Lanka's tourism industry has, more than many, been troubled by crisis incidents over the years. An internal military and para-military conflict plagued Sri Lanka over two decades. As a result, the country's tourism industry is no stranger to initiating crisis management measures in order to deal with the fallout on the industry at home and to handle the negative publicity that has been generated overseas.

However, an attack at Bandaranaike International Airport in July 2001 was especially severe and appeared to hit at the very heart of tourism itself. The airport is effectively the only entry point to the country for international tourists. The incident killed some 17 people and caused the airport to shut down for over 24 hours. International flights from Sydney, London, Berlin, Rome and the Middle East were diverted. The government had to appeal for calm and asked people in Colombo to remain in their homes. Such measures hit the international headlines and tourism collapsed.

Prior to the airport attack, Sri Lanka's tourism industry had been growing, reaching an alltime high in 1999. Numbers climbed from 302,000 in 1996, to 366,000 in 1997, 381,000 in 1998, 436,000 in 1999 and then dipped to 400,000 in 2000. The announcement of peace initiatives in the island encouraged the industry in early 2001 to adopt a new strategy to facilitate effective image and product repositioning, adopting an integrated approach with all stakeholders.

By June 2001, the first six months of the year had seen an increase of 17% on the same period in the previous year, with 227,205 arrivals. However, following the attack, the country's major leisure tourism markets in Europe, notably the UK and Germany, as well as Australia and the USA, saw huge reductions. Total arrivals fell by 14.1% in July, 54% in August, 62% in September and 52% in October; it was eleven months after the incident before growth resumed. The number of tourists travelling by SriLankan Airlines declined by 41% during the second half of 2001, recording a decline of 9% for the year as a whole. Charter flights to the country bringing in leisure tourists declined sharply, accounting for 3% of total traffic in 2001 compared with 7% the previous year.

The sequence of measures undertaken following 24 July 2001 fell into three phases: crisis management activity, damage control measures, and recovery strategies. Immediate action was undertaken to persuade foreign countries to withdraw travel warnings and lower the insurance risk premium imposed on foreign airlines and shipping companies. At the same time, an assessment was made to evaluate the impact in all areas including loss of income, employment and tourism revenue, and how to assist existing businesses through the crisis. The government introduced a relief package to cover temporary difficulties faced by companies through the rescheduling of loans and interest payments and difficulties were assessed on a case by case basis.

A press campaign was launched and familiarisation trips to the country were arranged. The lull in tourism activity was reportedly utilised to try to improve the tourism product and service standards. Four months after the crisis, a marketing campaign was undertaken entitled "Buy one, get one free" for FIT (Free Independent Traveller) customers over the November/December period.

The number of nights spent by foreign guests in tourist hotels decreased by 23 per cent in 2001. The industry responded to the difficulties by offering low rates and promotional packages and there was a considerable increase in the number of local guests, particularly in the Colombo city and hill country. This increase in domestic travel helped the hotel sector survive the crisis period.

Provisional figures show that employment in tourism declined significantly as a result of the events. It was estimated that in the case of both direct and indirect employment there was a fall of 6.6%, implying that some 2,500 direct jobs and 3,500 indirect jobs were lost. A substantial amount of casual labour in the industry also reportedly lost jobs. The cease-fire and initiation of peace talks have helped to boost Sri Lanka's international image. Coupled with aggressive marketing by tour operators and Sri Lanka Airlines as well as the hosting of international sporting events, this has helped to restore the country's reputation.

There has, in addition, been a significant increase in visits from expatriates - many of Tamil origin - taking advantage of the prevailing peace to visit the island. 2002 arrivals were up by almost 17% on 2001, with particularly strong increases coming from within the region. The vital European and US markets had, however, still to regain growth.

Severe Acute Respiratory Syndrome (SARS)

The outbreak of the Severe Acute Respiratory Syndrome (SARS), initially in China, in March 2003 provides an example of a need for crisis management in tourism. It also provides a stark reminder of the vulnerability of the travel industry to 'natural' crises, in addition to man-made security issues and the vagaries of the economic cycle.

Although SARS was a headline story in the world's press for a relatively short time, in reality it has dealt (and continues to deal) a severe blow to the tourism industry throughout the Asia/Pacific region, the effects of which may be felt for the remainder of 2003 at least. In ILO's paper established in May 2003, New Threats to Employment in the Travel and Tourism Industry - 2003,it was estimated that SARS together with other factors such as the continuous economic slump worldwide and travellers' security concerns in view of on going conflicts could result in a further 5 million job losses worldwide in the travel and tourism sector in 2003 which, on top of the 6.5 million already lost during the 2001-02 crisis, would take global jobs losses to 14% of direct employment in the industry since 2001.

SARS was especially threatening since its epidemiological characteristics were not yet fully understood by science. It thus had the potential of threatening travellers with danger, including the danger of the unknown, whether or not it had the potential to become a widespread epidemic in public health terms. The nature of the threat from SARS was therefore one of personal safety. It affected the confidence of potential travellers, touching the most sensitive area of the travel business. If people do not have to travel to an area where there is perceived to be such a threat, they will not do so, even if the threat is small in real terms of probability. As a consequence, the latter half of March and most of April and May 2003 saw drastic falls in tourism and travel activity throughout Asia and the Pacific. The region had escaped the worst of the 2001-02 downturn in international travel, but it saw its growth prospects destroyed by SARS. Typical estimates available in April 2003 included:

— a decline of one third in travel activity in March-April 2003 in the countries and areas directly affected-China, Singapore, Viet Nam and Taiwan, China;

— in Hong Kong, China, a growth of 19% in arrivals in the first half of March became a decline of 10% in the second half, with a 70% decline anticipated for April;

— a decline of perhaps 15% in the medium term in the rest of Asia and the main Pacific nations;

— a 30-40% drop in United States air bookings to the region, and almost a 30% drop in bookings on British Airways' Asian routes;

— 30% of flights to Hong Kong, China, cancelled;

— a 61% fall in arrivals in Singapore in the latter half of April;

— a 50% drop in arrivals in the Republic of Korea in April;

— hotel occupancy rates down to between 30% and single figures in some Asian destinations;

— predictions of a 40% decline in arrivals in Thailand for the April-June period;

— Australian hotel occupancy rates down by 20-30%, with a 30% decline in tour operators' bookings for the destination in May and 20% in June.

On 23 May the World Health Organisation lifted some of its advisories against travel to the region - 'freeing' Hong Kong, China, and Guangdong province of China among others. WHO's travel advisories against the other areas (Beijing, Hebei, Inner Mongolia, Shanxi, Tianjin and Taiwan, China) were lifted until 5 July. In most affected destinations, it is still too early to assess recovery measures, although in Hong Kong, China, the lifting of the WHO travel advisory has been used as an opportunity to re-launch the destination under the banner of 'Rediscover Hong Kong'.

The tourism authorities and the tourism industry were combining to generate positive messages about safety, coupled with the promotion of the destination by more traditional means such as special offers and price reductions. It is stressed that the recovery will take a considerable length of time and that the guard against SARS will need to be kept up, but the sector is also using well-recognised communications principles to deal with the situation in a professional manner.

The crisis illustrates the 'geographical blindness' on the part of many travellers, since there have been sharp declines in arrivals and in the level of business generally in countries within the region that have had no SARS cases. Even in other regions of the world, travel has been depressed as a result of the virus and of worries about how it might be spread through, for example, air travel. The fact that some such concerns may be scientifically ill-founded did nothing in the short-term to mitigate the effects.

Based on past experience, it is likely that the tourism markets most affected will recover by 2004. However, there is no sign yet that the outbreak is fully under control. Until that point is reached, SARS seems to have caused serious damage to tourism demand, and thus to employment prospects, throughout the region.

9

Tourism and Sustainable Development

The role of local authorities as facilitators in the development process is reinforced through municipal international cooperation (MIC). With globalisation, the governance challenges facing local authorities in different parts of the world have increased in their similarities, transcending the national political and economic systems upon which different communities rely.

These shared challenges of governance have instigated thousands of local authorities to establish municipal international cooperation projects and to join international local government organisations (LGOs) to advocate for local self-governance and control over the development process. Even prior to the UN Conference on Environment and Development, but particularly since the adoption of Agenda 21, many local authorities and their LGOs have focused on the unique challenges of governance for sustainable development.

At the local level, sustainable development is achieved by steering local development activities to simultaneously achieve three objectives:

— increased local social welfare;

— greater, and more equitably distributed, local economic wealth; and

— enhanced integrity of local ecosystems.

Thousands of local authorities, in partnership with their communities and supported by MIC activities, have instigated Local Agenda 21 processes to create a shared vision for local development that is consistent with the sustainable development concept. In response to these visions, local authorities have been adapting their practices and activities to steer local development along the sustainable development path.

Local Agenda 21 processes, in conjunction with decentralisation policies originating at the national level, are transforming local governance and reorienting the process of local development in communities throughout the world. A primary challenge of local governance, both today and in decades ahead, is to steer increasingly external, global forces on local development so that development achieves the shared vision of the local population.

In cities, towns and villages throughout the world, the primary responsibility for this steering process rests with the institution of local government and its diverse local authorities. As providers of social services, builders of economic infrastructure, regulators of economic activity, and managers of the natural environment, local authorities have many direct instruments at their disposal to influence development.

Yet in addition to their direct roles in the development process, perhaps the most important role that local authorities can play in a global economy is that of facilitator among the diverse interests seeking to influence the direction of local development. Only with such a facilitator can a community of diverse interests define a shared vision and act consistent with this vision.

Tourism is one of the many external forces influencing the direction and options for local development. The question of whether tourism can be sustainable-that is, whether it can contribute to local sustainable development-is rightfully addressed in the context of the Local Agenda 21 process.

A truly legitimate and practical discussion on sustainable tourism must take place in and with the communities that are being influenced by tourist industry development. It must create accountability of the tourism industry to locally-defined development visions.

The true proof of "sustainable tourism" will be the sustainable development of local communities that serve as tourist destinations. It is time for the sustainable tourism debate to focus on this challenge. Local authorities worldwide welcome the leadership of the UN Commission on Sustainable Development, and the interest of the tourism industry, to reduce tourism's negative impacts and to increase the positive contribution of tourism business and consumption activity to local sustainable development.

Problems in Tourism Industry

Tourism is a recognised global industry-one of the largest industries in the world. Like any global industry, tourist business activities can have considerable impact on local development trends. The local impacts of the tourism industry are diverse and are often unique to the tourism sector. Tourist activities, as traditionally defined by the tourism industry, fundamentally involve the transportation and hosting of the tourism consumer in a local community, i.e., "tourist destination," where the tourist product is consumed.

No other global industry structures itself in such a way that the consumer is brought to the product, rather than the product being delivered to the consumer in his or her own community. This structural difference produces unique social impacts upon the local tourist community, including the interruption of local customs and lifestyles, the spread of infectious diseases, changes in local demographics, and changes in local housing and labor markets. The primary product of tourism is not something produced by the industry.

The product is often the heritage, wealth, and expected legacy of the community that serves as the tourist destination. The business activity of the tourism industry is to promote the "salable" or appealing aspects of the community, transport non-residents into the community, manage the hospitality for and guidc the activities of these visitors, and provide them with goods and services to purchase during their stay. If these business activities degrade the community's heritage and wealth, then the community suffers more directly than the consumer, who can return to his or her own community without responsibility for or awareness of the impacts of his tourist activities.

Tourism activities can, in particular, degrade the social and natural wealth of a community. The intrusion of large numbers of uninformed foreigners into local social systems can undermine pre-existing social relationships and values. This is particularly a problem where tourism business is centered in traditional social systems, such as isolated communities or indigenous peoples. Tourism in natural areas, euphemistically called "eco-tourism," can be a major source of degradation of local ecological, economic and social systems.

The intrusion of large numbers of foreigners with high-consumption and high-waste habits into natural areas, or into towns with inadequate waste management infrastructure, can produce changes to those natural areas at a rate that is far greater than imposed by local residents. These tourism-related changes are particularly deleterious when local residents rely on those natural areas for their sustenance. Resulting economic losses can encourage socially deleterious economic activities such as prostitution, crime, and migrant and child labour.

Solutions to Adverse Tourism Impacts

Solutions to adverse tourism impacts are to be found in the shared interest of local communities, tourism businesses, and tourism consumers to maintain the natural wealth and social heritage of the tourist destination. In the first instance, therefore, an institutional mechanism must be established, relative to each destination, to articulate and develop this sense of shared interest.

To secure the legitimacy of these mechanisms, the participation of all interested local groups or interests must be guaranteed. Dialogue must take place in an open and transparent way. Experience demonstrates that if dialogue among interested parties is to have a real impact on development, it must generate accountability among these parties with regards to future investments, practices and policies. Consensus or decisions arising from dialogue must be reflected in institutional action.

Only through such accountability can interests maintain a commitment to continued dialogue and a common agenda for local tourism development. Experience demonstrates that this accountability should be reciprocal between individual or private interests and societal or public interests. Without such reciprocal accountability, local communities are typically forced to choose, in conflict, between private and public benefits, even if ample "win-win" development choices exist.

On the one hand, accountability requires that property owners are provided with opportunity to retain the economic value of their property, either through sale or income generating activity.On the other hand, private market relationships, including property ownership, do not provide sufficient basis for social accountability related to "public goods," including ecological integrity and social heritage. Private property titles do not recognise the concepts of ecological integrity or social heritage.

Excessive reliance upon private property ownership as a guide in development has in fact contributed to the deterioration of public goods. Within such a framework of accountability, numerous instruments are available to guide local tourist development on a sustainable path. These instruments include:

— heritage preservation requirements for site developments and building designs;

— programs to exchange land and development rights from non-suitable to suitable development areas;

— private heritage and green space stewardship programs;

— tax benefits accruing to property owners exercising sustainable development practices;

— tourism taxes and development fees to support construction and maintenance of required infrastructure.

However, without true commitment to the sustainable tourism agenda, these instruments are not themselves sufficient to prevent the steady erosion, by legally sanctioned private actions, of local natural wealth and social heritage. Therefore, support from the international, national, provincial and local levels of industry and government, is essential to the success of this agenda.

Fortunately, in more than 2,000 communities in 64 countries Local Agenda 21 partnership forums already exist to serve as a mechanism for sustainable tourism dialogue. Where these forums are weak or have not yet addressed tourism issues, the tourist industry, local government organisations (LGOs) and concerned NGOs can serve as a catalyst for dialogue.

A particular opportunity exists in those countries where Local Agenda 21 national campaigns (in more than 20 countries) or where National Councils for Sustainable Development (NCSDs-in about 70 countries) have been established. NCSDs can play a key role in providing country-level support to local review of the sustainable tourism agenda. Through their international facilitating body, the Earth Council, a comprehensive effort between industry, NGOs, LGOs and NCSDs can be established. Of additional interest at the local level is the potential role of local tourism offices or Convention and Visitor Bureaus (CVBs) that have been created through public-private partnerships to promote local tourist attractions.

Where motivated to support sustainable tourism development, the CVBs could serve as facilitators of working groups, within the context of Local Agenda 21 activities, on sustainable tourism development. Where CVBs or their related international body(ies) have made no express commitment to sustainable development, local authorities, as primary funders of CVBs, are in an excellent position to mobilise their awareness and support. Internationally, alliances between LGOs and various tourism industry trade associations, trade unions and consumer organisations can support awareness raising and local demonstration projects that may serve as models for other local communities on a country or regional basis.

Impact of Consumer Behaviour in Sustainable Tourism

Tourism-related consumption has three stages of impact. First, prior to departure, tourists purchase travel-related clothing and equipment, which may be produced under conditions that undermine the social and ecological sustainability of the producing communities. Second, when tourists travel long distances to tourist destinations, they create considerable atmospheric pollution and other impacts on the global environment. Third, upon arrival at the tourist destination, tourists often continue their accustomed habits of consumption, even though these destinations may not have the infrastructure required to manage those consumption patterns.

In addition to high altitude emissions from long distance air travel, air travel produces considerable negative local environmental impacts, including ground level emissions of VOCs and particulates, disposal of fuel, hazardous chemicals and solid waste, noise pollution, and wildlife and habitat disruption. Marine dumping of wastes from cruise ships is an increasing concern. However, with nearly 600 million international travelers in 1997, surprisingly little public information is available on the environmental and social impacts of long distance travel.

For instance, individual travelers receive far greater information about the impacts of their local automobile use than of their air or cruise ship transportation. Motor vehicle pollution is typically more highly regulated than aircraft and ship pollution. Following arrival at tourist destinations, the tourism industry typically strives to host tourists according to the standards and amenities of their country of origin. These hospitality standards mimic-and encourage-the high consumption lifestyles of developed countries.

For instance, luxury hotel rooms, with high levels of energy and water consumption, are given the highest rankings or "stars" in international hotel rankings. These "luxury" consumption standards, using current technologies, are themselves globally unsustainable. The most immediate observable impacts of introducing these high consumption practices into lower consumption communities are:

— degradation of local water and soil quality, with direct impacts on local health and economies, as a result of the lack of adequate water, drainage, waste water, and waste management infrastructure to manage the higher volumes of waste produced by higher levels of consumption;

— reduced access by local residents to land, housing and marine resources through, among other things, reallocation of these community resources to foreign tourist residents and inflation of local prices;

— destruction of traditional sources of income.

The most direct way to reduce the adverse impacts of tourism-related travel is to increase opportunities for people to engage in appealing tourism activities in their own cities, regions or countries. In various cities of the world, this local tourism concept is known as "green tourism." Green tourism-in contrast to "eco-tourism," which relies on travel to distant locations-seeks to provide recreational attractions and hospitality facilities to local people within their local regions, thereby reducing tourism-related travel.

While green tourism has the positive economic effect of stimulating local economic activity, it reduces the flow of foreign currency to developing nations- and any resulting economic benefits that may accrue to developing towns and cities from these revenue flows. However, short of definitive actions by the tourism industry and host countries/communities to reduce the negative environmental impacts of foreign travel and the negative social impacts of foreign tourist enclaves in developing nations, green tourism advocates will continue to build support among tourism consumers.

Solutions to tourism-related pollution in the travel and tourism industry are technologically available. Overcoming economic barriers to their implementation may require government regulation, the development of economic instruments, and industry self-regulation. The industry has every opportunity to institute voluntary initiatives and self-regulation to address green tourism advocates and those calling for government regulation.

The growing effort among international hotel chains, for instance, to offer guests the option of reusing their bedroom towels and linens demonstrates the ability of the industry to respond in one area of impact. However, more comprehensive efforts are required to tangibly resolve accelerating environmental and social impacts. In this regard, the establishment of formal environmental management systems (EMSs) in each business establishment provides a way for tourism businesses to identify their adverse social and environmental impacts and to institute a programme for continuous reductions of those impacts.

EMS registration programmes such as ISO 14001 and European EMAS regimes offer extensive guidance to tourism businesses, and deserve the active support of international tourism industry associations. Ultimately, the solution to adverse environmental impacts arising from local tourist consumption is the establishment of waste reduction programs and appropriate waste management systems and infrastructure, particularly in developing country destinations.

Again a choice exists between voluntary and regulatory measures. National governments and tourism businesses, which receive disproportional economic benefits from tourism, share an interest in maintaining tourismrelated hard currency inflows, and should either directly provide such infrastructure or ensure that funds are made available to local authorities for this purpose.

Without such support, powers should be provided to local authorities to increase local revenues from tourism, through local airport taxes, hotel and service taxes, and development fees, to finance infrastructure construction and maintenance. Only through such economic instruments can the public costs of tourism activity be "internalised" in the local tourist economy. Local revenue measures need to be carefully coordinated across municipal jurisdictions on a regional basis to ensure coordinated infrastructure development.

Without a coordinated regional infrastructure development approach, pollution from communities without infrastructure can undo the environmental benefits of infrastructure investments in neighboring communities. Where statutory regional planning bodies do not exist to provide coordination, Local Agenda 21 forums may provide a flexible mechanism for multi-jurisdictional coordination. Tourist businesses can make a significant voluntary contribution to resolving the social costs of tourism by:

— providing local resident employment and training opportunities, including in traditional trades and crafts;

— establishing purchasing guidelines that favor local goods and services procurement;

— making donations and investments in local recreational facilities, parks, cultural facilities and security operations (which also serve to improve local tourist amenities as well);

— establishing local profit-sharing arrangements.

Failing necessary voluntary measures, local governments can institute economic incentives and regulatory measures to reward best practices and prevent severe social impacts that need to be resolved at public expense. Ultimately, in the face of private establishments that demonstrate no long-term commitment to maintaining the preconditions for tourism-which include public safety, environmental quality, infrastructure maintenance, and economic justice-local authorities need to use all powers available to protect the cultural and environmental wealth that make an attractive tourist destination.

Agents and Partnerships for Change: A partnership approach to addressing negative impacts of tourism consumption requires, above all, assumption of responsibility and voluntary action by the tourism industry. For example, within the framework of a voluntary EMS approach, partnerships can be established between local governments, airport authorities, regional air quality agencies, airlines, trade unions, NGOs and resident associations to develop an action programme to reduce local airport pollution.

Following the model of the "Responsible Care" programme in the chemical industry, these partnerships could be supported by international travel and tourism organisations and related industry associations. Measures to reduce high altitude pollution by aircraft require similar initiatives by the industry and government at the national and international levels.

Of critical importance is the creation of mechanisms to inform and involve tourism consumers in making educated choices about their activities as tourists in distant tourist destinations. Ideally, these efforts would ensure that tourism consumers, as with industry, begin to recognise and understand tourist destinations as living communities that deserve their support and respect. Communications from tourism consumers to tourism industry and to local authorities about their desire to reduce the adverse impacts of their tourism activities can be essential to mobilising changes in industry and government practices.

International consumer advocacy organisations and trade unions can play an important role in informing consumers about tourism development activities that violate basic principles of sustainable development. Provision of such information to LGOs can facilitate local authority responsiveness to identified problems.

BROAD-BASED SUSTAINABLE TOURISM DEVELOPMENT

Many of the technologies and measures required for sustainable development in the tourism sector are clear. Resources exist within the tourism industry-which annually generates hundreds of billions of dollars-to apply these technologies and to make development within the sector more equitable. However, as the experiences of hundreds of local authorities demonstrate, through their engagement in broad-based sustainable development planning through Local Agenda 21, the appropriate application of technologies and resources requires effective and truly accountable development partnerships.

If industry and government are to protect and sustain the social, cultural and environmental wealth that attracts tourists, they must build more ambitious and committed partnerships to plan, manage and invest in this wealth. In this respect, the primary barrier to sustainable development through tourism is an over reliance on market mechanisms to guide tourism development and consumption decisions. The market-which treats cultural and environmental wealth as free, "public goods" and which responds to degradation of this wealth as a "free rider"-provides instruments to guide development, but is insensitive to many requirements of sustainable tourism.

Furthermore, in a global market such as tourism, the problem of "leakage", whereby the economic benefits of local tourism activity flow out of the local community and country back to a foreign corporate headquarters, is another indication of the inadequacy of simple market-driven approaches. Sustainable tourism development requires a partnership among the stakeholders of the local tourist destination. This partnership must use both market and non-market instruments to implement a shared sustainable development vision.

Without such a partnership, advocacy for sustainable development becomes a conflictive struggle between an industry which seeks to respond only to market forces and a public sector which, when accountable, acts to protect public goods and wealth for future generations. Therefore, the key problem at this stage of the "sustainable tourism" debate is the creation of tangible, working local partnerships. These local partnerships must be encouraged and supported by national governments and industry, and not undermined by "higher level" agreements.

To succeed, local residents and their local authorities need to more fully recognise the significant adverse impacts of tourism development and must be informed about opportunities for reducedimpact tourism development. Tourism businesses need to recognise and support the social conditions (e.g., security, public health) and the cultural and environmental wealth that make a community an attractive tourist destination.

The UN Commission on Sustainable Development has repeatedly recognised Local Agenda 21 planning as an effective partnership mechanism for implementing Agenda 21 in cities and local communities. Experience with Local Agenda 21 activities in hundreds of communities since 1990 has highlighted a number of principles for effective sustainable development planning.

These principles can also provide the basis for effective partnerships for sustainable tourism planning and development in local tourist destinations. These partnerships can be established either within or independent from existing Local Agenda 21 activities. The principles for Local Agenda 21 planning are as follows:

— Participation and Transparency, that involves local residents, representing all major groups of society, in Local Agenda 21 planning and makes information aboutsustainable development easily available to the general public.

— Partnerships that build collective responsibility for planning, decision making,problem solving, project implementation and evaluation.

— Accountability that holds all partners answerable for their actions.

— Systemic Approach that addresses the underlying causes of social, economic and ecological problems in an integrated way, focusing on the entire systems that are affected, rather than only problem symptoms.

— Ecological Limits, that are defined by Earth's carrying capacity and that serve as the limits for development.

— Equity and Justice, that are secured locally through the provision of equal opportunities and human rights, and globally through development cooperation partnerships between developed and developing nations.

— Concern for the Future, that requires long-term planning and action that addresses both immediate needs and long-term trends.

These principles can be applied, in working partnerships, to evaluate and improve efforts to address sensitive tourism development issues, such as:

— inequitable distribution of tourism revenues and "leakage" of revenues to foreign shores;

— displacement of pre-existing local settlements by tourism developments;

— equal access to local coastal and recreational resources and controversies over uses and long-term protection of those areas;

— concerns related to lack of foreign tourist sensitivity to cultural traditions and sites.

The primary partnerships for sustainable tourism development will be local partnerships, addressing the unique development goals and needs of each community. Where Local Agenda 21 activities are underway, a Sustainable Tourism Working Group could be established within the existing Local Agenda 21 planning structures to facilitate planning and action.

Notwithstanding the primacy of local partnerships, the transnational nature of tourism requires transnational partnerships to support sustainable tourism planning activities at the local and national levels. The Local Agenda 21 process has established a new mechanism for such transnational partnership, called "Local Agenda 21 Charters." Initiated by the Netherlands Ministry of Foreign Affairs, in cooperation with the International Union of Local Authorities, the International Council for Local Environmental Initiatives, and Towns & Development, the Local Agenda 21 Charters process provides a mechanism for local communities to factor issues of global responsibility within their Local Agenda 21 activities.

Two local authorities, typically on a North- South and East-West basis, establish a "Charter" agreement that specifies areas of mutual support to jointly address relevant issues of global equity and sustainability. Presently, 20 local authorities have established the first Local Agenda 21 Charters.

Ultimately, tourism consumers must be rallied to the sustainable tourism agenda, thereby shaping both the market and public policy. Tourism consumers in existing Local Agenda 21 communities may find the Local Agenda

21 Charters mechanism useful in supporting sustainable development in popular tourist destinations. Existing "twinning" or "sister city" relationships with cities that are located in tourist regions can provide the basis for a possible Local Agenda 21 Charters relationship.

Sustainable Coastal Tourism Development

Economic development activities in any sensitive natural area pose a particular challenge for sustainable development. Coastal areas host the most productive marine ecosystems and serve as spawning grounds for the oceans. The degradation of coastal areas in many countries, with the resulting impacts upon coastal settlements and fisheries, justifies strict local controls on further coastal development. Coastal zones are dynamic in nature, responding to daily tidal changes as well as long term events such as sea level rising.

This dynamic quality offers a defense from extreme weather events. Rigid infrastructure from coastal development can inhibit the ability of coastal ecosystems to respond to changes. Since coastal areas are the most highly populated regions on Earth, their protection requires unique attention and the effective management of numerous competing interests. In many coastal areas, tourism development is destroying or marginalising dwindling habitats for marine animals and spawning fish, as well as the livelihoods of traditional fishing families and villages.

Unregulated water sport activities and machinery are adding to this toll. Lack of effective waste water treatment for tourist facilities is making a significant contribution to coastal water pollution. Excessive private tourist development is denying equitable human access to beaches and coastal waters, cutting off local populations from their coastal heritage. Inappropriate development in high risk storm areas is costing families, local economies and governments billions of dollars annually.

As a first measure towards the sustainable management of coastal areas, governments at all levels, working in partnership with private foundations and investors, should establish designated coastal areas where development will be forever restricted. Protection of these areas should be stringently enforced.

In areas where coastal development can be socially and environmentally justified, tourism development should be designed as a form of low-impact economic activity relative to other development alternatives. The reputation and viability of the sustainable tourism concept depends upon the definition and implementation of clear management objectives for each coastal area. These objectives should clearly designate ecologically and socially/culturally sensitive areas as well as high risk areas.

Appropriate tourism uses should be designated for each area according to levels of sensitivity and risk. Education programs should be established to inform tourists about these management objectives. The aims of any sustainable tourism development in coastal areas should be to:

— recognise the economic value of existing coastal ecosystems, towns and heritage sites by providing opportunity for local revenue-generation through managed tourist use of these areas;

— design tourism developments, in cooperation with local stakeholders, to suit the unique ecological and social characteristics of each coastal site;

— use tourism investment to develop and upgrade the watershed, solid waste and waste water management systems for coastal cities and towns;

— ensure equitable access to coastal areas by all people, with a specific emphasis on using tourism development as a means to upgrade and manage traditional social uses, for example, through the designation of special natural/cultural heritage sites.

In addition sound planning and management to achieve the above aims, the following opportunities for low-impact tourism development could be considered:

— application of low-impact building and transportation designs, materials and technologies;

— control of waste production through recycling and efficiency measures;

— co-investment by the tourism industry, government and local residents to upgrade existing settlements and urban infrastructure, including drainage and sewerage infrastructure.

The planning and management of coastal development typically requires the cooperation of local stakeholders-including property owners, residents, local business groups, and local authorities-and government agencies at the national and sub-national levels. In general, some institutional mechanism will need to be established to facilitate cooperation and consensus-building among these actors.

As coastal areas typically extend beyond the jurisdictions of individual local authorities, regional coastal management agencies are often established through inter-municipal cooperation or sub-national action to provide effective multi-jurisdictional coordination. Alternatively, private foundations or regional/national NGOs have frequently been used as a mechanism for coastal area planning.

Under ideal circumstances, tourism industry representatives, including property owners, will be directly involved in coastal planning and management schemes. In such cases, the tourism industry, in particular transnational businesses, needs to make a good faith commitment not to circumvent local/regional planning and management discussions by directly lobbying national government for special permissions and considerations.

10

Initiatives for Sustainable Tourism

Tourism is not a clean and non-polluting industry. A major problem is the lack of a common understanding of what sustainable tourism or "ecotourism" means. This ambiguity leads to violations of environmental regulations and standards. Hence, the environmental problems evolving from tourism are manifold. First of all, the tourism industry is very resource and land intensive. Consequently, the interest of the tourism sector will often be in conflict with local resource and land use practices. The introduction of tourism will imply an increased stress on resources available. An influx of tourists into the area will lead to a competition for resources.

Employees working at the tourist sites compound this competition. Almost as a rule, tourists are supplied at the expense of the local population. Tourist activities imply an intensified utilisation of vulnerable habitats. Investors and tourists do not necessarily possess awareness on how to use natural resources sustainably, and subsequently this utilisation often leads to a degradation of resources.

Tourism is also a major generator of wastes. In most tourist regions of developing countries, sewage, wastewater and solid waste disposal are not properly managed or planned. Lastly, tourism is also responsible for a considerable proportion of increased volumes and mileage in global transport and hence the associated environmentally damaging pollutant emissions. The tourism industry has not shown sufficient willingness to (internalise or) compensate the cost of conservation of biodiversity in, for instance, protected areas, even though they can profit from it.

Tourism is a powerful agent of change. International tourism acts as a catalyst for the transition from traditional ways of life to so-called modern, Western forms of society. Accordingly, tourism often brings with it the introduction of new behaviour trends and norms. Very often, these are contrary to traditional norms existing in the host community, and can come into conflict with its cultural identity and threaten the traditional value systems there. The problem is that the investors seem to have a lack of cultural understanding of the invested society. There is a need for an increased awareness that establishment of new hotels etc. will have its consequences on the society and the people who live in it. Tourism has become associated with violation of human rights.

Many destination countries have experienced an increase in criminality, prostitution, alcohol and drug abuse as a consequence of tourism. Furthermore, child labour is commonplace in the tourism industry (particularly in the informal sector). According to estimates made by ILO (International Labour Organisation), between 3 and 19 million children and teenagers work in the tourism sector. A particularly abominable form of violation of human rights is child slavery and despicable abuse of children taking place in the booming sex industry in many countries. In these countries, tourism has led to an incredible increase in prostitution and also in the exploitation of children. The tourism industry has not yet come up with a general condemnation of these violations of human rights.

The tourism industry is characterised by a high degree of monopoly, which implies a concentration of services and profits into very few big transnational corporations. In many countries, tourism facilities mostly belong to foreigners. Furthermore, in local host communities in many countries a relatively small number of people are involved in the tourism industry in host communities in many developing countries. Very often, there is a lack of qualified manpower in the locality. Hence, most employees are recruited form the big cities, neighbouring countries or even from the country of origin of the investors.

Multiplier effects from tourism are less significant than is often assumed. One reason is that tourism industries purchase most of their inputs (materials, products or services) in their country of origin. As a result, a considerable amount of foreign exchange revenues leaks from the destination countries. The more goods, services, physical capital and human capital a country must import for its tourism services, the higher the leakage. Very often the investors are not approaching the local community to see what it actually can provide. In addition to this, the General Agreement on Trade in Services (GATS), with its liberalisation of global trade and services, is increasingly undermining the possibilities of individual countries and regions to control their tourism industries and the possible economic gains from tourism.

The tourism industry should engage in promoting sustainability as a hallmark for investors. More specifically, investors in tourism should strive to adopt environmentally sound technologies or other measures to minimise the consumption of local ground water. In the case of water utilisation, such measures might be water saving equipment, desalination systems and collecting and utilising rainwater. Using other types of resources in a sustainable manner is, of course, also crucial. There is a need to use ecological materials and installation of renewable sources of energy systems (solar energy) in all new buildings and new construction.

Furthermore there should be an acceleration of installation or solar/wind power in all public work projects of communities where tourism will be introduced. To prevent or minimise the impact of chemical inputs in soil, water and health, one should start utilising sound ecological methods, including IPM (Integrated Pest Management). Ecological methods need to be applied in all areas utilised for tourism, including in the maintenance of golf courts, gardens and recreational facilities. Pollution of ground and coastal waters must be prevented, and recommendations must be made (perhaps even legislation) for tourism investors to invest in proper sewage treatment facilities.

Appropriate waste disposal systems and ways to separate garbage into organic and non-organic waste should be developed. Organic waste can be composted and possibly reused on hotel gardens or even for local farming. This could be done through collaboration with local residents. Residents could organise themselves and manage the allocated dumping sites, and hence benefit from the system in receiving payment from the hotel for services rendered. A system to separate the different materials, and recycle some should be in place at the landfill site, thus reducing the waste even further. To avoid degradation of the natural environment, tourism projects can help finance protected areas and safeguard ecologically sensitive regions against further environmental deterioration.

By empowering local populations and have them participating in the entire process, sustainability will be ensured as it becomes accepted by and adjusted to the local communities. Also, a protected area might certainly be a suitable tourist-attraction, where tourists can experience amazing nature and learn about conservation and traditional uses of natural resources in the area. Investors in tourism should always respect the traditional land tenure system in the area and the traditional user-right systems of resources. In regard to this, the communication and consultation with the local communities about resource-use is important.

Tourism investors should not exclude local people from using local resources, and thus take away what they depend on for maintaining their well being. The tourism industry can and must take initiatives to implement that polluter(s) pay a principle (or other forms of internalisation of externalities) for pollution related to tourism operations. This may be organised and carried out through local tax systems or through funds established by the tourism industry for local community development. However, the paid principle should be applied for minor pollution only and should not be developed into a possibility for investors to pay a symbolic fine for imposed irreversible negative impacts on the local environment.

Inaccurate and/or mild environmental legislation in destination countries may possibly attract more foreign investors contributing to fast economic growth and development, but with environmental damage as a consequence. To avoid the dilemma, destination countries will have to choose between economic development and environmental protection international. Multinational enterprises must be committed to follow the environmental standards of their home country should these be stricter than those at the destinations.

The tourism industry should promote projects, which are compatible with the cultural identity of the local population's way of life. Furthermore, the tourism sector should always make sure it acts in accordance with the cultural heritage, and respect the cultural integrity of tourism destinations. This might be accomplished by defining codes of conduct for the industry and hence providing investors with a checklist for sustainable tourism projects. Establishing and developing tourist training programmes could be one way of managing codes of conducts for the tourists.

Here, tourists can be informed and educated about the destination for their travel both before and after their arrival at the site. At the site, tourist information centres can be established through funding from the investor. The information given to tourists should include codes of conduct regarding appropriate behaviour and clothing. It is reasonable to assume that people's offending behaviour is largely a consequence of ignorance rather than intention. Consequently, information and facts about the destination, ways of life, history, cultural heritage is crucial to help tourists get along.

It is an absolute must that tourism investors do not engage in or promote child labour and prostitution. Moreover, it is appropriate that the industry commit themselves to a global campaign against such and any other violation of human rights. Evaluating the sustainability of the tourism development, in regards to cultural and human rights aspects, is highly recommended for those responsible for the tourism projects. As with the case mentioned earlier of preventing environmental degradation, this must be carried out through communication and consultation with the local communities.

By devising local training programmes and establishing educational projects, the tourism industry can ensure that qualified local people are employed in their projects. One should train the local people instead of foreigners to become guides due to their knowledge of the area and resources. The investors should be responsive to the kind of knowledge, abilities and skills found in the local communities. Very often such knowledge and skills are well fitted to be used in tourist activities be it fishing trips, nature trails, souvenir sales or dancing courses for tourists etc. To constrain foreign exchange leakage, those responsible for the tourism projects should ensure that local inputs are purchased for their projects.

A proper examination of local resources available will be beneficial for both the industry and the local residents. Usually, there is considerable local willingness to start producing new products if a market for these products exists. The tourism sector should also adopt measures to prevent foreign exchange leakage by a commitment to re-investment of a fair share of the locally accrued profit. We have already mentioned protected areas, training programmes on codes of conduct for tourists, or possible training of local employees, as projects in need of funds.

Initiatives towards more local community development projects should also be appropriate. The tourism industry should promote the establishment of small and medium-sized tourism enterprises which, compared to large-scale hotels etc., have far more moderate impacts on the environment. It is the industry's responsibility to act as a model for communities to show that it is possible to do business whilst protecting natural resources.

The industry should also promote and support local communities to start tourism-related businesses and grant access to low interest loans. It is the responsibility of the tourism sector to ensure total transparency in all transactions, and to prevent tourism projects from being used as projects for laundering illicit money, as well as to refuse using bribes as a means to obfuscate or avoid government rules and regulations. There should be a global boycott against those investors involved in such or other types of illegal activities.

Empowerment of residents at tourist destinations, through local participation, may be facilitated by providing written and legally binding contracts between local people and tourism investors. The contracts will help to avoid broken promises, which too many examples and previous experience prove to be a huge problem. In addition to the mentioned examples (providing proper information for tourists and establishing training programmes for residents), the tourism industry, through for instance the WTTC or the WTO with NGOs in the selection panels, could issue awards especially for sustainable tourism projects as an encouragement for investors.

Within the industry, it is important that both small and large-scale tourism operators are included in the collaboration and that they participate in solving problems related to tourism development. A sustainable development of the tourism industry can only be ensured through participation of all local residents in the destination countries. There is a need for a willingness and ability for the partners to work with this kind of bottom-up approach.

Governments in both destination and countries of origin of tourists and investors are responsible for providing appropriate legislation for sustainable tourism development, and to follow up the tourism projects with sufficient monitoring and appropriate sanctioning. Exchange of successful experiences of sustainable tourism projects is an important factor in this connection. Lastly, an interdisciplinary approach to the problem is necessary: using local, regional and/or international consultative forums.

Consumer Behaviour in Tourism

International tourism plays an ambivalent role in contributing to cultural exchange and sustainable development. On the one hand, it involves a highly buffered, short-term consumer experience of other locales. Tourists can pay and leave, remaining isolated from negative impacts at the local level. On the other hand, tourism may increase recognition of the importance of respecting cultural diversity and developing an identity as a world citizen. It offers opportunities to educate consumers regarding responsible tourism and sustainable development.

Consumers can play a major role in the transformation of societies towards sustainability. While the mass tourism in the past was rather producer-driven, the industry today is becoming increasingly consumer-driven. In highly competitive tourism markets, well informed, responsible consumers can put increasing pressure on the industry to behave more responsibly. A number of official proclamations have affirmed every individual's right to rest and leisure including tourism. However, tourism remains an unobtainable luxury for the majority of the world's population. Tourists primarily originate from affluent industrialised societies where tourism has become a mass phenomenon.

Tourists' values, attitudes and behaviour are determined by their social environment, cultural identity and way of life which may be in conflict with local customs. Tourism is heterogeneous in nature, made up of many different types of traveller, seeking a wide range of tourism products. Demand is influenced by irrational factors, e.g. fashion and trends. Demand depends on the availability of time and money, on images, perceptions and attitudes. Tourists have various needs, desires and motivations, both of a 'push' and 'pull' nature.

While household incomes in major touristsending countries are declining, industry sales projections continue to grow, indicating increasing competition. The consumer mind is set on discount prices and "buy now/pay later" options. This poses serious threats, as prices already lag far behind any realistic accounting of tourism costs and impacts. Many of the demand patterns in tourism reflect the unsustainable lifestyles of industrialised consumer societies. Tourism acts as an agent in exporting these life-styles and consumerist attitudes to less industrialised societies via demonstration effects and modelling.

Tourism increases demand for imported consumer goods in the destinations, with detrimental effects on the environment, due to the ecological costs of transport and the high amount of waste generated. Increasing imports also reduce local/national economic gains, due to foreign exchange leakage. The over-consumption of resources by tourists and tourism infrastructure (e.g. the excessive use of water, firewood or food) is incompatible with sustainable development. The carrying capacity of natural environments is often exceeded with the addition of tourism demands.

Tourist demand for resources (land, water, energy, food) may also compete with the needs of local people and may increase social inequality, gender inequality and injustice. Tourist transport, especially air travel, is highly energy intensive and causes pollutant emissions. Many tourism activities such as skiing, boating, mountain hiking, motorised water-sports (e.g. jet skies), and trekking represent stress for fragile ecosystems. Tourists often lack information and awareness about their impact in a different culture and environment, about their impacts on socio-economic and socio-cultural development, and about the environmental costs of tourism.

While tourists may be open to learning, they are often unaware of inappropriate behaviour and have little guidance on how to improve them. Others may refuse to adapt to local life-styles (even when informed) insisting on their freedom to behave as they want. While the tourism industry may be willing to improve their products and services, there is a conflict between the industry's pursuit of economic gains and social and environmental responsibility. The industry lacks information on the requirements of sustainable tourism and on how to integrate economic forces with environmental and social requirements.

Tourists shopping for escapism generally abide by one fundamental consumer ethic: receipt upon payment. Consumer advocates may intervene where inferior customer service is delivered. However, the sustainability of corporate practices is self-regulated. This conflict of interest within the industry, and consumers' low awareness of tourism impacts, have led to a widespread abuse of 'green' labeling.

The mass media, especially television through films and reports about events, sights, etc. in other parts of the world, are increasingly influential on travel decisions and consumer behaviour in the destinations. However, these programmes often serve primarily as advertisements, painting images of destinations, rather than providing relevant information for potential travellers. There is a lack of reliable and appropriate (e.g. age and gender segregated) research data on the determinants of tourist demand, motivation and behaviour.

Few countries, whether tourist-sending or tourist-receiving, collect such data that are helpful under sustainable development criteria. Most studies of tourist behaviour focus on mainstream markets or market segments, rather than assessing or modelling sustainable alternatives. Governments in many tourist destinations and local communities have little or no information on what to expect from tourism and the incoming tourists, and how to influence and control tourism and guide tourist behaviour; They are controlled by international/global institutions, the industry and the consumers.

Governments of the affluent countries are only beginning to look at the issues of outgoing tourism. They are not yet sufficiently aware of their responsibility and methods to influence tourist behaviour by political and legal guidelines/criteria and appropriate planning and policies. Trade unions have fought successfully for shorter working hours and more vacation. However, they need to take more responsibility for helping to create a leisure industry that is more sustainable.

Consumer behaviour can and must be influenced by:

— Fighting unsustainable forms and aspects of tourism, at the various levels, by sanctioning unacceptable behaviour and discouraging inappropriate consumer behaviour.

— Promoting responsible and sustainable patterns of behaviour, at the various levels, by promoting best practises and encouraging responsible consumer behaviour. There are different types of instruments and remedial measures available:

a) Legal measures (rules, regulations, sanctions);

b) Market based instruments, such as taxes to influence market prices;

c) Promotion of and (financial) support for best practice;

d) Industry self-monitoring/codes of conduct;

e) Information, education and research.

Agents and Partnership

Consumer behaviour in tourism is both a product and cause of policies by government and industry. Therefore, a comprehensive approach is required to solve the problems associated with market-driven tourism. Tourism should be viewed as a major development issue that all stakeholders need to be actively engaged with. To develop effective partnerships, the imbalance of power between the different stakeholders needs to be addressed.

UN action

— Establish an NGO tourism advisory group for UN to provide technical support, analysis, and strategic advice;

— Create a 'best practices' information clearing-house, in order to collect consumer information useful to understanding and positively influencing consumer behaviour and to make documentation accessible on an equitable basis;

— Initiate a broad information and awareness campaign to highlight damaging forms of tourism and impacts, providing tools for informed decision-making. Initially, target participants in the CSD and CBD processes to clarify roles and responsibilities;

— Research and develop effective certification schemes, form a technical group under the CSD to assess how certification can be improved, e.g. through the review of voluntary codes set up by CSD1998;

— Designate an 'ombuds' office jointly between the CSD, CBD, and UN-CHR to encourage diligent self-regulation and compliance with international standards for sustainable tourism;

— Develop guidance on tourism as an issue within Local Agenda 21 processes.

Govermental actions

— Introduce and enforce legislation to abolish child prostitution, implement effective control mechanisms, conclude judicial assistance agreements;

— Regulate tourist access to ecologically fragile or stressed natural areas;

— Tourist-sending countries: develop policies on outgoing tourism from a development perspective;

— Provide frameworks for ecologically appropriate pricing by strictly applying the polluterpays-principle to internalise external costs. This includes ecological tax reforms including the taxation of aviation gasoline and oil, removal of subsidies/other economic incentives with negative environmental impacts.

— Improve conditions for sustainable consumer behaviour by providing/promoting sustainable tourism facilities;

— Promote environmentally friendly modes of transport and transport concepts, reduce tourism-related traffic, shift demand to less environmentally damaging modes of transport;

— Promote renewable sources of energy (such as solar power), reduce the use of non-renewable energy and of limited local resources, through more sustainable practices/consumption patterns.

— Develop information and education programmes in co-operation with local stakeholders ensuring all stakeholders' involvement (e.g. women's); provide information to tourists on appropriate behaviour, e.g. by establishing information centres in destinations, or by including briefing material for package tours;

— Take into account the specific information needs of various market segments, provide information to the local population on the opportunities and risks from tourism and on how to influence tourist behaviour;

— Adopt, observe, implement and promote codes of conduct, e.g. the planned WTO-OMT 'Global Code of Ethics for Tourism';

— Integrate sustainable development education including tourism in the curricula of schools at all levels, universities and training institutions, involving all stakeholder groups, create and promote open networks for information and research on sustainable tourism, disseminate and implement results;

Tourism industry action

— Promote sustainable tourism products, using market related instruments and incentives, such as contests, awards, certification, model projects, culturally sensitive quality labels covering both environmental and social sustainability;

— Reduce inappropriate consumption, use local resources in preference to imports in a sustainable manner; reduce and recycle waste, ensure safe waste disposal, develop and implement sustainable transport policies and systems, e.g. efficient public transport, walking, cycling in destinations;

— Provide tourists with authentic information, enabling them to understand all environmental and related aspects (e.g. human rights situation) of tourism when selecting any destination or holiday package; educate visitors in advance of arrival and give guidance on 'dos' and 'don'ts'; make tourists aware of their potential impact on and their responsibilities towards host societies;

— Provide information on respecting the cultural and natural heritage of destination areas; employ tour guides who portray societies honestly and dispel stereotypes;

— Ensure that the marketing of 'green' tourism reflects sound environmental policy and practice; use non-exploitative marketing strategies that respect people, communities and environments of destinations, dismantle stereotyping, integrate sustainable tourism principles when creating new marketing strategies;

— Train staff to foster tourist responsibility towards the destinations, encourage multi-cultural education and exchange;

— Actively discourage exploitative sex tourism, particularly sexual exploitation of children, and tourism which causes or contributes to social problems;

— Adopt, observe, implement and promote codes of conduct.

NGO action

— Disseminate information to a wide public about the complexity of tourism and about the objectives and criteria of sustainable tourism;

— Educate tourists to change consumption patterns and promote appropriate, environmentally and socially acceptable behaviour in the destinations;

— Launch broad awareness campaigns on the worst impacts of tourism, to be funded by international governmental and non-governmental agencies;

— Promote relevant research on tourism impacts, criteria for sustainable tourism and possibilities for implementation;

— Monitor tourism development, policy, industry initiatives, and local people's reaction to tourism development and policy, and implementation of stakeholder action.

Early tourism development has given little consideration to natural resource limitations, impacts on wildlife and indigenous cultures. The human environment and development has been largely ignored. Within the process of globalisation local communities' participation and nature conservation are threatened and often overlooked. If tourism is to be sustainable, it must improve the lives of local people, protect their environment and health, and offer them a better future.

In many instances, tourism can be seen as a vehicle to empower local communities and protect the environment through the development of new employment opportunities, the enhancement of local economies, preservation of indigenous knowledge and practices, public awareness and education. Sustainable tourism can create positive opportunities for community development in remote areas. The business sector can choose sustainable tourism over other more polluting ventures.

Long and short-term development plans should be developed so that tourism and its benefits are spread within the area. To develop tourism in a sustainable manner, it is necessary to define optimal tourism destinations in local areas and regions, ensuring enjoyment for the tourist and minimum impact or disruption for the environment and local communities. Complex and broad-based local communities' involvement in tourism development requires targeted investment strategies implemented by local decision-makers.

Those strategies do not exist in many areas and the development of tourism is not planned. Often, tourism investments are imposed from the outside, and the potential for sustainable forms of tourism is weakened. Alternatives to mass tourism (e.g. cultural and "ecotourism") can be influential in changing the nature of tourism. Tourism can benefit both tourists and local communities and allow for two-way interaction and education.

In order for tourism to become a sustainable industry, countries, states, regions, and individuals must work with new technology, natural resource management and marketing concepts. Ideally, participatory planning and implementation will be a part of Local Agenda 21 processes. To ensure community involvement and to safeguard local cultures, sustainable tourism development should therefore involve all stakeholders in tourism development at all appropriate levels, facilitate the development of tourism services that are planned, managed and reviewed by the host community in Local Agenda 21 processes. This will also ensure that tourism revenue stays in the host communities to enhance livelihoods and generate a profitable source of income, empower and motivate local groups to direct cross-cultural exchange in the way they wish and adopt practices which conserve, protect and preserve the environment.

Local and Regional Tourism Boards

These Boards should:

— promote sustainable tourism concepts in co-operation with local governments and all —stakeholders, in line with Local Agenda 21 priorities;

— work systematically to attract investment in sustainable tourism;

— help other institutions in developing marketing strategies and training programmes and developing educational materials;

— work together with different public institutions to involve all stakeholder groups in tourism activities, and bring greater benefits to the entire community; and

— co-operate with grass-roots organisations to develop employment strategies through sustainable tourism.

Institutional Action

The UN-CSD should:

— invite countries to integrate tourism into their sustainable development strategies for the 2002 review;

— ask the review progress in local communities involvement in tourism development in their country profiles to the preparatory meetings for Earth Summit III in 2002 as part of the review process;

— instruct DESA in co-operation with relevant UN agencies and convention secretariats, major groups and all stakeholders to develop indicators of sustainable tourism;

— invite convention secretariats and the Committee on the Environment of the WTO-OMC to report annually to the CSD;

— establish an international "ombuds" office to deal with human rights abuses and environmental destruction in tourism;.

— ask UNEP, through their Technology Industry and Economics Division, to work with industry associations at all levels, trade unions, local authorities and NGOs to develop a framework for 'good practice' and to develop a database on good practice, criteria, examples and analysis which should be accessible to governments and stakeholders alike;

— ask UNEP together with UNCHS, the Sustainable Cities Programme and relevant stakeholders to develop guidance notes on tourism within Local Agenda 21.

— ask the UN Regional Commissions to prepare a report for the preparatory meetings for Earth Summit III in 2002 on sustainable and community-based tourism activities within their region and to work with UNEP/WTO to develop regional agreements to address sustainable tourism.

— invite UNDP to share its work on guidelines for "good practice" and to involve indigenous peoples and local communities this work;

— ask the UNDP country offices to bring together UN agencies, bilateral donors and other stakeholders to work together on sustainable tourism, as well as involve the gender development programme in this process;

— ask UNDP to include sustainable tourism into its poverty alleviation strategies and programmes.

— ask the United Nations Conference on Trade and Development to integrate tourism into their development strategies and include a progress review on the role of indigenous and local communities' involvement in tourism for the Earth Summit III (year 2002) review, and to support community-owned and controlled initiatives in tourism and bio-diversity through its BIOTRADE initiative.

— invite environmental conventions and treaties secretariats to include community-based tourism in their action plans and programmes, and to promote it as an incentive for the conservation and sustainable use of bio-diversity.

Multilateral financing and assistance agencies should:

— provide funds for applied research through pilot projects to determine optimal mechanisms for tourism development in a range of differing circumstances;

— create small-scale credit lines to assist small enterprises to invest in tourism without excessive risk on personal property;

— support community controlled tourism initiatives that are directed to poverty alleviation, bio-diversity conservation and promotion of human rights;

— assess their projects' effectiveness on local, sub-national and national levels involving all stakeholders, and publish the results by the Earth Summit III in 2002;

— take part in a discussion forum on minimising leakage, with findings to be brought back to the finance discussion at CSD-8 in 20Possible outcomes include the development of a purchasing/procurement strategy for the tourism industry, local/ national investment strategies, improved mechanisms for informed choice by consumers, and a linking of aid with capacity building in tourism-dependent areas.

Governments should, at national level

— establish/clarify institutional and departmental responsibility for developing outgoing tourism and harmonise institutional interventions;

— initiate the use of tourism for local economic development by involving all sectors alongside the tourist ministry; to build the capacity to work at the destination level, including product development and effective management of existing destinations;

— facilitate research grants on sustainable tourism, methodologies, impacts and analysis of good practice; finance pilot schemes to develop 'good practice' and establish systems for ongoing evaluation and monitoring;

— establish sustainable tourism policies and regulations, ensuring responsibly zoned development; natural and cultural heritage and resource conservation and protection;

— review land ownership in potential tourism areas and where possible transfer ownership to local communities and provide the necessary training for them;

— include the perspective of local and indigenous communities into local and national sustainable development strategies;

— increase funding for local NGOs to enable them to engage in a dialogue on tourism;

— support public education programmes which encourage responsible consumption, natural resource use, environmental protection and local culture conservation;

— give priority to the following investment suggestions: create funds to help tour operators improve their technical capacity for sustainable tourism development; create funds to develop recreational facilities for the public;

— encourage local banks and other lending institutions to set up regional investment funding programmes, including micro-credit programmes;

— create Regional Tourism Boards, fully staffed, to help in planning, promoting, regulating, and expanding sustainable tourism;

— initiate special marketing programmes by local governments and Tourism Boards, in which local tourism programmes will be advertised in the media;

— initiate programmes to improve the management of eco-tourism in protected areas;

— set up training programmes for guides, tour operators, marketers, etc.

Governments should, at local level

— harmonise laws on tourism including regulations, fee standards, licensing, etc. so that they will be more favourable to sustainable tourism in the region;

— ensure that tourism development is in line with Local Agenda 21 priorities and land-use plans and that the public can participate in local and regional decision making;

— regulate tourism to ensure that profits benefit local people and conservation efforts;

— Develop and support programmes to revitalise the diverse aspects of local cultures.

The tourism industry should

— reduce financial leakage and support local economies by buying food and resources locally, develop long-term partnerships with local operators, businesses and suppliers;

— train and hire local staff and contract with local businesses, promote management opportunities for women;

— prefer accommodations owned, built and staffed by local people, promote locally made handicrafts and traditional products;

— encourage clients to study and understand their destinations, respect local cultures and co-ordinate visits with local communities, authorities and women's organisations, being aware of and being sensitive to local customary laws, regulations and traditions, whilst respecting historical heritage and scientific sites;

— educate staff to avoid negative environmental and cultural impacts and create incentive schemes to promote sustainable behaviour.

NGOs should:

— initiate stakeholder dialogue on community involvement in tourism development, recognising social and gender divisions in communities;

— promote consultation processes in tourism planning, involving local communities;

— launch educational and awareness programmes on tourism for local communities, support and promote history research and museums;

— promote the respect for indigenous peoples and local communities' self-determination, autonomy and social and cultural integrity;

—strengthen their efforts to empower disenfranchised groups (in particular women) to become involved in local tourism planning and management;

— develop participatory programmes to support the integrity of local cultures and economies;

— support the sustainable resource use and initiate environmental actions on different levels to conserve the environment while the tourism is developing;

— analyse the experience with sustainable tourism in different parts of the world, in order to disseminate methodology/positive examples of community involvement in tourism;

— support the use of traditional knowledge, practices and innovation systems relevant for the conservation and sustainable use of biological resources and promote actions on different levels to eradicate poverty, protect human rights and conserve the environment while working in tourism.

There is an urgency to constructively shape tourism in order to support local development and conservation goals.

UN bodies and institutions, governments, industry and civil society should co-operate to launch a dialogue process on sustainable tourism. This must be planned within the framework provided by the various UN treaties and declarations. All the stakeholders involved in and affected by tourism should be involved in the development of action plans for sustainable tourism. Identifying mechanisms to achieve sustainable development goals in tourism must be a priority for co-operation.

'Good practices' in conserving culture and nature while developing sustainable tourism should be collected worldwide, involving all stakeholders. This process should lead to a multi-stakeholder round-table on strategic planning of local community involvement in tourism to be organised by UNEP as a side event at the Preparatory meetings for Earth Summit III in 2002. There is an urgent need to assess the impacts of globalisation and the role of multilateral and bilateral development organisations in unsustainable tourism practices. An independent international assessment commission should be created under the CSD.

NGOs, indigenous peoples, women's organisations and local communities should be involved in this assessment process together with all other stakeholders. The UN Working Group on Indigenous Peoples should be invited to monitor impacts of tourism on indigenous peoples and local communities. The assessment is to be completed and published by the year 2002.

Coastal Tourism

The United Nations Commission on Sustainable Development in 1999 will address both Oceans and Seas and the review of SIDS. Therefore, it is recognising that: "The survival of small island developing States is firmly rooted in their human resources and cultural heritage, which are their most significant assets; those assets are under severe stress and all efforts must be taken to ensure the central position of people in the process of sustainable development." With these words, the Report of the Global Conference on the Sustainable Development of Small Island Developing States identifies the single most important issue to be borne in mind as we address the challenge of survival and development for our islands.

Article 25 of the Programme of Action from the United Nations Conference on the Sustainable Development of Small Island Developing States (SIDS) focuses our attention on another significant consideration: "Sustainable development in small island developing States depends largely on coastal and marine resources, because their small land area means that those States are effectively Costal entities" Tourism is one of many anthropogenic activities with a special focus on coastal areas.

The two most popular locations for holidaymakers are the mountains and the coast. The coastal area or zone (as it is often called) is hard to define as the area where fresh and salt waters mix, containing many complex, diverse and productive ecosystems on and offshore interacting with each other. New concepts including the whole watershed area seem to be the best approach, especially when aquatic pollution problems are considered. Most problems are related to conflicts between different uses and access restrictions. Tourism leads to increased traffic flow and overcrowding in already densely populated areas. Up to 130 tourists has been calculated per inhabitant in the most popular coastal regions. Therefore, tourism adds substantially to the following pressures:

— Pollution by waste water, garbage, heating, noise and traffic emissions;

— Encroachment of buildings, facilities and roads close to the coastline;

— Beach erosion due to building, dune removal and dredging;
— Excessive use of natural areas;
— Destruction of natural areas to accommodate tourism or other needs;
— Inter-sectorial competition and conflict over (marine and terrestrial) space;
— Exclusion of local communities from any role of significance in decision-making;
— The loss of natural and architectural heritage in the face of rapid expansion;
— Strain on public utilities and facilities;
— displacement of local population;
— Creation of restricted exclusive zones that are off-limits to the local people;

Additional typical tourism impacts are socio-economic conflicts as property and general costs of living increases, and social structure can be changed significantly, when summer guests overrun small communities. Foreign customs and expectations can create conflicts and a deterioration of cultural and regional values.

A major focus should be on the integration of tourism planning and operation of tourist facilities into local planning instruments. Local agenda 21 can play a key role here in ensuring the involvement of all stakeholders. Ideally, this would be done in the context of integrated coastal area management (ICAM). This instrument bridges sectorial approaches in order to avoid or mitigate user conflicts, and it ideally takes into account ecosystem features and physical, not man-made borders.

New tourism developments should be planned together with municipal, industrial, agri- / aqua-cultural and nature protection activities, to allow for multiple complementary uses and to segregate conflicting activities. Area development plans should inform sector plans which should then be incorporated into a coordinated national development plan. All planning should be accompanied by widespread public information dissemination and provide opportunity for discussion leading to integrated coastal zone management.

The tourism development strategy should protect local culture, respect local traditions and promote local ownership and management of programs and projects, so as to foster community stewardship of the natural resource base. Environmental Impact Assessment (EIA) on a strategic level as well as for projects is an invaluable tool for this stage. Criteria for planning and EIA should be:

— Strict environmental standards for solid, liquid and gaseous waste emissions;

— Taking the integrity of coastal values and resources into account;

— Enhancement of public transport infrastructure (train, boat, bike, bus);

— Locally adapted styles and maximum height/size limit for facilities;

— Setting of local/regional carrying capacities on a case-by-case basis;

— Limits to sale of property to foreigners;

— Maintenance of public access to the coastal strip;

— Safeguarding cultural values and customary uses.

During the operation of tourism facilities, several instruments can be applied to enable sustainable development. The details have to be developed according to the use, and together with the local community, the facility operator and local NGOs. Local Agenda 21 could play an important role here (They will be different for a diving site than for a big hotel complex). Modern instruments, which should be, and partly are, already applied in the tourism industry are:

— Introducing environmental management, (according to ISO 14.000 or the European EMAS Initiative);

— Increasing cultural and nature awareness of guests through interactions with local initiatives, guided nature walks, museums, etc.;

— Integrating the local economy by giving priority to local produce (e.g. fish, fruit, vegetables, furniture, and building materials).

However, all these efforts will be in vain, unless carrying capacity limits can be agreed upon in a dialogue and on a case-by-case basis. These limits have to follow sustainability criteria and have to come out of discussions on the development objectives and the natural and cultural values to be protected. They can be tiered in respect to nature used, number of beds and other facilities for guests, and amount of property to be sold to foreigners.

To diminish conflicts a better use of facilities over the year, instead of only in a short season of two to three months should be aimed at. These limits probably have to be stricter for "nature use". Here the introduction and implementation of ranger and guide systems together with limits, regarding the number of visitors, can lead to increased awareness and control at the same time. A simple example is the different approaches to beach litter: Instead of excessive beach cleaning of all organic matter, a plastic litter clean-up by volunteers plus hands-on teaching on the biota originally inhabiting the beach and its natural detritus (like algae and wood) could reinstate an appreciation of nature.

Institutional Actions

Actions on several levels are necessary. First and foremost, the historically grown sectorial approach to managing coastal issues, relating to tourism and other uses, has to be changed substantially. Under the lead of one coastal agency, all stakeholders, especially local people and NGOs, and also sectorial agencies, small and medium enterprises and industry representatives should meet regularly to promote sustainable development of their coastal area. The planning process and the operation of tourism developments should reflect the country's commitment to the guidelines set out in international accords such as Agenda 21 and the SIDS Program of Action.

Depending on the region, this could mean enhancing human resource development including public awareness building and training; institutional strengthening and networking. Lessons learned in one community should be accessible to others. This will start the ICAM process, which is a goal-directed planning and decision- making process. ICAM leads to inter-agency and inter-sectorial collaboration, resulting in operational decision-making with strong public participation and feedback mechanisms. ICAM could mean in practice:

— To start an environmental management initiative through an award scheme;

— To raise an environmental tax from visitors for small projects, e.g. for funding ranger;

— Training or environmental training for tourism staff;

— To start joint actions with local fishermen, farmers, hotels, or other local initiatives;

— To develop a tourism master plan for the region.

In the long term, a development plan should be devised and discussed thoroughly in order to achieve a common understanding on the objectives and necessary restrictions. As all coastal areas contain particularly sensitive sites, environmental protection has to feature strongly in this planning process, with representatives from government nature protection agencies and NGOs having an equal standing with all other participants. Depending on the nature of the coastline, regional and intergovernmental collaboration may be necessary in addition to local initiatives. For some issues, such as the reduction of pollution and especially "eutrophication", co-operation on a larger regional scale is necessary.

As integrated processes take time, tourism umbrella organisations should start with voluntary selfrestraint, until locally adapted objectives have been reached. In the north, which bears the brunt of world-wide tourism, a development of quality tourism should be the focus for the future instead of an increase in quantity. The term quality should include ecological and social carrying capacities at the same time as being economically sustainable.

Future of Tourism Industry

The tourism and recreation industry is confronted with serious and difficult choices about its future. The decisions made now will for decades affect the lifestyles and economic opportunity of residents in tourism destination areas. Many of these decisions are irreversible because once communities lose the character that makes them distinctive and attractive to nonresidents, they have lost their ability to vie for tourist-based income in an increasingly global and competitive marketplace.

One option is to continue the road of the past, focusing on delivering the service and retail sectors that have provided the bulk of economic benefit to local communities lodging, transportation, food and retail sales without considering the emerging concerns about the industry. This option is based on assumptions about stability in values and preferences of travelers, and it delays answers to vital questions about the tourism product, appropriate scale and type of development, sustainability, and hosts' quality of life. These assumptions are questionable in an era of rapid social change where the future is no longer a straight-line projection of the past.

Worldwide, tourism is undergoing fundamental change, from the experiences and settings travelers demand to the regulations governments impose to protect the environment. Signs of these shifts are everywhere, from tourism industry statements on the value of the environment to the demand for "ecotourism." This transformation of demand and values leaves the industry no alternative other than to pursue a different, yet difficult, course one that builds upon the key questions of purpose, objectives, values, and strategies.

Decisions about tourism development are difficult. The fundamental questions they imply such as the visions we have for our communities, how changes brought about by development will impact these visions, and how the community can absorb such changes have largely been ignored in the past. These decisions are controversial because they will prevent or diminish some traditional uses of natural resources and affect the people who have or who might have benefited from those uses.

Powerful economic forces entrenched in the current direction are reluctant to open dialogue. The decisions are essentially judgments reflecting divergent value systems and how those value systems will be integrated. Our clients, primarily the public, are communicating through changes in tastes and preferences and, consequently, they are demanding that the industry pursue sustainability and care of the environment. We need to systematically explore the linkage that exists, whether recognized or not, between tourism, the environment, and sustainability.

As we humans become more aware of our impact on the Earth and its life support systems, we increasingly look for examples of economic and community development other than unconstrained growth. Some have argued that gross national product or per capita income are incomplete measures of well-being. These measures may not accurately portray the distribution of economic benefits among people, they do not faithfully capture important quality of life factors, and they do not measure the temporal or social distribution of existing and anticipated costs and benefits of resource development programs.

Many argue for the development of "sustainable" economies as the new guidepost to deal with issues of growth, economic and community development, and environmental protection. Sustainable growth and natural resource development will help communities use natural resources more prudently and sensitively than in the past and ensure their continued survival. Sustainability contains the appeal of an attractive model for action but is difficult to implement practically or operationally. Sustainability is often associated with such terms as "sustainable development," "sustainable management," "sustainable agriculture," "sustainable forestry," and "sustainable tourism." In the tourism and recreation context, it is frequently associated with discussions of "ecotourism" and "nature-based tourism".

Sustainability has become an attractive ideal for both scientists and activists, but operational details, objectives, or actions provided by advocates are scarce. Discussions of sustainability are presented within the context of stability, particularly about communities (defined in a territorial versus an interest sense). We generally want our communities to be stable and predictable and to provide a sense of belonging. Sustainability goes beyond economic considerations and biophysical issues; it must deal with important concepts of social order, such as hierarchy, territory, and norms.

We must understand how tourism development may impact the distribution of wealth or power, may affect land uses and zoning laws, and may interject new behaviors or institutions. We must discuss the acceptability of tourism-based interventions in the normative social order: What do these changes mean for community stability? And we must consider factors affecting a community's capacity to deal with such interventions. In other words, how do the type and intensity of tourism-induced disturbances affect our social world?

Sustainability definitions also frequently speak to intra- and intergenerational equity and option maintenance. The tourism industry receives substantive criticism about the distribution of jobs and income. While job quality encompasses more than wages and monetary benefits, inequities in income are a major concern that residents hold about tourism development. Nearly 58 percent of the adult Montanans participating in the Martin and McCool study agreed that tourism industry jobs are low paying, and over 55 percent disagreed that their household standard of living was higher because of tourist expenditures. What is an equitable distribution of options and income?

Sustainable tourism allows visitors to enjoy an attraction, community or region with a volume and impact in such a way that the local culture and environment are unimpaired. Strictly speaking, tourism and recreation use always lead to some level of impairment in natural systems. The question is primarily how much change is acceptable. Despite the extensive discussion about sustainability since the 1987 report from the World

Commission on Environment and Development, which popularized the issue, few answers have been found. Entering sustainability-based management is essentially a value judgment, a decision that says that current management is inadequate or inappropriate.

Sustainability is a concept decision makers can use to assess the consequences of actions on human communities. A human focus is deliberately taken here because it is the human population that places values on social structure, cultural values and traditions, economic opportunity, and ecosystems and their species. Maintenance of ecosystems and the protection of individual species are human-based values and, therefore, can be described from only a human viewpoint.

Human communities are impacted in a variety of ways by tourism, including social structure and function, cohesiveness, economic and educational opportunity, community stability, provision of and payment for services (police protection, fire), physically (architecture, location and design of highways), competition in access to recreation opportunities and other services, and interaction with the natural environment and the non-commodity values it produces. The general concept is that sustainability is not only a goal for specific industries, but it is also an objective for the human communities that benefit and that are impacted from various economic development scenarios.

Industry sustainability goals are most likely physical output or net revenue goals, such as board feet of timber, room-nights occupancy, and skier visits. These sustainability goals, however, may not achieve broader community sustainability goals, goals that may be difficult to quantify and measure. Several other questions must be dealt with. At what spatial or social organizational scale do we want to measure sustainability globally, regionally, locally? We also are concerned about the temporal scale of sustainability tomorrow, next week, next year, and the next generation. We need to examine not only industry-specific sustainability, generally addressed by physical commodities, but also the impacts of distinctive economic development actions on the larger community.

Impacts of Tourism in the Environment

Environment is the travel industry's base product. While many tourism promotion efforts banner the climate, sun, warmth, and sand of particular destinations, tourism's dependency on environments, in particular, nature-dominated environments, does not appear to be well understood within the tourism and recreation industry. Cook and others, for example, focus more on how the tourism industry is meeting legal obligations for environmental protection (such as emissions) than the dependency of tourism on high-quality natural environments.

The importance of the environment in attracting vacation travel is significant, natural beauty and cultural heritage represent a competitive advantage for many areas. A place that takes care of its environment is very important in choosing a destination outside of the state. The linkage between environment as an attraction and economic impact can be substantial.

Bibliography

Burns, Peter, and Andrew Holden, *Tourism: A New Perspective.* London: Prentice Hall, 1995.

Burr, Steven W. "A Conceptual Model for Facilitating Rural Tourism Development," *Proceedings of the 1996 Northeastern Recreation Research Symposium,* March 31-April 2, 1996, Lake George in Bolton Landing, NY, 1997.

Gibson, Lay James. "The Potential for Tourism Development in Nonmetropolitan Areas," pp. 145-164, in David L. Barkley, ed., *Economic Adaptation.* Boulder, Colorado: Westview Press, 1993.

Jepson, Edward J., Jr., and David W. Marcouiller. Ethnic Variation in Leisure and Recreational Interests. Chicago: Council of Planning Librarians. *CPL Bibliography* No. 311. 1994.

Koth, Barbara, Glenn Kreag, and John Sem. *A Training Guide for Rural Tourism Development.* St. Paul, Minnesota: Rural Tourism Center, Minnesota Extension Service, 1995.

Long, Patrick T., and Jonelle S. Nuckolls. "Organizing Resources for Rural Tourism Development: The Importance of Leadership, Planning and Technical Assistance," *Tourism Recreation Research,* Vol. 19, No. 2, pp. 19-34, 1994.

Marcouiller, David W. *Tourism Planning.* Chicago: Council of Planning Librarians. CPL Bibliography No. 316, 1995.

Marcouiller, David W. "Toward Integrative Tourism Planning in Rural America," *Journal of Planning Literature,* Vol. 11, No. 3: pp. 337-357, 1997.

Weaver, Glenn. "TTRA Annual Conference Focuses on Rural Tourism Development Issues," *Rural Development News*, Vol. 15, No. 1: pp. 8-9, 1991.

Wilkerson, Mary L. "Developing a Rural Tourism Plan: The Major Publications," *Economic Development Review*, Vol. 14, No. 2: p. 79, 1996.

Willits, Fern K. "The Rural Mystique and Tourism Development: Data from Pennsylvania," *Journal of the Community Development Society*, Vol. 24, No. 2: pp. 159-174, 1993.

Woods, Mike. "Diversifying the Rural Economy: Tourism Development." *The Rural South: Preparing for the Challenges of the 21st Century*, No. 10: pp. 1-10. Jackson, Mississippi. Southern Rural Development Center, Mississippi State University, 2000.

Index

Air Traffic Control (ATC) 67
Air Traffic Management (ATM) 80
Airborne Collision Avoidance System (ACAS) 80
Airports Authority of India (AAI) 67
Automobiles 25
Aviation Turbine Fuel (ATF) 74

Bharat Heavy Electrical Limited (BHEL) 84
Bharatiya Janata Party (BJP) 23
Boosting tourism 31
Build-Own-Operate (BOO) 66
Bureau of Civil Aviation Security (BCAS) 81

Cargo, Insurance and Freight (CIF) 37
Central Training Establishment (CTE) 83
Civil Aviation Authority (CAA) 63
Civil Aviation Training College (CATC) 83
Coastal Tourism 261
Computerization 69
Controlled Flights Into Terrain (CFIT) 80
Convention and Visitor Bureaus (CVBs) 223

Digital cameras 117
Domestic tourism 28

Economic development strategy 10
Ecotourism 237
Electronic data interchange 77
Electronic guidebooks 118
Environmental Impact Assessment (EIA) 264
Export Promotion of Capital Goods Scheme (EPCG) 37

General Agreement on Trade in Services (GATS) 1
Global economy 59
Globalisation 173
Gross Domestic Product (DP) 171
Ground Proximity Warning System (GPWS) 80
Group of Ministers (GoM) 26

Hindustan Aeronautics Limited (HAL) 84
Human resources development 107
India Tourism Development Corporation (ITDC) 22
Indian Association of Tour Operators (IATO) 42

Indian Hotels and Restaurants Association (IHRA) 42
Indira Gandhi Rashtriya Uran Akademi (IGRUA) 83
Inland Air Travel Tax (IATT) 74
Integrated Coastal Area Management (ICAM) 263
International Civil Aviation Organisation (ICAO) 84
International Labour Organisation (ILO) 238
International Monetary Fund (IMF) 1

Jet Engine Overhaul Complex (JEOC) 83

Least Developed Countries (LDCs) 18
Local government organisations (LGOs) 217

Mass tourism 183
Minimum Safe Altitude Warning (MSAW) 80
Mobile technologies 107
Monopolies and Restrictive Trade Practices (MRTP) 41
Municipal International Cooperation (MIC) 217

National tourism policy 26
North East Council (NEC) 78

Photographicmaterials 100
Planning commission 23
Purchasing Power Parity (PPP) 171

Reserve Bank of India (RBI) 101

Sustainable development of tourism 100

Telecommunication 100
Tourism Satellite Accounting (TSA) 5
Travel Agents Association of India (TAAI) 42

Union Territory (U. T.) 100
United Nations Conference on Trade and Development (UNCTD)1

Value Added Tax (VAT) 183

World tourism ladder 22
World Tourism Organisation 21
World Travel and Tourism Council (WTTC) 1